Mathematics in Robot Control for Theoretical and Applied Problems

Mathematics in Robot Control for Theoretical and Applied Problems

Guest Editors

Paolo Mercorelli
Oleg Sergiyenko
Oleksandr Tsymbal

Basel • Beijing • Wuhan • Barcelona • Belgrade • Novi Sad • Cluj • Manchester

Guest Editors

Paolo Mercorelli
Institute for Production
Technology and Systems
Leuphana Universität
Lüneburg
Lüneburg
Germany

Oleg Sergiyenko
Department of Applied
Physics
Autonomous University of
Baja California
Mexicali
Mexico

Oleksandr Tsymbal
Department of
Computer-Integrated
Technologies
Kharkiv National University
of Radio Electronics
Kharkiv
Ukraine

Editorial Office
MDPI AG
Grosspeteranlage 5
4052 Basel, Switzerland

This is a reprint of the Special Issue, published open access by the journal *Mathematics* (ISSN 2227-7390), freely accessible at: https://www.mdpi.com/si/mathematics/robot_control.

For citation purposes, cite each article independently as indicated on the article page online and as indicated below:

Lastname, A.A.; Lastname, B.B. Article Title. *Journal Name* **Year**, *Volume Number*, Page Range.

ISBN 978-3-7258-3715-1 (Hbk)
ISBN 978-3-7258-3716-8 (PDF)
https://doi.org/10.3390/books978-3-7258-3716-8

© 2025 by the authors. Articles in this book are Open Access and distributed under the Creative Commons Attribution (CC BY) license. The book as a whole is distributed by MDPI under the terms and conditions of the Creative Commons Attribution-NonCommercial-NoDerivs (CC BY-NC-ND) license (https://creativecommons.org/licenses/by-nc-nd/4.0/).

Contents

About the Editors vii

Preface ix

Paolo Mercorelli, Oleg Sergiyenko and Oleksandr Tsymbal
Mathematics in Robot Control for Theoretical and Applied Problems
Reprinted from: *Mathematics* **2024**, *12*, 2240, https://doi.org/10.3390/math12142240 1

Sergio Palomino-Resendiz, Norma Lozada-Castillo, Diego Flores-Hernández, Oscar Octavio Gutiérrez-Frías and Alberto Luviano-Juárez
Adaptive Active Disturbance Rejection Control of Solar Tracking Systems with Partially Known Model
Reprinted from: *Mathematics* **2021**, *9*, 2871, https://doi.org/10.3390/math9222871 4

Oleksandr Tsymbal, Paolo Mercorelli and Oleg Sergiyenko
Predicate-Based Model of Problem-Solving for Robotic Actions Planning
Reprinted from: *Mathematics* **2021**, *9*, 3044, https://doi.org/10.3390/math9233044 24

Mikhail Babenko, Andrei Tchernykh, Bernardo Pulido-Gaytan, Arutyun Avetisyan, Sergio Nesmachnow, Xinheng Wang and Fabrizio Granelli
Towards the Sign Function Best Approximation for Secure Outsourced Computations and Control
Reprinted from: *Mathematics* **2022**, *10*, 2006, https://doi.org/10.3390/math10122006 37

Diego Cerrillo, Antonio Barrientos and Jaime Del Cerro
Kinematic Modelling for Hyper-Redundant Robots—A Structured Guide
Reprinted from: *Mathematics* **2022**, *10*, 2891, https://doi.org/10.3390/math10162891 59

Mario Ramírez-Neria, Jaime González-Sierra, Alberto Luviano-Juárez, Norma Lozada-Castillo and Rafal Madonski
Active Disturbance Rejection Strategy for Distance and Formation Angle Decentralized Control in Differential-Drive Mobile Robots
Reprinted from: *Mathematics* **2022**, *10*, 3865, https://doi.org/10.3390/math10203865 99

Carlos Escobar, Francisco J. Vargas, Andrés A. Peters and Gonzalo Carvajal
A Cooperative Control Algorithm for Line and Predecessor Following Platoons Subject to Unreliable Distance Measurements
Reprinted from: *Mathematics* **2023**, *11*, 801, https://doi.org/10.3390/math11040801 118

Haneul Jeon and Donghun Lee
Explicit Identification of Pointwise Terrain Gradients for Speed Compensation of Four Driving Tracks in Passively Articulated Tracked Mobile Robot
Reprinted from: *Mathematics* **2023**, *11*, 905, https://doi.org/10.3390/math11040905 136

Jian Sun, Jie Zhao, Xiaoyang Hu, Hongwei Gao and Jiahui Yu
Autonomous Navigation System of Indoor Mobile Robots Using 2D Lidar
Reprinted from: *Mathematics* **2023**, *11*, 1455, https://doi.org/10.3390/math11061455 152

Tan Kai Noel Quah, Yi Wei Daniel Tay, Jian Hui Lim, Ming Jen Tan, Teck Neng Wong and King Ho Holden Li
Concrete 3D Printing: Process Parameters for Process Control, Monitoring and Diagnosis in Automation and Construction
Reprinted from: *Mathematics* **2023**, *11*, 1499, https://doi.org/10.3390/math11061499 173

Sergey Nesteruk, Ilya Zherebtsov, Svetlana Illarionova, Dmitrii Shadrin, Andrey Somov, Sergey V. Bezzateev, et al.
CISA: Context Substitution for Image Semantics Augmentation
Reprinted from: *Mathematics* **2023**, *11*, 1818, https://doi.org/10.3390/math11081818 207

R. Peón-Escalante, Manuel Flota-Bañuelos, Roberto Quintal-Palomo, Luis J. Ricalde, F. Peñuñuri, B. Cruz Jiménez and J. Avilés Viñas
Neural Network Based Control of Four-Bar Mechanism with Variable Input Velocity
Reprinted from: *Mathematics* **2023**, *11*, 2148, https://doi.org/10.3390/math11092148 231

Vadym Savanevych, Sergii Khlamov, Oleksandr Briukhovetskyi, Tetiana Trunova and Iryna Tabakova
Mathematical Methods for an Accurate Navigation of the Robotic Telescopes
Reprinted from: *Mathematics* **2023**, *11*, 2246, https://doi.org/10.3390/math11102246 248

Hilton Tnunay, Kaouther Moussa, Ahmad Hably and Nicolas Marchand
Distributed Finite-Time Coverage Control of Multi-Quadrotor Systems with Switching Topology
Reprinted from: *Mathematics* **2023**, *11*, 2621, https://doi.org/10.3390/math11122621 267

About the Editors

Paolo Mercorelli

Paolo Mercorelli (Member, IEEE) received a PhD degree in systems engineering from the University of Bologna, Italy, in 1998. In 1997, he was a Visiting Researcher for one year in the Department of Mechanical and Environmental Engineering, University of California, Santa Barbara, CA, USA. From 1998 to 2001, he was a Postdoctoral Researcher at Asea Brown Boveri Corporate Research, Heidelberg, Germany, where he obtained three patents. From 2002 to 2005, he was a Senior Researcher at the Institute of Automation and Informatics, Wernigerode, Germany, where he was the leader of the control group. From 2005 to 2011, he was an Associate Professor of Process Informatics at the Ostfalia University of Applied Sciences, Wolfsburg, Germany. Since 2012, he has been a Full Professor and Chair of control and drive systems at the Institute for Production Technology and Systems, Leuphana University of Lueneburg, Germany. Since the winter semester of 2017/2018, he has been an International Distinguished Visiting Professor at the Institute of Automatic Control, Lodz University of Technology, Lodz, Poland, where he has been responsible for different courses in the field of robotic system control. From 1998 to 2001, Dr. Mercorelli was the recipient of a three-year scholarship from the Marie Curie Actions Research Fellowship Program, which is one of the most competitive and prestigious European awards sponsored by the European Commission. He received seven best international conference paper awards: IECON 2013, IECON 2014, CoDIT 2014, ICCC 2017, FedCSIS 2019, ACD 2019, ICCC 2020, and ICSTCC 2023. He has held thirteen plenary lectures during international conferences. In 2019, 2020, 2021, 2022, 2023, and 2024, he was listed in the top 2% scientists by Elsevier Database and the University of Stanford (USA). Since 2022, he has been Editor-in-Chief for the "Engineering Mathematics" Section in *Mathematics*, MDPI, Basel, Switzerland.

Oleg Sergiyenko

Oleg Sergiyenko received B.Sc. (Honoris Causa) and M.Ss. degrees from the Kharkiv National University of Automobiles and Highways, Kharkiv, Ukraine, in 1991 and 1993, respectively. He received a Ph.D. degree from Kharkiv National Polytechnic University with a specialty in "Tools and methods of non-destructive control" in 1997. He received a postdoctorate degree (DsC, or habilitation thesis) from the Kharkiv National University of Radioelectronics in 2018. He has been the author of 1 book, editor of 12 books, and writer of 23 book chapters; he has had 200 papers indexed in SCOPUS (h-index 25) and holds 5 patents of Ukraine and 2 patents of Mexico. He is currently the Head of Applied Physics Department of Engineering Institute of Baja California Autonomous University, Mexico, where he is the director of several master's and doctorate thesis programs. He was a member of the program committees of various international and local conferences, participating annually as Session Chair of IEEE ISIE and IECON conferences in 2014–2024. He is a recognized reviewer of *Elsevier*, constant reviewer *of IEEE Transaction on Industrial Electronics*, *Trans on Mechatronics*, etc. He is a member (Academician) of the Academy of Applied Radioelectronics of Ukraine, Russia and Belarus. He has previously received the "Best session presentation" award at IECON2014 in Dallas, USA, IECON2016 in Florence, Italy, and ISIE2019 in Vancouver, Canada. He also received, as a coauthor, the "Outstanding Paper" award at the 2017 Emerald Literati Network Awards for Excellence. He is member of CONACYT National Research System, currently ranked at level 3.

Oleksandr Tsymbal

Oleksandr Tsymbal received an M.Sc. degree from Karazin National University (Faculty of Radio Physics), Kharkiv, Ukraine, in 1992. He received a Ph.D. degree from the Technological Research Institute of Instrument-Building, Kharkiv, Ukraine, specializing in the "Automation of Technological processes and industries" and "Computer-Aided Design", in 1996. He received a postdoctorate degree (DsC, or habilitation thesis) from the Kharkiv National University of Radioelectronics in 2015. He has been the author and co-author of six textbooks and five monographs, and he has had 15 papers indexed in SCOPUS (h-index 3). He is currently the Professor of Computer-Integrated Technologies, Automation and Robotics at the Kharkiv National University of Radio Electronics, Kharkiv, Ukraine, where he works as a supervisor of master's and doctorate thesis programs. He was a member of program committees of various international and local conferences in 2014–2024.

Preface

Industrial robotic systems have already achieved wide consolidation in various sectors. Today, they are commonly used in paint shops, welding, the assembly of semi-finished and finished components, and the inspection and repair of failures in nuclear facilities or underwater environments, as well as having numerous applications in agriculture. Robotics presents both theoretical and practical challenges, particularly in replacing or augmenting physically demanding tasks, thus benefitting certain categories of at-risk workers. The endeavor to alleviate human burdens such as physical pain and fatigue has long been a driving force in science and technology, considered by some scholars as foundational to epistemology.

The history of robotics, up to the present day, is not a superfluous subject. It is intriguing to explore the original meaning of the word "robot." Some philologists suggest its derivation from the Latin root "robor-roboris," meaning "force." Regardless, the term "robot" was first introduced in 1921 by the Czech writer Karel Capek in his satirical work titled "Rossum's Universal Robots," where "robota" in Czech means "work." Capek's satire underscores the distinction between machines and humans, highlighting that robots never tire. Post-World War II, the necessity to handle radioactive materials led to the development of the first remotely controlled mechanical manipulators, known as Master–Slave systems, pioneered in laboratories such as Argonne and Oak Ridge (USA). These manipulators were operated by human controllers, whose movements were replicated on the manipulator through mechanical linkages. General Electric, in collaboration with General Mills, replaced these mechanical linkages with electrical couplings, coining the term "teleoperators."

This reprint contains 13 articles accepted for publication in the Special Issue "Mathematics in Robot Control for Theoretical and Applied Problems 2023" of the MDPI journal *Mathematics*. These chapters cover a broad spectrum of topics related to the theory and applications of robotic systems.

It is hoped that this reprint will be of interest and utility to those working in the field of robot control, as well as to those with a suitable mathematical background who wish to familiarize themselves with recent advances in engineering mathematics, particularly in mathematics for robot control, which has permeated nearly all sectors of human life and activity.

As Guest Editors of the Special Issue, we express our gratitude to the authors for their high-quality contributions, the reviewers for their valuable feedback that enhanced the submitted works, and the administrative staff of MDPI publications for their support in completing this project. Special thanks are due to the Managing Editor of this Special Issue, Ms. Emma He, for her excellent collaboration and valuable assistance.

Paolo Mercorelli, Oleg Sergiyenko, and Oleksandr Tsymbal
Guest Editors

Editorial

Mathematics in Robot Control for Theoretical and Applied Problems

Paolo Mercorelli [1,*], Oleg Sergiyenko [2] and Oleksandr Tsymbal [3]

[1] Institute for Production Technology and Systems (IPTS), Leuphana Universität Lüneburg, 21335 Lüneburg, Germany
[2] Department of Applied Physics, Autonomous University of Baja California, Mexicali 21100, Mexico; srgnk@uabc.edu.mx
[3] Department of Computer-Integrated Technologies, Automation and Mechatronics, Kharkiv National University of Radio Electronics, 61166 Kharkiv, Ukraine; oleksandr.tsymbal@nure.ua
* Correspondence: paolo.mercorelli@leuphana.de

1. Introduction to the Special Issue

Technological development has not only boosted the use of mechanical systems for industrial uses but above all has made it possible for them to be used in areas and sectors unimaginable until a few years ago. Mechatronics is the neologism which now indicates in general modern robotic systems which are to be equipped with sophisticated electronic control devices. Such devices are capable of helping systems to achieve high performance and allowing their use and disparate aspects of our daily life. It is a synergy set which can radically change some aspects of the production world. A growing interest toward robots, a special class of mechanical systems, as well as fear and perplexity in relation to the impact that these systems have in the world of productivity, and then ultimately their social impact, has be witnessed in recent years. Future robotics represent a tremendous challenge in the field of mathematics because of the central role their control plays in the context of this field. In fact, robot control is one of the most important and challenging topics for mathematicians, engineers, physicians, and practitioners. Mathematical issues are the kernel of the design of control of movements and performance of robots. This Special Issue aims to collect the latest advancements of mathematical methods for solving not only theoretical but also applied problems of classical and also modern robot structures, such as robotic manipulators, walking robots, flexible robots, haptic robots, and any kind of old and new mechanisms with all possible tasks, in grasp, manipulation, and motion for any kind of their possible issues and applications. Advances in robot control, tackling theoretical complexity as well as practical applications, have been given a considerable boost by the use of mathematical methodologies. The Special Issue titled "Mathematics in Robot Control for Theoretical and Applied Problems" where researchers share their discoveries summarizes the latest results of the application of mathematical insights in robotic field.

2. Presentation of the Research Papers

Trajectory tracking control of a solar tracking system is tackled by means of an adaptive active disturbance rejection control scheme as shown in Contribution 1. The state and disturbance estimation system is based on the combination of a time varying identification system and an adaptive observer.

To facilitate robotic problem-solving, especially in industrial settings, the authors of Contribution 2 develop a predicate-based logical paradigm. In addition to improving automation processes, this model also aids in the study of applications designed for problem-solving and intelligent agent-based manufacturing systems.

Using homomorphic encryption, in Contribution 3 authors discuss safe computing and control in robots. The ramifications of their approach to improving robot control system security are substantial, especially in settings where access to critical data is restricted.

For hyper-redundant robots, Contribution 4 provides a methodical manual for kinematic modeling. The evolution of hyper-redundant robot design and control is aided by this contribution's assistance in modeling these complex robots.

A Robust distance and orientation synchronization for differential-drive mobile robots is a topic explored in Contribution 5. As a result, the control accuracy and performance of mobile robotic systems may be greatly enhanced by using the proposed active disturbance rejection control technique.

To mitigate the effects of inaccurate distance estimations, the authors of Contribution 6 describe a cooperative control method for vehicle platoons. Their method improves the stability and dependability of platoon control systems, leading to more secure and productive vehicle traffic flow.

In Contribution 7 the authors discuss issues with tracked mobile robots and terrain navigation. To improve trajectory tracking and overall performance in difficult terrains, their kinematic technique incorporates speed adjustment based on pointwise terrain gradients.

In Contribution 8 2D Lidar technology is applied to the problem of improving autonomous navigation within buildings. This approach enhances the usefulness of autonomous mobile robots in confined locations by increasing the precision with which maps are constructed and routes are planned.

In their investigation into automation and construction, the authors of Contribution 9, as highlighted in references, place a significant emphasis on process control, monitoring, and diagnostics. Their focus revolves around the application of these principles in the context of concrete 3D printing. The study's findings shed light on the effective integration of mathematical techniques to improve robotic applications within the construction sector.

Contribution 10 deals with the lack of data in computer vision and offers a context replacement technique. The method illustrated in the contribution makes it possible for robotic systems to outsource calculations and control safely by making use of homomorphic encryption. This work offers crucial guidance for protecting robot control systems, especially in low-information environments.

A new method for regulating four-bar mechanisms with varied input velocities is presented in Contribution 11. The authors' approach is dynamic, allowing for fine-grained control over the movements that are produced. This development expands robotic systems' applicability and thereby increases their adaptability. All these aspects are very well analyzed.

The authors of Contribution 12 discuss how robotic telescopes can more reliably identify the sky. The quality of astronomical observations is enhanced as a result of their use of mathematical approaches to improve the navigation process. This work makes a major improvement to astronomical research by enhancing the automated telescopes' ability to navigate their surroundings.

The problem of centralized control of coverage in multi-quadrotor systems is investigated in Contribution 13. The authors provide a strategy for achieving finite-time convergence by adapting the goal function to meet consensus requirements. With this novel method, multi-quadrotor systems may function in a wide variety of network architectures without sacrificing economy or performance.

3. Conclusions

In summary, the Special Issue "Mathematics in Robot Control for Theoretical and Applied Problems" has presented a wide variety of research papers that together highlight the central importance of mathematics in defining the subject of robot control. Multi-quadrotor systems, telescopes, manipulators, computer vision, navigation, and building are only some of the areas covered in these publications. These works show how mathematics may be used to solve difficult problems and propel progress in our theoretical knowledge and practical use of robotic systems.

Conflicts of Interest: The authors declare no conflicts of interest.

List of Contributions

1. Palomino-Resendiz, S.I.; Lozada-Castillo, N.B.; Flores-Hernández, D.A.; Gutiérrez-Frías, O.O.; Luviano-Juárez, A. Adaptive Active Disturbance Rejection Control of Solar Tracking Systems with Partially Known Model. *Mathematics* **2021**, *9*, 2871. https://doi.org/10.3390/math9222871.
2. Tsymbal, O.; Mercorelli, P.; Sergiyenko, O. Predicate-Based Model of Problem-Solving for Robotic Actions Planning. *Mathematics* **2021**, *9*, 3044. https://doi.org/10.3390/math9233044.
3. Babenko, M.; Tchernykh, A.; Pulido-Gaytan, B.; Avetisyan, A.; Nesmachnow, S.; Wang, X.; Granelli, F. Towards the Sign Function Best Approximation for Secure Outsourced Computations and Control. *Mathematics* **2022**, *10*, 2006. https://doi.org/10.3390/math10122006.
4. Cerrillo, D.; Barrientos, A.; Cerro, J.D. Kinematic Modelling for Hyper-Redundant Robots—A Structured Guide. *Mathematics* **2022**, *10*, 2891. https://doi.org/10.3390/math10162891.
5. Ramírez-Neria, M.; González-Sierra, J.; Luviano-Juárez, A.; Lozada-Castillo, N.; Madonski, R. Active Disturbance Rejection Strategy for Distance and Formation Angle Decentralized Control in Differential-Drive Mobile Robots. *Mathematics* **2022**, *10*, 3865. https://doi.org/10.3390/math10203865.
6. Escobar, C.; Vargas, F.J.; Peters, A.A.; Carvajal, G. A Cooperative Control Algorithm for Line and Predecessor Following Platoons Subject to Unreliable Distance Measurements. *Mathematics* **2023**, *11*, 801. https://doi.org/10.3390/math11040801.
7. Jeon, H.; Lee, D. Explicit Identification of Pointwise Terrain Gradients for Speed Compensation of Four Driving Tracks in Passively Articulated Tracked Mobile Robot. *Mathematics* **2023**, *11*, 905. https://doi.org/10.3390/math11040905.
8. Sun, J.; Zhao, J.; Hu, X.; Gao, H.; Yu, J. Autonomous Navigation System of Indoor Mobile Robots Using 2D Lidar. *Mathematics* **2023**, *11*, 1455. https://doi.org/10.3390/math11061455.
9. Quah, T.K.N.; Tay, Y.W.D.; Lim, J.H.; Tan, M.J.; Wong, T.N.; Li, K.H.H. Concrete 3D Printing: Process Parameters for Process Control, Monitoring and Diagnosis in Automation and Construction. *Mathematics* **2023**, *11*, 1499. https://doi.org/10.3390/math11061499.
10. Nesteruk, S.; Zherebtsov, I.; Illarionova, S.; Shadrin, D.; Somov, A.; Bezzateev, S.V.; Yelina, T.; Denisenko, V.; Oseledets, I. CISA: Context Substitution for Image Semantics Augmentation. *Mathematics* **2023**, *11*, 1818. https://doi.org/10.3390/math11081818.
11. Peón-Escalante, R.; Flota-Bañuelos, M.; Quintal-Palomo, R.; Ricalde, L.J.; Peñuñuri, F.; Jiménez, B.C.; Viñas, J.A. Neural Network Based Control of Four-Bar Mechanism with Variable Input Velocity. *Mathematics* **2023**, *11*, 2148. https://doi.org/10.3390/math11092148.
12. Savanevych, V.; Khlamov, S.; Briukhovetskyi, O.; Trunova, T.; Tabakova, I. Mathematical Methods for an Accurate Navigation of the Robotic Telescopes. *Mathematics* **2023**, *11*, 2246. https://doi.org/10.3390/math11102246.
13. Tnunay, H.; Moussa, K.; Hably, A.; Marchand, N. Distributed Finite-Time Coverage Control of Multi-Quadrotor Systems with Switching Topology. *Mathematics* **2023**, *11*, 2621. https://doi.org/10.3390/math11122621.

Disclaimer/Publisher's Note: The statements, opinions and data contained in all publications are solely those of the individual author(s) and contributor(s) and not of MDPI and/or the editor(s). MDPI and/or the editor(s) disclaim responsibility for any injury to people or property resulting from any ideas, methods, instructions or products referred to in the content.

Article

Adaptive Active Disturbance Rejection Control of Solar Tracking Systems with Partially Known Model

Sergio Isai Palomino-Resendiz [1,†], Norma Beatriz Lozada-Castillo [2,*,†], Diego Alonso Flores-Hernández [2,†], Oscar Octavio Gutiérrez-Frías [2,†] and Alberto Luviano-Juárez [2,†]

1. Instituto Politécnico Nacional ESIME ZACATENCO, Ciudad de México 07738, Mexico; spalominor@ipn.mx
2. Instituto Politécnico Nacional UPIITA, Ciudad de México 07340, Mexico; dfloreshe@ipn.mx (D.A.F.-H.); ogutierrezf@ipn.mx (O.O.G.-F.); aluvianoj@ipn.mx (A.L.-J.)
* Correspondence: nlozadac@ipn.mx; Tel.: +52-5729-6000 (ext. 56918)
† These authors contributed equally to this work.

Abstract: In this article, the trajectory tracking control of a solar tracking system is tackled by means of an adaptive active disturbance rejection control scheme. The state and disturbance estimation system is based on the combination of a time varying identification system and an adaptive observer. The stability and robustness of the controller is mathematically tested by means of the second method of Lyapunov, and its effectiveness is experimentally tested in a robotic test bed, achieving both lower energy consumption and better tracking results with respect to a PID-based controller.

Keywords: trajectory tracking control; solar tracking systems; adaptive control; active disturbance rejection

Citation: Palomino-Resendiz, S.I.; Lozada-Castillo, N.B.; Flores-Hernández, D.A.; Gutiérrez-Frías, O.O.; Luviano-Juárez, A. Adaptive Active Disturbance Rejection Control of Solar Tracking Systems with Partially Known Model. *Mathematics* **2021**, *9*, 2871. https://doi.org/10.3390/math9222871

Academic Editors: Paolo Mercorelli, Oleg Sergiyenko and Oleksandr Tsymbal

Received: 17 October 2021
Accepted: 10 November 2021
Published: 11 November 2021

Publisher's Note: MDPI stays neutral with regard to jurisdictional claims in published maps and institutional affiliations.

Copyright: © 2021 by the authors. Licensee MDPI, Basel, Switzerland. This article is an open access article distributed under the terms and conditions of the Creative Commons Attribution (CC BY) license (https://creativecommons.org/licenses/by/4.0/).

1. Introduction

The tendency of using alternative energy sources has led to the solution of problems concerning a wide variety of collecting technologies, storage and management systems. In the case of solar energy, the increased efficiency of the collected energy has a close relation with the capacity to manipulate the collecting device (photovoltaic module, concentrating lens, etc.) such that the light incidence is normal to a specific area of interest (tilt angle control). The last aspect is especially important in Fresnel-lens-based concentration systems [1–3].

The aim to increase the benefits of energy collecting systems has led to the development of solar trackers [4,5], the efficiency of which can be improved through the use of optimal design technologies [6–9] and concurrent engineering tools [10] as well as highly accurate positioning control systems such as solar sensors [11–15].

The accuracy and energy consumption in the positioning policy are considered to be among the main aspects of the performance of a solar tracker. Both problems are directly related to the nature of the mechanism of the tracker, which can have uncertain dynamics or nonlinearities, and the operation may be affected by external disturbance elements such as wind disturbances, which can produce tracking errors, or high energy compensation actions reducing the energetic efficiency of the controller. Addressing both features concurrently demands robustness and an energy management adaptation.

Several control approaches are reported in the literature, and some comprehensive studies and reviews provide further information and specific features regarding existing control studies and implementations [16–19], in which the application may lead to specific precision demands (see [20]). Among recent studies, in [21], a comprehensive practical classification of active solar tracking systems is presented, focusing on the importance of the control law and the sensing technology used to achieve appropriate results in solar concentration tasks. In this sense, proportional integral derivative-based control (PID) is the most popular closed-loop strategy in active solar tracking systems (see [22,23]). This scheme is suitable for solar trackers that include a gear train transmission with a high gear ratio [24]. The strategy has a wide variety of tuning strategies, including optimal gain selection, that make this scheme the natural choice for practitioners [25].

Due to the high-gain nature of PID control, diverse tuning schemes to avoid overshooting effects are used. On one hand, some schemes based on set points or the internal model control principle have been developed [26,27]. Although these approaches are a precise alternative, some tests and several criteria are necessary to obtain the best results with the approach. In contrast, some adaptive variations of PID have been developed to ease the drawbacks of high gain by means of time-varying gain dynamics [28–31]. In [32], an adaptive gain PID controller is implemented for dual-axis sun tracker applications. The gains are normalized in terms of the tracking error, improving upon the classic PID control. However, most of the reported schemes lack time derivative measurements, which may affect the final result by using computationally costly platforms (for instance, matlab) or dirty derivative-based computation with high computational and energetic costs and possible measurement noise problems. Moreover, low gear ratio transmissions or the possible presence of nonlinearities in the mechanism or the actuator motivate robust adaptive strategies that deal with the original multivariable nonlinear tracker model.

Other control strategies include model predictive control [33,34], sliding mode control [35,36] and neural and fuzzy control [37–40]. Most of these schemes solve one of the aforementioned problems effectively, while the other important aspects are partially achieved due to the fact that optimizing strategies usually need exact information of the system and they usually work for linear models; on the other hand, robust strategies usually demand high energetic costs. This motivates the development of a control scheme that can strike a balance between robustness and adaptivity.

Active disturbance rejection control (ADRC) [41–46] represents a control paradigm in which the system can be simplified such that the main external disturbances and unknown dynamics are lumped into a generalized disturbance input to be estimated and further cancelled. This scheme provides some of the advantages of classic PID control while enhancing the performance by means of the use of extended state observers [47]. The possibility of estimating the generalized disturbance simplifies the control actions, obtaining accurate results in trajectory tracking tasks. One of the most popular approaches to active disturbance rejection is linear active disturbance rejection (LADRC) [48], which consists of the use of an extended state observer of the Luenberger type. This scheme is highly effective for the estimation of a large class of additive disturbances, and the high-gain nature of the strategy results in an easy-to-tune procedure. The high-gain nature of classic LADRC may be sensitive to noises and can increase the energy consumption in the control applications, and the compromise between robustness and low energy consumption can be improved by proposing alternative schemes that keep the estimation advantages of LADRC with some restrictions in the high-gain nature. To achieve robustness and low energy consumption, adaptive designs for the ADRC [49,50] provide accurate tracking, robustness and adaptivity, which make them suitable for solar tracking applications.

In this article, an adaptive active disturbance rejection control design is proposed to solve the problem of the trajectory tracking system in a two-axis solar tracking system. The proposed observer is based on the combination of a time-varying identification system and an adaptive observer. This combination is used for online generalized disturbance estimation, which is used in the control loop. The main contributions are listed as follows:

1. In contrast with the disturbance estimation approach proposed in [49], in this article, the disturbance is estimated in terms of both states and an additional constant term used to compensate possible offset errors and external components that are independent of the states.
2. The stability and robustness of the controller is mathematically tested by means of the second method of Lyapunov, and its effectiveness is experimentally tested in a robotic test bed.

3. Some numerical and experimental tests show that the proposed controller demands a low energy consumption, in contrast to a classic ADRC scheme, while keeping appropriate estimation and tracking results for the solar tracking application.

The remainder of the article is given as follows. Section 2 presents the class of systems and the control problem. Section 3 provides the adaptive observer design and the stability test. Then, Section 4 presents the experimental results in the tracking of a numerically generated solar trajectory. Finally, Section 5 provides some concluding remarks and a general discussion of the contribution.

2. Controller Design

Consider the model which describes a class of open kinematic chain robotic manipulators:

$$D(q)\ddot{q} + C(q,\dot{q})\dot{q} + g(q) = u + \eta(t) \quad (1)$$

where $D(q) \in \mathbb{R}^{n \times n}$ is the inertia matrix (positive definite), $C(q,\dot{q}) \in \mathbb{R}^{n \times n}$ is the coriolis matrix, $g(q) \in \mathbb{R}^n$ is the gravity vector, $u \in \mathbb{R}^n$ denotes the control input vector, and $\eta(t) \in \mathbb{R}^n$ denotes a vector of bounded external disturbances of unknown nature.

The last model can be represented as follows:

$$\begin{aligned} \dot{x}_a &= x_b \\ \dot{x}_b &= f(x) + G(x_a)u + \eta(t) \end{aligned} \quad (2)$$

where $x_a(t) := q(t)$, $x_b(t) := \dot{q}(t)$, $x \in \mathbb{R}^{2n}$, $x = [x_a^\top \ x_b^\top]^\top$ is the state vector, $G(x_a) := D(q)^{-1}$, which is always well defined from the positive definiteness condition on $D(q)$.

A direct consequence of the inertia matrix bounds property is the following inequality:

$$0 < g^- \leq \|G(\cdot)\| \leq g^+, g^-, g^+ \in \mathbb{R}^+ \quad (3)$$

Assuming a lack of knowledge of the terms f and η, both terms can be lumped into a generalized disturbance input $\xi(x,t) := f(x) + \eta(t)$. Then, system (2) can be rewritten as

$$\begin{aligned} \dot{x}(t) &= Ax(t) + B[G(x_a)u(t) + \xi(x,t)] \\ y(t) &= Cx(t) \end{aligned} \quad (4)$$

where $y \in \mathbb{R}^{n \times 1}$, $y = x_a$ denotes the measurable output. $A \in \mathbb{R}^{2n \times 2n}$, $B \in \mathbb{R}^{2n \times n}$, $C \in \mathbb{R}^{n \times 2n}$ with values given by

$$A = \begin{bmatrix} 0_{n \times n} & I_{n \times n} \\ 0_{n \times n} & 0_{n \times n} \end{bmatrix}, B = \begin{bmatrix} 0_{n \times n} \\ I_{n \times n} \end{bmatrix}, C := \begin{bmatrix} I_{n \times n} & 0_{n \times n} \end{bmatrix} \quad (5)$$

Disturbance approximation: In this article, the generalized disturbance input is proposed to be approximated by the time varying combination of the system states and an additionally constant term (to incorporate arising offset contributions):

$$\begin{aligned} \xi(x,t) &= \Lambda_1(t)x(t) + \Lambda_2(t) + \tilde{\xi}(x,t) \\ &= \Lambda(t)X(t) + \tilde{\xi}(x,t) \end{aligned} \quad (6)$$

where $\Lambda(t) \in \mathbb{R}^{n \times 2n+1}$ is the time varying approximation matrix, $\Lambda(t) = [\Lambda_1(t) \ \Lambda_2(t)]$, with $\Lambda_1(t) \in \mathbb{R}^{n \times 2n}$ denoting the approximation based on the state vector and $\Lambda_2(t) \in \mathbb{R}^{n \times 1}$ representing the offset adjustment. The vector $X \in \mathbb{R}^{2n+1 \times 1}$ is defined as $X := [x^\top \ 1]^\top$, and $\tilde{\xi} \in \mathbb{R}^n$ denotes the approximation error.

In this article, the approximation error is proposed to be minimized through a time window least squares criterion (see [49] for the single input-single output unbiased case).

3. Observer Design

The adaptive observer for the system (4) is proposed as

$$\dot{\hat{x}} = \hat{A}(t)\hat{x}(t) + B[\hat{\Lambda}_2(t) + G(x_a)u] + L(t)\varepsilon(t)$$
$$\varepsilon(t) = C(x(t) - \hat{x}(t))$$
$$\hat{A}(t) = \begin{bmatrix} 0_{n\times n} & I_{n\times n} \\ & \hat{\Lambda}_1(t) \end{bmatrix} \quad (7)$$

where $G(x_a)$ is used instead of $G(\hat{x}_a)$ since x_a is a measurable state. The term $\hat{x} \in \mathbb{R}^{2n}$ denotes the estimate of x, the matrix $C \in \mathbb{R}^{n\times 2n}$ maps the state vector to the measurable states x_a, $\varepsilon(t) \in \mathbb{R}^n$ denotes the injection error, and $L(t) \in \mathbb{R}^{2n\times n}$ is the time varying injection gain subject to an adaptation law of the form:

$$\dot{L}(t) = l_1 S(t)(L^* - L(t)) \quad (8)$$

where $l_1 \in \mathbb{R}^+$ is a positive constant, and $S(t) \in \mathbb{R}^{2n\times 2n}$, $P(t) \in \mathbb{R}^{2n\times 2n}$ positive definite time varying matrices which satisfy the following Riccati equations:

$$A_o^\mathsf{T}(t)P(t) + P(t)A_o(t) + \dot{P}(t) + P(t)N_4 P(t) + C^\mathsf{T} L^\mathsf{T}(t)N_2 L(t)C + Q_1 = 0 \quad (9)$$
$$A_c^\mathsf{T} S(t) + S(t)A_c + \dot{S}(t) + S(t)N_2^{-1}S(t) + A^\mathsf{T} N_1 A + Q_2 = 0 \quad (10)$$

where $A_c = A - BK^\mathsf{T}$, $A_o := A - L(t)C$, and $N_2 \in \mathbb{R}^{2n\times 2n}$, $N_2 = N_2^\mathsf{T} > 0$. The term L^* is a user defined parameter such that the matrix $A - L^*C$ is Hurwitz.

Control Law

Let $x^* \in \mathbb{R}^{2n}$ be a smooth reference trajectory for the state vector x. From the nominal dynamics (4) without the presence of disturbances, the feedforward input u^* can be defined such that the following relation is satisfied:

$$\dot{x}^*(t) = Ax^*(t) + BG(x_a)u^*(t) \quad (11)$$

which leads to

$$u^*(t) = G(x_a)^{-1}\dot{x}_b^* \quad (12)$$

The output-based control is proposed as

$$u(t) = u^*(t) - G(x_a)^{-1}[K^\mathsf{T}(\hat{x} - x^*) + \hat{\Lambda}(t)\hat{X}(t)] \quad (13)$$

where $K \in \mathbb{R}^{n\times 2n}$ is the control gain matrix and the last term of the control law stands for the estimate of the generalized disturbance input $\xi(x,t)$; that is, $\hat{\xi}(x,t) = \hat{\Lambda}(t)\hat{X}(t)$. Figure 1 shows a block diagram of the proposed control structure.

The following result states the convergence of the tracking and estimation errors, in an ultimate bound sense, of the output based adaptive control law:

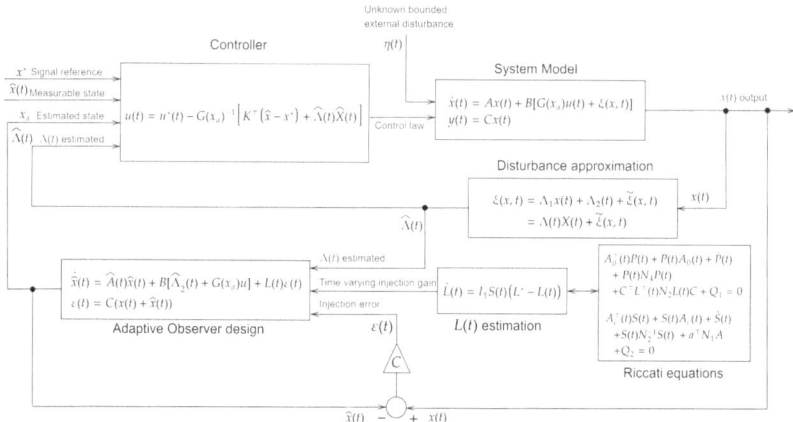

Figure 1. Schematic of the proposed adaptive active disturbance rejection controller.

Theorem 1. *Consider the class of partially known robotic systems (4), where the lumped disturbance input $\xi(x,t)$ satisfies the condition of being absolutely bounded given a reference trajectory $x^*(t)$ and an output feedback control (13) based on a linear time varying identification of the disturbance input, given by (16), and an adaptive observer (7), such that the control gain K forces the matrix $A - BK^\mathsf{T}$ to be Hurwitz. If there exist positive definite matrices $P(t), S(t) N_1, N_2, N_4, Q_1, Q_2 \in \mathbb{R}^{2n \times 2n}$, such that the time varying Riccati Equations (9) and (10) have positive definitive solutions, the state estimation and tracking errors $\Delta(t)$ and $\delta(t)$ are uniformly ultimate bounded.*

Proof. The estimation error obeys the following dynamics:

$$\dot{\Delta}(t) = (A - L(t)C)\Delta(t) + A\hat{x}(t) + B\tilde{\xi}(x,t)$$
$$= (A - L(t)C)\Delta(t) + A\delta(t) + Ax^*(t) + B\tilde{\xi}(x,t) \qquad (14)$$

Let define the difference between the estimate state $\hat{x}$ and the desired trajectory x^* as $\delta(t)$. The dynamics of $\delta(t)$ are computed as

$$\dot{\delta}(t) = (A - BK^\mathsf{T})\delta(t) + L(t)C\Delta(t) \qquad (15)$$

From the observer dynamics (7) and the disturbance approximation proposal (6), the time varying approximation matrix $\hat{\Lambda}(t)$ is proposed as the solution of the following optimization problem:

$$\hat{\Lambda}^*(t) = \arg\min_{\hat{\Lambda} \in \mathbb{R}^{n \times (2n+1)}} \left[\int_{t-\nu}^{t} \omega(\tau) - \hat{\Lambda}(\tau) X(\tau) d\tau \right]^2 \qquad (16)$$

where

$$\omega(t) = B^\mathsf{T}[\hat{x}(t) - \hat{x}(t-\nu)] - \left[\int_{t-\nu}^{t} G(x_a)u(\tau) + B^\mathsf{T} L(\tau)\varepsilon(\tau) d\tau \right] \qquad (17)$$

whose solution leads to the following dynamics [51]:

$$\hat{\Lambda}^\mathsf{T}(t) = [\int_{t-\nu}^{t} \hat{X}(\tau)\hat{X}^\mathsf{T}(\tau) d\tau]^{-1} [\int_{t-\nu}^{t} \omega(\tau)\hat{X}^\mathsf{T}(\tau) d\tau]^\mathsf{T} \qquad (18)$$

Now, let us propose the following quadratic Lyapunov candidate function:

$$V(\Delta, \delta, L, \rho, K^\mathsf{T}, t) = \Delta^\mathsf{T} P(t)\Delta + \delta^\mathsf{T} S(t)\delta + \mathrm{tr}\left\{ \frac{1}{2} l_1^{-1} \tilde{L}^\mathsf{T}(t) \tilde{L}(t) \right\} + \mathrm{tr}\left\{ \frac{1}{2} \rho^\mathsf{T}(t) \rho(t) \right\} \qquad (19)$$

where

$$\rho(t) = \int_0^t \left[\int_{\tau-\nu}^{\tau} \hat{x}(\sigma)\omega(\sigma) - \int_{\tau-\nu}^{\tau} \hat{x}(\sigma)\hat{x}^\mathsf{T}(\sigma)d\sigma \hat{\Lambda}(\tau) \right] d\tau \qquad (20)$$

$$\tilde{L}(t) = L^* - L(t) \qquad (21)$$

The time derivative of the Lyapunov candidate function (19) is given by

$$\dot{V}(\Delta, \delta, L, \rho, K^\mathsf{T}, t) = \Delta^\mathsf{T}\left[A_o^\mathsf{T}(t)P(t) + P(t)A_o(t) + \dot{P}(t)\right]\Delta + \mathrm{tr}\{\tilde{L}^\mathsf{T}(t)\dot{\tilde{L}}(t)\} +$$
$$+ \delta^\mathsf{T}\left[A_c^\mathsf{T}S(t) + S(t)A_c + \dot{S}(t)\right]\delta + \delta^\mathsf{T}A^\mathsf{T}P(t)\Delta + \Delta^\mathsf{T}P(t)A\delta + \Delta^\mathsf{T}C^\mathsf{T}L^\mathsf{T}(t)S(t)\delta$$
$$+ \delta^\mathsf{T}S^\mathsf{T}(t)L(t)C\Delta + (Ax^* + B\tilde{\varepsilon})^\mathsf{T}P(t)\Delta + \Delta^\mathsf{T}P(t)(Ax^* + B\tilde{\varepsilon}) + \mathrm{tr}\{\rho^\mathsf{T}(t)\dot{\rho}(t)\} \qquad (22)$$

From the lambda inequality [52], there exists a set of symmetric positive definite matrices $N_i \in \mathbb{R}^{2n \times 2n}, i = 1, 2, 3$, such that

$$\delta^\mathsf{T}A^\mathsf{T}P(t)\Delta + \Delta^\mathsf{T}P(t)A\delta \leq \delta^\mathsf{T}A^\mathsf{T}N_1 A\delta +$$
$$+ \Delta^\mathsf{T}P(t)N_1^{-1}P(t)\Delta \qquad (23)$$
$$\Delta^\mathsf{T}C^\mathsf{T}L^\mathsf{T}(t)S(t)\delta + \delta^\mathsf{T}S(t)L(t)C\Delta \leq \Delta^\mathsf{T}C^\mathsf{T}L^\mathsf{T}(t)N_2 L(t)C\Delta +$$
$$+ \delta^\mathsf{T}S(t)N_2^{-1}S(t)\delta \qquad (24)$$
$$(Ax^* + B\tilde{\varepsilon})^\mathsf{T}P(t)\Delta + \Delta^\mathsf{T}P(t)(Ax^* + B\tilde{\varepsilon}) \leq (Ax^* + B\tilde{\varepsilon})^\mathsf{T}N_3(Ax^* + B\tilde{\varepsilon}) +$$
$$+ \Delta^\mathsf{T}P(t)N_3^{-1}P(t)\Delta \qquad (25)$$

Using (23)–(25) in (22),

$$\dot{V}(\Delta, \delta, L, \rho, K^\mathsf{T}, t) = \Delta^\mathsf{T}\left[A_o^\mathsf{T}(t)P(t) + P(t)A_o(t) + \dot{P}(t) + P(t)N_1^{-1}P(t) + \right.$$
$$\left. + C^\mathsf{T}L^\mathsf{T}(t)N_2 L(t)C + P(t)N_3^{-1}P(t)\right]\Delta +$$
$$+ \delta^\mathsf{T}\left[A_c^\mathsf{T}S(t) + S(t)A_c + \dot{S}(t) + A^\mathsf{T}N_1 A + S(t)N_2^{-1}S(t)\right]\delta +$$
$$+ (Ax^* + B\tilde{\varepsilon})^\mathsf{T}N_3(Ax^* + B\tilde{\varepsilon}) + \mathrm{tr}\{\rho^\mathsf{T}(t)\dot{\rho}(t)\} + \mathrm{tr}\left\{\tilde{L}^\mathsf{T}(t)\dot{\tilde{L}}(t)\right\} \qquad (26)$$

Since N_1, N_2 are positive definite, the terms $A^\mathsf{T}N_1 A$, $C^\mathsf{T}L^\mathsf{T}(t)N_2 L(t)C$ are positive definite (see Section 7.1 of [53]). Then, to complete the time varying Riccati equations while ensuring the negative definiteness condition of the time derivative of V, let us add $\pm \Delta^\mathsf{T}(t)Q_1\Delta \pm \delta^\mathsf{T}Q_2\delta$, for symmetric positive definite matrices $Q_1, Q_2 \in \mathbb{R}^{2n \times 2n}$. Then, we obtain

$$\dot{V}(\Delta, \delta, L, \rho, K^\mathsf{T}, t) = \Delta^\mathsf{T}\left[A_o^\mathsf{T}(t)P(t) + P(t)A_o(t) + \dot{P}(t) + P(t)N_4 P(t) + \right.$$
$$\left. + C^\mathsf{T}L^\mathsf{T}(t)N_2 L(t)C + Q_1\right]\Delta + \delta^\mathsf{T}\left[A_c^\mathsf{T}S(t) + S(t)A_c + \dot{S}(t) + S(t)N_2^{-1}S(t) + \right.$$
$$\left. + A^\mathsf{T}N_1 A + Q_2\right]\delta + (Ax^* + B\tilde{\varepsilon})^\mathsf{T}N_3(Ax^* + B\tilde{\varepsilon}) + \mathrm{tr}\{\rho^\mathsf{T}(t)\dot{\rho}(t)\} +$$
$$+ \mathrm{tr}\left\{\tilde{L}^\mathsf{T}(t)\dot{\tilde{L}}(t)\right\} - \Delta^\mathsf{T}Q_1\Delta - \delta^\mathsf{T}Q_2\delta \qquad (27)$$

where $N_4 = N_1^{-1} + N_3^{-1}$. Using the dynamics (18), the following equality is obtained:

$$\int_{t-\nu}^{t} \hat{x}(\tau)\omega(\tau)d\tau - \int_{t-\nu}^{t} \hat{x}(\tau)\hat{x}^\mathsf{T}(\tau)d\tau \hat{\Lambda}(t) = 0 \qquad (28)$$

which implies that $\eta^\mathsf{T}(t)\dot{\eta}(t) = 0$ (see [49]). From (8),

$$\mathrm{tr}\left\{\tilde{L}^\mathsf{T}(t)\dot{\tilde{L}}(t)\right\} = -\mathrm{tr}\left\{\tilde{L}^\mathsf{T}(t)S(t)\tilde{L}(t)\right\} \tag{29}$$

Since $\tilde{L}^\mathsf{T}(t)S(t)\tilde{L}(t)$ is at least positive semidefinite (positive definite if $\tilde{L}(t)$ is full rank in columns), then (29) is negative or zero. Using (28) and (29) in (26), the following expression is obtained:

$$\begin{aligned}\dot{V}(\Delta,\delta,L,\rho,K^\mathsf{T},t) = \Delta^\mathsf{T}&\Big[A_o^\mathsf{T}(t)P(t) + P(t)A_o(t) + \dot{P}(t) + P(t)N_4P(t) + \\ &+ C^\mathsf{T}L^\mathsf{T}(t)N_2L(t)C + Q_1\Big]\Delta + \delta^\mathsf{T}\Big[A_c^\mathsf{T}S(t) + S(t)A_c + \dot{S}(t) + \\ &+ S(t)N_2^{-1}S(t) + A^\mathsf{T}N_1A + Q_2\Big]\delta + (Ax^* + B\tilde{\varepsilon})^\mathsf{T}N_3(Ax^* + B\tilde{\varepsilon}) - \\ &- \mathrm{tr}\left\{\tilde{L}^\mathsf{T}(t)S(t)\tilde{L}(t)\right\} - \Delta^\mathsf{T}Q_1\Delta - \delta^\mathsf{T}Q_2\delta\end{aligned} \tag{30}$$

Using the assumption of the positive definiteness of the solutions of the Equations (9) and (10),

$$\dot{V}(\Delta,\delta,L,\rho,K^\mathsf{T},t) = (Ax^* + B\tilde{\varepsilon})^\mathsf{T}N_3(Ax^* + B\tilde{\varepsilon}) - \mathrm{tr}\left\{\tilde{L}^\mathsf{T}(t)S(t)\tilde{L}(t)\right\} - \Delta^\mathsf{T}Q_1\Delta - \delta^\mathsf{T}Q_2\delta \tag{31}$$

Let define the vectors z and $\tilde{z}$ as

$$z := \begin{bmatrix}\Delta \\ \delta\end{bmatrix} \tag{32}$$

$$\tilde{z} := Ax^* + B\tilde{\varepsilon} \tag{33}$$

From the last definitions, (31) becomes

$$\dot{V}(z,L,K^\mathsf{T},t) = \tilde{z}^\mathsf{T}N_3\tilde{z} - \mathrm{tr}\left\{\tilde{L}^\mathsf{T}(t)S(t)\tilde{L}(t)\right\} - z^\mathsf{T}Q_3z \tag{34}$$

with

$$Q_3 := \begin{bmatrix}Q_1 & 0 \\ 0 & Q_2\end{bmatrix} \tag{35}$$

Using the Rayleigh inequality

$$\dot{V}(z,L,K^\mathsf{T},t) \leq -\lambda_{min}(Q_3)\|z\|^2 - \mathrm{tr}\left\{\tilde{L}^\mathsf{T}(t)S(t)\tilde{L}(t)\right\} + \lambda_{max}(N_3)\|\tilde{z}\|^2 \tag{36}$$

Let us introduce the auxiliary term $\theta \in (0,1)$. Rewriting (36),

$$\begin{aligned}\dot{V}(z,L,K^\mathsf{T},t) \leq &- (1-\theta)\lambda_{min}(Q_3)\|z\|^2 - \theta\lambda_{min}(Q_3)\|z\|^2 - \\ &- \mathrm{tr}\left\{\tilde{L}^\mathsf{T}(t)S(t)\tilde{L}(t)\right\} + \lambda_{max}(N_3)\|\tilde{z}\|^2\end{aligned} \tag{37}$$

Then,

$$\dot{V}(z,L,K^\mathsf{T},t) \leq -(1-\theta)\lambda_{min}(Q_3)\|z\|^2 - \mathrm{tr}\left\{\tilde{L}^\mathsf{T}(t)S(t)\tilde{L}(t)\right\} < 0;$$
$$\text{for all } \|z\|^2 \geq \frac{\lambda_{max}(N_3)\|\tilde{z}\|^2}{\theta\lambda_{min}(Q_3)}$$

From the last expression and using Definition 4.6 from [54], it is proven that the tracking and estimation errors are uniformly ultimately bounded. □

4. Case Study: A Two Degrees of Freedom Solar Tracker

Consider a two degrees of freedom solar tracking system in an azimuthal elevation configuration, the axis representation of which is given in Figure 2. The frames {0}, {1}, and {2} denote the inertia, the azimuth link, and the end effector frame, respectively. Variables m_i, $I_i = \text{diag}\{I_{xi}, I_{yi}, I_{zi}\}$ stand for the mass and Inertia tensor of the $i-th$ link (it is assumed to be diagonal since the links are assumed to besymmetric with respect to their center of mass). $\bar{g}$ denotes the gravity vector, l_{cmi} is the distance from the previous frame $(i-1)$ to the center of mass of the $i-th$ link, and l_i is the length of the $i-th$ link, respectively.

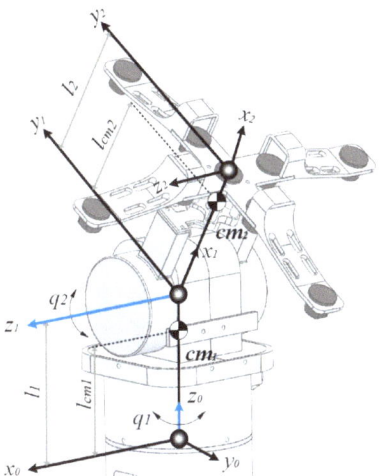

Figure 2. Schematic of the robotic system.

Using the Euler Lagrange procedure, the dynamic model of the system in the form (1) is given as follows [55]:

$$\begin{bmatrix} d_{11}(q_2) & 0 \\ 0 & d_{22} \end{bmatrix} \begin{bmatrix} \ddot{q}_1 \\ \ddot{q}_2 \end{bmatrix} + \begin{bmatrix} c_{11}(q_2,\dot{q}_2) & c_{12}(q_2,\dot{q}_1) \\ c_{21}(q_2,\dot{q}_1) & 0 \end{bmatrix} \begin{bmatrix} \dot{q}_1 \\ \dot{q}_2 \end{bmatrix} + \begin{bmatrix} 0 \\ g_2(q_2) \end{bmatrix} = \begin{bmatrix} u_1 \\ u_2 \end{bmatrix} \quad (38)$$

$$d_{11}(q_2) := \left(m_2 l_{cm2}^2 + I_{y2}\right)\cos^2(q_2) + I_{x2}\sin^2(q_2) + I_{y1}$$

$$d_{22} := m_2 l_{cm2}^2 + I_{z2}$$

$$c_{11}(q_2,\dot{q}_2) := \cos(q_2)\sin(q_2)\left(m_2 l_{cm2}^2 + I_{y2} - I_{x2}\right)\dot{q}_2$$

$$c_{12}(q_2,\dot{q}_1) := \left(I_{x2} - I_{y2} - m_2 l_{cm2}^2\right)\cos(q_2)\sin(q_2)\dot{q}_1$$

$$c_{21}(q_2,\dot{q}_1) := -c_{12}(q_2,\dot{q}_1)$$

$$g_2(q_2) := m_2 g_r l_{cm2}\cos(q_2)$$

where g_r stands for the gravity constant.

Let define the variables $x_a = \begin{bmatrix} x_{a1} & x_{a2} \end{bmatrix}^T := \begin{bmatrix} q_1 & q_2 \end{bmatrix}^T$, $x_b = \begin{bmatrix} x_{b1} & x_{b2} \end{bmatrix}^T := \begin{bmatrix} \dot{q}_1 & \dot{q}_2 \end{bmatrix}^T$. Then, the system (38) can be expressed as the class of systems (2) as follows:

$$\dot{x}_a = x_b \quad (39)$$
$$\dot{x}_b = f(x) + G(x_a)u \quad (40)$$

where

$$f(x) = \begin{bmatrix} -\dfrac{1}{d_{11}(x_{a2})}[c_{11}(x_{a2}, x_{b2})x_{b1} + c_{12}(x_{a2}, x_{b1})x_{b2}] \\ -\dfrac{1}{d_{22}}[c_{21}(x_{a2}, x_{b1})x_{b1} + g_2(x_{a2})] \end{bmatrix},$$

$$G(x_a) = \begin{bmatrix} \dfrac{1}{d_{11}(x_{a2})} & 0 \\ 0 & \dfrac{1}{d_{22}} \end{bmatrix}$$

4.1. System and Control Parameters

Since system (38) satisfies the class of systems to be controlled by the adaptive scheme (13), for this application, the following conditions were proposed:

- The parameters of the robotic system are provided in Table 1.

Table 1. Physical parameters of the robotic system.

Parameter	Value
l_1	100 mm
l_2	120 mm
l_{cm1}	61 mm
l_{cm2}	104 mm
m_1	0.908 Kg
m_2	0.290 Kg
I_{y1}	0.01 g·mm^2
I_{x2}	0.04 g·mm^2
I_{y2}	0.01 g·mm^2
I_{z2}	0.95 g·mm^2
g_r	9.81 Kg·m/s^2

- The reference trajectory is defined by the Cooper's algorithm [56], given by

$$\delta_r = 23.45° \sin\left(360\left(\dfrac{284 + n}{365}\right)\right)$$
$$q_2^* = \arcsin(\cos(\phi_r)\cos(\delta_r)\cos(\sigma_r)) + \sin(\phi_r)\sin(\delta_r))$$
$$q_1^* = \arccos\left(\dfrac{\sin(q_1^*)\sin(\phi_r) - \sin(\delta_r)}{\cos(q_2^*)\cos(\phi_r)}\right)$$

where $\sigma_r = (12 - t)(15°)$, δ_r is the solar declination, ϕ_r, L_{rc} are the longitude and latitude coordinates of the robot, n is the day number ($1 < n < 365$), and σ_r denotes the hour angle. In this case, $n = 93$, $\phi_r = -99.12°$, $L_{rc} = 19.12°$. The time interval, t, was set to be from 8 a.m. to 8 p.m.

- The controller gain parameters were set to be

$$l_1 = 0.1; \quad K^\mathsf{T} = \begin{bmatrix} 69 & 0 & 0.9 & 0 \\ 0 & 69 & 0 & 0.9 \end{bmatrix};$$

$$(L^*)^\mathsf{T} = \begin{bmatrix} 400 & 0 & 1.4 \times 10^4 & 0 \\ 0 & 400 & 0 & 4.5 \times 10^4 \end{bmatrix}$$

The choice of L^*, l_1, K^T was in the context of a set of a model matching with two decoupled, stable, second-order linear model references of the form $s^2 + 2\zeta_i \omega_{ni} s + \omega_{ni}^2$, $i = 1, 2$, $\zeta_i, \omega_{ni} > 0$. That is,

$$K^\mathsf{T} = \begin{bmatrix} 2\zeta_{1c}\omega_{n1c} & 0 & \omega_{n1c}^2 & 0 \\ 0 & 2\zeta_{2c}\omega_{n2c} & 0 & \omega_{n2c}^2 \end{bmatrix}$$

$$(L^*)^\mathsf{T} = l_1 \begin{bmatrix} 2\zeta_{1o}\omega_{n1o} & 0 & \omega_{n1o}^2 & 0 \\ 0 & 2\zeta_{2o}\omega_{n2o} & 0 & \omega_{n2o}^2 \end{bmatrix}$$

where $\zeta_{1c} = \zeta_{2c} = 36.3662$, $\omega_{n1c} = \omega_{n2c} = 0.9487$, $\zeta_{1c} = \zeta_{2c} = 0.5345$, $\omega_{n1c} = \omega_{n2c} = 37.4166$. This choice can be enhanced by optimization procedures [57], but this aspect is out of the scope of this work and will be considered in future research.

4.2. Numerical Results

To assess the behavior of the proposed controller, the trajectory tracking test was carried out in two conditions: without external disturbance and with a load on the end effector. Besides, in order to compare the results against reported active disturbance rejection controllers, two approaches were used for the test:

- A linear active disturbance rejection controller with an extended state observer was proposed [47];
- An adaptive active disturbance rejection control with disturbance approximation based on a linear state space combination (ASSC) [49].

Two different tests were carried out. The first test considered the robotic system without external disturbances, where the non-modeled dynamics were the only variable to compensate. The second test involved the application of a disturbance load of chaotic nature taken from the first state of a Chen system [58] with a normalization factor of 0.01. The observer injection gains of the LADRC were set such that the linear dominant dynamics were of the form $(s^2 + 2\zeta_{ai}\omega_{ani}s + \omega_{ani}^2)(s + p_{ai})$, $i = 1, 2$ with $\zeta_{a1} = \zeta_{a2}1$, $\omega_{an1} = \omega_{an2} = 14$, $p_{a1} = p_{a2} = 0.5$, and the control gains of the LADRC were set to match the linear stable dynamics of the form $s^2 + 2\zeta_{aci}\omega_{acni}s + \omega_{acni}^2$, with $\zeta_{ac} = \zeta_{ac2} = 0.08$, $\omega_{acn1} = \omega_{acn2} = 120$. In the case of the ASSC, the same parameters as the proposal in both the controller and observer were used. Figure 3 shows the trajectory tracking error of the proposals for the unperturbed case. Notice that the LADRC achieves a smaller error but the adaptive proposals keep a competitive error bound in the context of solar tracking applications. Figure 4 depicts the effect of the disturbance in the controllers; in this case, the LADRC is shown to be more robust than the other schemes. However, this action demands a larger energy consumption, as shown in Figures 5–8. The aggressive behavior of the control inputs in the LADRC, as shown in Figures 5 and 6, implies larger amplitude values, in contrast with the proposal. Figures 7 and 8 depict the energy consumption per actuator. Notice that the LADRC has around a five times larger consumption with respect to the proposal. The ASSC has a larger energy consumption (to a lesser extent) with respect to the proposal, which may be caused by the improvement in the generalized disturbance input. Finally, a cost function of the form

$$J(x, \hat{x}) = \int_0^t \|\Delta(\tau)\|^2 d\tau$$

is proposed to assess the quality of the state estimation by the observers. The behavior of the estimation error in the three cases denotes an ultimate bound behavior, which shows that the three strategies achieve good estimation results; in the case of the LADRC, it has the largest growing rate, which can be related to the high-gain nature, which has good results but some fluctuations that are accumulated in the integral term. Even so, the three schemes are, in general, good choices in the tracking task, and the proposal shows good estimation/tracking results and low energy consumption, and the LADRC shows the best robustness of the evaluated strategies. State estimation as Figure 9.

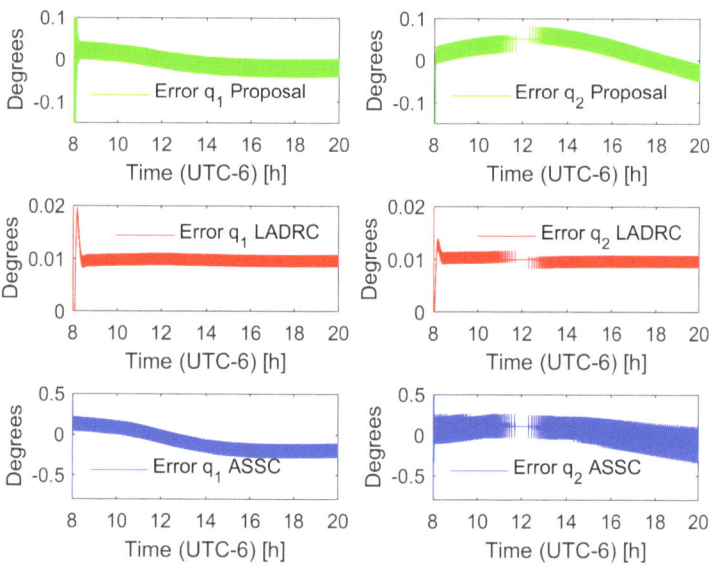

Figure 3. Tracking error behavior comparison (non-disturbed case) for azimuthal axis (q_1) and elevation axis (q_2). LADRC stands for linear active disturbance rejection control and ASSC for adaptive state space combination.

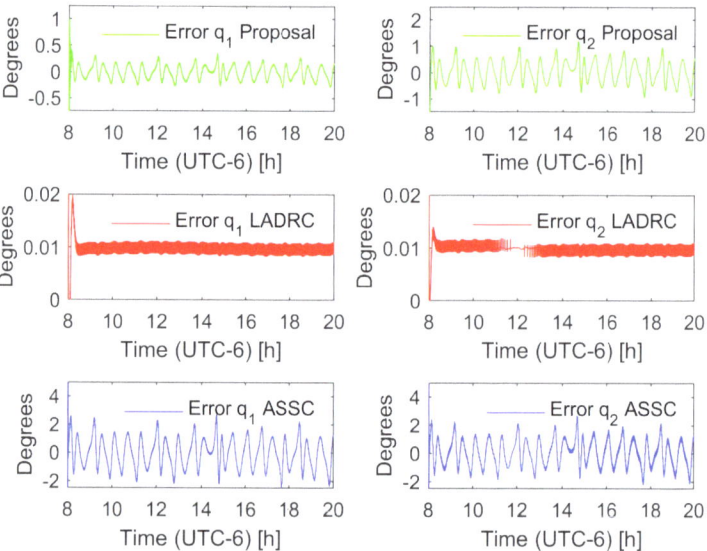

Figure 4. Tracking error behavior comparison (disturbed case) for azimuthal axis (q_1) and elevation axis (q_2). LADRC stands for linear active disturbance rejection control and ASSC for adaptive state space combination.

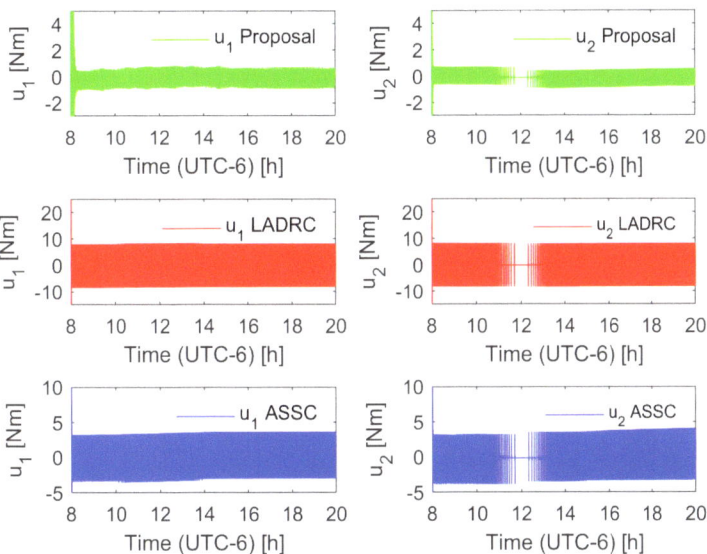

Figure 5. Control input behavior comparison (non-disturbed case).

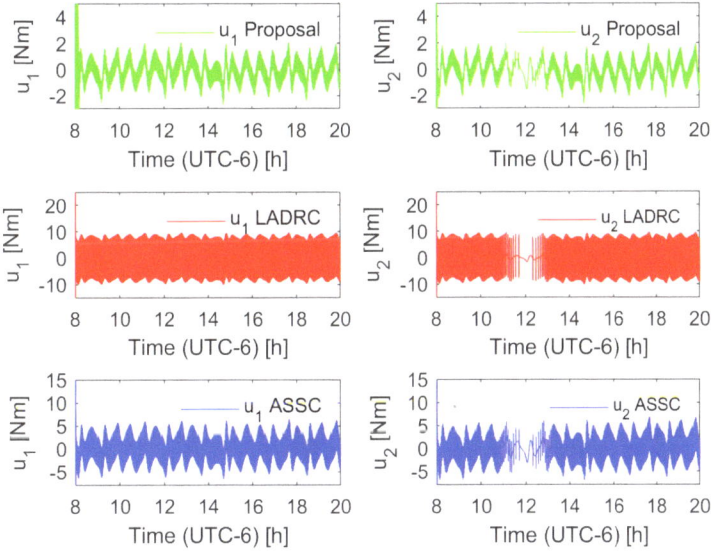

Figure 6. Control input behavior comparison (disturbed case).

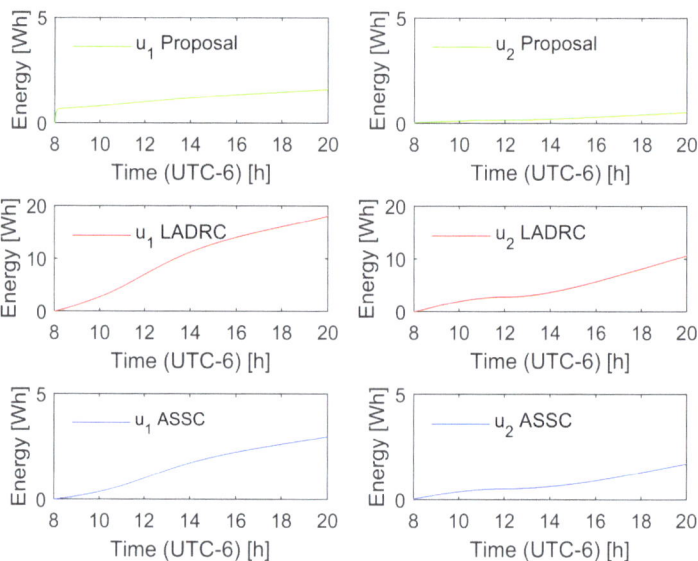

Figure 7. Energy consumption per actuator (unperturbed case).

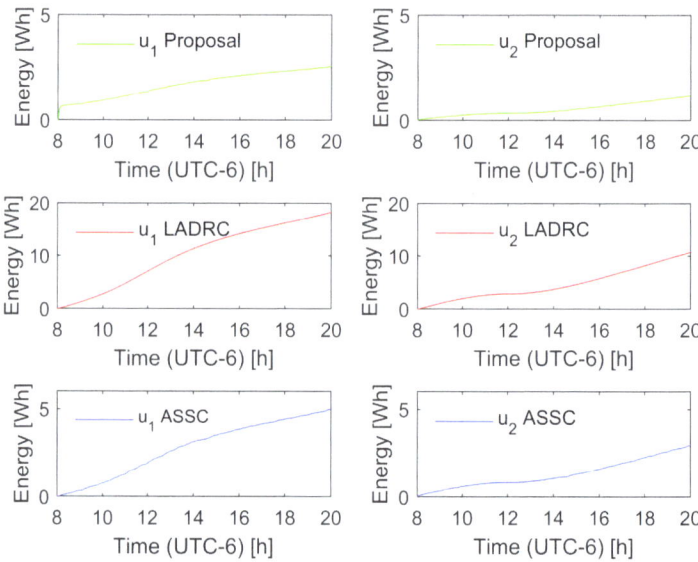

Figure 8. Energy consumption per actuator (perturbed case).

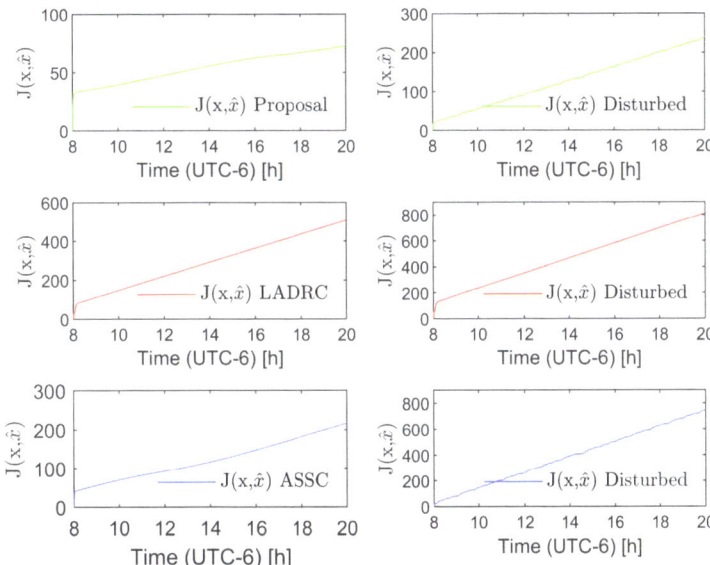

Figure 9. Performance index behavior of the state estimation. The graphics on the left side denote the case without disturbance and the graphics on the right side show the performance in presence of disturbance.

4.3. Experimental Results

Figure 10 shows the experimental robotic platform, whose parameters are listed in Table 1 and Figure 11 shows a general block diagram of the experimental platform including the user interface and the embedded system. The robotic system was actuated by means of two DC motors (Dongzen model 28JX20K139G/2838-1250S), with a nominal power of 2.9 W (12 V, 0.24 A), a geared transmission with a gear ratio of 1:139, and nominal torque of 9 Nm. The position sensors were incremental encoders with 1440 pulses per revolution. This information was sent to the microcontroller and decoded by means of two digital inputs implementing a gray code reading routine. The main control algorithm was programmed in a PC through the Waijung blockset simulink interface [59] and implemented through a STM32 Nucleo-F411RE microcontroller. The control law was implemented in the actuators by a PWM signal applied through a motor driver pololu model VNH5019. The numerical method used to implement the control was a fourth-order Runge–Kutta method with a sample time of 1 ms. In this case, the external disturbance $\eta(t)$ was due to the end effector consisting of a luminosity sensor with a nominal mass value of 0.12 Kg, which was not considered in the mathematical model, and the external wind load which presented variations from 0 to 12 Km/h according to the local weather report. Both signals were assumed as unknown external disturbances.

Figure 12 shows the tracking results for the azimuthal axis while Figure 13 shows the respective results for the elevation axis; the figures include the desired and actual trajectories and the error evolutions (with absolute bounds around 0.5 degrees). In order to assess the energy consumption with respect to the existing control approaches, a PID control was tuned such that it reached similar tracking results (see Figures 14 and 15 to observe the tracking behavior); then, the energy consumption of the controllers was measured to evaluate if there was an energetic consumption advantage of the proposed controller. To measure the controller energy during the tracking task, an HER-423 Wattmeter was used for the complete cycle, with the following results: for the adaptive controller, the azimuthal axis expenditure was 95.35 Wh, and for the elevation angle, the expenditure was 94.68 Wh. That is, the total control consumption was 189.46 Wh. In the same test, the energy consumption of the PID control for the azimuthal axis was 104.65 Wh, and for the elevation axis, the energy consumption of the control actions was 105.88 Wh, leading to a total energy consumption of 210.53 Wh. That is, the proposal achieves about a 10% energy saving with respect to a high-gain controller. Finally, Figures 16 and 17 show the time varying behavior of the observer gains associated with the azimuthal and elevation axes.

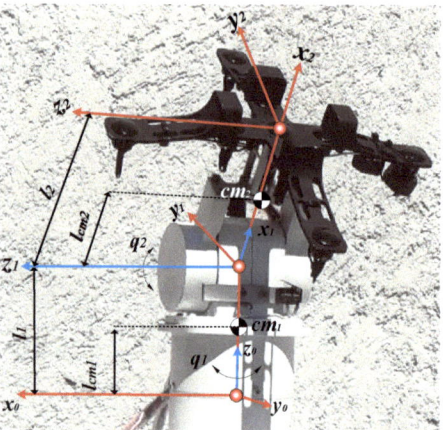

Figure 10. Experimental test bed of the solar tracking system.

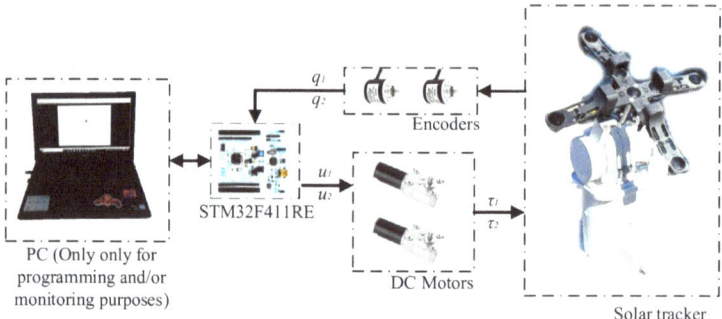

Figure 11. Block diagram of the experimental robotic system.

From the numerical and experimental results, the following advantages and drawbacks of the strategy can be stated:

- As advantages, the proposal provides low energy consumption, achieving acceptable results in trajectory tracking for solar tracking. It showed low energy consumption with respect to both classic PID control and robust control of the LADRC nature. The adaptation rule is suitable for an implementation in embedded systems, which ensures low energy consumption in contrast with other strategies that are tested in a PC-based controller. The adaptive nature of the system may be suitable for noisy measurements with respect to high-gain state estimators.
- As possible drawbacks, even when the proposed tuning process is of the same nature as the classic PID and LADRC controllers, the process is not as natural as the former controllers. The robustness of the scheme is lower than that shown by the LADRC, but in the case of solar trackers, the mechanism design can contribute to avoiding aggressive robust actions. Besides, even when the system was successfully implemented in an embedded processor, the computational cost of the scheme was larger in comparison to classic schemes.

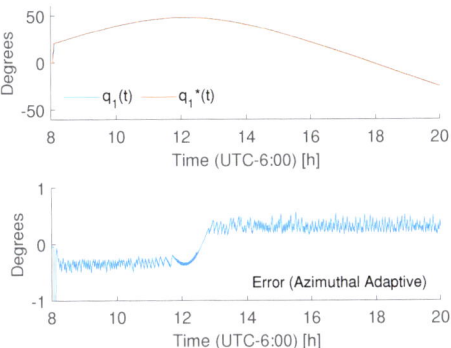

Figure 12. Tracking behavior for the azimuthal axis.

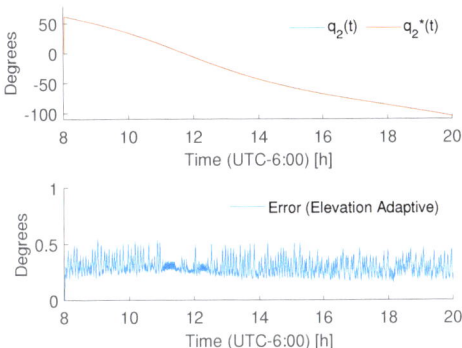

Figure 13. Tracking behavior for the elevation axis.

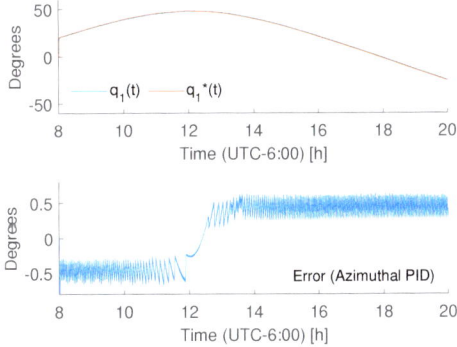

Figure 14. Tracking behavior for the azimuthal axis (PID control).

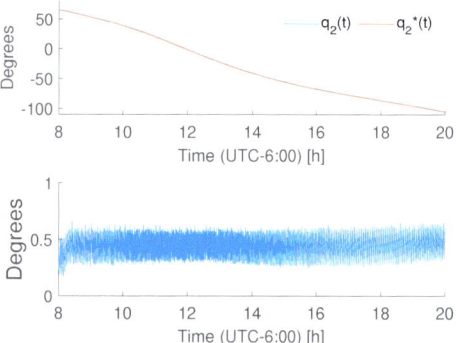

Figure 15. Tracking behavior for the elevation axis (PID control).

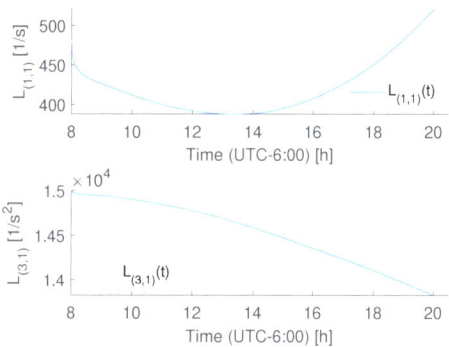

Figure 16. Observer gain behavior for the azimuthal axis injection.

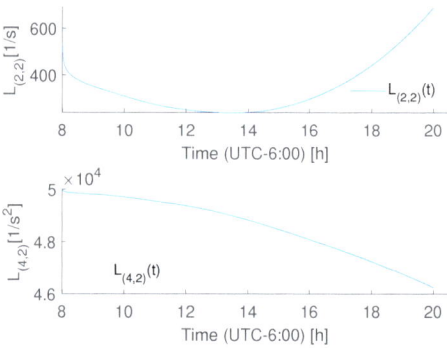

Figure 17. Observer gain behavior for the elevation axis injection.

5. Conclusions

The proposed controller is a robust, low energy consuming alternative for trajectory tracking control in solar tracking systems, but the general structure allows this approach to be implemented in a general family of robotic systems modeled by Euler Lagrange equations. Besides, this approach respects the multivariable nature of the system, which is suitable for low gear ratio transmissions. Future implementations are planned for other robotic structures for solar tracking systems such as parallel configurations. On the other hand, the proposed class of controllers can be used for mobile robots which need low energetic cost controls in order to improve their global autonomy, enhancing the operation time.

Author Contributions: Conceptualization, S.I.P.-R., N.B.L.-C., D.A.F.-H., O.O.G.-F. and A.L.-J.; Data curation, S.I.P.-R., N.B.L.-C., D.A.F.-H., O.O.G.-F. and A.L.-J.; Formal analysis, S.I.P.-R., N.B.L.-C., D.A.F.-H., O.O.G.-F. and A.L.-J.; Funding acquisition, S.I.P.-R., N.B.L.-C., D.A.F.-H., O.O.G.-F. and A.L.-J.; Investigation, S.I.P.-R., N.B.L.-C., D.A.F.-H., O.O.G.-F. and A.L.-J.; Methodology, S.I.P.-R., N.B.L.-C., D.A.F.-H., O.O.G.-F. and A.L.-J.; Project administration, S.I.P.-R., N.B.L.-C., D.A.F.-H., O.O.G.-F. and A.L.-J.; Resources, S.I.P.-R., N.B.L.-C., D.A.F.-H., O.O.G.-F. and A.L.-J.; Software, S.I.P.-R., N.B.L.-C., D.A.F.-H., O.O.G.-F. and A.L.-J.; Supervision, S.I.P.-R., N.B.L.-C., D.A.F.-H., O.O.G.-F. and A.L.-J.; Validation, S.I.P.-R., N.B.L.-C., D.A.F.-H., O.O.G.-F. and A.L.-J.; Visualization, S.I.P.-R., N.B.L.-C., D.A.F.-H., O.O.G.-F. and A.L.-J.; Writing—original draft, S.I.P.-R., N.B.L.-C., D.A.F.-H., O.O.G.-F. and A.L.-J.; Writing—review and editing, S.I.P.-R., N.B.L.-C., D.A.F.-H., O.O.G.-F. and A.L.-J. All authors have read and agreed to the published version of the manuscript.

Funding: This research was funded by Secretaría de Investigación y Posgrado IPN: 20210266, 20210259, 20210268, 20210269, 20212122; Secretaría de educación, ciencia, tecnología e innovación de la Ciudad de México SECTEI: SECTEI/249/2021.

Institutional Review Board Statement: Not applicable.

Informed Consent Statement: Not applicable.

Data Availability Statement: Not applicable.

Acknowledgments: This research was supported by the Secretaría de Investigación y Posgrado of the Instituto Politécnico Nacional (SIP-IPN) under the grants SIP-20210266, SIP-20210259, SIP-20210268, SIP-20210269 and SIP-20212122. In addition, the work team is grateful for the support provided to perform this research to the Secretaria de Educación, Ciencia, Tecnología e Innovación de la Ciudad de México with the project SECTEI/249/2021.

Conflicts of Interest: The authors declare no conflict of interest.

References

1. Ohkubo, T.; Yabe, T.; Yoshida, K.; Uchida, S.; Funatsu, T.; Bagheri, B.; Oishi, T.; Daito, K.; Ishioka, M.; Nakayama, Y.; et al. Solar-pumped 80 W laser irradiated by a Fresnel lens. *Opt. Lett.* **2009**, *34*, 175–177. [CrossRef] [PubMed]
2. Allil, R.C.; Manchego, A.; Allil, A.; Rodrigues, I.; Werneck, A.; Diaz, G.C.; Dino, F.T.; Reyes, Y.; Werneck, M. Solar tracker development based on a POF bundle and Fresnel lens applied to environment illumination and microalgae cultivation. *Sol. Energy* **2018**, *174*, 648–659. [CrossRef]
3. Hidayanti, F.; Rahmah, F.; Agusto, J. Design of Solar Tracker on Solar Panel with Fresnel Concentrator. *Int. J. Adv. Sci. Technol.* **2020**, *29*, 1014–1025.
4. Bentaher, H.; Kaich, H.; Ayadi, N.; Hmouda, M.B.; Maalej, A.; Lemmer, U. A simple tracking system to monitor solar PV panels. *Energy Convers. Manag.* **2014**, *78*, 872–875. [CrossRef]
5. Camacho, E.; Berenguel, M.; Rubio, F.; Martínez, D. *Control of Solar Energy Systems*; Advances in Industrial Control b; Springer: London, UK, 2012.
6. Fernández-Ahumada, L.; Ramírez-Faz, J.; López-Luque, R.; Varo-Martínez, M.; Moreno-García, I.; de la Torre, F.C. Influence of the design variables of photovoltaic plants with two-axis solar tracking on the optimization of the tracking and backtracking trajectory. *Sol. Energy* **2020**, *208*, 89–100. [CrossRef]
7. Alexandru, C.; Irina Tatu, N. Optimal design of the solar tracker used for a photovoltaic string. *J. Renew. Sustain. Energy* **2013**, *5*, 023133. [CrossRef]
8. Alexandru, C. Optimal design of the dual-axis tracking system used for a PV string platform. *J. Renew. Sustain. Energy* **2019**, *11*, 043501. [CrossRef]
9. Al Garni, H.Z.; Awasthi, A.; Ramli, M.A. Optimal design and analysis of grid-connected photovoltaic under different tracking systems using HOMER. *Energy Convers. Manag.* **2018**, *155*, 42–57. [CrossRef]
10. Alexandru, C.; Pozna, C. Simulation of a dual-axis solar tracker for improving the performance of a photovoltaic panel. *Proc. Inst. Mech. Eng. Part J. Power Energy* **2010**, *224*, 797–811. [CrossRef]
11. Ahmed, R.; Oh, S.J.; Mehmood, M.U.; Kim, Y.; Jeon, G.; Han, H.J.; Lim, S.H. Computer vision and photosensor based hybrid control strategy for a two-axis solar tracker-Daylighting application. *Sol. Energy* **2021**, *224*, 175–183. [CrossRef]
12. Diaz, A.; Garrido, R.; Soto-Bernal, J. A filtered sun sensor for solar tracking in HCPV and CSP systems. *IEEE Sens. J.* **2018**, *19*, 917–925. [CrossRef]

13. Ortega, P.; López-Rodríguez, G.; Ricart, J.; Domínguez, M.; Castañer, L.M.; Quero, J.M.; Tarrida, C.L.; García, J.; Reina, M.; Gras, A.; et al. A miniaturized two axis sun sensor for attitude control of nano-satellites. *IEEE Sens. J.* **2010**, *10*, 1623–1632. [CrossRef]
14. Saymbetov, A.; Mekhilef, S.; Kuttybay, N.; Nurgaliyev, M.; Tukymbekov, D.; Meiirkhanov, A.; Dosymbetova, G.; Svanbayev, Y. Dual-axis schedule tracker with an adaptive algorithm for a strong scattering of sunbeam. *Sol. Energy* **2021**, *224*, 285–297. [CrossRef]
15. Urbano, J.A.; Matsumoto, Y.; Asomoza, R.; Aceves, F.; Sotelo, A.; Jacome, A. 5 Wp PV module-based stand-alone solar tracking system. In Proceedings of the 3rd World Conference on Photovoltaic Energy Conversion, Osaka, Japan, 11–18 May 2003; Volume 3, pp. 2463–2465.
16. Lee, C.Y.; Chou, P.C.; Chiang, C.M.; Lin, C.F. Sun tracking systems: A review. *Sensors* **2009**, *9*, 3875–3890. [CrossRef]
17. Nsengiyumva, W.; Chen, S.G.; Hu, L.; Chen, X. Recent advancements and challenges in Solar Tracking Systems (STS): A review. *Renew. Sustain. Energy Rev.* **2018**, *81*, 250–279. [CrossRef]
18. Hafez, A.; Yousef, A.; Harag, N. Solar tracking systems: Technologies and trackers drive types—A review. *Renew. Sustain. Energy Rev.* **2018**, *91*, 754–782. [CrossRef]
19. Sumathi, V.; Jayapragash, R.; Bakshi, A.; Akella, P.K. Solar tracking methods to maximize PV system output—A review of the methods adopted in recent decade. *Renew. Sustain. Energy Rev.* **2017**, *74*, 130–138. [CrossRef]
20. Barbón, A.; Bayón-Cueli, C.; Bayón, L.; Ayuso, P.F. Influence of solar tracking error on the performance of a small-scale linear Fresnel reflector. *Renew. Energy* **2020**, *162*, 43–54. [CrossRef]
21. Fuentes-Morales, R.F.; Diaz-Ponce, A.; Peña-Cruz, M.I.; Rodrigo, P.M.; Valentín-Coronado, L.M.; Martell-Chavez, F.; Pineda-Arellano, C.A. Control algorithms applied to active solar tracking systems: A review. *Sol. Energy* **2020**, *212*, 203–219. [CrossRef]
22. Sidek, M.; Azis, N.; Hasan, W.; Ab Kadir, M.; Shafie, S.; Radzi, M. Automated positioning dual-axis solar tracking system with precision elevation and azimuth angle control. *Energy* **2017**, *124*, 160–170. [CrossRef]
23. Sabir, M.M.; Ali, T. Optimal PID controller design through swarm intelligence algorithms for sun tracking system. *Appl. Math. Comput.* **2016**, *274*, 690–699. [CrossRef]
24. Spong, M.; Hutchinson, S.; Vidyasagar, M. *Robot Modeling and Control*; John Wiley: Hoboken, NJ, USA, 2006.
25. Visioli, A. *Practical PID Control*; Springer Science & Business Media: Berlin/Heidelberg, Germany, 2006.
26. Shamsuzzoha, M.; Skogestad, S. The setpoint overshoot method: A simple and fast closed-loop approach for PID tuning. *J. Process. Control* **2010**, *20*, 1220–1234. [CrossRef]
27. Ali, A.; Majhi, S. PI/PID controller design based on IMC and percentage overshoot specification to controller setpoint change. *ISA Trans.* **2009**, *48*, 10–15. [CrossRef] [PubMed]
28. Li, K.; Boonto, S.; Nuchkrua, T. On-line self tuning of contouring control for high accuracy robot manipulators under various operations. *Int. J. Control Autom. Syst.* **2020**, *18*, 1818–1828. [CrossRef]
29. Nuchkrua, T.; Leephakpreeda, T. Fuzzy self-tuning PID control of hydrogen-driven pneumatic artificial muscle actuator. *J. Bionic Eng.* **2013**, *10*, 329–340. [CrossRef]
30. Roman, R.C.; Precup, R.E.; Petriu, E.M. Hybrid data-driven fuzzy active disturbance rejection control for tower crane systems. *Eur. J. Control* **2021**, *58*, 373–387. [CrossRef]
31. Hou, Z.; Xiong, S. On model-free adaptive control and its stability analysis. *IEEE Trans. Autom. Control* **2019**, *64*, 4555–4569. [CrossRef]
32. Safan, Y.M.; Shaaban, S.; El-Sebah, M.I.A. Performance evaluation of a multi-degree of freedom hybrid controlled dual axis solar tracking system. *Sol. Energy* **2018**, *170*, 576–585. [CrossRef]
33. Lashab, A.; Sera, D.; Guerrero, J.M.; Máthé, L.; Bouzid, A. Discrete model-predictive-control-based maximum power point tracking for PV systems: Overview and evaluation. *IEEE Trans. Power Electron.* **2017**, *33*, 7273–7287. [CrossRef]
34. Rubio, F.; Ortega, M.; Gordillo, F.; Lopez-Martinez, M. Application of new control strategy for sun tracking. *Energy Convers. Manag.* **2007**, *48*, 2174–2184. [CrossRef]
35. Kim, I.S. Robust maximum power point tracker using sliding mode controller for the three-phase grid-connected photovoltaic system. *Sol. Energy* **2007**, *81*, 405–414. [CrossRef]
36. Chu, C.C.; Chen, C.L. Robust maximum power point tracking method for photovoltaic cells: A sliding mode control approach. *Sol. Energy* **2009**, *83*, 1370–1378. [CrossRef]
37. Alata, M.; Al-Nimr, M.; Qaroush, Y. Developing a multipurpose sun tracking system using fuzzy control. *Energy Convers. Manag.* **2005**, *46*, 1229–1245. [CrossRef]
38. Al Nabulsi, A.; Dhaouadi, R. Efficiency optimization of a DSP-based standalone PV system using fuzzy logic and dual-MPPT control. *IEEE Trans. Ind. Inform.* **2012**, *8*, 573–584. [CrossRef]
39. Bahgat, A.; Helwa, N.; Ahmad, G.; El Shenawy, E. Maximum power point traking controller for PV systems using neural networks. *Renew. Energy* **2005**, *30*, 1257–1268. [CrossRef]
40. AL-Rousan, N.A.; Isa, N.A.M.; Desa, M.K.M. Efficient Single and Dual Axis Solar Tracking System Controllers Based on Adaptive Neural Fuzzy Inference System. *J. King Saud-Univ.-Eng. Sci.* **2020**, *32*, 459–469. [CrossRef]
41. Han, J. From PID to active disturbance rejection control. *IEEE Trans. Ind. Electron.* **2009**, *56*, 900–906. [CrossRef]
42. Gao, Z. Active disturbance rejection control: A paradigm shift in feedback control system design. In Proceedings of the American Control Conference, Minneapolis, MN, USA, 14–16 June 2006; IEEE: New York, NY, USA, 2006; pp. 2399–2405.

43. Chu, Z.; Wu, C.; Sepehri, N. Active disturbance rejection control applied to high-order systems with parametric uncertainties. *Int. J. Control. Autom. Syst.* **2019**, *17*, 1483–1493. [CrossRef]
44. Liu, F.; Li, H.; Liu, L.; Zou, R.; Liu, K. A Control Method for IPMSM Based on Active Disturbance Rejection Control and Model Predictive Control. *Mathematics* **2021**, *9*, 760. [CrossRef]
45. Patelski, R.; Dutkiewicz, P. On the stability of ADRC for manipulators with modelling uncertainties. *ISA Trans.* **2020**, *102*, 295–303. [CrossRef]
46. Madoński, R.; Herman, P. Survey on methods of increasing the efficiency of extended state disturbance observers. *ISA Trans.* **2015**, *56*, 18–27. [CrossRef]
47. Sira-Ramírez, H.; Luviano-Juárez, A.; Ramírez-Neria, M.; Zurita-Bustamante, E.W. *Active Disturbance Rejection Control of Dynamic Systems: A Flatness Based Approach*; Butterworth-Heinemann: Oxford, UK, 2017.
48. Ahi, B.; Haeri, M. Linear active disturbance rejection control from the practical aspects. *IEEE/ASME Trans. Mechatron.* **2018**, *23*, 2909–2919. [CrossRef]
49. Lozada-Castillo, N.; Luviano-Juárez, A.; Chairez, I. Robust control of uncertain feedback linearizable systems based on adaptive disturbance estimation. *ISA Trans.* **2019**, *87*, 1–9. [CrossRef]
50. Nuchkrua, T.; Leephakpreeda, T. Novel Compliant Control of Pneumatic Artificial Muscle Driven by Hydrogen Pressure under Varying Environment. *IEEE Trans. Ind. Electron.* **2021**. [CrossRef]
51. Escobar, J.; Poznyak, A. Time-varying matrix estimation in stochastic continuous-time models under coloured noise using LSM with forgetting factor. *Int. J. Syst. Sci.* **2011**, *42*, 2009–2020. [CrossRef]
52. Poznyak, A. *Advanced Mathematical Tools for Control Engineers: Volume 1: Deterministic Systems*; Elsevier: Amsterdam, The Netherlands, 2010.
53. Horn, R.; Johnson, C. *Matrix Analysis*; Cambridge University Press: Cambridge, UK, 2012.
54. Khalil, H. *Nonlinear Systems*; Prentice Hall: Upper Saddle River, NJ, USA, 2002.
55. Flores-Hernandez, D.; Palomino-Resendiz, S.; Luviano-Juárez, A.; Lozada-Castillo, N.; Gutierrez-Frias, O. A heuristic approach for tracking error and energy consumption minimization in solar tracking systems. *IEEE Access* **2019**, *7*, 52755–52768. [CrossRef]
56. Cooper, P. The absorption of radiation in solar stills. *Sol. Energy* **1969**, *12*, 333–346. [CrossRef]
57. da Silva Campos, V.C.; Nguyen, A.T.; Palhares, R.M. Adaptive gain-scheduling control for continuous-time systems with polytopic uncertainties: An LMI-based approach. *Automatica* **2021**, *133*, 109856. [CrossRef]
58. Sira-Ramirez, H.; Fliess, M. An algebraic state estimation approach for the recovery of chaotically encrypted messages. *Int. J. Bifurc. Chaos* **2006**, *16*, 295–309. [CrossRef]
59. Hmidet, A.; Hasnaoui, O. Waijung blockset-STM32F4 environment for real time induction motor speed control. In Proceedings of the 2018 IEEE 5th International Congress on Information Science and Technology (CiSt), Marrakech, Morocco, 21–27 October 2018; IEEE, New York, NY, USA, 2018; pp. 600–605.

Article

Predicate-Based Model of Problem-Solving for Robotic Actions Planning

Oleksandr Tsymbal [1,†], Paolo Mercorelli [2,*,†] and Oleg Sergiyenko [3,†]

1. Faculty of Automatics and Computerized Technologies, Kharkiv National University of Radio Electronics, Nauki Avenue 14, 61166 Kharkiv, Ukraine; oleksandr.tsymbal@nure.ua
2. Institute of Product and Process Innovation, Leuphana University of Lüneburg, Universitätsallee 1, D-21335 Lüneburg, Germany
3. Faculty of Engineering, Autonomous University of Baja California, Blvd. Benito Juárez, Mexicali 21280, Mexico; srgnk@uabc.edu.mx
* Correspondence: paolo.mercorelli@leuphana.de; Tel.: +49-4131-677-1896
† The authors contributed equally to this work.

Abstract: The aim of the article is to describe a predicate-based logical model for the problem-solving of robots. The proposed article deals with analyses of trends of problem-solving robotic applications for manufacturing, especially for transportations and manipulations. Intelligent agent-based manufacturing systems with robotic agents are observed. The intelligent cores of them are considered from point of view of ability to propose the plans of problem-solving in the form of strategies. The logical model of adaptive strategies planning for the intelligent robotic system is composed in the form of predicates with a presentation of data processing on a base of set theory. The dynamic structures of workspaces, and a possible change of goals are considered as reasons for functional strategies adaptation.

Keywords: adaptation; problem-solving; robotics; predicates; manufacturing system

Citation: Tsymbal, O.; Mercorelli, P.; Sergiyenko, O. Predicate-Based Model of Problem-Solving for Robotic Actions Planning. *Mathematics* **2021**, *9*, 3044. https://doi.org/10.3390/math9233044

Academic Editor: António M. Lopes

Received: 2 October 2021
Accepted: 19 November 2021
Published: 26 November 2021

Publisher's Note: MDPI stays neutral with regard to jurisdictional claims in published maps and institutional affiliations.

Copyright: © 2021 by the authors. Licensee MDPI, Basel, Switzerland. This article is an open access article distributed under the terms and conditions of the Creative Commons Attribution (CC BY) license (https://creativecommons.org/licenses/by/4.0/).

1. Introduction

Mobile robots are remarkable cases of highly developed technology and systems. The robot community has developed a complex analysis to meet the increased demands of the control challenges pertaining to the movement of robots. The research on mobile robots has attracted many researchers in recent years. In practical application, very often, the robot operating system (ROS) is used for the communication between the robot and its control system. Different control systems are applied in Robotino. For instance, in [1,2], a linear model predictive control is used for optimal motion control, with a great advantage obtained in terms of global optimality and in computational load.

This paper is an extension of work originally presented in SPEEDAM 2020 [3], which proposed an analysis of a computer-integrated system of mobile robots application for transportation and the manipulation of goods inside manufacturing workspaces, and connected to works of P. Mercorelli and O. Sergiyenko: the consideration of a set theory-based dynamic model to describe problem-solving processes in the execution of mobile robots' paths or manipulation tasks. The description of a logical model as a key element of the decision-making system for robotic applications was connected to works of O. Tsymbal.

Modern manufacturing systems are described by an intensive application of information technologies on the base of computer networks, artificial intelligence, and digital technologies, and must correspond to requirements of mobility, of fast responses to the changing quality of products, of small sizes, specific, individual, customer, and environmental demands. In the last two decades, industrial engineers and scientists have spent a substantial amount of time and effort in researching the advanced production systems and their influence in the global market [4,5].

The parts of the mentioned concepts of manufacturing systems are already widely applied in practice, and result in an essential decrease of designer time. Others are still at the research and conceptualization stage. In any case, the core element of manufacturing systems control is in the introduction of the manufacturing intelligence. The participation of numerous units of equipment, including technological, transportation, and warehouse units, as well as humans acting in workspaces, makes it possible to describe and simulate manufacturing systems as multi-agents, as well as their origins and functioning.

Robotic systems of the transportation and manipulation types are key points of manufacturing and other automated systems. The intelligence of robots is defined by their ability to observe the workspaces, to analyze them, to make decisions concerning the problems, and to execute transportation movements/manipulations to reach the proposed goals in industrials areas. In this view, decision-making systems for robotics are important for both theory and experiments.

The aim of this article is to propose the logical approach to the decision-making of robots for manufacturing workspaces, added with adaptation solutions to respond to the dynamics of industrial areas.

2. Agent-Based Systems and Role of Robots

The open architecture of multi-agent systems (MAS) has become the basic direction of distributed artificial intelligence development. From a practical point of view, these agents are considered as self-controlled software objects with self-estimation systems and independent problem-solving tools for their own needs, and for other agents (by requests) [4].

The conceptual agent model consists of four components:

- perception, which is a source for information about the external world;
- effector, which is the agent's interface to change the world or the agent's community;
- communication system, which is the tool for information exchange between other members of the agent's community;
- aims, which are the list of goals for the agent's execution.

Any manufacturing system can be considered as a sort of MAS because they consist of various kinds of technological equipment (with/without intelligent features), possibly including manipulation and transportation robots, and human personnel, which are united by an automated control system. Modern manufacturing systems (which are mainly decentralized) are typical applications of MAS. There are many benefits of such applications for manufacturing systems: distributed processing of information, in a way which is different from united big systems; quality increase, supplied by learning and interaction with objects; support of system integration.

For the condition of manufacturing, the agent is an object with a certain intelligent level, which can be considered as physical (worker, machine) or a logical object (task, directive, order). In this way, a robot with manipulation and transportation functions looks as an ideal manufacturing agent (MA). In [5,6], we can see presentation of such an agent.

The model of MA usually includes the library of procedures (the experience of the system in the form of actions) [6–8], inference drive (problem-solver) [9–12], knowledge base (more general than procedures), and a perception processor with the possibility to communicate with the sensors of robots [11,13]. MA concepts have found their implementations for robotic group tasks [13–17], for manufacturing problems [18–22], and also for social and collaborative robotic problems [23–27]. The simulation component allows the estimation of possible results for the activity of MA [13,14]. Like any computing systems, MA includes memory and communication units [15,16]. The coordination subsystem checks the internal functions of MA, and receives the queries for coordination from other MA [3]. According to the general structure of manufacturing, [7] proposes the architecture of the manufacturing system on an agent-based concept, whereas the core of the system can be based on a number of technologies, presented in [25,26,28–37]. Decision-making systems became an object of software development design in the works [38,39].

From the point of view of multi-agent manufacturing systems functioning, the interaction of agents at every level is not the only key point. Another important thing is the implementation of agents. Other important tasks are resource planning, technological processes design, and schedules development [10,13,18]. MA can be implemented in the forms of virtual (as an automated control system function set) or physical (as industrial or transport robot) agents, able to analyze the constructive and technological specifications of manufacturing for specific workplaces of the flexible manufacturing system (FMS), to monitor the production process, to check-up the manufacturing technology acceptance, to respond to predicted or unpredicted manufacturing situations, and to supply the selected functions of operative manufacturing control [10,11]. The paper is organized in the following way: Part 3 is dedicated to the formal description of strategies planning; Part 4 describes the decision-making model, based on predicates; in Part 5, the adaptation technique of the assembling planning is shown; Part 6 describes practical implementations. The paper closes with a discussion of the results.

3. Formal Description of Strategies Planning

From an analysis of the manufacturing agent conception, we can see the need to describe the creation and activity of the problem-solving component. Such a component must include: the set of operative procedures (actions) with common knowledge support; an inference engine as the core of problem-solving; and a dynamic database with information on the surrounding workspace of the manufacturing system [8]. The actions of the manufacturing robotic agent can be described in the form of procedures, which allow the transformation of states of the robotic platform and of the external workspace (WS) [9].

The robotic agent (RA) can be described by: number of sets, *X,D,S*; of platform states; of robotic system decisions; and of WS.

Correspondingly, $x_i \in X, d_i \in D, s_i \in S$ can be introduced as atoms for the model, which describes robotic agents and their WS. We can also introduce standard operations $\neg, \wedge, \vee, \rightarrow, \leftrightarrow$ and well-formed formulas on the base of them:

$$\neg x, x \wedge y, x \vee y, x \rightarrow y, x \leftrightarrow y$$

To describe the theory, sets *X,D,S*, the functions, and the predicates are introduced.
Transition of states for RA: $x_i = f(x_0, \ldots, x_{i-1})$, for *i*-th element of set *X*.
Transition of states for WS: $s_i = \psi(s_0, \ldots, s_{i-1})$.
To define the logics of the problem-solving system, the set of predicates (pt) is introduced:

$$pt(x_i), pt(s_i), pt(d_i), pt(x_i, s_i), pt(x_i, d_i), pt(d_i, s_i), pt(x_i, d_i, s_i)$$

These predicates define:

$pr(x_i, s_i) \subset pt$—states of the RA in the workspace (WS),
$ps(x_i, s_i) \subset pt$—states of the WS in the system of the RA,
$pa(x_i, s_i) \subset pt$—actions of the RA inside the WS,
$pg(pr, ps) \subset pt$—goals of the RA inside the WS.

Every goal of the RA is formulated as a new (or existing) state of the RA or WS:

$$pg(pr, ps) \leftarrow (pr(x_i, s_i) \vee ps(x_i, s_i))$$

The database of the RA is combined from:

$$pr(x_i), pr(x_i, s_i), ps(s_i), ps(x_i, s_i)$$

The knowledge base of the RA includes possible action *$pa(x_i, s_i)$*s of the RA in the WS.

Predicate $pa(x_i,s_i)$ is a strategy, which solves goal $(pr(x_i,s_i),ps(x_i,s_i))$, if there exists such a conjunction of RA actions $pa(x_i,s_i)$ (with n—total number of actions), which supplies $pg(pr(x_i,s_i), ps(x_i,s_i))$:

$$pg(pr(x_i,s_i),ps(x_i,s_i)) \leftarrow pa^0(x_i,s_i) \wedge pa^1(x_i,s_i) \wedge \ldots \wedge pa^{n-1}(x_i,s_i), \text{or} \\ pg(pr(x_i,s_i),ps(x_i,s_i)) \leftarrow \wedge_{i=0}^{n-1} pa^i(x_i,s_i), \qquad (1)$$

which defines, that for every robotic platform state x_i and state of workspace s_i, the goal state $pr(x_i,s_i)$ of the robotic agent or the state $ps(x_i,s_i)$ of the workspace can be reached by n-number of actions (upper indexes) and besides: $\exists f, f \in F: x_i = f_i(x_{i-1}, s_{i-1})$, $\exists \psi, \psi \in \Psi: x_i = \psi_i(x_{i-1}, s_{i-1})$, with F and Ψ—general sets of RA and WS transitions.

Therefore, $pa(x_i,s_i) = tr \| f_i + \psi_i \|$ and presents trace of norm.

The problem-solving process is the sequence of m-alternatives to reach the goals of the RA:

$$pg^0(pr,ps) \leftarrow pg_0^0(pr_0,ps_0,pa_0) \wedge pg_1^0(pr_1,ps_1,pa_1) \wedge \ldots \\ \wedge pg_{n-1}^0(pr_{n-1},ps_{n-1},pa_{n-1}) = \wedge_{i=0}^{n-1} pg_i^0(pr_i,ps_i,pa_i) \\ pg^m(pr,ps) \leftarrow pg_0^m(pr_0,ps_0,pa_0) \wedge pg_1^m(pr_1,ps_1,pa_1) \wedge \ldots \\ \wedge pg_{n-1}^m(pr_{n-1},ps_{n-1},pa_{n-1}) = \wedge_{i=0}^{n-1} pg_i^m(pr_i,ps_i,pa_i). \qquad (2)$$

As a result, the global (final) goal is defined as follows:

$$pg^{total}(pr, ps) \leftarrow \vee_{j=0}^{m-1} \wedge_{i=0}^{n-1} pg_i^m(pr_i, ps_i, pa_i). \qquad (3)$$

Every RA starts planning from the development of the initial plan of actions in the WS. It includes the next transitions:

$$pr(x_1,s_1) \leftarrow pa_0^0(pr(x_0,s_0) \vee ps(x_0,s_0)) \\ pr(x_2,s_2) \leftarrow pa_1^0(pr(x_1,s_1) \vee ps(x_1,s_1)) \\ pr(x_n=Y,s_n) \leftarrow pa_{n-1}^0(pr(x_{n-1},s_{n-1}) \vee ps(x_{n-1},s_{n-1})). \qquad (4)$$

Such transitions can be correct for a static WS, but become practically wrong if the WS is dynamic, with an impossibility to reach the desired state:

$$pr(x_i,s_i) \neq pa_i^0(pr(x_{i-1},s_{i-1}) \vee ps(x_{i-1},s_{i-1})). \qquad (5)$$

In this case, the strategy must be modified (signed with *):

$$pr(x_i,s_i) \leftarrow pa_i^*(pr(x_{i-1},s_{i-1}) \vee ps(x_{i-1},s_{i-1})), \\ pr(x_{i+1},s_{i+1}) \leftarrow pa_{i+1}^*(pr(x_i,s_i) \vee ps(x_i,s_i)), \qquad (6)$$

with the general result for m^* (modified) strategy:

$$pg^{m*}(pr,ps) \leftarrow pg_0^{m*}(pr_0,ps_0,pa_0) \wedge pg_1^{m*}(pr_1,ps_1,pa_1) \wedge \ldots \\ \wedge pg_{n-1}^{m*}(pr_{n-1},ps_{n-1},pa_{n-1}) = \wedge_{i=0}^{n-1} pg_i^{m*}(pr_i,ps_i,pa_i). \qquad (7)$$

4. Model of Robotic System Planning on Base of Predicates

Let's define RA states as set $X = \{X^0, X^1, \ldots, X^{n-1}\}$. In the process of the execution of the decision, the automated control system of the RA provides transformation of the initial state $state(x_0^0, x_1^0, x_2^0, \ldots, x_{n-1}^0)$ into a specific goal state $state(x_0^m, x_1^m, x_2^m, \ldots, x_{n-1}^m)$, with upper indexes for states, and lower indexes for different objects of the RA.

If the system (the RA and the WS around it) at the initial time is a set of arguments $x_0^0, \ldots, x_{n-1}^0$ and is characterized by a state $state(x_0^0, x_1^0, x_2^0, \ldots, x_{n-1}^0)$, then considering the discrete process of planning strategies, which consists of individual actions $action_0, \ldots, action_k$, we can indicate that the transition from one discrete state to another is a certain relationship between objects:

$$state\left(x_0^1, x_1^1, \ldots, x_{n-1}^1\right) \leftarrow action_0\left(state\left(x_0^0, x_1^0, \ldots, x_{n-1}^0\right)\right). \qquad (8)$$

Here, *state* is a relationship (predicate) that characterizes the state of the system as a whole, and *action (state)* means the action of transition from one state to another.

All activities related to the transitions from one state of the system to another (by executing a list of solutions) are sets of predicates:

$$\begin{aligned} state(X^1) &\leftarrow action_0(state(X^0)), \\ state(X^2) &\leftarrow action_1(state(X^1)), \\ state(X^{n-1}{=}Y) &\leftarrow action_{n-2}(state(X^{n-2})). \end{aligned} \quad (9)$$

Thus, the goal of a strategy planning system is to find the appropriate number of *action$_i$* that would satisfy the *state$_i$* conditions of the system. The choice of the *action$_i$* action to convert the *state(X^i)* to state *state(X^{i+1})* is made to ensure compatibility of the *action* arguments and the corresponding state X^{i+1}, which, in practice, will mean the possibility of implementing the state (local goal) X^{i+1} by the performing of *action*:

$$X^{i+1} \leftarrow action\left(X^i\right),$$

with X^{i+1} as a possible result of action *action* for the condition of state X^i.

The predicate scheme is adaptive if the components of the antecedent (right part of the predicate expression) and the result of the scheme (consequent) change depending on changes in the state of the robotic system (RS) and the workspace (WS):

$$state(Y) \leftarrow action(S_0), action(S_1), \ldots, action(S_{n-1}), \quad (10)$$

Here, *Y*—final goal of RA; $S_0, S_1, \ldots S_{n-1}$—the sequential states of the control system.

However, in case of the dynamics of the WS (world of robot), the state of the robot can also be transformed (such changes are not obligatory, but probable), and there are possible situations when, for some, state *state(X^{i-1})* action $action_{i-1}\left(state\left(X^{i-1}\right)\right)$ will not transform the system to state *state(X^i)*, thus:

$$state\left(X^i\right) \neq action_{i-1}\left(state\left(X^{i-1}\right)\right). \quad (11)$$

For this case, the initial solution is in the determination of predicate *action*, which satisfies the condition. However, the actual number of real actions is limited (unlike the number of states), and the solution can be found in search of the predicate vector $\vec{action}$, which satisfies the goal of system.

Therefore, if there is set *X* of the world's objects, and X^0 is a set of their initial states, then to supply goal state *X*, it is needed to compose a plan consisting of sequences of actions, expressed by predicate *action*, and with states of the system—by predicate *state*:

$$\begin{aligned} & state(X^0), \\ state(X^1) &\leftarrow action_0(state(X^0)), \\ state(Y) &\leftarrow action_{n-1}(state(X^{n-1})). \end{aligned} \quad (12)$$

If, at some step *i*, the state X^i is unobtainable, that $state\left(X^i\right) \neq action_{i-1}\left(state\left(X^{i-1}\right)\right)$, then the adaptive strategies planning system must generate the new order of action predicates $\vec{action}$, that will satisfy the changes of the WS:

$$state\left(X^{i1}\right) \leftarrow action_{n-1}^1\left(state\left(X^{i-1}\right)\right), \; state(Y) \leftarrow action_{n-1}^{m-1}\left(state\left(X^{n-1}\right)\right). \quad (13)$$

A similar situation is when the decision-making system (DMS) has information that the goal of system is changed. It means that the goal state *state(Y)* will be changed to some *state(Y^i)*. Here, two variants are possible:

(a) the information on the change of the goal comes at the moment when the system is in the state i—$state(x^i)$, and it is possible to generate plan $\vec{action}$ to transit from x^i to state y^i;

(b) the information on the change of the goal comes at the moment when the system is in the state i—$state(x^i)$, but the generation of plan $\vec{action}$ is possible only from state $state(x^{i-k})$, where $k \leq i$, so to generate the plan, the system must return to previous states, possibly up to state $state(x^0)$.

Again, it will need the generation of a new order of predicate actions.

According to definition, the plan of decision will consist of sets {$action_0, action_1, \ldots, action_n$}, and the entire plan (of all the plans), developed during the problem-solving. The adapted decision plan will be the expression:

$$plan^{adaptive}(Y) \leftarrow action_0(state(X^0), \\ action_1(state(X^1), \ldots, action_{n-1}(state(X^{n-1})))) \quad (14)$$

Such a plan is in the final decision of the adaptive DMS.

The developed plan will be changed up to the execution of the last subgoal of planned order, and the plan's adaptation can be considered as its essential specification.

Also, note the need to evaluate the actions proposed by the DMS in a sequence of predicates.

As is known, a predicate has verity value. In classics, it is a mapping of n arguments to verity value. Though the fuzzy sets theory directs to the possible introduction of a fuzzy predicate term [10,11], the classic predicate has only two values: *true* and *false*. At this point, the DMS transition from one state $state(X_{i-1})$ to state $state(X_i)$ also has values of *true* or *false*, so the system transfers to a new state or does not. Probably, it is difficult to predict the state of the whole system even in ideal cases, and more to give the simple system evaluation in binary values of *true* or *false*. Rather, the verity or falsity will describe the particular system parameters. As to predicated theory, the robot's world can be described as a relation set between the world's objects, for instance, *is_a*—membership to the object's type, *is_at*—one object positioning near the other, *stands*—object's being in some state, etc.

5. Planning for Assembling System and Its Adaptation

The flexible integrated assembling system (FIAS) contains assembling automatic (soldering) machines, assembling-transport robots, storehouses, defining set $q_i \in Eq$, $i = 0 \ldots n-1$. The aim of FIAS is the execution of assembling technological process (modules) of radio-electronic devices, in particular, for the printed circuit board M.

Here $M = < B, Ch, T, R, C, L, \ldots >$, where B—the printed circuit board, Ch—microchips, T—semiconductor devices, R—resistors, C—capacitors, L—inductances.

The configuration of the device is determined by its construction design M^G, which defines the purpose location of elements at the printed circuit board. Actually, the module (board) is a rectangular matrix, filled by elements of set M (shown at Figure 1).

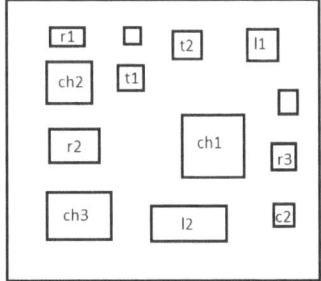

Figure 1. Workspace for manipulation task.

Initially, M_0 is zero matrix. FIAS generates decisions $d_k \in D, k=0,\ldots,l-1$, which are implemented by actions (technological transitions): $a_k \in A, k=0,\ldots,l-1$. Decision $\vec{D}$ for the order of assembling operations execution is a sequence of operations $a_i \in A, i=0\ldots l-1$, which are in the settings to board B of some elements from sets $Ch, T, R, C, L \ldots$, for example:

$$\vec{D} = \{Ch_0, Ch_1, T_0, T_1, R_0, Ch_3, C_0, L_0, \ldots\}$$

To reach the goal state M^G, there are transformations $M_i = f_i(Eq, D_i, M_{i-1})$:

$$M_0 \to M_1 \to M_2 \to \ldots \to M^G$$

The filling of M is defined by the order of assembling operations. Such an order is set by design project M^G, technological rules Tr, and the abilities of technological equipment E. Therefore, $\vec{D} = g(M^G, Tr, E)$. The purpose of the search is to find such a sequence of transitions $f_1, \ldots, f_n$, that provides transformation from initial state M_0 to goal M^G.

The strategies planning process is an act of constant comparison of the system's goal to the current state and current possibilities. The strategies planning process according to the discontinuity of operations also must be discrete, be correspondent to the goal's achievement, and implement the particular technological operations.

In general, the strategies planning process is a mapping of such a view:

$$F : D \times X \to Y, \tag{15}$$

that is, strategies planning process means an application of decision set $D = \{D_0, D_1, \ldots, D_n\}$ to the set $X_0, \ldots, X_{n-1}$, that formally is considered as a Cartesian product of sets $D \times X \to Y$, where Y is the set which defines ACS at the moment of goal achievement.

The transition of the robotic system (RS) from its initial state to goal is a sequence of the state's transformations, and has the view:

$$\begin{bmatrix} x_0^0 \\ x_1^0 \\ \ldots \\ x_{n0}^0 \end{bmatrix} \Rightarrow \begin{bmatrix} x_0^1 \\ x_1^1 \\ \ldots \\ x_{n1}^1 \end{bmatrix} \Rightarrow \begin{bmatrix} x_0^2 \\ x_1^2 \\ \ldots \\ x_{n2}^2 \end{bmatrix} \Rightarrow \ldots \Rightarrow \begin{bmatrix} x_0^n \\ x_1^n \\ \ldots \\ x_{nn}^n \end{bmatrix} \equiv \begin{bmatrix} y_0 \\ y_1 \\ \ldots \\ y_{nn} \end{bmatrix} \tag{16}$$

It corresponds to a real situation, when, in the process of generation and execution of the solution, there is an evolution of RS states.

However, the mentioned sequence of changes describes not only the problem-solving process, but also the dynamics of the system's changes in time. On strategies planning, the system's state changes in active mode, so, at every step, the strategies planning may change the characteristics of the RS. To consider the sequence of actions on strategies planning, there is need to define the function (vector) of problem-solving $\vec{D} = \{D_0, D_1, \ldots, D_{n-1}\}$.

Therefore, the application of decision D_i for every step of ACS functioning leads to a transformation of vector column $X_i^j \to X_{i+1}^j$ of RS states.

$$\begin{bmatrix} x_0^0 \\ x_1^0 \\ \ldots \\ x_{n0}^0 \end{bmatrix} *D_0 \Rightarrow \begin{bmatrix} x_0^1 \\ x_1^1 \\ \ldots \\ x_{n1}^1 \end{bmatrix} *D_1 \Rightarrow \ldots \begin{bmatrix} x_0^{n-1} \\ x_1^{n-1} \\ \ldots \\ x_{nn-1}^{n-1} \end{bmatrix} *D_{n-1} \Rightarrow \begin{bmatrix} x_0^n \\ x_1^n \\ \ldots \\ x_{nn}^n \end{bmatrix} \equiv \begin{bmatrix} y_0 \\ y_1 \\ \ldots \\ y_{nn} \end{bmatrix} \tag{17}$$

Note, that the case of adaptive strategies planning needs to take into account the effect of "third side", for example, of external world objects or rivals, which affects (positively or negatively) the strategies planning process. From one side, the effect of the external workspace may be direct, and, to take into account its existence and effect on the strategies planning process, we need to introduce the additional factor S of external WS states, containing the objects' set $S^i = \{s_0^i, s_1^i, \ldots, s_m^i\}$, with index i for discrete states of external WS:

$$\begin{bmatrix} x_0^0 \\ x_1^0 \\ \ldots \\ x_{n0}^0 \end{bmatrix} * \begin{bmatrix} s_0^1 \\ s_1^1 \\ \ldots \\ s_{m0}^1 \end{bmatrix} * D_0 \Rightarrow \ldots \begin{bmatrix} x_0^{n-1} \\ x_1^{n-1} \\ \ldots \\ x_{nn-1}^{n-1} \end{bmatrix} * \begin{bmatrix} s_0^{n-1} \\ s_1^{n-1} \\ \ldots \\ s_{mm}^{n-1} \end{bmatrix} * D_{n-1} \Rightarrow \begin{bmatrix} x_0^n \\ x_1^n \\ \ldots \\ x_{nn}^n \end{bmatrix} \equiv \begin{bmatrix} y_0 \\ y_1 \\ \ldots \\ y_{nn} \end{bmatrix} \quad (18)$$

The other way is in the introduction of functional dependence for particular acts of strategies planning of workspace's states:

$$F : D(S) \times X \to Y, \quad (19)$$

and, correspondingly:

$$\begin{bmatrix} x_0^0 \\ x_1^0 \\ \ldots \\ x_{n0}^0 \end{bmatrix} * D_0 \left(\begin{bmatrix} s_0^1 \\ s_1^1 \\ \ldots \\ s_{m0}^1 \end{bmatrix} \right) \Rightarrow \ldots \begin{bmatrix} x_0^{n-1} \\ x_1^{n-1} \\ \ldots \\ x_{nn-1}^{n-1} \end{bmatrix} * D_{n-1} \left(\begin{bmatrix} s_0^{n-1} \\ s_1^{n-1} \\ \ldots \\ s_{mm}^{n-1} \end{bmatrix} \right) \Rightarrow \begin{bmatrix} x_n^0 \\ x_n^1 \\ \ldots \\ x_n^{nn} \end{bmatrix} \equiv \begin{bmatrix} y_0 \\ y_1 \\ \ldots \\ y_{nn} \end{bmatrix} \quad (20)$$

Therefore, D_i, as the strategies planning act, depends on the state of external workspace objects.

The difference of both the ways is not very expressive, but the explanation can be inequal. In the first case, the strategies planning system directly interacts with WS, and such an interaction leads to changes on RTS states, and, therefore, the act of strategies planning relates to the system's state, affected by the WS. For the second case, the planning act depends on the WS state, and must take into account its effect during the definition of the decision's procedures (strategies), and the decision executor transforms the state of RTS being WS-dependent.

Therefore, the ACS goal at the stage of strategies planning for the given task is in determination of ordered set (vector) $\vec{D} \subset D$, as a set of problem-solving acts, implementing the transition of the robot's ACS from initial state X_0 to the goal Y as to expression $F : D \times X \to Y$.

The importance of adaptive problem-solving arises in the case of essential changes on the conditions of decision implementation. For cases of the robot's static workspace, the goal Y, as a state of RTS, is reached by the application of the possible action's set $\vec{D} = \{D_0, D_1, \ldots, D_{n-1}\}$, which transfers the systems from initial state X_0 to the goal $X_{n-1} = Y$. The set of selected actions $\vec{D}$ is considered as a decision plan.

For a static WS, an initial decision plan $\vec{D} = \{D_0^0, D_1^0, \ldots, D_{n-1}^0\}$ is developed, where the particular decision acts (strategies) are directly connected, and the application of local problem-solving act D_i to the current state X_i will transfer the system to the state X_{i+1}, which is, correspondingly, the goal for the decision act D_i. In its turn, the state X_{i+1} is initial for the new state D_{i+1}, which will transfer the system from state X_{i+1} to X_{i+2}, etc.

In the case of a WS dynamic state, the problem-solving system application of decision acts D_i can transfer the system to state X_{i+1}, which can be insufficient to implement action D_{i+1}, and will acquire the additional decision acts D'_{i+1}, D'_{i+1}, etc. Therefore, the changes of WS will lead to an indetermination of possible problem-solving tools.

6. Practical Implementations

Proposed mathematical models are used as a basis for development of decision-making systems for mobile and manipulation robots.

Initially implemented with Prolog language, the decision-making system (DMS), based on principles of proposed models, was added by graphical simulation procedures, and translated to C++/MFC. It had view of a classic STRIPS-like system, which describes the robotic workspace (such as for a transportation robot), consisting of rooms with boxes inside, and connected by opening/closing doors. The user's interface allows the selection of the agent of action (robot or boxes), the type of action (go/push (for boxes); open/close (for doors)), and, in this way, to set the task (goal) for the system. According to the formulated goal (if formulated correctly), the DMS finds the action scheme which satisfies the goal, automatically sets subgoals, and reaches them. Structurally, the DMS consists of a decision-maker procedure and action scheme procedures descriptions.

The decision-making procedure includes the stages:

- selection of the action scheme, compatible to the goal (subgoal);
- satisfaction of pre-conditions for the selected action scheme, possibly with recursive execution of subgoals;
- execution of post-conditions (for lists of deleted and added facts).

Correspondingly, every action scheme includes the parts of the action result, and of precondition and post-condition facts lists. Implementation of the DMS is shown in Figure 2.

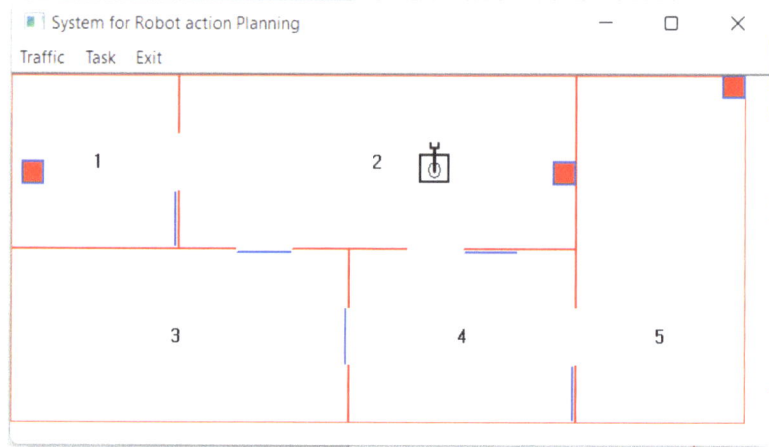

Figure 2. Decision-making system implementation.

This DMS deals with elements of sets, mentioned in Sections 3 and 4 of this article. Here, X includes the positions and states of the robot (such as is_at(robot, door45, now); or is_with(robot, box1, now)), S contains states of WS (such as stands(door12, closed, now); or is_in(box1, room1. now)), whereas D consists of a list of actions: "go_to";"open_door"; "take_box"; "push_box"; etc.

Later implementations of the DMS, based on the predicate's models, were included to projects with the NXT MindStorms mobile robot with a visual-guided control system, and, currently, with the Festo Robotino (version 2). These projects consider the predicate-based DMS as the upper level of decision making to plan actions within distributed workspaces, or for manipulations (if robots are equipped with manipulators), whereas lower decision-making levels are mostly based on path-optimized methods to plan movements within the discrete workspace of a particular work cell (e.g., as shown in Figure 3 for the Festo Robotino Robot).

The Festo Robotino is controlled by a two-level RPC (remote procedure call) protocol, which allows a program running on one computer to access the functions (procedures) of a program running on another computer.

To test the developed decision-making models, there is created a program to control the movements of the Festo Robotino. In this program, the task of the robot is set in the form of the final (target) robot position in 2D-space, for example, P (x, y). The possibility to reach the target position is analyzed, taking into account the information about the occupied and free areas of the robotic workspace provided by the visual monitoring system, implemented using a set of web-cameras. The check of the robot's position is provided by global cameras mounted above the workspace, and a local camera on board with the robot.

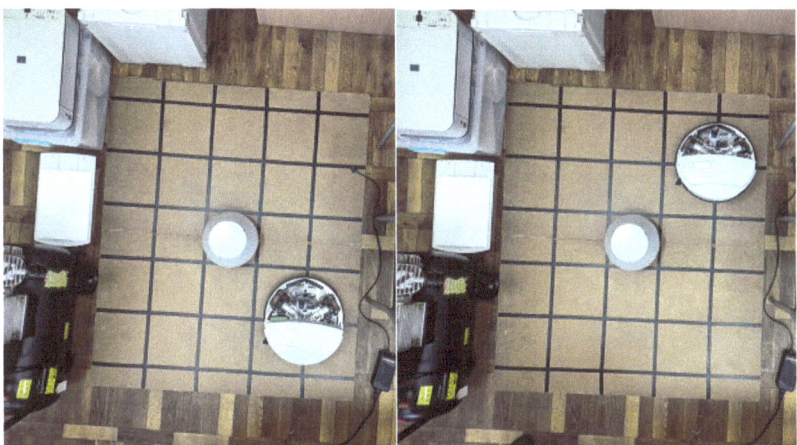

Figure 3. Example of discrete workspace for the Festo Robotino.

In a command mode, the developed program provides a number of modes, including determination of the robot's current position, a stop command, a setting of a target point, a setting of vector of long-distance movement, and opening and closing the robot's gripper.

In strategy planning mode, the user can set tasks for the robot. In particular, the next options can be specified: action agent–robot; current action, for example, "take object" or "take"; subject (or subjects) of action, such as "instrument".

DMS in this program is provided in the manner described in Section 3 of the article. The generation of the robot's route is supported by analyses of the objects and obstacles allocation in the robotic workspace with computer vision methods. After the decision is made, it is implemented by the control system of the Robotino robot.

The developed software allows the consideration of the robot as a multi-agent system, which includes: motion agent (robot motion control subsystem); vision agent (computer vision system robot); sensory agent (implemented by the sensor system of the mobile robot and information processing means); agent navigation (associated with the robot's motion control system and computer vision system); strategy planning agent.

7. Discussion

Therefore, the proposed article describes the formalization of strategies planning for the problem-solving component of a robotic control system. Such formalization includes the setting of a theory basis, the definition of predicates to describe the workspace, and the states, actions, and goals for the robotic system. Here, goals are reached as conjunctions of actions, with recursive definitions as sub-goals. The selection of the sequence of actions to reach the desired goal is defined as strategy, selected from several alternative plans. Such a definition makes it possible to implement a decision-making system in the form of an automatic problem-solver, efficient for closed workspaces or areas with advanced monitoring. This set of strategies can be considered as a knowledge base for particular robots or groups of robots, acting as manufacturing agents.

From the formal description of problem solving, the article shifts to the implementation of Prolog-similar predicate notation (Section 4), while also supporting the idea of a decision-making engine based on logics. The dynamics of the robotic workspace can lead to the re-formalization of strategies, which is also discussed as a requirement for plan modification. The proposed formalization of decision-making can be applied for transportation tasks of mobile robots, and for manipulations (Section 5 contains an example of the assembling system).

8. Conclusions

Action planning for robotic systems can be introduced into transportation and manipulation problems, and applied for the solution of manufacturing tasks [18–21], and also for social and collaboration tasks of robots [23,25,26,30]. For transportation problems in static workspaces, a solution can be effectively reached by computation methods. But, if the system has knowledge how to solve the problem, AI-methods become more effective, especially with the application of neural networks and genetic algorithms. More complex transportation problems appear for 3D systems of the warehouse type with vertical shelves, or for container terminals for seaports. However, with a different scale, the latter tasks look very similar to the 3D problems of robotic manipulators, especially if they make actions in a narrow space of obstacles [18,39]. Here, the knowledge of the system becomes more critical, and helps to solve the problems.

However, for conditions of dynamic space, the situation is more complicated. The motion of other objects (equipment, robots, vehicles, humans) can easily stop the execution of the best calculated plan (or strategy—in the terms of the proposed paper). In this case, the system must be adaptive to solve its problems, or come back to previous steps of the solution, to previous key points, or even to starting points [11,12]. In this case, robots, like humans, must be more logically intelligent (with experience in a greater number of operator's schemes), while combining computations, AI-methods, and group methods [13–16]. Possibly, in this way, we can find the combined solution for robots which aim to be intelligent.

In future works, the authors will try to expand the proposed model with the consideration of uncertain factors of robotic workspaces, with more detailed descriptions of robotic manipulations, and by modelling the group work of robots.

Author Contributions: Conceptualization, O.T., P.M. and O.S.; methodology, O.T., P.M. and O.S.; software, O.T.; validation, O.T., O.S. and P.M.; formal analysis, O.T. and O.S.; investigation, O.S.; resources, P.M.; data curation, O.T. and O.S.; writing—original draft preparation, O.T.; writing—review and editing, P.M. and O.S.; visualization, O.T.; supervision, P.M.; project administration, P.M.; funding acquisition, P.M. All authors have read and agreed to the published version of the manuscript.

Funding: This research received no external funding.

Institutional Review Board Statement: Not applicable.

Informed Consent Statement: Not applicable.

Data Availability Statement: Not applicable.

Conflicts of Interest: The authors declare no conflict of interest.

References

1. Mercorelli, P.; Voss, T.; Strassberger, D.; Sergiyenko, O.; Lindner, L. A model predictive control in robotino and its implementation using ROS system. In Proceedings of the International Conference on Electrical Systems for Aircraft, Railway, Ship Propulsion and Road Vehicles & International Transportation Electrification Conference (ESARS-ITEC), Toulouse, France, 2–4 November 2016; pp. 1–6. [CrossRef]
2. Mercorelli, P.; Voss, T.; Strassberger, D.; Sergiyenko, O.; Lindner, L. Optimal trajectory generation using MPC in robotino and its implementation with ROS system. In Proceedings of the 2017 IEEE 26th International Symposium on Industrial Electronics (ISIE), Edinburgh, Scotland, 19–21 June 2017; pp. 1642–1647. [CrossRef]
3. Tsymbal, O.; Bronnikov, A.; Mercorelli, P. Decision-making models for Robotic Warehouse. In Proceedings of the 2020 International Symposium on Power Electronics, Electrical Drives, Automation and Motion, Sorrento, Italy, 24–26 June 2020; pp. 546–551.
4. Mikhailov, E.; Remenyuk, B. Optimize the placement warehouse transport system. *J. Electrotech. Comput. Syst.* **2015**, *18*, 60–64.
5. Kerak, P. Novel trends in the intelligent manufacturing systems. In Proceedings of the 8th International Baltic Conference Industrial Engineering, Tallinn, Estonia, 19–21 April 2012.
6. Red'ko, V. Interaction between learning and evolution in population of autonomous agents. *Computing* **2013**, *12*, 42–47. [CrossRef]
7. Eiter, T.; Wolfgang, F.; Leone, N.; Pfeifer, G. A Logic Programming Approach to Knowledge-State Planning: Semantics and Complexity. *ACM Trans. Comput. Log.* **2004**, *5*, 206–263. [CrossRef]

8. Tsymbal, A.; Bronnikov, A.; Yerokhin, A. Adaptive Decision-making for Robotic adaptive tasks. In Proceedings of the IEEE 8th International Conference on Advanced Optoelectronics and Lasers (CAOL), Sozopol, Bulgaria, 6–8 September 2019; pp. 594–597. [CrossRef]
9. Nevliudov, I.; Tsymbal, O.; Bronnikov, A. Intelligent means in the system of managing a manufacturing agent. *Innov. Technol. Sci. Solut. Ind.* **2018**, *1*, 33–47. [CrossRef]
10. Nevliudov, O.; Tsymbal, A.; Andrusevitch, V.; Gopejenko. *Intelligent Decision-Making Support for Flexible Integrated Manufacturing*; ISMA: Riga, Latvia, 2020; 390p.
11. Bronnikov, A.; Nevliudov, I.; Tsymbal, O. Flexible manufacturing tendencies and improvements with visual sensing. *Eskiseh. Tech. Univ. J. Sci. Technol. Appl. Sci. Eng.* **2019**, *20*, 77–83.
12. Vacic, V.; Sobh, T. Vehicle routing problem with time windows. *Computing* **2004**, *3*, 72–80.
13. Sergiyenko, O.; Flores-Fuentes, W.; Mercorelli, P. (Eds.) *Machine Vision and Navigation*; Springer: Berlin/Heidelberg, Germany, 2019; 851p.
14. Sergiyenko, O.Y.; Ivanov, M.V.; Tyrsa, V.V.; Kartashov, V.M.; Rivas-López, M.; Hernández-Balbuena, D.; Flores-Fuentes, W.; Rodríguez-Quiñonez, J.C.; Hipólito, J.I.N.; Hernandez, W.; et al. Data transferring model determination in robotic group. *Robot. Auton. Syst.* **2016**, *83*, 251–260. [CrossRef]
15. Sergiyenko, O.Y.; Tyrsa, V.V. 3D Optical Machine Vision Sensors With Intelligent Data Management for Robotic Swarm Navigation Improvement. *IEEE Sens. J.* **2021**, *21*, 11262–11274. [CrossRef]
16. Ivanov, M.; Sergiyenko, O.; Tyrsa, V.; Lindner, L.; Flores-Fuentes, W.; Rodríguez-Quiñonez, J.C.; Hernandez, W.; Mercorelli, P. Influence of data clouds fusion from 3D real-time vision system on robotic group dead reckoning in unknown terrain. *IEEE/CAA J. Autom. Sin.* **2020**, *7*, 368–385. [CrossRef]
17. Palmieri, N.; Yang, X.; De Rango, F.; Santamaria, A.F. Self-adaptive decision-making mechanisms to balance the execution of multiple tasks for a multi-robots team. *Neurocomputing* **2018**, *306*, 17–36. [CrossRef]
18. Kangru, T.; Riives, J.; Otto, T.K.; Pohlak, M.; Mahmood, K. Intelligent Decision Making Approach for Performance Evaluation of a Robot-Based Manufacturing Cell. In Proceedings of the ASME 2018 International Mechanical Engineering Congress and Exposition, Pittsburgh, PA, USA, 9–15 November 2018; Volume 2: Advanced Manufacturing.
19. Hubmann, C.; Becker, M.; Althoff, D.; Lenz, D.; Stiller, C. Decision making for autonomous driving considering interaction and uncertain prediction of surrounding vehicles. In Proceedings of the 2017 IEEE Intelligent Vehicles Symposium (IV), Los Angeles, CA, USA, 11–14 June 2017; pp. 1671–1678. [CrossRef]
20. Guérin, J.; Thiery, S.; Nyir, E.; Gibaru, O. Unsupervised Robotic Sorting: Towards Autonomous Decision Making Robots. *Int. J. Artif. Intell. Appl.* **2018**, *9*, 81–98. [CrossRef]
21. Schwarting, W.; Alonso-Mora, J.; Rus, D. Planning and Decision-Making for Autonomous Vehicles. *Ann. Rev. Control Robot. Auton. Syst.* **2018**, *1*, 187–210. [CrossRef]
22. Popescu, G.; Valášková, K.; Majerova, J. Real-Time Sensor Networks, Advanced Robotics, and Product Decision-Making Information Systems in Data-driven Sustainable Smart Manufacturing. *Econ. Manag. Financ. Mark.* **2020**, *15*, 29–38.
23. Pérula-Martínez, R.; Castro-González, A.; Malfaz, M.; Alonso-Martín, F.; Salichs, M. Bioinspired decision-making for a socially interactive robot. *Cogn. Syst. Res.* **2019**, *54*, 287–301. [CrossRef]
24. Wang, B.; Rau, P.L.P. Influence of Embodiment and Substrate of Social Robots on Users' Decision-Making and Attitude. *Int. J. Soc. Robot.* **2019**, *11*, 411–421. [CrossRef]
25. Chen, M.; Nikolaidis, S.; Soh, H.; Hsu, D.; Srinivasa, S. Trust-Aware Decision Making for Human-Robot Collaboration: Model Learning and Planning. *J. Hum.-Robot Interact.* **2020**, *9*, 1–23. [CrossRef]
26. Ebert, J.; Gauci, M.; Nagpal, R. Multi-Feature Collective Decision Making in Robot Swarms. In Proceedings of the 17th International Conference on Autonomous Agents and MultiAgent Systems (AAMAS '18), Stockholm, Sweden, 10–15 July 2018; pp. 1711–1719.
27. WanLee, S.; Seymour, B. Decision-making in brains and robots—The case for an interdisciplinary approach. *Curr. Opin. Behav. Sci.* **2019**, *26*, 137–145.
28. Patle, B.K.; Pandey, A.; Jagadeesh, A.; Parhi, D.R. Path planning in uncertain environment by using firefly algorithm. *Def. Technol.* **2018**, *14*, 691–701. [CrossRef]
29. Joo, S.-H.; Manzoor, S.; Rocha, Y.G.; Bae, S.-H.; Lee, K.-H.; Kuc, T.-Y.; Kim, M. Autonomous Navigation Framework for Intelligent Robots Based on a Semantic Environment Modeling. *Appl. Sci.* **2020**, *10*, 3219. [CrossRef]
30. Unhelkar, V.; Li, S.; Shah, J. Decision-Making for Bidirectional Communication in Sequential Human-Robot Collaborative Tasks. In Proceedings of the 2020 ACM/IEEE International Conference on Human-Robot Interaction, Cambridge, UK, 23–26 March 2020; pp. 329–341.
31. Shi, H.; Lin, Z.; Zhang, S.; Li, H.; Hwang, F. An adaptive decision-making method with fuzzy Bayesian reinforcement learning for robot soccer. *Inf. Sci.* **2018**, *436–437*, 268–281. [CrossRef]
32. Sun, C.; Kingry, N.; Dai, R. A Unified Formulation and Nonconvex Optimization Method for Mixed-Type Decision-Making of Robotic Systems. *IEEE Trans. Robot.* **2021**, *37*, 831–846. [CrossRef]
33. Zafar, M.N.; Mohanta, J.C. Methodology for Path Planning and Optimization of Mobile Robots: A Review. *Procedia Comput. Sci.* **2018**, *133*, 141–152. [CrossRef]

34. Zagradjanin, N.; Pamucar, D.; Jovanovic, K. Cloud-Based Multi-Robot Path Planning in Complex and Crowded Environment with Multi-Criteria Decision Making Using Full Consistency Method. *Symmetry* **2019**, *11*, 1241. [CrossRef]
35. Wojtak, W.; Ferreira, F.; Vicente, P.; Louro, L.; Bicho, E.; Erlhagen, W. A neural integrator model for planning and value-based decision making of a robotics assistant. *Neural Comput. Appl.* **2021**, *33*, 3737–3756. [CrossRef]
36. Li, L.; Ota, K.; Dong, M. Humanlike Driving: Empirical Decision-Making System for Autonomous Vehicles. *IEEE Trans. Veh. Technol.* **2018**, *67*, 6814–6823. [CrossRef]
37. Upadhyay, J.; Rawat, A.; Deb, D.; Muresan, V.; Unguresan, M.-L. An RSSI-Based Localization, Path Planning and Computer Vision-Based Decision Making Robotic System. *Electronics* **2020**, *9*, 1326. [CrossRef]
38. Tsarouchi, P.; Spiliotopoulos, J.; Michalos, G.; Koukas, S.; Athanasatos, A.; Makris, S.; Chryssolouris, G. A Decision Making Framework for Human Robot Collaborative Workplace Generation. *Procedia CIRP* **2016**, *44*, 228–232. [CrossRef]
39. Agostini, A.; Torras, C.; Wörgötter, F. Efficient interactive decision-making framework for robotic applications. *Artif. Intell.* **2017**, *247*, 187–212. [CrossRef]

Article

Towards the Sign Function Best Approximation for Secure Outsourced Computations and Control

Mikhail Babenko [1,2], **Andrei Tchernykh** [2,3,4,*], **Bernardo Pulido-Gaytan** [3], **Arutyun Avetisyan** [2], **Sergio Nesmachnow** [5], **Xinheng Wang** [6] and **Fabrizio Granelli** [7]

1. North-Caucasus Center for Mathematical Research, North-Caucasus Federal University, 1 Pushkin Street, 355017 Stavropol, Russia; mgbabenko@ncfu.ru
2. Control/Management and Applied Mathematics, Ivannikov Institute for System Programming, 109004 Moscow, Russia; arut@ispras.ru
3. Computer Science Department, CICESE Research Center, Ensenada 22800, Mexico; lpulido@cicese.edu.mx
4. School of Electronic Engineering and Computer Science, South Ural State University, 454080 Chelyabinsk, Russia
5. Faculty of Engineering, Universidad de la República, Montevideo 11300, Uruguay; sergion@fing.edu.uy
6. Department of Mechatronics and Robotics, Xi'an Jiaotong-Liverpool University, Suzhou 215123, China; xinheng.wang@xjtlu.edu.cn
7. Department of Information Engineering and Computer Science, University of Trento, 38150 Trento, Italy; fabrizio.granelli@unitn.it
*   Correspondence: chernykh@cicese.mx; Tel.: +52-646-1786994

Abstract: Homomorphic encryption with the ability to compute over encrypted data without access to the secret key provides benefits for the secure and powerful computation, storage, and communication of resources in the cloud. One of its important applications is fast-growing robot control systems for building lightweight, low-cost, smarter robots with intelligent brains consisting of data centers, knowledge bases, task planners, deep learning, information processing, environment models, communication support, synchronous map construction and positioning, etc. It enables robots to be endowed with secure, powerful capabilities while reducing sizes and costs. Processing encrypted information using homomorphic ciphers uses the sign function polynomial approximation, which is a widely studied research field with many practical results. State-of-the-art works are mainly focused on finding the polynomial of best approximation of the sign function (PBAS) with the improved errors on the union of the intervals $[-1, -\epsilon] \cup [\epsilon, 1]$. However, even though the existence of the single PBAS with the minimum deviation is well known, its construction method on the complete interval $[-1, 1]$ is still an open problem. In this paper, we provide the PBAS construction method on the interval $[-1, 1]$, using as a norm the area between the sign function and the polynomial and showing that for a polynomial degree $n \geq 1$, there is (1) unique PBAS of the odd sign function, (2) no PBAS of the general form sign function if n is odd, and (3) an uncountable set of PBAS, if n is even.

Keywords: minimax approximate polynomial; Chebyshev polynomials of the second kind; Bernstein polynomial; sign function

MSC: 90C23; 12-08

1. Introduction

Comparing numbers in a homomorphic cipher causes the problem of finding the polynomial of best approximation of the sign function (PBAS). To approximate it, various approaches are used: rational functions [1], Bernstein polynomials [2], Chebyshev polynomials of the first kind [3,4], Fourier series expansions, artificial neural networks [5], least-squares [6–9], Newton–Raphson [10], etc. In these approaches, the noncontinuous sign function is replaced by a continuous function $s(x)$ equal to:

$$s(x) = \begin{cases} 1 & \text{if } x > \epsilon, \\ \frac{x}{\epsilon}, & \text{if } x \in [-\epsilon, \epsilon]. \\ -1 & \text{otherwise} \end{cases}$$

The main issue is that the approximation is considered on the union of two intervals $[-1, -\epsilon] \cup [\epsilon, 1]$. The smallest deviation of a polynomial from the sign function is used as a measure of quality. However, this measure has a maximum error close to 0.5 in the zero neighborhood regardless of the degree of the polynomial, which makes it inapplicable for approximating a polynomial on the complete interval $[-1, 1]$.

According to Chebyshev theory, there exists a single polynomial $f(x)$ for continuous function $s(x)$ with the minimum deviation $\min \max_{x \in [-1,1]} |s(x) - f(x)|$ [11], also known as minimax approximate polynomial or polynomial of best approximation.

The form of the minimax polynomial for the sign function approximation depends on ϵ. Various strategies for choosing ϵ for polynomial approximate $s(x)$ are proposed. However, the problem of constructing PBAS remains open.

In this paper, we consider the classical definition of the sign function:

$$sign(x) = \begin{cases} 1 & \text{if } x > 0, \\ 0 & \text{if } x = 0, \\ -1 & \text{if } x < 0. \end{cases}$$

To construct the PBAS, we use the norm as the area between the sign function and the polynomial $f(x)$, determined by the following formula.

$$\|f(x)\| = \int_{-1}^{0} |-1 - f(x)| dx + \int_{0}^{1} |1 - f(x)| dx = \int_{-1}^{0} |1 + f(x)| dx + \int_{0}^{1} |1 - f(x)| dx$$

This norm allows us to avoid dramatically increasing the least deviation of the polynomial from the sign function as a result in the zero neighborhood.

Let us formulate the problem of the PBAS construction.

It is required to find the polynomial $Q_n(x) = \sum_{i=0}^{n} a_i x^i$, where $\forall i = \overline{0, n}$: $a_i x^i$ is the i-th term, $a_i \in \mathbb{R}$ is a coefficient, x is a variable, and $\deg Q_n(x) \leq n$.

It is formally defined as follows:

$$\left\| \sum_{i=0}^{n} a_i^{(0)} x^i \right\| = \Delta = \inf_{a_0, a_1, \ldots, a_n} \left\| \sum_{i=0}^{n} a_i x^i \right\|$$

If $Q_n(x)$ exists, it is called the PBAS. In [11], p. 160, the theorem is proved that the PBAS exists. However, the number of PBAS and their form remains open. In this paper, we study these two problems.

The rest of the paper is organized as follows: Section 2 discusses the properties of the norm, which are then used in the proof. Section 3 discusses approximation of the sign function by Bernstein polynomials. It is shown that if $n \geq 1$ and $Q_n(x)$ is the PBAS, then $\|Q_n(x)\| \leq 1$. Section 4 discusses the PBAS properties. Section 5 discusses the number of the PBAS odd functions. Section 6 investigates the problem of the existence of the PBAS of general form. Section 7 contains a conclusion.

2. Norm and Its Properties

The section discusses the main properties of the norm used for the proof.

Property 1. *If $f(x)$ is an even function, then $\|f(x)\| \geq 2$.*

Proof. Since $f(x)$ is an even function, then $\int_{-1}^{0}|1+f(x)|dx = \int_{0}^{1}|1+f(x)|dx$; therefore:

$$\begin{aligned}\|f(x)\| &= \int_{0}^{1}|1+f(x)|dx + \int_{0}^{1}|1-f(x)|dx \\ &= \int_{0}^{1}|1+f(x)| + |1-f(x)|dx\end{aligned}$$

considering that $\forall x \in \mathbb{R}: |1+f(x)| + |1-f(x)| \geq 2$, then

$$\|f(x)\| \geq \int_{0}^{1} 2dx = 2$$

The property is proven. □

Let us consider an example of calculating the norm for $n = 0$.

Example 1.
(a) Calculate $\|a_0\|$; if $|a_0| \leq 1$, then $\int_{0}^{1}|1+a_0| + |1-a_0|dx = 2$.
(b) Calculate $\|a_0\|$; if $|a_0| > 1$, then $\int_{0}^{1}|1+a_0| + |1-a_0|dx = 2|a_0| > 2$.

From the data presented in Example 1, we can conclude that for $n = 0$, there is an uncountable number of PBAS, and they are given by $f(x) = a_0$, where $|a_0| \leq 1$.

Property 2. If $f(x)$ is an odd function, then $\|f(x)\| = 2\int_{0}^{1}|1-f(x)|dx$.

Proof. Since $f(x)$ is an odd function, then $\int_{-1}^{0}|1+f(x)|dx = \int_{0}^{1}|1-f(x)|dx$; therefore:

$$\|f(x)\| = 2\int_{0}^{1}|1-f(x)|dx$$

The property is proven. □

Property 3. If $f(x) = e(x) + o(x)$ is a general function, then $\|f(x)\| \geq \|o(x)\|$, where $e(x)$ is an even function and $o(x)$ is an odd function.

Proof.

$$\|f(x)\| = \int_{-1}^{0}|1+e(x)+o(x)|dx + \int_{0}^{1}|1-e(x)-o(x)|dx$$

Let $x = -t$, then:

$$\begin{aligned}\int_{-1}^{0}|1+e(x)+o(x)|dx &= -\int_{1}^{0}|1+e(-t)+o(-t)|dt \\ &= \int_{0}^{1}|1+e(t)-o(t)|dt\end{aligned}$$

Therefore,

$$\|f(x)\| = \int_{0}^{1}|1-e(x)-o(x)| + |1+e(x)-o(x)|dx \geq \int_{0}^{1}|2 - 2\cdot o(x)|dx = 2\int_{0}^{1}|1-o(x)|dx$$

According to Property 2 $\|o(x)\| = 2\int_{0}^{1}|1-o(x)|dx$, we find:

$$\|f(x)\| \geq \|o(x)\|$$

The property is proven. □

Property 4. $\forall \phi \in \left(0, \frac{\pi}{2}\right)$:

$$\|f(x) + g(x)\| \leq \sin^2\phi \|\frac{1}{\sin^2\phi} \cdot f(x)\| + \cos^2\phi \|\frac{1}{\cos^2\phi} \cdot g(x)\|.$$

Proof. By the definition,

$$\|f(x) + g(x)\| = \int_{-1}^{0} |1 + f(x) + g(x)| dx + \int_{0}^{1} |1 - f(x) - g(x)| dx$$

According to the basic trigonometric identity $\sin^2 \phi + \cos^2 \phi = 1$, then

$$|1 + f(x) + g(x)| = |\sin^2 \phi + f(x) + \cos^2 \phi + g(x)| \leq |\sin^2 \phi + f(x)| + |\cos^2 \phi + g(x)|$$
$$= \sin^2 \phi \left|1 + \frac{1}{\sin^2 \phi} \cdot f(x)\right| + \cos^2 \phi \left|1 + \frac{1}{\cos^2 \phi} \cdot g(x)\right|$$

$$|1 - f(x) - g(x)| = |\sin^2 \phi - f(x) + \cos^2 \phi - g(x)| \leq |\sin^2 \phi - f(x)| + |\cos^2 \phi - g(x)|$$
$$= \sin^2 \phi \left|1 - \frac{1}{\sin^2 \phi} \cdot f(x)\right| + \cos^2 \phi \left|1 - \frac{1}{\cos^2 \phi} \cdot g(x)\right|.$$

Therefore:

$$\|f(x) + g(x)\| \leq \sin^2 \phi \| \frac{1}{\sin^2 \phi} \cdot f(x)\| + \cos^2 \phi \| \frac{1}{\cos^2 \phi} \cdot g(x)\|$$

The property is proven. □

Corollary 1. $\forall \phi \in \left[0, \frac{\pi}{2}\right]$:

$$\|\sin^2 \phi \cdot f(x) + \cos^2 \phi \cdot g(x)\| \leq \sin^2 \phi \|f(x)\| + \cos^2 \phi \|g(x)\|.$$

Proof. According to Property 4 $\forall \phi \in \left(0, \frac{\pi}{2}\right)$: $\|\sin^2 \phi \cdot f(x) + \cos^2 \phi \cdot g(x)\| \leq \sin^2 \phi \|f(x)\| + \cos^2 \phi \|g(x)\|$. Let us show that the inequality holds in the case $\phi = 0$, then $\|g(x)\| \leq \|g(x)\|$ in the case $\phi = \frac{\pi}{2}$, then $\|f(x)\| \leq \|f(x)\|$.
The corollary is proven. □

Corollary 2. If $\|f(x)\| = \|g(x)\| = a$, then $\forall \phi \in \left[0, \frac{\pi}{2}\right]$:

$$\|\sin^2 \phi \cdot f(x) + \cos^2 \phi \cdot g(x)\| \leq a$$

Proof. According to Corollary 1, we get:

$$\|\sin^2 \phi \cdot f(x) + \cos^2 \phi \cdot g(x)\| \leq \sin^2 \phi \|f(x)\| + \cos^2 \phi \|g(x)\| = a \cdot \sin^2 \phi + a \cdot \cos^2 \phi = a$$

The corollary is proven. □

From Example 1, it follows that if $n = 0$, then there are infinitely many PBAS of the zero degree. If $f(x) = -1$ and $g(x) = 1$, then $Q_0(x) = \sin^2 \phi \cdot f(x) + \cos^2 \phi \cdot g(x) = \cos 2\phi$ defines every PBAS of degree zero.

Let us investigate the problem of the number of PBAS of degrees greater than or equal to one.

3. Approximation of the Sign Function by Bernstein Polynomials

Let us apply the Bernstein polynomials for an approximation of the sign function $f_n(x)$.

$$f_n(x) = \frac{2n+1}{4^n} \binom{2n}{n} \sum_{i=0}^{n} (-1)^i \cdot \frac{1}{2i+1} \cdot \binom{n}{i} \cdot x^{2i+1} \quad (1)$$

Since the function $f_n(x)$ is odd, using Property 2, we can calculate $\|f_n(x)\|$ using $\|f_n(x)\| = 2 \int_0^1 |1 - f_n(x)| dx$. Let us calculate the value $\int_0^1 |1 - f_n(x)| dx$, proving the following statement.

Statement 1. $\forall n \in \mathbb{Z}_+ : \int_0^1 |1 - f_n(x)| dx = \frac{2n+1}{(2n+2)4^n} \binom{2n}{n}$

Proof. Since the Bernstein polynomials on the interval $[-1, 1]$ have the property that $\forall n \in \mathbb{Z}_+, x \in [-1, 1] : |f_n(x)| \leq 1$,

$$\int_0^1 |1 - f_n(x)| dx = \int_0^1 1 - f_n(x) dx$$

Substituting—instead of $f_n(x)$—expression (1), we find

$$\int_0^1 |1 - f_n(x)| dx = \int_0^1 1 - \frac{2n+1}{4^n} \binom{2n}{n} \sum_{i=0}^n (-1)^i \cdot \frac{1}{2i+1} \cdot \binom{n}{i} \cdot x^{2i+1} dx$$

$$= \left(x - \frac{2n+1}{4^n} \binom{2n}{n} \sum_{i=0}^n (-1)^i \cdot \frac{1}{(2i+1)(2i+2)} \cdot \binom{n}{i} \cdot x^{2i+2} \right) \bigg|_0^1$$

$$= 1 - \frac{2n+1}{4^n} \binom{2n}{n} \sum_{i=0}^n (-1)^i \cdot \frac{1}{(2i+1)(2i+2)} \cdot \binom{n}{i}$$

We represent $\frac{1}{(2i+1)(2i+2)}$ in the form $\frac{1}{(2i+1)(2i+2)} = \frac{1}{2i+1} - \frac{1}{2i+2}$, and we find:

$$\int_0^1 |1 - f_n(x)| dx = 1 - \frac{2n+1}{4^n} \binom{2n}{n} \sum_{i=0}^n (-1)^i \cdot \frac{1}{2i+1} \cdot \binom{n}{i} + \frac{2n+1}{4^n} \binom{2n}{n} \sum_{i=0}^n (-1)^i \cdot \frac{1}{2i+2} \cdot \binom{n}{i}$$

Substitute

$$\sum_{i=0}^n (-1)^i \cdot \frac{1}{2i+1} \cdot \binom{n}{i} = \frac{4^n}{(2n+1)\binom{2n}{n}} \sum_{i=0}^n (-1)^i \cdot \frac{1}{2i+2} \cdot \binom{n}{i} = \frac{1}{2n+2}$$

Hence,

$$\int_0^1 |1 - f_n(x)| dx = \frac{2n+1}{(2n+2)4^n} \binom{2n}{n}$$

The statement is proven. □

Corollary 3. $\forall n \in \mathbb{Z}_+ : \|f_n(x)\| \leq \min\left(1, \frac{2}{\sqrt{3n+1}}\right)$

Proof. Since $f_n(x)$ is an odd function, according to Property 2:

$$\|f(x)\| = 2 \int_0^1 |1 - f(x)| dx$$

Let $n \geq 1$:

$$\|f_n(x)\| = 2 \cdot \frac{2n+1}{(2n+2)4^n} \binom{2n}{n} < \frac{2}{4^n} \binom{2n}{n} \leq \frac{2}{\sqrt{3n+1}} \leq 1$$

if $n = 0$, then $\|x\| = 1$; therefore $\forall n \in \mathbb{Z}_+ : \|f_n(x)\| \leq 1$.
The corollary is proven. □

From Property 1 and Corollary 3, we can conclude that if $n \geq 1$, the PBAS is not an even function.

4. Properties of the PBAS

Since the polynomial $Q_n(x)$ is a continuous function on the interval $[-1, 1]$, according to the Weierstrass theorem, it is bounded by this in interval and reaches the minimum and maximum values—that is, there are $x_m, x_M \in [-1, 1]$ such that $\forall x \in [-1, 1] : Q_n(x_m) \leq Q_n(x) \leq Q_n(x_M)$. Let us denote $m_Q = Q_n(x_m)$ and $M_Q = Q_n(x_M)$, and

$m_Q \leq M_Q$. Let us investigate the values of m_Q and M_Q for the PBAS $Q_n(x)$. The result is presented in the form of the following lemma.

Lemma 1. *If $n \geq 1$ and $Q_n(x)$ is the PBAS, then $m_Q \leq -1$ and $M_Q \geq 1$.*

Proof. We split the two-dimensional space $\mathbb{R}^2$ into subspaces using the curves $m_Q = \pm 1$ and $M_Q = \pm 1$ (see Figure 1).

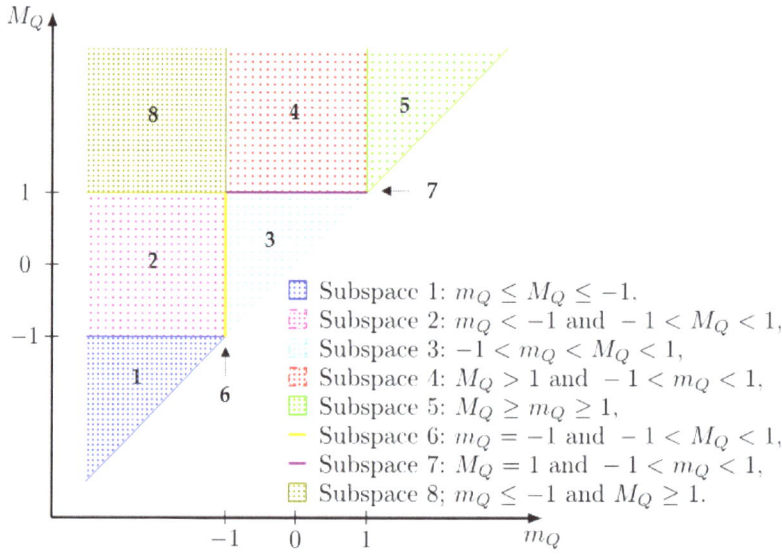

Figure 1. The set of possible values m_Q and M_Q.

In the following, we consider each subspace separately.

Subspace 1. Let us assume that PBAS $Q_n(x)$ satisfies the condition: $m_Q \leq M_Q \leq -1$ (see Figure 1, Subspace 1), then $\forall x \in [-1,1] : Q_n(x) \leq -1, 1 + Q_n(x) \leq 0, 1 - Q_n(x) \geq 0$; therefore:

$$\|Q_n(x)\| = \int_{-1}^{0} |1 + Q_n(x)| dx + \int_{0}^{1} |1 - Q_n(x)| dx$$
$$= \int_{-1}^{0} -1 - Q_n(x) dx + \int_{0}^{1} 1 - Q_n(x) dx = -\int_{-1}^{1} Q_n(x) dx \geq -\int_{-1}^{1} -1 dx = 2$$

From Corollary 3, it follows that for $n \geq 1$ the PBAS has the property $\|Q_n(x)\| \leq 1$. Therefore, we came to a contradiction and our assumption is not correct.

Subspace 2. Let us assume that the PBAS $Q_n(x)$ satisfies the condition: $m_Q < -1$ and $-1 < M_Q < 1$ (see Figure 1, Subspace 2), then $\forall x \in [-1,1] : 1 - Q_n(x) \geq 0$ and $1 - Q_n(x) \geq 0$:

$$\|Q_n(x)\| = \int_{-1}^{0} |1 + Q_n(x)| dx + \int_{0}^{1} 1 - Q_n(x) dx$$

We calculate $\|Q_n(x) + 1 - M_Q\|$ and find

$$\|Q_n(x) + 1 - M_Q\| = \int_{-1}^{0} |2 + Q_n(x) - M_Q| dx + \int_{0}^{1} M_Q - Q_n(x) dx$$

We subtract from $\|Q_n(x)\|$ the value $\|Q_n(x) + 1 - M_Q\|$ and find:

$$\|Q_n(x)\| - \|Q_n(x) + 1 - M_Q\| = \int_{-1}^{0} |1 + Q_n(x)| - |2 + Q_n(x) - M_Q| dx + 1 - M_Q$$
$$= \int_{-1}^{0} |1 + Q_n(x)| - |2 + Q_n(x) - M_Q| + 1 - M_Q dx$$

Considering that
$$\forall x \in [-1,0] : |2 + Q_n(x) - M_Q| \leq |1 + Q_n(x)| + |1 - M_Q| = |1 + Q_n(x)| + 1 - M_Q,$$
then
$$|1 + Q_n(x)| - |2 + Q_n(x) - M_Q| + 1 - M_Q \geq 0$$

Therefore, $\|Q_n(x)\| - \|Q_n(x) + 1 - M_Q\| \geq 0$. If $\|Q_n(x)\| - \|Q_n(x) + 1 - M_Q\| > 0$, then $Q_n(x)$ is not a PBAS, so $\|Q_n(x)\| - \|Q_n(x) + 1 - M_Q\| = 0$; then, $\forall x \in [-1,0] : 1 + Q_n(x) \geq 0$ and

$$\|Q_n(x)\| = \int_{-1}^{0} |1 + Q_n(x)| dx + \int_{0}^{1} 1 - Q_n(x) dx = 2 + \int_{-1}^{0} Q_n(x) dx - \int_{0}^{1} Q_n(x) dx$$

Let $\lambda = \frac{2}{1+M_Q} > 1$, then

$$\forall\, x \in [-1,0] : \lambda Q_n(x) + \frac{1-M_Q}{1+M_Q} + 1 = \lambda Q_n(x) + \lambda = \lambda(Q_n(x) + 1) \geq 0$$
$$\forall\, x \in [-1,0] : 1 - \lambda Q_n(x) - \frac{1-M_Q}{1+M_Q} = \lambda M_Q - \lambda Q_n(x) = \lambda(M_Q - Q_n(x)) \geq 0$$

Therefore,

$$\|\lambda Q_n(x) + \frac{1-M_Q}{1+M_Q}\| = \lambda \int_{-1}^{0} 1 + Q_n(x) dx + \lambda \int_{0}^{1} M_Q - Q_n(x) dx$$
$$= \lambda \cdot (1 + M_Q) + \lambda \left(\int_{-1}^{0} Q_n(x) dx - \int_{0}^{1} Q_n(x) dx \right) = 2 + \lambda \left(\int_{-1}^{0} Q_n(x) dx - \int_{0}^{1} Q_n(x) dx \right)$$

since $\lambda > 1$ и $\int_{-1}^{0} Q_n(x) dx - \int_{0}^{1} Q_n(x) dx \leq -1$, then

$$\lambda \left(\int_{-1}^{0} Q_n(x) dx - \int_{0}^{1} Q_n(x) dx \right) < \int_{-1}^{0} Q_n(x) dx - \int_{0}^{1} Q_n(x) dx$$

Therefore,
$$\|\lambda Q_n(x) + \frac{1 - M_Q}{1 + M_Q}\| < \|Q_n(x)\|$$

it means that $Q_n(x)$ is not a PBAS. We came to a contradiction.

Subspace 3. Let us assume that the PBAS $Q_n(x)$ satisfies the condition: $-1 < m_Q < M_Q < 1$ (see Figure 1, Subspace 3), then $\forall x \in [-1,1] : -1 < Q_n(x) < 1$, $1 + Q_n(x) > 0$, $1 - Q_n(x) > 0$. Let $M = \max(|m_Q|, |M_Q|) < 1$. If $M = 0$, then $Q_n(x) = 0$ and $\|Q_n(x)\| = 2$; from the other side, $\forall n \geq 1 : \|Q_n(x)\| \leq 1$. Therefore, we came to a contradiction and $M \neq 0$. Let $\lambda = \frac{1}{M} > 1$ and $\forall x \in [-1,1] : -1 \leq \lambda Q_n(x) \leq 1$, $1 + \lambda Q_n(x) > 0$, $1 - \lambda Q_n(x) > 0$. We calculate the value $\|Q_n(x)\|$ and find:

$$\|Q_n(x)\| = \int_{-1}^{0} 1 + Q_n(x) dx + \int_{0}^{1} 1 - Q_n(x) dx = 2 + \left(\int_{-1}^{0} Q_n(x) dx - \int_{0}^{1} Q_n(x) dx \right)$$

Since, according to the conditions of Theorem 1 and Corollary 3, $n \geq 1$ and $\|Q_n(x)\| \leq 1$. Hence,
$$\int_{-1}^{0} Q_n(x) dx - \int_{0}^{1} Q_n(x) dx \leq -1.$$

We calculate $\|\lambda \cdot Q_n(x)\|$ and find

$$\|\lambda \cdot Q_n(x)\| = \int_{-1}^{0} 1 + \lambda \cdot Q_n(x) dx + \int_{0}^{1} 1 - \lambda \cdot Q_n(x) dx = 2 + \lambda \left(\int_{-1}^{0} Q_n(x) dx - \int_{0}^{1} Q_n(x) dx \right)$$

Since $\lambda > 1$ и $\int_{-1}^{0} Q_n(x)dx - \int_{0}^{1} Q_n(x)dx \leq -1$,

$$\lambda\left(\int_{-1}^{0} Q_n(x)dx - \int_{0}^{1} Q_n(x)dx\right) < \int_{-1}^{0} Q_n(x)dx - \int_{0}^{1} Q_n(x)dx$$

Therefore,

$$2 + \lambda\left(\int_{-1}^{0} Q_n(x)dx - \int_{0}^{1} Q_n(x)dx\right) < 2 + \left(\int_{-1}^{0} Q_n(x)dx - \int_{0}^{1} Q_n(x)dx\right)$$

and

$$\|\lambda \cdot Q_n(x)\| < \|Q_n(x)\|$$

Therefore, we came to a contradiction and our assumption is not correct.

Subspace 4. Let us assume that the PBAS $Q_n(x)$ satisfies the condition: $M_Q > 1$ and $-1 < m_Q < 1$ (see Figure 1, Subspace 4).

$$\|Q_n(x)\| = \int_{-1}^{0} 1 + Q_n(x)dx + \int_{0}^{1} |1 - Q_n(x)|dx$$

we calculate $\|Q_n(x) - 1 - m_Q\|$ and get

$$\|Q_n(x) - 1 - m_Q\| = \int_{-1}^{0} Q_n(x) - m_Q dx + \int_{0}^{1} |2 - Q_n(x) + m_Q|dx$$

we subtract from $\|Q_n(x)\|$ the value $\|Q_n(x) - 1 - m_Q\|$ and get:

$$\|Q_n(x)\| - \|Q_n(x) - 1 - m_Q\| = 1 + m_Q + \int_{0}^{1} |1 - Q_n(x)| - |2 - Q_n(x) + m_Q|dx$$
$$= \int_{0}^{1} |1 - Q_n(x)| - |2 - Q_n(x) + m_Q| + 1 + m_Q dx$$

Considering that $\forall x \in [0,1] : |2 - Q_n(x) + m_Q| \leq |1 - Q_n(x)| + |1 + m_Q| = |1 - Q_n(x)| + 1 + m_Q$, then $\forall x \in [0,1] : |1 - Q_n(x)| - |2 - Q_n(x) + m_Q| + 1 + m_Q \geq 0$; therefore, $\|Q_n(x)\| - \|Q_n(x) - 1 - m_Q\| \geq 0$. If $\|Q_n(x)\| - \|Q_n(x) - 1 - m_Q\| > 0$, then $Q_n(x)$ is not a PBAS, so $\|Q_n(x)\| - \|Q_n(x) - 1 - m_Q\| = 0$ and $\forall x \in [0,1] : 1 - Q_n(x) \geq 0$ and

$$\|Q_n(x)\| = 2 + \int_{-1}^{0} Q_n(x)dx - \int_{0}^{1} Q_n(x)dx$$

let $\lambda = \frac{2}{1-m_Q} > 1$, then

$$\forall x \in [-1,0] : \lambda Q_n(x) - \frac{1+m_Q}{1-m_Q} + 1 = \lambda Q_n(x) - \lambda m_Q = \lambda(Q_n(x) - m_Q) \geq 0$$
$$\forall x \in [0,1] : 1 - \lambda Q_n(x) + \frac{1+m_Q}{1-m_Q} = \lambda - \lambda Q_n(x) = \lambda(1 - Q_n(x)) \geq 0$$

Therefore,

$$\|\lambda Q_n(x) - \frac{1+m_Q}{1-m_Q}\| = \lambda \int_{-1}^{0} Q_n(x) - m_Q dx + \lambda \int_{0}^{1} 1 - Q_n(x)dx$$
$$= 2 + \lambda\left(\int_{-1}^{0} Q_n(x)dx - \int_{0}^{1} Q_n(x)dx\right)$$

since $\lambda > 1$ and $\int_{-1}^{0} Q_n(x)dx - \int_{0}^{1} Q_n(x)dx \leq -1$, then

$$\left(\int_{-1}^{0} Q_n(x)dx - \int_{0}^{1} Q_n(x)dx\right) < \int_{-1}^{0} Q_n(x)dx - \int_{0}^{1} Q_n(x)dx$$

Therefore,

$$\|\lambda Q_n(x) - \frac{1+m_Q}{1-m_Q}\| < Q_n(x)$$

it means that $Q_n(x)$ is not a PBAS. We came to a contradiction.

Subspace 5. Let us assume that the PBAS $Q_n(x)$ satisfies the condition: $M_Q \geq m_Q \geq 1$ (see Figure 1, Subspace 5); therefore, $\forall x \in [-1,1] : Q_n(x) \geq 1$, $1 + Q_n(x) \geq 0$, $1 - Q_n(x) \leq 0$ means

$$\|Q_n(x)\| = \int_{-1}^{0} |1 + Q_n(x)| dx + \int_{0}^{1} |1 - Q_n(x)| dx$$
$$= \int_{-1}^{0} 1 + Q_n(x) dx + \int_{0}^{1} Q_n(x) - 1 dx = \int_{-1}^{1} Q_n(x) dx \geq \int_{-1}^{1} 1 dx = 2$$

From Corollary 3, it follows that for $n \geq 1$, the PBAS has the property $\|Q_n(x)\| \leq 1$. This means that we have come to a contradiction and our assumption is not correct.

Subspace 6. Let us assume that the PBAS $Q_n(x)$ satisfies the condition: $m_Q = -1$ and $-1 < M_Q < 1$ (see Figure 1, Subspace 6), then

$$\|Q_n(x)\| = \int_{-1}^{0} 1 + Q_n(x) dx + \int_{0}^{1} 1 - Q_n(x) dx = 2 + \int_{-1}^{0} Q_n(x) dx - \int_{0}^{1} Q_n(x) dx$$

Let $\lambda = \frac{2}{1+M_Q} > 1$, then

$$\forall x \in [-1,0] : \lambda Q_n(x) + \frac{1-M_Q}{1+M_Q} + 1 = \lambda + \lambda Q_n(x) = \lambda(1 + Q_n(x)) \geq 0$$
$$\forall x \in [0,1] : 1 - \lambda Q_n(x) - \frac{1-M_Q}{1+M_Q} = \lambda M_Q - \lambda Q_n(x) = \lambda(M_Q - Q_n(x)) \geq 0$$

Therefore,

$$\|\lambda Q_n(x) + \frac{1-M_Q}{1+M_Q}\| = \int_{-1}^{0} \lambda + \lambda Q_n(x) dx + \int_{0}^{1} \lambda M_Q - \lambda Q_n(x) dx$$
$$= 2 + \lambda\left(\int_{-1}^{0} Q_n(x) dx - \int_{0}^{1} Q_n(x) dx\right)$$

Since $\lambda > 1$ и $\int_{-1}^{0} Q_n(x) dx - \int_{0}^{1} Q_n(x) dx \leq -1$,

$$\lambda\left(\int_{-1}^{0} Q_n(x) dx - \int_{0}^{1} Q_n(x) dx\right) < \int_{-1}^{0} Q_n(x) dx - \int_{0}^{1} Q_n(x) dx$$

Therefore,

$$\|\lambda Q_n(x) + \frac{1-M_Q}{1+M_Q}\| < Q_n(x)$$

This means that $Q_n(x)$ is not a PBAS.

Subspace 7. Let us assume that $Q_n(x)$ satisfies the condition: $M_Q = 1$ and $-1 < m_Q < 1$ (see Figure 1, Subspace 7). Then,

$$\|Q_n(x)\| = \int_{-1}^{0} 1 + Q_n(x) dx + \int_{0}^{1} 1 - Q_n(x) dx = 2 + \int_{-1}^{0} Q_n(x) dx - \int_{0}^{1} Q_n(x) dx$$

Let $\lambda = \frac{2}{1-m_Q} > 1$, then

$$\forall x \in [-1,0] : \lambda Q_n(x) - \frac{1+m_Q}{1-m_Q} + 1 = \lambda Q_n(x) - \lambda m_Q = \lambda(Q_n(x) - m_Q) \geq 0$$
$$\forall x \in [0,1] : 1 - \lambda Q_n(x) + \frac{1+m_Q}{1-m_Q} = \lambda - \lambda Q_n(x) = \lambda(1 - Q_n(x)) \geq 0$$

Therefore,

$$\|\lambda Q_n(x) - \frac{1+m_Q}{1-m_Q}\| = \lambda \int_{-1}^{0} Q_n(x) - m_Q dx + \lambda \int_{0}^{1} 1 - Q_n(x) dx$$
$$= 2 + \lambda\left(\int_{-1}^{0} Q_n(x) dx - \int_{0}^{1} Q_n(x) dx\right)$$

Since $\lambda > 1$ and $\int_{-1}^{0} Q_n(x)dx - \int_{0}^{1} Q_n(x)dx \leq -1$,

$$\lambda \left(\int_{-1}^{0} Q_n(x)dx - \int_{0}^{1} Q_n(x)dx \right) < \int_{-1}^{0} Q_n(x)dx - \int_{0}^{1} Q_n(x)dx$$

Therefore,
$$\|\lambda Q_n(x) - \frac{1 + m_Q}{1 - m_Q}\| < Q_n(x)$$

This means that $Q_n(x)$ is not a PBAS.

Subspace 8. Since in all seven cases we have come to a contradiction, if $Q_n(x)$ is a PBAS, it satisfies the boundary conditions defining Subspace 8 (See, Figure 1).

Lemma 1 is proven. □

Lemma 2. *For $n \geq 1$, there exists the PBAS odd function $Q_n^1(x)$.*

Proof. The existence of the PBAS $Q_n(x)$ follows from Theorem [11] p. 160. Since for $n \geq 1$, the PBAS $Q_n(x)$ is not an even function, so $Q_n(x)$ is either a general function or an odd function.

Let us assume that $Q_n(x)$ is a general function; it can be represented in the form $Q_n(x) = Q_n^0(x) + Q_n^1(x)$, where $Q_n^0(x)$ is an even function and $Q_n^1(x)$ is an odd function. It follows from Property 3 that $\|Q_n(x)\| \geq \|Q_n^1(x)\|$. Considering that $Q_n(x)$ is the PBAS, $\|Q_n(x)\| = \|Q_n^1(x)\|$, so the odd function $Q_n^1(x)$ is the PBAS. Therefore, for any $n \geq 1$, there is the PBAS $Q_n(x)$, which is an odd function.

Lemma 2 is proven. □

Corollary 4. *Let $n \geq 1$, $Q_n^1(x)$ be a PBAS odd function, $M_Q > 1$, and $m_Q < -1$.*

Proof. We assume that PBAS is the odd function $Q_n^1(x)$ and $M_Q = -m_Q = 1$.

Let us consider the function $R(x) = \lambda Q_n^1(x)$, where $\lambda \in \mathbb{R}$. Since $Q_n^1(x)$ is an odd function, $R(x)$ is also an odd function. We calculate $\|Q_n^1(x)\|$ and $\|R(x)\|$ using Property 2 and find:

$$\|Q_n^1(x)\| = 2\int_0^1 1 - Q_n^1(x)dx \|R(x)\| = 2\int_0^1 \left|1 - \lambda Q_n^1(x)\right|dx$$

Let us show that there exists $\lambda > 1$, for which the inequality $\|Q_n^1(x)\| > \|R(x)\|$ is satisfied.

$$\int_0^1 1 - Q_n^1(x)dx > \int_0^1 \left|1 - \lambda Q_n^1(x)\right|dx \int_0^1 1 - Q_n^1(x) - \left|1 - \lambda Q_n^1(x)\right|dx > 0$$

We denote as G_+ a set of all $x \in [0,1]$ for which the inequality $1 - \lambda Q_n^1(x) \geq 0$ holds and G_- for which the inequality $1 - \lambda Q_n^1(x) \leq 0$ holds. We then find:

$$\int_0^1 1 - Q_n^1(x) - |1 - \lambda Q_n^1(x)| dx = \int_{G_+} \lambda Q_n^1(x) - Q_n^1(x) dx + \int_{G_-} 2 - Q_n^1(x) - \lambda Q_n^1(x) dx$$

$$= (\lambda - 1) \int_{G_+} Q_n^1(x) dx + \int_{G_-} 2 - Q_n^1(x) - \lambda Q_n^1(x) dx$$

$$= (\lambda - 1) \int_{G_+} Q_n^1(x) dx + \int_{G_-} 2 dx - \int_{G_-} Q_n^1(x) + \lambda Q_n^1(x) dx$$

$$= (\lambda - 1) \int_{G_+} Q_n^1(x) dx + 2|G_-| - (1 + \lambda) \int_{G_-} Q_n^1(x) dx$$

$$= \lambda \left(\int_{G_+} Q_n^1(x) dx - \int_{G_-} Q_n^1(x) dx \right) + 2|G_-| - \int_0^1 Q_n^1(x) dx$$

$$= \lambda \left(\int_0^1 Q_n^1(x) dx - 2 \int_{G_-} Q_n^1(x) dx \right) + 2|G_-| - \int_0^1 Q_n^1(x) dx$$

$$\geq \lambda \int_0^1 Q_n^1(x) dx - 2\lambda |G_-| + 2|G_-| - \int_0^1 Q_n^1(x) dx = (\lambda - 1) \left(\int_0^1 Q_n^1(x) dx - 2|G_-| \right)$$

where $|G_-|$ is the length of the set G_-.

We denote $g(\lambda) = \{|G_-| | G_- = \{x | 1 - \lambda Q_n^1(x) \leq 0 \ \& \ 0 \leq x \leq 1\}\}$.

Since $n \geq 1$ and $\forall x \in [0, 1]$: $Q_n^1(x) \leq 1$, then $g(1) = 0$ and $\forall \lambda > 1$: $g(\lambda) < 1$.

Let us consider two cases.

Case 1: If $\forall x \in [0, 1]$: $Q_n^1(x) < 1$, then there is such a number $x_a \in [0, 1]$ for which $\forall x \in [0, 1]$: $Q_n^1(x) \leq Q_n^1(x_a) = M_Q^a$ holds. If $M_Q^a \leq 0$, then $\int_0^1 1 - Q_n^1(x) dx \geq 1$; therefore, $\|Q_n^1(x)\| \geq 2 > 1$ so $Q_n^1(x)$ is not the PBAS. If $M_Q^a > 0$, we choose as λ the value $\lambda = \frac{1}{M_Q^a} > 1$, for which the inequality $\|Q_n^1(x)\| > \|R(x)\|$ holds, and $Q_n^1(x)$ is not a PBAS. Therefore, we came to a contradiction.

Case 2: If $M_Q^a = 1$, then $g(\lambda)$ is an increasing function; that is, $\xi > 1$, for which the inequality $\int_0^1 Q_n^1(x) dx - 2|G_-| = 0$ holds. Therefore, for any $\lambda \in (1, \xi)$, the following inequality holds:

$$\int_0^1 1 - Q_n^1(x) - |1 - \lambda Q_n^1(x)| dx > 0$$

Therefore, we came to a contradiction. If $M_Q = 1$ and $m_Q = -1$, then $\forall n \geq 1 : Q_n^1(x)$, which is not the PBAS.

The corollary is proven. □

5. The Number of PBAS Odd Functions

In Lemma 2, it is proved that for $n \geq 1$, the PBAS is an odd function, but the question of their number remains open. The following theorem will answer this question.

Theorem 1. *If $n \geq 1$, then there is only one odd function $Q_n^1(x)$ that is the PBAS. Depending on the n, the function $Q_n^1(x)$ is determined as follows:*

If n is odd, then

$$Q_n^1(x) = x \sum_{i=1}^{\frac{n+1}{2}} \frac{1}{\sin \frac{i \cdot \pi}{n+3}} \prod_{j=1, j \neq i}^{\frac{n+1}{2}} \frac{x^2 - \sin^2 \frac{j \cdot \pi}{n+3}}{\sin^2 \frac{i \cdot \pi}{n+3} - \sin^2 \frac{j \cdot \pi}{n+3}}$$

and

$$\|Q_n^1(x)\| = 2 \tan \frac{\pi}{2n+6};$$

If n is even, then

$$Q_n^1(x) = x \sum_{i=1}^{\frac{n}{2}} \frac{1}{\sin \frac{i \cdot \pi}{n+2}} \prod_{j=1, j \neq i}^{\frac{n}{2}} \frac{x^2 - \sin^2 \frac{j \cdot \pi}{n+2}}{\sin^2 \frac{i \cdot \pi}{n+2} - \sin^2 \frac{j \cdot \pi}{n+2}}$$

and
$$\|Q_n^1(x)\| = 2\tan\frac{\pi}{2n+4}.$$

Proof. Let us consider two cases.

Case 1. n is an odd number.

We consider the points $0 < x_1 < x_2 < \ldots < x_u \leq 1$ such that $\forall i = \overline{1,u}: Q_n^1(x_i) = 1$. According to Corollary, 4 the value M_Q^a satisfies the condition $M_Q^a > 1$. Considering that the function $Q_n^1(x)$ is an odd continuous function, then at least one point $x_1 \in [0,1]$ is such that $Q_n^1(x) = 1$ exists.

Let us consider the question of the number of zeroes of the function $F(x) = \frac{dQ_n^1(x_i)}{dx}$. Since the function $Q_n^1(x)$ is an odd continuous function, then $F(x)$ is an even function. The number of zeroes of $F(x)$ is less or equal to $n-1$, of which non-negative numbers are less than or equal to $\frac{n-1}{2}$. Therefore, the number of solutions to the equation $Q_n^1(x) = 1$ satisfying the question $x \in (0,1]$ is less than or equal to $\frac{n-1}{2} + 1 = \frac{n+1}{2}$. That is, $u \leq \frac{n+1}{2}$.

Let us consider the points $0 = y_0 < y_1 < y_2 < \ldots < y_v < y_{v+1} = 1$. In each of the points $y_1, y_2, \ldots, y_v$ the value of the function $f(x) = 1 - Q_{2v-1}^1(x) = 1 - \sum\limits_{i=0}^{v-1} a_{2i+1} x^{2i+1}$ changes its sign.

$$I_v = \frac{\|Q_{2v-1}^1(x)\|}{2} = \int_0^1 |1 - Q_n^1(x)|dx = \sum_{i=0}^{v}(-1)^i \int_{y_i}^{y_{i+1}} f(x)dx$$
$$= 2\sum_{i=1}^{v}(-1)^{i+1} F(y_i) + (-1)^v F(y_{v+1})$$

where $F(x) = x - \sum_{i=0}^{v-1} \frac{a_{2i+1}}{2i+2} x^{2i+2}$.

We calculate the values of the partial derivatives $\forall i = \overline{1,v}$:

$$\frac{\partial F(y_i)}{\partial y_i} = 1 - \sum_{i=0}^{v-1} a_{2i+1} y_i^{2i+1} - \sum_{i=0}^{v-1} \frac{\partial a_{2i+1}}{\partial y_i} \cdot \frac{y_i^{2i+2}}{2i+2}$$

Since $1 - \sum_{i=0}^{v-1} a_{2i+1} y_i^{2i+1} = 0$ by the definition, then:

$$\frac{\partial F(y_i)}{\partial y_i} = -\sum_{i=0}^{v-1} \frac{\partial a_{2i+1}}{\partial y_i} \cdot \frac{y_i^{2i+2}}{2i+2}$$

We calculate the values of the partial derivatives $\forall i \neq j$:

$$\frac{\partial F(y_i)}{\partial y_j} = -\sum_{i=0}^{v-1} \frac{\partial a_{2i+1}}{\partial y_j} \cdot \frac{y_i^{2i+2}}{2i+2}$$

The necessary condition for the value $\|Q_{2v+1}^1(x)\|$ to be minimal is: $\forall i = \overline{1,v}: \frac{\partial I_v}{\partial y_i} = 0$; therefore,

$$\frac{\partial I_v}{\partial y_i} = -2\sum_{j=1}^{v}(-1)^{j+1} \sum_{k=0}^{v-1} \frac{\partial a_{2k+1}}{\partial y_i} \cdot \frac{y_j^{2k+2}}{2k+2} - (-1)^v \sum_{k=0}^{v-1} \frac{\partial a_{2k+1}}{\partial y_i} \cdot \frac{1}{2k+2}$$
$$= -\sum_{k=0}^{v-1} \frac{\partial a_{2k+1}}{\partial y_i} \cdot \frac{1}{2k+2} \left(2\sum_{j=1}^{v}(-1)^{j+1} y_j^{2k+2} + (-1)^v\right)$$

Solving the system $\frac{\partial I_v}{\partial y_i} = 0$ [12], we find that $\forall k = \overline{0,v-1}$:

$$2\sum_{j=1}^{v}(-1)^{j+1} y_j^{2k+2} + (-1)^v = 0$$

Considering that $\forall\, i = \overline{1,v}$: $y_i > 0$; therefore, $\forall\, i = \overline{1,v}$: $y_i = \sin\frac{i\cdot\pi}{2v+2}$ [12].

Using the Lagrange interpolation formula, we calculate the value $Q^1_{2v-1}(x)$, and we find $Q^1_{2v-1}(x) = \sum_{i=1}^{v} l_i(x) - \sum_{i=1}^{v} \bar{l}_i(x)$, where

$$l_i(x) = \prod_{j=1}^{v}\frac{x+y_j}{y_i+y_j} \cdot \prod_{j=1,\, j\neq i}^{v}\frac{x-y_j}{y_i-y_j} \quad \bar{l}_i(x) = -\prod_{j=1,\, j\neq i}^{v}\frac{x+y_j}{y_i-y_j} \cdot \prod_{j=1}^{v}\frac{x-y_j}{y_i+y_j}$$

Then,

$$Q^1_{2v-1}(x) = \sum_{i=1}^{v}\left(\prod_{j=1}^{v}\frac{x+y_j}{y_i+y_j}\cdot\prod_{j=1,\,j\neq i}^{v}\frac{x-y_j}{y_i-y_j} + \prod_{j=1,\,j\neq i}^{v}\frac{x+y_j}{y_i-y_j}\cdot\prod_{j=1}^{v}\frac{x-y_j}{y_i+y_j}\right)$$

$$= \sum_{i=1}^{v}\prod_{j=1,\,j\neq i}^{v}\frac{x-y_j}{y_i-y_j}\prod_{j=1,\,j\neq i}^{v}\frac{x+y_j}{y_i+y_j}\cdot\left(\frac{x+y_i}{2y_i}+\frac{x-y_i}{2y_i}\right)$$

$$= x\sum_{i=1}^{v}\frac{1}{y_i}\prod_{j=1,\,j\neq i}^{v}\frac{x-y_j}{y_i-y_j}\prod_{j=1,\,j\neq i}^{v}\frac{x+y_j}{y_i+y_j}$$

$$= x\sum_{i=1}^{v}\frac{1}{y_i}\prod_{j=1,\,j\neq i}^{v}\frac{x^2-y_j^2}{y_i^2-y_j^2}$$

Let $F(x) = \sum_{i=1}^{v}\frac{a_i}{2i}x^{2i}$ and $\frac{dF(x)}{dx} = Q^1_{2v-1}(x)$, so I_v is equal to

$$I_v = \int_0^1 |1 - Q^1_{2v-1}(x)|\,dx = \sum_{i=0}^{v}(-1)^i\int_{\sin\frac{i\cdot\pi}{2v+2}}^{\sin\frac{(i+1)\cdot\pi}{2v+2}} 1 - Q^1_{2v-1}(x)\,dx$$

$$= 2\sum_{i=1}^{v}(-1)^{i+1}\sin\frac{i\cdot\pi}{2v+2} + (-1)^v + 2\sum_{j=1}^{v}(-1)^j F\left(\sin\frac{j\cdot\pi}{2v+2}\right) + (-1)^{v+1}F(1)$$

We calculate the value $2\sum_{j=1}^{v}(-1)^j F\left(\sin\frac{j\cdot\pi}{2v+2}\right) + (-1)^{v+1}F(1)$, and we obtain:

$$2\sum_{j=1}^{v}(-1)^j F\left(\sin\frac{j\cdot\pi}{2v+2}\right) + (-1)^{v+1}F(1) = 2\sum_{j=1}^{v}(-1)^j\sum_{i=1}^{v}\frac{a_i}{2i}\sin^{2i}\frac{j\cdot\pi}{2v+2} + (-1)^{v+1}\sum_{i=1}^{v}\frac{a_i}{2i}$$

$$= \sum_{i=1}^{v}\frac{a_i}{2i}\left(2\sum_{j=1}^{v}(-1)^j\sin^{2i}\frac{j\cdot\pi}{2v+2} + (-1)^{v+1}\right)$$

Considering that (2) holds, $\forall\, i = \overline{1,v}$: $2\sum_{j=1}^{v}(-1)^j\sin^{2i}\frac{j\cdot\pi}{2v+2} + (-1)^{v+1}$
$= -\left(2\sum_{j=1}^{v}(-1)^{j+1}\sin^{2i}\frac{j\cdot\pi}{2v+2} + (-1)^v\right) = 0$, then

$$2\sum_{j=1}^{v}(-1)^j F\left(\sin\frac{j\cdot\pi}{2v+2}\right) + (-1)^{v+1}F(x) = 0$$

and

$$I_v = \int_0^1 |1 - Q^1_{2v-1}(x)|\,dx = 2\sum_{i=1}^{v}(-1)^{i+1}\sin\frac{i\cdot\pi}{2v+2} + (-1)^v$$

If v is even, then

$$I_v = 2\sum_{i=1}^{v/2}\sin\frac{(2i-1)\cdot\pi}{2v+2} - 2\sum_{i=1}^{v/2}\sin\frac{i\cdot\pi}{v+1} + 1$$

Using the formula $\sin(\alpha - \beta) = \sin\alpha\cos\beta - \sin\beta\cos\alpha$, where $\alpha = \frac{2i\pi}{2v+2} = \frac{i\pi}{v+1}$ and $\beta = \frac{\pi}{2v+2}$, we have

$$\sum_{i=1}^{v/2} \sin\frac{(2i-1)\cdot\pi}{2v+2} = \sum_{i=1}^{v/2}\left(\sin\frac{i\pi}{v+1}\cos\frac{\pi}{2v+2} - \sin\frac{\pi}{2v+2}\cos\frac{i\pi}{v+1}\right)$$

$$= \cos\frac{\pi}{2v+2}\sum_{i=1}^{v/2}\sin\frac{i\pi}{v+1} - \sin\frac{\pi}{2v+2}\sum_{i=1}^{v/2}\cos\frac{i\pi}{v+1}$$

Since $\frac{1}{2} + \sum_{i=1}^{n}\cos ix = \frac{\sin\left(n+\frac{1}{2}\right)x}{2\sin\frac{1}{2}x}$ and $\sum_{i=1}^{n}\sin ix = \frac{\cos\frac{x}{2}-\cos\left(n+\frac{1}{2}\right)x}{2\sin\frac{1}{2}x}$ ([13] p. 2), where $n = \frac{v}{2}$ and $x = \frac{\pi}{v+1}$, we have:

$$\sum_{i=1}^{v/2}\cos\frac{i\pi}{v+1} = \frac{\sin\left(\frac{v}{2}+\frac{1}{2}\right)\frac{\pi}{v+1}}{2\sin\frac{\pi}{2v+2}} - \frac{1}{2} = \frac{1}{2\sin\frac{\pi}{2v+2}} - \frac{1}{2}$$

$$\sum_{i=1}^{v/2}\sin\frac{i\cdot\pi}{v+1} = \frac{\cos\frac{\pi}{2v+2}-\cos\left(\frac{v}{2}+\frac{1}{2}\right)\frac{\pi}{v+1}}{2\sin\frac{\pi}{2v+2}} = \frac{\cos\frac{\pi}{2v+2}}{2\sin\frac{\pi}{2v+2}}$$

Therefore,

$$I_v = 2\left(\cos\frac{\pi}{2v+2}\cdot\frac{\cos\frac{\pi}{2v+2}}{2\sin\frac{\pi}{2v+2}} - \sin\frac{\pi}{2v+2}\left(\frac{1}{2\sin\frac{\pi}{2v+2}} - \frac{1}{2}\right)\right) = \frac{\cos^2\frac{\pi}{2v+2}}{\sin\frac{\pi}{2v+2}} + 1 = \frac{\cos^2\frac{\pi}{2v+2}+\sin^2\frac{\pi}{2v+2}}{\sin\frac{\pi}{2v+2}} - \frac{\cos\frac{\pi}{2v+2}}{\sin\frac{\pi}{2v+2}}$$

Using the basic trigonometric identities $\cos^2 2\alpha + \sin^2 2\alpha = 1$ and $1 - \cos 2\alpha = 2\sin^2\alpha$, $\sin 2\alpha = 2\sin\alpha\cos\alpha$, where $\alpha = \frac{\pi}{4v+4}$ we obtain:

$$I_v = \frac{1-\cos\frac{\pi}{2v+2}}{\sin\frac{\pi}{2v+2}} = \frac{2\sin^2\frac{\pi}{4v+4}}{2\sin\frac{\pi}{4v+4}\cos\frac{\pi}{4v+4}} = \tan\frac{\pi}{4v+4}$$

If v is odd, then

$$I_v = 2\sum_{i=1}^{\frac{v+1}{2}}\sin\frac{(2i-1)\cdot\pi}{2v+2} - 2\sum_{i=1}^{\frac{v-1}{2}}\sin\frac{i\cdot\pi}{v+1} - 1$$

Using the formula $\sin(\alpha - \beta) = \sin\alpha\cos\beta - \sin\beta\cos\alpha$, where $\alpha = \frac{2i\pi}{2v+2} = \frac{i\pi}{v+1}$ and $\beta = \frac{\pi}{2v+2}$, we have

$$\sum_{i=1}^{\frac{v+1}{2}}\sin\frac{(2i-1)\cdot\pi}{2v+2} = \sum_{i=1}^{\frac{v+1}{2}}\left(\sin\frac{i\pi}{v+1}\cos\frac{\pi}{2v+2} - \sin\frac{\pi}{2v+2}\cos\frac{i\pi}{v+1}\right)$$

$$= \cos\frac{\pi}{2v+2}\sum_{i=1}^{\frac{v+1}{2}}\sin\frac{i\pi}{v+1} - \sin\frac{\pi}{2v+2}\sum_{i=1}^{\frac{v+1}{2}}\cos\frac{i\pi}{v+1}$$

Since $\sum_{i=1}^{n}\sin ix = \frac{\cos\frac{x}{2}-\cos\left(n+\frac{1}{2}\right)x}{2\sin\frac{1}{2}x}$ [13] p. 2, where $n = \frac{v+1}{2}$ and $x = \frac{\pi}{v+1}$ we find:

$$\sum_{i=1}^{\frac{v+1}{2}}\sin\frac{i\pi}{v+1} = \frac{\cos\frac{\pi}{2v+2}-\cos\left(\frac{v+1}{2}+\frac{1}{2}\right)\frac{\pi}{v+1}}{2\sin\frac{\pi}{2v+2}} = \frac{\cos\frac{\pi}{2v+2}-\cos\left(\frac{\pi}{2}+\frac{\pi}{2v+2}\right)}{2\sin\frac{\pi}{2v+2}}$$

According to the reduction formula $\cos\left(\frac{\pi}{2}+\frac{\pi}{2v+2}\right) = -\sin\frac{\pi}{2v+2}$, we have:

$$\sum_{i=1}^{\frac{v+1}{2}}\sin\frac{i\pi}{v+1} = \frac{\cos\frac{\pi}{2v+2}+\sin\frac{\pi}{2v+2}}{2\sin\frac{\pi}{2v+2}}$$

Using the formula $\frac{1}{2} + \sum_{i=1}^{n} \cos ix = \frac{\sin\left(n+\frac{1}{2}\right)x}{2\sin\frac{1}{2}x}$ [13] p. 2, where $n = \frac{v+1}{2}$ and $x = \frac{\pi}{v+1}$ we find:

$$\sum_{i=1}^{\frac{v+1}{2}} \cos\frac{i\pi}{v+1} = \frac{\sin\left(\frac{v+1}{2}+\frac{1}{2}\right)\frac{\pi}{v+1}}{2\sin\frac{\pi}{2v+2}} - \frac{1}{2} = \frac{\sin\left(\frac{\pi}{2}+\frac{\pi}{2v+2}\right)}{2\sin\frac{\pi}{2v+2}} - \frac{1}{2}$$

According to the reduction formula $\sin\left(\frac{\pi}{2}+\frac{\pi}{2v+2}\right) = \cos\frac{\pi}{2v+2}$, we obtain:

$$\sum_{i=1}^{\frac{v+1}{2}} \cos\frac{i\pi}{v+1} = \frac{\cos\frac{\pi}{2v+2}}{2\sin\frac{\pi}{2v+2}} - \frac{1}{2}$$

Since $\sum_{i=1}^{n} \sin ix = \frac{\cos\frac{x}{2}-\cos\left(n+\frac{1}{2}\right)x}{2\sin\frac{1}{2}x}$ [13] p. 2, where $n = \frac{v-1}{2}$ and $x = \frac{\pi}{v+1}$ we find:

$$\sum_{i=1}^{\frac{v-1}{2}} \sin\frac{i\cdot\pi}{v+1} = \frac{\cos\frac{\pi}{2v+2} - \cos\left(\frac{v-1}{2}+\frac{1}{2}\right)\frac{\pi}{v+1}}{2\sin\frac{\pi}{2v+2}} = \frac{\cos\frac{\pi}{2v+2} - \cos\left(\frac{\pi}{2}-\frac{\pi}{2v+2}\right)}{2\sin\frac{\pi}{2v+2}}$$

According to the reduction formula $\cos\left(\frac{\pi}{2}-\frac{\pi}{2v+2}\right) = \sin\frac{\pi}{2v+2}$, we find:

$$\sum_{i=1}^{\frac{v-1}{2}} \sin\frac{i\cdot\pi}{v+1} = \frac{\cos\frac{\pi}{2v+2} - \sin\frac{\pi}{2v+2}}{2\sin\frac{\pi}{2v+2}}$$

Therefore,

$$I_v = 2\left(\cos\frac{\pi}{2v+2}\cdot\frac{\cos\frac{\pi}{2v+2}+\sin\frac{\pi}{2v+2}}{2\sin\frac{\pi}{2v+2}} - \sin\frac{\pi}{2v+2}\left(\frac{\cos\frac{\pi}{2v+2}}{2\sin\frac{\pi}{2v+2}} - \frac{1}{2}\right)\right)$$
$$-2\frac{\cos\frac{\pi}{2v+2}-\sin\frac{\pi}{2v+2}}{2\sin\frac{\pi}{2v+2}} - 1 = \frac{1-\cos\frac{\pi}{2v+2}}{\sin\frac{\pi}{2v+2}} = \tan\frac{\pi}{4v+4}$$

Therefore, $\forall v \in N : \|Q_{2v-1}^1(x)\| = 2I_v = 2\tan\frac{\pi}{4v+4}$.

Since $\forall v \in N : I_{v-1} > I_v$, then the smallest value $\|Q_{2v-1}^1(x)\|$ at the maximum v, considering that $v \leq u \leq \frac{n+1}{2}$, then $v = \frac{n+1}{2}$ and $2v+2 = n+3$.

Case 2. If n is an even number, then the result is obtained similarly to case 1, except $v = \frac{n}{2}$ and $2v+2 = n+2$.

The theorem is proved. □

From Theorem 1, it follows that for $n \geq 1$, there is a unique odd function that is the PBAS, which is constructed using the Lagrange interpolation formula, and the interpolation nodes are an alternative to Chebyshev for Chebyshev polynomials of the second kind.

Example 2. *Construct the PBAS for $n = 3$ and $n = 4$, which are odd functions.*

Solution

If $n = 3$, then, according to Theorem 1, the PBAS is given by the following formula:

$$Q_3^1(x) = x \sum_{i=1}^{2} \frac{1}{\sin\frac{i\cdot\pi}{6}} \prod_{j=1, j\neq i}^{2} \frac{x^2 - \sin^2\frac{j\cdot\pi}{6}}{\sin^2\frac{i\cdot\pi}{6} - \sin^2\frac{j\cdot\pi}{6}}$$

$$= x\left(\frac{1}{\sin\frac{\pi}{6}}\cdot\frac{x^2-\sin^2\frac{\pi}{3}}{\sin^2\frac{\pi}{6}-\sin^2\frac{\pi}{3}} + \frac{1}{\sin\frac{\pi}{3}}\cdot\frac{x^2-\sin^2\frac{\pi}{6}}{\sin^2\frac{\pi}{3}-\sin^2\frac{\pi}{6}}\right) = 2x\left(-2x^2 + \frac{3}{2} + \frac{2\sqrt{3}}{3}x^2 - \frac{\sqrt{3}}{6}\right) = \frac{4\sqrt{3}-12}{3}x^3 + \frac{9-\sqrt{3}}{3}x$$

If $n = 4$, then, according to Theorem 1, the PBAS is given by the following formula:

$$Q_4^1(x) = x \sum_{i=1}^{2} \frac{1}{\sin\frac{i\cdot\pi}{6}} \prod_{j=1, j\neq i}^{2} \frac{x^2 - \sin^2\frac{j\cdot\pi}{6}}{\sin^2\frac{i\cdot\pi}{6} - \sin^2\frac{j\cdot\pi}{6}} = \frac{4\sqrt{3}-12}{3}x^3 + \frac{9-\sqrt{3}}{3}x$$

Let us pay attention to the fact that $Q_3^1(x) = Q_4^1(x)$. This fact can be generalized: if n is even and $n \geq 2$, then $Q_n^1(x) = Q_{n-1}^1(x)$.

6. The Number of PBAS of the Neither Function

Let us investigate the problem of the existence of PBAS $Q_n(x)$.

Theorem 2. *If $n \geq 1$, then the following statements are true:*
1. *If n is an odd number, then there is no PBAS $Q_n(x)$.*
2. *If n is an even number, then there is an infinite number of PBAS $Q_n(x)$.*

Proof. From Theorem 1, it follows that there is a unique odd function $Q_n^1(x)$ that is a PBAS. Let us show that there exists an even function $Q_n^0(x) \neq 0$, such that: $\|Q_n(x) = Q_n^1(x)\|$. For this, we calculate $\|Q_n(x)\| - \|Q_n^1(x)\|$ and find:

$$\|Q_n(x)\| - \|Q_n^1(x)\| = \int_0^1 \left|1 - Q_n^0(x) - Q_n^1(x)\right| + \left|1 + Q_n^0(x) - Q_n^1(x)\right| - 2\left|1 - Q_n^1(x)\right| dx$$

where $Q_n(x) = Q_n^0(x) + Q_n^1(x)$, $Q_n^0(x)$ is an even function, and $Q_n^1(x)$ is an odd function. $\|Q_n(x)\| - \|Q_n^1(x)\|$ is equal to zero only if the condition
$\forall x \in [0,1] : \left|1 - Q_n^0(x) - Q_n^1(x)\right| + \left|1 + Q_n^0(x) - Q_n^1(x)\right| - 2\left|1 - Q_n^1(x)\right| = 0$
holds, equivalent to:

$$\forall x \in [0,1] \text{ и } Q_n^1(x) \leq 1 : \begin{cases} 1 - Q_n^0(x) - Q_n^1(x) \geq 0, \\ 1 + Q_n^0(x) - Q_n^1(x) \geq 0; \end{cases} \Leftrightarrow Q_n^1(x) - 1 \leq Q_n^0(x) \leq 1 - Q_n^1(x)$$

and

$$\forall x \in [0,1] \text{ и } Q_n^1(x) \geq 1 : \begin{cases} 1 - Q_n^0(x) - Q_n^1(x) \leq 0, \\ 1 + Q_n^0(x) - Q_n^1(x) \leq 0; \end{cases} \Leftrightarrow 1 - Q_n^1(x) \leq Q_n^0(x) \leq Q_n^1(x) - 1$$

Therefore: $\forall x \in [0,1] : -\left|1 - Q_n^1(x)\right| \leq Q_n^0(x) \leq \left|1 - Q_n^1(x)\right|$.

Since $Q_n^1(x_i)$ is an odd-function PBAS, it follows from Theorem 1 that there are points $x_1, x_2, \ldots, x_u \in (0,1]$ such that $\forall i = \overline{1,u} : Q_n^1(x_i) = 1$. Since $Q_n^1(x_i)$ is an odd-function PBAS, it follows from the proof of Theorem 1 that if n is an odd number, then $u = \frac{n+1}{2}$. Otherwise, $u = \frac{n}{2}$.

Substituting $x_1, x_2, \ldots, x_u$ into the inequalities $-\left|1 - Q_n^1(x)\right| \leq Q_n^0(x) \leq \left|1 - Q_n^1(x)\right|$ we find $\forall i = \overline{1,u} : 0 \leq Q_n^0(x_i) \leq 0$; therefore, the necessary condition is $\forall i = \overline{1,u} : Q_n^0(x_i) = 0$. Since the function $Q_n^0(x)$ is an even function, $\forall i = \overline{1,u} : Q_n^0(-x_i) = 0$; therefore, $Q_n^0(x)$ is divisible by the polynomial $\prod_{i=1}^{u}(x^2 - x_i^2)$ and $\deg Q_n^0(x) \geq 2u$. Let us consider two cases.

Case 1. If n is an odd number, then $\deg Q_n^0(x) \geq 2u = n+1$. Therefore, there is no even polynomial satisfying the condition $\deg Q_n^0(x) \leq n$. Hence, if n is an odd number, there is no PBAS that is a function of general form.

Case 2. If n is an even number, then $\deg Q_n^0(x) \geq 2u = n$. From the other side, $\deg Q_n^0(x) \leq n$; therefore, $\deg Q_n^0(x) = n$. To construct the polynomial $Q_n^0(x)$ we consider the polynomial of the form:

$$Z_n(x) = \frac{Q_n^1(x) - 1}{\prod_{i=1}^{n/2}(x - x_i)}$$

where $\forall i = \overline{1, \frac{n}{2}} : x_i = \sin\frac{i\pi}{n+2}$.

We consider the equation $Q_n^1(x) - 1 = 0$, $\forall i = \overline{1, \frac{n}{2}} : Q_n^1(x_i) - 1 = 0$; therefore, according to Rolle's theorem, in each of the intervals (x_i, x_{i+1}), at least one point $\xi_i \in (x_i, x_{i+1})$ exists for which $F(\xi_i) = 0$, where $F(x) = \frac{d(Q_n^1(x) - 1)}{dx} = \frac{dQ_n^1(x)}{dx}$ and $i \in \overline{1, \frac{n}{2} - 1}$. Since $Q_n^1(x)$ is an odd function, $F(x)$ is an even function; therefore, $\forall i \in \overline{1, \frac{n}{2} - 1} : F(-\xi_i) = 0$.

Considering that $\deg F(x) = n - 2$, then, according to the main theorem of algebra, the equation $F(x) = 0$ over the field of real numbers can have at most $n - 2$ roots—considering their multiplicity—so $\pm \xi_i$ are roots of multiplicity one. Since $\pm \xi_i$ are roots of multiplicity one, the function $F(x)$ passing through $\pm \xi_i$ changes its sign; therefore, $\left(-\infty, -\xi_{\frac{n}{2}-1}\right)$, $\left(-\xi_{\frac{n}{2}-1}, -\xi_{\frac{n}{2}-2}\right), \ldots, (-\xi_2, -\xi_1), (-\xi_1, \xi_1), (\xi_1, \xi_2), \ldots, \left(\xi_{\frac{n}{2}-2}, \xi_{\frac{n}{2}-1}\right), \left(\xi_{\frac{n}{2}-1}, +\infty\right)$ are the intervals of the increase or decrease in the function $Q_n^1(x)$. Therefore, the equation $Q_n^1(x) - 1 = 0$ has at most one solution for each of the intervals. Taking into account that the intervals $(-\xi_1, \xi_1), (\xi_1, \xi_2), \ldots, \left(\xi_{\frac{n}{2}-2}, \xi_{\frac{n}{2}-1}\right), \left(\xi_{\frac{n}{2}-1}, +\infty\right)$, solutions of the equation $Q_n^1(x) - 1 = 0$ are respectively $x_1, x_2, \ldots, x_{\frac{n}{2}}$; therefore, $\psi \geq 0$ does not exist, and $\forall i = \overline{1, \frac{n}{2}}: \psi \neq x_i$ and $Q_n^1(\psi) - 1 = 0$.

Let us show that x_i is a root of multiplicity one of the equation $Q_n^1(x) - 1 = 0$. We suppose that there exists k, for which x_k is a root of multiplicity greater than one of $Q_n^1(x) - 1 = 0$; therefore, x_k is also a root of the equation $\forall i = \overline{1, \frac{n}{2} - 1}: \pm \xi_i$ and x_k.

Provided that $\deg F(x) = n - 2$, we have come to a contradiction. Therefore x_i is a root of multiplicity one of the equation $Q_n^1(x) - 1 = 0$, so if there exists $\gamma \in R$ for which the condition $Z_n(\gamma) = 0$ is satisfied, then $\gamma < 0$ and one of the two conditions $\forall x \geq 0: Z_n(x) > 0$ or $\forall x \geq 0: Z_n(x) < 0$ hold.

Since $Z_n(0) = \frac{Q_n^1(0) - 1}{\prod_{i=1}^{\frac{n}{2}}(-x_i)} = \frac{(-1)^{\frac{n}{2}+1}}{\prod_{i=1}^{\frac{n}{2}} x_i}$, then if $\frac{n}{2}$ is an even number, then $\forall x \geq 0: Z_n(x) < 0$, otherwise $\forall x \geq 0: Z_n(x) > 0$.

Let us consider the function $R_n(x)$, given by the following formula:

$$R_n(x) = \frac{Z_n(x)}{\prod_{j=1}^{\frac{n}{2}}(x + x_j)}$$

The function $R_n(x)$ is continuous on the interval $[0,1]$. According to the Weierstrass theorem, it is bounded; that is, there exist $x_m^R, x_M^R \in [0,1]$ such that $\forall x \in [0,1]: R_n(x_m^R) \leq R(x) \leq R_n(x_M^R)$. Considering that $\forall x \in [0,1]: \prod_{j=1}^{\frac{n}{2}}(x + x_j) > 0$, we find that if $\frac{n}{2}$ is even number, then $R_n(x_m^R) < R_n(x_M^R) < 0$. Otherwise, $0 < R_n(x_m^R) < R_n(x_M^R)$. If $\frac{n}{2}$ is even number, $\tau = -R_n(x_m^R)$; otherwise, $\tau = R_n(x_M^R)$ and we find the function $Q_n^0(x) = \tau \prod_{i=1}^{n/2}(x^2 - x_i^2)$ satisfying $\forall x \in [0,1]: -|1 - Q_n^1(x)| \leq Q_n^0(x) \leq |1 - Q_n^1(x)|$. Since $Q_n(x) = Q_n^0(x) + Q_n^1(x)$, it follows from Corollary 2 that $\forall \phi \in [0, \frac{\pi}{2}]: \sin^2 \phi \cdot Q_n(x) + \cos^2 \phi \cdot Q_n^1(x) = Q_n^1(x)$, so $Q_{\phi,n}(x) = \sin^2 \phi \cdot Q_n(x) + \cos^2 \phi \cdot Q_n^1(x)$ is the PBAS and $Q_{\phi,n}(x) = \sin^2 \phi \cdot Q_n(x) + \cos^2 \phi \cdot Q_n^1(x) = \sin^2 \phi \cdot Q_n^0(x) + Q_n^1(x)$. It is also worth noting that $\overline{Q}_n(x) = -Q_n^0(x) + Q_n^1(x)$ is a PBAS, so $\overline{Q}_{\phi,n}(x) = \sin^2 \phi \cdot \overline{Q}_n(x) + \cos^2 \phi \cdot Q_n^1(x) = -\sin^2 \phi \cdot Q_n^0(x) + Q_n^1(x)$ is the PBAS.

The theorem is proven. □

Example 3. *Construct the general form PBAS for $n = 4$.*

Solution follows from Example 2 that $Q_4^1(x) = \frac{4\sqrt{3}-12}{3}x^3 + \frac{9-\sqrt{3}}{3}x$. Calculating $Z_4(x)$, we have

$$Z_4(x) = \frac{Q_4^1(x) - 1}{\left(x - \frac{1}{2}\right)\left(x - \frac{\sqrt{3}}{2}\right)} = \frac{4\sqrt{3} - 12}{3}x - \frac{4\sqrt{3}}{3}$$

We calculate $R_4(x)$ and find:

$$R_4(x) = \frac{Z_4(x)}{\left(x + \frac{1}{2}\right)\left(x + \frac{\sqrt{3}}{2}\right)} = \frac{\frac{4\sqrt{3}-12}{3}x - \frac{4\sqrt{3}}{3}}{\left(x + \frac{1}{2}\right)\left(x + \frac{\sqrt{3}}{2}\right)} = \frac{\frac{4\sqrt{3}}{3}\left(x + \frac{1}{2}\right) - 4\left(x + \frac{\sqrt{3}}{2}\right)}{\left(x + \frac{1}{2}\right)\left(x + \frac{\sqrt{3}}{2}\right)} = \frac{\frac{4\sqrt{3}}{3}}{x + \frac{\sqrt{3}}{2}} - \frac{4}{x + \frac{1}{2}}$$

We calculate the derivative of the function $R_4(x)$ and find:

$$\frac{dR_4(x)}{dx} = -\frac{\frac{4\sqrt{3}}{3}}{\left(x+\frac{\sqrt{3}}{2}\right)^2} + \frac{4}{\left(x+\frac{1}{2}\right)^2}$$

Since there are no critical points on the segment $[0,1]$, the function $R_4(x)$ takes the maximum and minimum values at the ends of the segment. If we calculate $R_4(0)$ and $R_4(1)$, respectively, we have: $R_4(0) = -\frac{16}{3}$ and

$$R_4(1) = \frac{\frac{4\sqrt{3}-12}{3} - \frac{4\sqrt{3}}{3}}{\left(1+\frac{1}{2}\right)\left(1+\frac{\sqrt{3}}{2}\right)} = -\frac{16}{6+3\sqrt{3}}$$

Therefore, $\tau = \frac{16}{6+3\sqrt{3}}$ and

$$Q_{4,\mu}^0 = \mu\left(x^2 - \frac{1}{4}\right)\left(x^2 - \frac{3}{4}\right) = \mu\left(x^4 - x^2 + \frac{3}{16}\right) = \mu \cdot \frac{U_5(x)}{32 \cdot x}$$

where μ is any number satisfying the condition $\mu \in [-\tau, \tau]$, and $U_5(x)$ is a Chebyshev polynomial of the second kind. Thus, the PBAS has the form $Q_{4,\mu}(x) = \mu x^4 + \frac{4\sqrt{3}-12}{3}x^3 - \mu x^2 + \frac{9-\sqrt{3}}{3}x + \frac{3}{16}\mu$.

Lemma 3. *If n is an even number, then*

$$\forall i = \overline{1, \frac{n}{2}} : \alpha_i = \prod_{j=1, j\neq i}^{\frac{n}{2}} \left(\sin^2 \frac{i\cdot\pi}{n+2} - \sin^2 \frac{j\cdot\pi}{n+2}\right) = \frac{(-1)^{\frac{n}{2}-i}}{\frac{n+2}{2^n} \cdot \sin^2 \frac{2i\cdot\pi}{n+2}}$$

Proof. As $\forall x, y \in R : \sin^2 x - \sin^2 y = \sin(x-y) \cdot \sin(x+y)$, then

$$\alpha_i = \prod_{j=1, i\neq j}^{n/2} \sin\frac{(i+j)\pi}{n+2} \sin\frac{(i-j)\pi}{n+2}$$

Consider two cases.
Case 1: If $i = \frac{n}{2}$ then

$$\alpha_{\frac{n}{2}} = \prod_{j=1}^{\frac{n}{2}-1} \sin\frac{\left(\frac{n}{2}+j\right)\pi}{n+2} \sin\frac{\left(\frac{n}{2}-j\right)\pi}{n+2} = \frac{\prod_{j=1}^{n-1} \sin\frac{j\cdot\pi}{n+2}}{\sin\frac{n\cdot\pi}{2n+4}}$$

Because $\prod_{j=1}^{n+1} \sin\frac{j\cdot\pi}{n+2} = \frac{n+2}{2^{n+1}}$, we have

$$\alpha_{\frac{n}{2}} = \frac{n+2}{2^n \sin^2 \frac{2\pi}{n+2}}$$

Case 2. If $i \neq \frac{n}{2}$ then

$$\alpha_i = \frac{1}{\sin\frac{2i\pi}{n+2} \sin\frac{i\pi}{n+2}} \prod_{j=i-\frac{n}{2}}^{-1} \sin\frac{j\pi}{n+2} \prod_{j=1}^{i+\frac{n}{2}} \sin\frac{j\pi}{n+2}$$

54

Because $\sin\frac{j\pi}{n+2} = -\sin\frac{(n+2+j)\pi}{n+2}$, we obtain

$$\alpha_i = \frac{(-1)^{\frac{n}{2}-i}}{\sin\frac{2i\cdot\pi}{n+2}\sin\frac{i\cdot\pi}{n+2}} \prod_{j=i-\frac{n}{2}}^{-1} \sin\frac{(n+2+j)\pi}{n+2} \prod_{j=1}^{i+\frac{n}{2}} \sin\frac{j\cdot\pi}{n+2}$$

$$= \frac{(-1)^{\frac{n}{2}-i}}{\sin\frac{2i\cdot\pi}{n+2}\sin\frac{i\cdot\pi}{n+2}} \prod_{j=\frac{n}{2}+i+2}^{n+1} \sin\frac{j\cdot\pi}{n+2} \prod_{j=1}^{i+\frac{n}{2}} \sin\frac{j\cdot\pi}{n+2}$$

$$= \frac{(-1)^{\frac{n}{2}-i}}{\sin\frac{2i\cdot\pi}{n+2}\sin\frac{i\cdot\pi}{n+2}\sin\frac{(\frac{n}{2}+i+1)\pi}{n+2}} \prod_{j=1}^{n+1} \sin\frac{j\cdot\pi}{n+2}$$

As $\prod_{j=1}^{n+1}\sin\frac{j\cdot\pi}{n+2} = \frac{n+2}{2^{n+1}}$, $\sin\frac{(\frac{n}{2}+i+1)\pi}{n+2} = \cos\frac{i\cdot\pi}{n+2}$, and $2\cdot\cos\frac{i\cdot\pi}{n+2}\cdot\sin\frac{i\cdot\pi}{n+2} = \sin\frac{2i\cdot\pi}{n+2}$,

$$\alpha_i = \frac{(-1)^{\frac{n}{2}-i}}{\sin^2\frac{2i\cdot\pi}{n+2}}\cdot\frac{2^n}{n+2}$$

Lemma 3 is proven. □

Theorem 3. *If n is an even number, then PBAS is defined as*

$$Q_{\mu,n}(x) = \mu\prod_{i=1}^{n/2}\left(x^2 - x_i^2\right) + Q_n^1(x),$$

where $\mu \in [-\tau, \tau]$, $x_i = \sin\frac{i\cdot\pi}{n+2}$, and $\tau = \frac{2^{n+1}}{n+2}\tan\frac{\pi}{2n+4}$.

Proof. Using the theorem on the expansion of rational functions in the case of different roots [14], we represent $R_n(x)$ as partial fraction decomposition:

$$R_n(x) = \frac{Z_n(x)}{\prod_{j=1}^{n/2}(x+x_j)} = \sum_{j=1}^{n/2}\frac{b_j}{x+x_j},$$

where $\forall j = \overline{1,\frac{n}{2}} : b_j \in R$. Therefore, we have

$$Z_n(x) = \sum_{j=1}^{n/2} b_j \prod_{i=1,i\neq j}^{n/2}(x+x_i)$$

Calculating the values of $Z_n(x)$ at the point $x = -x_j$, we obtain:

$$Z_n(-x_j) = b_j \prod_{i=1,i\neq j}^{n/2}(x_i - x_j)$$

On the other hand, $Z_n(x) = \frac{Q_n^1(x)-1}{\prod_{i=1}^{n/2}(x-x_i)}$, hence

$$Z_n(-x_j) = \frac{-2}{\prod_{i=1}^{n/2}(-x_j-x_i)} = (-1)^{\frac{n}{2}+1}\cdot\frac{2}{\prod_{i=1}^{n/2}(x_j+x_i)}$$

Since $Z_n(-x_j) = b_j \prod_{i=1,i\neq j}^{n/2}(x_i - x_j) = (-1)^{\frac{n}{2}+1}\cdot\frac{2}{\prod_{i=1}^{n/2}(x_j+x_i)}$, it follows that

$$b_j = (-1)^{\frac{n}{2}+1}\cdot\frac{1}{x_j\prod_{i=1,i\neq j}^{\frac{n}{2}}\left(x_i^2 - x_j^2\right)} = \frac{1}{x_j\prod_{i=1,i\neq j}^{\frac{n}{2}}\left(x_j^2 - x_i^2\right)}.$$

Using Lemma 3, we find

$$b_j = (-1)^{\frac{n}{2}+j} \cdot \frac{2^n}{n+2} \cdot \frac{x_{2j}^2}{x_j}.$$

Therefore,

$$R_n(x) = (-1)^{\frac{n}{2}} \cdot \frac{2^n}{n+2} \sum_{j=1}^{\frac{n}{2}} (-1)^j \cdot \frac{x_{2j}^2}{x_j} \cdot \frac{1}{x+x_j} = (-1)^{\frac{n}{2}} \cdot \frac{2^{n+2}}{n+2} \sum_{j=1}^{\frac{n}{2}} (-1)^j \cdot \frac{x_j - x_j^3}{x+x_j}.$$

Calculating $\frac{dR_n(x)}{dx}$, we have

$$\frac{dR_n(x)}{dx} = -\sum_{j=1}^{\frac{n}{2}} \frac{b_j}{(x+x_j)^2}.$$

Let us show that $\forall x \in [0,1]: \frac{dR_n(x)}{dx} \neq 0$. Using the corollary of the Cauchy–Schwarz inequality $(\sum_{i=1}^n u_i v_i)^2 \leq (\sum_{i=1}^n v_i)(\sum_{i=1}^n u_i^2 v_i)$, we have

$$\left(\sum_{b_j>0} \frac{b_j}{x+x_j}\right)^2 \leq \left(\sum_{b_j>0} b_j\right)\left(\sum_{b_j>0} \frac{b_j}{(x+x_j)^2}\right) \left(\sum_{b_j<0} \frac{b_j}{x+x_j}\right)^2 \leq -\left(\sum_{b_j<0} b_j\right)\left(\sum_{b_j<0} \frac{b_j}{(x+x_j)^2}\right)$$

Therefore,

$$\frac{\left(\sum_{b_j>0} \frac{b_j}{x+x_j}\right)^2}{\sum_{b_j>0} b_j} \leq \sum_{b_j>0} \frac{b_j}{(x+x_j)^2} \qquad \frac{\left(\sum_{b_j<0} \frac{b_j}{x+x_j}\right)^2}{-\sum_{b_j<0} b_j} \leq \sum_{b_j<0} \frac{b_j}{(x+x_j)^2}$$

Let us add two inequalities:

$$\frac{\left(\sum_{b_j>0} \frac{b_j}{x+x_j}\right)^2}{\sum_{b_j>0} b_j} + \frac{\left(\sum_{b_j<0} \frac{b_j}{x+x_j}\right)^2}{-\sum_{b_j<0} b_j} \leq \sum_{j=1}^{n/2} \frac{b_j}{(x+x_j)^2}$$

As $\forall x \in [0,1]: \frac{\left(\sum_{b_j>0} \frac{b_j}{x+x_j}\right)^2}{\sum_{b_j>0} b_j} > 0$ and $\frac{\left(\sum_{b_j<0} \frac{b_j}{x+x_j}\right)^2}{-\sum_{b_j<0} b_j} > 0$ then $\sum_{j=1}^{n/2} \frac{b_j}{(x+x_j)^2} > 0$.

Therefore, $\frac{dR_n(x)}{dx}$ does not change sign on the interval $[0, 1]$. The minimum and maximum of the function $R_n(x)$ will be reached at the ends of the interval. Let us calculate the value of the function $R_n(x)$ at the points $x = 0$ and $x = 1$:

$$R_n(0) = (-1)^{\frac{n}{2}} \cdot \frac{2^{n+2}}{n+2} \sum_{j=1}^{n/2} (-1)^j \left(1 - x_j^2\right) \qquad R_n(1) = (-1)^{\frac{n}{2}} \cdot \frac{2^{n+2}}{n+2} \sum_{j=1}^{n/2} (-1)^j \left(x_j - x_j^2\right)$$

Considering that

$$\sum_{j=1}^{n/2} (-1)^j = \frac{-1 + (-1)^{n/2}}{2}, \sum_{j=1}^{n/2} (-1)^j x_j = \frac{(-1)^{n/2}}{2} - \frac{1}{2} \tan \frac{\pi}{2n+4}, \sum_{j=1}^{n/2} (-1)^j x_j^2 = \frac{(-1)^{n/2}}{2},$$

we have

$$R_n(0) = (-1)^{\frac{n}{2}+1} \cdot \frac{2^{n+1}}{n+2} \qquad R_n(1) = (-1)^{\frac{n}{2}+1} \cdot \frac{2^{n+1}}{n+2} \tan \frac{\pi}{2n+4}$$

As $\forall n \geq 2$ and $|n|_2 = 0 : |R_n(0)| > |R_n(1)|$, considering Theorem 2, we obtain

$$\tau = |R_n(1)| = \frac{2^{n+1}}{n+2} \tan \frac{\pi}{2n+4}.$$

The theorem is proven. □

7. Conclusions

Homomorphic encryption enables the computing of encrypted data without access to the secret key. It has become a promising mechanism for the secure computation, storage, and communication of confidential data in cloud services [15]. Practical scenarios include robot control systems, machine learning models, image processing, and many others [6–10,16–18]. A challenge of processing encrypted information is finding a cryptographically compatible sign function approximation.

State-of-the-art works have mainly focused on constructing the polynomial of best approximation of the sign function (PBAS) on the union of the intervals $[-1, -\epsilon] \cup [\epsilon, 1]$. In this paper, we provide a construction of the PBAS on the complete interval $[-1, 1]$ and prove that:

If $n = 0$, then PBAS has the form $Q_n(x) = a_0$, where $|a_0| \leq 1$.

If $n \geq 1$, then there is a unique PBAS odd function, which can be calculated using the zeros of the Chebyshev polynomial of the second kind.

If $n \geq 1$ and n is an odd number, then there are no PBAS of the general form.

If $n \geq 1$ and n is an even number, then there is an uncountable set of PBAS of the general form.

Future studies include assessing the accuracy and efficiency of PBAS on real systems, e.g., over privacy-preserving neural networks with homomorphic encryption, where the non-linear activation function is replaced with a PBAS to operate with encrypted data.

Author Contributions: Conceptualization, M.B., A.T., A.A. and F.G.; Data curation, B.P.-G. and F.G.; Formal analysis, M.B.; Investigation, M.B., A.T., B.P.-G., A.A., S.N., X.W. and F.G.; Methodology, A.A., S.N., X.W. and F.G.; Project administration, A.A.; Resources, S.N., X.W. and F.G.; Software, B.P.-G. and F.G.; Supervision, A.T. and A.A.; Validation, M.B., B.P.-G., S.N., X.W. and F.G.; Visualization, M.B. and B.P.-G.; Writing—original draft, M.B. and A.T.; Writing—review & editing, A.T. All authors have read and agreed to the published version of the manuscript.

Funding: This work was supported by the Ministry of Education and Science of the Russian Federation (Project 075-15-2020-915).

Institutional Review Board Statement: Not applicable.

Informed Consent Statement: Not applicable.

Data Availability Statement: Not applicable.

Conflicts of Interest: The authors declare no conflict of interest.

References

1. Cheon, J.H.; Kim, D.; Kim, D.; Lee, H.H.; Lee, K. Numerical Method for Comparison on Homomorphically Encrypted Numbers. *Lect. Notes Comput. Sci.* **2019**, *11922*, 415–445. [CrossRef]
2. Cheon, J.H.; Kim, D.; Kim, D. Efficient Homomorphic Comparison Methods with Optimal Complexity. *Lect. Notes Comput. Sci.* **2020**, *12492*, 221–256.
3. Chen, H.; Chillotti, I.; Song, Y. Improved Bootstrapping for Approximate Homomorphic Encryption. *Lect. Notes Comput. Sci.* **2019**, *11477*, 34–54.
4. Han, K.; Ki, D. Better bootstrapping for approximate homomorphic encryption. *Lect. Notes Comput. Sci.* **2020**, *12006*, 364–390. [CrossRef]
5. Boura, C.; Gama, N.; Georgieva, M. Chimera: A unified framework for B/FV, TFHE and HEAAN fully homomorphic encryption and predictions for deep learning. *IACR Cryptol. ePrint Arch.* **2018**, *2018*, 758.

6. Gilad-Bachrach, R.; Dowlin, N.; Laine, K.; Lauter, K.; Naehrig, M.; Wernsing, J. Cryptonets: Applying neural networks to encrypted data with high throughput and accuracy. In Proceedings of the 33rd International Conference on Machine Learning, New York, NY, USA, 19–24 June 2016; Volume 48, pp. 201–210. Available online: http://proceedings.mlr.press/v48/gilad-bachrach16.pdf (accessed on 10 April 2022).
7. Kim, M.; Song, Y.; Wang, S.; Xia, Y.; Jiang, X. Secure logistic regression based on homomorphic encryption: Design and evaluation. *JMIR Med. Inform.* **2018**, *6*, e19. [CrossRef] [PubMed]
8. Bonte, C.; Vercauteren, F. Privacy-preserving logistic regression training. *BMC Med. Genom.* **2018**, *11*, 86. [CrossRef] [PubMed]
9. Kim, A.; Song, Y.; Kim, M.; Lee, K.; Cheon, J.H. Logistic regression model training based on the approximate homomorphic encryption. *BMC Med. Genom.* **2018**, *11*, 83. [CrossRef] [PubMed]
10. Bajard, J.-C.; Martins, P.; Sousa, L.; Zucca, V. Improving the Efficiency of SVM Classification with FHE. *IEEE Trans. Inf. Forensics Secur.* **2019**, *15*, 1709–1722. [CrossRef]
11. Bakhvalov, N.S.; Zhidkov, N.P.; Kobelkov, G.M. *Numerical Methods*; Nauka: Moscow, Russia, 1987; p. 600.
12. Korkine, A.; Zolotareff, G. Sur un certain minimum. *Nouv. Ann. Mathématiques J. Candidats Écoles Polytech. Norm.* **1873**, *12*, 337–355. Available online: http://www.numdam.org/item/NAM_1873_2_12__337_0/ (accessed on 7 November 2019).
13. Zygmund, A. *Trigonometric Series*; Cambridge University Press: New York, NY, USA, 2002; Volume 1, p. 375.
14. Graham, R.L.; Knuth, D.E.; Patashnik, O. *Concrete Mathematics*; Addison-Wesley Publishing Company: Reading, MA, USA, 1994; p. 625.
15. Tchernykh, A.; Babenko, M.; Chervyakov, N.; Miranda-Lopez, V.; Avetisyan, A.; Drozdov, A.Y.; Rivera-Rodriguez, R.; Radchenko, G.; Du, Z. Scalable Data Storage Design for Nonstationary IoT Environment with Adaptive Security and Reliability. *IEEE Internet Things J.* **2020**, *7*, 10171–10188. [CrossRef]
16. Pulido-Gaytan, B.; Tchernykh, A.; Cortés-Mendoza, J.M.; Babenko, M.; Radchenko, G.; Avetisyan, A.; Drozdov, A.Y. Privacy-preserving neural networks with Homomorphic encryption: Challenges and opportunities. *Peer-to-Peer Netw. Appl.* **2021**, *14*, 1666–1691. [CrossRef]
17. Babenko, M.; Tchernykh, A.; Chervyakov, N.; Kuchukov, V.; Miranda-López, V.; Rivera-Rodriguez, R.; Du, Z.; Talbi, E.-G. Positional Characteristics for Efficient Number Comparison over the Homomorphic Encryption. *Program. Comput. Softw.* **2019**, *45*, 532–543. [CrossRef]
18. Cortes-Mendoza, J.M.; Radchenko, G.; Tchernykh, A.; Pulido-Gaytan, B.; Babenko, M.; Avetisyan, A.; Bouvry, P.; Zomaya, A. LR-GD-RNS: Enhanced Privacy-Preserving Logistic Regression Algorithms for Secure Deployment in Untrusted Environments. In Proceedings of the 2021 IEEE/ACM 21st International Symposium on Cluster, Cloud and Internet Computing (CCGrid), Melbourne, Australia, 10–13 May 2021; IEEE: Melbourne, Australia, 2021; pp. 770–775.

Article

Kinematic Modelling for Hyper-Redundant Robots—A Structured Guide

Diego Cerrillo *, Antonio Barrientos and Jaime Del Cerro

Centro de Automática y Robótica (UPM-CSIC), Universidad Politécnica de Madrid, José Gutiérrez Abascal, 2, 28006 Madrid, Spain
* Correspondence: d.cerrillov@alumnos.upm.es

Abstract: Obtaining mathematical equations to model the kinematics of a hyper-redundant robot is not intuitive and of greater difficulty than for traditional robots. Depending on the characteristics of the robot, the most appropriate methodology to approach the modelling may be one or another. This article provides a general overview of the different approaches there are when modelling a hyper-redundant cable-driven robot, while proposing a guide to help the novel researcher that approaches this field decide which methodology to apply when modelling a robot. After providing some definitions, a simple framework to understand all the underlying models is presented. Afterwards, the mathematical equations for the most important methods of modelling are developed. Finally, the proposal for a step-by-step tutorial is included, and it is exemplified by applying it to three real robots.

Keywords: hyper-redundant robots; kinematic modelling; forward and inverse kinematic; piecewise constant curvature

MSC: 70B15

Citation: Cerrillo, D.; Barrientos, A.; Del Cerro, J. Kinematic Modelling for Hyper-Redundant Robots—A Structured Guide. *Mathematics* 2022, 10, 2891. https://doi.org/10.3390/math10162891

Academic Editors: Paolo Mercorelli, Oleg Sergiyenko and Oleksandr Tsymbal

Received: 11 July 2022
Accepted: 6 August 2022
Published: 12 August 2022

Publisher's Note: MDPI stays neutral with regard to jurisdictional claims in published maps and institutional affiliations.

Copyright: © 2022 by the authors. Licensee MDPI, Basel, Switzerland. This article is an open access article distributed under the terms and conditions of the Creative Commons Attribution (CC BY) license (https://creativecommons.org/licenses/by/4.0/).

1. Introduction, Motivation and Definitions

In the 1960s, works with large robotic kinematic chains that involve a high number of degrees of freedom, also named hyper-redundant robots, had already started. The increase in the number of degrees of freedom allowed new configurations and innovative solutions for tasks. An example of the beginnings of hyper-redundant robotics was the Scripps Tensor Arm (1968) [1]. However, the increased difficulty in the control algorithms caused the investigation inside the field to stop in the 1970s. Once again, in the 1980s, Professor Hirose started developing new techniques and robots [2]. In 1990, the modal approximation method (based on approximating the robot's backbone to a mathematically describable curve) appeared [3].

Between the years 2000 and 2010, the investigation continued, both in the theoretical approach (for example, some works of Walker: [4–6]) and the applications, which can be found in the bibliography revisions made by Webster, Jones and Bryan [7]. Currently, the work that is being conducted in the hyper-redundant robotics field continues with this tendency. For example, new algorithms are being searched in order to efficiently solve their kinematics [8–12] while new applications are also being proposed [13,14].

The number of publications for the novel researcher in this field may be overwhelming. Some concepts might be confusing, due to the wide range of configurations that exist. There are many mathematical proposals to obtain different models, either spread around publications or treated without any apparent similarities. It is not difficult to imagine that some might wonder where to begin when modelling a hyper-redundant robotic arm. Some efforts are being made to provide a classification of the different kinematic models, comparing them through some benchmark studies [15] or providing a brief comparison between kinematic models for soft robots [16]. However, a framework for novel researchers is not provided, and they rely on some previous knowledge of how modelling is tackled.

Therefore, this article tries to give an overview of the most relevant and efficient techniques that currently exist and to provide a certain general framework to approach this task. It also proposes some criteria to select the most appropriate modelling methodology and applies them in some real examples.

To do so, a simple classification of hyper-redundant robots is adopted as one of the main criteria for choosing a certain method. Afterwards, some generalities on cable-driven hyper-redundant modelling are described. Then, these generalities are analysed on certain algorithms: Denavit–Hartenberg, the PCC (Piecewise Constant Curvature) method or the LSK (Linearised Segment Kinematics) equations. Additionally, and for completeness, a possible algorithm for solving the inverse kinematics is also explained: the Natural-CCD algorithm. Finally, the proposal of the flow diagram is explained and validated.

1.1. Definitions

In order to establish a kinematic model for "hyper-redundant robots", it must first be established what is considered as such. For this tutorial, the criterion proposed by Martin et al. [8] is accepted, which distinguishes between discreet robots, redundant robots and hyper-redundant robots. Other authors do not offer a numerical difference between such cases [17].

To completely define the position and orientation of a rigid body in a vector space defined in $\mathbb{R}^m$, the number of degrees of freedom required is given by Equation (1).

$$DOF_{\mathbb{R}^m} = \frac{m(m+1)}{2} \tag{1}$$

In particular, for the 2D space $\mathbb{R}^2$, $m = 2 \implies DOF = 3$, and for the 3D space $\mathbb{R}^3$, in which most robots work, $m = 3 \implies DOF = 6$.

Taking this into account, a possible classification of robots can be established:

- **Nonredundant robot:** Any robot whose degrees of freedom are fewer than or equal to $DOF_{\mathbb{R}^m}$, that is, the minimal number of degrees of freedom to completely define the position and orientation of the robot endpoint.
- **Redundant robot**: A robot with more than $DOF_{\mathbb{R}^m}$ degrees of freedom. They are ensured to be capable of reaching a certain state through different joint configurations since there are infinite solutions for each state.
- **Hyper-redundant robots**: A robot with more than twice the minimal degrees of freedom required to completely define the endpoint state ($DOF \geq 2 \cdot DOF_{\mathbb{R}^m}$).

This work focuses exclusively on hyper-redundant robots. However, given the exceptional breadth of this field, it exclusively refers to cable-driven hyper-redundant robots (from now on, CDHR). These particular robotic arms are formed by a series of sections delimited by discs, to some of which several cables are fixated. The modification of the cables' length, mostly achieved by motors, are the actuators responsible for the robot's movement. Hyper-redundancy is achieved by combining different sections with several cables attached to them.

1.2. Classification of CDHR

Once the concept of hyper-redundant cable-driven robots can be clearly delimited, it is desirable to establish a classification of which types can be found inside this set. To do so, several approaches could be adopted. Nevertheless, due to the final objective of achieving a step-by-step methodology to obtain a model for the robot, the following classification is used, which later makes it easier to find the desired equations for each case.

To do so, the concept of backbone should be introduced. The *backbone* of a CDHR is the internal support that joins the different discs together and that holds the weight of the robot itself. Using this new definition, three big sets of robots are suggested: discreet hyper-redundant robots, constant curvature continuous robots and other continuous robots. The features that distinguish each group are:

1. **Discreet Hyper-Redundant Robots:** The classical set of hyper-redundant robots and the most used in the origins of this field. Its main characteristic is that discreet robots are composed of a succession of rigid sections, joined together by, normally, one or two degree-of-freedom joints. The rigidity of the sections makes it possible to use traditional robotics techniques to obtain their kinematic model. MACH-I [14] (see Figure 1a) or Series II, X125 System from OC Robotics [18] are two examples of discreet hyper-redundant robots.

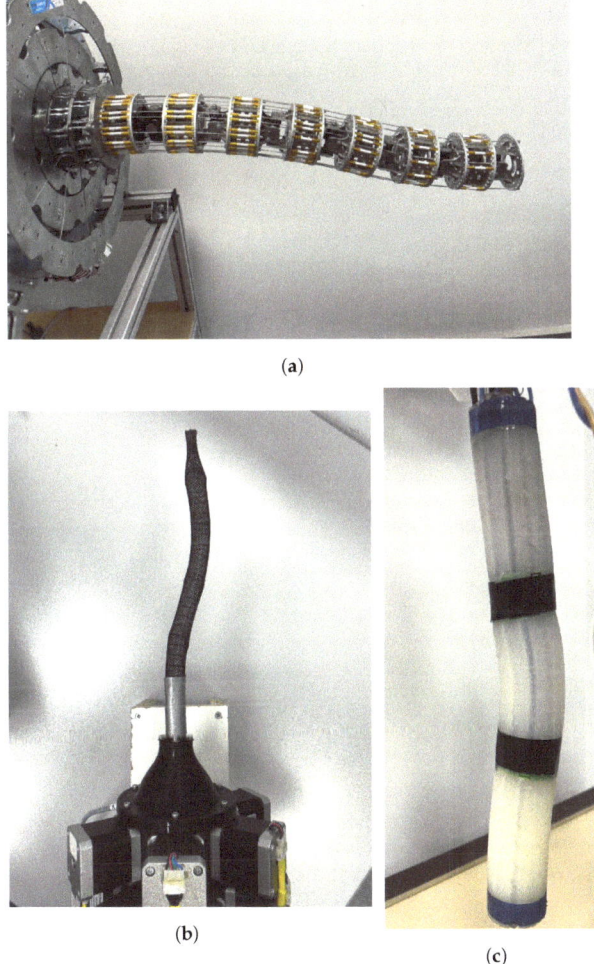

Figure 1. Three examples of CDHR exemplifying each category. (**a**) MACH-I: a discrete CDHR. (**b**) Pilory: a constant curvature CDHR. (**c**) Ruan: a soft CDHR.

2. **Constant Curvature Continuous Robots**: in this group, we include any robot whose sections' backbone can be mathematically modelled as a constant curvature segment. Therefore, actual continuous robots (soft robots, for example) might be included in

this group, but also robots with discreet joints and deformable sections that form a curve. They are mathematically more challenging, but due to the assumption of constant curvature, their equations can be analytically obtained. Examples of this group of robots are the Elephant Trunk by Hannan and Walker [19] or Pylori-I (see Figure 1b), a pivotal discs CDHR [20].

3. **Other Continuous Robots**: In some cases, due to an excess of forces either in the backbone of the robot (excessive distributed weight) or in the endpoint, the constant curvature hypothesis cannot be applied. These cases are more difficult to manage, and they often imply using numerical methods to solve the constitutive equations of the robot. However, since this is a dynamic condition, they are morphologically equivalent to constant curvature robots (either with joints and deformable sections or soft robots). Most soft robots (such as Ruan [21], see Figure 1c, or Kyma [22]), specially those made by polymeric materials, need this kind of kinematic model.

2. Kinematic Modelling Stages for CDHR

In order to have an adequate base for CDHR robots' kinematic modelling, several general aspects must be taken into account. Robot kinematics are affected by the characteristics they have. Once the previous classification is clear, general knowledge of the different steps for kinematic modelling is given so as to ease the introduction to the topic for newcomers.

2.1. Definitions and Nomenclature for the Kinematic Problem

The final objective of kinematic modelling is establishing the mathematical relationship between the state of the global robot's structure at time t with the cable lengths at the same time instant. In the end, the degrees of freedom that can be managed are the lengths of these cables, and through them, the robot is positioned.

Some basic definitions are needed for developing the mathematical equations for hyper-redundant robots:

- The definition of the whole robot's structure (the position of each of its points in space) is named the **robot configuration.**
- The discs (or equivalent physical structures) of the robot to which the cables are fixed are called **active discs.**
- The discs with no cables attached but that are crossed by them are called **passive discs**.
- Except as otherwise specified, the **section** of the robot is considered as the portion of the robot between two consecutive active discs.
- The determination of the position of each one of the infinite points of a certain section is named the **section's state**. It can be represented in different ways depending on the type of robot or the chosen model (a vector, a matrix, etc.).
- The **endpoint of a section** is the theoretical point that represents the ending of a certain section of the robot. Although it could be arbitrarily defined, in this work the usual convention of the geometric centre of the ending disc is chosen. The **endpoint of the robot** would then be the last section's endpoint.

Using these basic concepts, the kinematic problem can be mathematically presented as a transformation between reference systems. One global reference frame can be defined at the centre of the robot's first disc, with its z axis perpendicular to it and pointing towards the next disc. Afterwards, a reference frame can be defined for each active disc, as well as for the endpoint of the robot. As sections are delimited by active discs, these reference frames represent the beginning and the end of a certain section.

The transformation between these reference frames is the essential tool to solve the kinematics: the simplifying hypotheses of many models, by approximating the robot to a defined shape, enables representing the state of the whole section through the information of its endpoint relative to its origin.

In addition to these concepts and definitions, a general naming convention is presented here, which is maintained throughout the whole article:

- The total number of sections of the robot is named n.
- The index k is used when referring to any particular section.
- The total number of cables or tendons the robot uses is named f.
- The endpoint of the robot is indicated with a subindex e.

2.2. Direct Kinematics

Direct kinematics in CDHR robots tries to find the relationship between the existing degrees of freedom (cables' length) with the complete robot state at each moment. Let $\vec{x}_1, \vec{x}_2, \ldots, \vec{x}_n$ be the states of each of the sections for a CDHR, represented as vectors of parameters. Due to hyper-redundancy, finding a direct solution in one step (from $l_1, l_2, \ldots, l_n$ to $\vec{x}_1, \vec{x}_2, \ldots, \vec{x}_n$) is a very complex task. Often, either simplification hypotheses must be assumed or numerical methods are applied [8]. Therefore, in most cases, the simplification hypotheses allow dividing the model into several steps.

These simplifications usually make it possible to represent the state of the section with a finite set of intermediate parameters. For example, sometimes the pose (position and orientation) of the endpoint of a section is enough, considering a certain hypothesis, to represent the position of all its infinite points. The intermediate parameters can finally be inserted into a Homogeneous Transformation Matrix (HTM) between the origin of the section and its endpoint to have the mathematical representation of such section's state. The set of all the HTMs for each section then represents the robot configuration. Therefore, this is the system used throughout the paper (unless specifically stated otherwise), $^{i}A_j$ being the HTM for section j referenced to section i.

For this article, the schematic found in Figure 2 is used as a basis to classify the different direct-kinematic models. As stated, the last step of this theoretical framework is based on multiplying Homogeneous Transformation Matrices (HTMs) to obtain each section's state referenced to the global frame. The other two steps are conditioned by the simplification hypothesis applied to the robot.

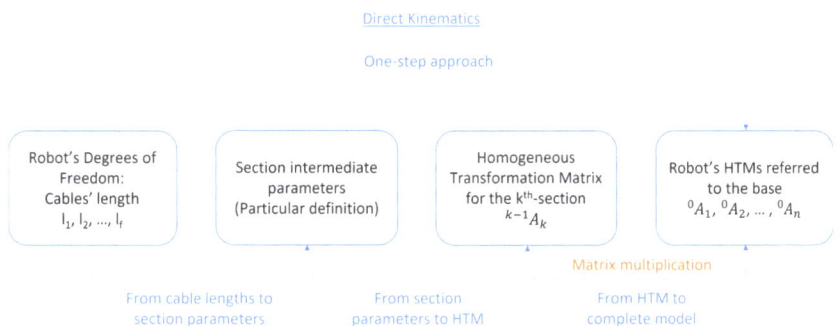

Figure 2. Summary of the different steps for direct kinematics.

Usually, the first step is completely dependent on the robot being modelled (and as such, it relies on the engineer's skills to obtain a mathematical relationship). The second step is frequently standard, and equations are already available in the bibliography. Throughout this paper, it is explained how each one of the mathematical hypothesis are fitted into this view of hyper-redundant kinematics.

2.3. Inverse Kinematics

The inverse kinematic problem consists in obtaining the necessary cable lengths required to achieve a certain robot configuration. As far as this article is concerned, inverse kinematics also involve determining a possible configuration for the robot when only the endpoint's position, given certain spatial coordinates, is known. Inverse kinematics are inherently complex in robots with a high number of serial degrees of freedom: the state or configuration of each joint (that is, the angle rotated by each DOF about a certain origin) affects the configuration of all subsequent joints. Due to the nature of hyper-redundant robots, which have many degrees of freedom, inverse kinematics is a challenge [7].

The first question that might be asked is which spatial coordinates should be used for the inverse kinematics. Representing the pose (position and orientation) of a rigid solid in space requires six degrees of freedom. However, most models presented here use certain hypotheses that reduce the number of degrees of freedom per section. Moreover, the most common robotic morphologies currently studied used, at most, three or four cables per section.

In this work, we use a three degrees of freedom standard as the input of the inverse kinematics. Many morphologies use three independent cables, and those who use four cables usually involve redundancies between them, effectively reducing this number. For simplicity, the three Cartesian coordinates are used ($\begin{bmatrix} x & y & z \end{bmatrix}^t$), but orientation parameters could also be considered. Geometric relationships could then be applied to transform the equations between these two cases. In robots with fewer degrees of freedom per section, further restrictions have to be applied, as addressed in Section 7.

To obtain the inverse kinematic equations, an equivalent process to that of the direct kinematics is followed. The global problem is divided into various steps, which are particularised depending on the chosen simplifying hypothesis (See Figure 3). Once again, this diagram is used as the main guideline throughout the article for inverse kinematics.

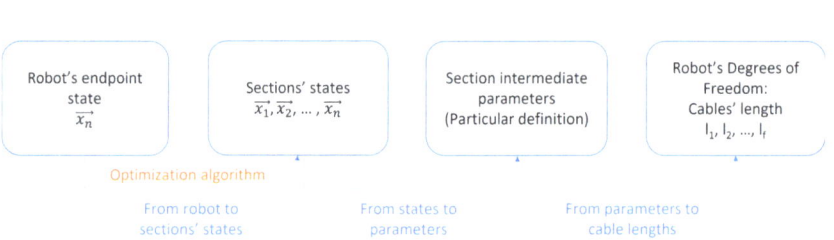

Figure 3. Summary of the different steps for inverse kinematics.

The first step, the optimisation algorithm, is completely independent of the other tasks. It has been thoroughly studied in many papers, using many different techniques ([23–25]). The objective is to obtain a series of orientations and positions for each robot section that allows the robot to reach the endpoint goal.

In general, this step uses algorithms that work independently of the robot's configuration definition (how the generalised coordinates are defined), since they model sections as reference systems and do not need specific information. Since the problem has infinite solutions, these algorithms typically try to optimise a certain value iteratively to obtain one solution. One example of such algorithms is the CCD algorithm or its improved version, the Natural-CCD [26], which is described further on. If the robot configuration is already given for a certain problem, this first step can be omitted.

The further steps depend on the chosen model for each particular robot. They are detailed for each hypothesis but include a transformation from the section's state (usually the endpoint's pose is enough, as stated in Section 2.1), to certain intermediate parameters. By using them, the cable lengths are found.

3. Discreet Hypothesis: Denavit–Hartenberg Method

3.1. Applying the Hypothesis

The first simplification hypothesis that is introduced is the discreet hypothesis. It is based on modelling the robot as a succession of perfectly distinguished 1 DOF or 2 DOF joints. It is the simplest of models, but it can be applied to many hyper-redundant robots. In particular, whenever the discreet hypothesis is acceptable, the Denavit–Hartenberg method is a very useful tool to obtain the equations: it is a systematic and well-known technique [27].

The method, which is briefly explained below, directly affects the second step for direct kinematics (see Figure 4). It fixes each of the joints' DOF as the section parameters, and it gives a relationship from state parameters to HTMs. Only the first step is left unspecified: as stated in Section 2.2, it is highly dependent on the specific geometry of the robot, and cannot be presented in a completely general method.

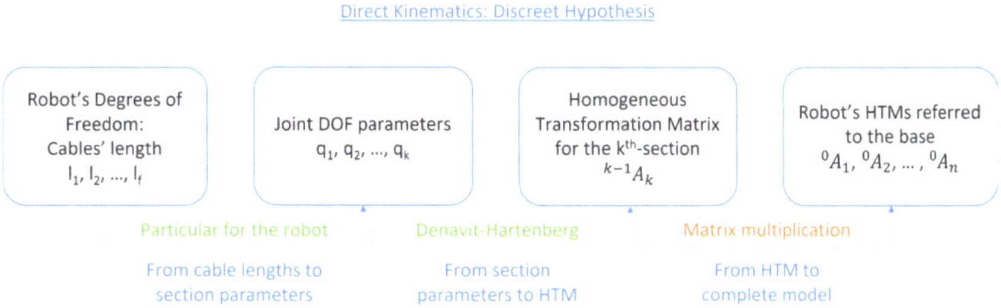

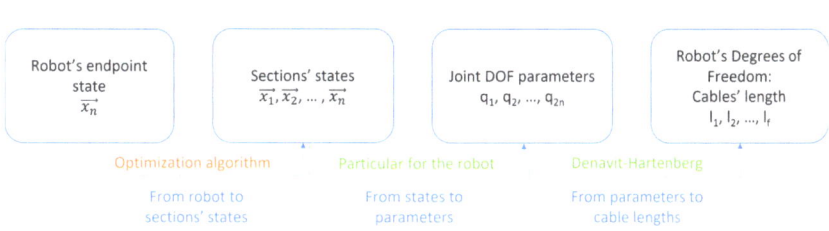

Figure 4. Direct kinematics for the discreet hypothesis.

Inverse kinematics are also affected by the discreet hypothesis, and the Denavit–Hartenberg method can also be used to obtain a procedure for inverse kinematics (see Figure 5). In this case, the relationship from states to parameters has to be obtained for the particular robot. However, once the parameters are available, the HTMs can be obtained for each section using the Denavit–Hartenberg method. Applying successive transformations to the cables' endpoints in each section gives their position in space, which can be used to deduce their lengths. This procedure is applied to an example in Section 8.1.

Figure 5. Inverse Kinematics for the discreet hypothesis.

3.2. Method Explanation

The Denavit–Hartenberg algorithm was proposed by Denavit and Hartenberg in the 20th century and used matrix linear algebra to obtain a kinematic model for a joint chain [27]. It is based on selecting a series of reference systems that have a simple relationship between them, reducing the six DOF of a 3-D space into four basic transformations. Using this method, a direct kinematic model can easily be found for a discreet succession of joints.

The key to applying this method is defining several reference systems: one for the robot's base and one for each of the links between joints. Then, the transformation between successive reference systems is obtained by the combination of four movements: rotation of θ around the z axis, translation of d along the z axis, translation of a along the x axis and rotation of α around the x axis. The variable affected by the joint would be θ in the case of a rotation joint or d for a translation joint, the other three parameters being dependent on the robot's geometry.

This algorithm is very popular in industrial robots, as serial configurations are very frequent in this field. The application to discreet hyper-redundant robots is direct since they are usually built as several serial one or two DOF joints. The method is independent of the final number of joints, and thus can be considered a general methodology for such discreet robots.

For the two DOF joints, it is common to divide it into two Denavit–Hartenberg reference systems but with the same origin (only the orientation would change). For each one DOF joint, a transformation matrix would then be obtained:

$$^{k-1}A_k = Rot_z(\theta_k)T(0,0,d_k)T(a_k,0,0)Rot_x(\alpha_k)$$

$$= \begin{bmatrix} \cos\theta_k & -\cos\alpha_k\sin\theta_k & \sin(\alpha_k)\sin\theta_k & a_k\cos\theta_k \\ \sin\theta_k & \cos\alpha_k\cos\theta_k & -\sin\alpha_k\cos\theta_k & a_k\sin\theta_k \\ 0 & \sin\alpha_k & \cos\alpha_k & d_k \\ 0 & 0 & 0 & 1 \end{bmatrix} \quad (2)$$

Afterwards, by multiplying the matrices for each joint one after the other, the various endpoints would be achieved. This is very useful since it allows to combine these matrices in different ways, so that positions or velocities might be directly transformed from an arbitrary joint to another one, only multiplying by the desired transformations.

Since the Denavit–Hartenberg method is extensively described in the academic world (for example, in Ref. [28] or in Ref. [7]), the method is not thoroughly explained here. However, a simple example is shown, and it could be easily extended for discreet hyper-redundant robots. A robot with two joints, each of them with two DOF, would be then modelled as seen in Figures 6a,b.

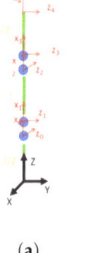

θ	d	a	α
q_1	0	0	$-\pi/2$
q_2	0	l	$\pi/2$
q_3	0	0	$-\pi/2$
q_4	0	$l/2$	0

(a) \qquad\qquad (b)

Figure 6. Example of Denavit–Hartenberg application for a two 2-DOF joint robot. (a) Schematic figure for the application of the Denavit–Hartenberg algorithm to a simple kinematic joint chain. (b) Denavit–Hartenberg parameters for such robot.

With these parameters, the different equations for the reference systems would be obtained:

$$^BA_0 = T(0,0,l/2)Rot_y(-\pi/2)$$
$$^0A_1 = Rot_z(q_1)T(0,0,0)T(0,0,0)Rot_x(-\pi/2)$$
$$^1A_2 = Rot_z(q_2)T(0,0,l)T(0,0,0)Rot_x(\pi/2)$$
$$^2A_3 = Rot_z(q_3)T(0,0,0)T(0,0,0)Rot_x(-\pi/2)$$
$$^3A_4 = Rot_z(q_4)T(0,0,l)T(0,0,0)Rot_x(0)$$
$$^BA_4 = {}^BA_0 \cdot {}^0A_1 \cdot {}^1A_2 \cdot {}^2A_3 \cdot {}^3A_4 \quad (3)$$

As stated before, this method is perfectly valid when joints can be easily distinguished, therefore classifying the robot as a discreet hyper-redundant robot. However, continuous robots such as Ruan [22] need further mathematical mechanisms to model their state.

4. PCC Hypothesis—Piecewise Constant Curvature

Piecewise Constant Curvature (PCC) kinematics is based on the assumption that the robot can be divided into a finite number of constant curvature arcs [7]. This is a desirable hypothesis in continuous hyper-redundant robots and can be successfully applied to many of them. Generally, the conditions for accepting such a hypothesis are, firstly, negligible effects of the gravity force and secondly, assuming the sections to which cables are attached are fixed to the backbone, allowing the robot to bend and producing a negligible friction [29].

Each of the robot's constant curvature arcs is called the robot's sections (as opposed to slices, which refer to the area defined by the slice of the robot at a certain point of the backbone). These sections usually correspond to the extent of the robot between two active slices.

4.1. Direct Kinematics

In Figure 7, the application of the PCC hypothesis to the theoretical framework previously established for direct kinematics is presented. The first determination that can be made is the parameters for the hypothesis. When accepting the constant curvature hypothesis, each of the robot's sections can be modelled through three values: curvature κ, azimuthal angle ϕ and the arc length l.

Having determined the section parameters, the two transformations that are left are a robot-dependent transformation (from cable lengths to section parameters), highly dependent on the morphology, and some robot-independent equations (from state parameters to HTM) that are valid for any robot. Both are examined in more detail.

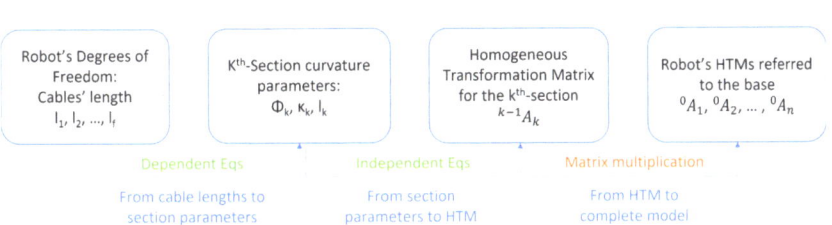

Figure 7. Direct kinematics for PCC.

4.1.1. Independent Transformation—Geometric Method

In this section, the second transformation is obtained: the mathematical equations for the kinematic model of a single section k are found by using geometrical relationships [7,30], even though alternative methods could be used to reach the same mathematical result (as seen in the next section). For clarity, given these formulae refer to a single section, the subindex k is omitted in the equations.

A 3-D arc can be defined in space, with the origin O of the reference system located in the centre of its inferior base (see Figure 8). The z axis is defined as orthogonal to such section, tangent to the curve of the arc. It would be desirable that the x axis is pointed to the centre of the arc, as in the S_{rotate} reference frame in Figure 8, but this is not always possible in all instances. Therefore, to not lose generality, the x axis can be arbitrarily defined, as long as it is orthogonal to the z axis. The y axis is then obtained by the cross product, maintaining the requirements of orthogonality.

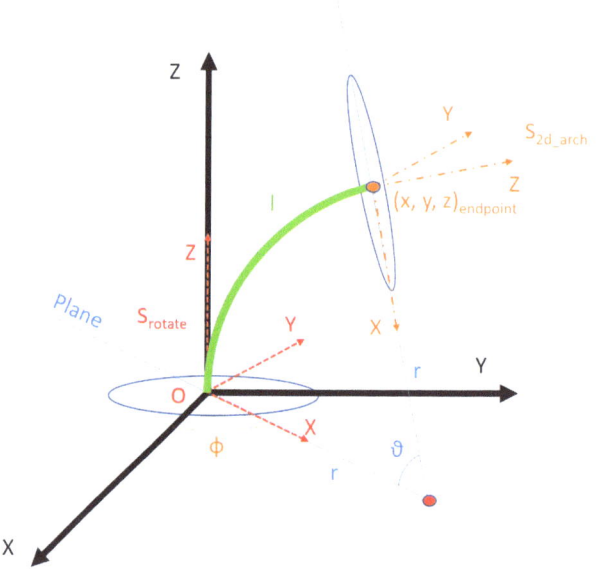

Figure 8. Schematic drawing for direct kinematics calculations—PCC.

The arch itself uses geometric parameters: its length l, the curvature κ (which is easily transformed into the angle θ) and the orientation of the plane that contains the arch defined by the angle ϕ. The problem consists of obtaining the relationships between curvature parameters κ, ϕ and l and the endpoint of the arc x_e, y_e and z_e.

This objective may be achieved by combining two movements (see Equation (4)): firstly, a rotation of ϕ degrees around the Z axis can be applied, therefore obtaining the desired S_{rotate} reference frame. Afterwards, the second transformation includes both a translation and a rotation alongside the arch. The translation sets the endpoint in the final point of the section, while the rotation leaves the Z axis tangent to the section and the X axis pointing to the centre of rotation.

$$^{k-1}A_k = T_{rotate}(\phi) \cdot T_{2d\_arch}(\phi, \kappa, l) \quad (4)$$

Obtaining $T_{rotate}(\phi)$ is simple, since it is a rotation matrix around the z axis of ϕ_k degrees:

$$T_{rotate} = \begin{bmatrix} \cos\phi & -\sin\phi & 0 & 0 \\ \sin\phi & \cos\phi & 0 & 0 \\ 0 & 0 & 1 & 0 \\ 0 & 0 & 0 & 1 \end{bmatrix} \quad (5)$$

As far as the plane arch representation is concerned, a homogeneous transformation between two reference frames can be used. Following the arch means translating the origin of the transformed reference frame to its endpoint, while also rotating the axis so that z is kept parallel to the arch's tangent and x points to its centre. In order to represent the whole arch, and not only its endpoint, a new variable s is defined: $s \in [0, l]$.

The arch contained in the plane has a radius that can be obtained from its curvature ($r = \frac{1}{\kappa}$), and the total angle it rotates around the positive axis y (see θ in Figure 9) would be defined as in Equation (6).

$$\theta = \kappa s \qquad (6)$$

Using these two parameters, and seeing the geometry in Figure 9, the total translation could then be geometrically obtained:

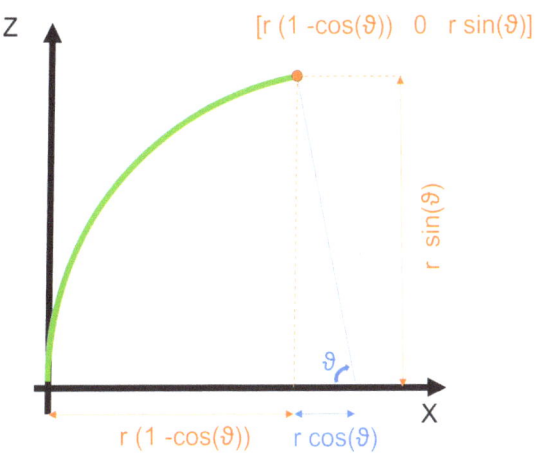

Figure 9. Deduction of translation movement for the endpoint.

$$t = \begin{bmatrix} r(1-\cos\theta) & 0 & r\sin\theta \end{bmatrix} = \begin{bmatrix} \frac{1-\cos\kappa s}{\kappa} & 0 & \frac{\sin\kappa s}{\kappa} \end{bmatrix} \qquad (7)$$

Combining both the translation and the rotation in the same homogeneous transformation matrix:

$$T_{2d\_arch} = \begin{bmatrix} \cos\kappa s & 0 & \sin\kappa s & \frac{1-\cos\kappa s}{\kappa} \\ 0 & 1 & 0 & 0 \\ -\sin\kappa s & 0 & \cos\kappa s & \frac{\sin\kappa s}{\kappa} \\ 0 & 0 & 0 & 1 \end{bmatrix} \qquad (8)$$

The resulting kinematic equations are then given by multiplying matrices resulting from Equations (7) and (8), giving a general matrix $^{k-1}A_k$, that can be particularised at l:

$$^{k-1}A_k(l) = \begin{bmatrix} \cos\phi\cos\kappa l & -\sin\phi & \cos\phi_k\sin\kappa l & \frac{\cos\phi(1-\cos\kappa l)}{\kappa} \\ \sin\psi\cos\kappa l & \cos\phi & \sin\phi\sin\kappa l & \frac{\sin\phi(1-\cos\kappa l)}{\kappa} \\ -\sin\kappa l & 0 & \cos\kappa l & \frac{\sin\kappa l}{\kappa} \\ 0 & 0 & 0 & 1 \end{bmatrix} \qquad (9)$$

4.1.2. Alternatives to Geometric Method

When assuming the PCC hypothesis, it is possible to apply the Denavit–Hartenberg method in order to obtain the equations, even though there are no discreet joints in the kinematic chain [7]. A recent example from the National University of Singapore has successfully used the Denavit–Hartenberg algorithm to estimate a flexible and continuous robot's kinematic model actuated by cables [9]. In this work, MATLAB was used to calculate the mathematical equations through this method, demonstrating its efficiency and simplicity.

To do so, it is necessary to define a series of virtual joints that, altogether, allow to express the same mathematical model as the geometric method. Using these fictitious joints, it is possible to find a group of transformations following the rules of Denavit–Hartenberg which, through a finite number of parameters, represent the robotic section. As an example, several alternatives can be studied [5,7].

In order to show some continuity, and since this parameter definition allows the obtention of the same transformation as Equation (9), this section presents the Walker and Hannan proposal [31], modified by Webster [7] to match the previously stated reference systems. In it, five virtual joints are defined per section, which in Figure 10 are represented as different reference systems:

1. The first transformation is used to transform the problem in a two-dimensional curve, using the rotation ϕ.
2. The second transformation represents a rotation of $\theta_2 = \frac{1}{2}\kappa s$ degrees, which is used to obtain a reference system pointing to the section's endpoint.
3. The third transformation introduces the translation from the origin to the endpoint of the section curve $d_3 = \frac{2}{\kappa} \sin \frac{\kappa s}{2}$.
4. The fourth transformation rotates again $\theta_4 = \frac{1}{2}\kappa s$ degrees to return the tangency to the curve in the endpoint.
5. Finally, the fifth transformation undoes the first transformation, returning to a three-dimensional problem.

Having defined these transformations, the Denavit–Hartenberg table can easily be filled, as seen in Figure 10f. Afterwards, the mathematical equations (the full transformation matrix) can be obtained by applying these parameters to the same method explained in Section 3.

In addition to this method, several additional algorithms can be used to obtain the same result: using differential geometry [19], Frenet's curvature [7], the integral method [3], etc. In each of these methods, an equivalent matrix transformation would be obtained, as Webster's article presents [7], which is why they can also be considered as PCC methods. Afterwards, the same relationship between cables and section curvature parameters as previously obtained must be added, in order to obtain a complete kinematic model.

This perfect equivalency between methods when obtaining the equations implies that choosing the deduction method is indifferent. The mathematical equations that conform the kinematic model are all valid, and the only difference when studying all these processes may be the reference systems. Therefore, it is possible to choose the most intuitive method for the designer.

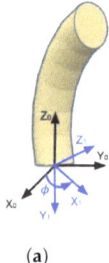

(a)

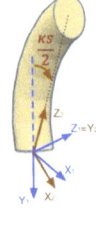

(b)

Figure 10. *Cont.*

(c)   (d)

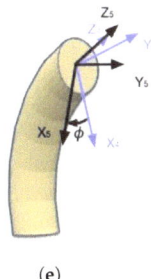

Transf.	θ	d	a	α
T_1	ϕ	0	0	$-\pi/2$
T_2	$\kappa s/2$	0	0	$\pi/2$
T_3	0	$2/\kappa \sin \kappa s/2$	0	$-\pi/2$
T_4	$\kappa s/2$	0	0	$\pi/2$
T_5	$-\phi$	0	0	0

(e)   (f)

Figure 10. Application of Denavit–Hartenberg's method to a robotic section of constant curvature. (**a**) T_1. (**b**) T_2. (**c**) T_3. (**d**) T_4. (**e**) T_5. (**f**) Section's parameter for Denavit–Hartenberg's method.

4.1.3. Dependent Transformation

The other required transformation is the one dependent on the robot's geometry, that is, the transformation from the cables' length to the curvature parameters, which is particular for each robot. This means that a completely general method for any hyper-redundant continuous robot cannot be given. However, for some of the most frequent cases, such as three or four cables per section robots (a higher number would not allow additional DOF) symmetrically distributed around the section; the equations have already been thoroughly studied and obtained in various articles. For example, the three-cable section placed equidistant to the backbone (forming an equilateral triangle) can be obtained following [5]. In ref. [7], this is explained for three and four cables with a similar mathematical process.

In this section, this last procedure is explained. Let us suppose a robot in which every section has three active cables, homogeneously and equidistantly distributed around the section's centre, with a radius d (see Figure 11a). In that same robot's section, several passive discs are used to guide the cables alongside the backbone (which follows the constant curvature hypothesis; therefore, the PCC model provides the position of each of the discs' centres). These cables are modelled with the hypothesis that they join these passive discs with a straight line (see Figure 11b).

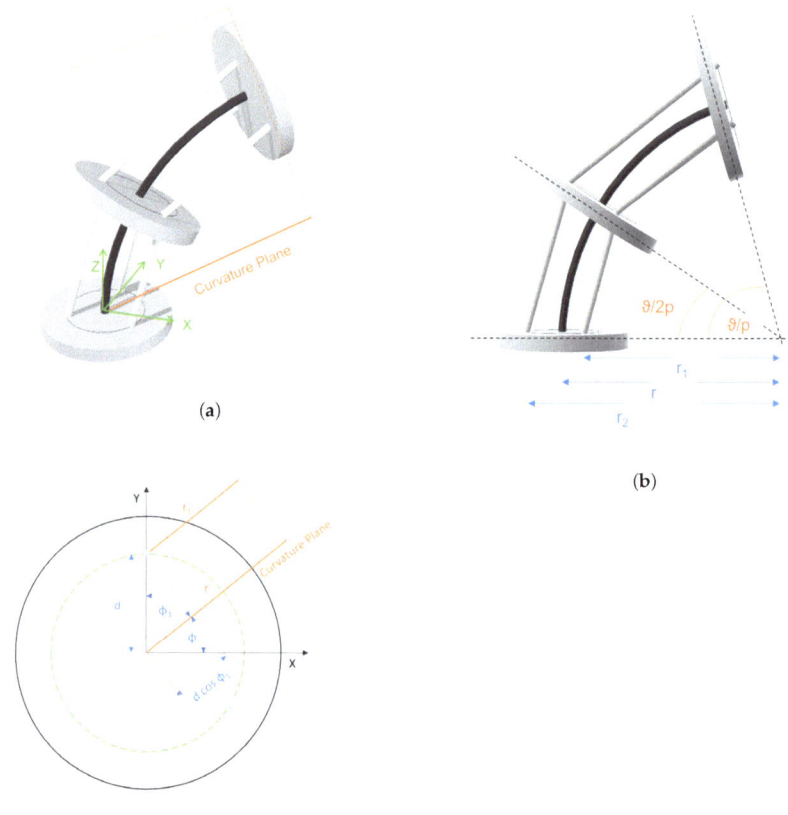

Figure 11. Auxiliary figures for the cables' kinematic relationships. (**a**) Three-dimensional image of the proposed robot. (**d**) Geometric hypothesis to obtain the kinematic equations for the cables. (**c**) Bird's-eye view of the robot's section, including the curvature plane projection.

In Figure 11c, the projection in the plane of one of the section's discs can be observed. In it, the curvature plane (which contains the circumference sector the backbone draws in space) can be seen, as well as the parallel plane that contains the curve that cable 1 follows (both in orange). If the three cables (grey) are equidistant to the section centre with a radius d, and homogeneously distributed, each of the cables i can be positioned by the angle ϕ_i. It can be easily deduced from the figure that:

$$r_i = r - d \cos \phi_i \tag{10}$$

The demonstration that these relationships are valid independently of the number of cables is simple, as long as the robot is compliant with the hypothesis of equidistant and homogeneous distribution.

Turning back to Figure 11b, the expressions for the hypothetical length of the section's backbone (l_c) as well as the length of each of the cables l_i can be derived; p being the number of passive discs in a section:

$$l_c = 2 \cdot p \cdot r \sin(\theta/2p) \tag{11}$$

$$l_i = 2 \cdot p \cdot r_i \sin(\theta/2p) \tag{12}$$

Multiplying Equation (10) by $2p\sin(\theta/2p)$, substituting in Equations (11) and (12), and solving it, the following expression is obtained:

$$l_c = l_i + d2p \cdot \sin(\theta/2p) \cdot \cos(\phi_i) \tag{13}$$

From this last expression, an important property can be deduced. Since cables are homogeneously distributed around the circumference, the total sum of angles ϕ_i is zero. Using trigonometric relations, if Equation (13) is added for each of the cables, then the total length of the backbone could be calculated as the arithmetic average of the real cables' lengths (independently of the number of cables that section has f_k).

$$l_c = \sum_{i=1}^{f_k} \frac{l_i}{f_k} \tag{14}$$

Going back to the three-cable example, applying Equation (13) to two cables and given that they must give the same l_c, then Equation (15) is obtained.

$$d2p\sin(\theta/2p) = (l_2 - l_1)/(\cos\phi_1 - \cos\phi_2) \tag{15}$$

This same step can be applied to cables two and three. Afterwards, joining together both expressions:

$$\phi = \tan^{-1}\left(\frac{\sqrt{3}(l_2 + l_3 - 2l_1)}{3(l_2 - l_3)}\right) \tag{16}$$

Finally, the curvature parameters are obtained through Equations (11) and (12) by which:

$$\sin(\theta/2p) = l_c/2pr = l_i/2pr_i \tag{17}$$

Then, for each cable i:

$$r_i = \frac{l_i}{\kappa l_c} \tag{18}$$

If Equation (10) is applied, then:

$$\kappa = \frac{(l_c - l_i)}{l_c d \cos(\phi_i)} \tag{19}$$

Given the reference that has previously been defined:

$$\kappa = \frac{l_2 + l_3 - 2l_1}{(l_1 + l_2 + l_3)d\sin(\phi)} \tag{20}$$

An expression that calculates κ using the problem's data can be deduced if substituting ϕ with Equation (16) and the trigonometric expression $\sin(\tan^{-1}(y/x)) = y/\sqrt{x^2 + y^2}$ is applied:

$$\kappa = \frac{2\sqrt{l_1^2 + l_2^2 + l_3^2 - l_1 l_2 - l_1 l_3 - l_2 l_3}}{d(l_1 + l_2 + l_3)} \tag{21}$$

To obtain the actual length of the curve (only the cable length has been calculated), applying the geometric definitions to Equation (11):

$$l = \frac{2p}{\kappa}\sin^{-1}\left(\frac{l_c \kappa}{2p}\right) \tag{22}$$

Finally, applying Equations (21) and (14):

$$l = \frac{pd(l_1 + l_2 + l_3)}{2\sqrt{l_1^2 + l_2^2 + l_3^2 - l_1 l_2 - l_1 l_3 - l_2 l_3}} \sin^{-1}\left(\frac{\sqrt{l_1^2 + l_2^2 + l_3^2 - l_1 l_2 - l_1 l_3 - l_2 l_3}}{3pd}\right) \quad (23)$$

Combining the two steps (cables → curvature parameters and curvature parameters → robot state), a direct kinematic model is completely defined for a hyper-redundant continuous robot with PCC hypothesis. If the expression for a multisection robot is desired, then the different transformations for the series of sections should be combined. Nevertheless, it must be taken into account that some corrections may be needed in these cases, since some sections may affect the others. Iterative algorithms [32] or optimisation may be used to improve the model [33].

4.2. Inverse Kinematics

In this section, a possible approach to inverse kinematics is explained. The methodology assumes that the state for each section is already fixed (that is, the optimisation algorithm has already been applied). The objective when applying these equations is, therefore, once the sections have been positioned in space for a certain configuration, to obtain the geometric parameters and translate them to cable lengths that each section requires.

Mathematically this is translated as obtaining $l_1, l_2, \ldots, l_f$ when introducing $\begin{bmatrix} x & y & z \end{bmatrix}^t$ into the equations. The reason for using the Cartesian coordinates was discussed in Section 2.3: the PCC hypothesis describes the configuration of a section using three curvature parameters. Therefore, there are three degrees of freedom with which both the position and the orientation are perfectly defined. Choosing the Cartesian coordinates is an arbitrary decision, but the orientation could also be used (and the geometric transformations could be found analytically).

As in previous models, once the section state has been defined, two transformations are needed (see Figure 12). One of them is the geometric definition of the curvature parameters to extract them from the sections' states. Afterwards, a robot-dependent transformation is needed, equivalent to that in direct kinematics. The relationship between curvature parameters and cable lengths is not general for all cases and must be examined individually.

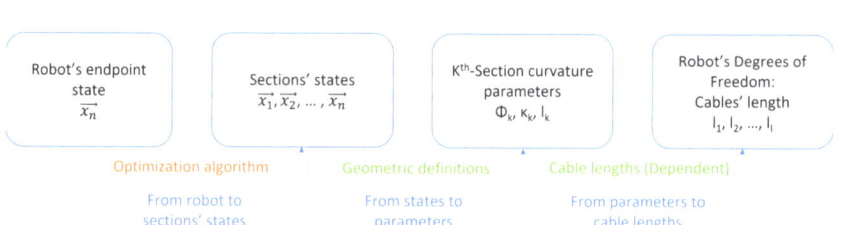

Figure 12. Inverse kinematics for PCC.

Firstly, and given the assumption of the constant curvature hypothesis, it is necessary to obtain the curvature parameters given a certain endpoint $\begin{bmatrix} x & y & z \end{bmatrix}^t$ for each robot section. Orientation is fixed when three parameters are given, as curvature parameters imply the robot only has three degrees of freedom per section. To do so, the method in [30] is followed. Beginning with the azimuthal angle ϕ, it can be obtained by a simple relationship:

$$\phi = \tan^{-1}\left(\frac{y}{x}\right) \quad (24)$$

Curvature is then obtained by analysing the robot's arch in the vertical plane that contains it and searching for its radius (because $\kappa = 1/r$). In this case, the endpoint of the section can be found in coordinates $x' = \sqrt{x^2 + y^2}$, $z' = z$. Then, the radius can be equalled to the distance from the centre of the arch to its endpoint.

$$(\sqrt{x^2 + y^2} - r)^2 + z^2 = r^2$$

Finding r and inverting:

$$\kappa = \frac{2\sqrt{x^2 + y^2}}{x^2 + y^2 + z^2} \qquad (25)$$

Finally, to obtain the value of the arch's length l, the θ angle must be used. Analysing again the arch contained in a plane, the following values can be extracted:

$$\theta = \begin{cases} \cos^{-1}(1 - \kappa\sqrt{x^2 + y^2}), & z > 0 \\ 2\pi - \cos^{-1}(1 - \kappa\sqrt{x^2 + y^2}), & z \leq 0 \end{cases} \qquad (26)$$

Lastly, the transformation to obtain l is purely geometrical: $l = r\theta = \theta/\kappa$.

When obtaining an inverse kinematic model, it is essential to pay attention to the possible singularities such a model might have, which may cause further problems when trying to apply the equations. In this case, singularities for both κ and ϕ appear when the endpoint is located in the vertical axis [30]:

- ϕ: Vertical axis z corresponds to the set of points in which $x = 0$ and $y = 0$, so that in those cases when the robot's endpoint is in the z axis, any value of ϕ can be set.
- κ: In this case, two possibilities must be taken into account. Whenever $z \neq 0$, then $\kappa = 0$ and $l = z$ can be used, as long as the robot's length can be varied and z has a positive value (other cases should be studied individually). On the other hand, if $z = 0$, then the robot's endpoint should be located precisely in the origin, thus forming a perfect circle. There could be many mathematical solutions to do so, choosing, as an example, $\kappa = 0$, $\phi = 0$ and $\theta = 2\pi$. It should be noted, though, that this situation is, in most cases, mechanically impossible to reach.

After obtaining the curvature parameters of a section, the following step would be to obtain the cables' length that are required to achieve such configuration. As said before, it is a robot-dependant transformation, so the following equations must not be taken as true for every robot. However, in order to complete the kinematic model, the three-cable robot is studied. To do so, it is enough to combine Equations (12) and (13), presented in Section 4.1, which defined the cables' length. Doing so, it is obtained that:

$$l_i = 2 \cdot p \cdot r_i \sin(\theta/2p) \qquad (27)$$

In the bibliography, other approaches to obtain this equation can be found through a different geometric deduction, which can afterwards be transformed into this expression through the definition of r_i [5]:

$$l_i = 2 \cdot p \cdot \sin\left(\frac{\theta}{2p}\right) \cdot \left(\frac{1}{\kappa} - d\sin(\phi + \phi_i)\right) \qquad (28)$$

Another aspect that should be taken into account when working with the inverse kinematic model is relative to multisection robots. The extension of these equations of the cables' length can be made with those relationships, as long as the strict order of the sections is followed when calculating the cables' lengths. This is due to the fact that, whenever a cable crosses a certain section, its length through it should also be obtained (as a passive cable) with such sections' curvature parameters.

This is justified when looking at Figure 13. In it, a two-section robot is modelled. The second section $S2$ has a slightly reduced radius, while its cables have been rotated about those in section S1 to allow their simultaneity. Clearly, if the second section is to be positioned, in order to establish the cables' length, both the segment of cable that is active in section S2 and the passive segment that goes through S1 should be taken into account.

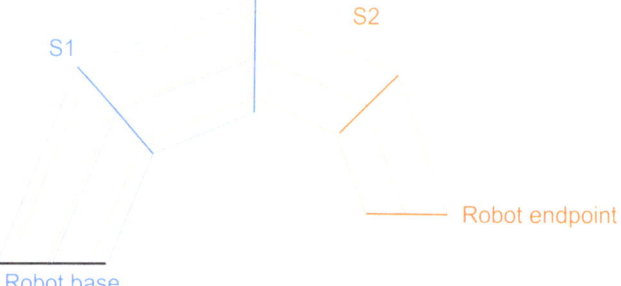

Figure 13. Cables' length for multisection robots.

As an example, for the robot in Figure 13, with l_{ik} being the length of cable i for section k:

$$l_{i1} = 2 \cdot p_1 \cdot \sin\left(\frac{\theta_1}{2p_1}\right) \cdot \left(\frac{1}{\kappa_1} - d_1 \sin(\phi + \phi_i)\right) \tag{29}$$

$$l_{i'2} = 2 \cdot p_1 \cdot \sin\left(\frac{\theta_1}{2p_1}\right) \cdot \left(\frac{1}{\kappa_1} - d_1 \sin(\phi + \phi_{i'})\right) + 2 \cdot p_2 \cdot \sin\left(\frac{\theta_2}{2p_2}\right) \cdot \left(\frac{1}{\kappa_2} - d_2 \sin(\phi + \phi_{i'})\right) \tag{30}$$

In particular, the previous formulae should be applied thrice. Once to calculate the S1 cables' length, directly as it was explained above (as a single-section robot). Then, and still using curvature parameters for S1 but changing d and ϕ_i, they should be applied again to the S2 cables. Finally, to that length, the values obtained by applying the formulae to an "isolated" S2 must be added.

Generalising for n sections, it can be easily verified that, in the first section of the robot, the formulae must be applied for each of the cables that manage the whole n sections. In the second section, they must be applied again to all but one section. Extrapolating this to all sections and assuming f_k cables per section, the total number of operations that must be computed for n sections is:

$$f_k(n + (n-1) + \cdots + 2 + 1) = f_k \sum_{j=1}^{n} j = f_k \frac{n(n+1)}{2}$$

It should be noted, though, that even if these equations have been obtained geometrically (and therefore should be applicable to any robot that follows the constant curvature hypothesis) they cannot be directly applied to all robots. Currently, much work is being put into variable-length robots, that is, that can grow larger or become smaller depending on the task being done. Other robots, such as soft continuous robots, can retract to diminish their length. In these cases, it may be possible to work with the inverse kinematics hereby presented but with some adjustments being made.

On the other hand, most current continuous robots have a rigid backbone, which implies that the length between sections must be practically constant. In these cases, it must be taken into account that the state space is not completely controllable. One of its degrees of freedom (the length between sections) is already fixed, and therefore the 3-D space is not completely reachable. As a result, these restrictions must be included in the kinematic equations for similar reasons to those explained in Section 2.2.

Finally, another effect should be considered. The coupling of sections may affect changes in shape in sections next to the base when trying to modify further segments of the robot. Although they may sometimes be neglected, a tangle/untangle algorithm designed by Jones and Walker may be used to improve accuracy [32].

4.3. Differential Kinematics

The differential model is the one that relates the velocities of the global reference system with those for each of the actionable degrees of freedom. That is, it would relate the change rate of the cables' lengths to the velocities of the robot's joints. It is an alternative to the direct kinematic model, as its integration would also give the position and orientation of the robot.

The obtention of a differential kinematic model can be achieved in two different ways. The first option could be deriving the direct kinematic model equations. However, it is frequently not desirable to use this method, as derivation is not computationally efficient. This could be solved with a similar method as the ones already explained, which separates the independent kinematics and those equations that explicitly depend on the robot being used.

Therefore, the most common solution is to derive separately the two transformations already described in Figure 7. This would lead to a specific expression of the relationship between the curvature's parameters rate change and the section's curvature parameter velocities, and another one between the curvature and the joints' speeds.

There are several ways of obtaining the first Jacobian matrix. Some works, such as [31], do so by using the direct transformation matrices of the Denavit–Hartenberg method. The main problem with using traditional calculations (see [34]) for differential real-time kinematics is the extremely high number of operations they involve, especially when the reference points of the robot are constantly changing (due to its reconfigurable feature) [35]. The most common alternative approach uses screw theory to obtain a more computationally efficient representation [36].

However, in a work by Chembrammel and Kesavadas [35], a novel algorithm for calculating the Jacobian of a manipulator is proposed while applying it to a hyper-redundant robot. It is based on decomposing the Jacobian as the product of two matrices: L and P. Although it is directly applied to discreet robots, it can easily be adjusted to be useful in our PCC method. The article demonstrates the algorithm and applies it to a 2-DOF robot. In this work, the needed adaptation is explained.

In order to use the algorithm, the Kronecker product for matrices must be defined:

$$A \otimes B = \begin{bmatrix} a_{11} & \cdots & a_{1n} \\ \cdots & \cdots & \cdots \\ a_{m1} & \cdots & a_{mn} \end{bmatrix} \otimes \begin{bmatrix} b_{11} & \cdots & b_{1n'} \\ \cdots & \cdots & \cdots \\ b_{m'1} & \cdots & b_{m'n'} \end{bmatrix} = \begin{bmatrix} a_{11}B & \cdots & a_{1n}B \\ \cdots & \cdots & \cdots \\ a_{m1}B & \cdots & a_{mn}B \end{bmatrix} = \begin{bmatrix} a_{11}b_{11} & \cdots & a_{11}b_{1n'} & \cdots & a_{1n}b_{11} & \cdots & a_{1n}b_{1n'} \\ \cdots & & \cdots & & \cdots & & \cdots \\ a_{11}b_{m'1} & \cdots & a_{11}b_{m'n'} & \cdots & a_{1n}b_{m'1} & \cdots & a_{1n}b_{m'n'} \\ \cdots & & \cdots & & \cdots & & \cdots \\ a_{m1}b_{11} & \cdots & a_{m1}b_{1n'} & \cdots & a_{mn}b_{11} & \cdots & a_{mn}b_{1n'} \\ \cdots & & \cdots & & \cdots & & \cdots \\ a_{m1}b_{m'1} & \cdots & a_{m1}b_{m'n'} & \cdots & a_{mn}b_{m'1} & \cdots & a_{mn}b_{m'n'} \end{bmatrix} \quad (31)$$

To be more clear, I_2 being the identity of dimension 2×2 and A another 2×2 matrix:

$$I_2 \otimes A = \begin{bmatrix} 1 \cdot a_{11} & 1 \cdot a_{12} & 0 \cdot a_{11} & 0 \cdot a_{12} \\ 1 \cdot a_{21} & 1 \cdot a_{22} & 0 \cdot a_{21} & 0 \cdot a_{22} \\ 0 \cdot a_{11} & 0 \cdot a_{12} & 1 \cdot a_{11} & 0 \cdot a_{12} \\ 0 \cdot a_{21} & 0 \cdot a_{22} & 1 \cdot a_{21} & 0 \cdot a_{22} \end{bmatrix} = \begin{bmatrix} a_{11} & a_{12} & 0 & 0 \\ a_{21} & a_{22} & 0 & 0 \\ 0 & 0 & a_{11} & a_{12} \\ 0 & 0 & a_{21} & a_{22} \end{bmatrix} \quad (32)$$

Having defined the Kronecker product, to begin the algorithm, the transformation matrix from the base to the endpoint of the section is needed. It was calculated in Equation (9). The three variables that are used to calculate the differential equations are l, ϕ and κ. Afterwards, the matrices L_i are calculated using:

$$L_i = \frac{\partial T_{indep}(q)}{\partial q_i} \quad (33)$$

q_i being the generalised coordinates already mentioned. The three matrices are:

$$L_l = \begin{bmatrix} -\kappa\cos\phi\sin\kappa l & 0 & \kappa\cos\phi\cos\kappa l & \cos\phi\sin\kappa l \\ -\kappa\sin\phi\sin\kappa l & 0 & \kappa\sin\phi\cos\kappa l & \sin\phi\cos\kappa l \\ -\kappa\cos\kappa l & 0 & -\kappa\sin\kappa l & \cos\kappa l \\ 0 & 0 & 0 & 0 \end{bmatrix} \quad (34)$$

$$L_\phi = \begin{bmatrix} -\sin\phi\cos\kappa l & -\cos\phi & -\sin\phi\sin\kappa l & ((\cos\kappa l - 1)\sin\phi)/\kappa \\ \cos\phi\cos\kappa l & -\sin\phi & \cos\phi\sin\kappa l & -((\cos\kappa l - 1)\cos\phi)/\kappa \\ 0 & 0 & 0 & 0 \\ 0 & 0 & 0 & 0 \end{bmatrix} \quad (35)$$

$$L_\kappa = \begin{bmatrix} -l\cos\phi\sin\kappa l & 0 & l\cos\phi\sin\kappa l & (\cos\phi(\cos\kappa l - 1))/\kappa^2 + l\cos\phi\sin\kappa l/\kappa \\ -l\sin\phi\sin\kappa l & 0 & l\sin\phi\sin\kappa l & (\sin\phi(\cos\kappa l - 1))/\kappa^2 + l\sin\phi\sin\kappa l/\kappa \\ -l\cos\kappa l & 0 & -l\sin\kappa l & (l\cos\kappa l)/\kappa - \sin\kappa l/\kappa^2 \\ 0 & 0 & 0 & 0 \end{bmatrix} \quad (36)$$

Then, the matrix L is built by joining the three submatrices:

$$L = \begin{bmatrix} L_l & L_\phi & L_\kappa \end{bmatrix} \quad (37)$$

In the work by Chembrammel and Kesavadas [35], the algorithm is general for any point in the reference frame. In this case, the endpoint is used, defined as the origin vector when transformed by T_{indep}:

$$p = \begin{bmatrix} 0 & 0 & 0 & 1 \end{bmatrix}^T \quad (38)$$

The algorithm proposed divides the Jacobian into two parts: the linear velocity Jacobian and the angular velocity Jacobian. To start with the linear part, the matrix P_{linear} is obtained using the Kronecker product with the identity:

$$P_{lin} = I_3 \cdot p = \begin{bmatrix} 0 & 0 & 0 & 1 & 0 & 0 & 0 & 0 & 0 & 0 & 0 & 0 \\ 0 & 0 & 0 & 0 & 0 & 0 & 0 & 1 & 0 & 0 & 0 & 0 \\ 0 & 0 & 0 & 0 & 0 & 0 & 0 & 0 & 0 & 0 & 0 & 1 \end{bmatrix}^T \quad (39)$$

For the angular part, another P_{ang} must be obtained as the inverse of the original transformation matrix (or T_{indep}). Finally, each of the Jacobians (both linear and angular) can be found by multiplying both matrices for each part:

$$J_{lin} = LP_{lin} = \begin{bmatrix} \cos\phi\sin\kappa l & (\sin\phi(\cos\kappa l - 1))/\kappa & (\cos\phi(\cos\kappa l - 1))/\kappa^2 + l\cos\phi\sin\kappa l/\kappa \\ \sin\phi\sin\kappa l & -(\cos\phi(\cos\kappa l - 1))/\kappa & (\sin\phi(\cos\kappa l - 1))/\kappa^2 + l\sin\phi\sin\kappa l/\kappa \\ \cos\kappa l & 0 & (l\cos\kappa l)/\kappa - \sin\kappa l/\kappa^2 \end{bmatrix} \quad (40)$$

The angular Jacobian is obtained somewhat differently. For each generalised coordinate q_i, the product $L_i P$ is calculated. For each coordinate, a different component of the product $L_i P$ is obtained:

$$J_\omega = \begin{bmatrix} (L_1 P)_{(3,2)} & (L_2 P)_{(3,2)} & (L_3 P)_{(3,2)} \\ (L_1 P)_{(1,3)} & (L_2 P)_{(1,3)} & (L_3 P)_{(1,3)} \\ (L_1 P)_{(2,1)} & (L_2 P)_{(2,1)} & (L_3 P)_{(2,1)} \end{bmatrix} = \begin{bmatrix} -\kappa\sin\phi & 0 & -l\sin\phi \\ \kappa\cos\phi & 0 & l\cos\phi \\ 0 & 1 & 0 \end{bmatrix} \quad (41)$$

With this, the conventional Jacobian could be obtained by combining the two matrices in one:

$$J = \begin{bmatrix} J_{lin} \\ J_\omega \end{bmatrix} \quad (42)$$

This represents the differential model for the curvature parameters, that is, the independent part of the robot. The work by Chembrammel and Kesavadas [35] also uses further expressions to calculate the derivative of the Jacobian, allowing for numeric integration over time. These expressions are not particularised for the example that was developed here but can be easily calculated:

$$\dot{L} = \frac{\partial L}{\partial q_i} \tag{43}$$

$$\dot{J}_{lin} = \sum_{i=1}^{n} \frac{\partial J_{lin}}{\partial q_i} \dot{q}_i = \sum_{i=1}^{n} \frac{\partial L}{\partial q_i} P \dot{q}_i \tag{44}$$

$$\dot{J}_\omega = \sum_{i=1}^{n} \frac{\partial J_\omega}{\partial q_i} \dot{q}_i \tag{45}$$

$$\frac{\partial J_{\omega,i}}{\partial q_j} (\begin{bmatrix} (L_i P)_{(3,2)} & (L_i P)_{(1,3)} & (L_i P)_{(2,1)} \end{bmatrix})^T \tag{46}$$

$$\frac{\partial L_i P}{q_j} = \left(\frac{\partial L_i}{\partial q_j} - L_i T^{-1}_{indep} L_j \right) T^{-1}_{indep} \tag{47}$$

As said, this would be a partial differential model: it would only take into account the independent part of the robot, and thus it is completely general for any PCC-compliant robot. However, this method for obtaining Jacobians would also be plausible using the complete equations. The only necessary steps would be substituting the relationships between cables and curvature parameters (such as Equations (21) and (16)) in the transformation matrix (Equation (9)). Then, the process would be repeated using $l_1, l_2, \ldots, l_n$ as generalised coordinates. This would return a complete differential model.

5. LSK—Linearised Segment Kinematics

PCC kinematics presents some problems when applied to certain applications. One of them is the great computational cost it represents when enlarging the number of sections of a robot, due to the number of operations already seen in the inverse kinematics. This means that using it for real-time applications in robots might not be enough, so work is being conducted to find alternative methods that evade these limitations. One example is Linearised Segment Kinematics, which also eliminates the PCC singularities [37].

As a derived method from the PCC, its general diagram is quite similar (see Figure 14). The main change the LSK method provides is the linearisation equations for cable lengths. It is indeed a dependent method on the geometry of the robot. However, the fact that many of the hyper-redundant robots are quite similar in their functional morphology makes it easy to find linearised equations for many robots. Only the inverse kinematics figure is shown, but linearised equations for cable lengths can be applied both to direct and inverse kinematics.

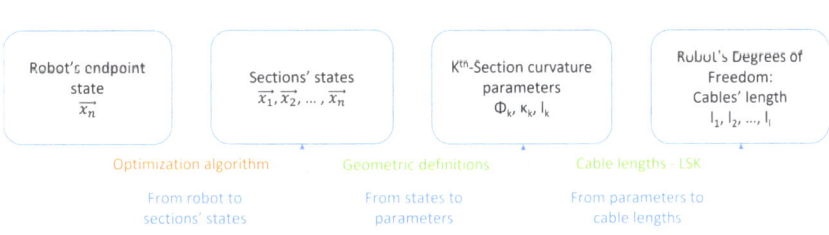

Figure 14. Inverse kinematics for LSK.

This method is based on linearising the kinematic equations for each cable, simplifying the equations of each section, and therefore, the robot's kinematic model. To do so, an adapted expression of the PCC formulae is used, combining Equations (10) and (13) and applying trigonometric relationships:

$$l_i = 2 \cdot \sin\left(\frac{\theta}{2p}\right) \cdot \left(\frac{l_c p}{\theta} - r_c \sin(\phi + \phi_i)\right) \tag{48}$$

To avoid the computational cost of calculating sines, to eliminate the dividing by zero ($\theta = 0$) singularity, and in order to reduce the number of necessary iterations when the number of sections increases, linearisation can be applied to this equation.

In the work presented in [37], whether this linearisation is necessary or not is firstly justified. To do so, it begins by calculating the neutral fibre of the robot, which becomes an example for further calculations:

$$l \geq 2 \cdot \sin\left(\frac{\theta}{2p}\right) \cdot \left(\frac{l_c p}{\theta} - r_c \sin(\phi)\right)$$

Cables are considered to work with tensile stress and do not offer resistance to compression. This way, any point that requires less cable length could be potentially reached, which forces the apparition of an inequality. Afterwards, the Maclaurin series for θ is applied (Taylor series when $\theta = 0$), and as a result:

$$l \approx l' \geq l_c - r_c \frac{\theta}{p} \tag{49}$$

If linearisation were to be applied to the whole range of possible angles of the robot, it could be verified that linearising for a certain point (such as the origin), in those points excessively far apart from those points, would present excessive errors in the equations. However, assuming several segments exist in a single section (passive discs), this total turning angle is divided among them, therefore reducing the subsequent error, which becomes acceptable. From this perspective, Barrientos and Dong demonstrate that the maximum error this development shows is 0.7%.

Linearising the equations for each cable l_i and applying the Maclaurin series again, the following relationship appears:

$$l'_i \geq -p \cdot r_c \cdot \theta \cdot (\cos(\phi_i) \cdot \cos(\phi) + \sin(\phi_i) \cdot \sin(\phi)) + l_c \tag{50}$$

Since what is actually needed is the increment of cable length with reference to a neutral position, the constant can be eliminated, thus expressing the equation as a difference of lengths. Apart from that, it can be observed that the system is left as a product between a certain scale factor $K(\theta)$, a matrix that only depends on the robot geometry $\mathbf{A}(\phi_i)$ and the trigonometric variables that use ϕ:

$$\begin{bmatrix} \Delta l_1 \\ \Delta l_2 \\ \dots \\ \Delta l_f \end{bmatrix} \gtrapprox K(\theta) \mathbf{A}(\phi_i) \begin{bmatrix} \cos(\phi_i) \\ \sin(\phi_i) \end{bmatrix} = -r_c \theta \begin{bmatrix} \cos(\phi_1) & \sin(\phi_1) \\ \cos(\phi_2) & \sin(\phi_2) \\ \dots & \dots \\ \cos(\phi_{np}) & \sin(\phi_{np}) \end{bmatrix} \begin{bmatrix} \cos(\phi_i) \\ \sin(\phi_i) \end{bmatrix} \tag{51}$$

This would then represent the inverse kinematic model for a single section. To obtain the direct kinematics, as long as the length increments are coherent, it could be inferred that:

$$\begin{bmatrix} \cos(\phi_i) \\ \sin(\phi_i) \end{bmatrix} \lessapprox -\frac{1}{r_c \theta} \begin{bmatrix} \cos(\phi_1) & \sin(\phi_1) \\ \cos(\phi_2) & \sin(\phi_2) \\ \dots & \dots \\ \cos(\phi_{np}) & \sin(\phi_{np}) \end{bmatrix}^T \begin{bmatrix} \Delta l_1 \\ \Delta l_2 \\ \dots \\ \Delta l_f \end{bmatrix} \tag{52}$$

6. Kinetic Robot Modelling Using Elastic Properties

Modelling hyper-redundant robots without the constant curvature hypothesis is mostly performed by kinetic modelling techniques, using elasticity parameters and taking the different strains that apply to the robot system into account [15]. They are more precise but more complex models, and solving them requires more computational power.

One of the reasons why the PCC hypothesis might not always be accurate enough to represent a certain robot can be if its specific weight is too high. When it has a continuous backbone of a certain material, including its dynamic properties in the model might provide more accuracy to the results of the kinematic model.

In particular, two models are briefly described in this section. The equations are not derived as thoroughly as the previous models, although the cited articles contain the detailed procedure. The main difference between the two models is the continuity of the backbone properties: the first model (Pseudorigid Body—PRB) uses lumped parameters [15] (they are a finite set of parameters) while the second model (Cosserat Rod Theory—CRT) requires an infinite number of parameters to characterise it.

6.1. Pseudorigid Body

The Pseudorigid Body is a model that allows the calculation of large deflections in beams through modelling them as combination of rotation joints and springs. In particular, the most used model for backbones in hyper-redundant robots is the one proposed by Su in 2009 [38] (see Figure 15). It proposes using four rigid and straight segments (in orange) joined by three pin joints with three torsion springs (in blue) to model the portion of the robot between two consecutive discs (in green). It should be noted that, being a kinetic model, it uses forces instead of lengths as an input parameter (see Figure 16). Moreover, as it characterises the backbone's dynamic parameters, it is oriented to robots with a continuous backbone of a homogeneous material.

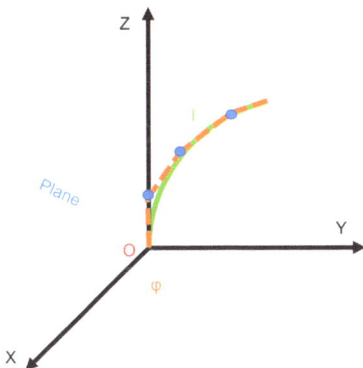

Figure 15. PRB conceptual diagram.

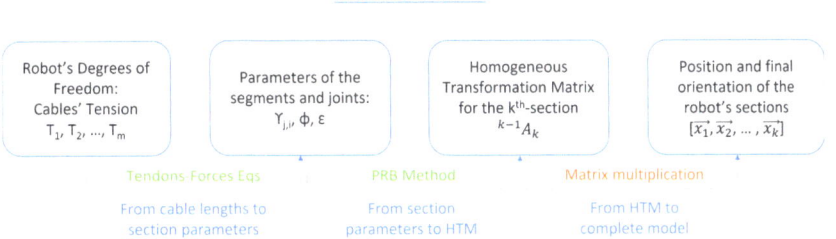

Figure 16. Inverse kinematics for PRB.

The PRB proposes using four parameters optimised by Chen in [39]: $\gamma_0 = 0.125$, $\gamma_1 = 0.35$, $\gamma_2 = 0.388$ and $\gamma_3 = 0.136$ as the ratio of each of the four segments to the total length of the section. Now, if the angle $\theta_{k,i}$ is the angle of link i in section k, the transformation matrix in the plane of section k becomes:

$$T_{k,i} = \begin{bmatrix} \cos(\theta_{k,i}) & 0 & \sin(\theta_{k,i}) & \gamma_{k,i} l_j \sin(\theta_{k,i}) \\ 0 & 1 & 0 & 0 \\ -\sin(\theta_{k,i}) & 0 & \cos(\theta_{k,i}) & \gamma_{k_i} l_j \cos(\theta_{k,i}) \\ 0 & 0 & 0 & 1 \end{bmatrix} \tag{53}$$

The section is finally modelled as the combination of the rotation to the plane (a rotation around z, R_z), the successive links and the rotation to undo the first turn. One final turn is added to represent a possible twist:

$$^k A_{k+1} = R_z(\phi_j) T_{k,0} T_{k,1} T_{k,2} T_{k,3} R_z(-\phi_j) R_z(\epsilon) \tag{54}$$

Several aspects should be taken into account at this point. When Huang et al. proposed this model, they only considered one-segment robots without external forces [40]. However, Rao et al. proposed a modified model which contains these possibilities too, and as such, it is the one developed [15].

First of all, and using as input the tension $\tau_{j,i}$ of the cables over disc i, the force of cable j over the last disk n is calculated, using the vector $\overrightarrow{P_{j,n} P_{j,n-1}}$ between the origin of the cable at two consecutive discs:

$$\vec{F}_{j,n} = \tau_{j,n} \frac{\overrightarrow{P_{j,n} P_{j,n-1}}}{\|\overrightarrow{P_{j,n} P_{j,n-1}}\|} \tag{55}$$

For other disks i, the equation ends up as:

$$\vec{F}_{j,i} = \tau_{j,i} \frac{\overrightarrow{P_{j,i} P_{j,i-1}}}{\|\overrightarrow{P_{j,i} P_{j,i-1}}\|} + \tau_{j,i+1} \frac{\overrightarrow{P_{j,i+1} P_{j,i}}}{\|\overrightarrow{P_{j,i+1} P_{j,i}}\|} \tag{56}$$

The total force over a certain disc is then obtained when adding up external forces (typically on the tip of the robot, therefore accounted in the last disk), n being the last disk, i a generic disc and f the total number of cables:

$$\vec{F}_n^T = \sum_{j=1}^{f} \vec{F}_{j,n} + \vec{F}_{ext} \tag{57}$$

$$\vec{F}_i^T = \sum_{j=1}^{f} \vec{F}_{j,i} + \vec{F}_{i+1} \qquad i < n \tag{58}$$

From this, the involved moments are derived. Naming $\overrightarrow{O_i O_{q,i}}$ as the vector that joins the base of the disk i and the theoretical joint q, $\overrightarrow{M_{i,q}}$ as the total moment applied to disk i by joint q and $\overrightarrow{M_{j,i}^c}$ the tension that cable j applies to disk i:

$$\vec{M}_{n,q} = \sum_{j=1}^{f} \overrightarrow{M_{n,j}^c} + \overrightarrow{O_n O_{q,n}} \times \vec{F}_n^T \tag{59}$$

$$\vec{M}_{i,q} = \sum_{j=1}^{f} \overrightarrow{M_{i,j}^c} + \overrightarrow{O_i O_{q,i}} \times \vec{F}_i^T + \vec{M}_{i+1,q} \qquad i < n \tag{60}$$

The total moment for the section $\overrightarrow{M_i^T}$ is calculated as:

$$\vec{M}_n^T = \sum_{j=1}^{f} \overrightarrow{M_{n,j}} + \overrightarrow{O_{n-1} O_n} \times \vec{F}_n^T \tag{61}$$

$$\vec{M}_i^T = \sum_{j=1}^f \vec{M}_{i,j} + \overrightarrow{O_{i-1}O_i} \times \vec{F}_i^T + \vec{M}_{i+1}^T \qquad i < n \qquad (62)$$

Taking this vector, the angle ϕ can be calculated by knowing that the vector $\vec{y}_i$, perpendicular to the plane, is colinear with $\vec{M}_i^T - \vec{M}_i^T \cdot \vec{z}_i^T$. Once this angle has been calculated, only the joints' angles are missing to have a complete set of equations. To obtain these angles, the relationship used is:

$$||\vec{M}_i^T - \vec{M}_i^T \cdot \vec{z}_i^T|| = K_{\Theta_q} \frac{EI}{l_i} \theta_q \qquad (63)$$

EI being the characterising parameters for the material, l the length of the section and K_{Θ_q} certain parameters that were also optimised as: $K_{\Theta_1} = 3.25$, $K_{\Theta_2} = 2.84$ and $K_{\Theta_3} = 2.95$ [39]. The last equation needed is used to obtain the twist parameter ϵ:

$$GJ\epsilon_i = l_i(^{i-1}T_i \vec{M}_i) \vec{z}_B \qquad (64)$$

There is a great complexity to solve these equations. There are five independent kinematic variables per section ($\theta_{1,i}, \theta_{2,i}, \theta_{3,i}, \phi_i$ and ϵ_i) and three independent dynamic variables per section ($M_{x,i}^T, M_{y,i}^T$ and M_{z-i}^T). There are also eight equations available per section (three equations in (62) where all the other terms are kinematic-dependent or known, three equations in (63) for the three joints, one equation for the colinearity condition and one equation in (64)). However, all sections must be solved at once due to the interdependence of sections, and it is a highly nonlinear system. Therefore, numerical methods must be used [41].

6.2. Cosserat Rod Theory

The Cosserat theory for elastic rods (CRT) is one of the most common techniques to model continuous beams and can be used to establish the backbone. This theory assigns six degrees of freedom to each point of the robot's backbone while establishing some boundary conditions it must meet using kinetic equations [42]. This technique has been applied to several kinematic problems, each for a different robot configuration [24,43,44]. All these works present slightly different proposals, with the integration information needed to solve the problem.

In particular, the Cosserat Theory provides the relationship between the forces (or strains) applied to the robot and the position of the backbone at each of its points. Once again, taking into account this is a kinetic model, the inputs for the model are the strains suffered by the robotic arm. In particular, the development used by Jones [43] is presented below.

Using the definitions seen in Figure 17, the position and orientation of section i are defined by a position vector $\vec{p}(i)$ and a rotation matrix $^{i-1}A_i$. If we define $\vec{v}(i)$ as the linear velocity of an infinitesimal section from the rigid body, expressed in body coordinates, and $\vec{u}(i)$ as the infinitesimal rotation of the frame $^{i-1}A_i$, then the derivatives take the form:

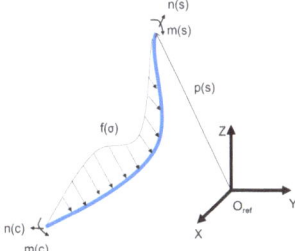

Figure 17. Section of a rod to explain the CRT.

$$\vec{p} = {}^{i-1}A_i \cdot \vec{v} \tag{65}$$

$${}^{i-1}\dot{A}_i = {}^{i-1}A_i \cdot \begin{bmatrix} 0 & -u_z & u_y \\ u_z & 0 & -u_x \\ -u_y & u_x & 0 \end{bmatrix} \tag{66}$$

Now, six more variables are introduced: $\vec{v}^*$ and $\vec{u}^*$ represent the linear and angular velocity of the default (nondeformed) state of the rod; $\vec{m}(i)$ and $\vec{n}(i)$ represent the internal moment and force vectors, respectively; $\vec{f}$ is the applied force distribution; and $\vec{l}$ is the distributed moment. Then, applying equilibrium and using $\vec{m}(i)$ and $\vec{n}(i)$ as state variables:

$$\vec{n}' = -\vec{f} \tag{67}$$

$$\vec{m}' = -\vec{p}' \times \vec{n} - \vec{l} \tag{68}$$

Finally, we need to introduce the material characterisation:

$$K_{se}(i) = \begin{bmatrix} GA(i) & 0 & 0 \\ 0 & GA(i) & 0 \\ 0 & 0 & EA(i) \end{bmatrix} \qquad K_{bt}(i) = \begin{bmatrix} EI_{xx}(i) & 0 & 0 \\ 0 & EI_{yy}(i) & 0 \\ 0 & 0 & EI_{zz}(i) \end{bmatrix} \tag{69}$$

To obtain a complete model, these matrices are introduced by the Constitutive Laws:

$$\vec{v} = K_{se}^{-1}\,{}^{i-1}A_i^T \vec{n} + \vec{v}^* \tag{70}$$

$$\vec{u} = K_{bt}^{-1}\,{}^{i-1}A_i^T \vec{m} + \vec{u}^* \tag{71}$$

Cosserat Theory per se is composed of Equations (65)–(68), (70) and (71). However, the theory of tendons and cables can also be coupled, taking into account that both the forces and the moments have an external ($\vec{f}_e$, $\vec{l}_e$) and a tendon-caused ($\vec{f}_t$, $\vec{l}_t$) component [44]. For brevity, the whole development is not added here, but tendon forces and moments are derived in the article from the tension of each cable τ_j. For the solution, the operator $\hat{w}$ is introduced as:

$$\hat{\vec{w}} = \begin{bmatrix} 0 & -w_z & w_y \\ w_z & 0 & -w_x \\ -w_y & w_x & 0 \end{bmatrix} \tag{72}$$

With this tool, and defining $\vec{r}_j$ as the vector from the origin of the attached frame to the tendon's origin, the equations that relate forces to tendons can be found below (do not confuse scalar f, the total number of cables with vectorial $\vec{f}$, which are forces):

$$\vec{f}_t = -\sum_{j=1}^{f} \tau_j \frac{\hat{\vec{p}}_j^{\,2}}{\|\vec{p}_j'\|^3} \vec{p}_j' \tag{73}$$

$$\vec{l}_t = -\sum_{j=1}^{f} \tau_j ({}^{i-1}A_i \vec{r}_j) \frac{\hat{\vec{p}}_j^{\,2}}{\|\vec{p}_j'\|^3} \vec{p}_j' \tag{74}$$

These equations use the derivatives, which can be expressed in terms of kinematic variables:

$$\vec{p}_j' = {}^{i-1}A_i(\hat{\vec{u}}\vec{r}_j + \vec{r}_j' + \vec{v}) \tag{75}$$

$$\dot{\vec{p}}_j' = {}^{i-1}A_i(\hat{\vec{u}}(\hat{\vec{u}}\vec{r}_j + \vec{r}_j' + \vec{v}) + \hat{\dot{\vec{u}}}\vec{r}_j + \hat{\vec{u}}\vec{r}_j' + \vec{r}_j' + \vec{v}) \tag{76}$$

This would constitute an implicit set of equations for hyper-redundant robots with tendons. The article goes on to develop the expression in order to give an explicit state system. However, the idea of the CRT is clear in this excerpt, including the complexity of the model compared with the previous ones and the need to explicitly know the continuous expressions of forces and moments.

7. Optimization Algorithm—CCD and Natural CCD Algorithms

In previous sections, different models and hypotheses to simplify hyper-redundant robot modelling were described in detail. They form the basis for choosing the right equations for every robot. However, as seen in the general stages of kinematic hyper-redundant modelling, there are two steps that are completely general to all methods. One of them is the matrix multiplication for combining all the HTMs involved and has no further difficulty. Apart from that, an optimisation method is required to place each of the robot's sections in space, in order to reach a certain endpoint.

So, as to have completeness in the kinematic models, a particular algorithm is proposed here as a possible solution to the problem. Of course, there are many alternative methods (numeric methods, neural networks, genetic algorithms or the pseudoinverse Jacobian). However, the algorithm of Natural CCD aims to obtain a computationally efficient solution, with high precision, that may be used in a Real-Time System (RTS) [26] and seems to fit in the proposed methodology (see Figure 18).

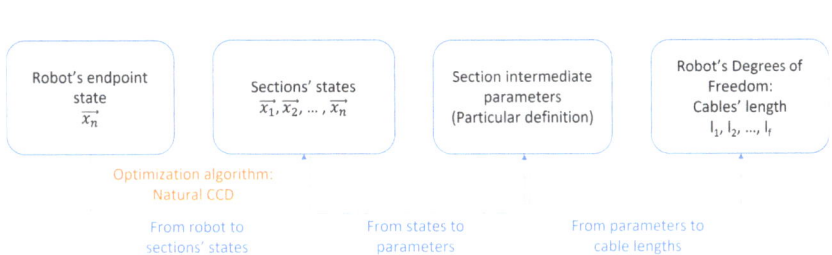

Figure 18. Inverse kinematics using CCD.

The CCD algorithm, which means Cyclic Coordinate Descent, is a method that, without using derivatives, finds a local minimum for a function. It is based on the concept that when minimising using generalised coordinates one by one on each iteration, the whole function is minimised in the end [25]. Applying this to inverse kinematics, the function to minimise is the euclidean distance between the robot's endpoint and the desired destination or objective.

Modelling the robot as a kinematic chain of spherical joints, in [26], it is expressed how to directly apply this CCD algorithm to the inverse kinematics of hyper-redundant robots. In order to simplify the other steps of the modelling process, it is important to note that how these spherical joints are positioned in the robot affects the shape of the reachable space. To understand this, an example with discrete robots is provided. Since most algorithms return the pose of the spherical joints, it can be intuitively proposed to fix them to each section's endpoint (their pose would then already be determined).

Two possible reachable spaces are defined, depending on the position of the joints relative to the studied section. If the physical joint in a discrete robot is placed in the endpoint of a section (in the centre of an active disc), a certain workspace is defined. However, if the robot has a rigid union between joints, which are placed inside a passive disc, the possible endpoint positions are conditioned by the orientation of the previous straight segment. (See Figure 19a).

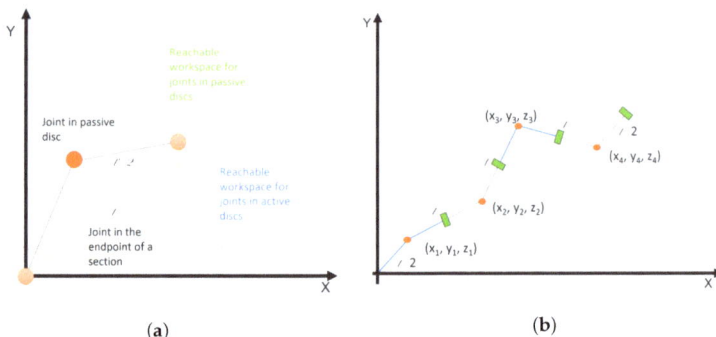

Figure 19. Defining virtual sections for inverse kinematic modelling. (**a**) Differences between work spaces. (**b**) Discreet sections for inverse kinematic modelling.

In discreet robots, it is clear that virtual joints should be modelled to represent the physical reality of the robot. Most hyper-redundant robots have joints placed in the middle of the section, inside passive discs, and as such, that model is more accurate. In fact, in Figure 19b, the possible model for a discreet robot can be found. Green rectangles represent the endpoint of a certain section, and orange circles are the symbols for joints. As it can be seen, the transition between sections is performed by straight segments and, as such, the orientation of its endpoint depends directly on the previous joint. Calling the joints' positions $\begin{bmatrix} x_k & y_k & z_k \end{bmatrix}^t$ and $\begin{bmatrix} x_{ek} & y_{ek} & z_{ek} \end{bmatrix}^t$ the endpoints, Equation (77) represents this transformation.

$$\begin{bmatrix} x_{ek} \\ y_{ek} \\ z_{ek} \end{bmatrix} = \begin{bmatrix} \frac{x_{k+1} - x_k}{2} \\ \frac{y_{k+1} - y_k}{2} \\ \frac{z_{k+1} - z_k}{2} \end{bmatrix} \tag{77}$$

On the other hand, continuous robots are modelled equivalently, with joints and straight lines, but the definition of these virtual elements is not straightforward. In fact, any of the two models seen in Figure 19a may be applied, as they are exchangeable through an additional degree of freedom (sections' length) and the definition of another constraint. A common approach used in continuous robots is extending the concepts from discreet robots to continuous configurations, thus using the same definitions (virtual joints in the middle of the section in order to position the endpoint). However, this could be particular for each case, depending on the physical robot's characteristics.

It must be reminded, however, that the simplifying hypothesis might introduce new equations that reduce the degrees of freedom. For example, the PCC hypothesis requires the length of the backbone to be constant, thus reducing the reachable space. These restrictions must be programmed into the optimisation algorithm.

After having decided how to define the kinematic chain for the robot, the actual CCD algorithm is now tackled. To do so, three points are defined (see Figure 20): p_c as the joint that is moved in a certain moment, or Current Joint; p_e as the endpoint of the robot, or End-Effector; and finally p_f as the final position that represents the objective for our inverse kinematic problem.

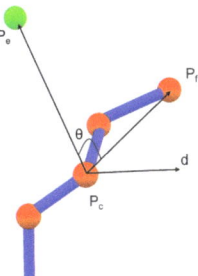

Figure 20. Vector definition for the CCD algorithm.

Using these three vectors, it can easily be deduced that in order to minimise the distance $||\overrightarrow{p_e p_f}||$, the vectors $\overrightarrow{p_c p_e}$ and $\overrightarrow{p_c p_f}$ should become aligned. This rotation could be represented by an angle θ and a direction $\vec{d}$ to indicate the rotation axis. The expressions for each of these values are:

$$\theta = \cos^{-1}\left(\frac{p_e - p_c}{||\overrightarrow{p_c p_e}||} \cdot \frac{p_f - p_c}{||\overrightarrow{p_c p_f}||}\right) \tag{78}$$

$$\vec{d} = \frac{p_e - p_c}{||\overrightarrow{p_c p_e}||} \cdot \frac{p_f - p_c}{||\overrightarrow{p_c p_f}||} \tag{79}$$

Successively applying these equations to joints $i = 1, 2, \ldots, n$, several angles θ_i and the directions around which they must turn in order to achieve the endpoint's final position are found. Afterwards, it is necessary to use the geometric relationships, given the hypothesis that joints are virtually linked together by a straight segment, so as to find the final position vector for each of the sections. Once these points are defined, the second step for the inverse kinematic can be applied.

As it was already stated in Section 2.3, one of the main advantages of this method, apart from its computational efficiency and its precision, is that it is a method that can be applied independently of the robot's morphology, due to the fact that the particularisation for each type of robot is easily achieved, having already stated common models for the robots.

However, this method also presents several disadvantages which must be taken into account [26]. Kinematic singularities that might appear due to the design of the robot are not even considered in the CCD algorithm. Moreover, it does not include any collision manager, not even with itself. This might result in a planned movement that is impossible to carry out. Finally, operating with high values of θ can be quite demanding for the robot's joints.

In order to solve, or at least mitigate these inconveniences (which might negatively affect the CCD algorithm usage), the Natural-CCD was developed [26]. Natural-CCD is an algorithm derived directly from CCD which obtains better results and more natural movements for the robot. This modification solves the CCD problems one by one:

- To tackle the possibility of a singularity, two viable alternatives can be used. In some cases, it would be enough to change to another joint (the movement of one of the joints might exit by itself the singularity that the first joint caused). However, in some cases where the singularity affects the whole robot (as when the robot is perfectly colinear and pointing to the goal), the Natural-CCD algorithm assigns a random d and θ that exit the position and allow it to continue.
- Collision management with itself is solved by designing an angle θ_{max} that represents a maximum bound for the possible range of the joint. This way, the angle can be defined

so the segment can never collide with its predecessor. To do so, Martín et al. in [26] define θ_{max} as the supplementary angle to the interior angle of an N-sided polygon, N being the number of the robot's joints.

- Finally, to minimise the effect of abrupt movements to the joints, Natural-CCD limits by a coefficient k the value of θ_i for the rotation. Particularly, the inverse of the distance between the robot's endpoint and the desired position is suggested as a possible coefficient. However, k must be superiorly bounded by 1 in order for the algorithm to converge.

$$k = \frac{1}{|\overrightarrow{p_e p_f}|} \quad 0 > k \geq 1 \quad \theta^* = k\theta$$

Another possible definition for the coefficient k is based on trying to obtain a specific number of cycles for a certain movement. To do so with N being the number of joints and C a positive constant:

$$k = \frac{C}{N|\overrightarrow{p_e p_f}|} \quad 0 > k \geq 1 \quad \theta^* = k\theta$$

These modifications are the basis of the final Natural-CCD algorithm. In Figure 21 a graphical summary can be found with said procedure.

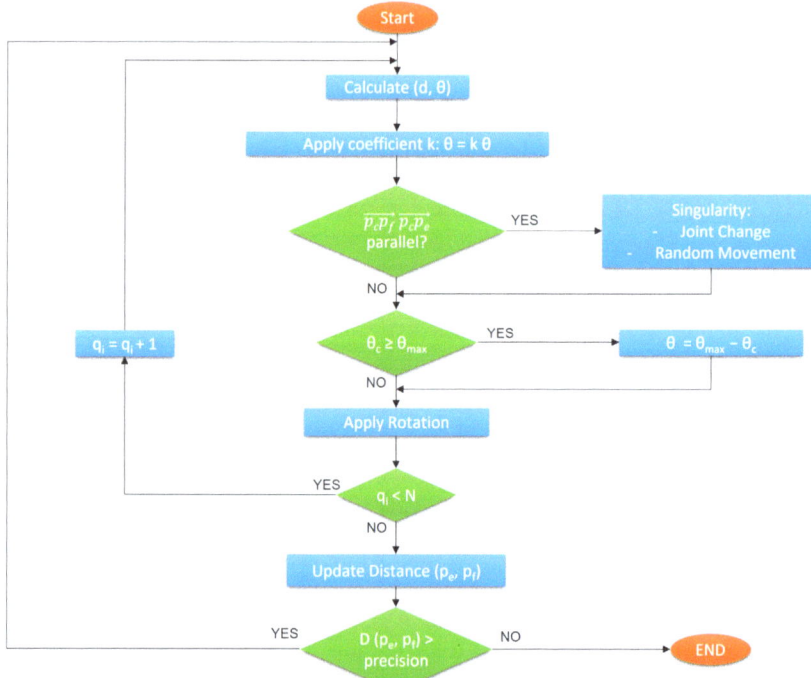

Figure 21. Graphical summary for the Natural-CCD algorithm, produced based on [26].

Using this algorithm implies some interesting consequences. Firstly, from Natural-CCD more natural movements are obtained, with fewer sudden movements. In fact, Natural-CCD can be considered to produce a certain biomimetic action [26]. Moreover, modifying the algorithm by changing the chosen points for its development (p_e, p_c, and p_f) surprisingly develops certain behaviours that, autonomously, might represent a functionality such as folding around itself, straightening, moving away from a point, etc. [45].

In this work, the Natural-CCD algorithm is suggested as a possible algorithm for section positioning due to its simplicity and the advantages it presents regarding computational efficiency and its real-time behaviour. However, many alternatives exist that are being used for hyper-redundant kinematics.

To show this, the inverse kinematic problem could be presented as trying to minimise the distance of the robot's endpoint to the objective, while verifying certain restrictions. This, at its core, is an optimisation problem. Therefore, to solve the section positioning problem, any optimisation algorithm could be used, including Neural Networks or Deep Learning techniques. The choice between these alternatives might depend on the computational power available, the response-time requirements or even the designer's personal preferences ([23–25]).

8. Tutorial for Hyper-Redundant Robot Modelling

Once some of the most important techniques for hyper-redundant kinematic modelling have been revised, this paper aims to offer some guidelines for the engineer that first approaches this topic. The proposal uses the classification given in Section 1.2 to make decisions between the existing alternatives.

A graphical summary is presented in Figure 22 as it is the basis for the explanations given in this section. In the following subsections, the different steps that are proposed in the procedure are explained in further detail. For example, it is reviewed how to decide whether or not a robot is discreet or continuous and how to determine if the backbone is constant or variable.

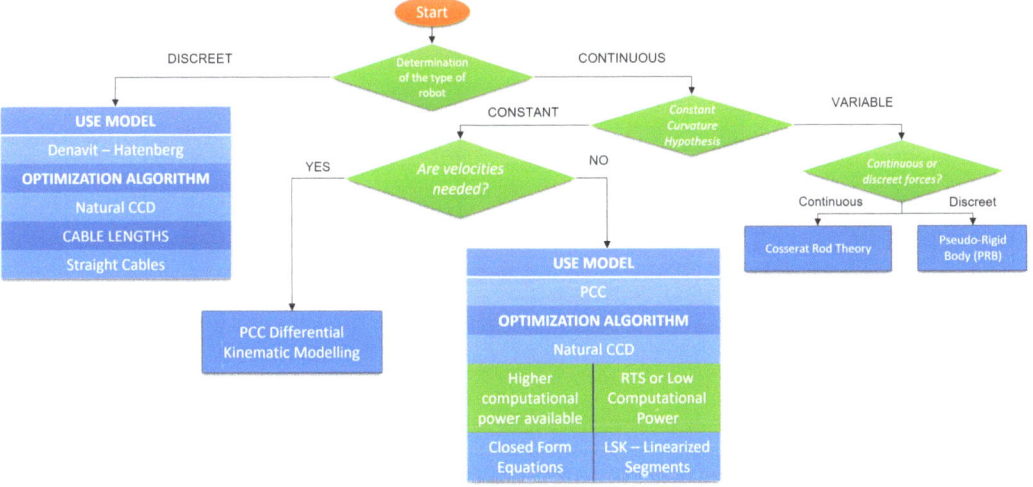

Figure 22. Graphical summary—kinematic modelling of hyper-redundant robots.

8.1. Determination of the Type Of Robot

The first step in order to conceive the kinematic model of a hyper-redundant robot is to determine the type of robot that will be modelled. As it has been stated throughout the revision of the different methods, it is an essential factor when deciding which approach is best for a certain robot.

The main difference in the model selection is the discreetness or continuousness of the robot's joints. If the robot is a kinematic chain of several joints with one or two DOF, then the Denavit–Hartenberg method would be perfect for obtaining the kinematic equations. However, if the backbone is purely continuous, then other factors must be considered when modelling.

Cable lengths also depend on this decision. In fact, it is a very determining factor. When the robot is continuous (or can be approximated as such) cable lengths are far more difficult to model, and usually PCC and Closed Forms equations are needed so as to include the intermediate passive discs in the mathematical expressions.

Moreover, if there are no passive discs, cables would form a straight line between sections, and the Denavit–Hartenberg method could be directly applied (it has already been stated that this method could be used to obtain curvature parameters).

8.2. Example of Discreet Robot: MACH-I

An example of a discreet robot is MACH-I. It can clearly be seen that it consists of several discreet joints between sections (see Figure 23a,b). In fact, cables do follow a straight line between sections. The only thing that must be taken into account is that sections do have a certain width that must also be added to the cable length.

(a)   (b)

Figure 23. Details of MACH-I that suggest the discreet CDHR classification. (**a**) Detail of joints and straight cables between sections. (**b**) Detail of sections and cables with curved robot.

Having classified MACH-I as a discreet CDHR, the kinematic modelling technique that is proposed is the Denavit–Hartenberg method. It is fairly simple and can be used with the Natural-CCD algorithm to enable inverse kinematics. Some particularities of the robot should be taken into account, such as the straight segment of cable there is between sections.

In fact, the choice of the Denavit–Hartenberg parameters is quite similar to that made in Section 3. The defined reference frames can be seen in Figure 24a, while the parameters are in Figure 24b. In addition to these transformations, the base and endpoint reference frames must also be added through two rotations (Equations (80) and (81)):

$$^{B}A_0 = T(0,0,L+H/2)Rot_y(-\pi/2) \tag{80}$$

$$^{2}A_F = Rot_y(\pi/2)Rot_z(\pi/2) \tag{81}$$

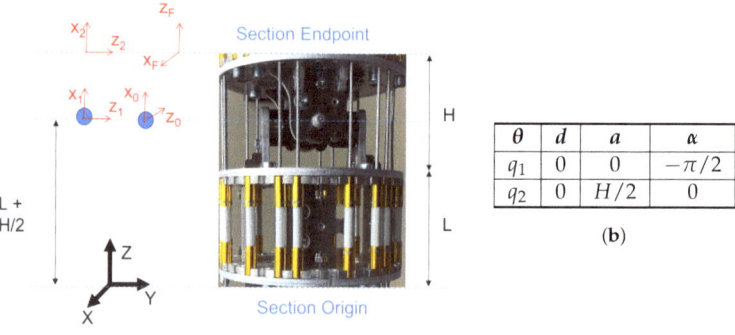

(a)

Figure 24. DH method for MACH-I. (**a**) Schematic figure for the application of the Denavit–Hartenberg algorithm to MACH-I. (**b**) Denavit–Hartenberg parameters for such a robot.

Therefore, the simple section transformation is found in Equation (82) by multiplying all the correspondent matrices obtained by the Denavit–Hartenberg method.

$$S_i = T(0,0,L+H/2)Rot_y(-\pi/2)^1A_2^2A_3Rot_y(\pi/2)Rot_z(\pi/2) \tag{82}$$

Each section endpoint can be found by multiplying all the preceding sections' matrices.

$$S_n = S_1 \cdot S_2 \cdot \cdots \cdot S_{n-1} \cdot S_n \tag{83}$$

Having achieved this, inverse kinematics demonstrate themselves to be quite easy. The first step would involve using the Natural-CCD algorithm to locate the endpoint reference frame for each section. Defining the two degrees of freedom of each joint as said parameters q_1 and q_2 would directly return these values for each section. Then, transforming this information into cable lengths is easy, since the transformation matrices would already be available. However, further geometric reasoning is needed (see Figure 25)

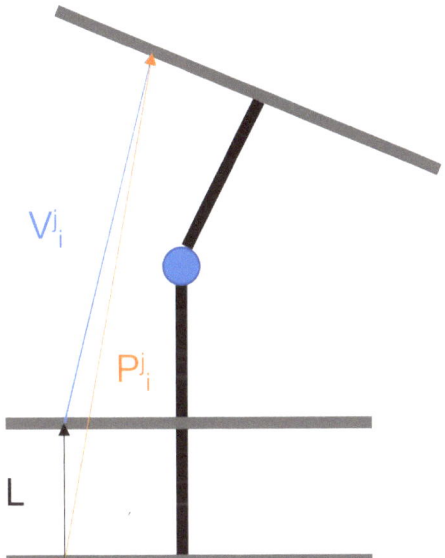

Figure 25. Geometrical reasoning for cables' lengths.

For each section, the endpoint position of each of the cables can be easily calculated by applying the transformation matrix of said section to the origin of the cable. For example, for section j, knowing cable i is located in point $(0,d,0)$, its end (P_i^j) would be located at:

$$P_i^j = S_1 \cdot \begin{bmatrix} 0 \\ d \\ 0 \end{bmatrix} \tag{84}$$

It must be taken into account that this vector includes both the fixed length of the cable (L) and the variable length (V_i^j) due to the current position. Therefore, the fixed part is subtracted knowing the current vector is obtained in section coordinates, and the section always starts oriented towards the z axis:

$$V_i^j = P_i^j - \begin{bmatrix} 0 \\ 0 \\ L \end{bmatrix} \tag{85}$$

The final length is then obtained using the sum of the fixed and the variable part:

$$l_i^j = L + \|V_i^j\| \tag{86}$$

Recursively calculating each section's cable lengths allows to add up the total length of each cable. Another alternative is to use increments of cable, for which fewer operations are needed. A complete inverse kinematic model is available for the MACH-I with these equations.

In case a direct kinematic model is needed, the relationships between the lengths of the cables and the degrees of freedom used in Denavit–Hartenberg's equations (the angles around x and y axis) would be required. As a parallel robot PPP-3S, the calculations are not direct, and would require either numerical algorithms or artificial intelligence to obtain them [46].

8.3. Constant Curvature Hypothesis

When considering continuous robots, the determining step (which might not be as easy as it seems) is deciding whether the constant curvature hypothesis applies to the robot to be modelled. The consequences of this dilemma directly affect the difficulty of the modelling process.

No robot actually complies perfectly with the constant curvature hypothesis. Therefore, the definitive criteria for rejecting the constant curvature hypothesis would be the empiric trials to determine whether the error is excessive, and thus the model must be rejected if the error is negligible or if it can be corrected by the controller.

As stated in Section 6, some of the reasons for the hypothesis not being applicable include an excessive weight of the robotic structure or not enough stiffness in the material. In these cases, a dynamic model is necessary. Whenever this is the case, a further question could be asked: whether or not the forces applied to the robot can be considered continuous (therefore using the CRT method) or discreet (where the PRB model is useful).

8.4. Example of Non-PCC Robot: Ruan

A good example of a robot which could be excluded from the constant curvature hypothesis is the previously introduced Ruan Robot. Ruan is a soft robot (see Figure 26). It can easily be stated that it does not belong to the discreet category, which directly excludes Denavit–Hartenberg method as applied to MACH-I.

Ruan being a soft robot implies that the constant curvature hypothesis may not be accurate enough when establishing its mathematical equations. Therefore, other alternatives such as the PRB or the Crosserat Rod Theory could be tried, depending on the knowledge of internal and external strains and forces. In the case of this soft robot, due to the fact that SMA threads act upon the discreet discs, the PRB method is proposed. Numerical methods, such as Finite Element Methods are also very common for soft robotics.

As said, the PRB method can be applied to this case. It is a three-disc robot, so three sections for the PRB need to be considered. Equations can be found in Figure 27. In addition to these equations, some general expressions must be added in order to transform some variables into known information (external forces and the tension of the cables).

This lot of equations would then have to be inserted into a nonlinear solver in order to update the position of the robot at each time, according to the PRB robot.

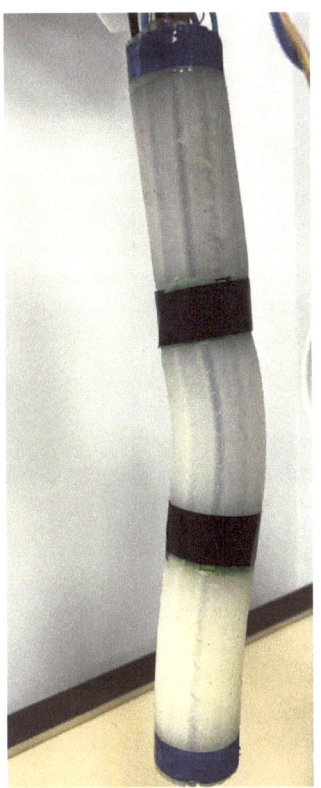

Figure 26. Ruan, a soft robot.

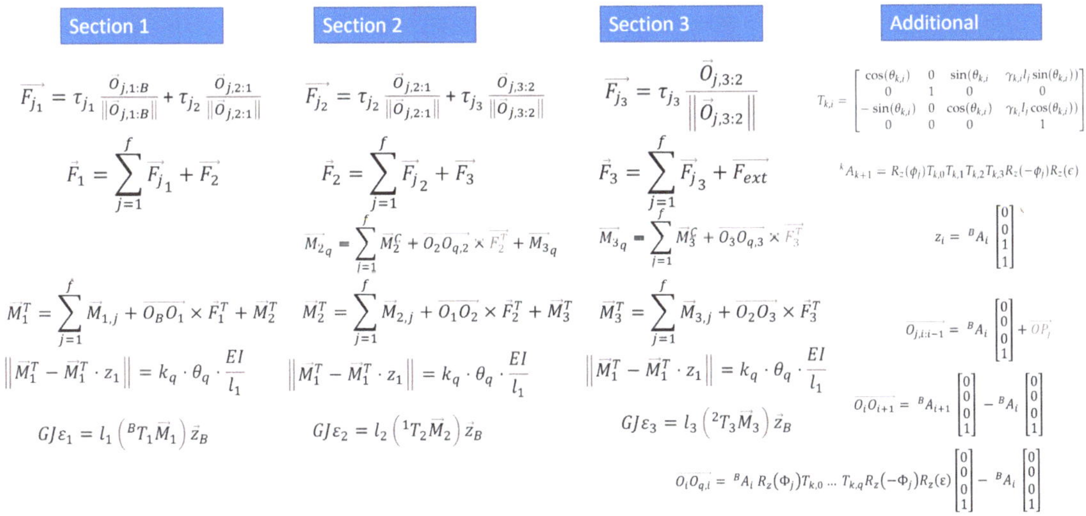

Section 1

$$\vec{F_{j_1}} = \tau_{j_1} \frac{\vec{O_{j,1:B}}}{\|\vec{O_{j,1:B}}\|} + \tau_{j_2} \frac{\vec{O_{j,2:1}}}{\|\vec{O_{j,2:1}}\|}$$

$$\vec{F_1} = \sum_{j=1}^{f} \vec{F_{j_1}} + \vec{F_2}$$

$$\vec{M_1^T} = \sum_{j=1}^{f} \vec{M_{1,j}} + \vec{O_B O_1} \times \vec{F_1^T} + \vec{M_2^T}$$

$$\|\vec{M_1^T} - \vec{M_1^T} \cdot z_1\| = k_q \cdot \theta_q \cdot \frac{EI}{l_1}$$

$$GJ\varepsilon_1 = l_1 \left(^B T_1 \vec{M_1}\right) \vec{z}_B$$

Section 2

$$\vec{F_{j_2}} = \tau_{j_2} \frac{\vec{O_{j,2:1}}}{\|\vec{O_{j,2:1}}\|} + \tau_{j_3} \frac{\vec{O_{j,3:2}}}{\|\vec{O_{j,3:2}}\|}$$

$$\vec{F_2} = \sum_{j=1}^{f} \vec{F_{j_2}} + \vec{F_3}$$

$$\vec{M_{2q}} = \sum_{j=1}^{f} \vec{M_2^C} + \vec{O_2 O_{q,2}} \times \vec{F_2^T} + \vec{M_{3q}}$$

$$\vec{M_2^T} = \sum_{j=1}^{f} \vec{M_{2,j}} + \vec{O_1 O_2} \times \vec{F_2^T} + \vec{M_3^T}$$

$$\|\vec{M_1^T} - \vec{M_1^T} \cdot z_1\| = k_q \cdot \theta_q \cdot \frac{EI}{l_1}$$

$$GJ\varepsilon_2 = l_2 \left(^1 T_2 \vec{M_2}\right) \vec{z}_B$$

Section 3

$$\vec{F_{j_3}} = \tau_{j_3} \frac{\vec{O_{j,3:2}}}{\|\vec{O_{j,3:2}}\|}$$

$$\vec{F_3} = \sum_{j=1}^{f} \vec{F_{j_3}} + \vec{F_{ext}}$$

$$\vec{M_{3q}} = \sum_{j=1}^{f} \vec{M_3^C} + \vec{O_3 O_{q,3}} \times \vec{F_3^T}$$

$$\vec{M_3^T} = \sum_{j=1}^{f} \vec{M_{3,j}} + \vec{O_2 O_3} \times \vec{F_3^T}$$

$$\|\vec{M_1^T} - \vec{M_1^T} \cdot z_1\| = k_q \cdot \theta_q \cdot \frac{EI}{l_1}$$

$$GJ\varepsilon_3 = l_3 \left(^2 T_3 \vec{M_3}\right) \vec{z}_B$$

Additional

$$T_{k,i} = \begin{bmatrix} \cos(\theta_{k,i}) & 0 & \sin(\theta_{k,i}) & \gamma_{k,i} l_i \sin(\theta_{k,i}) \\ 0 & 1 & 0 & 0 \\ -\sin(\theta_{k,i}) & 0 & \cos(\theta_{k,i}) & \gamma_{k,i} l_i \cos(\theta_{k,i}) \\ 0 & 0 & 0 & 1 \end{bmatrix}$$

$$^k A_{i+1} = R_z(\phi_j) T_{k,0} T_{k,1} T_{k,2} T_{k,3} R_z(-\phi_j) R_z(\epsilon)$$

$$z_i = {}^B A_i \begin{bmatrix} 0 \\ 0 \\ 1 \\ 1 \end{bmatrix}$$

$$\vec{O_{j,i:i-1}} = {}^B A_i \begin{bmatrix} 0 \\ 0 \\ 0 \\ 1 \end{bmatrix} + OP_j$$

$$\vec{O_i O_{i+1}} = {}^B A_{i+1} \begin{bmatrix} 0 \\ 0 \\ 0 \\ 1 \end{bmatrix} - {}^B A_i \begin{bmatrix} 0 \\ 0 \\ 0 \\ 1 \end{bmatrix}$$

$$\vec{O_i O_{q,i}} = {}^B A_i R_z(\Phi_j) T_{k,0} \ldots T_{k,q} R_z(-\Phi_j) R_z(\epsilon) \begin{bmatrix} 0 \\ 0 \\ 0 \\ 1 \end{bmatrix} - {}^B A_i \begin{bmatrix} 0 \\ 0 \\ 0 \\ 1 \end{bmatrix}$$

Figure 27. Equations applied to Ruan robot.

8.5. Inside the PCC Model

Apart from the aforementioned factors, there are some considerations that might help to choose a particular set of equations for a hyper-redundant robot that complies with the PCC hypothesis. For example, whenever the velocities are relevant information for the model (either because the sensors capture them or because the researcher is interested in developing a speed control system), the right choice would be to develop a differential model.

Computational power should also be taken into account. Hyper-redundant robots with many sections greatly increase the number of operations that are needed to solve the kinematic equations. Therefore, a less costly technique is more advisable than Closed-Form Equations. When a Real-Time System is also desirable, it also helps to reduce the number of operations. Linearisation allows faster computation and substantially less memory required for each DOF, thus being the best option when resources are scarce.

For example, MACH-I is designed to work with a computer next to it, which sends the instructions and can calculate simultaneously. Since a standard PC has enough computational power, even having several cores for parallel computing, it could implement the classical equations without worrying much about the scarcity of resources.

8.6. Example of PCC Robot: Pilory

As an application example for this decision, the Pilory robot can be used (see Figure 28). Beginning again with the classification process, the Pilory robot has a disc structure where one disc pivots over the following. It has four sections, with 20, 12, 12 and 8 discs each [20]. Every section is then actuated by four cables. There are no distinguishable discreet joints, and between sections, there are many intermediate passive discs. Therefore, the Denavit–Hartenberg method for discreet robots is immediately discarded.

Figure 28. Pilory, a continuous hyper-redundant robot.

Pilory has no backbone, therefore it has no problems with elasticity. It is quite lightweight since it has been built with 3-D-printed discs. These features account for trying to apply the constant curvature hypothesis before proceeding to more complex models, since it is not a soft robot, and the mathematical model might be good enough.

Inside the PCC model, the decisions can be considered more arbitrary. In this case, the simplest model is sought after, and velocities are not considered a must. This is why a differential model is not a requirement, and a simpler and more intuitive model is chosen.

The final decision in the proposed tutorial is whether or not the robot has low computational power, or if it is designed for real-time operation. The robot is managed through some hardware drivers that translate the instructions to the necessary electrical impulses, but the control is completely calculated by an external computer, which is connected to the hardware by a USB serial. The external computer has enough calculation power to use the complete model. Moreover, the robot is academically used and has no need for RTS features. Therefore, it is decided not to use the LSK method.

Therefore, the proposed model for Pilory (see Figure 29) is using PCC equations (as obtained in Section 4) for direct kinematics. Additionally, closed-form equations combined with the Natural CCD algorithm would be used for inverse kinematics.

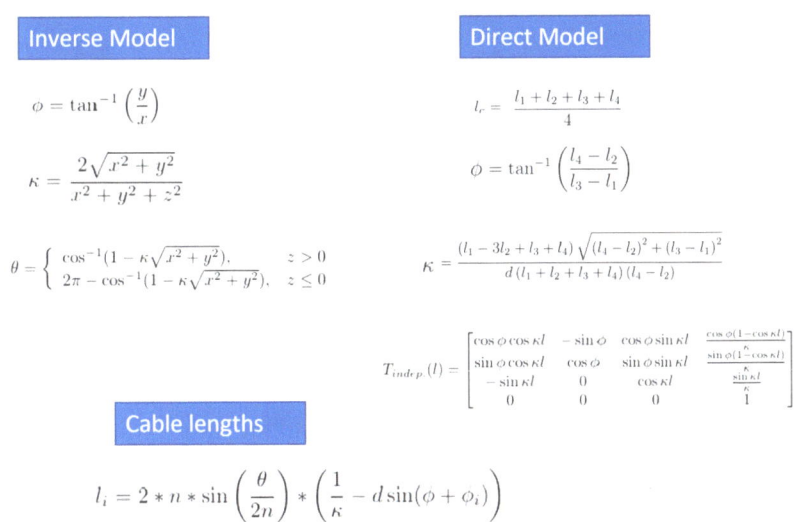

Figure 29. Equations for the Pilory robot, as deduced in Section 4.

9. Conclusions

As it has been revised in this work, hyper-redundant robotics is a growing sector that can be approached from different perspectives. Some mathematical alternatives are offered to the novel researcher, although it might be confusing to further reflect on some of them due to the large amount of work being published.

This article offers some guidelines to understand the current bibliography: It develops a simple scheme to conceptually fit all the models that are presented here, using several transformations to obtain both the direct and inverse kinematics for hyper-redundant robots. It also suggests a possible route in order to decide which mathematical expressions can be more useful depending on some of the robot's characteristics. This would simplify the approximation to the topic for newcomers while showing some of the most important differences between the methods available.

The proposal of a method of decision when tackling hyper-redundant robot modelling was applied to some examples of real robots, which also helps to clarify the concepts, and it provides a practical case for the novel researcher that approaches this topic.

Author Contributions: Conceptualisation, D.C. and A.B.; methodology, D.C. and A.B.; formal analysis, D.C.; investigation, D.C.; resources, A.B.; writing—original draft preparation, D.C.; writing—review and editing, A.B.; visualisation, D.C. and A.B.; supervision, A.B.; project administration, A.B.; funding acquisition, A.B. and J.D.C. All authors have read and agreed to the published version of the manuscript.

Funding: This work has received funding from the RoboCity2030-DIH-CM Madrid Robotics Digital Innovation Hub "Robótica aplicada a la mejora de la calidad de vida de los ciudadanos, fase IV"; S2018/NMT-4331), funded by "Programas de Actividades I+D en la Comunidad de Madrid" and cofunded by Structural Funds of the EU. The research has also been cofunded by Universidad Politécnica de Madrid (Becas-Colaboración de Formación Curso 2021-22) grant number D380.

Institutional Review Board Statement: Not applicable.

Informed Consent Statement: Not applicable.

Data Availability Statement: Not applicable.

Acknowledgments: This article has been possible thanks to the contribution of Iván Rodríguez and Andrés Martín as designers of the MACH-I robot, Silvia Terrile as the main creator of Ruan and Elena Muñoz as constructor of Pilory.

Conflicts of Interest: The authors declare no conflict of interest. The funders had no role in the design of the study; in the collection, analyses, or interpretation of data; in the writing of the manuscript, or in the decision to publish the results.

Abbreviations

The following abbreviations are used in this manuscript:

CDHR	Cable-Driven Hyper-Redundant Robot
DOF	Degrees Of Freedom
HTM	Homogeneous Transformation Matrix
PCC	Piecewise Constant Curvature
LSK	Linearised Segment Kinematics
PRB	Pseudorigid Body
CRT	Cosserat Rod Theory
CCD	Cyclic Coordinate Descent

References

1. Moran, M.E. Evolution of robotic arms. *J. Robot. Surg.* **2007**, *1*, 103–111. [CrossRef] [PubMed]
2. Hirose, S. *Biologically Inspired Robots: Snake-Like Locomotors and Manipulators*; Oxford University Press: Oxford, UK, 1993; p. 282.
3. Burdick, J.W. A Modal Approach to Hyper-Redundant Manipulator Kinematics. *IEEE Trans. Robot. Autom.* **1994**, *10*, 343–354. [CrossRef]
4. Hannan, M.W.; Walker, I.D. Novel Kinematics for Continuum Robots. In *Advances in Robot Kinematics*; Springer: Berlin/Heidelberg, Germany, 2000; pp. 227–238. [CrossRef]
5. Jones, B.A.; Walker, I.D. Kinematics for multisection continuum robots. *IEEE Trans. Robot.* **2006**, *22*, 43–55. [CrossRef]
6. Gravagne, I.A.; Rahn, C.D.; Walker, I.D. Large Deflection Dynamics and Control for Planar Continuum Robots. *IEEE/ASME Trans. Mechatronics* **2003**, *8*, 299–307. [CrossRef]
7. Webster, R.J.; Jones, B.A. Design and kinematic modeling of constant curvature continuum robots: A review. *Int. J. Robot. Res.* **2010**, *29*, 1661–1683. [CrossRef]
8. Martín Barrio, A. Design, Modelling, Control and Teleoperation of Hyper- Redundant Robots. Ph.D. Thesis, Universidad Politécnica de Madrid, Madrid, Spain, 2020. [CrossRef]
9. Kim, S.; Xu, W.; Ren, H. Inverse kinematics with a geometrical approximation for multi-segment flexible curvilinear robots. *Robotics* **2019**, *8*, 48. [CrossRef]
10. Xanthidis, M.; Kyriakopoulos, K.J.; Rekleitis, I. Dynamically efficient kinematics for hyper-redundant manipulators. In Proceedings of the 24th Mediterranean Conference on Control and Automation, MED 2016, Athens, Greece, 21–24 June 2016; pp. 207–213. [CrossRef]
11. Gallardo-Alvarado, J.; Tinajero-Campo, J.H.; Sánchez-Rodríguez, Á. Kinematics of a configurable manipulator using screw theory. *Rev. Iberoam. Automática E Inform. Ind.* **2020**, *18*, 58. [CrossRef]
12. Zaplana, I.; Hadfield, H.; Lasenby, J. Closed-form solutions for the inverse kinematics of serial robots using conformal geometric algebra. *Mech. Mach. Theory* **2022**, *173*, 104835. [CrossRef]
13. Kane, S.N.; Mishra, A.; Dutta, A.K. Towards extending Forward Kinematic Models on Hyper-Redundant Manipulator to Cooperative Bionic Arms. *J. Phys. Conf. Ser.* **2016**, *755*, 011001. [CrossRef]
14. Martín-Barrio, A.; Roldán-Gómez, J.J.; Rodríguez, I.; Del Cerro, J.; Barrientos, A. Design of a hyper-redundant robot and teleoperation using mixed reality for inspection tasks. *Sensors* **2020**, *20*, 2181. [CrossRef] [PubMed]
15. Rao, P.; Peyron, Q.; Lilge, S.; Burgner-Kahrs, J. How to Model Tendon-Driven Continuum Robots and Benchmark Modelling Performance. *Front. Robot. AI* **2021**, *7*, 1–20. [CrossRef] [PubMed]
16. Xu, F.; Wang, H. Soft Robotics: Morphology and Morphology-inspired Motion Strategy. *IEEE/CAA J. Autom. Sin.* **2021**, *8*, 1500–1522. [CrossRef]

17. Chirikjian, G.S. Theory and Applications of Hyper-Redundant Robotic Manipulators. Ph.D. Thesis, California Institute of Technology, Pasadena, CA, USA, 1992. Available online: https://resolver.caltech.edu/CaltechETD:etd-11082006-132210 (accessed on 30 June 2022).
18. Robotics, O. Series II, X125 System. 2015. Available online: https://www.ocrobotics.com/technology-/series-ii-x125-system/ (accessed on 15 May 2022).
19. Hannan, M.W. *Theory and Experimentation with an 'Elephant's Trunk' Robotic Manipulator*; Oxford University Press: Oxford, UK, 2002; p. 649.
20. Muñoz Sánchez, E. Construccion y Control de un Robot Continuo de Cables con Discos Pivotantes. Bachelor's Thesis, Universidad Politécnica de Madrid, Madrid, Spain, 2022. Available online: https://oa.upm.es/69811/ (accessed on 2 July 2022).
21. Terrile, S. Soft Robotics: Applications , Desing and Control. Ph.D. Thesis, Universidad Politécnica de Madrid, Madrid, Spain, 2021. [CrossRef]
22. Martin-Barrio, A.; Terrile, S.; Diaz-Carrasco, M.; del Cerro, J.; Barrientos, A. Modelling the Soft Robot Kyma Based on Real-Time Finite Element Method. *Comput. Graph. Forum* **2020**, *39*, 289–302. [CrossRef]
23. Paez-Grandos, D.; Gualdron, O.E.; Valencia Ramón, J.L. Aprendizaje de la cinemática en robots redundantes utilizando mapas de bézier. *Rev. Tecnol. J. Technol.* **2015**, *14*, 23–32. [CrossRef]
24. Dehghani, M.; Moosavian, S.A.A. Modeling and control of a planar continuum robot. In Proceedings of the IEEE/ASME International Conference on Advanced Intelligent Mechatronics, AIM, Budapest, Hungary, 3–7 July 2011; pp. 966–971. [CrossRef]
25. Tommy Wang, L.C.; Cheng Chen, C. A Combined Optimization Method for Solving the Inverse Kinematics Problem of Mechanical Manipulators. *IEEE Trans. Robot.* **1991**, *7*, 489–499. [CrossRef]
26. Martín, A.; Barrientos, A.; Del Cerro, J. The natural-CCD algorithm, a novel method to solve the inverse kinematics of hyper-redundant and soft robots. *Soft Robot.* **2018**, *5*, 242–257. [CrossRef]
27. Denavit, J.; Hartenberg, R. A Kinematic Notation for Lower-Pair Mechanisms Based on Matrices. *ASME J. Appl. Mech.* **1955**, *22*, 215–221. [CrossRef]
28. Barrientos Cruz, A.; Peñín, L.F.; Balaguer, C.; Aracil, R. *Fundamentos de Robótica*; McGraw-Hill: New York, NY, USA, 2007.
29. Simaan, N.; Taylor, R.; Flint, P. A dexterous system for laryngeal surgery. In Proceedings of the IEEE International Conference on Robotics and Automation, ICRA '04, New Orleans, LA, USA, 26 April–1 May 2004; Volume 2004, pp. 351–357. [CrossRef]
30. Neppalli, S.; Csencsits, M.A.; Jones, B.A.; Walker, I.D. Closed-form inverse kinematics for continuum manipulators. *Adv. Robot.* **2009**, *23*, 2077–2091. [CrossRef]
31. Hannan, M.W.; Walker, I.D. Kinematics and the implementation of an elephant's trunk manipulator and other continuum style robots. *J. Robot. Syst.* **2003**, *20*, 45–63. [CrossRef] [PubMed]
32. Jones, B.A.; McMahan, W.; Walker, I.D. Practical kinematics for real-time implementation of continuum robots. In Proceedings of the 2006 IEEE International Conference on Robotics and Automation, ICRA, Orlando, FL, USA, 15–19 May 2006; Volume 2006, pp. 1840–1847. [CrossRef]
33. Camarillo, D.B.; Carlson, C.R.; Salisbury, J.K. Configuration Tracking for Continuum Manipulators with Coupled Tendon Drive. *Springer Tracts Adv. Robot.* **2009**, *54*, 271–280. [CrossRef]
34. Orin, D.E.; Schrader, W.W. Efficient Computation of the Jacobian for Robot Manipulators. *Int. J. Robot. Res.* **1984**, *3*, 66–75. [CrossRef]
35. Chembrammel, P.; Kesavadas, T. A new implementation for online calculation of manipulator Jacobian. *PLoS ONE* **2019**, *14*, 1–16. [CrossRef] [PubMed]
36. Webster, R.J.; Swensen, J.P.; Romano, J.M.; Cowan, N.J. Closed-Form Differential Kinematics for Concentric-Tube Continuum Robots with Application to Visual Servoing. *Springer Tracts Adv. Robot.* **2009**, *54*, 485–494. [CrossRef]
37. Barrientos-Diez, J.; Dong, X.; Axinte, D.; Kell, J. Real-Time Kinematics of Continuum Robots: Modelling and Validation. *Robot. Comput.-Integr. Manuf.* **2021**, *67*, 102019. [CrossRef]
38. Su, H.J. A pseudorigid-body 3r model for determining large deflection of cantilever beams subject to tip loads. *J. Mech. Robot.* **2009**, *1*, 1–9. [CrossRef]
39. Chen, G.; Xiong, B.; Huang, X. Finding the optimal characteristic parameters for 3R pseudo-rigid-body model using an improved particle swarm optimizer. *Precis. Eng.* **2011**, *35*, 505–511. [CrossRef]
40. Huang, S.; Meng, D.; Wang, X.; Liang, B.; Lu, W. A 3D Static Modeling Method and Experimental Verification of Continuum Robots Based on Pseudo-Rigid Body Theory. In Proceedings of the IEEE International Conference on Intelligent Robots and Systems, Macau, China, 4–8 November 2019; pp. 4672–4677. [CrossRef]
41. Yuan, H.; Zhou, L.; Xu, W. A comprehensive static model of cable-driven multi-section continuum robots considering friction effect. *Mech. Mach. Theory* **2019**, *135*, 130–149. [CrossRef]
42. Altenbach, H.; Eremeyev, V.A.; Morozov, N.F. On the Influence of Residual Surface Stresses on the Properties of Structures at the Nanoscale. In *Surface Effects in Solid Mechanics 2013*; Springer: Berlin/Heidelberg, Germany, 2013; pp. 21–32. [CrossRef]
43. Jones, B.A.; Gray, R.L.; Turlapati, K. Three dimensional statics for continuum robotics. In Proceedings of the 2009 IEEE/RSJ International Conference on Intelligent Robots and Systems, IROS 2009, St. Louis, MO, USA, 10–12 October 2009; pp. 2659–2664. doi: 10.1109/IROS.2009.5354199. [CrossRef]

44. Renda, F.; Laschi, C. A general mechanical model for tendon-driven continuum manipulators. In Proceedings of the IEEE International Conference on Robotics and Automation, St Paul, MN, USA, 14–18 May 2012; pp. 3813–3818. [CrossRef]
45. Martín-Barrio, A.; del Cerro, J.; Barrientos, A.; Hauser, H. Emerging behaviours from cyclical, incremental and uniform movements of hyper-redundant and growing robots. *Mech. Mach. Theory* **2021**, *158*, 104198. [CrossRef]
46. Merlet, J.P. Parallel robots. In *Part of Series: Solid Mechanics and Its Applications*; Springer: Berlin/Heidelberg, Germany, 2006; Volume 128, pp. 1–413. ISBN 978-1-4020-4132-7. [CrossRef]

Article

Active Disturbance Rejection Strategy for Distance and Formation Angle Decentralized Control in Differential-Drive Mobile Robots

Mario Ramírez-Neria [1], Jaime González-Sierra [2], Alberto Luviano-Juárez [3], Norma Lozada-Castillo [3] and Rafal Madonski [4,*]

1. InIAT Institute of Applied Research and Technology, Universidad Iberoamericana Ciudad de México, Prolongación Paseo de la Reforma 880, Colonia Lomas de Santa Fé, Ciudad de México 01219, Mexico
2. Unidad Profesional Interdisciplinaria de Ingeniería Campus Hidalgo, Instituto Politécnico Nacional, Carretera Pachuca-Actopan Kilómetro 1+500 Ciudad del Conocimiento y la Cultura Educación, San Agustín Tlaxiaca 42162, Mexico
3. Unidad Profesional Interdisciplinaria en Ingeniería y Tecnologías Avanzadas, Instituto Politécnico Nacional, Av. IPN 2580, Col. Barrio La Laguna Ticomán, Ciudad de México 07340, Mexico
4. Energy and Electricity Research Center, Jinan University, Zhuhai 519070, China
* Correspondence: rafal.madonski@jnu.edu.cn

Abstract: The important practical problem of robust synchronization in distance and orientation for a class of differential-drive mobile robots is tackled in this work as an active disturbance rejection control (ADRC) problem. To solve it, a kinematic model of the governed system is first developed based on the distance and formation angle between the agents. Then, a special high-order extended state observer is designed to collectively estimate the perturbations (formed by longitudinal and lateral slipping parameters) that affect the kinematic model. Finally, a custom error-based ADRC approach is designed and applied assuming that the distance and orientation between the agents are the only available measurements. The proposed control strategy does not need time-derivatives of the reference trajectory, which increases the practical appeal of the proposed solution. The experimental results, obtained in laboratory conditions with a set of differential-drive mobile robots operating in a leader–follower configuration, show the effectiveness of the proposed governing scheme in terms of trajectory tracking and disturbance rejection.

Keywords: active disturbance rejection control (ADRC); differential-drive mobile robots; multi-robot control; formation control; extended state observer (ESO); robust control

MSC: 70E60

Citation: Ramírez-Neria, M.; González-Sierra, J.; Luviano-Juárez, A.; Lozada-Castillo, N.; Madonski, R. Active Disturbance Rejection Strategy for Distance and Formation Angle Decentralized Control in Differential-Drive Mobile Robots. *Mathematics* **2022**, *10*, 3865. https://doi.org/10.3390/math10203865

Academic Editors: Paolo Mercorelli, Oleg Sergiyenko and Oleksandr Tsymbal

Received: 28 September 2022
Accepted: 17 October 2022
Published: 18 October 2022

Publisher's Note: MDPI stays neutral with regard to jurisdictional claims in published maps and institutional affiliations.

Copyright: © 2022 by the authors. Licensee MDPI, Basel, Switzerland. This article is an open access article distributed under the terms and conditions of the Creative Commons Attribution (CC BY) license (https://creativecommons.org/licenses/by/4.0/).

1. Introduction

1.1. Motivation

The coordination of multiple mobile robots has been widely studied in recent years by both academic researchers and industry practitioners, as shown in surveys [1,2]. The progress made in this field allowed the development of important real-world applications, including surveillance, home services, and logistics [3]. The multiple mobile robots coordination problem extends the classical control, related to point convergence and trajectory tracking of a single mobile robot, to the case of collective behaviors, like the convergence to formation patterns, formation tracking, dispersion, containment, and inter-robot collision avoidance, among others.

The most basic scheme of multi-robot formation tracking is the case of two robots, where a leader agent follows a desired trajectory while the follower agents must keep a desired position and orientation with respect to the leader [4–6]. In a decentralized scheme, the multi-robot control methodology depends on the local measurements of distance and direction or absolute orientation [7]. From the vast area of decentralized multi-robot control, our work focuses on the challenge of robust formation control for differential-drive mobile robots or first order agents.

1.2. Related Works

To address the issue of decentralized formation control, different solutions have been proposed so far. For instance, a decentralized feedback law was presented in the pioneer work [8]. A control law that only depends on the distance and/or bearing angle measurements was proposed in [9–12]. In [13], a control law was developed using the gradient vector field based approach. An adaptive dynamic feedback with an immersion and invariance estimation-based second order sliding mode control was designed in [14]. A control strategy that combines kinematic controller based on Lyapunov theory with a dynamic controller based on sliding mode was proposed in [15]. It is worth pointing out that in [9,10], even though the control strategy is designed to be robust, there are still oscillations in the distances between the agents. Moreover, if there is noise in the measurement, the distances between agents start to oscillate. In [11], the main drawback is that the leader stays static. On the other hand, in [9,10,12,14,15] it is assumed that the leader's velocity is constant or it moves with a low velocity. Furthermore, none of the cited references consider perturbations that affect the kinematic model, and most of them only present simulation results. On the other hand, the existing physical systems are often affected by various types of uncertainties, like information delays, external disturbances, non-modeled dynamics, low energy storage in the agents, and/or possible unexpected frictions. This motivates to look for actual robust control schemes, that would allow the use of models with only partial system knowledge and could handle scenarios in which the robots are subject to uncertainties.

Another problem that arises when performing formation control in a multi-agent system is related to communication. In the first instance, there is a central computer where the control inputs are calculated and sent, via radio frequency, Bluetooth, or WiFi, to each of the agents. It is well known that wireless communication systems often have time delays and loss of information [16]. However, in recent years, different communication protocols have been developed [17,18] and have presented improvements in sending/receiving data as well as minimal information loss [19,20].

To address the above limitations of current control designs, an active disturbance rejection control (ADRC, [21,22]) scheme can be applied to solve the robust formation control for differential-drive mobile robots. The relative tuning simplicity of ADRC, together with its desirable features for practical applications [23,24], have made it an attractive alternative to standard controllers (e.g., PID-type) for tackling real-world control problems [25]. The ADRC, as a control philosophy, is based on the simplification of the control system, such that it can be represented as the control of a disturbed chain of integrators, in which the *total disturbance* aggregates all the internal and external disturbing effects, which are estimated by an extended state observer (ESO; see [26–28] for a comprehensive review of the topic) and further canceled out in the control law.

In light of the above advantages, there has been a considerable effort in the last few years to utilize ADRC in mobile robotics. The concept of ADRC has been previously considered for the trajectory tracking control of differentially flat mobile robots, particularly omnidirectional, which have the advantage of being of holonomic nature in contrast with the differential ones. For example, ADRC with high-order observer has been proposed in [29]. A combination of ADRC, model predictive control, and friction compensation was introduced in [30]. In [31], an ADRC-based trajectory tracking control was designed for an omnidirectional mobile manipulator operating in the presence of parameter uncertainties and external disturbances. The combination of ADRC and flatness is specially useful for mobile robots since flatness trivializes the trajectory planning task [32], allowing to ensure a robust trajectory tracking behavior. However, even when ADRC-based schemes are robust with minimal information of the system to control, the flatness-based ADRC requires the knowledge of the high order time derivatives of the reference trajectory, which, for the case of leader–follower schemes, is not regularly available.

1.3. Contribution

In this work, a special version of ADRC is proposed for differential-drive mobile robots. It relies on an error-based modification of ADRC, introduced in [33] (later generalized and proved in [24]). The main idea behind it is to make the implementation of ADRC resemble that of those currently used industrial solutions (like PID), hence making it easier to implement in real applications or to swiftly replace the existing control algorithm. This error-based adaptation already found itself useful in various control scenarios, like robust tracking in an under-actuated mass-spring system [34], altitude/attitude control of a quadrotor UAV [35], and motion control in robotic manipulators [36,37].

To summarize, the contribution of this paper is the proposition of a robust control strategy to solve the formation control problem based on the distance and formation angle between differential-drive mobile robots. The main distinctive features of the proposed control solution are as follows:

- It utilizes the robust ADRC scheme (with a custom error-based high-order ESO) that allows the follower agent to keep a desired distance and formation angle with respect to its own leader in spite the external disturbances, i.e., linear and lateral slipping parameters as well as unknown leader dynamics and velocities.
- It only depends on the distance and formation angle measurements.
- It is developed using solely a kinematic model based on the distance and the formation angle between a pair of robots, taking into account the front point of the differential-drive mobile robots.

To the authors' best knowledge, such an approach has not been yet presented in the available literature.

2. Leader–Follower Problem

2.1. Considered Class of Systems

Let $N = \{R_1, \ldots, R_n\}$ be a set composed of n differential-drive mobile robots moving in the horizontal plane, as depicted in Figure 1.

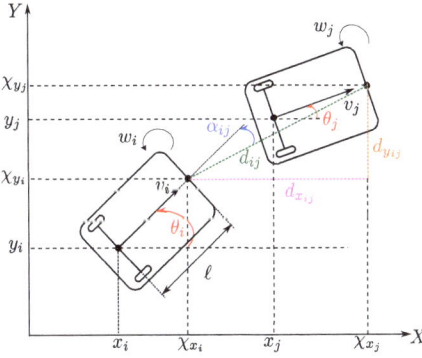

Figure 1. Schematic diagram of two differential-drive wheeled mobile robots in the leader–follower configuration.

The set of equations that describe the perturbed kinematic motion of the differential-drive mobile robots is defined as

$$\dot{\xi}_i = G(\theta_i)\mathbf{u}_i + \boldsymbol{\varphi}_i(t), \quad i = 1, \ldots, n, \tag{1}$$

where R_n is the leader agent while $R_1, \ldots, R_{n-1}$ are the followers and $G(\theta_i)$ is the system matrix, defined by

$$G(\theta_i) = \begin{bmatrix} \cos\theta_i & 0 \\ \sin\theta_i & 0 \\ 0 & 1 \end{bmatrix},$$

where $\boldsymbol{\xi}_i = \begin{bmatrix} x_i & y_i & \theta_i \end{bmatrix}^\top \in \mathbb{R}^3$ is the state vector with $x_i \in \mathbb{R}$, $y_i \in \mathbb{R}$ as the position in the plane of the i-th agent, $\theta_i \in \mathbb{R}$ is the orientation with respect to the horizontal axis, $\mathbf{u}_i = \begin{bmatrix} v_i & \omega_i \end{bmatrix}^\top$ is the control input vector, where $v_i \in \mathbb{R}$ represents the longitudinal velocity and $\omega_i \in \mathbb{R}$ is the angular velocity; $\boldsymbol{\varphi}_i = \begin{bmatrix} \varphi_{x_i} & \varphi_{y_i} & 0 \end{bmatrix}^\top$ is the disturbance vector, which corresponds to the lateral and longitudinal slipping parameters of the wheels (this class of disturbance does not affect the orientation angle [38,39]). It is well known that when one tries to control the coordinates x_i, y_i, from (1), the system cannot be stabilized with a continuous and time-invariant control law due to singularities in the controller [40]. In order to avoid such singularities, it is proposed to study the kinematics of a point χ_i, located at a distance l from the midpoint of the wheels' axle of the mobile robot, defined as

$$\chi_i = \begin{bmatrix} \chi_{x_i} \\ \chi_{y_i} \end{bmatrix} = \begin{bmatrix} x_i + l\cos\theta_i \\ y_i + l\sin\theta_i \end{bmatrix}.$$

The kinematics of the point χ_i is computed as

$$\dot{\chi}_i = A_i(\theta_i, l)\mathbf{u}_i + \boldsymbol{\varphi}_i, \qquad (2)$$

with $A_i = \begin{bmatrix} \cos\theta_i & -l\sin\theta_i \\ \sin\theta_i & l\cos\theta_i \end{bmatrix}$ being the decoupling matrix, which is non-singular since $\det(A_i) = l \neq 0$.

Assumption 1. *The perturbations $\boldsymbol{\varphi}_i$ are smooth and bounded, where $\sup_t |\varphi_{x_i}| \leq K_x$ and $\sup_t |\varphi_{y_i}| \leq K_y$, with K_x and K_y being sufficiently large, positive, real numbers.*

Remark 1. *The studied class of systems is of passive nature and with bounds of inertia [41]; hence, Assumption 1 is practically justified and can be found in various robotic systems [42].*

Remark 2. *The capacity of the system to reject perturbations and disturbances is closely related to the fact that the flatness property (which involves the controllability) is preserved, which implies that the rolling lacks slipping conditions [43] (for instance, when there is a wheel skidding due to slippery floor). This condition represents the relation between the angular movement of the wheels' axes and the generated tangential movement of the wheels in contrast with slipping conditions due to external disturbances that are to be compensated by the control scheme. Thus, the controllability condition in each wheel is assumed to be satisfied in this work.*

2.2. Problem Statement

The considered problem can be divided into two subproblems: modeling and control. For the first one, a kinematic model of a pair of differential-drive mobile robots, based on distance and formation angle between agents, has to be developed by taking into account the front point χ_i, i.e.,

$$\dot{\boldsymbol{\eta}}_{ij} = \begin{bmatrix} \dot{d}_{ij} & \dot{\alpha}_{ij} \end{bmatrix}^\top = f(\boldsymbol{\eta}_{ij}, \theta_i, \theta_j, \mathbf{u}_i, \mathbf{u}_j),$$

where $d_{ij} \in \mathbb{R}^+$ is the Euclidean distance measured from the front point of R_i to the front point of R_j, with $\mathbb{R}^+$ as the set of all positive real numbers, $d_{x_{ij}}$ and $d_{y_{ij}} \in \mathbb{R}^+$ are the components of the distance vector $\vec{d}_{ij}$ with respect to a global frame, $\alpha_{ij} \in \mathbb{R}$ is the formation angle measured from the distance vector $\vec{d}_{ij}$ to a local frame attached to the follower agent, as is shown in Figure 1. Once the model is obtained, the second subproblem has to be solved. A robust feedback control law has to be designed, such that:

- Leader tracks a prescribed trajectory, i.e.,

$$\lim_{t \to \infty} (\chi_n - \chi^*) = 0,$$

where $\chi^* = \begin{bmatrix} \chi_x^* & \chi_y^* \end{bmatrix}^\top \in \mathbb{R}^2$ is the desired trajectory;

- Agent R_i maintains a desired distance d_{ij}^* and a desired formation angle α_{ij}^* with respect to the agent R_j, i.e.,

$$\lim_{t \to \infty} (\eta_{ij} - \eta_{ij}^*) = 0,$$

where $\eta_{ij}^* = \begin{bmatrix} d_{ij}^* & \alpha_{ij}^* \end{bmatrix}^\top$ is the vector that contains the desired distance d_{ij}^* and the desired formation angle α_{ij}^*.

It is worth pointing out that both control tasks have to be realized effectively despite the influence of perturbations such as the lateral and longitudinal slipping parameters of the wheels, sensor noises, and/or measurement errors.

3. Proposed Control System

3.1. Leader–Follower Scheme Based on Distance and Formation Angle between the Agents

Before designing the control law, the kinematic model based on distance and formation angle between the agents has to be obtained. Based on Figure 1, the distance d_{ij} and the angle α_{ij} are defined as

$$d_{ij} = |\vec{d}_{ij}| = \sqrt{d_{x_{ij}}^2 + d_{y_{ij}}^2}, \tag{3a}$$

$$\alpha_{ij} = \theta_i - \tan^{-1}\left(\frac{d_{y_{ij}}}{d_{x_{ij}}}\right), \tag{3b}$$

where $d_{x_{ij}} = \chi_{x_j} - \chi_{x_i}$ and $d_{y_{ij}} = \chi_{y_j} - \chi_{y_i}$. The time-derivative of (3) is calculated as

$$\dot{d}_{ij} = \frac{d_{x_{ij}} \dot{d}_{x_{ij}} + d_{y_{ij}} \dot{d}_{y_{ij}}}{d_{ij}}, \tag{4a}$$

$$\dot{\alpha}_{ij} = \dot{\theta}_i - \frac{d_{x_{ij}} \dot{d}_{y_{ij}} - d_{y_{ij}} \dot{d}_{x_{ij}}}{d_{ij}^2}, \tag{4b}$$

where

$$\dot{d}_{x_{ij}} = v_j \cos\theta_j - v_i \cos\theta_i - l\omega_j \sin\theta_j + l\omega_i \sin\theta_i + \varphi_{x_j} - \varphi_{x_i}, \tag{5a}$$

$$\dot{d}_{y_{ij}} = v_j \sin\theta_j - v_i \sin\theta_i + l\omega_j \cos\theta_j - l\omega_i \cos\theta_i + \varphi_{y_j} - \varphi_{y_i}. \tag{5b}$$

Substituting (5) into (4) and considering $d_{x_{ij}} = d_{ij}\cos(\theta_i - \alpha_{ij})$ and $d_{y_{ij}} = d_{ij}\sin(\theta_i - \alpha_{ij})$, the kinematics of d_{ij} and α_{ij} can be expressed as follows

$$\dot{\eta}_{ij} = A_{ij}(\theta_i, \theta_j, \eta_{ij})\mathbf{u}_j - B_{ij}(\eta_{ij})\mathbf{u}_i + \varphi_{ij}, \tag{6}$$

with

$$A_{ij} = \begin{bmatrix} \cos(\alpha_{ij} - \theta_i + \theta_j) & -l\sin(\alpha_{ij} - \theta_i + \theta_j) \\ -\frac{\sin(\alpha_{ij} - \theta_i + \theta_j)}{d_{ij}} & -\frac{l}{d_{ij}}\cos(\alpha_{ij} - \theta_i + \theta_j) \end{bmatrix},$$

$$B_{ij} = \begin{bmatrix} \cos\alpha_{ij} & -l\sin\alpha_{ij} \\ -\frac{\sin\alpha_{ij}}{d_{ij}} & -\left(1 + \frac{l}{d_{ij}}\cos\alpha_{ij}\right) \end{bmatrix},$$

$$\varphi_{ij} = \begin{bmatrix} \cos(\theta_i - \alpha_{ij}) & \sin(\theta_i - \alpha_{ij}) \\ \frac{1}{d_{ij}}\sin(\theta_i - \alpha_{ij}) & -\frac{1}{d_{ij}}\cos(\theta_i - \alpha_{ij}) \end{bmatrix}\begin{bmatrix} \varphi_{x_j} - \varphi_{x_i} \\ \varphi_{y_j} - \varphi_{y_i} \end{bmatrix}.$$

Proposition 1. *Matrix B_{ij} is non singular for all $\cos\alpha_{ij} \neq -\frac{l}{d_{ij}}$ and $j \neq i$.*

Proof. The determinant of matrix B_{ij} is given by

$$\det(B_{ij}) = -\left(\frac{l}{d_{ij}} + \cos\alpha_{ij}\right).$$

It becomes evident that a singularity will appear when $\cos\alpha_{ij} = -\frac{l}{d_{ij}}$. Since l and $d_{ij} > 0$, the singularity can appear when

$$\alpha_{ij} \in \left(-\frac{3}{2}\pi, -\frac{\pi}{2}\right) \cup \left(\frac{\pi}{2}, \frac{3}{2}\pi\right) \tag{7}$$

With these values of α_{ij}, it means that the leader agent is outside of the field of view of the follower. On the other hand, one can select d_{ij} sufficiently larger than l to ensure the follower do not collide with his own leader. □

Let us now define the tracking error as $\mathbf{e}_{ij} = \eta_{ij} - \eta_{ij}^*$, with its dynamics given by

$$\dot{\mathbf{e}}_{ij} = A_{ij}(\theta_i, \theta_j, \eta_{ij})\mathbf{u}_j - B_{ij}(\eta_{ij})\mathbf{u}_i + \varphi_{ij} - \dot{\eta}_{ij}^*. \tag{8}$$

Note that (8) can be simplified to a perturbed error system

$$\dot{\mathbf{e}}_{ij} = -B_{ij}(\eta_{ij})\mathbf{u}_i + \Phi_{ij}(t), \tag{9}$$

where $\Phi_{ij}(t)$ is the *total disturbance* vector (that affects the R_i agent), which has to be estimated and its influence cancelled. For the considered system, it is defined as

$$\Phi_{ij}(t) = A_{ij}(\theta_i, \theta_j, \eta_{ij})\mathbf{u}_j + \varphi_{ij} - \dot{\eta}_{ij}^*.$$

The term $\Phi_{ij}(t)$ lumps: (i) the effects of neglected internal and external kinematics given by $A_{ij}(\theta_i, \theta_j, \eta_{ij})$, as well as the lateral and longitudinal slipping parameters of the wheels φ_{ij}; (ii) the unknown velocities, such as the control input $\mathbf{u}_j$, and (iii) the desired nominal velocities $\dot{\eta}_{ij}^*$.

3.2. Followers Control Strategy

Let us now consider the kinematic model error given in (9). In order to design the control strategy for the followers, an extended state space is proposed, with $\mathbf{z}_{ij} = \Phi_{ij}$

$$\dot{\mathbf{e}}_{ij} = -B_{ij}(\eta_{ij})\mathbf{u}_i + \mathbf{z}_{ij}, \tag{10a}$$

$$\dot{\mathbf{z}}_{ij} = \psi_{ij} \approx 0. \tag{10b}$$

For the above extended system, a following high-order ESO (also known as generalized proportional-integral observer, or GPIO) in the error domain is proposed to estimate the follower *total disturbance*

$$\dot{\hat{\mathbf{e}}}_{ij} = -B_{ij}(\boldsymbol{\eta}_{ij})\mathbf{u}_i + \hat{\mathbf{z}}_{ij} + \Lambda_i\big(\mathbf{e}_{ij} - \hat{\mathbf{e}}_{ij}\big), \tag{11a}$$

$$\dot{\hat{\mathbf{z}}}_{ij} = \Gamma_i\big(\mathbf{e}_{ij} - \hat{\mathbf{e}}_{ij}\big), \tag{11b}$$

where $\Lambda_i = \mathrm{diag}\{\lambda_{x_i}, \lambda_{y_i}\} \in \mathbb{R}^{2\times 2}$ and $\Gamma_i = \mathrm{diag}\{\gamma_{x_i}, \gamma_{y_i}\} \in \mathbb{R}^{2\times 2}$ are positive diagonal matrices. Let us define the follower estimation error $\tilde{\mathbf{e}}_{ij} = \mathbf{e}_{ij} - \hat{\mathbf{e}}_{ij}$, whose time-derivative is obtained from (10) and (11) as follows

$$\ddot{\tilde{\mathbf{e}}}_{ij} + \Lambda_i \dot{\tilde{\mathbf{e}}}_{ij} + \Gamma_i \tilde{\mathbf{e}}_{ij} = \boldsymbol{\Phi}_{ij}. \tag{12}$$

In order to tune the observer gains, the characteristic polynomials of the follower estimation error are matched with Hurwitz polynomials as

$$I_2 s^2 + \Lambda_i s + \Gamma_i = I_2 s^2 + 2\mathbf{Z}_i \mathbf{W}_i s + \mathbf{W}_i^2,$$

where I_2 is the 2×2 identity matrix while the follower observer gain matrices are chosen as

$$\Lambda_i = 2\mathbf{Z}_i \mathbf{W}_i, \quad \Gamma_i = \mathbf{W}_i^2. \tag{13}$$

The proper selection of gains (13) allows to estimate the perturbations of the model, i.e., $\hat{\boldsymbol{\Phi}}_{ij}(t) \to \boldsymbol{\Phi}_{ij}(t)$. Based on this relation, the ADRC law can be designed as

$$\mathbf{u}_i = B_{ij}^{-1}(\boldsymbol{\eta}_{ij})\big(K_i \mathbf{e}_{ij} + \hat{\boldsymbol{\Phi}}_{ij}(t)\big). \tag{14}$$

Since $\hat{\boldsymbol{\Phi}}_{ij}(t) \to \boldsymbol{\Phi}_{ij}(t)$, the closed-loop tracking error dynamics (9)–(14) yields

$$\dot{\mathbf{e}}_{ij} + K_i \mathbf{e}_{ij} = \boldsymbol{\Phi}_{ij}(t) - \hat{\boldsymbol{\Phi}}_{ij}(t). \tag{15}$$

The gain matrix K_i can be selected using a representation of (15) in frequency domain [44], where the closed-loop tracking error characteristic polynomials can be matched with some Hurwitz polynomials

$$s I_2 + K_i := s I_2 + \bar{\mathbf{W}}_i^2,$$

where $\bar{\mathbf{W}}_i = \mathrm{diag}\{\bar{w}_{x_i}, \bar{w}_{y_i}\} \in \mathbb{R}^{2\times 2}$ is a positive diagonal matrix, which are design parameters. Therefore, the specific control gains can be calculated as

$$K_i = \bar{\mathbf{W}}_i^2. \tag{16}$$

3.3. Leader Control Strategy

It is expected that the leader agent tracks a desired trajectory $\boldsymbol{\chi}^* = \begin{bmatrix} \chi_x^* & \chi_y^* \end{bmatrix}^T$ independently of the follower agents. Hence, let us define the trajectory leader error as $\mathbf{e}_{\chi_n} = \boldsymbol{\chi}_n - \boldsymbol{\chi}^*$, whose kinematics is given by

$$\dot{\mathbf{e}}_{\chi_n} = A_n(\theta_n, l)\mathbf{u}_n + \boldsymbol{\varphi}_n - \dot{\boldsymbol{\chi}}^*. \tag{17}$$

The error dynamics (17) can be expressed as a simplified perturbed system defined as

$$\dot{\mathbf{e}}_{\chi_n} = A_n(\theta_n, l)\mathbf{u}_n + \boldsymbol{\Phi}_n, \tag{18}$$

with $\boldsymbol{\Phi}_n$ as the *total disturbance* of the leader agent

$$\boldsymbol{\Phi}_n = \boldsymbol{\varphi}_n - \dot{\boldsymbol{\chi}}^*. \tag{19}$$

To design the leader control strategy, an extended state space, with $\mathbf{z}_n = \boldsymbol{\Phi}_n$, is first introduced as

$$\dot{\mathbf{e}}_{\chi_n} = A_n(\theta_n, l)\mathbf{u}_n + \mathbf{z}_n, \tag{20a}$$
$$\dot{\mathbf{z}}_n = \boldsymbol{\psi}_n \approx 0, \tag{20b}$$

for which an error-based GPIO can be designed to estimate the leader *total disturbance*, as follows

$$\dot{\hat{\mathbf{e}}}_{\chi_n} = A_n(\theta_n, l)\mathbf{u}_n + \hat{\mathbf{z}}_n + \Lambda_n(\mathbf{e}_{\chi_n} - \hat{\mathbf{e}}_{\chi_n}), \tag{21a}$$
$$\dot{\hat{\mathbf{z}}}_n = \Gamma_n(\mathbf{e}_{\chi_n} - \hat{\mathbf{e}}_{\chi_n}), \tag{21b}$$

where $\Lambda_n = \text{diag}\{\lambda_{x_n}, \lambda_{y_n}\}$ and $\Gamma_n^L = \text{diag}\{\gamma_{x_n}, \gamma_{y_n}\} \in \mathbb{R}^{2\times 2}$ are positive diagonal matrices. The leader estimation error is defined as $\tilde{\mathbf{e}}_n = \mathbf{e}_{\chi_n} - \hat{\mathbf{e}}_{\chi_n}$ and its dynamics are obtained from (20) and (21) as follows

$$\ddot{\tilde{\mathbf{e}}}_n + \Lambda_n \dot{\tilde{\mathbf{e}}}_n + \Gamma_n \tilde{\mathbf{e}}_n = \dot{\boldsymbol{\Phi}}_n. \tag{22}$$

In order to select the observer gains, the characteristic polynomials of leader estimation error are matched with Hurwitz polynomials

$$I_2 s^2 + \Lambda_n s + \Gamma_n = I_2 s^2 + 2\mathbf{Z}_n \mathbf{W}_n s + \mathbf{W}_n^2,$$

where the follower observer gain matrices are chosen as

$$\Lambda_n = 2\mathbf{Z}_n \mathbf{W}_n, \quad \Gamma_n = \mathbf{W}_n^2. \tag{23}$$

The proper selection of gains (23) allows to estimate the perturbations of the model, i.e., $\hat{\boldsymbol{\Phi}}_n(t) \to \boldsymbol{\Phi}_n(t)$. Based on this concept, the ADRC for the leader can be designed as

$$\mathbf{u}_n = -A_n^{-1}(\theta_n, l)\left(K_n \mathbf{e}_{\chi_n} + \hat{\boldsymbol{\Phi}}_n(t)\right). \tag{24}$$

Since the *total disturbance* $\boldsymbol{\Phi}_n$ can be estimated (which is valid since it can be expressed in terms of the input signal, the output signal, and the algebraic combination of their finite time derivatives), then, the closed-loop tracking error dynamics (18)–(24) yields

$$\dot{\mathbf{e}}_n + K_n \mathbf{e}_n = \boldsymbol{\Phi}_n(t) - \hat{\boldsymbol{\Phi}}_n(t). \tag{25}$$

The gain matrix K_n can be selected using a representation of (25) in frequency domain, where the closed-loop tracking leader error characteristic polynomials are matched with Hurwitz polynomials as follows

$$s I_2 + K_n := s I_2 + \bar{\mathbf{W}}_n^2, \tag{26}$$

where $\bar{\mathbf{W}}_n = \text{diag}\{\bar{w}_{x_n}, \bar{w}_{y_n}\} \in \mathbb{R}^{2\times 2}$ are the design parameters. The specific control gains can be calculated as

$$K_n = \bar{\mathbf{W}}_n^2. \tag{27}$$

In the next section, the above proposed control system will be verified in a practical environment utilizing a set of laboratory mobile robots.

4. Experimental Validation

In this section, the experimental results are validated. In the first step, the experimental platform is described. Then, two experiments are performed. In the former one, a comparison between the proposed approach and a PI controller is developed, while in the second case, a platform with a slope is added, which acts as a disturbance to the robots, to verify the robustness of the proposed approach.

4.1. Experimental Platform

To perform real-time experiments, laboratory differential-drive mobile robots were constructed (see Figure 2a). They use two 12V POLOLU 37D gear motors, each with a gear ratio of 1:30, and a built-in encoder with a resolution of 64 counts per revolution. An STM32F4 Discovery board is used as a data acquisition card, and the communication between the computer and the robot is realized in real-time using a publicly available "waijung1504" MATLAB/Simulink library, Bluetooth connection, and an ESP32 microcontroller as is shown in Figure 3. The setup runs inside a controlled environment with a set of 10 infrared cameras manufactured by VICON© with a precision of 0.5 [mm] that measure the position and orientation of each robot in an area of 5×4 [m^2] with a sample time of 0.005 s. Each robot has several reflective markers with different patterns to be detectable by the TRACKER© cameras' software (see Figure 2b).

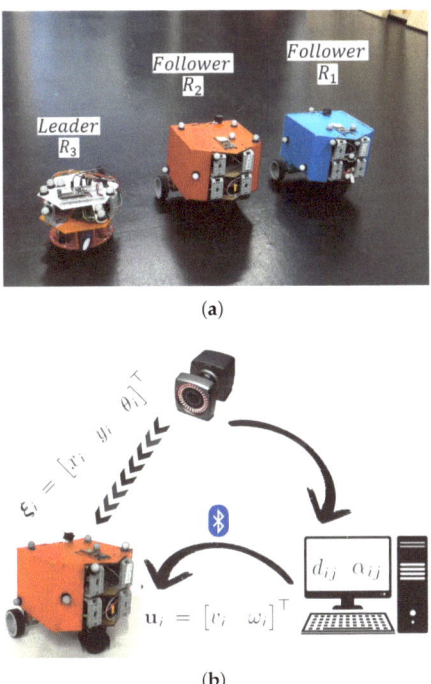

Figure 2. Overview of the experimental setup. (**a**) Differential-drive wheeled robots used in the test. (**b**) Communication flow chart.

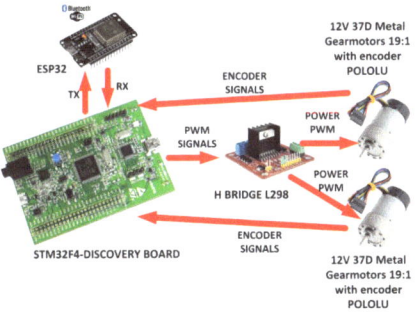

Figure 3. General scheme of the experimental platform (differential-drive robot).

Remark 3. *The communication between the computer and the differential-drive mobile robots is made through Bluetooth. In this work it is assumed that the wireless communication errors are assumed to be so small that they do not affect the performance of the robots. This may be because the GPIO estimates these errors and compensates them in the control law. The study of the errors that may occur due to wireless communication is out of scope of this work; however, it is considered for future work.*

The tested control strategies are implemented in MATLAB/Simulink. The leader observer gains (23) are set to $\mathbf{Z}_3 = \text{diag}\{7,7\}$ and $\mathbf{W}_3 = \text{diag}\{40,40\}$ while the control gains for the leader (27) are set to $\bar{\mathbf{W}}_3 = \text{diag}\{1.2, 1.2\}$. On the other hand, the follower observer gains (13) are set to $\mathbf{Z}_1 = \mathbf{Z}_2 = \text{diag}\{4,4\}$ and $\mathbf{W}_1 = \mathbf{W}_2 = \{30, 30\}$, while the control gains (16) are set to $\bar{\mathbf{W}}_1 = \bar{\mathbf{W}}_2 = \text{diag}\{1.2, 1.2\}$.

To verify the robustness of the proposed GPIO approach, a Proportional-Integral (PI) control strategy is applied to the system (9) and (17). In this sense, the control strategies given in (14) and (24) are modified as follows

$$\mathbf{u}_{i_{PI}} = B_{ij}^{-1}(\eta_{ij})\left(K_{i_{PI}}\mathbf{e}_{ij} + K_{ii_{PI}}\int_0^t \mathbf{e}_{ij}(\tau)d\tau\right),$$

$$\mathbf{u}_{n_{PI}} = -A_n^{-1}(\theta_n, l)\left(K_{n_{PI}}\mathbf{e}_{\chi_n} + K_{ni_{PI}}\int_0^t \mathbf{e}_{\chi_n}(\tau)d\tau\right),$$

for the followers and the leader, respectively. The PI gain matrices are chosen as

$$K_{i_{PI}} = 2\mathbf{W}_{i_{PI}}, \quad K_{ii_{PI}} = \mathbf{W}_{i_{PI}}^2, \quad \mathbf{W}_{i_{PI}} = \frac{\bar{\mathbf{W}}_i^2}{2}.$$

$$K_{n_{PI}} = 2\mathbf{W}_{n_{PI}}, \quad K_{ni_{PI}} = \mathbf{W}_{n_{PI}}^2, \quad \mathbf{W}_{n_{PI}} = \frac{\bar{\mathbf{W}}_i^2}{2}.$$

For a fair comparison, the gains of the GPIO and PI controllers where chosen with the same $\bar{\mathbf{W}}_i = \text{diag}\{1.2, 1.2\}$.

4.2. First Experiment

The trajectory in the plane of the three differential-drive robots is depicted in Figure 4, where the leader (blue line) is tracking a circular trajectory of radius 0.5 m, which is accomplished in 30 s, while the first follower (depicted in red line) and the second follower (depicted in green line) maintain a desired distance $d_{12}^* = d_{23}^* = 0.25$ [m] and a desired formation angle $\alpha_{12}^* = \alpha_{23}^* = \frac{\pi}{2}$ [rad] for $t = [0, 15]$ [s] and $\alpha_{12}^* = \alpha_{23}^* = \frac{\pi}{4}$ [rad] for $t = [15, 30]$ [s]. Specifically, Figure 4a shows the trajectory in the plane with the GPIO approach while Figure 4b shows the trajectory in the plane with a PI controller.

Figure 5a illustrates a comparison between the GPIO and the PI of the leader's trajectory while Figure 5b shows the leader's position error. Such errors are oscillating around zero (± 0.001 m in steady-sate) therefore, the leader reaches its desired trajectory. It becomes evident that the performance of both control strategies is quite similar.

The distance and formation angle among the mobile robots is shown in Figure 6. It can be noticed that when using the GPIO approach, the agents converge to the desired distance between them, i.e., $d_{12} \approx d_{12}^*$ and $d_{23} \approx d_{23}^*$. In the same way, the formation angles converge to the desired angle, i.e., $\alpha_{12} \approx \alpha_{12}^*$ and $\alpha_{23} \approx \alpha_{23}^*$ with $\alpha_{12}^* = \alpha_{23}^* = \frac{\pi}{2}$ [rad] for $0 \leq t < 15$ [s]. Furthermore, when the desired formation angle changes to $\alpha_{12}^* = \alpha_{23}^* = \frac{\pi}{4}$ [rad] for $15 \leq t \leq 30$ [s], the control is able to keep the distances between the agents. On the other hand, when using the PI controller, oscillations of greater amplitude are presented. This behavior is also seen in Figure 7, where the distance and formation angle errors are displayed. One can note that the errors are closer to zero with the GPIO approach.

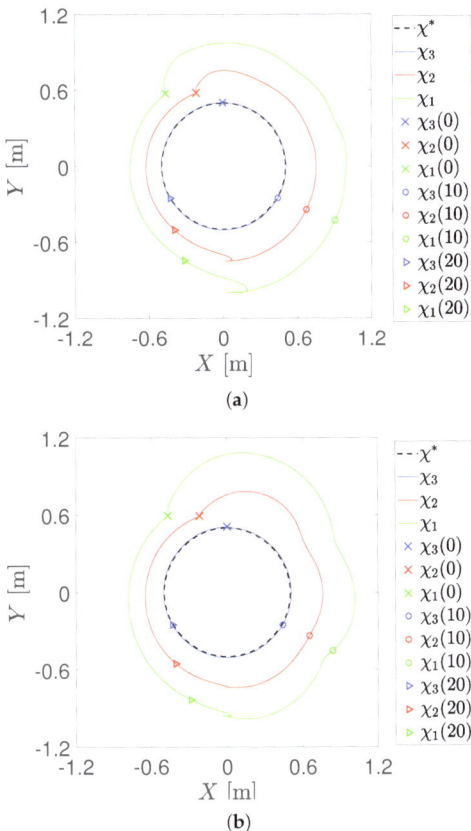

Figure 4. Trajectory in the plane of the mobile robots for the first experiment. (**a**) Trajectory in the plane with the GPIO approach. (**b**) Trajectory in the plane with the PI approach.

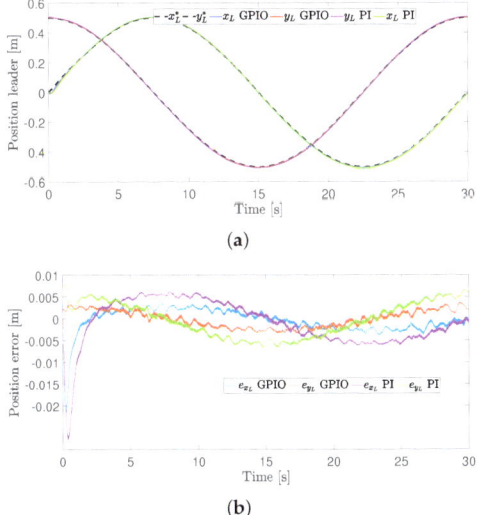

Figure 5. Leader trajectory tracking performance. (**a**) Leader tracking for the first experiment. (**b**) Leader trajectory error.

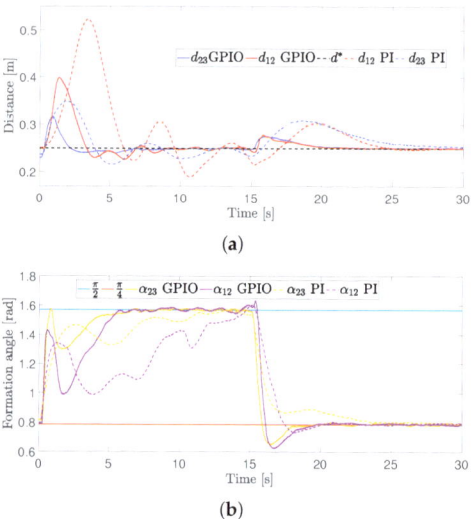

Figure 6. Distances and formation angles between the robots for the first experiment. (**a**) Distances between the robots. (**b**) Formation angles between the robots.

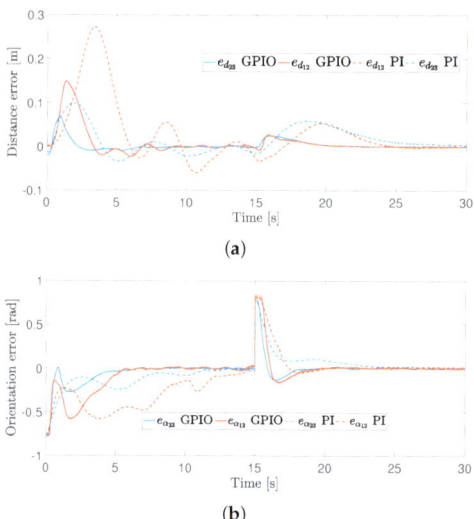

Figure 7. Distances and orientation angles errors for the first experiment. (**a**) Distance error. (**b**) Orientation error.

A comparison, between the control inputs, given by the GPIO approach and the PI controller, is given in Figure 8. One can note oscillations of greater amplitude with the PI controller.

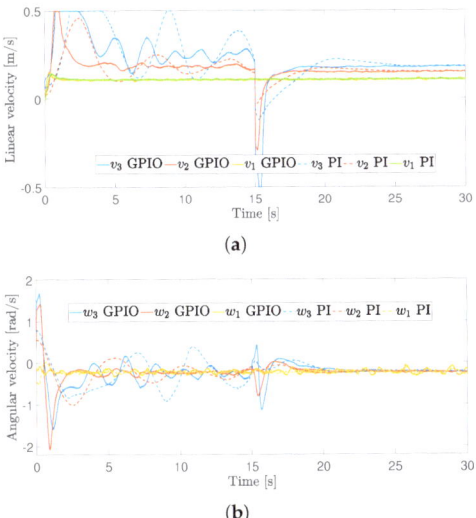

Figure 8. Control inputs for the robots for the first experiment. (**a**) Longitudinal velocities. (**b**) Angular velocities.

4.3. Second Experiment

For the second experiment, we used an uneven surface with 10 degrees of slope that is collocated such that it acts as a disturbance to the agents (see Figure 9). Furthermore, the parameters are the same as in the previous experiment.

Figure 9. Uneven surface as a disturbance experimental test.

The trajectory in the three-dimensional space of the three differential-drive robots is depicted in Figure 10, while the trajectory in the plane is shown in Figure 11. Specifically, Figure 11a shows the trajectory in the plane with the GPIO approach, while Figure 11b shows the trajectory in the plane with a PI controller.

Figure 12a illustrates a comparison between the GPIO and the PI of the leader's trajectory, while Figure 12b shows the leader's position error. Note that when the leader enters the uneven surface, the position error increases. However, the GPIO approach can deal with these perturbations, while with the PI controller, the position error has oscillations of greater amplitude.

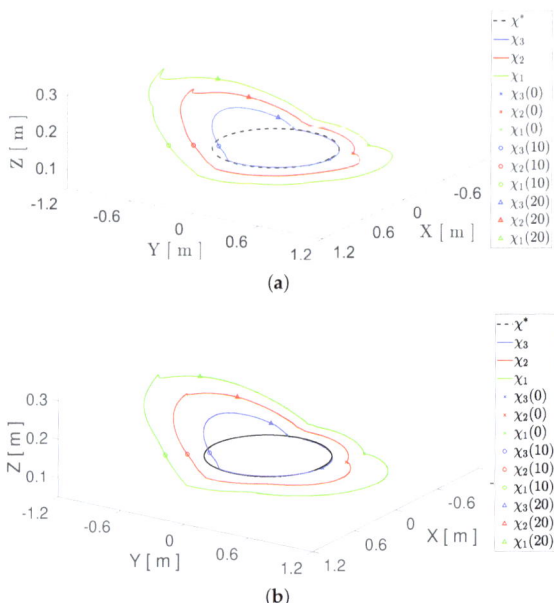

Figure 10. Trajectory in the three dimensional space of the mobile robots for the second experiment. (**a**) Trajectory in the three dimensional space with the GPIO approach. (**b**) Trajectory in the three dimensional space with the PI approach.

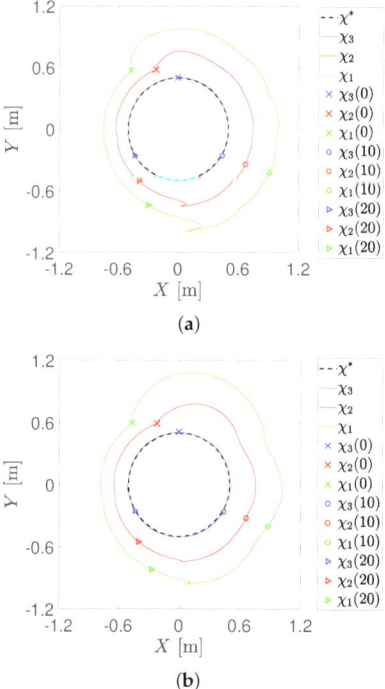

Figure 11. Trajectory in the plane of the mobile robots for the second experiment. (**a**) Trajectory in the plane with the GPIO approach. (**b**) Trajectory in the plane with the PI approach.

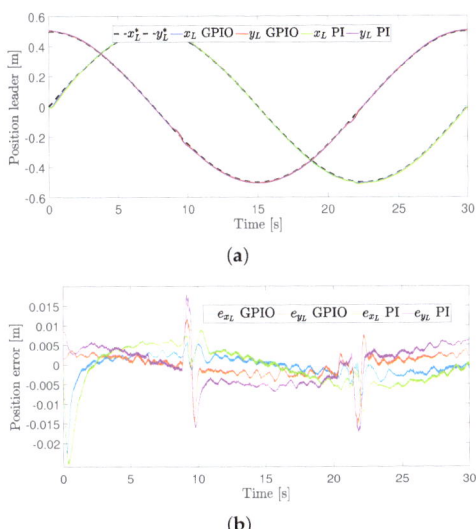

Figure 12. Leader trajectory tracking performance for the second experiment. (**a**) Leader tracking. (**b**) Leader trajectory error.

The distance and formation angle among the mobile robots is shown in Figure 13. It can be noticed that when using the GPIO approach, the agents converge to the desired distance and formation angle, even in the presence of the uneven surface. Otherwise, with the PI controller, which is not capable of dealing with the disturbance, in addition to presenting oscillations of greater amplitude. This behavior is also seen in Figure 14, where the distance and formation angle errors are displayed.

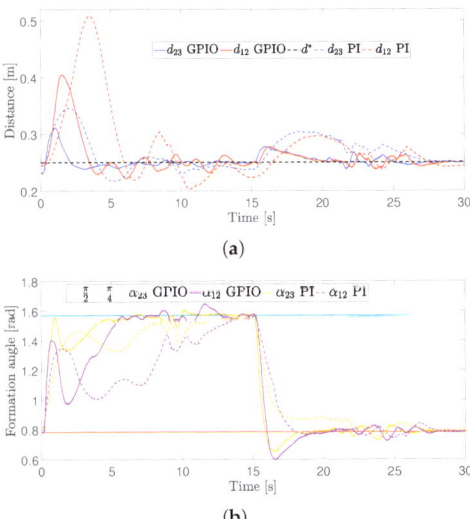

Figure 13. Distances and formation angles between the robots for the second experiment. (**a**) Distances between the robots. (**b**) Formation angles between the robots.

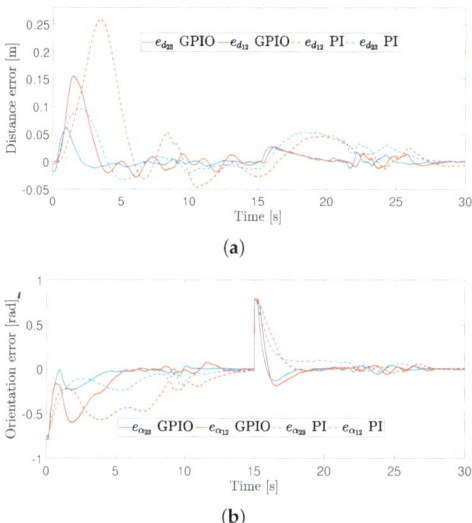

(a)

(b)

Figure 14. Distances and orientation angles errors for the second experiment. (**a**) Distance error. (**b**) Orientation error.

A comparison between the control inputs, given by the GPIO approach and the PI controller, is given in Figure 15.

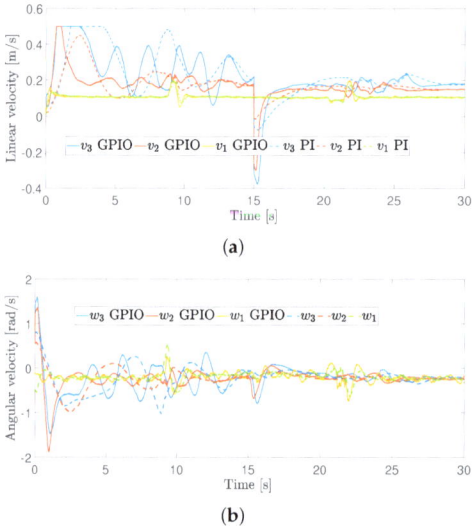

(a)

(b)

Figure 15. Control inputs for the robots for the second experiment. (**a**) Longitudinal velocities. (**b**) Angular velocities.

Finally, Figure 16 presents the disturbance estimation of each agent, which was used for the disturbance cancellation effects.

Remark 4. *It is worth mentioning that similar results will be obtained despite having different initial conditions regarding the distance between agents. However, the restriction given in (7) must be considered. This implies that the leader agent must be in line of sight of the follower agent. Furthermore, the initial distances of the robots are defined from their initial positions according to Equation (3a).*

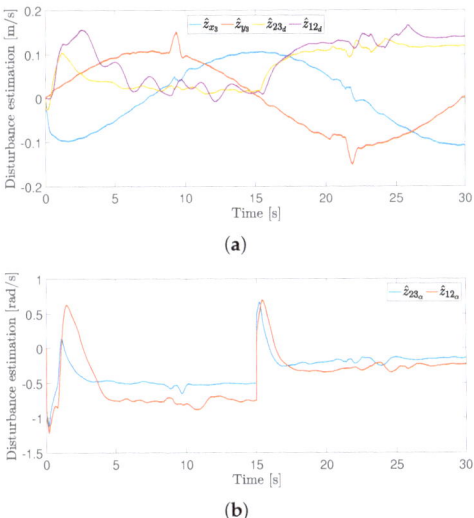

Figure 16. On line total disturbance estimation. (**a**) Total disturbance estimation of the longitudinal velocity. (**b**) Total disturbance estimation of angular velocity.

A real time experiment of the performance of the differential-drive robots can be watched on the link in Supplementary Material.

5. Conclusions

In this work, the problem of designing an ADRC for differential-drive mobile robots operating in a leader–follower configuration is solved by firstly developing a kinematic model based on distance and formation angle between agents. A specific case of trajectory tracking is considered without the use of signal time-derivatives in the controller. The utilized control task reformulation to error-domain allowed the unmeasured time-derivatives to be conveniently reconstructed with a custom observer, which benefits the practical appeal of the proposed control scheme.

Mobile robots are usually exposed to time delays in communication. This can be overcome by predictor-based schemes (e.g., [22]) or making the delay as part of the control design (e.g., [45,46]). The ADRC could be thus combined in the future with such methods to increase their performance.

Supplementary Materials: Some evidence of the experimental results is provided in the following video: https://www.youtube.com/watch?v=J0qHcUQ-17o (accessed on 17 October 2022).

Author Contributions: Conceptualization, M.R.-N. and J.G.-S.; methodology, R.M., N.L.-C. and A.L.-J.; software, M.R.-N. and R.M.; validation, M.R.-N., J.G.-S. and R.M.; formal analysis, J.G.-S., R.M., N.L.-C. and A.L.-J.; investigation, M.R.-N., J.G.-S., R.M., N.L.-C. and A.L.-J.; resources, M.R.-N., J.G.-S., R.M., N.L.-C. and A.L.-J.; data curation, M.R.-N., J.G.-S. and R.M.; writing—original draft preparation, M.R.-N., J.G.-S., R.M., N.L.-C. and A.L.-J.; writing—review and editing, M.R.-N., J.G.-S., R.M., N.L.-C. and A.L.-J.; visualization, M.R.-N., J.G.-S., R.M., N.L.-C. and A.L.-J.; supervision, M.R.-N., R.M. and A.L.-J.; project administration, M.R.-N., J.G.-S., R.M., N.L.-C. and A.L.-J.; funding acquisition, M.R.-N. and A.L.-J. All authors have read and agreed to the published version of the manuscript.

Funding: This research was funded by Secretaría de Investigación y Posgrado SIP IPN under grants 20220623, 20220633, and by the Universidad Iberoamericana Ciudad de México, División de Investigación y Posgrado (DINVP), Ciudad de México, México, under Grant 25.

Data Availability Statement: Not applicable.

Conflicts of Interest: The authors declare no conflict of interest.

Abbreviations

The following abbreviations are used in this manuscript:

ADRC   Active Disturbance Rejection Control
PID   Proportional Integral Derivative Control
ESO   Extended State Observer
GPIO   Generalized Proportional Integral Observer

References

1. Yan, Z.; Jouandeau, N.; Cherif, A.A. A survey and analysis of multi-robot coordination. *Int. J. Adv. Robot. Syst.* **2013**, *10*, 399. [CrossRef]
2. Feng, Z.; Hu, G.; Sun, Y.; Soon, J. An overview of collaborative robotic manipulation in multi-robot systems. *Annu. Rev. Control* **2020**, *49*, 113–127. [CrossRef]
3. Ren, W.; Beard, R.W. *Distributed Consensus in Multi-Vehicle Cooperative Control*; Springer: Berlin/Heidelberg, Germany, 2008.
4. Wang, X.; Li, S.; Yu, X.; Yang, J. Distributed active anti-disturbance consensus for leader-follower higher-order multi-agent systems with mismatched disturbances. *IEEE Trans. Autom. Control* **2016**, *62*, 5795–5801. [CrossRef]
5. González-Sierra, J.; Hernández-Martínez, E.G.; Ferreira-Vazquez, E.D.; Flores-Godoy, J.J.; Fernandez-Anaya, G.; Paniagua-Contro, P. Leader-follower control strategy with rigid body behavior. *IFAC-PapersOnLine* **2018**, *51*, 184–189. [CrossRef]
6. Wang, X.; Liu, W.; Wu, Q.; Li, S. A Modular Optimal Formation Control Scheme of Multiagent Systems With Application to Multiple Mobile Robots. *IEEE Trans. Ind. Electron.* **2022**, *69*, 9331–9341. [CrossRef]
7. Hernández-Martínez, E.G.; Aranda-Bricaire, E. Trajectory tracking for groups of unicycles with convergence of the orientation angles. In Proceedings of the IEEE Conference on Decision and Control, Atlanta, GA, USA, 15–17 December 2010; pp. 6323–6328.
8. Desai, J.P.; Ostrowski, J.P.; Kumar, V. Modeling and control of formations of nonholonomic mobile robots. *IEEE Trans. Robot. Autom.* **2001**, *17*, 905–908. [CrossRef]
9. Deghat, M.; Shames, I.; Anderson, B.D.O.; Yu, C. Localization and Circumnavigation of a Slowly Moving Target Using Bearing Measurements. *IEEE Trans. Autom. Control* **2014**, *59*, 2182–2188. [CrossRef]
10. Shames, I.; Dasgupta, S.; Fidan, B.; Anderson, B.D.O. Circumnavigation Using Distance Measurements Under Slow Drift. *IEEE Trans. Autom. Control* **2012**, *57*, 889–903. [CrossRef]
11. Shao, J.; Tian, Y.P. Multi-target localization and circumnavigation control by a group of moving agents. In Proceedings of the IEEE International Conference on Control Automation, Ohrid, Macedonia, 3–6 July 2017; pp. 606–611.
12. Boccia, A.; Adaldo, A.; Dimarogonas, D.V.; di Bernardo, M.; Johansson, K.H. Tracking a mobile target by multi-robot circumnavigation using bearing measurements. In Proceedings of the IEEE Conference on Decision and Control, Melbourne, Australia, 12–15 December 2017; pp. 1076–1081.
13. Zhong, H.; Miao, Y.; Tan, Z.; Li, J.; Zhang, H.; Fierro, R. Circumnavigation of a Moving Target in 3D by Multi-agent Systems with Collision Avoidance. An Orthogonal Vector Fields-based Approach. *Int. J. Control Autom. Syst.* **2019**, *17*, 212–224. [CrossRef]
14. Shen, D.; Sun, Z.; Sun, W. Leader-follower formation control without leader's velocity information. *Sci. China Inf. Sci.* **2014**, *57*, 1–12. [CrossRef]
15. Zhao, Y.; Zhang, Y.; Lee, J. Lyapunov and Sliding Mode Based Leader-follower Formation Control for Multiple Mobile Robots with an Augmented Distance-angle Strategy. *Int. J. Control Autom. Syst.* **2019**, *17*, 1314–1321. [CrossRef]
16. Hua, C.C.; Liu, X.P. Delay-Dependent Stability Criteria of Teleoperation Systems with Asymmetric Time-Varying Delays. *IEEE Trans. Robot.* **2010**, *26*, 925–932. [CrossRef]
17. Saha, O.; Dasgupta, P. A comprehensive survey of recent trends in cloud robotics architectures and applications. *Robotics* **2018**, *7*, 47. [CrossRef]
18. Toris, R.; Kammerl, J.; Lu, D.V.; Lee, J.; Jenkins, O.C.; Osentoski, S.; Wills, M.; Chernova, S. Robot web tools: Efficient messaging for cloud robotics. In Proceedings of the IEEE/RSJ International Conference on Intelligent Robots and Systems (IROS), Hamburg, Germany, 28 September–3 October 2015; pp. 4530–4537.
19. Diddeniya, I.; Wanniarachchi, I.; Gunasinghe, H.; Premachandra, C.; Kawanaka, H. Human–Robot Communication System for an Isolated Environment. *IEEE Access* **2022**, *10*, 63258–63269. [CrossRef]
20. Panchi, F.; Hernández, K.; Chávez, D. MQTT Protocol of IoT for Real Time Bilateral Teleoperation Applied to Car-Like Mobile Robot. In Proceedings of the 2018 IEEE Third Ecuador Technical Chapters Meeting (ETCM), Cuenca, Ecuador, 15–19 October 2018; pp. 1–6.
21. Han, J. From PID to active disturbance rejection control. *IEEE Trans. Ind. Electron.* **2009**, *56*, 900–906. [CrossRef]
22. Sira-Ramírez, H.; Luviano-Juárez, A.; Ramírez-Neria, M.; Zurita-Bustamante, E.W. *Active Disturbance Rejection Control of Dynamic Systems: A Flatness Based Approach*; Butterworth-Heinemann: Oxford, UK, 2018.
23. Herbst, G. Practical Active Disturbance Rejection Control: Bumpless Transfer, Rate Limitation, and Incremental Algorithm. *IEEE Trans. Ind. Electron.* **2016**, *63*, 1754–1762. [CrossRef]
24. Madonski, R.; Shao, S.; Zhang, H.; Gao, Z.; Yang, J.; Li, S. General error-based active disturbance rejection control for swift industrial implementations. *Control Eng. Pract.* **2019**, *84*, 218–229. [CrossRef]

25. Gao, Z.; Zheng, Q. Active disturbance rejection control: Some recent experimental and industrial case studies. *Control Theory Technol.* **2018**, *16*, 301–313.
26. Madonski, R.; Herman, P. Survey on methods of increasing the efficiency of extended state disturbance observers. *ISA Trans.* **2015**, *56*, 18–27. [CrossRef]
27. Wu, Z.H.; Zhou, H.C.; Guo, B.Z.; Deng, F. Review and new theoretical perspectives on active disturbance rejection control for uncertain finite-dimensional and infinite-dimensional systems. *Nonlinear Dyn.* **2020**, *101*, 935–959. [CrossRef]
28. Zhang, X.; Zhang, X.; Xue, W.; Xin, B. An overview on recent progress of extended state observers for uncertain systems: Methods, theory, and applications. *Adv. Control Appl.* **2021**, *3*, e89. [CrossRef]
29. Sira-Ramírez, H.; López-Uribe, C.; Velasco-Villa, M. Linear Observer-Based Active Disturbance Rejection Control of the Omnidirectional Mobile Robot. *Asian J. Control* **2013**, *15*, 51–63. [CrossRef]
30. Ren, C.; Liu, R.; Ma, S.; Hu, C.; Cao, L. ESO Based Model Predictive Control of an Omnidirectional Mobile Robot with Friction Compensation. In Proceedings of the Chinese Control Conference, Wuhan, China, 25–27 July 2018; pp. 3943–3948.
31. Ren, C.; Zhang, M.; Ma, S.; Wei, D. Trajectory Tracking Control of an Omnidirectional Mobile Manipulator Based on Active Disturbance Rejection Control. In Proceedings of the World Congress on Intelligent Control and Automation, Changsha, China, 4–8 July 2018; pp. 1537–1542.
32. Fliess, M.; Lévine, J.; Martin, P.; Rouchon, P. Flatness and defect of non-linear systems: Introductory theory and examples. *Int. J. Control* **1995**, *61*, 1327–1361. [CrossRef]
33. Michalek, M.M. Robust trajectory following without availability of the reference time-derivatives in the control scheme with active disturbance rejection. In Proceedings of the American Control Conference, Boston, MA, USA, 6–8 July 2016; pp. 1536–1541.
34. Ramirez-Neria, M.; Madonski, R.; Shao, S.; Gao, Z. Robust tracking in underactuated systems using flatness-based ADRC with cascade observers. *J. Dyn. Syst. Meas. Control* **2020**, *142*, 091002. [CrossRef]
35. Stankovic, M.; Madonski, R.; Manojlovic, S.; Lechekhab, T.E.; Mikluc, D. Error-Based Active Disturbance Rejection Altitude/Attitude Control of a Quadrotor UAV. In *Advanced, Contemporary Control*; Springer: Berlin/Heidelberg, Germany, 2020; pp. 1348–1358.
36. Chen, S.; Chen, Z.; Zhao, Z. An error-based active disturbance rejection control with memory structure. *Meas. Control* **2021**, *54*, 724–736. [CrossRef]
37. Ramírez-Neria, M.; Madonski, R.; Luviano-Juárez, A.; Gao, Z.; Sira-Ramírez, H. Design of ADRC for Second-Order Mechanical Systems without Time-Derivatives in the Tracking Controller. In Proceedings of the American Control Conference, Denver, CO, USA, 1–3 July 2020; pp. 2623–2628.
38. Cui, M.; Huang, R.; Liu, H.; Liu, X.; Sun, D. Adaptive tracking control of wheeled mobile robots with unknown longitudinal and lateral slipping parameters. *Nonlinear Dyn.* **2014**, *2014*, 1811–1826. [CrossRef]
39. Wang, D.; Low, C.B. Modeling and Analysis of Skidding and Slipping in Wheeled Mobile Robots: Control Design Perspective. *IEEE Trans. Robot.* **2008**, *24*, 676–687. [CrossRef]
40. Li, Z.; Canny, J. *Nonholonomic Motion Planning*; Springer Science & Business Media: Berlin/Heidelberg, Germany, 1993.
41. Spong, M.W.; Hutchinson, S.; Vidyasagar, M. *Robot Modeling and Control*; John Wiley & Sons: Hoboken, NJ, USA, 2020.
42. Fareh, R.; Khadraoui, S.; Abdallah, M.Y.; Baziyad, M.; Bettayeb, M. Active disturbance rejection control for robotic systems: A review. *Mechatronics* **2021**, *80*, 102671. [CrossRef]
43. Rouchon, P.; Fliess, M.; Lévine, J.; Martin, P. Flatness and motion planning: The car with n trailers. In Proceedings of the ECC'93, Groningen, The Netherlands, 28 June–1 July 1993; pp. 1518–1522.
44. Gao, Z. Scaling and bandwidth-parameterization based controller tuning. In Proceedings of the American Control Conference, Denver, CO, USA, 4–6 June 2003; Volume 6, pp. 4989–4996.
45. Ochoa-Ortega, G.; Villafuerte-Segura, R.; Luviano-Juárez, A.; Ramírez-Neria, M.; Lozada-Castillo, N. Cascade Delayed Controller Design for a Class of Underactuated Systems. *Complexity* **2020**, *2020*, 2160743. [CrossRef]
46. Villafuerte, R.; Mondié, S.; Garrido, R. Tuning of proportional retarded controllers: Theory and experiments. *IEEE Trans. Control Syst. Technol.* **2012**, *21*, 983–990. [CrossRef]

Article

A Cooperative Control Algorithm for Line and Predecessor Following Platoons Subject to Unreliable Distance Measurements

Carlos Escobar [1], Francisco J. Vargas [1,*], Andrés A. Peters [2] and Gonzalo Carvajal [1]

[1] Departamento de Electrónica, Universidad Técnica Federico Santa María, Valparaíso 2390123, Chile
[2] Faculty of Engineering and Sciences, Universidad Adolfo Ibáñez, Santiago 7941169, Chile
* Correspondence: francisco.vargasp@usm.cl

Abstract: This paper uses a line-following approach to study the longitudinal and lateral problems in vehicle platooning. Under this setup, we assume that inter-vehicle distance sensing is unreliable and propose a cooperative control strategy to render the platoon less vulnerable to these sensing difficulties. The proposed control scheme uses the velocity of the predecessor vehicle, communicated through a Vehicle-to-Vehicle technology, to avoid significant oscillations in the local speed provoked by tracking using unreliable local distance measurements. We implement the proposed control algorithm in the RUPU platform, a low-cost experimental platform with wireless communication interfaces that enable the implementation of cooperative control schemes for mobile agent platooning. The experiments show the effectiveness of the proposed cooperative control scheme in maintaining a suitable performance even when subject to temporal distortions in local measurements, which, in the considered experimental setup, arise from losing the line-of-sight of the local sensors in paths with closed curves.

Keywords: multi-agent systems; path-following; experimental platform; vehicle platooning; MIMO control

MSC: 93C85

Citation: Escobar, C.; Vargas, F.J.; Peters, A.A.; Carvajal, G. A Cooperative Control Algorithm for Line and Predecessor Following Platoons Subject to Unreliable Distance Measurements. *Mathematics* 2023, 11, 801. https://doi.org/10.3390/math11040801

Academic Editor: Ivan Lorencin

Received: 30 December 2022
Revised: 18 January 2023
Accepted: 1 February 2023
Published: 4 February 2023

Copyright: © 2023 by the authors. Licensee MDPI, Basel, Switzerland. This article is an open access article distributed under the terms and conditions of the Creative Commons Attribution (CC BY) license (https://creativecommons.org/licenses/by/4.0/).

1. Introduction

In Cooperative Adaptive Cruise Control (CACC) applications, a platoon of vehicles coordinates its actions to navigate along a predefined path while maintaining the desired distance between vehicles [1–3]. Considering a platoon of vehicles traveling on a highway, the collective behavior can be achieved through the local control of each vehicle based on its own perception of the environment but also with information received from other vehicles through Vehicle-to-Vehicle (V2V) and Vehicle-to-Infrastructure (V2I) [4] communication. Vehicle platooning applications are expected to provide a backbone for future Intelligent Transportation Systems (ITS) technologies [5], bringing significant improvements in safety, congestion management, energy efficiency, reduction of emissions, etc. [6–8].

In practical scenarios representative of urban roads and highways, the drivable sections are marked with lanes delimited with painted lines. Each vehicle is then required to detect the lanes and determine its relative position and orientation with respect to the lanes to calculate a smooth path to traverse while staying within the delimited drivable region. Extending the scenario to a platoon configuration introduces the requirement for each vehicle to maintain a predefined distance from its predecessor. With the previous considerations, the control problem of path-following platooning can be seen as a dual problem [9]: (i) the *lateral problem*, which requires each vehicle to move along a predefined path [10]; and (ii) the *longitudinal problem*, which requires each vehicle to maintain a predefined distance from its predecessor [11]. Simultaneously addressing both control problems for each vehicle is challenging since achieving one goal may harm the other due to the coupled dynamics. This interplay between control objectives is receiving attention in the context of individual autonomous vehicles [12–14] and, more recently, in platooning [15–17].

Path-following applications are typically preceded by a path-planning stage in which each vehicle defines a trajectory to move smoothly along the delimited region of the road [18,19]. This requires each vehicle to be equipped with sensors and computing capabilities to perceive the lane ahead and disturbances such as obstacles or changes in road conditions. The rapid proliferation of technologies associated with Advanced Driving Assistance Systems (ADASs) has pushed the development of multiple techniques for lane-keeping and optimal path-planning, which generally project the path to follow using a single virtual line along the center of the lane. Nowadays, autonomous vehicle path-planning algorithms remain an active research topic [19–21], and there are also commercial solutions already available in modern cars [22,23]. In the case of platoon formations, each vehicle can address the lateral problem by either implementing its own lane-keeping system or following the state of the leading vehicle; however, additional challenges arise due to the coupling with the longitudinal problem.

A fundamental aspect of safe vehicular navigation is the reliability of environment perception [24]. Control algorithms for path-following platoons rely on an appropriate measure of the inter-vehicle distances. In practice, distance sensing could be unreliable due to, for example, the inaccuracy of sensing devices [25], the effect of turns that may affect the path-planning stage yielding cutting-corner phenomena [16], and temporal interference in the line of sight of the ranging sensors due to curves, inclinations, and obstacles in the road [26]. The latter case is critical for distance tracking since the vehicle cannot detect the predecessor. Although unreliable distance measurement is part of the underlying platooning navigation problem in a natural environment, it remains a mostly unexplored research topic in path-following platooning control. Most of the related research is focused on collision avoidance [27], string stabilization [28,29], which is also relevant for smooth navigation, and recently on communication issues in the network that connects vehicles, such as noisy channels or data dropouts, [30,31]. Strategies that deal with these problems may help to cope with intermittent distance measurement loss.

On the other hand, evaluating control algorithms for platooning considering curved paths, non-reliable communication, and other challenges requires testing them in real scenarios where non-modeled interactions may arise, especially for large formations. Major commercial conglomerates have implemented and tested platooning configurations using real-scale vehicles and road infrastructure [32]. However, these experiments are targeted as industrial technological demonstrators, and the data and results are not openly available for scrutiny and academic research. Moreover, the high costs of these experiments preclude experimental research on new control algorithms for large platoons. A suitable alternative for experimental evaluation is the use of scaled-down platforms that capture the essence and challenges of control problems in path-following platooning, allowing for quick and safe testing of new control algorithms.

In this paper, we introduce the approach of *line-following platooning* to study the fundamental control problems arising in path-following platooning. In this approach, we assume that the navigation is carried on an established road and that the path-planning stage in each vehicle is properly working, such that the target path can be represented through a single line painted on the floor. The proposed framework avoids the required hardware and software necessary for lane detection and path planning in an experimental setup while still capturing the essence of the underlying longitudinal and lateral control problems, allowing us to observe and study relevant aspects of platooning such as string stability, cooperative schemes, and sensing and communication challenges. We use this approach to evaluate a line-following platoon with a predecessor-following communication topology, i.e., each vehicle has access to its own information but also some data from its predecessor obtained via V2V communication. The main contribution of this paper is the proposal and experimental evaluation of a cooperative control algorithm to deal with both lateral and longitudinal problems in line-following platooning where local measurements of inter-vehicle distance are unreliable. The control algorithm consists of a set of controllers in a multi-input multi-output (MIMO) scheme, enhanced by a non-linear function that limits the vehicle speed based on that of the predecessor. We test the proposed algorithm using the RUPU experimental platform, consisting of a set of scaled-down vehicles with wireless communication interfaces that we specifically designed to study platooning problems. Experimental results using the proposed cooperative control scheme show that the platoon is less vulnerable to unreliable distance measurements when contrasted with its non-cooperative counterpart.

The rest of the paper is organized as follows: Section 2 presents the line-following platooning control problem. The RUPU experimental platform is described in Section 3, while the proposed control algorithm is in Section 4. Section 5 presents the experimental results obtained from the case studies, and Section 6 summarizes the conclusions and future work.

2. The Line-Following Platooning Control Problem

Modern ADASs in commercial self-driving vehicles implement path-planning algorithms that project the path to follow as a virtual line along the road [23]. In this work, we assume that the platoon navigates on an established road with properly marked lanes and that the path-planning stage in each vehicle provides a single line to follow. Isolating the path-planning stage from the main control problems simplifies the analysis and evaluation of the platooning formation, reducing the more general path-following platooning problem to a line-following platooning configuration. At the same time, the configuration still retains the essence and challenges associated with the lateral and longitudinal control problems. The proposed approach presents the following advantages:

- Individual vehicles may adapt existing techniques from line-following robot literature to help deal with the lateral problem (see e.g., [33,34]).
- Despite the simplification in the setup, the configuration retains fundamental challenges that arise in control of platoon formations, such as dealing with unreliable distance measurement, designing string stabilizing controllers, and considering communication issues, among others.
- The decoupling of the path-planning stage relieves the mathematical treatment from analytically studying platooning for more than one-dimensional paths, allowing to concentrate on the primary control problems.
- Enables the development of low-cost experimental platforms to evaluate platooning formations using low-cost sensors for line-following applications (e.g., infrared sensors), without requiring sophisticated hardware and software support for cameras or lidars that are normally required for the path-planning stage [16,20].

Indeed, considering the growing interest in ITS technology, the infrastructure must be adapted to support autonomous navigation at a large scale. In this context, it is reasonable to assume that roads will have predefined marked lines and signaling to facilitate platooning and autonomous navigation in a similar fashion to the proposed line-following configuration.

Figure 1 shows a representation of the variables involved in both lateral and longitudinal control problems arising in line-following platoons. The figures consider the example of a vehicle identified with the index i, with $i = 1, \ldots N - 1$, where N is the total number of vehicles in the platoon. The vehicle with index $i = 0$ represents the platoon leader. Figure 1a represents the lateral control problem for vehicle i. This setup requires each vehicle to determine its position and orientation with respect to the reference line and, based on such information, to position itself in the desired way on the road. The red dashed line represents the desired path along the road, $\delta_i(t)$ denotes the perpendicular distance from the line to be followed to the middle point of the wheel axle, and the angle $\theta_i(t)$ represents the orientation respect to the desired moving direction. An appropriate position for navigation is when both $\delta_i(t)$ and $\theta_i(t)$ are close to zero. Figure 1b represents the longitudinal control problem for a set of vehicles. The distance between vehicle i and its predecessor $i - 1$ is denoted by $d_i(t)$. Note that we represent the inter-vehicle distance as the shortest path between the front part of a vehicle and the rear of the preceding vehicle along the reference line to follow. Here, the goal is to achieve $d_i(t) = r_i(t)$, where $r_i(t)$ is a given desired distance.

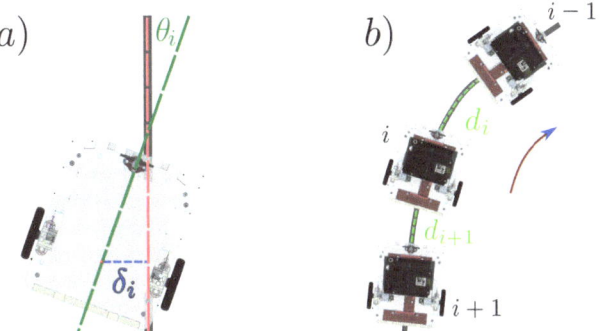

Figure 1. Line-following control: (**a**) lateral problem (**b**) longitudinal problem.

The overall platooning control scheme requires simultaneously addressing both the lateral and the longitudinal problems. So, we can view each vehicle as a multi-input, multi-output (MIMO) feedback control system [35]. Figure 2 shows a general diagram of the control loop, where G_i represents the MIMO dynamical model of the vehicle, C_i is the MIMO controller, $r_i(t)$ denotes the desired inter-vehicle distance, $w_i(t)$ represents a vector with the information obtained from other vehicles, $z_i(t)$ is a vector with the variables to be controlled, that is, $\theta_i(t)$, $\delta_i(t)$ and $d_i(t)$, and $u_i(t)$ is a control signal that manipulates the steering, acceleration, and braking of the vehicle. When each vehicle is initially positioned on the line, an appropriate controller design should perform so that $\delta_i(t) \approx 0$ most of the time. Thus, considering an initial routine to position each agent on the line path, it is reasonable to assume that $\delta_i(t) = 0$ and the problem reduces to controlling both $\theta_i(t)$ and $d_i(t)$.

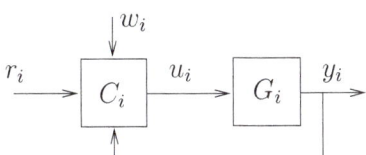

Figure 2. General feedback control loop of each vehicle.

The general feedback control system in Figure 2 can be tailored to deal with specific frameworks, such as considering different linear or non-linear controllers and dynamical models. We could assume the desired distance $r_i(t)$ to be constant or time-variant, allowing the inclusion of time headway policies for inter-vehicle distance [28]. Furthermore, we can study the control problem in continuous-time, discrete-time, or frequency domains. We could also consider that each controller uses only local information (i.e., $w_i(t) = 0$) or a cooperative framework in which the vehicles exchange data via V2V communication, which would require specifying a network topology [36]. Several communication topologies can be explored, with one of the most common being the one in which each vehicle shares some information with its immediate follower (predecessor–follower topology) [37].

We consider that the whole platoon is governed in a distributed but coordinated fashion through the local MIMO controllers in each vehicle. We do not consider the case where a single control unit uses the information of the whole platoon and computes the control signals for every vehicle in a centralized manner. Although such centralized control approach is normally expected to perform better than the distributed approach, it is not representative of real-world platooning scenarios, where each vehicle is autonomous and locally controlled.

For the control problem, the primary goal of each vehicle is to keep the tracking error signal $e_i(t)$ close to zero most of the time. The error is defined by

$$e_i(t) = \begin{bmatrix} e_{d_i}(t) \\ e_{\theta_i}(t) \end{bmatrix} = \begin{bmatrix} r_i(t) - d_i(t) \\ \theta_i(t) \end{bmatrix}. \tag{1}$$

The essential requirement is the design of stabilizing MIMO controllers and achieving zero steady-state error for each vehicle. Additional properties such as string stability and robustness against unreliable sensor measurements are important research topics.

In this paper, we propose a cooperative control algorithm for line-following platooning with unreliable distance measurements. To focus on the relevant aspects of the control problems, we assume a predecessor–follower topology and that vehicles communicate through an ideal communication channel. We validate the proposed approach using an experimental platform whose capabilities and dynamical model are described next.

3. Description of the RUPU Platform

The RUPU platform is a novel experimental platform that comprises two elements: (i) a surface with a customizable path to follow and (ii) a set of electromechanical mobile agents equipped with sensing and computing hardware necessary to follow the line in the path and track its immediate predecessor with a desired safety distance. We have designed and built the RUPU platform specifically to study platooning and multiagent problems. Figure 3 shows a general overview of a sample surface and three mobile agents.

Figure 3. Overview of the RUPU experimental platform.

Each agent is implemented as a differential drive mobile robot (DDMR) that can move autonomously through two active wheels, which are controlled independently to allow agents to move forward, backward, rotate, turn, or maintain a curved trajectory. Regarding sensing capabilities, each agent is equipped with a time-of-flight distance sensor located in the front, which allows the vehicle to measure the distance from the front of the agent to some object ahead. The orientation of each agent with respect to the white line in the path is measured with two arrays of eight infrared sensors located at the bottom of each agent. The infrared sensors allow for determining if the line is below the agent and measuring the orientation with respect to its axis of translation. The agents can implement initialization routines to get themselves aligned with the line to follow before performing experiments. Finally, the speed of the agents is measured through two Hall-effect encoders located within each DC motor, which collect data on the angular position, sense of rotation, and the rotational speed of each wheel. The central processing core for each agent is an

ESP32 embedded development board, which possesses an integrated WiFi module for wireless communication. Additional user-interface devices provide support for monitoring purposes and online interaction. Figure 4 shows two views of an agent.

Figure 4. Top and bottom views for a single assembled agent.

3.1. Dynamical Model for Control Synthesis

This section presents a simple linear dynamical model derived for each agent in the platoon moving along a straight line. To ease notation, in this section, we consider an arbitrary agent and omit the index i referring to the agent's position within the platoon.

The agent has two control inputs, which are the right and left motors voltages, denoted by $u_{mr}(t), u_{ml}(t)$, respectively. The angular positions of the right and left wheels of the agent are denoted by $\phi_r(t), \phi_l(t)$, respectively. The signals of interest are the linear velocity $v(t)$, the position $p(t)$, and the angular position $\theta(t)$ with respect to the line, which can be modeled as

$$v(t) = \frac{r}{2}(\dot{\phi}_r(t) + \dot{\phi}_l(t)), \tag{2}$$

$$p(t) = \frac{r}{2}(\phi_r(t) + \phi_l(t)), \tag{3}$$

$$\theta(t) = \frac{r}{2l}(\phi_r(t) - \phi_l(t)). \tag{4}$$

Based on an Euler–Lagrange modeling considering the dynamics of the motor and the geometry of the chassis, we perform standard parameter estimation techniques (see, for instance, [38] and the references therein) to obtain the following model, which is presented in the frequency domain:

$$\underbrace{\begin{bmatrix} V(s) \\ P(s) \\ \Theta(s) \end{bmatrix}}_{Z(s)} = \underbrace{\begin{bmatrix} G_{11}(s) & G_{12}(s) \\ G_{21}(s) & G_{22}(s) \\ G_{31}(s) & G_{32}(s) \end{bmatrix}}_{G(s)} \underbrace{\begin{bmatrix} U_{mr}(s) \\ U_{ml}(s) \end{bmatrix}}_{U(s)} \tag{5}$$

where $V(s), P(s), \Theta(s), U_{mr}(s)$, and $U_{ml}(s)$ are the Laplace transforms of $v(t), p(t), \theta(t), u_{mr}(t)$, and $u_{ml}(t)$ respectively, and

$$G_{11}(s) = G_{12}(s) = \frac{120020}{(s+4592)(s+7.187)}, \tag{6}$$

$$G_{21}(s) = G_{22}(s) = \frac{120020}{s(s+4592)(s+7.187)}, \tag{7}$$

$$G_{31}(s) = -G_{32}(s) = \frac{24962}{s(s+4591)(s+8.372)}. \tag{8}$$

The structure of the transfer matrix $G(s)$ is due to the symmetry in the agent construction and also because the agent velocity is the derivative of the position, explaining the deficient rank for $G(s)$. Thus, the model is essentially a two-input, two-output model since the distance and velocity are not independent variables. Indeed, we can write

$$G(s) = \begin{bmatrix} G_{11}(s) & 0 \\ G_{11}(s)/s & 0 \\ 0 & G_{31}(s) \end{bmatrix} \underbrace{\begin{bmatrix} 1 & 1 \\ 1 & -1 \end{bmatrix}}_{M_u} \quad (9)$$

allowing a static decoupling of the MIMO model through M_u for control design [35].

It is important to note that the obtained model is valid for a single agent. However, since each vehicle has the same dynamical model for a homogeneous platoon, we can write the relative output between agents simply as $z_{i-1}(t) - z_i(t)$, where the indexes i and $i-1$ refer to a given agent and its predecessor, respectively. Therefore, since the model is linear, the same transfer function matrix $G(s)$ can be used to describe the interaction between two consecutive agents, specifically to consider the inter-vehicle distance $d(t)$ as part of the model output. In the real implementation, the distance $d(t)$ may not be available due to unreliable sensing; hence we denote $d^m(t)$ as the distance measured by the local sensor and maintain $d(t)$ as the true distance.

3.2. Distance Measurement Issues

As mentioned in the previous section, the framework considers that distance measurements obtained from the ranging sensors may be unreliable. In the context of the experimental setup based on the RUPU platform, the main factor that affects the reliability of the distance sensors is the temporary loss of the line of sight when the vehicles move along a curve. Without having a vehicle in the line of sight, the measurement will be relative to the closest object in the environment. Figure 5 shows an example situation that illustrates the difficulty, where the last two agents do not have a preceding vehicle in the line of sight of its ranging sensor (shown with a yellow line). Therefore, the measured distance using the sensor, $d^m(t)$, and used by the controller, will not always be equal to the true inter-vehicle distance $d(t)$.

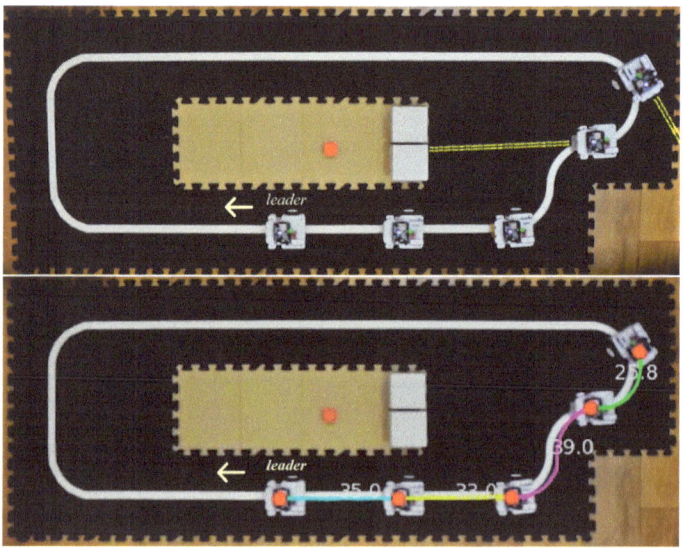

Figure 5. Top: Unreliable measurement of the distance sensor, $d^m(t)$. **Bottom:** offline estimation of the true distance $d(t)$ along the path.

To evaluate the performance of the proposed control strategy, we implemented an offline algorithm to estimate an approximate value for $d(t)$ using computer-vision techniques. The outcome of the algorithm for an example scenario is depicted in the bottom picture in Figure 5, where the same scenario shown in the top part now includes estimated values for all inter-vehicle distances, emphasized with different colors. The algorithm calculates the inter-vehicle distance as the shortest path along the line between two markers in consecutive agents. Assuming that the agents are similar and the markers are positioned at the same point on each vehicle, we can then obtain the shortest distance by subtracting the length of an agent from the value delivered by the algorithm. It is important to highlight that $d(t)$ is not employed online for control purposes and only serves as a reference value to evaluate the control performance using a reliable and consistent measurement of the distance tracking error.

4. Cooperative Control Strategy

The proposed cooperative strategy to design local controllers aims to deal with the lateral and longitudinal problems in line-following platooning and also provide robustness against unreliable distance measurements generated, for instance, in curved paths. The proposed controller is based on the dynamical model of the RUPU platform; however, the underlying cooperative control technique can be adapted and employed for different models.

We maintain here the simplified notation, omitting the index i. The proposed control exploits the structure of the system model in Equation (5), considering the inter-vehicle distance as an output, and it can include in the control loop the velocity of the predecessor vehicle, which is received using wireless communication. Indeed, from Equation (9), we note that it is possible to include the matrix M_u as a part of the controller and define a new input vector as

$$\begin{bmatrix} U_d(s) \\ U_\theta(s) \end{bmatrix} = \underbrace{\begin{bmatrix} 1 & 1 \\ 1 & -1 \end{bmatrix}}_{M_u} U(s) = \begin{bmatrix} U_{mr}(s) + U_{ml}(s) \\ U_{mr}(s) - U_{ml}(s) \end{bmatrix}. \tag{10}$$

This yields $V(s) = G_{11}(s)U_d(s)$, $D(s) = G_{21}(s)U_d(s)$ and $\theta(s) = G_{31}(s)U_\theta(s)$. Since we can only manipulate two variables ($U_d(s)$ and $U_\theta(s)$) we cannot control $V(s)$ and $D(s)$ independently. Indeed, when controlling the distance $D(s)$, we implicitly control $V(s)$, since $G_{11}(s) = sG_{21}(s)$.

In our proposed cooperative algorithm, we exploit the communication topology to enhance the control scheme, including an inner loop to manipulate the speed using the velocity of the predecessor agent. This inner loop allows us to perform speed control in case the distance sensing is unreliable. Moreover, we should recall that the true distance $d(t)$ is assumed to be known to derive the model; however, the controller uses the distance measured by the local sensor $d^m(t)$, which may not be equal to $d(t)$. Consequently, we use the control loop depicted in Figure 6, where $C_1(s)$, $C_2(s)$, and $C_3(s)$ are SISO controllers to be designed with integral action, where M_u^{-1} allows for recovering the true voltage signals given that

$$U_{mr}(s) = (U_d(s) + U_\theta(s))/2 \tag{11}$$
$$U_{ml}(s) = (U_d(s) - U_\theta(s))/2. \tag{12}$$

The cooperative feature of this control technique affects the inner loop controlling the velocity. We explicitly use the information of the predecessor's velocity as a part of a function to limit the speed reference of the agent, which is represented in Figure 6 by the block denoted by S. The inputs of S are the output of the dynamic controller $C_1(s)$, denoted by u_1, and the velocity of the predecessor agent, which is denoted by w and is transmitted wirelessly. The signal z is the output of S, and given by

$$z(t) = \begin{cases} S_u(t) & \text{for} \quad u_1(t) \geq S_u(t) \\ u_1(t), & \text{for} \quad S_l(t) < u_1(t) < S_u(t) \\ S_l(t), & \text{for} \quad u_1(t) \leq S_l(t) \end{cases} \quad (13)$$

where $S_u(t)$ and $S_l(t)$ are functions that depend on w and represent the upper and lower limits of u_1, respectively. The limiting functions are chosen to be

$$S_u(t) = \alpha\, w(t) + \epsilon, \quad S_l(t) = \beta\, w(t) - \epsilon, \quad \text{for} \quad w(t) \geq 0 \quad (14)$$
$$S_u(t) = \beta\, w(t) + \epsilon, \quad S_l(t) = \alpha\, w(t) - \epsilon, \quad \text{for} \quad w(t) < 0 \quad (15)$$

where $\alpha \geq 1$, $0 < \beta \leq 1$, and $\epsilon > 0$, are parameters to be chosen such that $S_u(t)$ and $S_l(t)$ are close to the predecessor's velocity. A natural choice in a practical scenario is α and β being close to 1, and ϵ being close to 0.

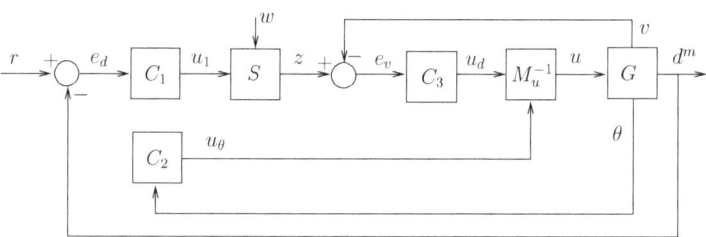

Figure 6. Cooperative control scheme with speed saturation.

Given the control scheme, $z(t)$ can be viewed as a speed reference for the agent, which is governed by the distance tracking error and limited by the predecessor's speed. This allows the agent to keep a velocity close to the predecessor's, but not necessarily equal, allowing it to perform the distance tracking properly. The values of α, β, and ϵ can be adjusted to achieve a desired transient response. In steady-state, distance and velocity tracking should be equal to zero due to the integral action. Note that, for high values of ϵ, the saturation may not affect, and thus this case is not a cooperative case since the predecessor's speed $w(t)$ is not playing any role.

This strategy makes the controller less vulnerable to vigorous speed changes provoked by temporary distance sensing issues such as those due to curved paths since the inner control loop and the saturation policy prioritize speed control when distance measurement is unreliable.

5. Experimental Results

This section presents the experimental results of two case studies. The first case is a non-cooperative one, without considering the saturation stage where the predecessor's speed is important. The second one is the cooperative case, where saturation is considered.

For the experimental setup, we use the path given in Figure 5, which has straight and curved sections and a group of five agents (one leader and four followers). We label the leader with the index 0, while the remainder agents are labeled with index $i = 1, 2, 3, 4$. Before the experiments, the agents perform an initialization routine to position themselves aligned along a straight section of the line to follow (starting with an orientation angle error around zero) and at a predefined distance from the predecessors. During the experiments, the leader receives its velocity reference remotely from an external user. The remaining vehicles follow the leader's trajectory but aim to maintain the inter-vehicle distance constant at 25 cm, regardless of the speed changes of the leader. For precaution, we limit the speed of each agent to 30 cm/s.

For illustrative purposes, we choose the controllers to be Proportional–Integral–Derivative (PID) for C_1 and C_2, and Proportional–Integral (PI) for C_3. In particular, we select

$$C_1(s) = -8 - 5.6\frac{1}{s} - 1.01s, \qquad C_2(s) = -2760 + 6250\frac{1}{s} + 304s$$

$$C_3(s) = -20.3 - 145\frac{1}{s}.$$

We use the same controllers C_1, C_2, and C_3 for both the cooperative and the non-cooperative setups. Thus, the comparison is not with this specific controller's performance but with the effect of incorporating the cooperative-based limiting speed stage on the platoon's behavior.

5.1. Offline-Distance Measurement Results

We start by showing the performance of the offline algorithm to estimate the true distances $d_i(t)$, as described in Section 3.2. As an example, Figure 7 shows the distances between the first follower and the leader, including the distance measured with the ranging sensors $d_1^m(t)$ and the estimated true distance $d_1(t)$ obtained from the offline algorithm based on computer vision techniques. The reference inter-vehicle distance is 25 cm. In the periods where $d_1^m(t)$ is close to 25 cm, the vehicles are moving along a straight section of the path; however, during curved sections, the measured distance deviates significantly from the target due to the temporal loss of the line of sight of the sensor, making the measurements unreliable and not representative of the actual inter-vehicle distance. On the other hand, the estimated distance $d_1(t)$ from the offline algorithm matches $d_1^m(t)$ during straight path periods but also provides reliable measurements during curves. Similar behavior is verified for different agents, speeds, and distance references.

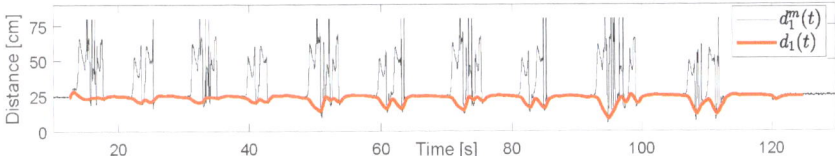

Figure 7. Offline video-based distance measurement performance.

For the distance tracking analysis in the following sections, we use $d_i(t)$ instead of $d_i^m(t)$. However, we recall that $d_i(t)$ is obtained offline for validation purposes and is not used for the control tasks. The implemented controllers use $d_i^m(t)$ to perform the experiments.

5.2. Experimental Results for the Non-Cooperative Case

In this case, we consider that the saturation block in the control scheme in Figure 6 is not present, and thus, the predecessor's speed does not play any role. The control is implemented based only on the measured distance $d_i(t)$. The dynamic behavior of the platoon is summarized in Figures 8–11. A video of the experiment showing the operational conditions and the platoon behavior is available here: https://youtu.be/JvotmTYlXOY (accessed on 16 January 2023).

The plots in Figure 8 show the velocity of each agent. The leader receives an external stair-type velocity reference, which is tracked without problems. The rest of the agents do not receive an external reference but generate an internal one through distance control. We can see that the agent velocities $v_i(t)$ follow the corresponding references $z_i(t)$, although with some transient errors. The main observation in this plot is that the velocity references $z_i(t)$ are erratic as a consequence of tracking the unreliable distance d_i^m. During curves, the measured distances $d_i^m(t)$ are higher than the real value (see Figure 7), and thus the controller increases the speed vigorously to reach the desired inter-vehicle distance. At some point, the agent leaves the curve and enters a straight section, and the distance sensor suddenly detects the predecessor, which is closer than expected, and therefore, the follower moves in the opposite direction. Actually, in this experiment, some $z_i(t)$ change abruptly from 30 cm/s to -30 cm/s, provoking an oscillatory behavior. Indeed, the last agent collides with its predecessors at approximately 100 s and moves out from the path. The experiment finishes a few seconds later. For higher speeds of the leader, agents are less sensitive to unreliable distance measures since the periods on curved sections are shorter, but at a low leader speed, the influence of the curves is aggravated.

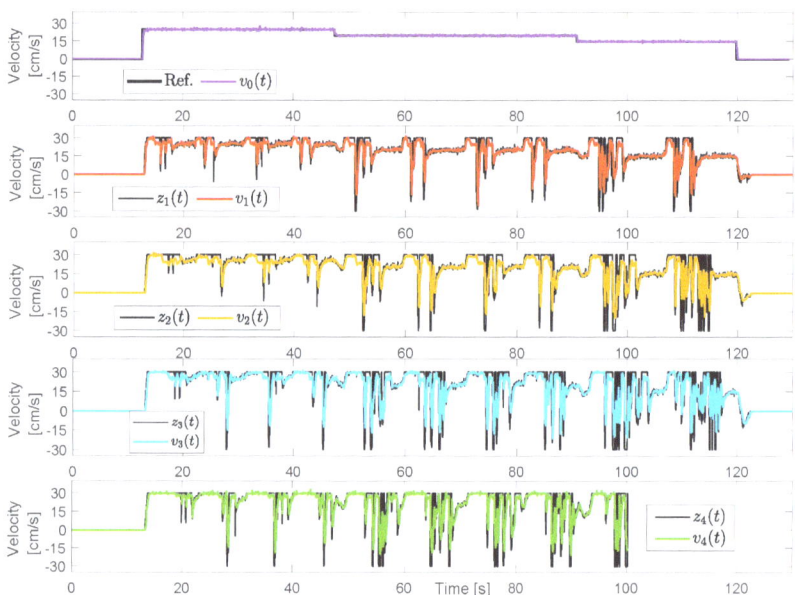

Figure 8. Velocity tracking using the non-cooperative strategy.

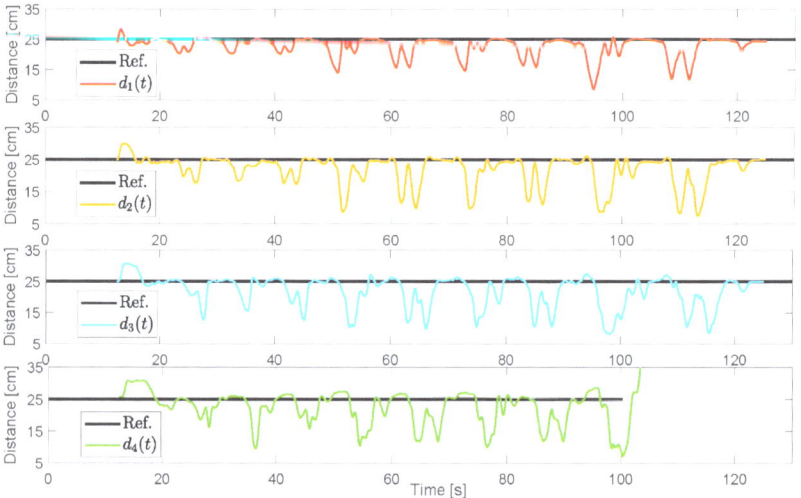

Figure 9. Distance tracking using the non-cooperative strategy.

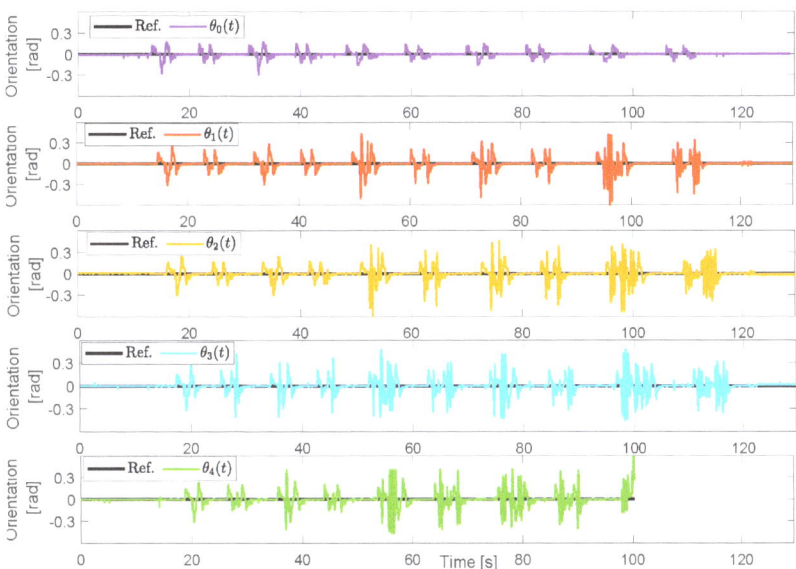

Figure 10. Angle tracking using the non-cooperative strategy.

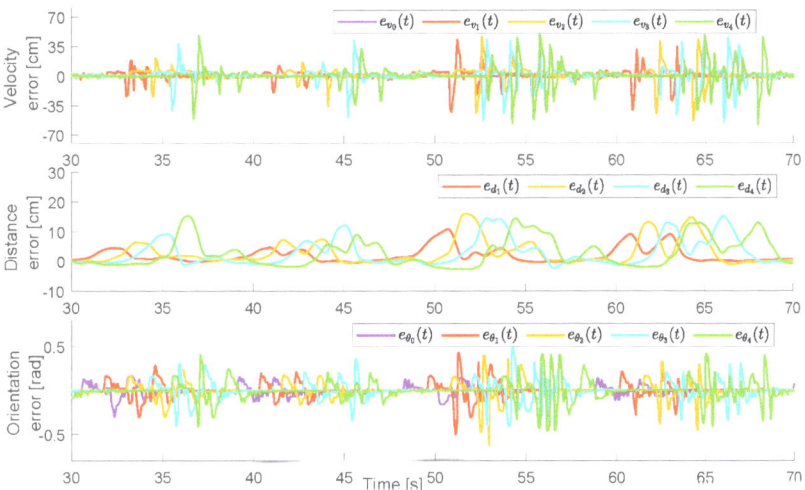

Figure 11. Errors in a time window of the experiment using the non-cooperative strategy.

The distance tracking is shown in Figure 9 for each agent, except for the leader. Clearly, agents can be considerably closer than expected during curves due to the behavior mentioned above, yielding the worst performance for the last agent, which ultimately collides with its predecessor. On the other hand, errors in the orientation measurement are also associated with curved paths. In this case, errors are not related to a sensing issue but rather an intrinsic disturbance due to the alignment of the infrared sensors that detect the line in the path. This can be aggravated by erratic behavior due to improper distance tracking. This behavior is illustrated in Figure 10, where the orientation angles for each vehicle are plotted, which also correspond to the orientation error since $\theta_i = e_{\theta_i}$ (see Equation (1)). The leader presents an acceptable performance in terms of orientation with respect to the line, achieving zero error during straight sections of the path and maintaining low transient deviation angles during curves; however, such a performance level is not reached by the followers, whose orientation errors are considerably higher when moving along curves. We also note that such angles are higher at lower velocities and, actually, near $t = 100$, we observe peak values around $\pm 0.6[\text{rad}] \approx \pm 34°$. Figure 11 presents a zoomed-in version of a region of interest for all plots in Figure 10, which also include the corresponding graphs of the velocity and distance tracking errors. The magnification of the plots is on a time window where a change of speed from 25 cm/s to 20 cm/s is performed by the leader. We can see that the errors increase as the disturbance propagates from the first agent to the last one, suggesting that the controller performs in a string-unstable fashion [37]. This could be corrected by changing the controller parameters; however, string stabilization is not within the scope of this paper.

5.3. Experimental Results for the Cooperative Case

In this case, we include the saturation stage of the proposed control scheme with $\epsilon = 1$, $\alpha = 1.1$, and $\beta = 0.9$, for each agent. The velocity of the predecessor is transmitted wirelessly. The rest of the control scheme, including the controller C_1, C_2, and C_3, is the same as in the previous experiment. By incorporating the saturation stage, each follower uses the internal signal z_i as a velocity reference, which now strongly depends on the estimated predecessor velocity. Implementing this control scheme requires inter-agent communication so that each vehicle can communicate its local velocity to its follower. The experimental results are given in Figures 12–15. The video of the reported experiment is available here: https://youtu.be/uK39YJ0bv1M (accessed on 16 January 2023).

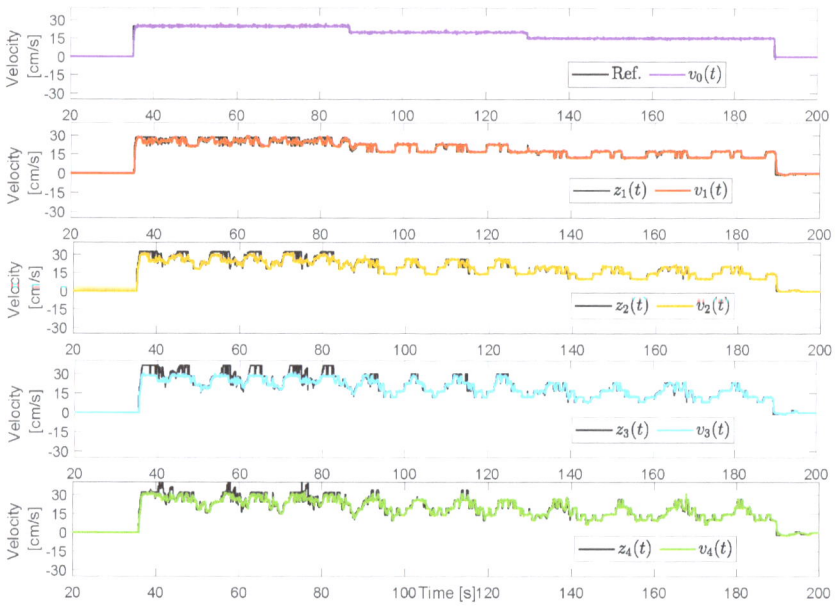

Figure 12. Velocity tracking using the cooperative strategy.

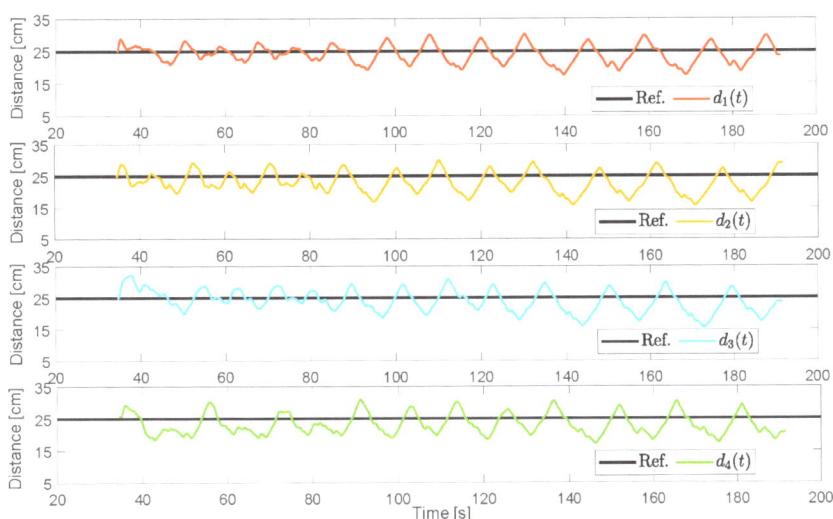

Figure 13. Distance tracking using the cooperative strategy.

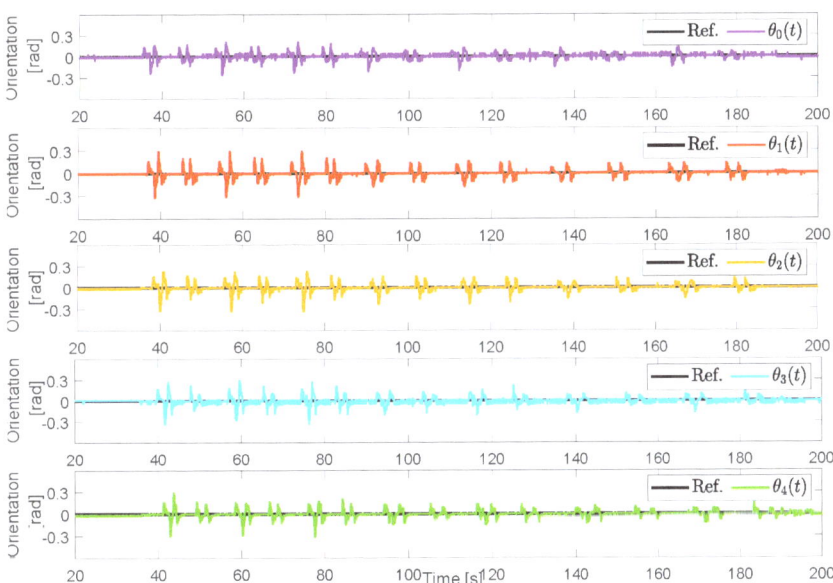

Figure 14. Angle tracking using the cooperative strategy.

The velocity tracking results are presented in Figure 12. In this case, the experiment is more extended since, unlike the non-cooperative case, it is not aborted due to agent collisions. In this case, the leader and the followers adequately follow their corresponding velocity reference. A key difference, in this case, is that the internal references z_i are now less vigorous due to the effect of the saturation stage. We recall that the measured distances $d_i^m(t)$ are still erratic as the ones in Figure 7; however, the effect provoked by such unreliable measurement is considerably reduced by the limits imposed by the predecessors' velocities. In this case, none of the agents have negative velocities; thus, the group of agents always moves forward. Figure 13 shows the distance tracking results. Distance tracking is also affected by curves, and we can note that a close-to-zero tracking error is not achieved most of the time; however, the cooperative case performs better than the non-cooperative case, where agents could be too close. Although agents do not behave abruptly as in the previous case, settling times may be slower due to saturation, which explains why tracking errors are not zero most of the time during straight sections of the path. Nevertheless, the platoon movement is much more fluent and avoids collisions see https://youtu.be/uK39YJ0bv1M (accessed on 16 January 2023).

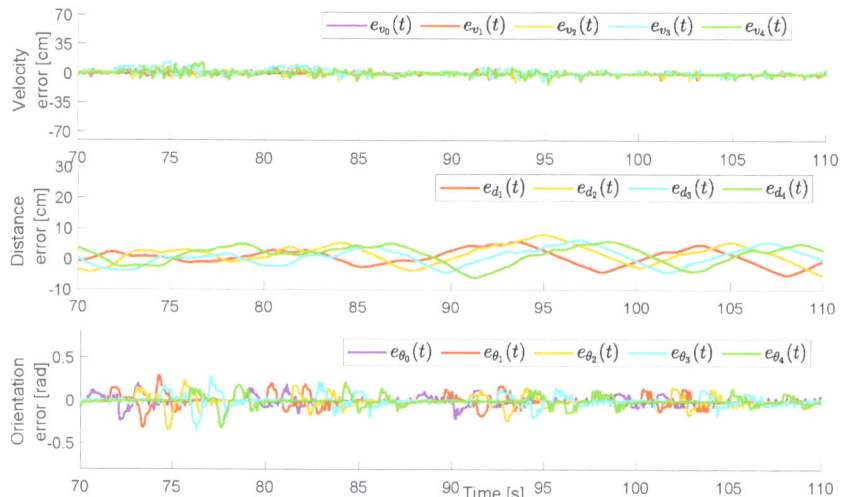

Figure 15. Errors in a time window of the experiment with the cooperative strategy.

Figure 14 summarizes results related to the orientation control (angle tracking). Clearly, the controller follows the reference with transient errors during the curves, but the performance is considerably better than in the non-cooperative case. Indeed, the control strategy effectively maintains the angle around zero with oscillations in the range ± 0.3[rad] $\approx \pm 17°$ at the beginning of the experiment, which decreases as the velocity decreases. This behavior is the opposite of the non-cooperative case in Figure 10. Figure 15 shows a more detailed view of the transient behavior during the time window that encloses the change in the leader's velocity reference from 25 cm/s to 20 cm/s. The plots in Figure 15 can be directly compared with the ones in Figure 11, where we can observe that velocity, distance, and orientation errors are considerably lower in the cooperative case compared to the non-cooperative case.

We can also visually inspect the global performance of the platoon in the provided videos, where we observe a notable improvement in the cooperative scheme. Figure 16 shows an example of an equivalent relevant scenario considering both non-cooperative and cooperative control schemes. Specifically, we considered the leader to be the independent and common subject and took a frame when the leader leaves the first curve after changing its velocity from 20 cm/s to 15 cm/s. The platoon performs poorly in the non-cooperative case, even with collisions in the last vehicles. In an equivalent scenario, the cooperative case shows better tracking of the inter-vehicle distance for all vehicles.

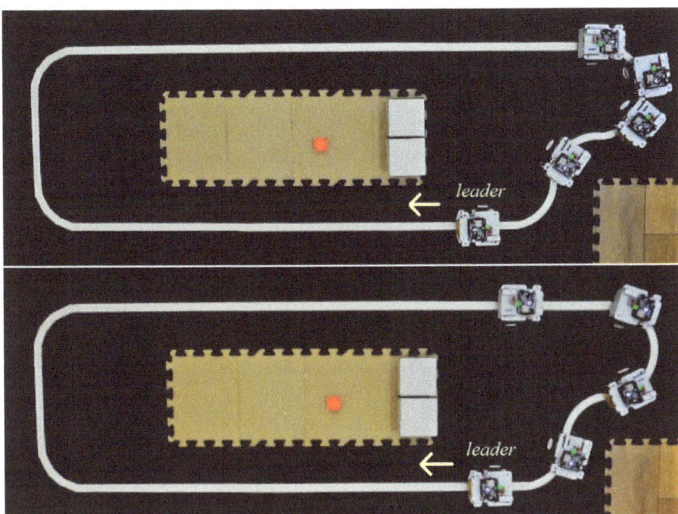

Figure 16. Visual comparison of the performance with the non-cooperative case (**top**) and the cooperative case (**bottom**).

6. Conclusions

We presented a cooperative control scheme to deal with unreliable measurements of the inter-vehicle distance in line-following platooning problems. In this control strategy, the velocity of a predecessor is used to limit the speed of the vehicles, avoiding vigorous reactions due to the temporary erroneous sensing derived from the limited line-of-sight of ranging sensors. We used the RUPU experimental platform to test the proposed control algorithm and compare it to a non-cooperative strategy. The RUPU platform is a low-cost platform specifically designed for testing different cooperative platooning schemes and related problems of relevance. The experimental results illustrate the proposed control algorithm's effectiveness in dealing with unreliable distance sensing and also showcase the capabilities of the experimental platform.

Future work includes the analytical study for string stabilizing control design in the proposed setup, the exploration of new control architectures in line-following platooning, and the usage of new cooperative policies to deal with practical issues that may arise in large platoon formations, such as sensing and communication issues.

Author Contributions: Conceptualization, F.J.V.; methodology, F.J.V.; software, C.E. and A.A.P.; validation, C.E.; formal analysis, C.E. and F.J.V.; investigation, all authors; resources, all authors; data curation, all authors; writing—original draft preparation, all authors; writing—review and editing, all authors.; visualization, all authors; supervision, F.J.V., A.A.P. and G.C.; project administration, F.J.V.; funding acquisition, F.J.V., G.C. and A.A.P. All authors have read and agreed to the published version of the manuscript.

Funding: This work has been funded by UTFSM internal project PI-LII-2020-38, ANID FONDECYT 11221365 grant, and CORFO Project 14ENI2-26865.

Informed Consent Statement: Not applicable.

Data Availability Statement: Not applicable.

Conflicts of Interest: The authors declare no conflict of interest.

References

1. Dey, K.C.; Yan, L.; Wang, X.; Wang, Y.; Shen, H.; Chowdhury, M.; Yu, L.; Qiu, C.; Soundararaj, V. A review of communication, driver characteristics, and controls aspects of cooperative adaptive cruise control (CACC). *IEEE Trans. Intell. Transp. Syst.* **2015**, *17*, 491–509. [CrossRef]
2. Wang, Z.; Wu, G.; Barth, M.J. A Review on Cooperative Adaptive Cruise Control (CACC) Systems: Architectures, Controls, and Applications. In Proceedings of the 2018 21st International Conference on Intelligent Transportation Systems (ITSC), Maui, HI, USA, 4–7 November 2018; pp. 2884–2891. [CrossRef]
3. Wang, C.; Gong, S.; Zhou, A.; Li, T.; Peeta, S. Cooperative adaptive cruise control for connected autonomous vehicles by factoring communication-related constraints. *Transp. Res. Part Emerg. Technol.* **2020**, *113*, 124–145. [CrossRef]
4. Li, S.E.; Zheng, Y.; Li, K.; Wu, Y.; Hedrick, J.K.; Gao, F.; Zhang, H. Dynamical Modeling and Distributed Control of Connected and Automated Vehicles: Challenges and Opportunities. *IEEE Intell. Transp. Syst. Mag.* **2017**, *9*, 46–58. [CrossRef]
5. Guerrero-Ibáñez, J.; Zeadally, S.; Contreras-Castillo, J. Sensor technologies for intelligent transportation systems. *Sensors* **2018**, *18*, 1212. [CrossRef] [PubMed]
6. Turri, V.; Besselink, B.; Johansson, K.H. Cooperative look-ahead control for fuel-efficient and safe heavy-duty vehicle platooning. *IEEE Trans. Control Syst. Technol.* **2016**, *25*, 12–28.
7. Thormann, S.; Schirrer, A.; Jakubek, S. Safe and efficient cooperative platooning. *IEEE Trans. Intell. Transp. Syst.* **2020**, *2*, 1368–1380. [CrossRef]
8. Jia, D.; Lu, K.; Wang, J.; Zhang, X.; Shen, X. A survey on platoon-based vehicular cyber-physical systems. *IEEE Commun. Surv. Tutor.* **2015**, *18*, 263–284. [CrossRef]
9. Bergenhem, C.; Shladover, S.; Coelingh, E.; Englund, C.; Tsugawa, S. Overview of platooning systems. In Proceedings of the 19th ITS World Congress, Vienna, Austria, 22–26 October 2012.
10. Jiang, J.; Astolfi, A. Lateral Control of an Autonomous Vehicle. *IEEE Trans. Intell. Veh.* **2018**, *3*, 228–237. [CrossRef]
11. Swaroop, D.; Hedrick, J.K.; Choi, S.B. Direct adaptive longitudinal control of vehicle platoons. *IEEE Trans. Veh. Technol.* **2001**, *50*, 150–161.
12. Dang, D.; Gao, F.; Hu, Q. Motion planning for autonomous vehicles considering longitudinal and lateral dynamics coupling. *Appl. Sci.* **2020**, *10*, 3180. [CrossRef]
13. Chebly, A.; Talj, R.; Charara, A. Coupled longitudinal/lateral controllers for autonomous vehicles navigation, with experimental validation. *Control Eng. Pract.* **2019**, *88*, 79–96. [CrossRef]
14. Zhou, H.; Jia, F.; Jing, H.; Liu, Z.; Güvenç, L. Coordinated longitudinal and lateral motion control for four wheel independent motor-drive electric vehicle. *IEEE Trans. Veh. Technol.* **2018**, *67*, 3782–3790. [CrossRef]
15. Latrech, C.; Chaibet, A.; Boukhnifer, M.; Glaser, S. Integrated Longitudinal and Lateral Networked Control System Design for Vehicle Platooning. *Sensors* **2018**, *18*, 3085. [CrossRef]
16. Bayuwindra, A.; Ploeg, J.; Lefeber, E.; Nijmeijer, H. Combined Longitudinal and Lateral Control of Car-Like Vehicle Platooning With Extended Look-Ahead. *IEEE Trans. Control Syst. Technol.* **2020**, *28*, 790–803. [CrossRef]
17. Yu, L.; Bai, Y.; Kuang, Z.; Liu, C.; Jiao, H. Intelligent Bus Platoon Lateral and Longitudinal Control Method Based on Finite-Time Sliding Mode. *Sensors* **2022**, *22*, 3139. [CrossRef]
18. Badue, C.; Guidolini, R.; Carneiro, R.V.; Azevedo, P.; Cardoso, V.B.; Forechi, A.; Jesus, L.; Berriel, R.; Paixão, T.M.; Mutz, F.; et al. Self-driving cars: A survey. *Expert Syst. Appl.* **2021**, *165*, 113816. [CrossRef]
19. Bautista-Camino, P.; Barranco-Gutiérrez, A.I.; Cervantes, I.; Rodríguez-Licea, M.; Prado-Olivarez, J.; Pérez-Pinal, F.J. Local Path Planning for Autonomous Vehicles Based on the Natural Behavior of the Biological Action-Perception Motion. *Energies* **2022**, *15*, 1769. [CrossRef]
20. Claussmann, L.; Revilloud, M.; Gruyer, D.; Glaser, S. A Review of Motion Planning for Highway Autonomous Driving. *IEEE Trans. Intell. Transp. Syst.* **2020**, *21*, 1826–1848. [CrossRef]
21. Gupta, A.; Anpalagan, A.; Guan, L.; Khwaja, A.S. Deep learning for object detection and scene perception in self-driving cars: Survey, challenges, and open issues. *Array* **2021**, *10*, 100057. [CrossRef]
22. Ingle, S.; Phute, M. Tesla autopilot: Semi autonomous driving, an uptick for future autonomy. *Int. Res. J. Eng. Technol.* **2016**, *3*, 369–372.
23. The New York Times. What Riding in a Self-Driving Tesla Tells Us about the Future of Autonomy. 2022. Available online: https://www.nytimes.com/interactive/2022/11/14/technology/tesla-self-driving-flaws.html (accessed on 16 January 2023).
24. Rosique, F.; Navarro, P.J.; Fernández, C.; Padilla, A. A Systematic Review of Perception System and Simulators for Autonomous Vehicles Research. *Sensors* **2019**, *19*, 648. [CrossRef] [PubMed]
25. Sybis, M.; Rodziewicz, M.; Wesołowski, K. Influence of Sensor Inaccuracies and Acceleration Limits on IEEE 802.11p-Based CACC Controlled Platoons. In Proceedings of the 2020 IEEE 91st Vehicular Technology Conference (VTC2020-Spring), Antwerp, Belgium, 25–28 May 2020; pp. 1–6.
26. Lengyel, H.; Tettamanti, T.; Szalay, Z. Conflicts of Automated Driving With Conventional Traffic Infrastructure. *IEEE Access* **2020**, *8*, 163280–163297. [CrossRef]
27. Yin, S.; Yang, C.; Kawsar, I.; Du, H.; Pan, Y. Longitudinal Predictive Control for Vehicle-Following Collision Avoidance in Autonomous Driving Considering Distance and Acceleration Compensation. *Sensors* **2022**, *22*, 7395. [CrossRef] [PubMed]
28. Stüdli, S.; Seron, M.; Middleton, R. From vehicular platoons to general networked systems: String stability and related concepts. *Annu. Rev. Control* **2017**, *44*, 157–172. [CrossRef]
29. Feng, S.; Zhang, Y.; Li, S.E.; Cao, Z.; Liu, H.X.; Li, L. String stability for vehicular platoon control: Definitions and analysis methods. *Annu. Rev. Control* **2019**, *47*, 81–97. [CrossRef]

30. Gordon, M.A.; Vargas, F.J.; Peters, A.A. Comparison of Simple Strategies for Vehicular Platooning with Lossy Communication. *IEEE Access* **2021**, *9*, 103996–104010. [CrossRef]
31. Gordon, M.A.; Vargas, F.J.; Peters, A.A. Mean square stability conditions for platoons with lossy inter-vehicle communication channels. *Automatica* **2023**, *147*, 110710. [CrossRef]
32. Ensemble. Available online: https://platooningensemble.eu (accessed on 16 January 2023).
33. Widyotriatmo, A.; Siregar, P.I.; Nazaruddin, Y.Y. Line following control of an autonomous truck-trailer. In Proceedings of the 2017 International Conference on Robotics, Biomimetics, and Intelligent Computational Systems (Robionetics), Bali, Indonesia, 23–25 August 2017; pp. 24–28.
34. Sezgin, A.; Çetin, Ö. Design and Implementation of Adaptive Fuzzy PD Line Following Robot. In *Intelligent and Fuzzy Techniques in Big Data Analytics and Decision Making, Proceedings of the INFUS 2019 Conference, Istanbul, Turkey, 23–25 July 2019*; Springer: Cham, Switzerland, 2019; pp. 106–114.
35. Albertos, P.; Sala, A. *Multivariable Control Systems: An Engineering Approach*; Springer Science & Business Media: Berlin/Heidelberg, Germany, 2006.
36. Wu, L.; Lu, Z.; Guo, G. Analysis, synthesis and experiments of networked platoons with communication constraints. *Promet Traffic Traffico* **2017**, *29*, 35–44. [CrossRef]
37. Seiler, P.; Pant, A.; Hedrick, K. Disturbance propagation in vehicle strings. *IEEE Trans. Autom. Control* **2004**, *49*, 1835–1842. [CrossRef]
38. Siwek, M.; Panasiuk, J.; Baranowski, L.; Kaczmarek, W.; Prusaczyk, P.; Borys, S. Identification of Differential Drive Robot Dynamic Model Parameters. *Materials* **2023**, *16*, 683. [CrossRef] [PubMed]

Disclaimer/Publisher's Note: The statements, opinions and data contained in all publications are solely those of the individual author(s) and contributor(s) and not of MDPI and/or the editor(s). MDPI and/or the editor(s) disclaim responsibility for any injury to people or property resulting from any ideas, methods, instructions or products referred to in the content.

Article

Explicit Identification of Pointwise Terrain Gradients for Speed Compensation of Four Driving Tracks in Passively Articulated Tracked Mobile Robot

Haneul Jeon and Donghun Lee *

Mechanical Engineering Department, Soongsil University, Seoul 06978, Republic of Korea
* Correspondence: dhlee04@ssu.ac.kr

Abstract: Tracked mobile robots can overcome the limitations of wheeled and legged robots in environments, such as construction and mining, but there are still significant challenges to be addressed in terms of trajectory tracking. This study proposes a kinematic strategy to improve the trajectory-tracking performance of a PASTRo (Passively Articulated Suspension based Track-typed mobile robot), which comprises four tracks, two rockers, a differential gear, and a main body. Due to the difficulties in explicitly identifying track-terrain contact angles, suspension kinematics is used to identify track-terrain contact angles (TTCA) in arbitrarily rough terrains. Thus, the TTCA-based driving velocity projection method is proposed in this study to improve the maneuverability of PASTRo in arbitrarily rough terrains. The RecurDyn-Simulink co-simulator is used to examine the improvement of PASTRo compared to a tracked mobile robot non-suspension version. The results indicate that PASTRo has a 33.3% lower RMS(Root Mean Square) distance error, 56.3% lower RMS directional error, and 43.2% lower RMS offset error than the four-track skid-steer mobile robot (SSMR), even with planar SSMR kinematics. To improve the maneuverability of PASTRo without any information on the rough terrain, the TTCA is calculated from the suspension kinematics, and the TTCA obtained is used for both TTCA-based driving velocity projection methods. The results show that PASTRo, with the TTCA-based driving velocity projection method, has a 39.2% lower RMS distance error, 57.9% lower RMS directional error, and 51.9% lower RMS offset error than the four-track SSMR.

Keywords: skid-steer mobile robot; terrain gradient; velocity propagation; track typed mobile robot; passively articulated suspension

MSC: 70B15

Citation: Jeon, H.; Lee, D. Explicit Identification of Pointwise Terrain Gradients for Speed Compensation of Four Driving Tracks in Passively Articulated Tracked Mobile Robot. *Mathematics* **2023**, *11*, 905. https://doi.org/10.3390/math11040905

Academic Editors: Paolo Mercorelli, Oleg Sergiyenko and Oleksandr Tsymbal

Received: 11 January 2023
Revised: 7 February 2023
Accepted: 8 February 2023
Published: 10 February 2023

Copyright: © 2023 by the authors. Licensee MDPI, Basel, Switzerland. This article is an open access article distributed under the terms and conditions of the Creative Commons Attribution (CC BY) license (https://creativecommons.org/licenses/by/4.0/).

1. Introduction

For several decades, there have been many studies on MRs in rough terrains in aerospace [1,2], industry [3,4], and military [5–8] applications. A disaster rescue robot [9] has consistently been developed for a mission at the scene of accidents, and the DARPA robotics challenge was held to motivate the development of disaster robots that could do "complex tasks in dangerous, degraded, human-engineered environments" instead of humans [10,11].

The MRs driving on rough, rugged, "nd u'even terrains can be classified into wheel, leg, and track-typed MRs in terms of their locomotion mechanisms. Over the past decade, numerous research projects on legged robots have been carried out. Especially the two famous quadrupedal robots, Spot of the Boston Dynamics [6] and Cheetah of MIT, started showing remarkable results in their quadrupedal locomotion. Additionally, the most noteworthy characteristic of such quadrupedal MRs would be the possibility of various gait pattern generation.

However, despite such advantages of quadrupedal locomotion, wheel and track-driven MRs are still being studied because securing posture stability in steering control of quadrupedal locomotion is evaluated to be somewhat more complicated than the wheel and track-driven MRs. The Mars rover Curiosity, composed of six wheels with rocker-bogie suspension, has already shown remarkable results in NASA's Mars missions [2]. The Packbot of the iRobot [7] for reconnaissance missions is composed of two tracks for driving, and two tilting tracks for both driving and overcoming obstacles. In particular, several MRs with passively or actively articulated suspensions for driving stabilities on rough terrains have been presented [12,13]. The rocker-bogie suspension used in the Mars rovers, and the Shrimp suspension proposed by Siegwart [12] is the most popular passively articulated suspension structures.

In the case of the rocker-bogie system, it is possible to reduce the motion of the main body when surmounting sizable obstacles by pitching the motion of a rocker and bogie mounted on each side of the rover. However, there are no rolling joints in the rockers, bogies, and wheels to passively and independently adapt their orientations to the ground surfaces inclined in the transverse direction. Then, the lack of rolling joints may lead to loss of traction between the wheel and ground at specific postures due to improper contact. According to simulation results performed in our laboratory, it is confirmed that the inappropriate contact of a driving wheel with the ground may lead to peak torques in the other driving wheels and poor driving performances during the entire driving. In designing MR for driving on such unknown terrains, it is natural for a designer to think of the peak torque and the torque distribution as one of the most critical factors in selecting the driving motors. Therefore, in an aspect of the mechanical design, the effect of the passive rolling joints in the suspensions, or driving modules should be considered for improving driving performances on rough terrains. Especially as the four tracks are supposed to passively maximize the contact area between operating modules and the grounds.

In control of the skid-steer MR, the linear and angular velocities of MR are typically expressed in an inertial coordinate frame under the assumption of the coplanar contact of all driving wheels or tracks with grounds. Under this assumption, Caracciolo, Luca et al. [14]; Kozłowski, Krzysztof, and Dariusz Pazderski [15]; and Shuang, Gao et al. [16] calculated the velocity control input of a skid-steering MRs by solving kinematics in XY-plane of the inertial coordinate. However, the motion of MRs on rough terrains should be described in three-dimensional space due to geometric complexities of the ground. Especially in cases of the MRs with passively articulated suspensions for connecting the main body and four driving tracks, each driving track may have arbitrary orientations relative to the main body. That is, it is evident that the MR kinematics should not be enough for precise posture tracking control due to no consideration of the tilting angle of the driving track.

In previous research, Tarokh, Mahmoud et al. [17] proposed a kinematic model for the Mars rover that can estimate the wheel-terrain contact angle of driving modules by considering the 6-DOF motion of the rocker-bogie suspension. However, the research only focused on reducing the effects of slippage for given elevation maps by compensating for differences between wheel-terrain contact points. Thus, in case of insufficient information on the elevation map of the ground, such an elevation map-dependent method should not be used to expect satisfactory trajectory tracking performances in unknown terrains.

Thus, a new MR mechanism named PASTRo (passively articulated suspension-based track-typed MR), which was previously published [18,19] by this author, is composed of four tiltable driving tracks, two rockers, a main body, and a differential gear module connecting two rockers are proposed. Moreover, the main contributions of this study include the following:

1. The suspension kinematics-based speed compensation methods are newly proposed to successfully calculate the track-terrain contact angles (TTCA) at any arbitrary rough terrains without a pointwise terrain elevation map.
2. Then, the uncertainties in the kinematic parameters of MR kinematics and the relative orientation of the driving track can be successfully removed.

3. The proposed algorithm is evaluated through simulation and experimental results, demonstrating improved trajectory tracking performance compared to traditional control methods.
4. Additionally, the paper includes an analysis of the robustness and stability of the proposed algorithm under different operating conditions.
5. Overall, this research aims to contribute to the advancement of tracked mobile robot technology and its potential applications in various fields.

This paper is organized as follows: Section 2 describes the design of a track-typed MR composed of four tracks, and passively articulated suspensions similar to the rocker. Section 3 describes MR kinematics for posture tracking control of MR on rough terrains. Primarily, the suspension kinematics to estimate the inclination of driving tracks on arbitrary rough terrains is described. Then, a way to compensate for the gradient effect by considering the inclination of driving tracks obtained by the suspension kinematics is described. In Section 4, the locomotive simulation to verify improvements in posture tracking performances by applying the proposed gradient effect compensator is conducted in a virtual environment in RecurDyn -Simulink co-simulator. Additionally, the results of posture tracking performances impro

2. A New Quad-Tracked Mobile Robot with Passively Articulated Suspensions

This section describes all details regarding the new track-typed mobile mechanism with passively articulated suspension for improving its mobility in rough terrains. The proposed MR comprises the main body, four passively tiltable driving tracks, two rockers, a differential gear, and passive pitch-roll joints between the rocker and the driving track. The differential gear enables relative pitching of the left and right suspensions and induces the same pitching on the left and right with respect to the chassis, resulting in the chassis' posture stability and the track's ground contact smoothly. By passive motions dependent on the contact geometry of the rough terrains, the pose of each driving track can be properly and independently determined to maximize the contact areas between driving modules and the grounds, as shown in Figure 1. Thus, this MR can always secure the proper contact with the ground in all driving tracks without any additional control efforts.

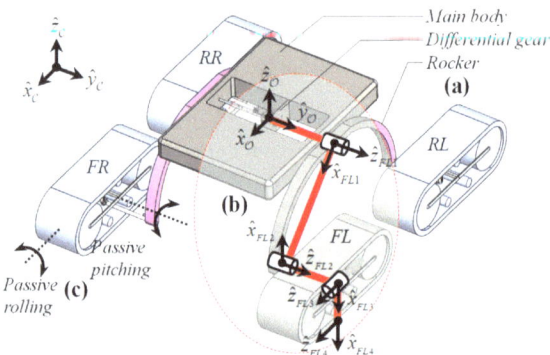

Figure 1. Proposed quad-tracked MR: (**a**) four driving tracks connected with main body with rocker, (**b**) joint coordinate frames assigned to the front left suspension as an example of suspension kinematics, (**c**) 2-dof pitch-roll joints for passively connecting rockers and driving tracks.

As shown in Figure 1, the instantaneous center of rotation (ICR) frame and the center of mass(COM) frame are denoted as $\mathcal{C} - xyz$ and $\mathcal{O} - xyz$ in this paper, respectively. The 2-dof passive joint between rocker and track is assembled in the order of pitch and roll to maintain z axes of the driving tracks to be parallel with heading axis of the main body on any arbitrary rough terrains. For securing orientation stabilities of all driving tracks at any arbitrary contact terrains, the intersecting points of pitch and roll axes should be located at middle of the tracks in transverse direction and slightly lower down from center of the tracks in height direction. Each passive joint has intentional ±20° joint limits, which prevents the decline of orientation stability of MR due to excessive tilting on steep slope. When the difference of height between left and right side on terrain is significantly large, differential-gear make the main body retain stability by having average pitch angle between left and right rocker.

3. MR Kinematics for Rough Terrains

This section describes the overall posture tracking control strategy of the proposed MR on arbitrary rough terrains as shown in Figure 2. In Section 3.1, the planar kinematics of the skid-steer mobile robot (SSMR) is described first to calculate the required track angular speeds for the desired linear velocity and angular velocity of the MR. Section 3.2 describes the suspension kinematics to calculate the driving tracks' poses relative to the main body on arbitrary rough terrains. Then, gradient effect compensator (GEC) for considering the unavoidably varying driving tracks' attitudes will be detailed in Section 3.3. In updating the driving speed consecutively calculated from planar SSMR kinematics and the GEC, a critical violation of the assumption about driving speeds obtained from the SSMR kinematics inevitably occurred. The violation may lead to slippage in the contact area due to differences in front and rear driving velocities on the same side. Additionally, the front or rear track can be tilted up and unintentionally lose contact with the ground due to the differences in driving speed. Thus, at the end of Section 3.3, the backward velocity propagation of the updated front driving velocity to the rear driving track is proposed to prevent the undesired track pitching phenomena.

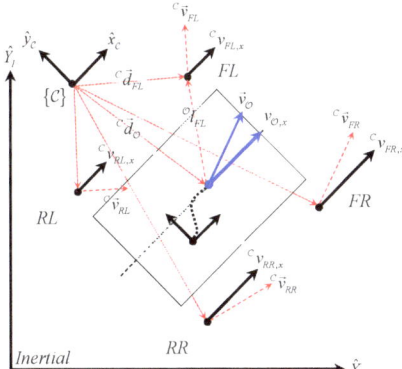

Figure 2. Coordinate frames of conventional planar SSMR kinematics defined on the inertial XY plane. The z axes of the frame $\{C\}$ and $\{O\}$ are all out of the page.

3.1. Planar SSMR Kinematics

As shown in Figure 2, in the planar SSMR kinematics, the frame $\{O\}$ and frame $\{pq\}$ located at the center of mass (COM) of MR and the driving tracks, respectively are expressed in the XY-plane of the frame $\{C\}$ located at the instantaneous center of rotation. Here, $p \in \{F, R\}$, $q \in \{L, R\}$, FR (front right), FL (front left), RR (rear right), and RL (rear left) are indices for defining the suspension kinematics and driving track positions, respectively. The linear and angular velocities of the frame $\{O\}$ is also expressed in the frame $\{C\}$, as shown in Figure 2.

For given desired linear and angular velocities of the main body in its steering motions, the driving track speeds can be calculated using following Equations (1) and (2):

$$\frac{\|v_{pq,x}\|}{\|{}^C d_{pq,y}\|} = \frac{\|v_{O,x}\|}{\|{}^C d_{O,y}\|} = |\omega_O| \qquad (1)$$

where,

$$^C\vec{d}_O = [x_O, y_O, 0]^T \tag{2}$$

where, $^C\vec{d}_O$ denotes position of origin of the frame $\{O\}$ relative to the frame $\{C\}$. For given linear velocity of the main body in x-direction and angular velocity of the main body, the radius of instantaneous center of rotation, y_O, can be calculated with following Equation (3):

$$y_O = \frac{v_{O,x}}{\omega_O} \tag{3}$$

For given input $^Cv_{O,x}$ and $^C\omega_{O,z}$ expressed in frame $\{C\}$, the linear track speeds can be calculated as follows:

$$\begin{bmatrix} ^Cv_{pL,x} \\ ^Cv_{pR,x} \end{bmatrix} = \begin{bmatrix} 1 & -^Ol_{pL,y} \\ 1 & ^Ol_{pR,y} \end{bmatrix} \cdot \begin{bmatrix} ^Cv_{O,x} \\ ^C\omega_{O,z} \end{bmatrix} \tag{4}$$

From Equations (1)–(4), the following equality constraint between the front and rear driving speeds on the same side can be obtained with the assumption of identical driving speed on the same side. $^Cv_{pL,x}$ and $^Cv_{pR,x}$ denote the linear speeds of the left and right driving tracks, respectively.

$$\begin{cases} ^Cv_{pL,x} = {^Cv_{FL,x}} = {^Cv_{RL,x}} \\ ^Cv_{pR,x} = {^Cv_{FR,x}} = {^Cv_{RR,x}} \end{cases} \tag{5}$$

3.2. Suspension Kinematics

As shown in Figure 1, the frame $\{O\}$ is chosen as a common reference frame for four cases of the suspension kinematics. Table 1 represents the screw axes expressed in the frame $\{O\}$ for the suspension kinematics at its zero position. The zero position means that all joint values set equal to zero. The l_1, l_2, l_3, and l_4 parameters are the constant link parameters of the suspension structure.

Table 1. Screw axes $(\_^O)S\_(pq,i) = (\omega\_i, v\_(pq,i))$ expressed in the frame $\{O\}$ for the suspension kinematics from main body.

i	ω_i	$v_{FL,i}$	$v_{FR,i}$	$v_{RR,i}$	$v_{RL,i}$
1	(0, 1, 0)	$(0, l_1, 0)$	$(0, -l_1, 0)$	$(0, -l_1, 0)$	$(0, l_1, 0)$
2	(0, 1, 0)	$(l_2 \cdot c\theta_s, l_1, -l_2 \cdot s\theta_s)$	$(l_2 \cdot c\theta_s, -l_1, -l_2 \cdot s\theta_s)$	$(-l_2 \cdot c\theta_s, -l_1, -l_2 \cdot s\theta_s)$	$(-l_2 \cdot c\theta_s, l_1, -l_2 \cdot s\theta_s)$
3	(1, 0, 0)	$(l_2 \cdot c\theta_s, l_1 + l_3, -l_2 \cdot s\theta_s)$	$(l_2 \cdot c\theta_s, -l_1 - l_3, -l_2 \cdot s\theta_s)$	$(-l_2 \cdot c\theta_s, -l_1 - l_3, -l_2 \cdot s\theta_s)$	$(-l_2 \cdot c\theta_s, l_1 + l_3, -l_2 \cdot s\theta_s)$
4	(1, 0, 0)	$(l_2 \cdot c\theta_s, l_1 + l_3, -l_2 \cdot s\theta_s - l_4)$	$(l_2 \cdot c\theta_s, -l_1 - l_3, -l_2 \cdot s\theta_s - l_4)$	$(-l_2 \cdot c\theta_s, -l_1 - l_3, -l_2 \cdot s\theta_s - l_4)$	$(-l_2 \cdot c\theta_s, l_1 + l_3, -l_2 \cdot s\theta_s - l_4)$

Equation (6) represents the product of exponentials (PoE) formula describing the suspension kinematics from $\{O\}$ to $\{pq4\}$. All screw axes in Equation (6) are expressed in the frame $\{O\}$ as Table 1.

$$^O_{pq4}T = e^{[S_{pq,1}]\theta_1} e^{[S_{pq,2}]\theta_2} e^{[S_{pq,3}]\theta_3} e^{[S_{pq,4}]\theta_4} {^O_{pq4}M} = \begin{bmatrix} ^O_{pq4}R & ^O_{pq4}\vec{l} \\ 0_{1\times 3} & 1 \end{bmatrix} \tag{6}$$

where θ_1 denotes angular displacement of differential gear that connects right and left side rockers. θ_2 and θ_3 denote pitch and roll of the driving tracks, respectively. θ_4 is set to zero, because the transformation from $\{pq3\}$ to $\{pq4\}$ is pure translation. The positive rotation about these axes is by the usual right-hand rule. $e^{[S]\theta}$ represents the matrix exponential of the $[S]\theta \in se(3)$. The $[S] \in \mathbb{R}^{4\times 4}$ denotes 4×4 matrix representation of unit screw axis $\mathcal{S} \in \mathbb{R}^6$, and θ is the joint angle. $^{\mathcal{O}}_{pq4}M$ denotes the configuration of the frame $\{pq4\}$ relative to the frame $\{\mathcal{O}\}$ when the suspension is in its zero position. The relative position $^{\mathcal{O}}\vec{l}_{pq4} \in \mathbb{R}^3$ and orientation $^{\mathcal{O}}_{pq4}R \in SO(3)$ of the frame $\{pq4\}$ relative to the frame $\{\mathcal{O}\}$ can be obtained from the following suspension kinematics.

As shown in Equation (7), the obtained $^{\mathcal{O}}\vec{l}_{pq4}$ and $^{\mathcal{O}}_{pq4}R$ are used to calculate the driving speed $^{\mathcal{O}}v_{pq4,x} \in \mathbb{R}$ with considering the relative pose between the main body and the pq driving track.

$$
\begin{aligned}
^{\mathcal{C}}v_{pq,x} &= {^{\mathcal{C}}\mathbf{S}_X} \cdot \left\{ {^{\mathcal{C}}\vec{\omega}_{\mathcal{O}}} \times \left({^{\mathcal{C}}\vec{d}_{\mathcal{O}}} + {^{\mathcal{C}}_{\mathcal{O}}R} \cdot \left({^{\mathcal{O}}\vec{l}_{pq4}} \right) \right) \right\} \\
&= v_{\mathcal{O},x} - \omega_{\mathcal{O},z}(l'_{pq4,y})
\end{aligned}
\quad (7)
$$

The driving speed vector $^{\mathcal{C}}\vec{v}_{pq}$ can be calculated by the cross product of $^{\mathcal{C}}\vec{\omega}_{\mathcal{O}}$ and $^{\mathcal{C}}\vec{d}_{pq4}$. The selection vector $^{\mathcal{C}}\mathbf{S}_X$ is then applied, so as to extract the heading component of the driving velocity $^{\mathcal{C}}v_{pq,x}$. By applying Equation (6) to FL, RL, RR, and FR driving tracks, an explicit relationship between the track speed $^{\mathcal{C}}\mathbf{v}_{track}$ and the MR velocity $^{\mathcal{C}}\mathbf{V}$ can be clarified as follows:

$$
^{\mathcal{C}}\mathbf{v}_{track} = ^{\mathcal{C}}\begin{bmatrix} v_{FL,x} \\ v_{RL,x} \\ v_{RR,x} \\ v_{FR,x} \end{bmatrix} = \begin{bmatrix} 1 & -l'_{FL4,y} \\ 1 & -l'_{RL4,y} \\ 1 & -l'_{RR4,y} \\ 1 & -l'_{FR4,y} \end{bmatrix} \underbrace{\begin{bmatrix} ^{\mathcal{C}}v_{\mathcal{O},x} \\ ^{\mathcal{C}}\omega_{\mathcal{O},z} \end{bmatrix}}_{\text{Compensator input}} = \Psi {^{\mathcal{C}}\mathbf{V}}
\quad (8)
$$

$$
\text{where, } l'_{pq4,y} = \begin{bmatrix} 0 & 1 & 0 \end{bmatrix} \cdot {^{\mathcal{C}}_{\mathcal{O}}R} \cdot {^{\mathcal{O}}\vec{l}_{pq4}}
$$

where, the matrix Ψ denotes a Jacobian matrix for mapping linear and angular velocity of the frame $\{\mathcal{O}\}$ to the desired driving speeds. The reason why the distance vector $l'_{pq4,y}$ is included in Equations (6) and (8) is the distance from origin of the frame $\{\mathcal{O}\}$ to origin of the $pq4$ frame vary with passive rolling motion of driving track relative to the rockers as shown in Figure 3.

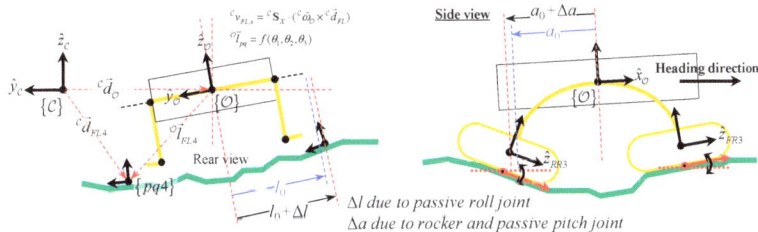

Figure 3. Variation of the transverse distances between the main body and driving track due to passive rolling motion of the driving track.

3.3. GEC Based Terrain Gradient Identification and Backward Velocity Propagation

The driving tracks are mechanically assembled with the main body through the passively articulated suspension. Thus, it is clear that the track driving speeds calculated from the planar SSMR kinematics cannot guarantee good posture tracking the performance of the MR at any arbitrary rough terrains, as shown in Figure 3, since the ICR changes according to the change in the relative pose of the driving track with respect to the main chassis. This can be referred to as the gradient effect (GE), inevitably caused by variations of the track-terrain contact angle (TTCA) in the rough terrain control.

3.3.1. Driving Speed Compensation

Figure 4 shows the overall GEC framework including feedback information from the suspension kinematics and MR. While the $^{\mathcal{C}}\mathbf{v}_{track} \in \mathbb{R}^4$ obtained from Equation (8) is a track speed to achieve the $^{\mathcal{C}}v_{\mathcal{O},x}$ and $^{\mathcal{C}}\omega_{\mathcal{O},z}$, it does not still include the relative orientation between the driving track and XY-plane of the frame $\{\mathcal{C}\}$.

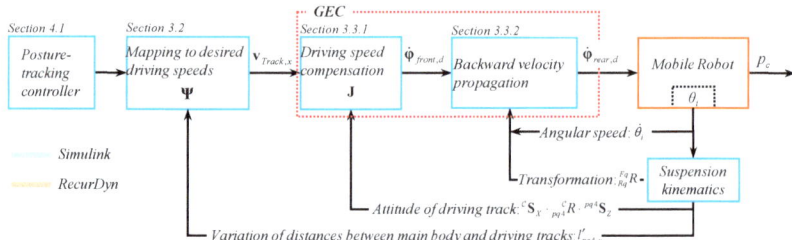

Figure 4. Detailed block diagram of the posture tracking control strategy of the proposed MR including the GEC with backward velocity propagation and feedbacks from the suspension kinematics.

For each driving track, the track angular speed $\dot{\varphi}_{pq}$ for the desired $^{\mathcal{C}}v_{pq,x}$ can be calculated through following Equation (9) considering the track-terrain contact angle (TTCA) relative to the frame $\{\mathcal{C}\}$.

$$^{\mathcal{C}}\mathbf{S}_x \cdot \left(^{\mathcal{C}}_{pq4}R^{pq4}\begin{bmatrix}0 & 0 & r\dot{\varphi}_{pq}\end{bmatrix}^T\right) = {}^{\mathcal{C}}v_{pq,x} \tag{9}$$

$$\text{Obtained from Eq.(6)}$$

where, r denotes an effective track radius and $^{\mathcal{C}}_{pq4}R$ denotes orientation of the driving track relative to the frame $\{\mathcal{C}\}$. Equation (9) can be rearranged to the following form:

$$\dot{\varphi}_{pq} = \left(r^{-1} \cdot \frac{1}{^{\mathcal{C}}\mathbf{S}_X \cdot {}^{\mathcal{C}}_{pq4}R \cdot {}^{pq4}\mathbf{S}_Z}\right) \cdot {}^{\mathcal{C}}v_{pq4,x} \tag{10}$$

The term $^{\mathcal{C}}\mathbf{S}_X \cdot {}^{\mathcal{C}}_{pq4}R$ denotes a direction cosine of the relative orientation of frame $\{pq4\}$ with respect to the frame $\{\mathcal{C}\}$ as shown in Figure 3. Then, by integrating Equations (8) and (10), a GE-compensated track angular speed $\dot{\varphi}_{pq}$ can be directly calculated from the $^{\mathcal{C}}\mathbf{V}$ As follows:

$$\dot{\varphi}_{pq} = (rK)^{-1}\begin{bmatrix}1 & -l'_{pq4,y}\end{bmatrix}\begin{bmatrix}^{\mathcal{C}}v_{\mathcal{O},x}\\ ^{\mathcal{C}}\omega_{\mathcal{O},z}\end{bmatrix} \tag{11}$$
$$\text{where, } K = {}^{\mathcal{C}}\mathbf{S}_X \cdot {}^{\mathcal{C}}_{pq4}R \cdot {}^{pq4}\mathbf{S}_Z$$

As a result, by applying Equation (11) to all driving tracks, the resultant relationship between the desired track angular speed vector $\dot{\varphi}$ and the MR velocity $^{\mathcal{C}}\mathbf{V}$ can be packaged as follow Equation (12).

$$\dot{\varphi} = \begin{bmatrix}\dot{\varphi}_{FL}\\ \dot{\varphi}_{RL}\\ \dot{\varphi}_{RR}\\ \dot{\varphi}_{FR}\end{bmatrix} = \begin{bmatrix}a_{FL} & -a_{FL}l'_{FL4,y}\\ a_{RL} & -a_{RL}l'_{RL4,y}\\ a_{RR} & -a_{RR}l'_{RR4,y}\\ a_{FR} & -a_{FR}l'_{FR4,y}\end{bmatrix} \cdot \begin{bmatrix}^{\mathcal{C}}v_{\mathcal{O},x}\\ ^{\mathcal{C}}\omega_{\mathcal{O},z}\end{bmatrix} = J{}^{\mathcal{C}}\mathbf{V} \tag{12}$$

$$\text{where, }\begin{cases}a_{pq} = (rK)^{-1}\\ ^{\mathcal{C}}_{pq4}R = {}^{\mathcal{C}}R_{\mathcal{O}}{}^{\mathcal{O}}R_{pq4} \in \mathbb{R}^{3\times 3}\end{cases}$$

Here, J denotes a Jacobian matrix for mapping the MR velocity expressed in frame $\{\mathcal{C}\}$ to the desired track angular speed vector.

3.3.2. Backward Velocity Propagation for Preventing Undesired Track Pitching

According to Equation (12), it is confirmed that the speeds of four driving tracks can be independently calculated for given MR velocity with respect to the frame $\{\mathcal{C}\}$. That is, when the postures of the driving track relative to the frame $\{\mathcal{C}\}$ are obtained from the suspension kinematics, the loss of driving speed due to the differences in attitude between the XY-plane of the frame $\{\mathcal{C}\}$, which is the reference frame of the planar SSMR kinematics, and the z-axis of the frame $\{pq4\}$ of the driving tracks can be successfully compensated. However, if the front and rear driving track on the same side are in different attitudes each other, the driving speeds obtained from Equation (11) will violate the SSMR kinematic assumptions in Equation (4). Additionally, this violation eventually leads to slippage in the ground due to differences in front and rear driving speeds on the same side. Then, either front or rear track can be unintentionally lifted up and lost their tractions between tracks and ground due to the inherent structural characteristics of the proposed MR.

An Intuitive way to resolve this issue inherently occurred in the passively tiltable structure is to impose new rear driving speeds dependent to the GEC-based front driving speeds, while maintaining to impose the GEC-based driving speeds to the front driving tracks and keep the holonomic constraints between the driving tracks and grounds. To calculate the rear driving speed generated by the front driving speed, we now choose the velocity propagation method in backward direction. A schematic diagram is detailed with a virtual single rigid link connecting two joints located in origins of the $\{Fq3\}$ and $\{Rq3\}$ in Figure 5. For given linear velocity of origin of the frame $\{Fq3\}$ and angular velocity of the link connecting $\{Fq3\}$ and $\{Rq3\}$, the linear velocity of origin of the frame $\{Rq3\}$ expressed in the frame $\{Rq3\}$ itself can be calculated by the backward velocity propagation in Equations (13)–(16). The linear velocity $^{Fq3}v_{Fq3}$ represents the front driving velocity obtained by the GEC. However, because it is impossible to directly calculate the angular velocity of the virtual link connecting $\{Fq3\}$ and $\{Rq3\}$ in Figure 5, a suspension based kinematic model from $\{Fq3\}$ to $\{Rq3\}$ should be developed for the actual backward velocity propagation. The coordinate frame assignment of the kinematic model is well detailed at Figure 5.

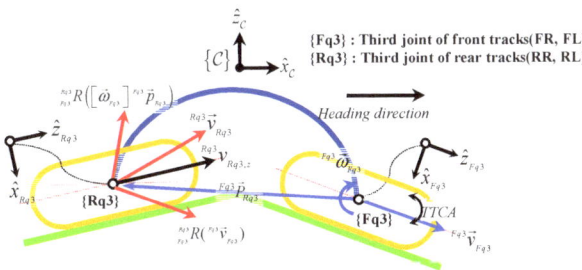

Figure 5. Schematic diagram of backward velocity propagation for calculating the rear driving speed in terms of the front driving speed.

To calculate the linear velocity of origin of the frame $\{Rq3\}$ expressed in the frame $\{Rq3\}$, we will now use Equation (13), starting from the frame $\{Fq3\}$, which is a based frame in this backward velocity propagation process, and has its linear velocity obtained from Equations (9)–(11). The linear velocity of the origin of frame $\{i+1\}$ is the same as that of the origin of frame $\{i\}$, plus additional velocity component caused by the angular velocity of the link connecting joint $\{i\}$ and $\{i+1\}$ as follows:

$$^{i}\vec{v}_{i+1} = {}^{i}\vec{v}_i + \vec{\omega}_i \times {}^{i}\vec{p}_{i+1} = {}^{i}\vec{v}_i + \left[\vec{\omega}_i\right] {}^{i}\vec{p}_{i+1} \tag{13}$$

Here, $^{i}v_{i+1}$ and $^{i}v_i$ denotes the linear velocity of the origin of frame $\{i+1\}$ and $\{i\}$ with respect to the frame $\{i\}$, respectively. $^{i}P_{i+1}$ is the position of the origin of frame

$\{i+1\}$ and $\{i\}$ with respect to the frame $\{i\}$. The matrix $\left[\vec{\omega}_i\right]$ is a 3×3 skew-symmetric matrix representation of the angular velocity vector ω_i of the link expressed in frame $\{i\}$. Then, the linear velocity of the origin of frame $\{Rq3\}$ relative to the frame $\{Fq3\}$ can be calculated as follows:

$$^{Fq3}\vec{v}_{Rq3} = {}^{Fq3}\vec{v}_{Fq3} + \left[\vec{\omega}_{Fq3}\right]{}^{Fq3}\vec{p}_{Rq3} \tag{14}$$

As mentioned earlier, because it is impossible to directly calculate the angular velocity of the link connecting $\{Fq3\}$ and $\{Rq3\}$ in Figure 5, a following formula using $SO(3)$ transformation from $\{Fq3\}$ to $\{Rq3\}$ is used to calculate the angular velocity. Then, the angular velocity can be calculated by multiplying a time derivative of the $SO(3)$ matrix by its transpose as follows:

$$\left[\vec{\omega}_{Fq3}\right] = \begin{bmatrix} 0 & -\omega_{Fq3,z} & \omega_{Fq3,y} \\ \omega_{Fq3,z} & 0 & -\omega_{Fq3,x} \\ -\omega_{Fq3,y} & \omega_{Fq3,x} & 0 \end{bmatrix} = {}^{Fq3}\dot{R}_{Rq3}{}^{Fq3}R_{Rq3}^T \tag{15}$$

After multiplying both sides of Equation (14) by $^{Fq3}_{Fq2}R^T$, the track angular speed can be obtained by the inner product of $^{Rq3}v_{Rq3}$ and $^{Rq3}S_Z = \begin{bmatrix} 0 & 0 & 1 \end{bmatrix}^T$ as follows:

$$\dot{\varphi}_{Rq3} = r_{track}^{-1} \left\{ S_{Rq3,z} \cdot {}^{Fq3}R_{Rq3}^T \left({}^{Fq3}\vec{v}_{Fq3} + \left[\vec{\omega}_{Fq3}\right]{}^{Fq3}\vec{p}_{Rq3} \right) \right\} \tag{16}$$

4. Verification of the Single GEC and Backward Velocity Propagation Combined GEC

4.1. Posture Tracking Controller

The reference velocity q_r and error posture p_e expressed in the ICR frame are selected as control inputs for the posture tracking controller, as shown in Figure 6. Since the position and the orientation of the MR can be measured with respect to the inertial frame using GPS and AHRS sensors, the following coordinate transformation should be conducted as shown in Equation (17):

$$^C p_e = {}^C \begin{bmatrix} x_e \\ y_e \\ \theta_e \end{bmatrix} = {}^C_I R \cdot {}^I (p_r - p_c) = {}^C_I R \cdot {}^I \begin{bmatrix} x_r - x_c \\ y_r - y_c \\ \theta_r - \theta_c \end{bmatrix} \tag{17}$$

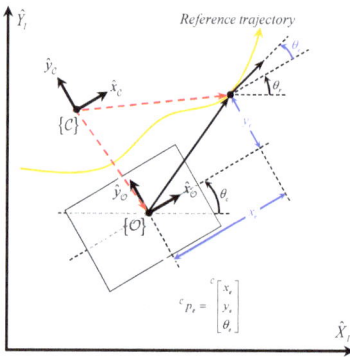

Figure 6. Posture error for the posture tracking controller.

The control algorithm shown in Equation (18) for posture tracking control is applied in this study as follows: The stability of the proposed posture tracking controller is based on the Lyapunov stability theorem, which provides a mathematical proof of the stability of the system. The stability of the proposed controller was already evaluated through both simulation and experimental results [20], which showed that the controller was able to maintain stability in a variety of operating conditions.

$$^C\mathbf{V} = \begin{bmatrix} ^Cv_{O,x} \\ ^C\omega_{O,x} \end{bmatrix} = C \begin{bmatrix} v_r \cos \theta_r + K_x x_e \\ \omega_r + v_r(K_y y_e + K_\theta \sin \theta_e) \end{bmatrix} \quad (18)$$

where K_x, K_y, and K_θ are positive constants, position error gains, and orientation error gains, respectively. The design of the controller gains was based on extensive testing and tuning, with the goal of finding the optimal balance between stability and performance.

4.2. Simulation

As shown in Figure 7, the performances of posture tracking control of the PASTRo with the proposed gradient effect compensator are verified in the RecurDyn-Simulink co-simulator. In this research, the maneuverability is chosen as the performance index for the posture-tracking control on rough terrain. All mechanical parameters of the PASTRo in the RecurDyn simulator are represented in Table 2.

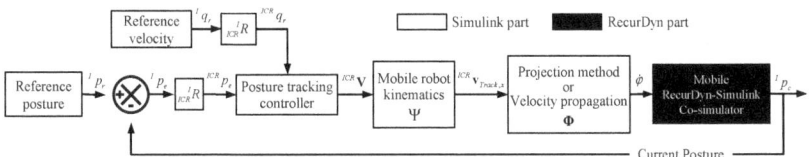

Figure 7. Overall simulation framework to verify the performance of the (1) TTCA-based driving velocity projection method and (2) velocity propagation driving velocity projection method based on the RecurDyn-Simulink co-simulator.

Table 2. Mechanical dimensions of 3D model of PASTRo for proposed simulation.

	Symbol	Unit	Value
Total mass		kg	1400.7
Main body mass		kg	512.8
Track mass		kg	470
Center of Mass	COM, x		0.03
	COM, y	mm	−0.12
	COM, z		−236.80
Total height	H1	mm	612
Total width	W1	mm	1670
Total length	L	mm	1760
Wheelbase	W2	mm	1377
Track diameter	D	mm	267.6
Track height	H2	mm	314.5
Track width	W3	mm	291
Roll joint height	H3	mm	90

The terrain and reference trajectory in these simulations are shown in Figure 8. The amplitude of the sinusoidal-shaped terrain is set to 629 mm, four times the driving track's height, and two times the total height of PASTRo, as shown in Table 3. The reference velocity remains constant at 1 m/s, the reference trajectory is set to a straight line, and its heading direction is set to an axis rotated 20 degrees about the z-axis of the inertial frame from the x-axis of the inertial frame, as shown in Figure 8. That is, the MR will traverse the sinusoidal terrain in diagonal with zero initial posture errors.

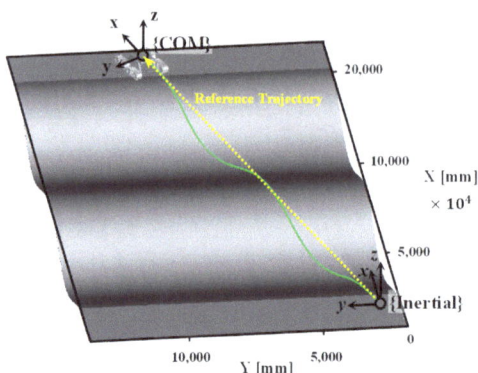

Figure 8. Reference trajectory and coordinate frames in the RecurDyn simulation model.

Table 3. Parameters of rough terrain and posture tracking controller for simulation.

Terrain	Total length	22,000 mm
	Total width	14,000 mm
	Amplitude	629 mm
	Period	8800 mm
Reference (in inertial frame)	Velocity	1000 mm/s
	Trajectory	Straight Line
Initial Posture (in inertial frame)	Position	Origin (0,0)
	Orientation	$\theta = 0$
Simulation	Sampling time	1 ms (Total 22 s)
	Step	22,000
Posture error gain	K_x	1
	K_y	10^{-6}
	K_θ	10^{-3}
Track Friction Coefficient	Dynamic	1
	Static	1.4

4.3. Performance Indices

Table 4 shows three conventional performance indices for the terrainability, maneuverability, and trafficability proposed by D. Apostopoulos [21], and these have been widely used to evaluate the performance of MRs.

Table 4. Previous works for evaluation of mobile robot mechanisms.

Author	Performance Index	Analysis Model	Driving Terrain
Takafumi Haji et al. [22]	Maneuverability	Dynamics model in 3D space	Flat ground
Michaud, S., & Richter, L [23]	Terrainability Trafficability	Dynamics model in 3D space	Stairs and blocks
Zhang, Peng et al. [24]	Terrainability Trafficability	Dynamics model in 3D space	blocks
Ding, Liang et al. [25]	Terrainability Maneuverability Trafficability	Dynamics model in 3D space	Rough terrains

Table 4. Cont.

Author	Performance Index	Analysis Model	Driving Terrain
Thueer, T., and Siegwart, R [26]	Terrainability	Dynamics model in 3D space	Stairs and blocks
Deng, Zongquan et al. [27]	Trafficability	Statics and kinematics model in 2D plane	Stairs and blocks
Gupta, A. K., & Gupta, V. K [28]	Terrainability Maneuverability	Dynamics model in 3D space	Stairs and slope
Nathaniel Steven Michaluk [29]	ESLV CESLV	Dynamics model in 2D plane	Blocks and slope
Paez, L., and Melo, K [30]	Terrainability, Maneuverability, Trafficability and Efficiency	Statics and kinematics model in 2D plane	Flat ground

These previous studies have shown that maneuverability is the most appropriate index to evaluate the posture-tracking performance of MRs. Haji [23] proposed maneuverability, distance, and heading angle error measures between the reference and actual trajectory in the XY-plane, and the two Haji indices and a position error in the y-direction were chosen as the performance indices in this study. The Haji indices are renamed as a distance error and a direction error, and the position error in the y-direction can be considered an offset distance error from the reference trajectory. The performance indices are described in the following Figure 9.

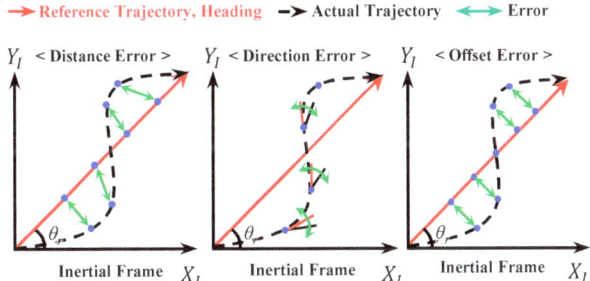

Figure 9. Definitions of the distance, direction and offset error for the maneuverability evaluation.

4.4. Simulation Results

For the comparison in this study, all parameters in the posture tracking control are equal. The distance, direction, and offset errors of a non-suspension version of the four-track SSMR and PASTRo are examined to verify the usefulness of the articulated suspension, as shown in Figure 10 and Table 5. While both the four-track SSMR and PASTRo show oscillatory behavior in all errors due to the terrain's sinusoidal geometries, all errors in PASTRo are confirmed to be much smaller than those of the non-suspension version of a four-track SSMR. The root-mean-square (RMS) values of the distance, direction, and offset errors and their percentage differences are presented in Table 5 for comparison.

Table 5. Maneuverability performance value.

Performance Index	4-Track SSMR	4-Track SSMR with Suspension	
RMS distance error [mm]	130.8	87.2	43.6 [33.3%]
RMS direction error [Deg]	4.8	2.1	2.7 [56.3%]
RMS offset error [mm]	111.3	63.2	48.1 [43.2%]

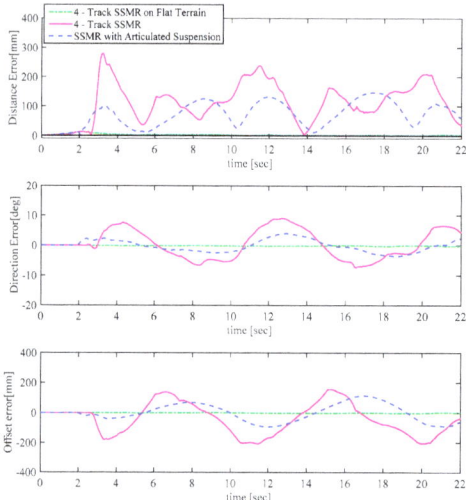

Figure 10. Comparison results of distance, direction, and offset errors of a non-suspension version of four track SSMR and PASTRo on flat and sinusoidal terrain: distance error, direction error, and offset error.

As shown in Table 5, the RMS distance, direction, and offset errors for PASTRo are 33.3, 56.3, and 43.2 percent smaller than the non-suspension version of the four-track MR, respectively. The proposed structural combination of a rocker and 2-DOF passive pitch-roll joints can improve posture tracking performance by maintaining a proper orientation in the driving tracks over rough terrain.

The distance, direction, and offset errors for PASTRo on the sinusoidal terrain are examined to compare the performance of the (1) TTCA-based driving velocity projection method and (2) velocity propagation-based driving velocity projection method. In addition, the three errors are also examined with conventional planar SSMR kinematics for comparison, as shown in Figure 11.

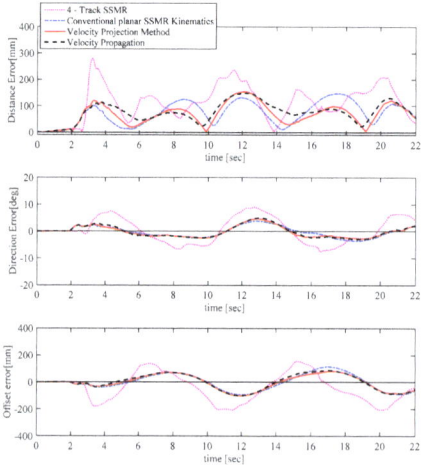

Figure 11. Comparison of maneuverability performances of the PASTRo in terms of the conventional SSMR kinematics, TTCA based driving velocity projection, and velocity propagation-based driving velocity projection methods on sinusoidal terrain: distance error, direction error, and offset error.

Table 6 shows that the RMS distance, direction, and offset errors of the TTCA driving velocity projection method are 8.8%, 3.8%, and 15.4%, smaller than those with conventional SSMR kinematics. The RMS distance, direction, and offset errors of the velocity propagation-based method are 3.31%, −3.33%, and 11.84% percent smaller than those with conventional SSMR kinematics, respectively. While the distance errors for both proposed methods in the downhill section are larger than those for conventional SSMR kinematics, the TTCA-based driving velocity projection-based method significantly improves the distance and offset errors.

1. No suspension + planar SSMR kinematics;
2. Suspension + planar SSMR kinematics;
3. Suspension + GEC w/o backward propagation;
4. Suspension + GEC w/backward propagation.

Table 6. Maneuverability performance value.

RSM Error	Four Track SSMR	PASTRo				
		Conventional Planar SSMR Kinematics	TTCA Based Driving Velocity Projection		Velocity Propagation Based Driving Velocity Projection	
Distance error [mm]	130.8	87.2 [** 33.3%]	79.5	[** 39.2%, * 8.8%]	84.3	[** 35.5%, * 3.3%]
Direction error [deg]	4.8	2.1 [** 56.3%]	2.0	[** 57.9%, * 3.8%]	2.2	[** 54.8%, * −3.3%]
Offset error [mm]	111.3	63.2 [** 43.2%]	53.5	[** 51.9%, * 15.4%]	55.7	[** 49.9%, * 11.8%]

* Percentage differences of RMS errors compared with the conventional planar SSMR kinematics. ** Percentage differences of RMS errors compared with results of the four track SSMR.

In fact, both velocity projection-based methods generate driving velocities larger than the planar SSMR kinematics to compensate for the tilting effects of driving tracks, and larger driving velocities in downhill sections lead to significant slippage and poor performance in terms of the distance and offset errors. On the contrary, the larger driving velocities in uphill sections lead to improved performance in the distance and offset errors.

In the case of the RMS direction error, the geometrical concept of the TTCA is the angle between the axes in the heading directions, so any information to compensate for errors in the heading direction is not included in both velocity projection-based methods. As a result, both methods do not show a significant performance improvement compared to the RMS direction error, even though the velocity propagation-based method shows a poor RMS direction error relative to planar SSMR kinematics. That is, any significant improvements in the maneuverability performance of PASTRo cannot be obtained from additional consideration of the violation of the assumption in Equation (4) of Section 3.1.

5. Discussion and Conclusions

This study compares the posture tracking performance for four-track SSMR and PASTRo in terms of the distance, direction, and offset errors under the RecurDyn-Simulink co-simulation framework. The posture-tracking errors for PASTRo are much smaller than those of the non-suspension version of a four-track mobile. Table 6 shows that PASTRo achieves a 33.3% lower RMS distance error, 56.3% lower RMS directional error, and 43.2% lower RMS offset error than the four-track SSMR, even with planar SSMR kinematics. Thus, these results confirm that the proposed structural combination of the rocker and passive pitch-roll joints can improve the posture-tracking performance on rough terrain.

The TTCA is calculated from the suspension kinematics to improve the posture tracking the performance of PASTRo without any further information on the rough terrain, and the obtained TTCA is used in both methods discussed in this study. The results indicate that PASTRo, with the TTCA-based driving velocity projection, achieves 39.2% lower RMS distance error, 57.9% lower RMS directional error, and 51.9% lower RMS offset error than the four-track SSMR. Additionally, PASTRo with velocity propagation-based driving velocity projection shows a 35.5% lower RMS distance error, 54.8% lower RMS directional error, and 49.9% lower RMS offset error than four track SSMR. The velocity propagation is confirmed to compensate for differences in front and rear driving velocities without significantly improving performance over the first method. In the case of the RMS direction error, the improvements in the direction error are not a result of either method but are due to the suspension structure of PASTRo.

The simulation results indicate that the TTCA-based driving velocity projection method used in this study can improve the RMS distance, direction, and offset errors of the four-track MR with a passively articulated suspension. In particular, when tracking the reference trajectories on arbitrarily rough terrain with a high elevation gap, the contribution of the first method and PASTRo will continue to increase as the elevation gap increases.

Author Contributions: Conceptualization, D.L.; methodology, D.L.; software, H.J.; validation, H.J.; formal analysis, D.L.; data curation, H.J.; writing—original draft preparation, D.L.; writing—review and editing, D.L.; visualization, H.J.; supervision, D.L. All authors have read and agreed to the published version of the manuscript.

Funding: This research was supported by the Basic Science Research Program through the National Re-search Foundation of Korea (NRF) funded by the Ministry of Education (NRF-2022 R1F1A1074704); Institute of Information & communications Technology Planning & Evaluation (IITP) grant funded by the Korea government (MSIT) (No. 2022-0-00218); the MSIT (Ministry of Science and ICT), Korea, under the Innovative Human Resource Development for Local Intellectualization support program (IITP-2022-RS-2022-00156360) supervised by the IITP (Institute for Information & communications Technology Planning & Evaluation); Korea Institute for Advancement of Technology (KIAT) grant funded by the Korea Government (MOTIE) (N000P0017033) and (N000P0017123).

Informed Consent Statement: Not applicable.

Data Availability Statement: Data sharing not applicable.

Conflicts of Interest: The authors declare no conflict of interest.

References

1. Lindemann, R.; Reid, L.; Voorhees, C. Mobility Sub-System for the Exploration Technology Rover. 1999. Available online: https://trs.jpl.nasa.gov/bitstream/handle/2014/17115/99-0537.pdf?sequence=1 (accessed on 8 January 2022).
2. NASA, Mars Rover Curiosity. 2015. Available online: http://www.nasa.gov/mission_pages/msl/index.html/ (accessed on 15 June 2022).
3. Lee, D.; Lee, S.; Ku, N.; Lim, C.; Lee, K.-Y.; Kim, T.-W.; Kim, J.; Kim, S.H. Development of a mobile robotic system for working in the double-hulled structure of a ship. *Robot. Comput. Integr. Manuf.* **2010**, *26*, 13–23. [CrossRef]
4. Kim, H.; Kim, D.; Yang, H.; Lee, K.; Seo, K.; Chang, D.; Kim, J. Development of a wall-climbing robot using a tracked wheel mechanism. *J. Mech. Sci. Technol.* **2008**, *22*, 1490–1498. [CrossRef]
5. Raibert, M.; Blankespoor, K.; Nelson, G.; Playter, R. Bigdog, the rough-terrain quadruped robot. *IFAC Proc. Vol.* **2008**, *41*, 10822–10825. [CrossRef]
6. Ma, J.; Susca, S.; Bajracharya, M.; Matthies, L.; Malchano, M.; Wooden, D. Robust multi-sensor, day/night 6-DOF pose estimation for a dynamic legged vehicle in GPS-denied environments. In Proceedings of the 2012 IEEE International Conference on Robotics and Automation, Saint Paul, MN, USA, 14–18 May 2012; pp. 619–626.
7. Yamauchi, B.M. PackBot: A versatile platform for military robotics. In Proceedings of the Unmanned Ground Vehicle Technology VI, Bellingham, WA, USA, 13–15 April 2004; pp. 228–237.
8. Lee, W.; Kang, S.; Kim, M.; Park, M. ROBHAZ-DT3: Teleoperated mobile platform with passively adaptive double-track for hazardous environment applications. In Proceedings of the 2004 IEEE/RSJ International Conference on Intelligent Robots and Systems (IROS) (IEEE Cat. No. 04CH37566), Sendai, Japan, 28 September–2 October 2004; pp. 33–38.
9. Zhang, D.; Gao, Z. Hybrid head mechanism of the groundhog-like mine rescue robot. *Robot. Comput.-Integr. Manuf.* **2011**, *27*, 460–470. [CrossRef]
10. DARPA. DARPA Robotics Challenge Program: 2012 to 2015. Available online: https://www.youtube.com/watch?v=mpsXQCHrAlM/ (accessed on 25 September 2015).
11. DARPA. DARPA Robotics Challenge 2015 Finals. Available online: https://www.youtube.com/watch?v=dv9Wm20UrcU/ (accessed on 6 October 2015).
12. Siegwart, R.; Lamon, P.; Estier, T.; Lauria, M.; Piguet, R. Innovative design for wheeled locomotion in rough terrain. *Robot. Auton. Syst.* **2002**, *40*, 151–162. [CrossRef]
13. Thueer, T.; Krebs, A.; Siegwart, R. Comprehensive locomotion performance evaluation of all-terrain robots. In Proceedings of the 2006 IEEE/RSJ International Conference on Intelligent Robots and Systems, Beijing, China, 9–15 October 2006; pp. 4260–4265.

14. Caracciolo, L.; De Luca, A.; Iannitti, S. Trajectory tracking control of a four-wheel differentially driven mobile robot. In Proceedings of the 1999 IEEE International Conference on Robotics and Automation (Cat. No. 99CH36288C), Detroit, MI, USA, 10–15 May 1999; pp. 2632–2638.
15. Kozłowski, K.; Pazderski, D. Modeling and control of a 4-wheel skid-steering mobile robot. *Int. J. Appl. Math. Comput. Sci.* **2004**, *14*, 477–496.
16. Shuang, G.; Cheung, N.C.; Cheng, K.E.; Lei, D.; Xiaozhong, L. Skid steering in 4-wheel-drive electric vehicle. In Proceedings of the 2007 7th International Conference on Power Electronics and Drive Systems, Bangkok, Thailand, 27–30 November 2007; pp. 1548–1553.
17. Tarokh, M.; McDermott, G.J. Kinematics modeling and analyses of articulated rovers. *IEEE Trans. Robot.* **2005**, *21*, 539–553. [CrossRef]
18. Kim, J.; Jeong, H.; Lee, D. Performance optimization of a passively articulated mobile robot by minimizing maximum required friction coefficient on rough terrain driving. *Mech. Mach. Theory* **2021**, *164*, 104368. [CrossRef]
19. Jeong, H.; Yu, J.; Lee, D. Track HM Design for Dynamic Analysis of 4-tracked Vehicle on Rough Terrain Using Recurd. *Trans. Korean Soc. Mech. Eng. A* **2021**, *45*, 275–283. [CrossRef]
20. Kanayama, Y.; Kimura, Y.; Miyazaki, F.; Noguchi, T. A stable tracking control method for an autonomous mobile robot. In Proceedings of the 1990 IEEE International Conference on Robotics and Automation, Cincinnati, OH, USA, 13–18 May 1990; pp. 384–389.
21. Apostolopoulos, D.S. *Analytical Configuration of Wheeled Robotic Locomotion*; Carnegie Mellon University: Pittsburgh, PA, USA, 2001.
22. Haji, T.; Kinugasa, T.; Yoshida, K.; Amano, H.; Osuka, K. Maneuverability of flexible mono-tread mobile track (FMT). In Proceedings of the 2009 ICCAS-SICE, Fukuoka, Japan, 18–21 August 2009; pp. 3427–3432.
23. Michaud, S.; Richter, L.; Thueer, T.; Gibbesch, A.; Huelsing, T.; Schmitz, N.; Weiss, S.; Krebs, A.; Patel, N.; Joudrier, L. Rover chassis evaluation and design optimisation using the RCET. In Proceedings of the ASTRA, 9th ESA Workshop on Advanced Space Technologies for Robotic and Automation, Noordwijk, The Netherlands, 28–30 November 2006.
24. Zhang, P.; Deng, Z.; Hu, M.; Gao, H. Mobility performance analysis of lunar rover based on terramechanics. In Proceedings of the 2008 IEEE/ASME International Conference on Advanced Intelligent Mechatronics, Xi'an, China, 2–5 July 2008; pp. 120–125.
25. Ding, L.; Gao, H.; Deng, Z.; Song, P.; Liu, R. Design of comprehensive high-fidelity/high-speed virtual simulation system for lunar rover. In Proceedings of the 2008 IEEE Conference on Robotics, Automation and Mechatronics, Chengdu, China, 21–24 September 2008; pp. 1118–1123.
26. Thueer, T.; Siegwart, R. Mobility evaluation of wheeled all-terrain robots. *Robot. Auton. Syst.* **2010**, *58*, 508–519. [CrossRef]
27. Deng, Z.; Fan, X.; Gao, H.; Ding, L. Influence analysis of terramechanics on conceptual design of manned lunar rover's locomotion system. In Proceedings of the 2011 International Conference on Electronic & Mechanical Engineering and Information Technology, Heilongjiang, China, 12–14 August 2011; pp. 645–648.
28. Gupta, A.K.; Gupta, V.K. Design and development of six-wheeled Multi-Terrain Robot. In Proceedings of the 2013 International Conference on Control, Automation, Robotics and Embedded Systems (CARE), Jabalpur, India, 16–18 December 2013; pp. 1–6.
29. Michaluk, N. *Design Methods for Cost-Effective Teams of Mobile Robots in Uncertain Terrain*; Massachusetts Institute of Technology: Cambridge, MA, USA, 2014.
30. Paez, L.; Melo, K. A preliminary review on metrics for modular snake robots locomotion. In Proceedings of the 4th Annual IEEE International Conference on Cyber Technology in Automation, Control and Intelligent, Hong Kong, China, 4–7 June 2014; pp. 539–545.

Disclaimer/Publisher's Note: The statements, opinions and data contained in all publications are solely those of the individual author(s) and contributor(s) and not of MDPI and/or the editor(s). MDPI and/or the editor(s) disclaim responsibility for any injury to people or property resulting from any ideas, methods, instructions or products referred to in the content.

Article

Autonomous Navigation System of Indoor Mobile Robots Using 2D Lidar

Jian Sun [1], Jie Zhao [2], Xiaoyang Hu [3,*], Hongwei Gao [2,4,*] and Jiahui Yu [5,*]

[1] School of Graduate, Shenyang Ligong University, Shenyang 110158, China
[2] School of Automation and Electrical Engineering, Shenyang Ligong University, Shenyang 110158, China
[3] School of Equipment Engineering, Shenyang Ligong University, Shenyang 110158, China
[4] China State Key Laboratory of Robotics, Shenyang Institute of Automation, Chinese Academy of Sciences, Shenyang 110017, China
[5] Department of Biomedical Engineering, Zhejiang University, Hangzhou 310058, China
* Correspondence: xiaoyang_hu@163.com (X.H.); ghw1978@sohu.com (H.G.); jiahui.yu@zju.edu.cn (J.Y.)

Abstract: Significant developments have been made in the navigation of autonomous mobile robots within indoor environments; however, there still remain challenges in the face of poor map construction accuracy and suboptimal path planning, which limit the practical applications of such robots. To solve these challenges, an enhanced Rao Blackwell Particle Filter (RBPF-SLAM) algorithm, called Lidar-based RBPF-SLAM (LRBPF-SLAM), is proposed. In LRBPF, the adjacent bit poses difference data from the 2D Lidar sensor which is used to replace the odometer data in the proposed distribution function, overcoming the vulnerability of the proposed distribution function to environmental disturbances, and thus enabling more accurate pose estimation of the robot. Additionally, a probabilistic guided search-based path planning algorithm, gravitation bidirectional rapidly exploring random tree (GBI-RRT), is also proposed, which incorporates a target bias sampling to efficiently guide nodes toward the goal and reduce ineffective searches. Finally, to further improve the efficiency of navigation, a path reorganization strategy aiming at eliminating low-quality nodes and improving the path curvature of the path is proposed. To validate the effectiveness of the proposed method, the improved algorithm is integrated into a mobile robot based on a ROS system and evaluated in simulations and field experiments. The results show that LRBPF-SLAM and GBI-RRT perform superior to the existing algorithms in various indoor environments.

Keywords: mobile robots; path planning; RBPF-SLAM; Lidar sensor; ROS system

MSC: 70B15

1. Introduction

In recent years, the widespread use of mobile robots for a variety of applications, such as rescue operations [1], household cleaning [2], and food service [3], has been facilitated by their high stability and affordability. To meet the needs of these applications, mobile robots require acquiring poses from Lidar sensors and building maps for environmental awareness, and then using path planning algorithms to determine travel trajectories. Mobile robots typically have three main functions: map building, positional estimation, and path planning. The main task of SLAM (Simultaneous Localization and Mapping) is to obtain real-time data from the robot's sensors in an unknown environment and construct a map, while also completing autonomous localization [4]. Moreover, after the localization and map building is completed, it is not feasible to manually set the walking path, which limits the robot's autonomy. Thus, we use SLAM technology to provide environmental information for path planning, helping mobile robots autonomously perform complex navigation tasks.

SLAM plays a crucial role in the field of mobile robotics, serving as a key precondition for the autonomous behavior and intelligence of mobile robots. The solution to SLAM can be mainly divided into two categories: the graph optimization [5–7] and the probabilistic estimation method [8]. The classical graph optimization algorithm is Karto SLAM [9], which solves the optimization problem through graph representation. Karto consists of three parts: front-end graph matching, back-end graph optimization, and loop closure detection. The loop closure detection reduces the drift of the map and ensures global consistency by recognizing loops and accordingly optimizing. Graph Optimization SLAM has the advantage of slow error accumulation and high robustness, but its disadvantages include a slow loop closure detection speed and the possibility of false loop closures. In addition to graph optimization, probabilistic estimation methods are also utilized to solve SLAM problems. Extended Kalman Filters (EKFs) are commonly applied by linearizing the system through a first-order Taylor expansion to address weakly nonlinear conditions [10]. However, EKFs can result in an erroneous pose and map estimates, especially under conditions of linearization error accumulation. On the other hand, Particle Filters (PF) can effectively handle nonlinear non-Gaussian probability estimation [11], but their complexity significantly increases as the spatial dimensionality increases. The RBPF SLAM [12] is a particle filter-based solution to SLAM problems that improves runtime by utilizing an accurate proposal distribution and selective resampling strategy [13], reducing the number of required particles. GMapping [14] is a probabilistic estimation algorithm that inputs odometry information and Lidar sensor measurements, producing the robot's pose and occupancy grid maps. The prediction of the proposed distribution function in RBPF-SLAM is based on odometry data, making it difficult to incorporate additional information in the Monte Carlo localization framework. Furthermore, the instability of the proposed distribution function, based on odometry, makes it challenging to eliminate motion uncertainty in large environments and long-term tasks. To address these challenges, some studies have proposed FastSlam [15], a combination of RBPF and EKF, to improve particle distribution.

Path planning is a critical component of mobile robot navigation [16], and its goal is to determine a feasible and optimal path for the robot to travel from a starting position to a goal position while avoiding obstacles in its environment. Path planning algorithms are mainly divided into graph-based search algorithms and sampling-based algorithms. Graph-based search algorithms use a graph representation of the search space to plan paths for mobile robots. These algorithms perform a search of the graph to find the optimal path from the starting position of the robot to the goal position while avoiding obstacles. The most common graph-based search algorithms are A* [17], Dijkstra [18], and D* [19]. The A* algorithm is a heuristic search algorithm that finds the shortest path from the starting position to the goal position by using a heuristic function to evaluate the next state. However, the A* algorithm requires additional storage space to maintain a set of open points, which can result in memory overhead. The Dijkstra algorithm is a classic shortest-path algorithm that finds the shortest path between any two points in a graph. The algorithm works by gradually relaxing the edge weights and updating the distance estimates of vertices. However, the time complexity of the Dijkstra algorithm is $O(n^2)$, where n is the number of vertices in the graph, and when the graph is large, the efficiency of the algorithm can be severely affected. The D* algorithm combines the advantages of the A* algorithm and the Dijkstra algorithm. The algorithm is capable of re-planning in real time according to the changing environment, which makes it well suited for dynamic and uncertain environments.

The sampling-based algorithm is an algorithm that finds the optimal path by random sampling method. This algorithm finds the optimal path by randomly selecting a point in space as the starting or ending point, and then continues expanding the nodes in space when the expansion reaches the target point. The rapidly exploring random tree (RRT) [20] algorithm is a popular and efficient algorithm in the field of sampling-based path planning. The RRT algorithm uses a random sampling method to explore the search space, so it can effectively avoid local optimum problems [21]. However, RRT requires sampling and searching the entire graph, and many redundant random nodes are generated near each node, increasing the corresponding search time and leading to slower convergence. One of the main advantages of the bidirectional rapidly exploring random tree (Bi-RRT) [22,23] algorithm is its efficiency compared to RRT algorithms. Since the trees are simultaneously expanded in both directions, the search space can be reduced by half, which can significantly reduce the search time. However, the Bi-RRT algorithm may not be able to find the optimal solution in complex environments with high-dimensional state spaces. This is because the algorithm relies on the random sampling method, which may not effectively cover all parts of the state space and may not promptly find the optimal solution. Many scholars have proposed improved methods based on the Bi-RRT algorithm; Xu et al. presented a post-processing fusion algorithm [24], which combines PRM and P-Bi-RRT algorithms. Compared to RRT, Bi-RRT, and P-Bi-RRT algorithms, this algorithm has shown improved results in terms of planning time, path length, and the number of path nodes. Yi et al. proposed the 1-0Bg-RRT algorithm [25], which uses a biased probability of 1 and 0 changes to construct a tree, resulting in shorter computation time and paths compared to traditional RRT algorithms. Jiankun Wang et al. presented a kino dynamically constrained Bi-RRT with efficient branch pruning algorithm [26]. This algorithm extends the Bi-RRT method by incorporating kino dynamic constraints, leading to improved performance. Grothe et al. presented the Space-Time RRT (ST-RRT*) algorithm [27]; ST-RRT* can effectively handle unbounded time-space and optimize arrival time in environments with moving obstacles on known trajectories. Huanjie Zhao. et al. proposed an Improved Bi-RRT algorithm based on Gaussian sampling [28]. This algorithm introduces heuristic search ideas based on bidirectional search, sample points with a Gaussian distribution constrained with a certain probability near the start, and goal points to reduce the blind search and improve search efficiency. Guojun Ma et al. presented a new algorithm for path planning named Probabilistic Smoothing Bi-RRT (PSBi-RRT) [29]. The proposed algorithm utilizes a θ-cut mechanism to optimize the path toward the global optimal solution, reducing the possibility of getting stuck in local optima. In comparison to the traditional Bi-RRT algorithm, PSBi-RRT exhibits a significant reduction in runtime with improved performance.

Based on the above analysis, we propose improvements to the simultaneous SLAM algorithm and the path planning algorithm. The distribution function in RBPF is susceptible to external factors such as robot tire skidding, resulting in suboptimal map construction. In contrast, Lidar navigation is highly stable because it is highly resistant to environmental noise. For this reason, we propose the LRBPF-SLAM algorithm, where the odometer data in the distribution function are replaced with the bit pose differences of adjacent moments from the 2D Lidar to improve the stability and accuracy of map construction. In addition, the Bi-RRT algorithm ignores the redundant computation due to the selection of random nodes. We improve the Bi-RRT algorithm by using target bias sampling to reduce invalid searches and combining the path reorganization strategy to minimize redundant path points and generate smooth trajectories. In summary, the contributions of this paper are as follows:

1. We embed the proposed algorithm into the ROS system [30] to verify the effectiveness of the algorithm;
2. In order to improve the stability and accuracy of the SLAM system, an algorithm called LRBPF-SLAM is proposed. In this algorithm, the odometer data in the distribution function is replaced by the 2D Lidar adjacent moment bit pose difference;
3. The GBI-RRT algorithm is proposed, which employs target bias sampling to reduce the negative impact of random sampling on path quality, and then optimizes the initial paths through a path reorganization strategy to eliminate redundant paths;
4. Extensive simulations were conducted to evaluate the improved algorithms, and the proposed algorithms were also ported to a mobile robot for real scenario experiments. The results of these experiments demonstrate that the proposed method exhibits

excellent performance compared to other algorithms in both simulation and real scenarios.

2. Robot Components and System Framework

The system we use is an advanced mobile robot navigation system equipped with sensors for environmental perception and data measurement. The main hardware used in this system is the NVIDIA Jetson Nano, which has sufficient processing capabilities to perform task planning. Additionally, it is equipped with an OpenCRP controller based on the STM32F4 core and an MPU6050 Inertial Measurement Unit (IMU) sensor that can be updated through ISP serial and implements closed-loop control for four DC motors. The robot is also equipped with the SICK A1 TK edition Lidar, with a range of 12 m and a measurement frequency of 8000 times per second, as well as an encoder that converts analog signals into electrical signals to obtain distance and angle data. The size of the mobile robot for navigation is 28 cm × 12 cm × 12 cm and weighs 2.3 kg, rated power is 60 W, and the linear velocity and acceleration are 1.2 m/s and 0.5 m/s, respectively. The physical structure of the robot is shown in Figure 1.

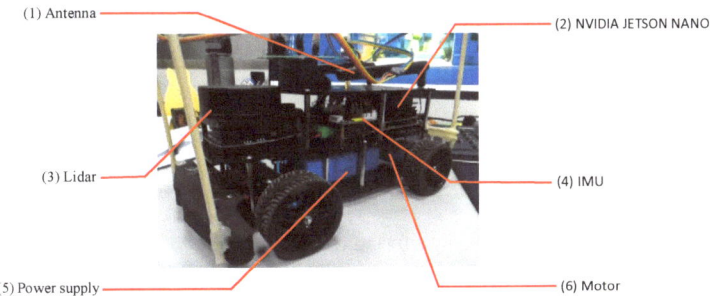

Figure 1. The physical structure of the robot. (1) The "Antenna" is utilized for transmission of communication protocols. (2) The "NVIDIA JETSON NANO" is utilized for receiving commands from the PC and running algorithms. (3) The "Lidar" is utilized for sensing the surrounding environment. (4) The "IMU" is utilized for acquiring the current attitude angles. (5) The "Power supply" sustains the operation of the moving robot by providing electrical energy. (6) The "Motor" is utilized for driving the movement of the robot.

The system control structure of the robot is shown in Figure 2.

1. The PC Module: The PC terminal uses a laptop and connects to the host computer on the same LAN via SSH (Secure Shell). Commands can be directly sent from the PC to the mobile robot host computer to achieve SLAM and navigation functions;
2. The Decision Module: The decision module is the host computer of the robot, namely NVIDIA Jetson Nano, which has an SSH tool installed with the ROS system to receive commands from the PC and run algorithms. It receives Lidar data through a USB interface, communicates I/O with the lower computer, and acquires sensor data connected to the lower computer;
3. The Execution Module: The execution module is a controller with STM32F4 as its core, which receives commands from the decision-making module, acquires data from the IMU and encoders, and controls motor drive operations;
4. The Sensor Module: The sensor module includes 2D Lidar for detecting the surrounding environment, IMU for estimating the motion posture of the robot, and encoders for estimating the robot's motion distance and rotation angle;
5. The Power Module: The power voltage is 12 V with a total capacity of 1200 mAh. The power expansion board can expand the 12 V power and 5 V output to facilitate the expansion of robot functions;
6. The Motor Drive Module: The motor drive module is responsible for controlling the movement of the robot, receiving control commands, and driving the motor

through current control. It includes the drive circuit, current sensor, and control circuit, ensuring the precise and stable movement of the robot.

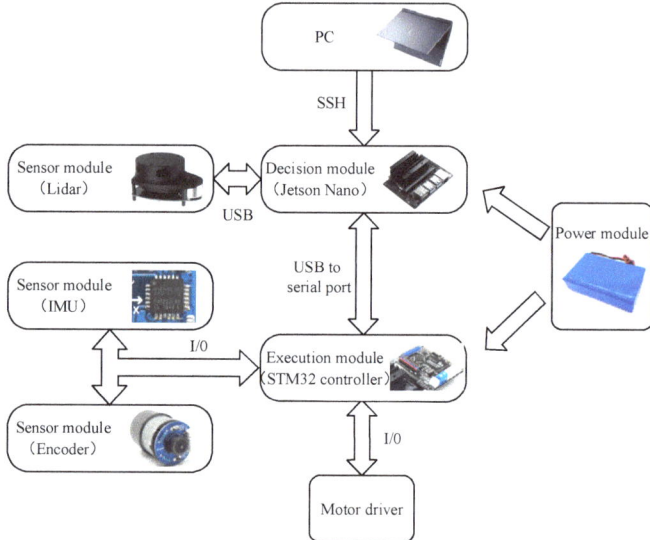

Figure 2. The system control structure of robot.

In the design of a robot navigation system, multiple critical steps are covered, including data conversion, SLAM mapping, and path planning. We designed a comprehensive robot navigation system framework to realize the navigation capability. This framework implements distributed communication through the ROS system, thereby enabling the collaboration between SLAM mapping and navigation path planning, and allowing for node publication and subscription, further improving the efficiency and reliability of the system. The flow of the robot navigation system framework is illustrated in Figure 3. The robot navigation can be divided into the following four steps:

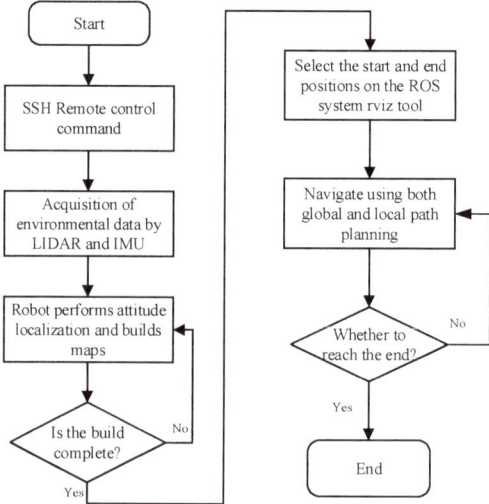

Figure 3. Framework flow of robot navigation system.

1. Install the Ubuntu operating system and ROS system on the robot and PC side, use the SSH remote control tool to realize the connection between the PC and the robot, and control the robot through PC input commands;
2. After receiving the PC command, the robot locates and builds a map using the data from the Lidar, and when the mapping is completed, the map is saved in the robot;
3. After starting the navigation command, the starting point and the end point are selected on the Rviz (a 3D visualization tool) visualization tool of ROS, and the robot autonomously plans the navigation path using the data from Lidar. The global path planning realizes safe and reliable path planning, and local path planning realizes real-time obstacle avoidance;
4. When the robot arrives at the destination, the navigation ends. If it does not reach the destination, it continues to navigate using the data from Lidar until it reaches the destination.

3. Algorithm Improvement

3.1. LRBPF-SLAM Algorithm

To better understand the proposed LRBPF-SLAM, we briefly review the basic principles of the RBPF. The RBPF-SLAM is an improved version of the particle filter. RBPF is a technique for reducing computational costs by lowering the dimensionality of the state space through the use of the chain rule. This is achieved by factoring the joint distribution of the variables into conditional distributions, which can be separately updated, resulting in improved computational efficiency. The problem of SLAM for RBPF involves the estimation of the posterior probability and posterior probability as shown in Equation (1).

$$p(m, x_{1:t}|z_{1:t}, u_{1:t}) = p(x_{1:t}|z_{1:t}, u_{1:t-1})p(m|x_{1:t}, z_{1:t}) \tag{1}$$

Where $p(m, x_{1:t}|z_{1:t}, u_{1:t})$ is the posterior probability, the estimated joint posterior probability $p(x_{1:t}|z_{1:t}, u_{1:t})$ represents the distribution of the motion trajectory of a mobile robot, $p(m|x_{1:t}, z_{1:t})$ is the posterior map generated by particles using the occupancy grid mapping algorithm to create a two-dimensional planar map of the environment. m represents the grid map of the environment, $x_{1:t}$ denotes the motion trajectory of the mobile robot, $z_{1:t}$ is the sensor observations from 1 to t moments, $u_{1:t}$ is the odometry measurements in the odometer. The estimation of the robot's true pose can be achieved using the $z_{1:t}$ and $u_{1:t}$ parameters. The specific steps of RBPF are shown below:

1. Sampling: The particle at the previous moment $x^i_{1:t-1}$ is sampled from the distribution function to acquire new particles $x^i_{1:t}$. The distribution function obtained by the sensor is often termed the proposed distribution:

$$\pi(x^i_t|x^i_{1:t-1}, z_{1:t}, u_{1:t-1}) \tag{2}$$

2. Importance weighting: Each particle x^i_t is assigned a weight ω^i_t, which is computed as the ratio of the posterior distribution to the proposal distribution (based on the probabilistic odometry motion model). The higher the weight, the more the particle's pose matches the true value. The importance weighting can be defined using Formula (3).

$$\omega^i_t = \frac{p(x^i_{1:t}|z_{1:t}, u_{1:t-1})}{\pi(x^i_{1:t}|z_{1:t}, u_{1:t-1})} \tag{3}$$

3. Resampling: Particles with smaller weights are discarded and replaced by resampled particles, but the total number of particles remains constant.
4. Map updating: Each particle's map is updated using the optimized pose represented by the particle and the current observations.

RBPF can effectively reduce the dimensionality of the state space and improve the particle quality. However, the proposed distribution based on odometry may suffer from increasing errors over time. As the Lidar signal has a single-peak characteristic and a small variance coefficient, it is more suitable to use it as the input to the proposed distribution function. To improve the accuracy of the proposed distribution, we augment the original odometry data by adding the position differences derived from the 2D Lidar data at adjacent time steps. The RBPF algorithm usually uses odometer data as the proposed distribution function:

$$\pi(x_t^i | x_{1:t-1}^i, z_{1:t}, u_{1:t-1}) = p(x_t^i | x_{t-1}^i, u_{t-1}) \tag{4}$$

IMU is a sensor used for attitude estimation. Typically consisting of an accelerometer, gyroscope, and magnetometer, it measures the acceleration, angular velocity, and magnetic field strength of an object in three axes. In attitude estimation, the IMU plays a key role by providing real-time attitude information that allows us to track the position, orientation, and motion of the object. However, the odometer data from the IMU can be affected by robot vibration, drift, and sliding. Lidar can provide higher spatial resolution and accuracy to ensure the accuracy of attitude estimation. LRBPF uses the Lidar positional difference as a distribution function, as shown in Equations (5) and (6).

$$p(x_t^i | x_{t-1}^i, z_t) = x_{t-1}^i + h_t(z_t, z_{t-1}) \tag{5}$$

$$h_t = z_t - z_{t-1} \tag{6}$$

where h_t is the Lidar attitude difference between adjacent moments.

3.2. GBI-RRT Algorithm

To gain a better understanding of the proposed algorithm, it is necessary to first review the RRT and the Bi-RRT algorithms. Figure 4 shows the planning process of the RRT algorithm, where q_{init} and q_{goal} represent the start and target nodes of the random tree, q_{rand} is the random node generated by each sampling point, and q_{near} is the closest node to q_{rand} on the tree, q_{new} is a new node obtained after collision detection, which is obtained by growing from q_{near} to q_{rand} with step size ε. The RRT principle diagram is shown in Figure 4.

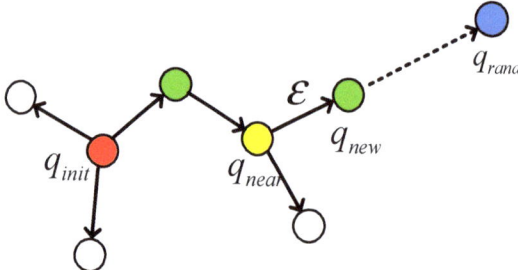

Figure 4. RRT principle diagram.

The RRT algorithm begins by selecting the q_{init} as the root node of the random tree growth. Next, q_{rand} is generated within the safe space. Then, the algorithm searches for the node q_{near} that is closest to q_{rand}, with q_{near} initially set to q_{init}. Starting from q_{near}, the random tree moves ε steps in the direction of q_{rand} to obtain a new node q_{new}. This process is repeated until the Euclidean distance between q_{init} and q_{goal} is less than a predetermined threshold, at which point the search is terminated. The resulting path is the extended tree path from the initial node q_{init} to the target node q_{goal}. The expansion rule for the new node in the RRT algorithm is expressed by Equation (7).

$$q_{new} = q_{near} + \varepsilon \frac{q_{rand} - q_{near}}{\|q_{rand} - q_{near}\|} \tag{7}$$

where $q_{rand} - q_{near}$ represents the normalization of two vectors, and $\|q_{rand} - q_{near}\|$ represents the Euclidean distance between two points. When the target node q_{goal} is added to the random tree or the number of iterations exceeds the specified threshold of iterations, the path planning will end with the corresponding result.

Although the RRT algorithm is better than the traditional algorithm in complex environments, its one-way search approach implies that it takes longer to reach the endpoint. To address this issue, the Bi-RRT algorithm was developed, which enables a two-way search. The Bi-RRT algorithm is shown in Figure 5:

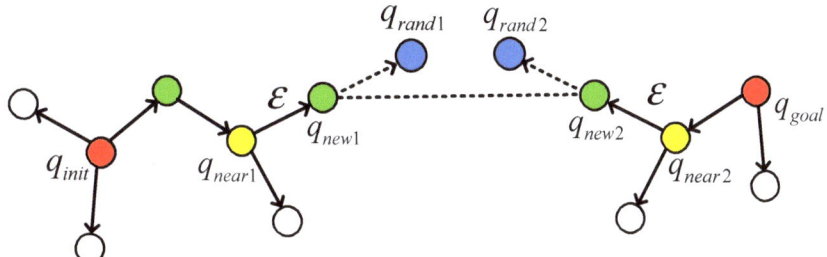

Figure 5. Bi-RRT principle diagram.

The Bi-RRT algorithm constructs two random trees T_1 and T_2 in the environment state space, using the same node generation method as the basic RRT algorithm. T_1 has the root node as the initial node, while T_2 has the target point as the initial node. The Bi-RRT algorithm process is shown in Algorithm 1.

Algorithm 1 presents the fundamental Bi-RRT algorithm. First, the algorithm initializes the random tree T_1 using q_{init} and then initializes the random tree T_2 using q_{goal}. To extend the random tree outward, the *Sample*() function is designed to return a sample point q_{rand}. Then, the *Extend*() function searches for the nearest node in the random tree and grows toward node q_{rand} in steps ε, generating a new node q_{new}. Subsequently, if q_{new} passes collision detection, it is added to the random tree T. If q_{new} is the same for both random trees, then the loop terminates.

Compared with the RRT algorithm, the Bi-RRT algorithm reduces the search time while retaining the advantages of the RRT algorithm. However, both algorithms have a common drawback: both randomly generate expansion points, resulting in poor search path quality [31]. Based on this, we propose an improved Bi-RRT algorithm to reduce the algorithm's blindness in the node expansion phase by introducing target bias sampling, generating random points with a higher probability towards the target point. Additionally, we propose a path reorganization strategy to address the low-quality generated paths by removing redundant nodes and optimizing the path state.

Algorithm 1: BI-RRT(q_{init}, q_{goal})

1 $T_1.add(q_{init}); T_2.add(q_{goal}); i = 0;$
2 while($i < N$)
3    $q_{rand1} = $ Sample();
4    $q_{rand2} = $ Sample(); $i++;$
5    $q_{new1} = Extend(T_1, q_{rand1})$
6    $q_{new2} = Extend(T_2, q_{rand2})$
7   if $q_{new1} = q_{new2}$ then
8   return Path(T_1, T_2)
9   Swap(T_1, T_2)

---

1. Target bias sampling

The random sampling process of the Bi-RRT algorithm employs a global random search strategy, which generates a significant number of redundant random points and increases the length of the robot movement path. The path planning process can only be accelerated when the random tree grows toward the target point, so the target point can be considered as the sampling point. However, if the target point is selected as the only sampling point, the generated random tree may become trapped in a dead loop around the obstacles. To address this issue, we propose a target bias sampling that combines random search and target-oriented search. This strategy effectively guides the random tree to grow towards the target with a higher probability while avoiding interference from obstacles.

Figure 6 illustrates the GBI-RRT algorithm, which begins by selecting an initial point q_{init}. During each iteration, the system generates a random number p_{rand}. If p_{rand} is less than the given threshold p_{bias}, the algorithm generates a random point within the safe space $SampleFree()$. Otherwise, the random point is set to the target point coordinates. To implement the target bias sampling, we use Equation (8), which effectively guides the random tree to grow towards the target with a higher probability while avoiding obstacles.

$$q_{rand} = \begin{cases} q_{goal}, & \text{if } p_{rand} > p_{bias} \\ q_{SampleFree()}, & \text{else} \end{cases} \tag{8}$$

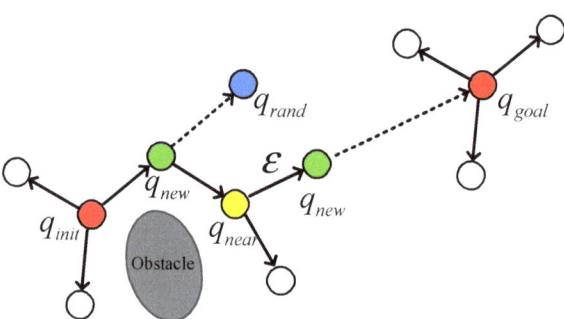

Figure 6. Bi-RRT random tree constructed by adding target bias sampling. The direction of the dashed line represents the random tree growth direction.

In the above Equation (8), P_{bias} represents the target bias threshold, P_{rand} represents that the random sampling probability range is (0, 1), and $q_{SampleFree()}$ represents the random point generated by the safe space.

Once the random node q_{rand} is obtained, we use a target bias sampling to guide the extension of the random tree towards the target point with a growth step of ε. This strategy promotes an explicit expansion direction for the random tree, which preserves the global expansion property of the RRT algorithm and allows the node expansions to spread across the state space. Moreover, the target bias sampling enables the preservation of local node properties on top of the global expansion properties, increasing the likelihood that the random tree will expand towards the target point. However, choosing an appropriate value for the threshold P_{bias} is crucial. A value that is too large can result in an expansion probability towards the target point that is too small to have a significant effect on the expansion speed, while a value that is too small can result in an overly large expansion probability towards the target point that is prone to local minima in environments with many obstacles. After experimental analysis, we set P_{bias} to 0.5.

The random growth function for the random tree to expand towards the target direction is shown in Equation (9).

$$X(n) = \varepsilon \frac{q_{near} - q_{goal}}{\|q_{near} - q_{goal}\|} \tag{9}$$

where ε denotes the step size when expanding towards the target point and $\|q_{near} - q_{goal}\|$ denotes the Euclidean distance between q_{near} and q_{goal}.

In addition, the random growth function $Y(n)$ for the random tree to randomly expand and avoid obstacles in the safe space is given by:

$$Y(n) = \varepsilon \frac{q_{SampleFree()} - q_{near}}{\|q_{SampleFree()} - q_{near}\|} \quad (10)$$

Therefore, by combining Equations (8)–(10), we can obtain the equation for generating a new node using the target bias sampling as follows:

$$q_{new} = \begin{cases} q_{near} + X(n), & \text{if } p_{rand} > p_{bias} \\ q_{near} + Y(n), & \text{else} \end{cases} \quad (11)$$

At this point, the calculation of the new node q_{new} not only takes into account the influence of the random sampling node q_{rand}, but also the gravitation of the target point q_{goal}. The threshold value P_{bias} plays a crucial role in determining the expansion direction. When the generated random sampling point is close to an obstacle, it may cause the newly generated node to collide with the obstacle, leading to expansion failure and getting stuck in a dead loop. If P_{rand} is larger than P_{bias}, the selected random point P_{rand} satisfies the requirement of expanding towards the target point and enables the system to approach the target point more quickly. On the other hand, when P_{rand} is smaller than P_{bias}, the selected random point q_{rand} no longer satisfies the requirement of expanding directly towards the target point, and random sampling points will be generated for expansion. By doing so, the expanded tree can bypass obstacles and reach the end point more efficiently.

2. Path reorganization strategy

In the Bi-RRT algorithm, the nearest tree node is determined by calculating the Euclidean distance from a random point to a tree node. However, this approach may result in zigzag node paths for the concatenated tree nodes, and such unsmooth paths are not optimal for mobile robot travel because they increase unnecessary steering time [32]. Even with a target bias sampling incorporated, the paths generated by the Bi-RRT algorithm may still contain many redundant nodes. Therefore, path reorganization strategies are needed to optimize the generated paths and obtain higher quality paths.

As shown in Figure 7, in path planning with multiple nodes, the distance through path $q_{init} \to b$ is less than the distance through $q_{init} \to a \to b$; the distance through $b \to d$ is less than the distance through $b \to c \to d$; and the distance through $d \to q_{goal}$ is less than the distance through $d \to e \to f \to q_{goal}$. Therefore, in the final path planning process, the redundant nodes a, c, e, and f can be removed. The node $q_{init} \to b \to d \to q_{goal}$ forms the optimal path, which only has a few key points, and thus improves the smoothness of the path and shortens the travel time of the mobile robot.

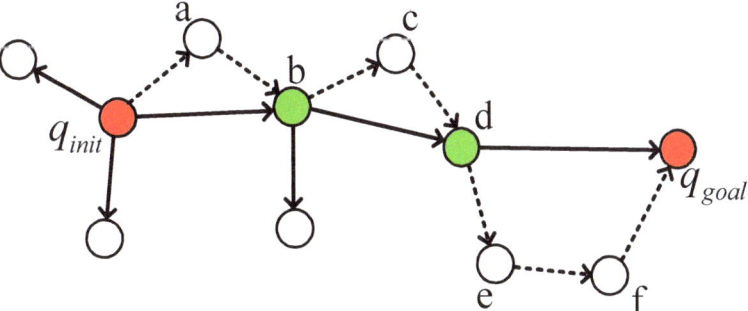

Figure 7. Path reorganization strategy.

The process of the path reorganization strategy is shown in Algorithm 2, where $keypoints$ represents the set of key points. Starting from the initial node q_{init}, we traverse its children nodes for collision detection. Only the node q_{temp} closest to the end point q_{goal} is kept and added to the *keypoints*. Then, q_{temp} is used as the initial node for the next traversal.

Algorithm 2: *GetKeyPoints(path)*

---
1 $q_{temp} = q_{init}$;
2 $while(q_{temp}! = q_{goal})$
3    $for(x = q_{temp}; q! = q_{init}; x = q_{temp}.child)$
4      $if\ CheckLine(x, q_{temp})$
5        $q_{temp} = x$;
6        $keypoints.add(q_{temp})$;

---

4. Simulation Experiments of Robots

In this section, we compare and analyze two common SLAM algorithms and two path planning algorithms in a simulated environment. To visualize the performance of the algorithms, we construct maps using Rviz.

4.1. Simulation Platform

To evaluate the effectiveness of the LRBPF-SLAM algorithm in terms of mapping accuracy, we conducted simulation experiments on the Gazebo platform [33] using Ubuntu 18.04 and ROS systems. The study focused on three simulated indoor environments and used the TurtleBot3 Burger virtual robot model. The simulated sensor data included Lidar, odometer, and IMU data. The simulation was carried out on a laptop computer equipped with an Intel i7-11800H processor and 16 GB DDR4 3200 MHz memory. The simulation environment was designed to replicate realistic physical characteristics, making it a reliable reference for real-world application environments. Environment modeling of the Gazebo simulation platform is shown in Figure 8.

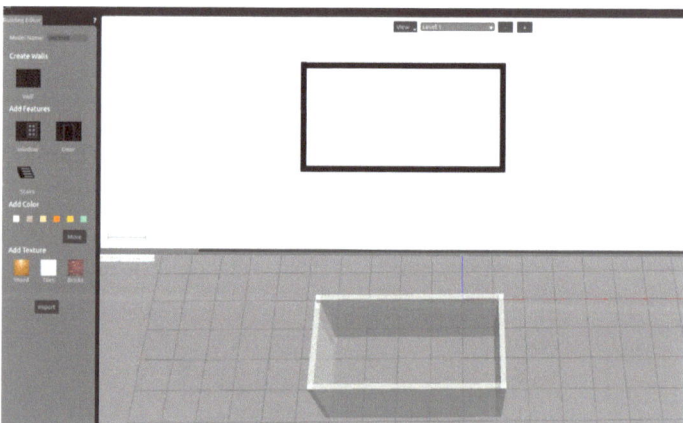

Figure 8. Environment modeling of Gazebo simulation platform.

4.2. Simulation Experiment of SLAM Algorithm

The simulation experiments of SLAM were constructed on Gazebo with three environments of different complexity for map building simulation. The different environment experiments could more accurately reflect the building effect and generalization ability of the proposed algorithm. Simulation environment 1 had a length and width of 11.25 m × 6.75 m, with regular surroundings and geometrical wall obstacles inside, to test the algorithm's building effect on geometrically shaped objects. Simulation environment 2 was 13.5 m × 8.5 m in length and width, and there were right-angle wall obstacles inside, which were used to test the algorithm's effect on building the details of corner-shaped objects. The overall simulation environment 3 was 11.85 m × 9.75 m, surrounded by irregular walls, and the internal obstacle objects were also irregular, testing the algorithm for the irregular walls and the building effect of the objects that account for the object. We compared the proposed algorithm with the Gmapping and Karto algorithms and visualized the map building results using the Rviz tool. The results of the SLAM simulation experiments for building maps are shown in Figure 9.

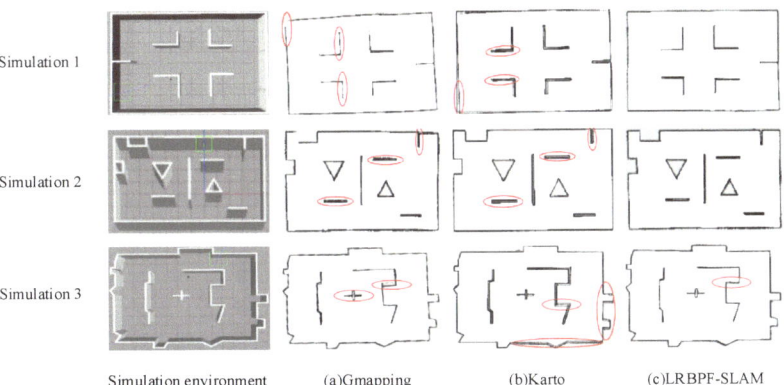

Figure 9. SLAM simulation results of three algorithms.

It can be seen from the three groups of simulation experiments that (a) the Gmapping algorithm distorts and makes a lot of noise in the wall and vertical obstacle construction, which is mainly caused by using single odometer data as the input of the distribution function. The (b) Karto algorithm is relatively good in the overall drawing effect, but in some details, the problem of wall overlap will appear. This is because the Karto algorithm is a graph optimization algorithm, which requires multiple loopback detection to optimize the result of graph construction. The (c) LRBPF-SLAM algorithm achieves satisfactory performance in the overall mapping effect and details, which benefits from using the Lidar data bit pose difference as the input of the distribution function, thus improving the mapping accuracy.

In addition to the subjective evaluation, we selected several feature points of the simulation environment for dimensional measurements and then compared the errors. The error results of the SLAM simulation experiments are analyzed in Table 1.

Based on the comparison of the feature locations between the actual and measured values by the three algorithms, we obtained the error of each feature location, as shown in Table 1. From the table, we can see that the average errors of simulation 1, simulation 2, and simulation 3 of the Gmapping algorithm are 10.4 cm, 6.4 cm, and 17.59 cm, respectively, which are relatively large and become larger as the length of the measured object increases. Simulation 1, simulation 2, and simulation 3 of the Karto algorithm have average errors of 9.34 cm, 7.64 cm, and 19.45 cm, respectively, the error of the Karto algorithm in measuring the feature size is larger. The average errors of simulation 1, simulation 2, and simulation 3 of the improved algorithm are 6.9 cm, 2.85 cm, and 11.27 cm, respectively. It can be seen that the improved algorithm always maintains smaller errors in terms of error control and has higher accuracy than the other algorithms.

Table 1. SLAM simulation experiment error results analysis.

Simulation	Feature Point	Actual Value/cm	Gmapping		Karto		LRBPF-SLAM	
			Measured Value/cm	Absolute Error/cm	Measured Value/cm	Absolute Error/cm	Measured Value/cm	Absolute Error/cm
1	1	100.00	97.99	2.01	98.48	1.52	100.86	0.86
	2	175.00	188.15	13.15	185.60	10.60	182.33	7.33
	3	325.00	341.03	16.03	340.91	15.91	337.50	12.50
	Mean	-	-	10.40	-	9.34	-	6.90
2	1	200.00	208.29	8.29	208.57	8.57	201.72	1.72
	2	225.00	216.00	9.00	231.32	6.32	228.88	3.88
	3	200.00	196.71	3.29	204.78	4.78	197.84	2.16
	4	125.00	131.14	6.14	136.52	11.52	128.02	3.02
	5	175.00	169.71	5.29	182.02	7.02	178.45	3.45
	Mean	-	-	6.40	-	7.64	-	2.85
3	1	300.00	316.00	16.00	315.74	15.74	312.05	12.05
	2	225.00	252.80	27.80	249.47	24.47	2370	12.00
	3	350.00	367.35	17.35	378.11	28.11	363.40	13.40
	4	300.00	316.00	16.00	319.64	19.64	308.10	8.10
	5	400.00	410.8	10.80	409.29	9.29	410.80	10.80
	Mean	-	-	17.59	-	19.45	-	11.27

4.3. Simulation Experiment of GBI-RRT Algorithm

In order to verify the effectiveness and search efficiency of the proposed GBI-RRT algorithm, we conducted simulations in three different environments using MATLAB2019. The simulated maps are represented with black for obstacles and white for safe space. We compared the performance of the RRT algorithm, the Bi-RRT algorithm, and the GBI-RRT algorithm by simulating each algorithm 30 times with the same parameters, including a fixed step size of 14 and identical start and end point locations. The simulated map had a horizontal coordinate range of (0, 500) and a vertical coordinate range of (0, 500).

Figure 10 presents the path planning results obtained from the (a) RRT, (b) Bi-RRT, and (c) GBI-RRT algorithms in the three simulated environments. Figure 10 indicates that the RRT and Bi-RRT algorithms produce a large number of unnecessary nodes scattered throughout the simulated map, resulting in discontinuous path curvature. However, the GBI-RRT algorithm generates a smoother planning path with fewer turning points.

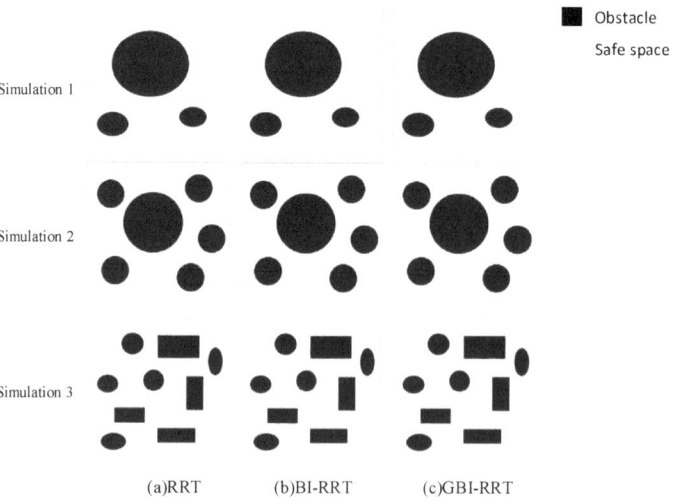

Figure 10. Results of path planning simulation experiment.

Table 2 shows the path planning times and lengths obtained using the RRT, Bi-RRT, and GBI-RRT algorithms. The results indicate that the RRT algorithm requires a much longer time to plan the path in all three simulation environments than the other two methods, especially in the complex obstacle simulated environment 3 where the longest planning time reaches 110.5 s. This is mainly due to the blindness of the expansion of the RRT algorithm. In contrast, Bi-RRT uses bi-directional search for speed optimization, which reduces the planning time to some extent. However, using the same random expansion strategy as RRT does not significantly improve the final path length, with only about a 6 m improvement in simulated environment 1.

Table 2. Comparison of the results of 30 experiments averaged over three path planning algorithms. The bold font indicates the optimal value.

Simulation	Algorithm	Time/s	Length/m
1	RRT	58.79	860.24
	Bi-RRT	16.18	854.30
	GBI-RRT	**5.08**	**674.45**
2	RRT	98.88	880.39
	Bi-RRT	13.19	859.37
	GBI-RRT	**5.46**	**679.21**
3	RRT	110.50	803.90
	Bi-RRT	5.28	777.35
	GBI-RRT	**4.84**	**594.14**

It is worth noting that the GBI-RRT algorithm probabilistically grows towards the target point with the help of the proposed target bias sampling, resulting in a significant reduction in planning time compared to the previous two. It performs well in all three environments with an average planning time of about 5 s. The path length is further optimized by using a path reorganization strategy for the already planned paths, with an average reduction of about 181 m compared to the previous two.

Figures 11 and 12 show the line graphs depicting the planning time and planning paths obtained by the GBI-RRT algorithm in 30 experiments across three environments. From the plots, it can be observed that the planning time is generally stable within a certain range, while the planning path length fluctuates within a certain range, indicating good performance.

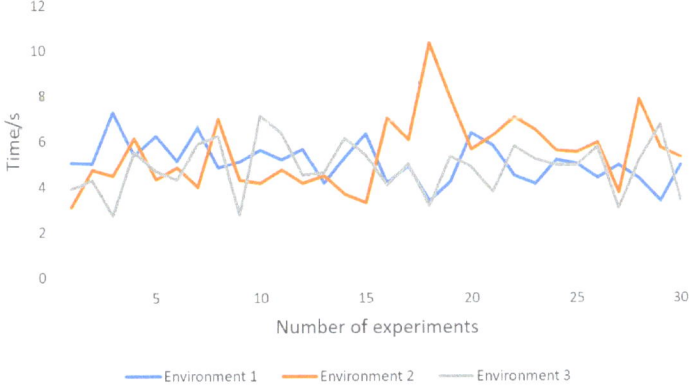

Figure 11. Planning time of 30 times GBI-RRT algorithm in three environments.

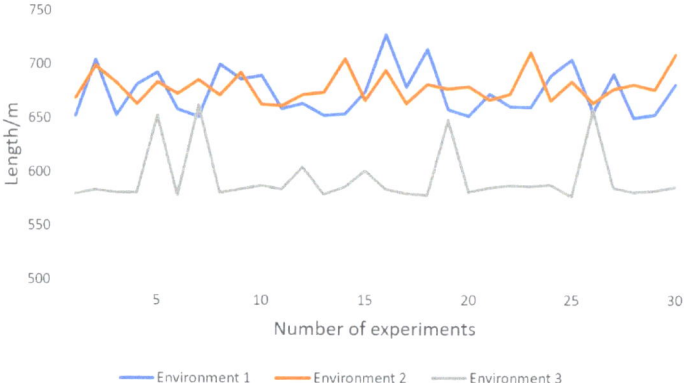

Figure 12. Planning path length of 30 times GBI-RRT algorithm in three environments.

5. Real Scenario Experiments for Robots

5.1. Real Scenario Experiment Setup

We use the distributed framework of the ROS platform to perform robotic tasks. The framework enables communication between nodes through a loosely coupled approach and is able to run on different computers. The robot and the computer must be on the same LAN to enable remote control of the robot via SSH commands. In addition, we provide a visual interface to make the control of the robot more intuitive by operating it from the computer terminal. This configuration greatly improves the flexibility and operability of the robot tasks.

Our specific configuration is as follows:

1. Host controller Jetson Nano and laptop are connected to the same network. A hotspot network on the phone is used to cover the robot's movement area.
2. The "ifconfig" command is used to check the IP addresses of the Jetson Nano and the laptop.
3. In the Ubuntu system of the laptop, the environment variables "ROS_MASTER_URI" and "ROS_HOSTNAME_URI" are added to the "bashrc" file. "ROS_MASTER_URI" points to the IP address of the Jetson Nano, while "ROS_HOSTNAME_URI" points to the IP address of the Ubuntu system on the laptop.
4. Finally, the robot is remotely accessed using SSH commands in the Ubuntu system terminal for visual remote control. This remote access method makes the robot more visible and makes it easier for the operator to control. These configuration measures greatly improved the efficiency and flexibility of the robot's tasks.

5.2. Experiment of SLAM Algorithm

In our practical experimental study, we conducted SLAM experiments in three real scenarios. Environment 1 is an indoor bedroom measuring 4.5 × 4.5 m, featuring obstacles such as cabinets, refrigerators, and tables. Environment 2 is a corner corridor with a total length of 15 m and a width of 2.5 m, containing obstacles such as regular wooden doors and irregular walls. Environment 3 is a conference room with a space of 4.5 × 6 m, featuring obstacles such as tables, chairs, uneven walls, and monitor stands. This scene is characterized by a high obstacle density. By performing experiments in these diverse real scenarios, we can more effectively evaluate the proposed method's effectiveness.

According to the experimental results in Figure 13, it can be seen that the (a) Gmapping algorithm underperforms in all three scenes with low building accuracy, blurred obstacle contours, the ghosting phenomenon in local details, incomplete wall building, and an inability to identify support legs of many chairs. In comparison, the (b) Karto algorithm can build complete maps in all three scenes, but with average reconstruction of local details. However, the (c) LRBPF-SLAM algorithm outperforms both algorithms with the best overall map-building effect in all three scenes without the ghosting phenomenon. In the complex conference room environment, the algorithm can fully scan wall contours, recognize chair support legs with high accuracy, and build highly precise detailed maps.

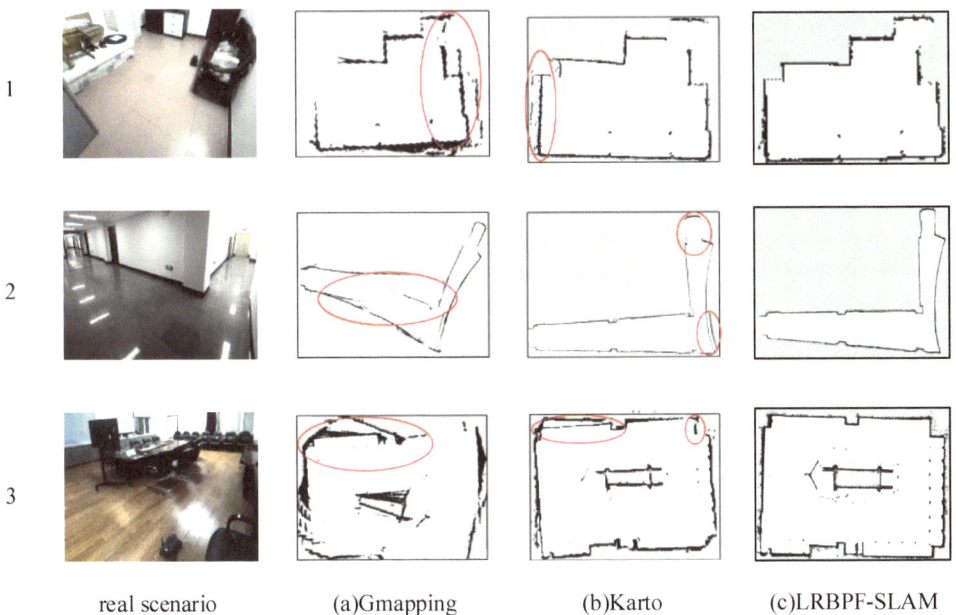

Figure 13. SLAM results of three algorithms in real scenarios.

Furthermore, we selected several typical feature locations in the real scenarios and compared their real values with the measured values, producing error results analysis tables.

According to the data in Table 3, it can be found that the average error of the Gmapping algorithm in the three different environments is 3.44 cm, 8.95 cm, and 6.74 cm, respectively. It is worth noting that the maximum error of the algorithm in feature location 3 of experiment 3 reaches 12.9 cm; in comparison, the average error of the Karto algorithm in these three environments is 3.83 cm, 6.04 cm, and 5.86 cm. The LRBPF-SLAM algorithm, on the other hand, exhibits the best accuracy, with average errors of 2.63 cm, 4.33 cm, and 2.74 cm in the three environments, and the maximum error is only 7.5 cm in feature 1 of experiment 2. The algorithm is also able to accurately reconstruct the details of the environment. The experimental results show that the proposed LRBPF-SLAM algorithm has a small overall error and high accuracy in map building, and can effectively reconstruct the overall state of the environment. From these data, it can be concluded that the LRBPF-SLAM algorithm has significant advantages, especially in complex environments that show better performance.

Table 3. SLAM experimental error results analysis in real scenes. The bold font indicates the optimal value.

Experiment	Feature Point	Gmapping			Karto		LRBPF-SLAM	
		Actual Value/cm	Measured Value/cm	Absolute Error/cm	Measured Value/cm	Absolute Error/cm	Measured Value/cm	Absolute Error/cm
1	1	42.00	45.30	**3.30**	45.48	3.48	46.92	4.92
	2	41.00	47.11	6.11	50.94	9.94	46.92	4.92
	3	50.00	48.92	1.08	49.12	0.88	50.55	0.55
	4	112.00	108.72	3.28	110.98	1.02	111.89	0.11
	Mean	-	-	3.44	-	3.83	-	2.63
2	1	139.00	151.00	12.00	149.60	8.30	146.50	7.50
	2	115.00	126.40	11.40	124.35	7.35	121.00	6.00
	3	84.00	92.60	5.60	93.00	3.20	89.40	2.40
	4	104.00	114.80	10.80	112.90	5.70	111.20	5.10
	5	115.00	131.30	7.80	127.70	8.50	118.60	3.60
	6	57.00	63.10	6.10	60.20	3.20	58.40	1.40
	Mean	-	-	8.95	-	6.04	-	4.33
3	1	57.00	64.30	5.30	53.60	3.40	59.10	2.10
	2	41.00	47.80	6.80	45.60	7.60	42.50	1.50
	3	370.00	382.90	12.90	379.80	9.80	378.70	5.20
	4	43.00	46.50	3.50	39.90	3.10	44.80	1.80
	5	39.00	42.20	5.20	43.50	4.50	42.10	3.10
	Mean	-	-	6.74	-	5.68	-	2.74

5.3. Experiment of Path Planning Algorithm

We compare the path planning results of the RRT, Bi-RRT and GBI-RRT algorithms in three different real scenarios.

As Figure 14 shows, the map of the three experimental sites obtained from the experiments in the previous section, the starting and ending points of the mobile robot are set. Table 4 shows the experimental data of path planning for the three algorithms RRT, Bi-RRT, and GBI-RRT. To minimize the error, the experimental data represent the average value of 20 experiments.

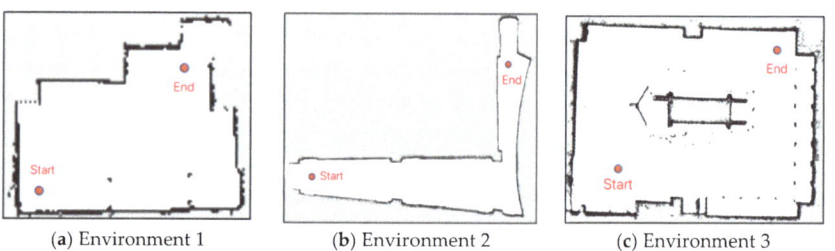

(a) Environment 1 (b) Environment 2 (c) Environment 3

Figure 14. Three experimental maps.

As shown in Table 4, the 20 experiments were conducted for three real scenarios, and then their averages were taken for path planning quality analysis.

In the simple Environment 1, the RRT and Bi-RRT algorithms require an average of 2.65 and 2.5 turns, respectively, while GBI-RRT requires only 0.45 turns on average, and the other two metrics (time and length) differ less among the three algorithms. In Environment 2, the number of turns increases for all three algorithms. Nevertheless, GBI-RRT outperforms the other two algorithms in terms of path planning time and length, with 5.1 and 3.75 s less time than RRT and Bi-RRT, respectively, and less difference in planning length between the three algorithms. In Environment 3, compared with Bi-RRT, the path planning time of GBI-RRT is reduced by 3.15 s, the path planning length is reduced by 2.35 m, and the number of turns is reduced by 2.2 turns. These results show that the GBI-RRT algorithm can quickly generate a smooth and optimal path from the origin to the destination.

Table 4. Quality analysis of three algorithms for path planning in three different environments. The bold font indicates the optimal value.

Environment	Algorithm	Time/s	Length/m	No. of Turns
1	RRT	6.95	5.97	2.65
	Bi-RRT	6.90	5.96	2.50
	GBI-RRT	**4.55**	**5.24**	**0.45**
2	RRT	31.25	18.14	7.55
	Bi-RRT	29.90	17.31	7.20
	GBI-RRT	**26.15**	**16.42**	**4.75**
3	RRT	17.95	11.29	4.85
	Bi-RRT	17.70	11.05	4.70
	GBI-RRT	**14.55**	**8.70**	**2.50**

5.4. Robot Navigation Process

Figure 15 depicts the autonomous navigation process of the robot, which is conducted within a known map constructed by SLAM. Connect to the computer through the ssh command to control the robot, run the navigation command and select the map path, and then start the visualization tool Rviz.

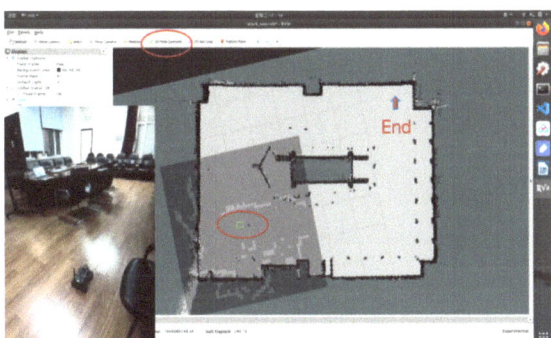

Figure 15. Initial position and pose of navigation robot.

As shown in Figure 15, the lower left corner depicts the pose of the robot in the real environment. The red circle located on the top menu bar is the 2D Pose Estimate that is utilized to determine the robot's initial pose, with the red circle marked on the map representing the determined initial pose. The shaded square surrounding the robot denotes the local cost map, which represents the area for local path planning. By selecting the navigation endpoint in the upper right corner of the map, the robot can execute autonomous navigation operations.

Figure 16 is the robot's initial pose and planning information during the movement process. The yellow line segment situated in front of the robot represents the local path planning Dynamic Window Approach (DWA) algorithm [34]. Whenever the robot approaches an obstacle, the DWA algorithm executes obstacle avoidance processing by selecting a safe path around the obstacle. Meanwhile, the long red line segment indicates the path planned by the global path planning GBI-RRT. Finally, in Figure 17, the robot arrives at its destination, concluding the navigation.

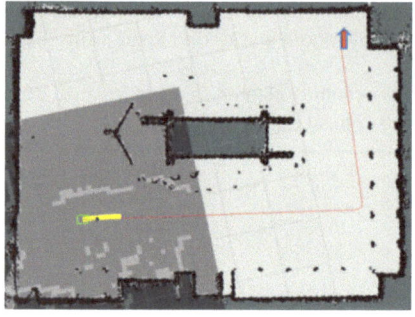 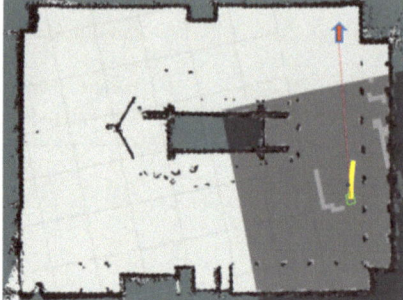

(**a**) Initial planning information. (**b**) Motion process planning information.

Figure 16. Mobile Robot Status Information.

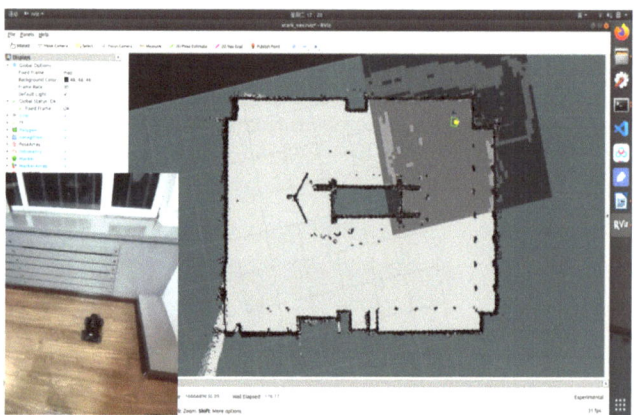

Figure 17. End point posture.

6. Conclusions

This study proposes an enhanced LRBPF-SLAM and GBI-RRT path planning algorithm to improve the navigation of autonomous mobile robots in indoor environments. LRBPF-SLAM overcomes the limitations of traditional distribution functions by utilizing Lidar data, resulting in more accurate pose estimation of the robot. GBI-RRT incorporates target bias sampling to efficiently guide nodes towards the goal, reducing ineffective searches. The path reorganization strategy further improves navigation efficiency by eliminating low-quality nodes and improving path curvature. The proposed method is evaluated in simulations and field experiments, and the results demonstrate superior performance compared to existing algorithms. Future research could focus on applying the currently proposed methods to more complex environments to better address the challenges of the real world. Researchers can also consider how to improve model speed and accuracy more effectively, and apply these algorithms to other fields.

Author Contributions: Conceptualization, J.S., J.Y. and X.H.; methodology, J.S. and J.Z.; software, J.Z.; validation, J.Z.; formal analysis, J.S.; investigation, H.G.; resources, H.G.; data curation, J.Z.; writing—original draft preparation, J.S.; writing—review and editing, X.H.; visualization, J.S.; supervision, J.Y.; project administration, X.H.; funding acquisition, X.H. All authors have read and agreed to the published version of the manuscript.

Funding: This work was supported by the [Liaoning Province Higher Education Innovative Talents Program #1] under Grant [number LR2019058] and [Liaoning Province Joint Open Fund for Key Scientific and Technological Innovation Bases #2] under Grant [number 2021-KF-12-05].

Data Availability Statement: Data sharing not applicable, No new data were created or analyzed in this study. Data sharing is not applicable to this article.

Acknowledgments: The authors would like to acknowledge support from the following projects: Liaoning Province Higher Education Innovative Talents Program Support Project (Grant No. LR2019058), Liaoning Province Joint Open Fund for Key Scientific and Technological Innovation Bases (Grant No.2021-KF-12-05) and Zhejiang Provincial Natural Science Foundation of China (LQ23F030001).

Conflicts of Interest: The authors declare no conflict of interest.

References

1. Py, F.; Robbiani, G.; Marafioti, G.; Ozawa, Y.; Watanabe, M.; Takahashi, K.; Tadokoro, S. SMURF software architecture for low power mobile robots: Experience in search and rescue operations. In Proceedings of the 2022 IEEE International Symposium on Safety, Security, and Rescue Robotics (SSRR), Sevilla, Spain, 8–10 November 2022; pp. 264–269. [CrossRef]
2. Sui, L.; Lin, L. Design of Household Cleaning Robot Based on Low-cost 2D LIDAR SLAM. In Proceedings of the 2020 International Symposium on Autonomous Systems (ISAS), Guangzhou, China, 6–8 December 2020; pp. 223–227. [CrossRef]
3. Farooq, M.U.; Eizad, A.; Bae, H.-K. Power solutions for autonomous mobile robots: A survey. *Robot. Auton. Syst.* **2023**, *159*, 104285. [CrossRef]
4. Ismail, H.; Roy, R.; Sheu, L.-J.; Chieng, W.-H.; Tang, L.-C. Exploration-Based SLAM (e-SLAM) for the Indoor Mobile Robot Using Lidar. *Sensors* **2022**, *22*, 1689. [CrossRef]
5. Gao, L.; Dong, C.; Liu, X.; Ye, Q.; Zhang, K.; Chen, X. Improved 2D laser slam graph optimization based on Cholesky decomposition. In Proceedings of the 2022 8th International Conference on Control, Decision and Information Technologies (CoDIT), Istanbul, Turkey, 17–20 May 2022; Volume 1, pp. 659–662.
6. Hampton, B.; Al-Hourani, A.; Ristic, B.; Moran, B. RFS-SLAM robot: An experimental platform for RFS based occupancy-grid SLAM. In Proceedings of the 2017 20th International Conference on Information Fusion (Fusion), Xi'an, China, 10–13 July 2017.
7. Juric, A.; Kendes, F.; Markovic, I.; Petrovic, I. A Comparison of Graph Optimization Approaches for Pose Estimation in SLAM. In Proceedings of the 2021 44th International Convention on Information, Communication and Electronic Technology (MIPRO), Opatija, Croatia, 27 September–1 October 2021; pp. 1113–1118. [CrossRef]
8. Dhaoui, R.; Rahmouni, A. Mobile Robot Navigation in Indoor Environments: Comparison of Lidar-Based 2D SLAM Algorithms. In *Design Tools and Methods in Industrial Engineering II: Proceedings of the Second International Conference on Design Tools and Methods in Industrial Engineering, ADM 2021, Rome, Italy, 9–10 September 2021*; Springer International Publishing: Berlin/Heidelberg, Germany, 2021; pp. 569–580.
9. Konolige, K.; Grisetti, G.; Kümmerle, R.; Burgard, W.; Limketkai, B.; Vincent, R. Efficient sparse pose adjustment for 2D map-ping. In Proceedings of the 2010 IEEE/RSJ International Conference on Intelligent Robots and Systems, Taipei, Taiwan, 18–22 October 2010; pp. 22–29.
10. Ribeiro, M.I. Kalman and extended kalman filters: Concept, derivation and properties. *Inst. Syst. Robot.* **2004**, *43*, 3736–3741.
11. Talwar, D.; Jung, S. Particle filter-based Localization of a mobile robot by using a single Lidar sensor under SLAM in ROS environment. In Proceedings of the 2019 19th International Conference on Control, Automation and Systems (ICCAS), Jeju, Republic of Korea, 15–18 October 2019; Volume 43, pp. 3736–3741. [CrossRef]
12. Cai, Y.; Qin, T. Design of Multisensor Mobile Robot Vision Based on the RBPF-SLAM Algorithm. *Math. Probl. Eng.* **2022**, *2022*, 1518968. [CrossRef]
13. Dai, Y.; Zhao, M. Grey Wolf Resampling-Based Rao-Blackwellized Particle Filter for Mobile Robot Simultaneous Localization and Mapping. *J. Robot.* **2021**, *2021*, 4978384. [CrossRef]
14. Tee, Y.K.; Han, Y.C. Lidar-based 2D SLAM for mobile robot in an indoor environment: A review. In Proceedings of the 2021 International Conference on Green Energy, Computing and Sustainable Technology (GECOST), Miri, Malaysia, 7–9 July 2021; pp. 1–7. [CrossRef]
15. Maziarz, B.; Domański, P.D. Customized fastSLAM algorithm: Analysis and assessment on real mobile platform. *Nonlinear Dyn.* **2022**, *110*, 669–691. [CrossRef]
16. Muhammad, A.; Ali Mohammed, A.H.; Turaev, S.; Abdulghafor, R.; Shanono, I.H.; Alzaid, Z.; Alruban, A.; Alabdan, R.; Dutta, A.K.; Almotairi, S. A Generalized Laser Simulator Algorithm for Mobile Robot Path Planning with Obstacle Avoidance. *Sensors* **2022**, *22*, 8177. [CrossRef]
17. LaValle, S.M. Rapidly-exploring random trees: A new tool for path planning. *Annu. Res. Rep.* **1998**.
18. Dijkstra, E.W. A Note on Two Problems in Connexion with Graphs. In *Edsger Wybe Dijkstra: His Life, Work, and Legacy*; ACM: New York, NY, USA, 2022; pp. 287–290. [CrossRef]
19. Jin, J.; Zhang, Y.; Zhou, Z.; Jin, M.; Yang, X.; Hu, F. Conflict-based search with D* lite algorithm for robot path planning in unknown dynamic environments. *Comput. Electr. Eng.* **2023**, *105*, 108473. [CrossRef]
20. Liu, B.; Liu, C. Path planning of mobile robots based on improved RRT algorithm. *J. Phys. Conf. Ser.* **2022**, *2216*, 012020. [CrossRef]
21. Pohl, I. *BI-Directional and Heuristic Search in Path Problems*; Stanford Linear Accelerator Center: Menlo Park, CA, USA, 1969.
22. Li, Z.; Li, L.; Zhang, W.; Wu, W.; Zhu, Z. Research on Unmanned Ship Path Planning based on RRT Algorithm. *J. Phys. Conf. Ser.* **2022**, *2281*, 012004. [CrossRef]

23. Zhang, X.; Zhu, T.; Du, L.; Hu, Y.; Liu, H. Local Path Planning of Autonomous Vehicle Based on an Improved Heuristic Bi-RRT Algorithm in Dynamic Obstacle Avoidance Environment. *Sensors* **2022**, *22*, 7968. [CrossRef] [PubMed]
24. Xu, J.; Tian, Z.; He, W.; Huang, Y. A fast path planning algorithm fusing PRM and P-BI-RRT. In Proceedings of the 2020 11th International Conference on Prognostics and System Health Management (PHM-2020 Jinan), Jinan, China, 23–25 October; pp. 503–508.
25. Gan, Y.; Zhang, B.; Ke, C.; Zhu, X.F.; He, W.M.; Ihara, T. Research on Robot Motion Planning Based on RRT Algorithm with Nonholonomic Constraints. *Neural Process. Lett.* **2021**, *53*, 3011–3029. [CrossRef]
26. Wang, J.; Li, B.; Meng, M.Q.-H. Kinematic Constrained Bi-directional RRT with Efficient Branch Pruning for robot path planning. *Expert Syst. Appl.* **2020**, *170*, 114541. [CrossRef]
27. Grothe, F.; Hartmann, V.N.; Orthey, A.; Toussaint, M. ST-RRT*: Asymptotically-Optimal Bidirectional Motion Planning through Space-Time. *arXiv* **2022**, arXiv:2203.02176.
28. Zhao, H. Path Planning of Mobile Robots Based on Improved Bi-RRT Algorithm. In Proceedings of the 2022 IEEE 5th International Conference on Automation, Electronics and Electrical Engineering (AUTEEE), Shenyang, China, 18–20 November 2022; pp. 1043–1050. [CrossRef]
29. Ma, G.; Duan, Y.; Li, M.; Xie, Z.; Zhu, J. A probability smoothing Bi-RRT path planning algorithm for indoor robot. *Future Gener. Comput. Syst.* **2023**, *143*, 349–360. [CrossRef]
30. Choi, J.; Jeong, B.; Theotokatos, G.; Tezdogan, T. Approach an autonomous vessel as a single robot with Robot Operating System in virtual environment. *J. Int. Marit. Saf. Environ. Aff. Shipp.* **2022**, *6*, 50–66. [CrossRef]
31. Kang, J.-G.; Lim, D.-W.; Choi, Y.-S.; Jang, W.-J.; Jung, J.-W. Improved RRT-Connect Algorithm Based on Triangular Inequality for Robot Path Planning. *Sensors* **2021**, *21*, 333. [CrossRef] [PubMed]
32. Zhang, Y.; Wang, H.; Yin, M.; Wang, J.; Hua, C. Bi-AM-RRT*: A Fast and Efficient Sampling-Based Motion Planning Algorithm in Dynamic Environments. *arXiv* **2023**, arXiv:2301.11816.
33. Platt, J.; Ricks, K. Comparative Analysis of ROS-Unity3D and ROS-Gazebo for Mobile Ground Robot Simulation. *J. Intell. Robot. Syst.* **2022**, *106*, 80. [CrossRef]
34. Li, Y.; Li, J.; Zhou, W.; Yao, Q.; Nie, J.; Qi, X. Robot Path Planning Navigation for Dense Planting Red Jujube Orchards Based on the Joint Improved A* and DWA Algorithms under Laser SLAM. *Agriculture* **2022**, *12*, 1445. [CrossRef]

Disclaimer/Publisher's Note: The statements, opinions and data contained in all publications are solely those of the individual author(s) and contributor(s) and not of MDPI and/or the editor(s). MDPI and/or the editor(s) disclaim responsibility for any injury to people or property resulting from any ideas, methods, instructions or products referred to in the content.

Review

Concrete 3D Printing: Process Parameters for Process Control, Monitoring and Diagnosis in Automation and Construction

Tan Kai Noel Quah, Yi Wei Daniel Tay, Jian Hui Lim, Ming Jen Tan, Teck Neng Wong and King Ho Holden Li *

Singapore Centre for 3D Printing, School of Mechanical & Aerospace Engineering, Nanyang Technological University, 50 Nanyang Avenue, Singapore 639798, Singapore; m190057@ntu.edu.sg (T.K.N.Q.)
* Correspondence: holdenli@ntu.edu.sg

Citation: Quah, T.K.N.; Tay, Y.W.D.; Lim, J.H.; Tan, M.J.; Wong, T.N.; Li, K.H.H. Concrete 3D Printing: Process Parameters for Process Control, Monitoring and Diagnosis in Automation and Construction. *Mathematics* **2023**, *11*, 1499. https://doi.org/10.3390/math11061499

Academic Editors: Paolo Mercorelli, Oleg Sergiyenko and Oleksandr Tsymbal

Received: 20 February 2023
Revised: 8 March 2023
Accepted: 13 March 2023
Published: 19 March 2023

Copyright: © 2023 by the authors. Licensee MDPI, Basel, Switzerland. This article is an open access article distributed under the terms and conditions of the Creative Commons Attribution (CC BY) license (https://creativecommons.org/licenses/by/4.0/).

Abstract: In Singapore, there is an increasing need for independence from manpower within the Building and Construction (B&C) Industry. Prefabricated Prefinished Volumetric Construction (PPVC) production is mainly driven by benefits in environmental pollution reduction, improved productivity, quality control, and customizability. However, overall cost savings have been counterbalanced by new cost drivers like modular precast moulds, transportation, hoisting, manufacturing & holding yards, and supervision costs. The highly modular requirements for PPVC places additive manufacturing in an advantageous position, due to its high customizability, low volume manufacturing capabilities for a faster manufacturing response time, faster production changeovers, and lower inventory requirements. However, C3DP has only just begun to move away from its early-stage development, where there is a need to closely evaluate the process parameters across buildability, extrudability, and pumpability aspects. As many parameters have been identified as having considerable influence on C3DP processes, monitoring systems for feedback applications seem to be an inevitable step forward to automation in construction. This paper has presented a broad analysis of the challenges posed to C3DP and feedback systems, stressing the admission of process parameters to correct multiple modes of failure.

Keywords: Concrete 3D Printing; sustainability; process control; diagnosis systems; feedback systems; feedback control; computer vision; monitoring systems; in-situ monitoring; ex-situ monitoring

MSC: 00A27

1. Introduction

In Singapore, there is an increasing need for independence from manpower within the Building and Construction (B&C) Industry [1]. Currently, the preferred construction approach in Singapore's high-density urban landscape is the use of Prefabricated Prefinished Volumetric Construction (PPVC). The Building and Construction Authority (BCA) in Singapore has supported this construction method by implementing regulatory channels to utilize its extensive network, mainly driven by benefits in environmental pollution reduction, improved productivity, quality control, and customizability [2,3]. The off-site fabrication capabilities of this technique also enable furnishings, finishes, and fittings prior to its deployment to the site. In turn, these benefits positively affect manpower costs and safety ratings on-site. However, overall cost savings have been counterbalanced by new cost drivers such as modular precast moulds, transportation, hoisting, manufacturing & holding yards, and supervision costs [3]. Case studies of two pilot projects carried out at North Hill, Nanyang Technological University and Changi Crown Plaza Hotel reported more than 15% increase in costs compared to traditional cast methods, largely attributed to these cost drivers [3].

Concrete 3D Printing (C3DP) is an additive manufacturing approach that deposits a mixture of concrete slurry or cement using a layer-by-layer methodology to form a structure without the use of traditional formwork. Potentially, the emergence of C3DP can improve sustainability by reducing material wastage, costs, and construction risks, with the reduction of labor intensive processes [4,5]. The highly modular requirements for PPVC places concrete additive manufacturing in an advantageous position due to its high customizability and low volume manufacturing capabilities for a faster manufacturing response time, faster production changeovers, and lower inventory requirements [4]. The inherent characteristics of 3D printing may seem advantageous, but C3DP has only just begun to move away from early-stage development and its success rate in the real-world environment is still being evaluated, as buildability, extrudability, and pumpability concerns persists. These current challenges in C3DP have been attributed to numerous parameters that include environmental, material, and process parameters [6].

Objective

This review paper will attempt to discuss the importance of process control parameters. The introduction has provided a brief overview of the building and construction industry in Singapore. This covered the research gap in C3DP and a brief description of the existing issues. Section 2 will give an overview of 3D printing's characteristics, exploring, and listing current challenges and solutions in the C3DP process. At the same time, a short discussion will be given of the parameters involved for the respective research challenges. Section 3 will specify and describe the need for monitoring systems to complement the requirements for a complete diagnosis system. Section 4 will discuss and describe the core requirements of a diagnosis system for C3DP applications and provide a correlation explanation for the previous two chapters. Section 5 displays existing systems that utilize machine vision technologies for diagnosis of varying aspects in traditional construction workspaces. Finally, Section 6 offers a conclusion and a future vision for feedback systems in C3DP.

2. Parameter Classification in C3DP Structural Faults

Ma et al. observed an eightfold increase in Concrete 3D Printing research from 2017 to 2020. The authors reported that about 80% of all research in the field was dedicated to material optimization studies, while the remainder were distributed between processing (10%), software (9%), and building integration (1%) [7]. A greater focus on material related studies was reported. Research conducted to implement optimization via process control for this field is sparse, which is an indicator that the research direction is still in its early-stage development, as process control is one of the considerations for later-stage or end-stage development.

Process control and automation falls under the branch of processing. This includes the study of process parameters in C3DP, such as material flow rate, nozzle travel speed, and nozzle stand-off distance [8–10]. Generally, these parameters are estimated and calibrated as an open-loop process prior to the print, which may introduce errors and could affect the print quality, and any unexpected in-process developments require manual intervention. Currently, several researchers are investigating a closed-loop control for these parameters to achieve an improved printing performance and outcome. However, these process control augmentations tend to require substantial developmental time and costs, which may discourage research in the area. Hence, this chapter attempts to focus on the importance of assessment for process parameters and process control.

With the current development, these parametric studies are independently defined within their own research scope. Solutions derived from these issues can appear subjective when two or more parametric categories are involved in the issue. In this section, the current issues and challenges encountered in C3DP will be classified according to their attributed parameters. This paper references the parameters classified in several literature sources and simplifies these technical parameters according to Figure 1, summarized into process, material, and environmental parameters [6,11–14].

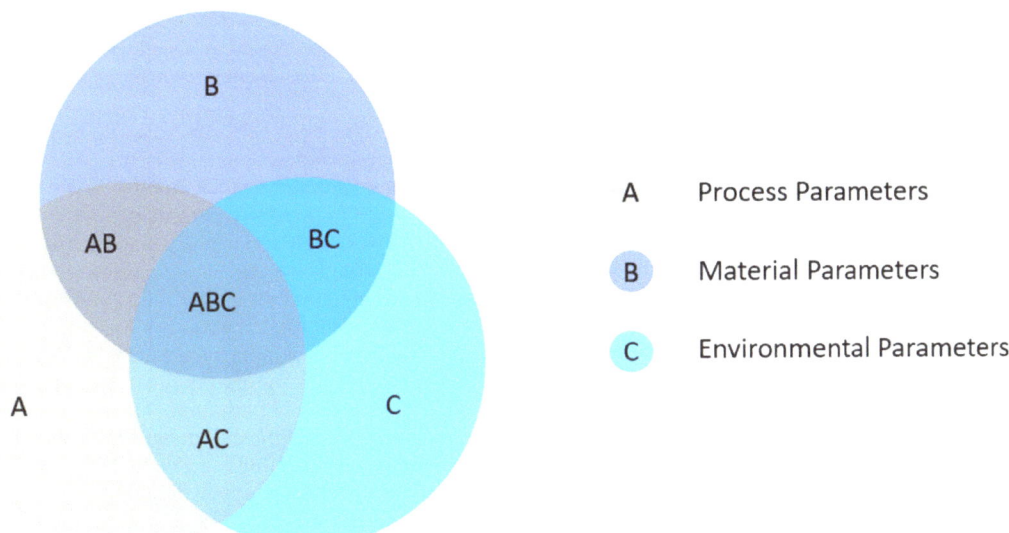

Figure 1. Venn Diagram of Parameters in Concrete 3D Printing.

We can refer to the table below to categorically define these parameters, based on the factors currently known. In this paper, qualified parameters are considered as observable qualitative or quantitative factors that can influence the printing outcome. This categorization includes pre- and post-process, in-situ and ex-situ measured parameters, and is non-exhaustive. The classification is sorted and organized according to current research findings and will distinguish and emphasize the importance of process parameters in process control, along with the following sections. Table 1 displays a list of parameters in their respective categories.

Table 1. List of Parameters Sorted into Respective Categories [6,13,15–24].

	Nozzle Travel Speed, Material Extrusion Rate
Process Parameter	Layer Height, Layer Width, Nozzle Diameter, Corner Travel Radius, Nozzle Shape/Geometry
	Extrusion Pressure/Force, Layer Cycle Time
Environmental Parameter	Temperature, Humidity, Winds, Freeze-Thaw Cycles
Material Parameter	Yield Stress (Static, Dynamic), Structuration Rate, Curing Rate, Density, Plastic Viscosity, Slump Ratio, Aggregate Size, Compressive Strength, Thixotropy, Open Time, Setting Time, Structural Build Up, Water-to-cement ratio, Hydration Rate

2.1. Weak Interlayer Bond

Weak interfacial bond strength has been considered by several researchers in the following areas: (a) porosity and saturation state of the substrate, (b) moisture condition of the surface, (c) magnitude of plastic shrinkage, (d) varying yield stress and/or plastic viscosities of the deposited material and substrate [17]. To date, this remains one of the biggest challenges n C3DP, as requires a deep understanding of material and machine parameters.

2.1.1. Porosity and Moisture Conditions

Microstructure discrepancies occur due to entrapped air pockets. In C3DP, air pockets within the extruded filament mainly appear due to the lack of formwork and vibration, which are prevalent methods in traditional construction to densify the concrete [25]. However, recent evidence suggests that the interconnected porosity within a 3D printed filament is much more complex, when compared to pores found in casted concrete, which poses a postponed fatal cracking facility [25–28]. Fundamental knowledge indicates that air entrapment begins in mixing and occurs between layers during deposition [29]. Air entrapment also occurs at the interlayer during deposition [17,27,28,30,31]. Both occurrences are typically assessed collectively in porosity tests such as Scanning Electron Microscope (SEM), Mercury intrusion porosimetry (MIP), and Computed tomography (CT) imaging [31].

Nerella et al. observed and categorized four cases of porosity in poor interlayer bond strength: (1) weakly bonded, (2) weakly bonded under process and curing conditions, (3) temporarily weakly bonded, and (4) strongly bonded. Case 1 indicates long and wide separation between layers that cannot be connected by hydration constituents before 28 days assessment. Case 2 is caused by air entrapped by process and curing parameters such as drying shrinkage, moisture conditions, or printing parameters that cannot undergo proper hydration. Situations of Case 3 are usually the least porous compared to the other cases and are likely to be self-healed overtime via hydration. Finally, case 4 indicates well-bonded regions [17]. The presence of porosity reveals poor densification within the C3DP structure, for which Shakor et al. stated that this was due to limited moisture and the presence of fine particles that decrease wettability of powder [32].

2.1.2. Plastic Shrinkage

3D printed concrete is extremely susceptible to plastic shrinkage cracks. The lack of formwork, low bleeding water, low aggregate to binder ratio and high quantities of fine aggregates are the material-based constraints that allow fresh concrete to retain its extrudability and buildability. These material properties are vulnerable to early age water evaporation that can result in volumetric shrinkage. Physical restraints lead to increased tension that causes plastic shrinkage cracking [33]. The combination of high surface-to-volume ratio and dry environment conditions also fosters an undesirable effect [34,35]. Aside from its aesthetic damage, the presence of cracks can increase the likelihood of water seepages and water penetration in the structure, which can cause corrosion in steel reinforcements, and crack propagation may occur from thermal expansion of water in varied environmental conditions, such as saltwater penetration and freeze–thaw cycles [24,36–39]. Plastic shrinkage appears to cause interlayer slips and leads to poor interlayer bond strength and structural durability [34].

2.1.3. Yield Stress Evolution Rates and Deposition Speed

The uninterrupted vertically assembled manufacturing process of 3DPC determines that synchronic curing methods pose a challenge in mitigating poor interlayer bond effects, as curing methods are typically implemented as a post-process procedure [40]. Panda et al. [41] determined that interlayer tensile bond is not dependent on the material hardening rate. Instead, the author's experiment suggests that the tensile bond strength of the interlayers can be optimized by adjusting the printing parameters, such as nozzle travel speed. Tay et al. [42] also studied the interlayer bond strength and both authors noted that a decrease in printing time gap enhances the interlayer tensile strength, but also inversely affects the structural stability due to the increase in printing speed. Hence, Panda et al. suggested that there must be an optimal printing parameter for all concrete variants and 3D printing designs [41,43]. Figure 2 shows the qualitative observation of interlayer bond with varying printing speeds.

This section has established a correlation to the effects of poor interlayer bond strength between different research studies. We summarized the above effects into Table 2, based on a handful of research articles.

Figure 2. Qualitative Observation of Interlayer Bond with Varying Printing Speeds: (**a**) 1-min time-gap, (**b**) 5 min time-gap, (**c**) 10-min time-gap and (**d**) 20-min time-gap [42].

Table 2. Parameters Involved in Poor Interlayer Bond Strength.

Process Parameter	Printing Time Gap, Nozzle Travel Speed, Nozzle Standoff Distance, Mixing, deposition method, Air Entrapment, Surface-to-Volume Ratio	[23,27–31,41,42,44–50]
Environmental Parameter	Temperature, Humidity, Hydration Rate, Saltwater Penetration, Freeze-Thaw Cycles	[23,24,30,34–39,44,45,51–57]
Material Parameter	Aggregate-to-Binder Ratio, Additives, Void distribution, Permeability, Drying Shrinkage, Plastic Shrinkage, Moisture,	[32,34,44,54,58–68]

2.2. Buildability

2.2.1. Plastic Collapse and Elastic Buckling

Plastic collapse is caused by the weight load at the bottom-most layer exceeding the maximum yield strength of the printing material. Suiker et al. describe this phenomenon as accumulated vertical deformation, where the influence on the critical height of the wall was studied in various supported structures [13,14]. Ashrafi et al. [43] reveal that the deformation of the base layer is not only a result of the weight of the subsequent layers, but is also caused by the extrusion pressure (Figure 3). It was demonstrated in the experiment that layer deformation can be reduced by extending the printing time gap between layers and the number of base layers used to reduce filament deformation. The author's methodology also aligns with the observations made by Panda et al. [41] and Tay et al. [42], that machine parameters should be controlled to optimize the time gap between layers.

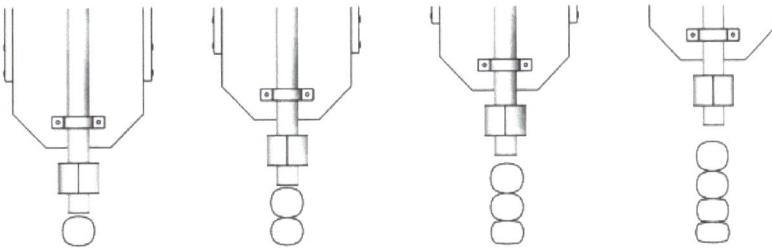

Figure 3. Layer-wise Deformation Illustration by Ashrafi et al. [43].

Elastic failure is an out-of-plane deflection failure mode that occurs before the maximum yield strength is reached. As opposed to plastic collapse, this phenomenon may also be caused by environmental or machine parameters. Suiker et al. describe this as lateral deformation, concluding that the filament width and the material curing rate have a significant influence on elastic buckling, with insignificant results from poor layer-wise deposition. The author's further work also validates the model with accelerators [13,14]. Nguyen-Van et al. also concluded that wider filament widths and lower printing speeds improve buildability and constructability [69]. Studies related to filament widths and printing speeds have been conducted by many researchers, where process control parameters indicate some degree of influence in this failure mode [6,70,71]. However, the extent of the parametric influence appears to be confounded between the two failure modes among these studies, the outcome of which leads to a convoluted discussion in research, with the use of terms such as "collapse", "deformation" or "shape stability" as a generalized encapsulation of both failure modes [41,69,71]. The need to isolate (or combine) and study the two effects will be further revealed in the next chapter as a thin wall process control solution.

2.2.2. Rapid Setting

Rapid setting binders can be used in concrete slurry to increase yield strength for the prevention of plastic collapse and elastic buckling. However, activators increase the initial yield strength in the mixing process, reducing pumpability and risking material build up in the printer. Set-on-demand has since been a method to perform activation near the nozzle end. This includes the modification of process parameters that moderates the feed rate of the accelerator [72]. It should be noted that this is a relatively new method to enhance buildability, with only limited research, pursued by Muthukrishnan et al. [72–74].

2.2.3. Reinforcements

Integration of reinforcements remains one of the central challenges in concrete 3D printing. Reinforcement methods are mainly used to enhance tensile strength and ductility. For C3DP, the method includes the use of bars, meshes, fibers or cables that can be incorporated, usually in one of three printing process stages (pre-process (mixing), in-process (printing), and post-process (cured/pre-wired) stages).

- Pre-process

A significant amount of research has been focused on adding synthetic fiber reinforcements to the concrete matrix. Addition of steel [75], polymer [76–79], glass [79–82], and plant-based fibers [83–86] has been explored over the years. Incorporating different fiber types has been a long-standing research topic in pursuit of Ultra High-Performance Concrete (UHPC). Chun et al. [83] assessed different fibers in concrete paste and uncovered different performances between a few notable fiber types; (1) Structural performance of fiber-reinforced concrete is still subject to the printability, nozzle travel speed, and printing direction of the process, (2) inorganic fibers, in comparison to organic fibers, tend to deter adhesion in the geopolymer matrix. Stiff materials, such as steel fibers, prevent complete adhesion to the interlayer bond strength due to increased porosity. For short fiber reinforcement methods, there is an overall improvement in ductility and tensile strength within the concrete filament but little to no improvement in the interlayer region [87–90]. Apart from the abovementioned reinforcements, research on other unique fiber configurations, such as thermoplastic composites and recyclable materials, are also being explored as a prospective expansion of UHPC materials for 3D printing [91–95].

- In-process

Extrusion of cementitious material fed with steel cables at the center of the extruded filament is a relatively common approach, despite scarcity in this area of research [96]. Pull-out tests and four-point bending tests were conducted by Bos et al. [97] to observe performance difference in different wire types. Bos observed an increase in ductility and post-crack resistance. However, cable slips were noted as a phenomenon, with smooth cables embedding inducing poor bond strength between the materials. Li et al. [96] agree that the inclusion of a metal cable exhibited a ductile failure mode during four-point bending tests. However, the authors also noted that cable reinforcements showed weaker interlayer bonding strength as compared to that without reinforcements, due to reduced contact area at the interlayer. Hojati et al. [98] attempted to mitigate cable slips via barbed-wire reinforcements. The inclusion of barbs alleviated cable slips but introduced a larger scale presence of voids surrounding the barbed protrusions. Hojati also highlighted that further investigation of barb frequency, cable types, and varying barb configuration is needed to optimize these findings. Xiao et al. [99] also explored the perpendicular insertion of steel cables to decrease the flexural anisotropy of concrete printed structures and noted a 10 times improvement in flexural capacity.

Alternatively, other methods of in-process installation include bolting of metal brackets in layered intervals within concrete filaments, developed by Simon and Sungwoo [100], and U-nail insertion into several layers of concrete filament to reduce the effects of poor interlayer bond, carried out by Wang et al. [101]. Both methods showed improved tensile strength in the steel reinforcement support. While these options offer promising methods for tensile strength improvement from a material study standpoint, scaling to a structural reinforcement system proves to be a challenge.

- Post-process

The definition of post-process printing in this section is defined by prior work done to the structure before addition of concrete or wires. There are currently two approaches to this process. (1) Mesh wires, cables, or bars are fitted into a completed 3D printed concrete structure, (2) Concrete is extruded around a pre-installed configuration of wires, cables, or bars.

(1) Asprone et al. [102] developed an external anchor connection design approach to install an out-of-plane reinforcement system in a 3D printed structure. Local fractures arise from shear forces between segments and steel–concrete anchors. Salet et al. [103] conceptualized post-tensioning reinforcements in which concrete structures are built with design considerations to sandwich C3DP slabs as an assembly, where the middle slab design allows cable passthrough. These parts are then pressed together by post-tensioned prestressing tendons. The method showed much promise, as the prototype passed all structural regulations in assembly trials (Figure 4).

Figure 4. Meshed wires or cable implementation to C3DP bridge structures [102,103].

(2) For a pre-configured wire mesh approach (Figure 5), Marchment et al. [104] introduced a nozzle design that enables printing about the mesh. Liu et al. [105] later developed a U-shaped wire mesh (USWM) configuration, where concrete is extruded at an inclined angle around the mesh wire. This configuration showed significant improvement in tensile strength. Table 3 shows the parameters involved in buildability.

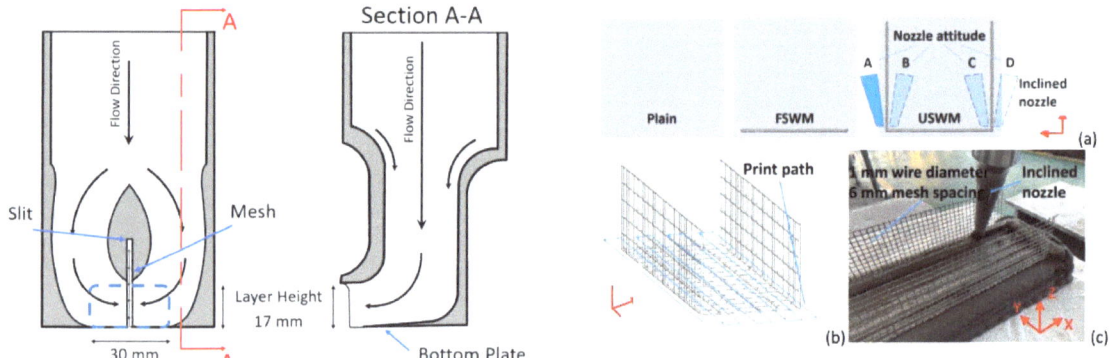

Figure 5. A pre-configured wire mesh approach, for concrete deposition around existing mesh layout [104,105]. (**a**–**c**) shows the process flow for a pre-configured wire mesh approach with an inclined angle deposition.

Table 3. Parameters Involved in Buildability.

Process Parameter	Printing Time Gap, Nozzle Travel Speed, Nozzle Standoff Distance, Filament Width, Structure Height, Nozzle Width, Vertical Building Rate, Total Construction Time, Nozzle Geometry, Peripheral Parameters (Activator Feed Rate)	[6,12–14,43,69–71,104–106]
Environmental Parameter		
Material Parameter	Aggregate-to-Binder Ratio, Curing Rate, Additives, Accelerator Ratio, Static & Dynamic Yield Stress, Open Time, Setting Time, Structural Build Up, Hydration Rate, Ductility,	[13,14,69,72–74,96,106]

2.3. Extrudability

Extrudability in C3DP is defined as the process of transporting material through the feedpipe and the print head. Good extrudability is defined as the ability to extrude filaments consistently. Nozzle blockage, filament tearing, and filament buckling can occur from poor process control and mixture composition. However, as cementitious material hardens with time, pumpability can be used to manage the printability of the material [107]. These factors were studied by Liu et al. and it was observed that a change in flow rate over time can improve the overall print and structural quality [108]. Furthermore, Tay et al. noted that pump flow rate and nozzle travel speed have similar significance in quality control for 3DCP [109,110]. Figure 6 shows the relationship between pump flow rate and nozzle travel speed in quality control.

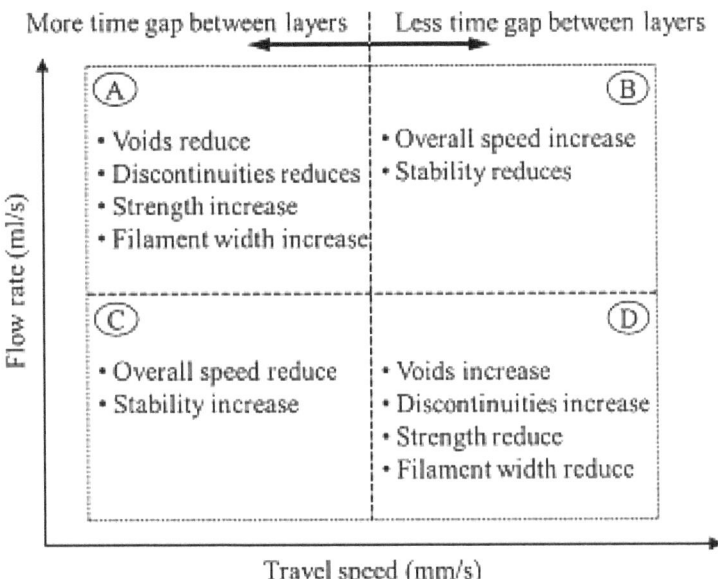

Figure 6. Relationship between pump flow rate and nozzle travel speed in quality control. (Image by Tay et al. [109]). (**A**–**D**) represents the regions when optimization between the two parameters are imbalanced, (**A**) high flow rate and low travel speed, (**B**) high flow rate and travel speed, (**C**) low flow rate and travel speed, (**D**) high travel speed and low flow rate.

Khalil et al. concluded that a diameter ratio, or the nozzle geometry, of $D_{nozzle}/D_{particle}$ should be larger than 4 for continuous flow to occur [111–113]. Multiple evidence also suggests that constituents of concrete, such as admixtures, water, binders, and cement, directly affect its flowability, stability and self-levelling. These factors have been associated with aggregate size, yield stress, plastic viscosity and open time [107,111–114]. Malaeb et al. [10] identified that good flowability can be optimized by reducing sand and increasing cement. Hence, both material and process parameters are attributed to the effects of poor extrudability [115]. These effects are amplified along sharp corners in the C3DP process when extrusion rate remains inconsistent within the nozzle geometry. A difference in curvature exists between the inner and outer radii of the filament, where the inner and outer radiuses exhibit overflow and underflow effects, respectively, if a corner rotation is sharp. Liu et al. determined that rheological properties have little significance in this occurrence, which is associated with the corner radius, nozzle travel speed, and nozzle geometry [116–118]. Large-scale implementation has also been shown to cause accelerated hardening due to friction caused by prolonged pumping, causing reduced workability, potentially causing clogs in the extruder, and quickening the effects of filament tearing and buckling [118].

Researchers conduct extrudability tests to assess the printability of a setup. It is still a common practice to conduct extrudability tests via visual inspection of single layer extrudate of a fixed length for any filament tearing or buckling in the sample [20,119]. Recent work conducted by Ting et al. attempts to leverage the manual inspection method with an instance segmentation model by quantifying surface defects with real-time in-situ monitoring [93]. It is relatively clear that filament tearing and bucking are qualitatively distinguished, time-dependent parameters that lead to nozzle blockage with material influence, and can be controlled by process parameters. Table 4 lists all parameters listed in this section.

Table 4. Parameters Involved in Extrudability.

Process Parameter	Corner Radius, Nozzle Travel Speed, Material Flow Rate, Extrusion Pressure, Nozzle Geometry (Diameter Ratio), Peripheral Parameters (Vibration at nozzle, etc)	[109,111–113,116–118,120–123]
Environmental Parameter		
Material Parameter	Sand-to-Cement Ratio, Curing Rate, Static & Dynamic Yield Stress, Plastic Viscosity, Lubrication Layer, Storage Modulus, Open Time, Setting Time, Structural Build Up, Hydration Rate, Aggregate Size	[10,120,123–134]

3. Process Monitoring for Fault Detection

The chapter above provided a summary of the current challenges in C3DP and discussed the parameters involved. Each challenge presented above has an established significance for process parameters. As cementitious material exhibits unpredictable mechanisms in the printing process, feedback systems make sense for process parametric adjustments in C3DP in place of manual observations and interventions [18,42,135–137]. However, from a process control standpoint, managing process parameters in a C3DP application for a closed loop feedback is challenging due to the required interdisciplinary understanding of material behaviour, computer vision, and fault diagnosis. Consequentially, feedback systems investigation in C3DP research is relatively uncommon compared to other branches of research. Generally, the process flow for a feedback system is listed as follows: Data Acquisition, Pre-Processing, Feature Extraction, Classification, and Diagnosis at a desired interval [138–140]. Several methods can be used as classification tools (this will be discussed in a later section). Depending on the classification methods used, pre-processing and feature extraction steps will typically be adjusted accordingly. This chapter attempts to breakdown the requirements needed in process monitoring for fault diagnosis (refer to Figure 7).

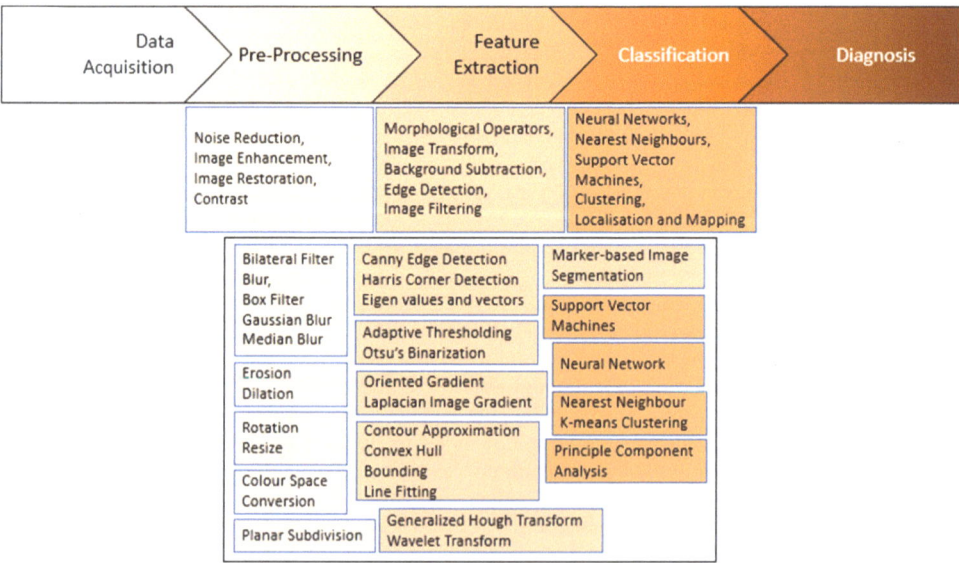

Figure 7. Categorization of computer vision methods and a non-exhaustive list of methods for pre-processing, feature extraction and classification [141].

3.1. Data Acquisition

Feedback systems in C3DP require an input data stream. These data inputs can be obtained with various arrays in one-dimensional to three-dimensional streams of data, often acquired in the form of an image with color spaces, such as HSI [142], HSV [143], Binary [144,145], Greyscale [18] and RGB [146]. Data obtained can then be interpreted for monitoring applications, such as safety monitoring [147], Building Information Modelling (BIM) [148], Structural Health Monitoring (SHM), and process monitoring [149]. A camera layout is typically installed, based on in-situ or ex-situ configurations, and depends greatly on the attention to detail needed for the operation. In this paper, in-situ and ex-situ monitoring systems will be defined as the measurement or camera sensor planted inside and outside the work envelop of the 3D printer, respectively (refer to Figure 8).

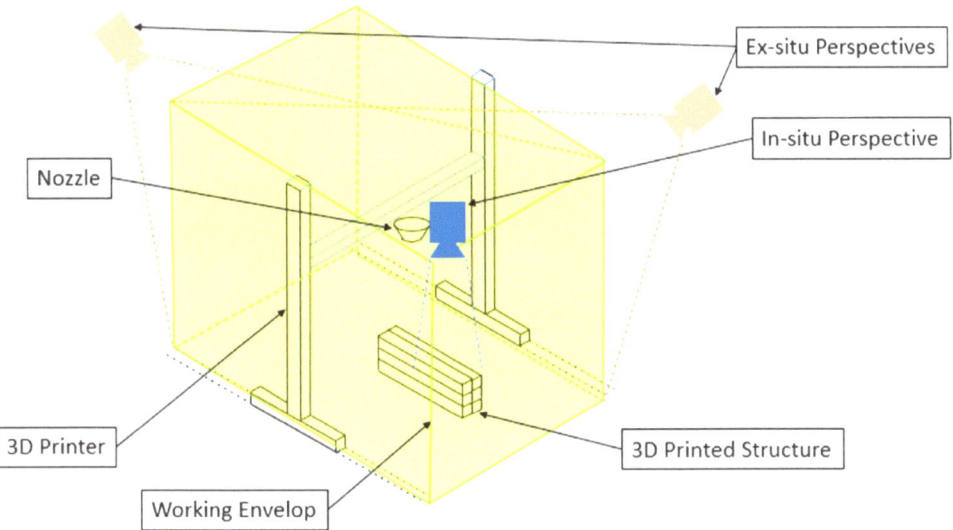

Figure 8. Illustration of Data Acquisition Sensor Layouts in C3DP.

Concrete 3D printed structures are generally large, thus varying environmental conditions, such as indoor or outdoor C3DP, can considerably affect sensor inputs. Noise, such as ambient light, temperature, and weather conditions, can easily impact the accuracy of the data acquired and the general outcome of the resulting diagnosis. Apart from a clear line of sight for the sensor, factors such as object cleanliness, reflectivity of the object, and occlusions in scanning path should also be considered. Depending on the sensor used, the calibration process, including lens distortion, bundled adjustment, and unit scaling for instance, must be regarded [150–152]. The visual cues for geometrical capture are dependent on lens/sensor perspective, object occlusion, and shading. In other words, computer vision tools are strongly affected by perspective and illumination strategies [153]. Refer to Figure 9 for examples of illustration strategies.

Further categorization can also be achieved by monitoring the print through in-process and post-process methods for process control [18,135–137,154–156]. The following research consists of monitoring techniques that have been, or will be, used in feedback for process monitoring. These publications indicate the progress made towards autonomy in C3DP. As of now, implementation has been largely discussed as future work and these solutions have not been fully realized, as the experimentation has been conducted in a fully controlled environment. The extent of the effectiveness of computer vision feedback control has not been thoroughly established, but has been successful in detection in most cases. It can be understood that post-process feedback applications are not thoroughly explored due to the scarcity of environmental input for long-term assessment in C3DP structures at the current time. Refer to Table 5 for examples of monitoring architectures with computer vision implementation.

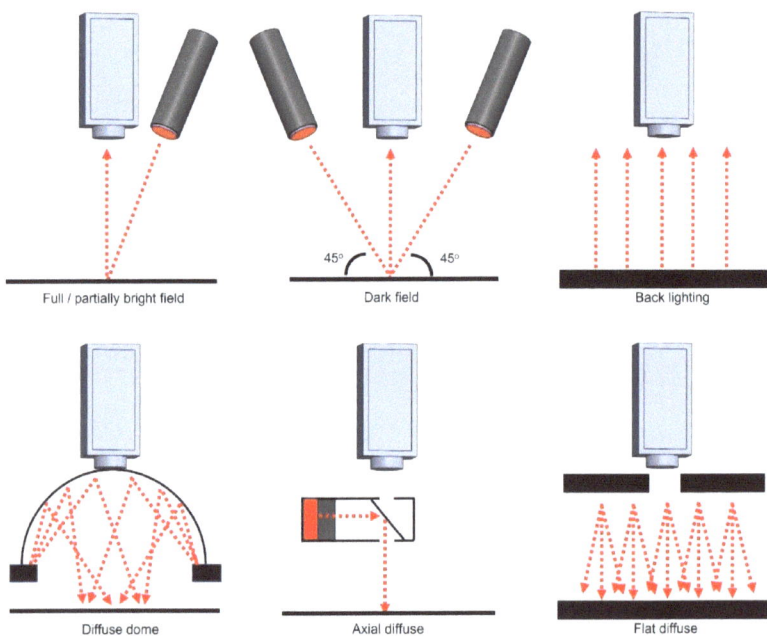

Figure 9. Examples of Illumination Strategies for Image Acquisition.

Table 5. Latest Applications for Machine Vision in C3DP separated by pre-process, in-process, and post-process factors (red indicates feedback application is successful, blue indicates intentions to implement a feedback system, black does not indicate intentions for feedback implementation).

Monitoring	Config	Parameter/Analysis	Publication(s)	Sensor/Method	Comments
In-process	In-Situ	Nozzle Height	[135]	1D ToF Distance Sensor/Direct Measurement	Feedback with sensor for Proof of Concept.
	In-Situ	Flow Rate, Width	[18]	Camera Sensor/ Binarization	Material flow for over and under extrusion.
	Ex-Situ	Surface Quality, Layer Width	[157]	Camera Sensor/ Gaussian Filter	Imaging Techniques to measure surface smoothness from side profile.
	In-Situ	Robot Collision	[158,159]	Camera Sensor, ArUco markers	Robot collision with 2 vision feedback methods for estimation and precision.
Post-Process	In-Situ	Layer Deformation	[146]	Camera Sensor/ Semantic Segmentation	Slump Inspection.
	In-Situ	Extrusion Quality	[136]	Camera Sensor/ U-VGG19	Side profile evaluation of layer quality to observe qualitatively.
	In-Situ	Texture Quality	[160]	Camera Sensor/ Thresholding	Entropy variation analysis to assess layer quality from a side profile.
	Ex-Situ	Geometric Inspection in C3DP Assembly	[161]	3D Laser Scanner/ Photogrammetry	Case Study Inspection

3.2. Pre-Processing and Feature Extraction

Pre-processing and feature extraction in computer vision applications are necessary steps to clean up and enhance acquired data in the C3DP workspace. Raw image data obtained directly from a camera sensor may face a variety of obstacles that could hinder the classification result. Pre-processing methods are commonly used in vision-based process systems to mitigate such errors early in the process [144,162–168]. In this paper's definition, pre-processing methods can be redefined into two groups: corrections are required to change the artifacts in the image prior to feature extraction, enhancements are utilized to augment key features for ease of classification in later steps.

- Corrections: Sensor Corrections, Lighting Corrections, Noise, Geometric Corrections, Color Corrections.
- Enhancements: Blur and Focus, Illumination, Thresholding. Edge Enhancement, Morphology, Segmentation, Region Processing, Color Space Conversions.

Despite the need for a robust illumination strategy as described earlier [169], features of interest in C3DP may still be suppressed by external factors, such as ambient light conditions and occlusions. The C3DP monitoring process flow would face difficulties replicating isolated environments, as seen in other disciplines such as metal additive manufacturing process monitoring [165–167,170,171]. Splatters, residuals, light, reflection, and shadow interferences can be observed on the substrate while printing. While it may not compromise the 3D printing process, it can cause a camera sensor's erroneous reading that may lead to poor diagnosis (Refer to Figure 10). Hence, digital corrections are essential to minimize the negative effects of the environment and setup. Kazemian et al. [18] have noted this effect in a feedback control process. The authors noted stray detections of concrete filament due to obstructed lighting conditions, hence developing an approach to conduct frame drops to minimize the erroneous readings.

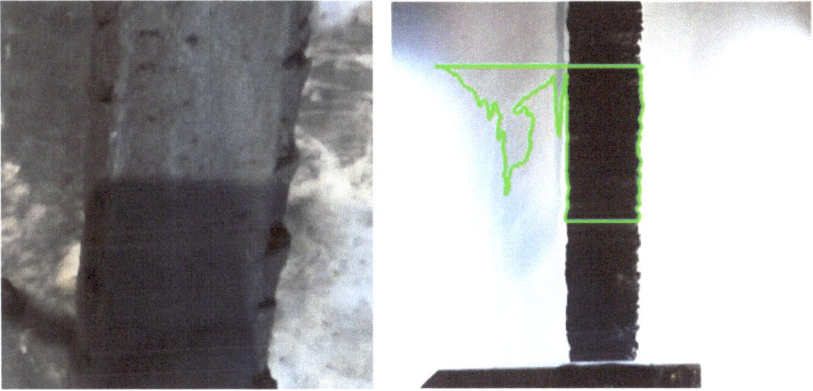

Figure 10. Left: Image sample by SC3DP taken by a camera attached to the nozzle, displaying background noise (splatters and residuals of concrete). **Right**: Error in feature extraction where background features were highlighted with a green outline (inclusive of the concrete filament), resulting in a discarded image (Image from Kazemian et al. [18]).

Enhancement, or feature extraction, methods such as morphological operators [142], image cropping, frame selection [18,136], filters, blurs, rotation, resizing, and color space conversion (refer to Figure 7), are some of the functions used to digitally enhance, modify, or amplify desired characteristics in a dataset, specific to any machine learning algorithms. Generally, supervised classification methods such as Deep Neural Networks require a model with numerous variations. Images are typically obtained and labelled manually, which are then fed into a training model. Pre-processing methods are used to expand the dataset variations in order to enhance the model, such as image augmentations for rotation, flipping, or contrast [145,146,172,173], whereas, in typical unsupervised machine learning techniques, pre-processing methods, such as binarization, image blurring, thresholding, contour extraction, and edge detection, are used to de-noise prior to classification [18,136,161]. Correction and enhancement methods can be interchangeably used for all classification methods and are not specific to a single use case. Davtalab et al. [146] utilized pre-processing methods for thresholding and binarization to provide a binary mask image as ground truth reference for a SegNet DNN model. This resulted in a post-process, in-situ monitoring method for observing deformities on the printed layers from a side profile (Figure 11).

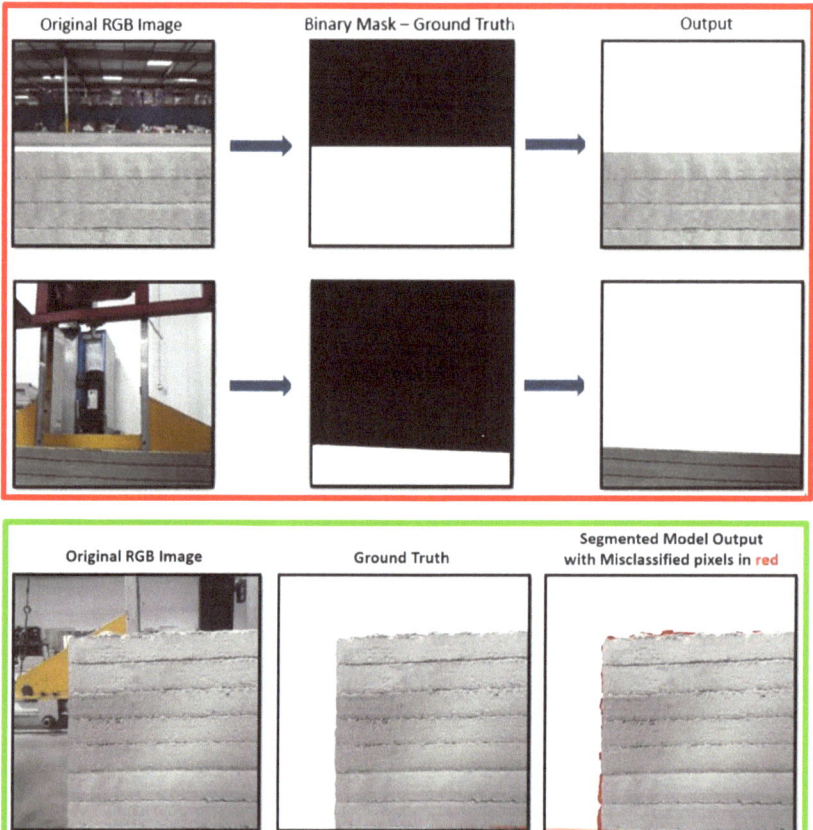

Figure 11. In red: pre-processing methods utilising thresholding and binarization for training dataset. In green: training data fed into a pixel-wise segmentation via DNN model to remove background noise [146].

3.3. Classification

Classification consists of categorization and labelling groups of pixels or variables within a dataset. These classification methods can be divided into four categories: Supervised, Semi-supervised, Reinforced, and Unsupervised systems, as shown in Figure 12 [174]. Supervised learning requires a training dataset that includes the input and ideal output data. Classification and regression algorithms are used to allow the model to learn over time. A loss function is used to measure its accuracy and recycled for the next iteration or dataset to an acceptable margin of error [145,172,173]. Unsupervised machine learning is typically used when labelled data is unknown or scarce [18,160,175]. Techniques used are normally based on clustering data samples, leaning towards a probabilistic model in which the output data may reside. A reinforced learning algorithm employs trial and error to identify a solution to a problem. The algorithm will be rewarded or penalized when it performs an action until it achieves its goals [176,177].

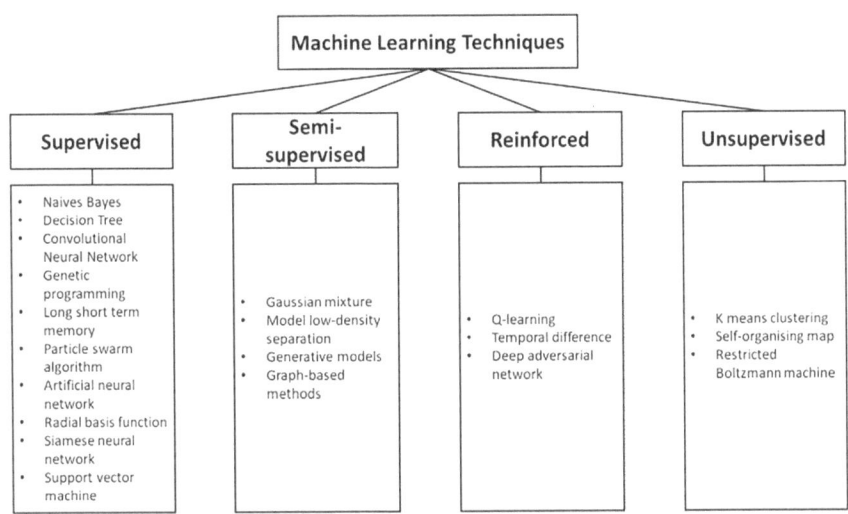

Figure 12. Categorized List of Machine Learning Techniques [174].

Object recognition tasks typically focus on high-resolution images (megapixel range), with few constraints on the viewing angle. Depending on the array size of the image and the number of pre-process methods used for classification, accuracy and performance should be considered, especially for real-time assessment [141,175,178,179].

Here, we can assess some image-based techniques used to optimize data acquisition, with some possible suggestions for implementation with C3DP (Table 6). This list is non-exhaustive, as a vast number of implementations are being developed over time. However, it intends to provide information useful for vision techniques in feedback. Some of the challenges in detection are related to noise, processing speed, and translation to control.

Table 6. List of innovations in computer vision that can be used in C3DP.

Work Conducted	Publication(s)	Method	Author(s)	Potential Relevance to C3DP
High-temperature measurement	[173]	Denoising Convolutional Neural Network	Wang J. et al.	Denoising can be useful in removing splatters from nozzle during printing.
Occlusion and illumination	[180]	Panoptic Segmentation	Hua X. et al.	Illumination and occlusions may occur during construction especially with a camera setup positioned to observe the overview of the site.
3D Detection	[181]	Mask R-CNN + RPN Optimization	Tao C. et al.	3D detection could have useful applications in depth detection for depth of printed filament, elastic buckling and plastic collapse etc. Additionally, depth perception can allow better control for machine control.
Point-based Single Stage Methods	[182]	3D Single Stage Object Detector	Yang Z. et al.	
LiDAR 3D Point Cloud Detection	[183]	VoxelNet	Zhou Y. et al.	
3D Detection with Stereo Images	[184]	Disp R-CNN		
Accuracy and Speed improvements	[185,186]	YOLOv3, YOLOv4	Redmon J. et al. Bochkovskiy A. et al.	Application for optimized real time detection for C3DP features.

4. Discussion of Process Control and Fault Diagnosis Systems

The earlier chapter focused on fault detection with computer vision for C3DP. Fault detection and diagnosis is an essential element to operations management in automatic systems [187]. A fault is defined as an event or occurrence outside of the acceptable range of observable parameters in the process [188]. This definition, by extension, implies that symptoms such as plastic collapse or elastic bucking (in Section 2) are considered anomalies. The underlying failure(s), basic event(s), or root cause(s)—to date—are associated with the printing time gap, nozzle standoff distance, curing rate, etc., (as observed in Table 3). Some of these features, such as nozzle standoff distance, can be acquired through sensor inputs, e.g., the 1D Time-of-Flight Sensor by Wolfs et al. [135]. Taking the model of Suiker et al. [12,13] as reference for plastic collapse and elastic bucking, the diagnosis model will inherit the parameters, boundary conditions, interactions, and assumptions defined by the author. Failure arising beyond the scope of these restrictions are deemed as exogenous factors, and can be expanded to a malfunction of the process, the sensor, and/or the actuator.

Based on this categorization, researchers in C3DP have extensively studied structural faults, though identification of faults in sensors and actuators are not commonly discussed in C3DP publications, largely due to incomplete, on-going, or proof-of-concept implementations for these process control systems. We attempt to breakdown the requirements for fault diagnostics in C3DP applications. Fault diagnostics is a comprehensive topic in a premature field in C3DP. Hence, we limit the categorizations to the components that should be considered. This chapter will discuss the performance vs. speed trade-off, isolation, robustness, novelty identifiability, classification estimate adaptability, explanation facility, and modelling requirements for the purpose of C3DP systems.

4.1. Detection Speeds/Diagnosis Performance

Detection speed in fault diagnosis refers to the time taken for the system to detect objects of interest. Diagnosis performance refers to accuracy in identifying the intended features. These are important considerations for real-time applications that require rapid processing and decision making. High speed and reliable accuracy in a diagnosis system is ideal but unrealistic [189]. These chokepoints can stem from software, where different architectures exhibit varying performances depending on situation. Clear examples have been given in a comparative study of unsupervised classical computer vision techniques conducted by Hussain et al. [190], who noted varying accuracies and computational speeds for the different techniques. Hardware limitations such as camera sensor resolution are a factor in computational efficiency. A clear example can be observed in the experimentations conducted by Yaacob and Fahmi [191] for object tracking tasks. For C3DP processes, the trade-off between detection speeds and diagnosis performance can be an important consideration when selecting a process monitoring method. For example, in-process monitoring would require speed-sensitive computational performance, whereas a post-process assessment can focus on better diagnosis performance measures.

4.2. Fault Isolation

Fault isolation is defined as the ability of the system to identify and set apart the specific causes of faults in a system. This refers to the diagnostic classifiers' capability to generate an output statistically independent of faults that are beyond the scope of the classifier. Process monitoring, data analysis, and root cause analysis are some of the methods employed for isolability. In C3DP, correction of properties for material and environmental changes are limited during the printing cycle. Hence, any unforeseeable changes are most likely dependent on adjustments made to process parameters. However, it is observable that there are common process parameters that contribute to all faults identified in Section 2. Root cause identifiability of current faults is still an ongoing pursuit, as post-process assessment is the current quantifiable evaluation mode. There is a gap in data points obtainable during in-process printing. Several researchers have attempted this via in- and ex-situ monitoring methods to obtain quantifiable results, such as layer height and layer width. However, reliability and standardization remain uncertain. This is critical as there is a trade-off between fault isolation and rejection of modelling uncertainties. Strict fault isolation requirements can incur false rejection of modelling uncertainties, and vice versa.

4.3. Robustness

A well-defined boundary condition in a robust diagnosis system should be impartial to noise and uncertainties. Failure in robustness will invalidate any diagnosis performance. Hence, ideally, there should be a proportional loss of performance in exchange for better robustness in the system. Monitoring systems that are based on neural networks pose a fundamental flaw for robustness, which is unstable and unusable for high-stakes applications [192]. Several studies have reported adversarial attacks on neural networks [192–195]. The image below is an example of an adversarial attack. Su et al. [196] modified a single pixel of an image. The resulting prediction provided high confidence with incorrect labels, showing that neural networks involving image-based systems are not spared from this limitation (Figure 13).

Figure 13. One Pixel Attacks Evaluated by Su et al. [196]. Images Labelling Format: Correct Label (Predicted Label).

Its relevance is dominant once in-process monitoring with neural networks i used for correcting critical processes. Researchers are still uncertain to an extent, regarding the cause and effect of adversarial robustness. However, the current consensus studied by Ilyas et al. [193] shows that adversarial attacks are not bugs, but instead are highly predictive non-robust features caused by human interpretation during model training. Hence, stable representations for DNN should be improved by introducing a human prior, for the elimination of human biases, to secure monitoring and printer head manipulation in C3DP feedback systems.

4.4. Novelty Identifiability

An abnormal behaviour in a process could be an indicator of a malfunction. If sufficient data is collected to validate any unknown malfunction, this can be known as novel identifiability. In cases with some available data for the unknown malfunction, the diagnosis system should be adequately robust to model the abnormal regions correctly without misclassification. Sparsity of abnormal data points could contribute to poor classification, which poses a challenge in novel identifiability. Ideally, unknown faults should not be misclassified as other known malfunctions.

Tay et al. [42] identified the importance of time gap effects on the interlayer bond strength, whereby a low modulus is required to bond the two printed layers sufficiently. The authors also specified that the opposite is required to maintain strength in the support of subsequent layers. Research [41,197] has indicated that effects of nozzle printing speeds and nozzle standoff distance have an influence on the interlayer bond strength. Post-process assessment methods mentioned above were able to identify root causes that define poor interlayer bond strength. However, as the requirement to manage the printing time gap between layers can be dynamic based on design, a monitoring or management process is needed to identify and handle the process. There is yet to be a classification method for poor interlayer voids with monitoring methods. However, there have been studies related to managing extrusion rates to avoid structural failure [6,13,17,108]. Hence, poor interlayer voids can be grouped as an unknown malfunction class in a monitoring or management method.

4.5. Classification Error Estimate

A diagnostic system should be able to provide an error estimate to project the confidence levels to the user on a practical basis for ease of facilitation and management of the existing errors. In computer vision, these classification estimates are akin to comparison to ground truth images. Many AI and machine learning techniques refer to this standardized test for error estimation [160,172,175,189–191]. Each method used in this manner can be fairly evaluated for its effectiveness. Additionally, complementary scores and matrices are often used as a quantitative assessment, such as Mean Average Precision (*mAP*), Intersection-over-Union (*IoU*), and F-Score. Each of these assessment methods utilize *Precision* and *Recall* parameters, which consist of True Positive (*TP*), True Negative (*TN*), False Positive (*FP*), and False Negative (*FN*) regions in classified data and provide a metric for comparison and evaluation [198–202]. These functions (*TP, FP, FN*) can be summarized with Ground Truth (*GT*) and Segmentation Mask Values (*S*) (Refer to Table 7). These metrics can enable the user or machine to make decisions on the ground for corrective measures or safety evaluation in C3DP applications.

Table 7. Example of Formula Used for Machine Learning Assessment.

$TP = GT \times S$ $FP = (GT + S) - GT$ $FN = (GT + S) - S$	$Precision = \frac{TP}{TP+FP}$ $Recall = \frac{TP}{TP+FN}$	$mAP = \frac{1}{11} \sum_{Recall_i} Presicion(Recall)$
		$IoU = \frac{TP}{(TP+FP+FN)}$
		$F - Score = \frac{Precision \times Recall}{Precision + Recall} = \frac{TP}{TP + \frac{1}{2}(FP+FN)}$

4.6. Adaptability

A system's process can be dependent on more than just noise and outliers. Different environmental conditions or process parameters can occur. Optimally, the diagnosis system should be able to adapt to these changes though gradual implementations during emerging issues. Kazemain et al. [18] (Section 3.2) represent an example of gradual implementation on unaccounted and unexpected issues with environmental lighting effects. This resulted in an occasional erroneous reading. Implementation was made to the algorithm to adjust accordingly by introducing frame drops. As of now, there are only a handful of researchers recruiting vision-based techniques for quantification and evaluation, and even less so for feedback implementations with vision-based systems (refer to Table 5). The lack of research interest in this area undermines the development of adaptable systems.

4.7. Explanation Facility

To provide an explanation in a diagnosis of an identified malfunction is critical for a support system. This should be able to provide cause and effects and justify its recommendations to the user. As only a handful of feedback systems have been developed in the field, there are limited examples for explanation. Wolfs et al. [135] developed a 1D time-of-flight sensor implementation, which was able to control the nozzle height as a feedback system, preventing buckling and collapse. The explanation facility dynamics for this application were the height values provided by the sensor, subsequently providing a recommendation to the machine to adjust the nozzle height upon deviation from the ideal elevation. As observed, the explanation facility provides critical support for the machine to respond to changes, failure of which would invalidate the diagnosis action and system.

4.8. Modelling Requirements

The model should be designed appropriately to optimize performance requirements. For an in-situ diagnostic system, modelling effort should be lightweight to reduce computational load for machine-based parameters. In supervised learning techniques, various network architectures can be used to optimize the process according to the application requirements: Mobilenet, Regnet, and Efficientnet, for example, are designed with detection speeds in mind, whereas ResNet and DenseNet are intent on better diagnosis performance with less focus on detection speeds [203]. As mentioned in the above section, modelling requirements should factor in human priors to eliminate predictive non-robust features. This addition will also increase the computational load in the feedback system. Hence, it is important to find an optimal operation rate to enable fluidity within the process.

5. Current and Potential Applications

Feedback implementations regarding C3DP applications are far from ready for deployment in industrial projects. However, similar diagnostic applications have already been implemented broadly in the construction industry. This section will consider the current and potential applications in diagnosis systems for C3DP based on existing technologies in the construction field.

5.1. Safety Monitoring

Camera equipped Unmanned Aerial Vehicles (UAVs) can be an inexpensive option to real-time monitoring and documenting of data. Fernandaz Galarreta et al. [204] developed a UAV monitoring system that uses point cloud assessment and object-based image analysis to inspect facades and roofs (Figure 14). Unfortunately, due to the early development of the technology, the data acquired misaligns with the requirements of ground-based Building Damage Assessments. The authors noted that feature extraction should be further developed to improve image characterization for damaged facades.

Figure 14. Wire Mesh Diagram with Cracks (in red) and Holes/Indentations (in Yellow), extracted in Object-Based Image Anaylsis [204].

On the other hand, Jhonattan et al. designed and developed an aerial monitoring system that utilizes Unmanned Aerial Systems (UAS) to inspect the workplace for common safety hazards such as worker distractions, signal interference, or workplace obstruction. There are some limitations in regulatory, safety, and technical aspects that can be problematic in UAS deployment. Some of the discussed problems reside in flight spaces, flying time reduction, data collection optimization, and battery life coverage in large workspaces. The research team is also leaning towards utilizing a computer vision algorithm to autonomize data collection (Figure 15) [147].

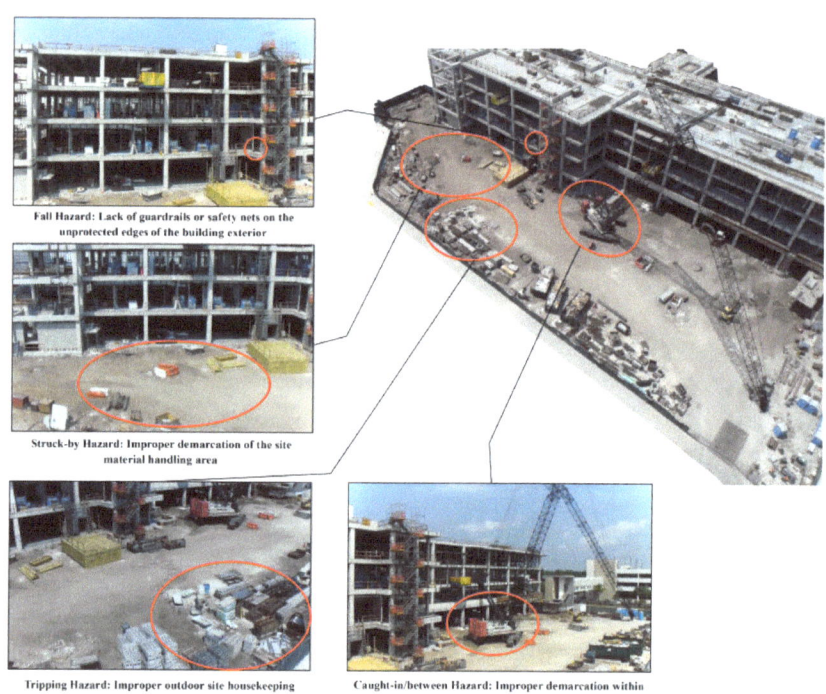

Figure 15. An example of Workplace Safety Inspection with UAS [147].

Lei et al. proposed a k-means clustering machine vision system to analyze construction sites for long term workplace safety, as opposed to a filter membrane that was used to collect the same data. The weight of the filter membrane had to be recorded before and at the end of the experiment, which is labor intensive and inefficient. Thick construction dust emissions that obscure the optical lens are detected with the k-means clustering algorithm in an HSV-formatted image. This method provided some levels of automation at the construction site that could streamline construction monitoring processes, reduced workload, and improved responsiveness to dangerous environmental changes. From a technical standpoint however, the authors expressed challenges in classifying low dust concentration levels and distinguishing between low and high dust concentration levels (Figure 16) [163].

5.2. Building Information Modelling

Photogrammetry was also used in documenting cultural heritage and gathering physical information, due to its low-cost feasibility. Documentation of cultural heritage can assist in protection, restoration, and renovation. However, accuracy and best practices are not well established for proper implementation on-site [205].

Figure 16. High Dust Concentration (**Left**) and Low Dust Concentration (**Right**) [163].

Yastikli [206] coupled laser scanning with photogrammetry to improve the accuracy of the documentation of cultural heritage sites. A ranged laser scanner was utilized to measure and compute the distance between the laser and the object while using a high-resolution camera to enhance the image feature quality. The combination of both techniques enabled the autonomous generation of high-quality images using a processing software, RiSCAN PRO. This allows all scans and images to be registered onto the reference coordinated system using reflectors in the scan area. With a series of images taken from multiple perspectives and angles, an RGB color value was assigned to every scanned 3D point. The images in Figure 17 show the results.

Figure 17. 3D point clouds of the Dolmabahce Palace. (Reprinted/adapted with permission. 2023, Yastikli) [206].

Implementing digitalization and BIM in the early phase of construction projects helps to establish a new method for process optimization. BIM can be useful for documenting progress information on a site, providing evidence that the work has been completed on-site and in accordance with the architectural design. Braun and Borrmann [207] proposed a solution to capture the construction process by taking photographs at regular intervals at different viewpoints. When sufficient images are taken, a 3D point cloud can be reconstructed with the help of photogrammetry methods (Figure 18).

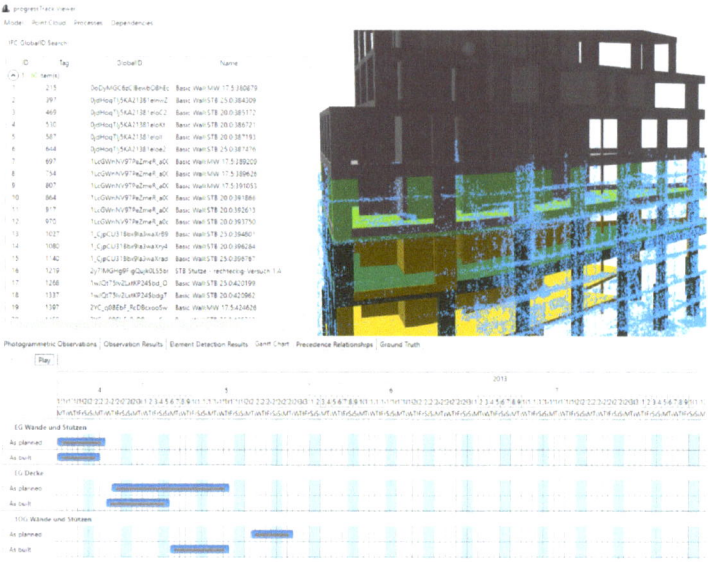

Figure 18. BIM viewer with detection states and point cloud from observations [207].

5.3. Structural Health Monitoring

5.3.1. Computer Vision

Computer vision has also been used in buildings to monitor structural health [137]. Cracks that undermine traditional construction methods can propagate due to tropical or cold weather conditions and can be attributed to poor hydration processes [208,209]. Small cracks are typically identified with electron microscopy and optical fluorescent microscopy [210–212]. Talab et al. [144] applied and compared several image filters (see Figure 19) to qualitatively scrutinize cracks in an image. Concrete surfaces exhibit noise, especially with Otsu's Method and the Kittler Met Method when processed individually. The experiment found that foreground and background features can be distinguished when concatenating more than one threshold method.

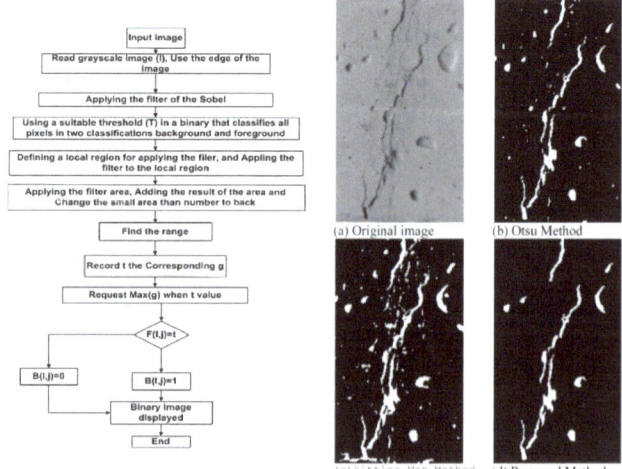

Figure 19. Process Flow (**Left**) of the Proposed Method Used by Talab et al. [144].

Dung et al. used VGG16-based convolutional neural network architecture to detect cracks on the surface of concrete (Figure 20) [162]. The model was able to detect cracks and crack density, proposing individual segmentation methods. While the proposed method is not in real time, it provided about 99.9% accuracy in classification. The experiment found that Otsu's thresholding and segmentation method can work well in both convoluted and non-complicated backgrounds.

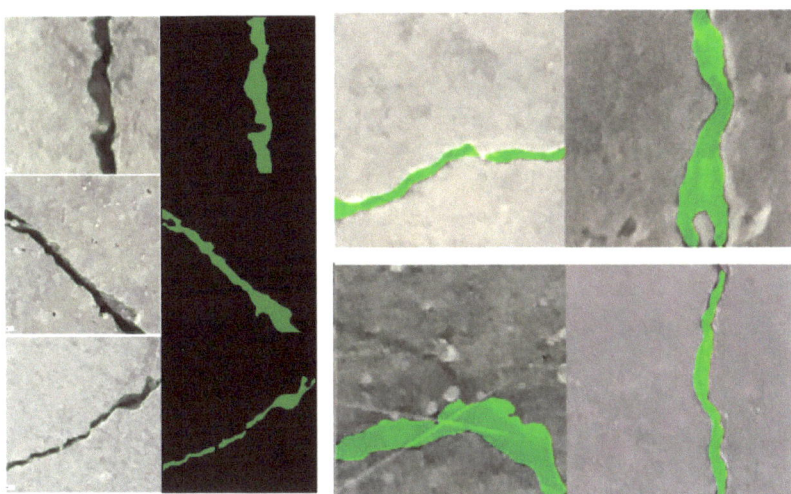

Figure 20. Actual and Annotated Crack Images (**Left**), Segmentation Results for Test Images (**Right**) [162].

The crack detection methods showed the different capabilities of computer vision approaches to surface detection in construction. Both methods could identify crack methods generally well. The classical method can produce levels of convoluted data in distinguishing any desired features with little training, while neural networks can be more accurate but time consuming, as a large dataset is generally needed to train the model. Collecting datasets can also be a challenge in analyzing 3D printed concrete, due to the lack of relevant research.

5.3.2. Sensor Embedment

Alternatively, SHM methods can also be used to characterize the internal properties of concrete structures. Sensor embedment can carry out various long term non-destructive tests as an early-detection and early-prevention measure to preserve structural integrity [213–216]. Some of these methods include the embedding of piezoresistive materials and piezoelectric sensors within the concrete structure during the fabrication process [217–221]. The mechanical reactions to internal structural changes can be picked up by the piezoresistive materials via electromechanical translation. This has enabled access to previously non-accessible analyses, such as damage assessments [222,223], strain logging [224–227], electromechanical interference shielding [228,229], corrosion sensing [230,231], and self-heating [232]. However, one of the pending challenges with sensor embedment is the high fabrication cost and poor material lifecycle in full scaled construction applications [220,221].

5.4. Progress Tracking

Bayrak and Kaka [149] discussed the use of photogrammetry to monitor the construction process from photos taken periodically during construction. The 3D model created can then be used to compare and track the measurements of the construction progress. The approach has shown to improve productivity in traditional construction and provided a better flow of information to all involved personnel. However, the CAD model is unable to obtain details of the plastering, electrical systems, and pipes. The method proves that a photogrammetric system can collect information, despite limitations at the time, and was able to monitor the general layout in the early stages of construction (Figure 21).

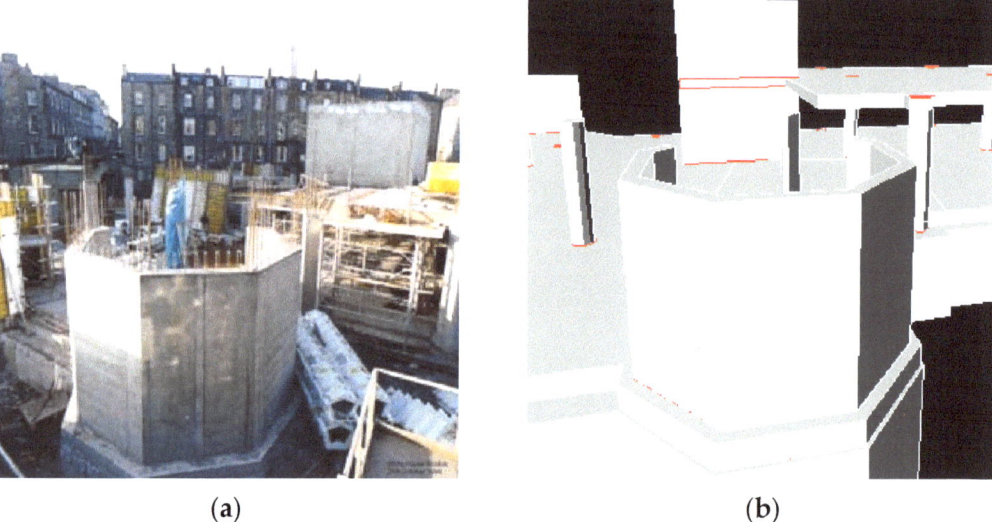

Figure 21. (**a**) Construction onsite progress. (**b**) Generation of 3D model with AutoCAD [149].

Despite the recent advancements in monitoring and management systems for Building Information Modelling (BIM) in the construction industry, the traditional approach that utilizes manual paperwork and recording of on-site activity is still prevalent in the industrial workflow [148]. Case studies of intra-production construction have been carried out to identify potential deviations from the intended construction schedule. Any deviations observed will activate an automatic notification system that is sent by email to inform the key decision makers [148]. Omar et al. [148] proposed a monitoring system that can achieve a significant improvement in accuracy and automation. However, occlusions are found to be one of the largest limitations in the advanced monitoring system. Exposure to static and dynamic obstructions present in construction sites are often deemed inevitable.

5.5. Sustainability

Sustainable technologies are described as self-sustaining efforts to improving overall quality of life, with little compromises to current technological efficiency and cost measures [233]. The heatmap of sustainability has been growing for the construction industry, as it contributes to approximately 40% of current world energy usage based on the 2019 Global Status Report for Buildings and Construction [234]. C3DP has a likely potential to significantly reduce the heavy reliance on natural resources and could introduce a robust circular economy framework with reusable materials and sustainable structural designs [235,236]. According to the Brundtland Commission (formerly known as the World Commission on Environment and Development), sustainability can be fragmented into economic, societal, and environmental factors [237].

C3DP researchers have been advocating for economic and environmental sustainability measures using industrial waste materials [80,85,86,93,238,239]. Operational benefits can also be achieved with a reallocation of manpower, with automated C3DP on-site [240]. Other sources within the construction industry have discussed the societal, economic, and environmental benefits of green buildings, where usage of natural resources (such as energy, water, material, waste, toxicity, and air quality) throughout the lifecycle of the building remains efficient [241]. Unfortunately, practical implementation studies related to sustainability in C3DP is not yet well documented, as challenges remain on a technical and process level, as described in Section 2 [236,242,243].

6. Conclusions and Future Vision

Currently, the preferred construction approach in Singapore's high-density urban landscape is the use of PPVC. This method is mainly driven by benefits in environmental pollution reduction, improved productivity, quality control, and customizability. However, its overall cost savings have been counterbalanced by new cost drivers, such as modular precast moulds, transportation, hoisting, manufacturing and holding yards, and supervision costs. The highly modular requirements for PPVC place additive manufacturing in an advantageous position due to its high customizability and low volume manufacturing capabilities for a faster manufacturing response time, faster production changeovers, and lower inventory requirements. As C3DP technology moves away from its early-stage development, there is a need to closely evaluate the process parameters across buildability, extrudability, and pumpability aspects.

As process parameters have been identified to have considerable influence in C3DP processes, monitoring systems for feedback applications seem to be an inevitable step forward towards automation in construction. This paper has presented a broad analysis of the challenges posed to C3DP and feedback systems, stressing the admission of similar parameters, evaluated and used for multiple failure modes that potentially confound the fault diagnosis processes. This paper covers some aspects of technicality and fundamental groundwork to develop a diagnosis system that consists of three parts.

- Existing parameter studies on various effects/challenges,
- Monitoring systems for fault diagnosis,
- Fault diagnosis principles in the context of C3DP.

Much work needs to be done to fully implement fault diagnosis methods for C3DP applications as a feedback system, as researchers must understand the material, the process, and the feedback methodologies. This paper hopes to contribute as a bridge between the complex branches of each aspect of C3DP for ease of understanding and further development of diagnosis systems in C3DP.

Author Contributions: Conceptualization, T.K.N.Q. and J.H.L. Resources, M.J.T., T.N.W. and K.H.H.L. Data Curation, T.K.N.Q. and J.H.L. Writing-Original Draft, T.K.N.Q. and Y.W.D.T. Writing-Review and Editing, T.K.N.Q. and K.H.H.L. Visualization, T.K.N.Q. and J.H.L. Supervision, T.N.W. and K.H.H.L. Project Administration, M.J.T., T.N.W. and K.H.H.L. Funding Acquisition, T.N.W. and K.H.H.L. All authors have read and agreed to the published version of the manuscript.

Funding: This research received no external funding.

Data Availability Statement: No new data were created or analyzed in this study. Data sharing is not applicable to this article.

Acknowledgments: This research is supported by the National Research Foundation, Prime Minister's Office, Singapore under its Medium-Sized Centre funding scheme, National Additive Manufacturing Innovation Cluster, Singapore Centre for 3D Printing, Enviro Sand Pty Ltd., and Chip Eng Seng Corporation Ltd.

Conflicts of Interest: The authors declare no conflict of interest.

References

1. S'pore's Construction Sector Faces Manpower, Materials Roadblocks with Future Uncertain. The Straits Times. Available online: https://www.straitstimes.com/singapore/spores-construction-sector-faces-manpower-materials-roadblocks-with-future-uncertain (accessed on 28 June 2022).
2. Prefabricated Prefinished Volumetric Construction (PPVC). Building and Construction Authority (BCA). Available online: https://www1.bca.gov.sg/buildsg/productivity/design-for-manufacturing-and-assembly-dfma/prefabricated-prefinished-volumetric-construction-ppvc (accessed on 24 April 2021).

3. Kong, H.; Managing, M.; Jien, L.; Director, P. *Pre-Fabricated Pre-Finished Volumetric Construction (PPVC) For Residential Projects*; Threesixty Cost Management Pte Ltd.: Singapore, 2018.
4. Chua, C.K.; Leong, K.F. *3D Printing and Additive Manufacturing: Principles and Applications*, 4th ed.; World Scientific Publishing Co.: Singapore, 2014. [CrossRef]
5. Khoshnevis, B.; Hwang, D. Contour Crafting. *Rapid Prototyp.* **2006**, *6*, 221–251. [CrossRef]
6. Carneau, P.; Mesnil, R.; Baverel, O.; Roussel, N. Layer pressing in concrete extrusion-based 3D-printing: Experiments and analysis. *Cem. Concr. Res.* **2022**, *155*, 106741. [CrossRef]
7. Ma, G.; Buswell, R.; da Silva, W.R.L.; Wang, L.; Xu, J.; Jones, S.Z. Technology readiness: A global snapshot of 3D concrete printing and the frontiers for development. *Cem. Concr. Res.* **2022**, *156*, 106774. [CrossRef]
8. Xu, J.; Ding, L.; Cai, L.; Zhang, L.; Luo, H.; Qin, W. Volume-forming 3D concrete printing using a variable-size square nozzle. *Autom. Constr.* **2019**, *104*, 95–106. [CrossRef]
9. Bos, F.; Wolfs, R.; Ahmed, Z.; Salet, T. Additive manufacturing of concrete in construction: Potentials and challenges of 3D concrete printing. *Virtual Phys. Prototyp.* **2016**, *11*, 209–225. [CrossRef]
10. Malaeb, Z.; AlSakka, F.; Hamzeh, F. 3D Concrete Printing: Machine Design, Mix Proportioning, and Mix Comparison between Different Machine Setups. In *3D Concrete Printing Technology*; Elsevier: Amsterdam, The Netherlands, 2019; pp. 115–136. [CrossRef]
11. Souza, M.T.; Ferreira, I.M.; de Moraes, E.G.; Senff, L.; de Oliveira, A.P.N. 3D printed concrete for large-scale buildings: An overview of rheology, printing parameters, chemical admixtures, reinforcements, and economic and environmental prospects. *J. Build. Eng.* **2020**, *32*, 101833. [CrossRef]
12. Suiker, A.S.J. Mechanical performance of wall structures in 3D printing processes: Theory, design tools and experiments. *Int. J. Mech. Sci.* **2018**, *137*, 145–170. [CrossRef]
13. Suiker, A.S.J. Effect of accelerated curing and layer deformations on structural failure during extrusion-based 3D printing. *Cem. Concr. Res.* **2022**, *151*, 106586. [CrossRef]
14. Suiker, A.S.J.; Wolfs, R.J.M.; Lucas, S.M.; Salet, T.A.M. Elastic buckling and plastic collapse during 3D concrete printing. *Cem. Concr. Res.* **2020**, *135*, 106016. [CrossRef]
15. Buswell, R.A.; de Silva, W.R.L.; Jones, S.Z.; Dirrenberger, J. 3D printing using concrete extrusion: A roadmap for research. *Cem. Concr. Res.* **2018**, *112*, 37–49. [CrossRef]
16. Lao, W.; Li, M.; Wong, T.N.; Tan, M.J.; Tjahjowidodo, T. Improving surface finish quality in extrusion-based 3D concrete printing using machine learning-based extrudate geometry control. *Virtual Phys. Prototyp.* **2020**, *15*, 178–193. [CrossRef]
17. Nerella, V.N.; Hempel, S.; Mechtcherine, V. Effects of layer-interface properties on mechanical performance of concrete elements produced by extrusion-based 3D-printing. *Constr. Build. Mater.* **2019**, *205*, 586–601. [CrossRef]
18. Kazemian, A.; Yuan, X.; Davtalab, O.; Khoshnevis, B. Computer vision for real-time extrusion quality monitoring and control in robotic construction. *Autom. Constr.* **2019**, *101*, 92–98. [CrossRef]
19. Kashani, A.; Ngo, T.D. Optimisation of mixture properties for 3D printing of geopolymer concrete. In Proceedings of the International Symposium on Automation and Robotics in Construction, New Orleans, LA, USA, 2–4 April 2018; IAARC Publications: Chennai, India, 2018.
20. Le, T.T.; Austin, S.A.; Lim, S.; Buswell, R.A.; Gibb, A.G.F.; Thorpe, T. Mix design and fresh properties for high-performance printing concrete. *Mater. Struct. Mater. Constr.* **2012**, *45*, 1221–1232. [CrossRef]
21. Almusallam, A.A. Effect of Environmental Conditions on the Properties of Fresh and Hardened Concrete. Available online: www.elsevier.com/locate/cemconcomp (accessed on 14 January 2021).
22. Ji, G.; Xiao, J.; Zhi, P.; Wu, Y.C.; Han, N. Effects of extrusion parameters on properties of 3D printing concrete with coarse aggregates. *Constr. Build. Mater.* **2022**, *325*, 126740. [CrossRef]
23. Geng, Z.; She, W.; Zuo, W.; Lyu, K.; Pan, H.; Zhang, Y.; Miao, C. Layer-interface properties in 3D printed concrete: Dual hierarchical structure and micromechanical characterization. *Cem. Concr. Res.* **2020**, *138*, 106220. [CrossRef]
24. Ma, Z.; Wittmann, F.H.; Xiao, J.; Zhao, T. Influence of freeze-thaw cycles on properties of Integral Water Repellent Concrete. *J. Wuhan Univ. Technol. Mater. Sci. Ed.* **2016**, *31*, 851–856. [CrossRef]
25. Danish, A.; Khurshid, K.; Mosaberpanah, M.A.; Ozbakkaloglu, T.; Salim, M.U. Microstructural characterization, driving mechanisms, and improvement strategies for interlayer bond strength of additive-manufactured cementitious composites: A review. *Case Stud. Constr. Mater.* **2022**, *17*, e01217. [CrossRef]
26. Moini, R.; Baghaie, A.; Rodriguez, F.B.; Zavattieri, P.D.; Youngblood, J.P.; Olek, J. Quantitative microstructural investigation of 3D-printed and cast cement pastes using micro-computed tomography and image analysis. *Cem. Concr. Res.* **2021**, *147*, 106493. [CrossRef]
27. Balapour, M.; Thway, T.; Moser, N.; Garboczi, E.J.; Hsuan, Y.G.; Farnam, Y. Engineering properties and pore structure of lightweight aggregates produced from off-spec fly ash. *Constr. Build. Mater.* **2022**, *348*, 128645. [CrossRef]
28. Liu, J.; Setunge, S.; Tran, P. 3D concrete printing with cement-coated recycled crumb rubber: Compressive and microstructural properties. *Constr. Build. Mater.* **2022**, *347*, 128507. [CrossRef]
29. Ramachandran, V.S. *Concrete Admixtures Handbook: Properties, Science, and Technology*; William Andrew: Norwich, NY, USA, 1995; p. 1153.

30. Marchment, T.; Sanjayan, J.G.; Nematollahi, B.; Xia, M. Interlayer Strength of 3D Printed Concrete: Influencing Factors and Method of Enhancing. *3D Concr. Print. Technol.* **2019**, 241–264. [CrossRef]
31. Micro-and Macroscopic Investigations on the Interface between Layers of 3D-Printed Cementitious Elements. Available online: https://www.researchgate.net/publication/319504633_MICRO-AND_MACROSCOPIC_INVESTIGATIONS_ON_THE_INTERFACE_BETWEEN_LAYERS_OF_3D-PRINTED_CEMENTITIOUS_ELEMENTS (accessed on 1 January 2023).
32. Shakor, P.; Sanjayan, J.; Nazari, A.; Nejadi, S. Modified 3D printed powder to cement-based material and mechanical properties of cement scaffold used in 3D printing. *Constr. Build. Mater.* **2017**, *138*, 398–409. [CrossRef]
33. Le, T.T.; Austin, S.A.; Lim, S.; Buswell, R.A.; Law, R.; Gibb, A.G.F.; Thorpe, T. Hardened properties of high-performance printing concrete. *Cem. Concr. Res.* **2012**, *42*, 558–566. [CrossRef]
34. Moelich, G.M.; Kruger, J.; Combrinck, R. Plastic shrinkage cracking in 3D printed concrete. *Compos. Part B Eng.* **2020**, *200*, 108313. [CrossRef]
35. Shahmirzadi, M.R.; Gholampour, A.; Kashani, A.; Ngo, T.D. Shrinkage behavior of cementitious 3D printing materials: Effect of temperature and relative humidity. *Cem. Concr. Compos.* **2021**, *124*, 104238. [CrossRef]
36. Cheewaket, T.; Jaturapitakkul, C.; Chalee, W. Concrete durability presented by acceptable chloride level and chloride diffusion coefficient in concrete: 10-year results in marine site. *Mater. Struct. Mater. Et Constr.* **2014**, *47*, 1501–1511. [CrossRef]
37. Zheng, X.; Liu, F.; Luo, T.; Duan, Y.; Yi, Y.; Hua, C. Study on Durability and Pore Characteristics of Concrete under Salt Freezing Environment. *Materials* **2021**, *14*, 7228. [CrossRef] [PubMed]
38. Wang, L.; Xiao, W.; Wang, Q.; Jiang, H.; Ma, G. Freeze-thaw resistance of 3D-printed composites with desert sand. *Cem. Concr. Compos.* **2022**, *133*, 104693. [CrossRef]
39. Assaad, J.J.; Hamzeh, F.; Hamad, B. Qualitative assessment of interfacial bonding in 3D printing concrete exposed to frost attack. *Case Stud. Constr. Mater.* **2020**, *13*, e00357. [CrossRef]
40. Bos, F.P.; Menna, C.; Pradena, M.; Kreiger, E.; da Silva, W.L.; Rehman, A.; Weger, D.; Wolfs, R.; Zhang, Y.; Ferrara, L.; et al. The realities of additively manufactured concrete structures in practice. *Cem. Concr. Res.* **2022**, *156*, 106746. [CrossRef]
41. Panda, B.; Paul, S.C.; Mohamed, N.A.N.; Tay, Y.W.D.; Tan, M.J. Measurement of tensile bond strength of 3D printed geopolymer mortar. *Measurement* **2018**, *113*, 108–116. [CrossRef]
42. Tay, Y.W.D.; Ting, G.H.A.; Qian, Y.; Panda, B.; He, L.W.; Tan, M.J. Time gap effect on bond strength of 3d printed concrete. *Virtual Phys. Prototyp.* **2019**, *14*, 104–113. [CrossRef]
43. Ashrafi, N.; Nazarian, S.; Meisel, N.A.; Duarte, J.P. Experimental prediction of material deformation in large-scale additive manufacturing of concrete. *Addit. Manuf.* **2021**, *37*, 101656. [CrossRef]
44. Yao, H.; Xie, Z.; Li, Z.; Huang, C.; Yuan, Q.; Zheng, X. The relationship between the rheological behavior and interlayer bonding properties of 3D printing cementitious materials with the addition of attapulgite. *Constr. Build. Mater.* **2022**, *316*, 125809. [CrossRef]
45. Slavcheva, G.S. Drying and shrinkage of cement paste for 3D printable concrete. *IOP Conf. Ser. Mater. Sci. Eng.* **2019**, *481*, 012043. [CrossRef]
46. Lu, B.; Qian, Y.; Li, M.; Weng, Y.; Leong, K.F.; Tan, M.-J.; Qian, S.; Lu, B.; Qian, Y.; Li, M.; et al. Designing spray-based 3D printable cementitious materials with fly ash cenosphere and air entraining agent. *Constr. Build. Mater.* **2019**, *211*, 1073–1084. [CrossRef]
47. Ma, G.; Zhang, J.; Wang, L.; Li, Z.; Sun, J. Mechanical characterization of 3D printed anisotropic cementitious material by the electromechanical transducer. *Smart Mater. Struct.* **2018**, *27*, 075036. [CrossRef]
48. Yu, S.; Xia, M.; Sanjayan, J.; Yang, L.; Xiao, J.; Du, H. Microstructural characterization of 3D printed concrete. *J. Build. Eng.* **2021**, *44*, 102948. [CrossRef]
49. Anleu, P.C.B. Quantitative Micro XRF Mapping of Chlorides: Possibilities, Limitations, and Applications, from Cement to Digital Concrete. Ph.D. Thesis, ETH Zurich, Zürich, Switzerland, March 2019. [CrossRef]
50. van der Putten, J.; Azima, M.; Heede, P.V.D.; Van Mullem, T.; Snoeck, D.; Carminati, C.; Hovind, J.; Trtik, P.; De Schutter, G.; Van Tittelboom, K. Neutron radiography to study the water ingress via the interlayer of 3D printed cementitious materials for continuous layering. *Constr. Build. Mater.* **2020**, *258*, 119587. [CrossRef]
51. Wang, L.; Tian, Z.; Ma, G.; Zhang, M. Interlayer bonding improvement of 3D printed concrete with polymer modified mortar: Experiments and molecular dynamics studies. *Cem. Concr. Compos.* **2020**, *110*, 103571. [CrossRef]
52. Hosseini, E.; Zakertabrizi, M.; Korayem, A.H.; Xu, G. A novel method to enhance the interlayer bonding of 3D printing concrete: An experimental and computational investigation. *Cem. Concr. Compos.* **2019**, *99*, 112–119. [CrossRef]
53. Sanjayan, J.G.; Nematollahi, B.; Xia, M.; Marchment, T. Effect of surface moisture on inter-layer strength of 3D printed concrete. *Constr. Build. Mater.* **2018**, *172*, 468–475. [CrossRef]
54. Moelich, G.M.; Kruger, P.J.; Combrinck, R. A plastic shrinkage cracking risk model for 3D printed concrete exposed to different environments. *Cem. Concr. Compos.* **2022**, *130*, 104516. [CrossRef]
55. Alchaar, A.S.; Al-Tamimi, A.K. Mechanical properties of 3D printed concrete in hot temperatures. *Constr. Build. Mater.* **2021**, *266*, 120991. [CrossRef]
56. Gonen, T.; Yazicioglu, S.; Demirel, B. The influence of freezing-thawing cycles on the capillary water absorption and porosity of concrete with mineral admixture. *KSCE J. Civ. Eng.* **2015**, *19*, 667–671. [CrossRef]
57. Salet, T.A.M.; Ahmed, Z.Y.; Bos, F.P.; Laagland, H.L.M. 3D Concrete Printing: A Systematic Review of Rheology, Mix Designs, Mechanical, Microstructural, and Durability Characteristics. *Materials* **2021**, *14*, 3800. [CrossRef]

58. Marchment, T.; Sanjayan, J.; Xia, M. Method of enhancing interlayer bond strength in construction scale 3D printing with mortar by effective bond area amplification. *Mater. Des.* **2019**, *169*, 107684. [CrossRef]
59. Wolfs, R.J.M.; Bos, F.P.; Salet, T.A.M. Hardened properties of 3D printed concrete: The influence of process parameters on interlayer adhesion. *Cem. Concr. Res.* **2019**, *119*, 132–140. [CrossRef]
60. Tsivilis, S.; Tsantilas, J.; Kakali, G.; Chaniotakis, E.; Sakellariou, A. The permeability of Portland limestone cement concrete. *Cem. Concr. Res.* **2003**, *33*, 1465–1471. [CrossRef]
61. Tatsuhiko, S. "EFFECT OF CARBONATION ON CHLORIDE PENETRATION IN CONCRETE," RILEM, Bagneux, Franc, 2005. Available online: https://www.rilem.net/images/publis/pro038-025.pdf (accessed on 20 February 2023).
62. Ye, H.; Jin, X.; Fu, C.; Jin, N.; Xu, Y.; Huang, T. Chloride penetration in concrete exposed to cyclic drying-wetting and carbonation. *Constr. Build. Mater.* **2016**, *112*, 457–463. [CrossRef]
63. Liu, B.; Shi, J.; Zhou, F.; Shen, S.; Ding, Y.; Qin, J. Effects of steam curing regimes on the capillary water absorption of concrete: Prediction using multivariable regression models. *Constr. Build. Mater.* **2020**, *256*, 119426. [CrossRef]
64. Abyaneh, S.D.; Wong, H.S.; Buenfeld, N.R. Computational investigation of capillary absorption in concrete using a three-dimensional mesoscale approach. *Comput. Mater. Sci.* **2014**, *87*, 54–64. [CrossRef]
65. Abyaneh, S.D.; Wong, H.S.; Buenfeld, N.R. Simulating the effect of microcracks on the diffusivity and permeability of concrete using a three-dimensional model. *Comput. Mater. Sci.* **2016**, *119*, 130–143. [CrossRef]
66. Akhavan, A.; Shafaatian, S.M.H.; Rajabipour, F. Quantifying the effects of crack width, tortuosity, and roughness on water permeability of cracked mortars. *Cem. Concr. Res.* **2012**, *42*, 313–320. [CrossRef]
67. Basheer, L.; Kropp, J.; Cleland, D.J. Assessment of the durability of concrete from its permeation properties: A review. *Constr. Build. Mater.* **2001**, *15*, 93–103. [CrossRef]
68. Gardner, D.; Jefferson, A.; Hoffman, A. Investigation of capillary flow in discrete cracks in cementitious materials. *Cem. Concr. Res.* **2012**, *42*, 972–981. [CrossRef]
69. Nguyen-Van, V.; Nguyen-Xuan, H.; Panda, B.; Tran, P. 3D concrete printing modelling of thin-walled structures. *Structures* **2022**, *39*, 496–511. [CrossRef]
70. Kruger, J.; Zeranka, S.; van Zijl, G. 3D concrete printing: A lower bound analytical model for buildability performance quantification. *Autom. Constr.* **2019**, *106*, 102904. [CrossRef]
71. Lee, J.H.; Kim, J.H. Matric suction of fine sand and its effect on the shape stability of 3D printed cement mortar. *Constr. Build. Mater.* **2022**, *341*, 127618. [CrossRef]
72. Muthukrishnan, S.; Ramakrishnan, S.; Sanjayan, J. Set on demand geopolymer using print head mixing for 3D concrete printing. *Cem. Concr. Compos.* **2022**, *128*, 104451. [CrossRef]
73. Muthukrishnan, S.; Ramakrishnan, S.; Sanjayan, J. Effect of microwave heating on interlayer bonding and buildability of geopolymer 3D concrete printing. *Constr. Build. Mater.* **2020**, *265*, 120786. [CrossRef]
74. Muthukrishnan, S.; Ramakrishnan, S.; Sanjayan, J. In-line activation of geopolymer slurry for concrete 3D printing. *Cem. Concr. Res.* **2022**, *162*, 107008. [CrossRef]
75. Pham, L.; Tran, P.; Sanjayan, J. Steel fibres reinforced 3D printed concrete: Influence of fibre sizes on mechanical performance. *Constr. Build. Mater.* **2020**, *250*, 118785. [CrossRef]
76. Nematollahi, B.; Vijay, P.; Sanjayan, J.; Nazari, A.; Xia, M.; Nerella, V.N.; Mechtcherine, V. Effect of Polypropylene Fibre Addition on Properties of Geopolymers Made by 3D Printing for Digital Construction. *Materials* **2018**, *11*, 2352. [CrossRef] [PubMed]
77. Weng, Y.; Li, M.; Liu, Z.; Lao, W.; Lu, B.; Zhang, D.; Tan, M.J. Printability and fire performance of a developed 3D printable fibre reinforced cementitious composites under elevated temperatures. *Virtual Phys. Prototyp.* **2019**, *14*, 284–292. [CrossRef]
78. Zheng, W.; Luo, B.; Wang, Y. Microstructure and mechanical properties of RPC containing PP fibres at elevated temperatures. *Mag. Concr. Res.* **2015**, *66*, 397–408. [CrossRef]
79. Christ, S.; Schnabel, M.; Vorndran, E.; Groll, J.; Gbureck, U. Fiber reinforcement during 3D printing. *Mater. Lett.* **2015**, *139*, 165–168. [CrossRef]
80. Panda, B.; Paul, S.C.; Tan, M.J. Anisotropic mechanical performance of 3D printed fiber reinforced sustainable construction material. *Mater. Lett.* **2017**, *209*, 146–149. [CrossRef]
81. Li, L.G.; Xiao, B.F.; Fang, Z.Q.; Xiong, Z.; Chu, S.H.; Kwan, A.K.H. Feasibility of glass/basalt fiber reinforced seawater coral sand mortar for 3D printing. *Addit. Manuf.* **2021**, *37*, 101684. [CrossRef]
82. Shakor, P.; Nejadi, S.; Paul, G.; Gowripalan, N. Effects of Different Orientation Angle, Size, Surface Roughness, and Heat Curing on Mechanical Behavior of 3D Printed Cement Mortar with/without Glass Fiber in Powder-Based 3DP. *3D Print Addit. Manuf.* **2021**, *0*, 1–10. [CrossRef]
83. Lv, C.; Shen, H.; Liu, J.; Wu, D.; Qu, E.; Liu, S. Properties of 3D Printing Fiber-Reinforced Geopolymers Based on Interlayer Bonding and Anisotropy. *Materials* **2022**, *15*, 8032. [CrossRef] [PubMed]
84. Kong, X.; Dai, L.; Wang, Y.; Qiao, D.; Hou, S.; Wang, S. Influence of kenaf stalk on printability and performance of 3D printed industrial tailings based geopolymer. *Constr. Build. Mater.* **2022**, *315*, 125787. [CrossRef]
85. Long, W.J.; Tao, J.-L.; Lin, C.; Gu, Y.-C.; Mei, L.; Duan, H.-B.; Xing, F. Rheology and buildability of sustainable cement-based composites containing micro-crystalline cellulose for 3D-printing. *J. Clean. Prod.* **2019**, *239*, 118054. [CrossRef]
86. Sinka, M.; Zorica, J.; Bajare, D.; Sahmenko, G.; Korjakins, A. Fast Setting Binders for Application in 3D Printing of Bio-Based Building Materials. *Sustainability* **2020**, *12*, 8838. [CrossRef]

87. Nam, Y.J.; Hwang, Y.K.; Park, J.W.; Lim, Y.M. Fiber-Reinforced Cementitious Composite Design with Controlled Distribution and Orientation of Fibers Using Three-Dimensional Printing Technology. In *3D Concrete Printing Technology*; Elsevier: Amsterdam, The Netherlands, 2019; pp. 59–72. [CrossRef]
88. Hambach, M.; Volkmer, D. Properties of 3D-printed fiber-reinforced Portland cement paste. *Cem. Concr. Compos.* **2017**, *79*, 62–70. [CrossRef]
89. Nematollahi, B.; Xia, M.; Sanjayan, J.; Vijay, P. Effect of Type of Fiber on Inter-Layer Bond and Flexural Strengths of Extrusion-Based 3D Printed Geopolymer. *Mater. Sci. Forum* **2018**, *939*, 155–162. [CrossRef]
90. Lesovik, V.; Fediuk, R.; Amran, M.; Alaskhanov, A.; Volodchenko, A.; Murali, G.; Uvarov, V.; Elistratkin, M. 3D-Printed Mortars with Combined Steel and Polypropylene Fibers. *Fibers* **2021**, *9*, 79. [CrossRef]
91. Moustafa, A.; Elgawady, M.A. Mechanical properties of high strength concrete with scrap tire rubber. *Constr. Build. Mater.* **2015**, *93*, 249–256. [CrossRef]
92. Ghabezi, P.; Flanagan, T.; Harrison, N. Short basalt fibre reinforced recycled polypropylene filaments for 3D printing. *Mater. Lett.* **2022**, *326*, 132942. [CrossRef]
93. Ting, G.H.A.; Quah, T.K.N.; Lim, J.H.; Tay, Y.W.D.; Tan, M.J. Extrudable region parametrical study of 3D printable concrete using recycled glass concrete. *J. Build. Eng.* **2022**, *50*, 104091. [CrossRef]
94. Bai, G.; Wang, L.; Ma, G.; Sanjayan, J.; Bai, M. 3D printing eco-friendly concrete containing under-utilised and waste solids as aggregates. *Cem. Concr. Compos.* **2021**, *120*, 104037. [CrossRef]
95. Ting, G.H.A.; Tay, Y.W.D.; Qian, Y.; Tan, M.J. Utilization of recycled glass for 3D concrete printing: Rheological and mechanical properties. *J. Mater. Cycles Waste Manag.* **2019**, *21*, 994–1003. [CrossRef]
96. Li, Z.; Wang, L.; Ma, G. Mechanical improvement of continuous steel microcable reinforced geopolymer composites for 3D printing subjected to different loading conditions. *Compos. B Eng.* **2020**, *187*, 107796. [CrossRef]
97. Bos, F.; Ahmed, Z.; Jutinov, E.; Salet, T. Experimental Exploration of Metal Cable as Reinforcement in 3D Printed Concrete. *Materials* **2017**, *10*, 1314. [CrossRef] [PubMed]
98. Hojati, M.; Memari, A.M.; Zahabi, M.; Wu, Z.; Li, Z.; Park, K.; Nazarian, S.; Duarte, J.P. Barbed-wire reinforcement for 3D concrete printing. *Autom. Constr.* **2022**, *141*, 104438. [CrossRef]
99. Xiao, J.; Chen, Z.; Ding, T.; Zou, S. Bending behaviour of steel cable reinforced 3D printed concrete in the direction perpendicular to the interfaces. *Cem. Concr. Compos.* **2022**, *125*, 104313. [CrossRef]
100. Austin, S.; Buswell, R.; Le, T.; Wackrow, R.; Austin, S.; Gibb, A.; Thorpe, T. Development of a viable concrete printing process. In Proceedings of the 28th International Symposium on Automation and Robotics in Construction (ISARC 2011), Seoul, Republic of Korea, 29 June–2 July 2011; pp. 665–670. [CrossRef]
101. Wang, L.; Ma, G.; Liu, T.; Buswell, R.; Li, Z. Interlayer reinforcement of 3D printed concrete by the in-process deposition of U-nails. *Cem. Concr. Res.* **2021**, *148*, 106535. [CrossRef]
102. Asprone, D.; Auricchio, F.; Menna, C.; Mercuri, V. 3D printing of reinforced concrete elements: Technology and design approach. *Constr. Build. Mater.* **2018**, *165*, 218–231. [CrossRef]
103. Salet, T.A.M.; Ahmed, Z.Y.; Bos, F.P.; Laagland, H.L.M. Design of a 3D printed concrete bridge by testing. *Virtual Phys. Prototyp.* **2018**, *13*, 222–236. [CrossRef]
104. Marchment, T.; Sanjayan, J. Mesh reinforcing method for 3D Concrete Printing. *Autom. Constr.* **2020**, *109*, 102992. [CrossRef]
105. Liu, M.; Wang, L.; Ma, G.; Li, W.; Zhou, Y. U-type steel wire mesh for the flexural performance enhancement of 3D printed concrete: A novel reinforcing approach. *Mater. Lett.* **2023**, *331*, 133429. [CrossRef]
106. Kruger, J.; Cho, S.; Zeranka, S.; Viljoen, C.; van Zijl, G. 3D concrete printer parameter optimisation for high rate digital construction avoiding plastic collapse. *Compos. B Eng.* **2020**, *183*, 107660. [CrossRef]
107. Tripathi, A.; Nair, S.A.O.; Neithalath, N. A comprehensive analysis of buildability of 3D-printed concrete and the use of bi-linear stress-strain criterion-based failure curves towards their prediction. *Cem. Concr. Compos.* **2022**, *128*, 104424. [CrossRef]
108. Liu, Z.; Li, M.; Wong, T.N.; Tan, M.J. Towards additive manufacturing: Pumping flow rate with time-dependent material rheology in 3d cementitious material printing. *Mater. Sci. Forum* **2018**, *941*, 2131–2136. [CrossRef]
109. Tay, Y.W.D.; Li, M.Y.; Tan, M.J. Effect of printing parameters in 3D concrete printing: Printing region and support structures. *J. Mater. Process. Technol.* **2019**, *271*, 261–270. [CrossRef]
110. Tay, Y.W.D.; Qian, Y.; Tan, M.J. Printability region for 3D concrete printing using slump and slump flow test. *Compos. B Eng.* **2019**, *174*, 106968. [CrossRef]
111. el Cheikh, K.; Rémond, S.; Khalil, N.; Aouad, G. Numerical and experimental studies of aggregate blocking in mortar extrusion. *Constr. Build. Mater.* **2017**, *145*, 452–463. [CrossRef]
112. Khalil, N.; Aouad, G.; el Cheikh, K.; Rémond, S. Use of calcium sulfoaluminate cements for setting control of 3D-printing mortars. *Constr. Build. Mater.* **2017**, *157*, 382–391. [CrossRef]
113. Zuriguel, I.; Garcimartín, A.; Maza, D.; Pugnaloni, L.A.; Pastor, J.M. Jamming during the discharge of granular matter from a silo. *Phys. Rev. E* **2005**, *71*, 051303. Available online: https://www.academia.edu/16258758/Jamming_during_the_discharge_of_granular_matter_from_a_silo (accessed on 27 November 2022). [CrossRef] [PubMed]
114. Perrot, A.; Lanos, C.; Melinge, Y.; Estellé, P. Mortar physical properties evolution in extrusion flow. *Rheol. Acta* **2007**, *46*, 1065–1073. [CrossRef]

115. Jayathilakage, R.; Rajeev, P.; Sanjayan, J. Rheometry for Concrete 3D Printing: A Review and an Experimental Comparison. *Buildings* **2022**, *12*, 1190. [CrossRef]
116. Liu, Z.; Li, M.; Weng, Y.; Qian, Y.; Wong, T.N.; Tan, M.J. Modelling and parameter optimization for filament deformation in 3D cementitious material printing using support vector machine. *Compos. B Eng.* **2020**, *193*, 108018. [CrossRef]
117. Liu, Z.; Li, M.; Tay, Y.W.D.; Weng, Y.; Wong, T.N.; Tan, M.J. Rotation nozzle and numerical simulation of mass distribution at corners in 3D cementitious material printing. *Addit. Manuf.* **2020**, *34*, 101190. [CrossRef]
118. Ahmed, Z.Y.; Bos, F.P.; Wolfs, R.J.M.; Salet, T.A.M. Design considerations due to scale effects in 3D concrete printing. In Proceedings of the 8th International Conference of the Arab Society for Computer Aided Architectural Design (ASCAAD 2016), London, UK, 7–8 November 2016.
119. Ma, G.; Li, Z.; Wang, L. Printable properties of cementitious material containing copper tailings for extrusion based 3D printing. *Constr. Build. Mater.* **2018**, *162*, 613–627. [CrossRef]
120. Nair, S.A.O.; Panda, S.; Santhanam, M.; Sant, G.; Neithalath, N. A critical examination of the influence of material characteristics and extruder geometry on 3D printing of cementitious binders. *Cem. Concr. Compos.* **2020**, *112*, 103671. [CrossRef]
121. Kaplan, D.; de Larrard, F.; Sedran, T. Design of Concrete Pumping Circuit. *Mater. J.* **2005**, *102*, 110–117. [CrossRef]
122. Perrot, A.; Mélinge, Y.; Estellé, P.; Lanos, C. Vibro-extrusion: A new forming process for cement-based materials. *Adv. Cem. Res.* **2009**, *21*, 125–133. [CrossRef]
123. Mohan, M.K.; Rahul, A.V.; van Tittelboom, K.; de Schutter, G. Rheological and pumping behaviour of 3D printable cementitious materials with varying aggregate content. *Cem. Concr. Res.* **2021**, *139*, 106258. [CrossRef]
124. de Schutter, G.; Feys, D. Pumping of Fresh Concrete: Insights and Challenges. *RILEM Tech. Lett.* **2016**, *1*, 76–80. [CrossRef]
125. Le, H.D.; Kadri, E.H.; Aggoun, S.; Vierendeels, J.; Troch, P.; de Schutter, G. Effect of lubrication layer on velocity profile of concrete in a pumping pipe. *Mater. Struct. Mater. Constr.* **2015**, *48*, 3991–4003. [CrossRef]
126. Mechtcherine, V.; Bos, F.; Perrot, A.; da Silva, W.L.; Nerella, V.; Fataei, S.; Wolfs, R.; Sonebi, M.; Roussel, N. Extrusion-based additive manufacturing with cement-based materials—Production steps, processes, and their underlying physics: A review. *Cem. Concr. Res.* **2020**, *132*, 106037. [CrossRef]
127. Roussel, N. Rheological requirements for printable concretes. *Cem. Concr. Res.* **2018**, *112*, 76–85. [CrossRef]
128. Srinivasan, R.; DeFord, D.; Shah, S. The use of extrusion rheometry in the development of extruded fiber-reinforced cement composites. *Concr. Sci. Eng.* **1999**, *1*, 26–36.
129. Kuder, K.G.; Shah, S.P. Rheology of Extruded Cement-Based Materials. *Mater. J.* **2007**, *104*, 283–290. [CrossRef]
130. Menna, C.; Mata-Falcón, J.; Bos, F.P.; Vantyghem, G.; Ferrara, L.; Asprone, D.; Salet, T.; Kaufmann, W. Opportunities and challenges for structural engineering of digitally fabricated concrete. *Cem. Concr. Res.* **2020**, *133*, 106079. [CrossRef]
131. Rahul, A.V.; Narayan, S.P.A.; Neithalath, N.; Santhanam, M. A thermodynamic framework for modelling thixotropic yield stress fluids: Application to cement pastes. *J. Non Newton. Fluid Mech.* **2020**, *281*, 104318. [CrossRef]
132. Jiang, Q. Effects of air entrainment on rheology. *Mater. J.* **2004**, *101*, 448–456. Available online: https://www.researchgate.net/publication/288569745 (accessed on 20 February 2023).
133. Qian, Y.; de Schutter, G. Enhancing thixotropy of fresh cement pastes with nanoclay in presence of polycarboxylate ether superplasticizer (PCE). *Cem. Concr. Res.* **2018**, *111*, 15–22. [CrossRef]
134. Qian, Y.; Ma, S.; Kawashima, S.; de Schutter, G. Rheological characterization of the viscoelastic solid-like properties of fresh cement pastes with nanoclay addition. *Theor. Appl. Fract. Mech.* **2019**, *103*, 102262. [CrossRef]
135. Wolfs, R.J.M.; Bos, F.P.; van Strien, E.C.F.; Salet, T.A.M. A real-time height measurement and feedback system for 3D concrete printing. In *High Tech Concrete: Where Technology and Engineering Meet: Proceedings of the 2017 fib Symposium, Held in Maastricht, The Netherlands, 12–14 June 2017*; Springer International Publishing: Berlin/Heidelberg, Germany, 2017; pp. 2474–2483. [CrossRef]
136. Rill-García, R.; Dokladalova, E.; Dokládal, P.; Caron, J.-F.; Mesnil, R.; Margerit, P.; Charrier, M. Inline monitoring of 3D concrete printing using computer vision. *Addit. Manuf.* **2022**, *60*, 103175. [CrossRef]
137. Dong, C.-Z.; Catbas, F.N. A review of computer vision–based structural health monitoring at local and global levels. *Struct. Health Monit.* **2021**, *20*, 692–743. [CrossRef]
138. Nor, N.M.; Hussain, M.A.; Hassan, C.R.C. Fault diagnosis and classification framework using multi-scale classification based on kernel Fisher discriminant analysis for chemical process system. *Appl. Soft Comput.* **2017**, *61*, 959–972. [CrossRef]
139. Burdzik, R. A comprehensive diagnostic system for vehicle suspensions based on a neural classifier and wavelet resonance estimators. *Measurement* **2022**, *200*, 111602. [CrossRef]
140. Kang, Z.; Catal, C.; Tekinerdogan, B. Product failure detection for production lines using a data-driven model. *Expert Syst. Appl.* **2022**, *202*, 117398. [CrossRef]
141. Image Pre-Processing. Available online: https://www.embedded-vision.com/sites/default/files/apress/computervisionmetrics/chapter2/9781430259299_Ch02.pdf (accessed on 11 January 2023).
142. Nair, S.A.O.; Sant, G.; Neithalath, N. Mathematical morphology-based point cloud analysis techniques for geometry assessment of 3D printed concrete elements. *Addit. Manuf.* **2022**, *49*, 102499. [CrossRef]
143. Mneymneh, B.E.; Abbas, M.; Khoury, H. Vision-Based Framework for Intelligent Monitoring of Hardhat Wearing on Construction Sites. *J. Comput. Civ. Eng.* **2018**, *33*, 04018066. [CrossRef]
144. Talab, A.M.A.; Huang, Z.; Xi, F.; HaiMing, L. Detection crack in image using Otsu method and multiple filtering in image processing techniques. *Optik* **2016**, *127*, 1030–1033. [CrossRef]

145. Garfo, S.; Muktadir, M.A.; Yi, S. Defect Detection on 3D Print Products and in Concrete Structures Using Image Processing and Convolution Neural Network. *J. Mechatron. Robot.* **2020**, *4*, 74–84. [CrossRef]
146. Davtalab, O.; Kazemian, A.; Yuan, X.; Khoshnevis, B. Automated inspection in robotic additive manufacturing using deep learning for layer deformation detection. *J. Intell. Manuf.* **2022**, *33*, 771–784. [CrossRef]
147. Martinez, J.G.; Albeaino, G.; Gheisari, M.; Issa, R.R.A.; Alarcón, L.F. iSafeUAS: An unmanned aerial system for construction safety inspection. *Autom. Constr.* **2021**, *125*, 103595. [CrossRef]
148. Omar, H.; Mahdjoubi, L.; Kheder, G. Towards an automated photogrammetry-based approach for monitoring and controlling construction site activities. *Comput. Ind.* **2018**, *98*, 172–182. [CrossRef]
149. Bayrak, T.; Kaka, A. Evaluation of digital photogrammetry and 3D CAD modelling applications in construction management. In Proceedings of the 20th Annual ARCOM Conference, Edinburgh, UK, 1–3 September 2004.
150. Aldao, E.; González-Jorge, H.; Pérez, J.A. Metrological comparison of LiDAR and photogrammetric systems for deformation monitoring of aerospace parts. *Measurement* **2021**, *174*, 109037. [CrossRef]
151. Cucci, D.A.; Rehak, M.; Skaloud, J. Bundle adjustment with raw inertial observations in UAV applications. *ISPRS J. Photogramm. Remote Sens.* **2017**, *130*, 1–12. [CrossRef]
152. Kume, H.; Sato, T.; Yokoya, N. Bundle adjustment using aerial images with two-stage geometric verification. *Comput. Vis. Image Underst.* **2015**, *138*, 74–84. [CrossRef]
153. Marschner, S. Light Reflection and Illumination, CS 4620 Lecture 23 Cornell CS4620. 2014. Available online: https://www.cs.cornell.edu/courses/cs4620/2014fa/lectures/23reflection.pdf (accessed on 20 February 2023).
154. Aicardi, I.; Chiabrando, F.; Lingua, A.M.; Noardo, F. Recent trends in cultural heritage 3D survey: The photogrammetric computer vision approach. *J. Cult. Herit.* **2018**, *32*, 257–266. [CrossRef]
155. Fang, W.; Ma, L.; Love, P.E.D.; Luo, H.; Ding, L.; Zhou, A. Knowledge graph for identifying hazards on construction sites: Integrating computer vision with ontology. *Autom. Constr.* **2020**, *119*, 103310. [CrossRef]
156. Golnabi, H.; Asadpour, A. Design and application of industrial machine vision systems. *Robot. Comput. Integr. Manuf.* **2007**, *23*, 630–637. [CrossRef]
157. Lao, W.; Li, M.; Tjahjowidodo, T. Variable-geometry nozzle for surface quality enhancement in 3D concrete printing. *Addit. Manuf.* **2021**, *37*, 101638. [CrossRef]
158. Zhang, X.; Li, M.; Lim, J.H.; Weng, Y.; Tay, Y.W.D.; Pham, H.; Pham, Q.-C. Large-scale 3D printing by a team of mobile robots. *Autom. Constr.* **2018**, *95*, 98–106. [CrossRef]
159. Printing-While-Moving: A New Paradigm for Large-Scale Robotic 3D Printing. Available online: https://www.researchgate.net/publication/327835498_Printing-while-moving_a_new_paradigm_for_large-scale_robotic_3D_Printing (accessed on 17 April 2021).
160. Senthilnathan, S.; Raphael, B. Using Computer Vision for Monitoring the Quality of 3D-Printed Concrete Structures. *Sustainability* **2022**, *14*, 15682. [CrossRef]
161. Buswell, R.; Kinnell, P.; Xu, J.; Hack, N.; Kloft, H.; Maboudi, M.; Gerke, M.; Massin, P.; Grasser, G.; Wolfs, R.; et al. Inspection Methods for 3D Concrete Printing. In *Second RILEM International Conference on Concrete and Digital Fabrication: Digital Concrete*; Springer International Publishing: Berlin/Heidelberg, Germany, 2020; Volume 28, pp. 790–803. [CrossRef]
162. Dung, C.V.; Anh, L.D. Autonomous concrete crack detection using deep fully convolutional neural network. *Autom. Constr.* **2019**, *99*, 52–58. [CrossRef]
163. Lei, F.; Ma, X.; Dong, X. Automatic Identification of Construction Dust Based on Improved K-Means Algorithm Automatic Identification of Construction Dust Based on Improved K-Means Algorithm. *IOP Conf. Ser. Earth Environ. Sci.* **2021**, *647*, 012017. [CrossRef]
164. Baumgartl, H.; Tomas, J.; Buettner, R.; Merkel, M. A deep learning-based model for defect detection in laser-powder bed fusion using in-situ thermographic monitoring. *Prog. Addit. Manuf.* **2020**, *5*, 277–285. [CrossRef]
165. Land, W.S.; Zhang, B.; Ziegert, J.; Davies, A. In-Situ Metrology System for Laser Powder Bed Fusion Additive Process. *Procedia Manuf.* **2015**, *1*, 393–403. [CrossRef]
166. Zhang, B.; Ziegert, J.C.; Ii, W.S.L.; Ziegert, J.; Davies, A. In Situ Monitoring of Laser Powder Bed Fusion Additive Manufacturing Using Digital Fringe Projection Technique. 2015. Available online: https://www.researchgate.net/publication/283097423 (accessed on 29 March 2021).
167. Altenburg, S.J.; Straße, A.; Gumenyuk, A.; Maierhofer, C. In-situ monitoring of a laser metal deposition (LMD) process: Comparison of MWIR, SWIR and high-speed NIR thermography. *Quant. InfraRed Thermogr. J.* **2022**, *19*, 97–114. [CrossRef]
168. Azar, E.R.; McCabe, B. Automated Visual Recognition of Dump Trucks in Construction Videos. *J. Comput. Civ. Eng.* **2011**, *26*, 769–781. [CrossRef]
169. LED Lighting Vendors Diversify Their Product Offerings. Vision Systems Design. Available online: https://www.vision-systems.com/cameras-accessories/article/16739336/led-lighting-vendors-diversify-their-product-offerings (accessed on 29 March 2021).
170. Zhang, Y.; Fuh, J.Y.H.; Ye, D.; Hong, G.S. In-situ monitoring of laser-based PBF via off-axis vision and image processing approaches. *Addit. Manuf.* **2019**, *25*, 263–274. [CrossRef]
171. Nassar, A.R.; Starr, B.; Reutzel, E.W. Process monitoring of directed-energy deposition of Inconel-718 via plume imaging. In *2014 International Solid Freeform Fabrication Symposium*; University of Texas at Austin: Austin, TX, USA, 2015.

172. Nefs, K.; Menkovski, V.; Bos, F.P.; Suiker, A.S.J.; Salet, T.A.M. Automated image segmentation of 3D printed fibrous composite micro-structures using a neural network. *Constr. Build. Mater.* **2023**, *365*, 130099. [CrossRef]
173. Wang, J.; Tang, Y.; Zhang, J.; Yue, M.; Feng, X. Convolutional neural network-based image denoising for synchronous measurement of temperature and deformation at elevated temperature. *Optik* **2021**, *241*, 166977. [CrossRef]
174. Goh, G.D.; Sing, S.L.; Yeong, W.Y. A review on machine learning in 3D printing: Applications, potential, and challenges. *Artif. Intell. Rev.* **2021**, *54*, 63–94. [CrossRef]
175. Manda, M.P.; Kim, H.S. A fast image thresholding algorithm for infrared images based on histogram approximation and circuit theory. *Algorithms* **2020**, *13*, 207. [CrossRef]
176. Lee, Y.S.; Vuong, N.; Adrian, N.; Pham, Q.C. Integrating Force-based Manipulation Primitives with Deep Learning-based Visual Servoing for Robotic Assembly. Available online: https://openreview.net/forum?id=01lfX8qrh1O (accessed on 20 February 2023).
177. Vuong, N.; Pham, H.; Pham, Q.C. Learning Sequences of Manipulation Primitives for Robotic Assembly. In Proceedings of the 2021 IEEE International Conference on Robotics and Automation, Xi'an, China, 30 May–5 June 2021; pp. 4086–4092. [CrossRef]
178. Murcia-Gómez, D.; Rojas-Valenzuela, I.; Valenzuela, O. Impact of Image Preprocessing Methods and Deep Learning Models for Classifying Histopathological Breast Cancer Images. *Appl. Sci.* **2022**, *12*, 11375. [CrossRef]
179. Duff, M.J.B.; Levialdi, S. An Analysis of Computational Cost in Image Processing: A Case Study. *IEEE Trans. Comput.* **1978**, *27*, 904–910. [CrossRef]
180. Hua, X.; Wang, X.; Rui, T.; Shao, F.; Wang, D. Cascaded panoptic segmentation method for high resolution remote sensing image. *Appl. Soft Comput.* **2021**, *109*, 107515. [CrossRef]
181. Tao, C.; He, H.; Xu, F.; Cao, J. Stereo priori RCNN based car detection on point level for autonomous driving. *Knowl. Based Syst.* **2021**, *229*, 107346. [CrossRef]
182. Yang, Z.; Sun, Y.; Liu, S.; Jia, J. 3DSSD: Point-based 3D Single Stage Object Detector. In Proceedings of the IEEE Computer Society Conference on Computer Vision and Pattern Recognition, Seattle, WA, USA, 13–19 June 2020; pp. 11037–11045. Available online: https://arxiv.org/abs/2002.10187v1 (accessed on 31 July 2021).
183. Zhou, Y.; Tuzel, O. VoxelNet: End-to-End Learning for Point Cloud Based 3D Object Detection. In Proceedings of the IEEE Conference on Computer Vision and Pattern Recognition, Salt Lake City, UT, USA, 18–22 June 2018.
184. Sun, J.; Chen, L.; Xie, Y.; Zhang, S.; Jiang, Q.; Zhou, X.; Bao, H. Disp R-CNN: Stereo 3D Object Detection via Shape Prior Guided Instance Disparity Estimation. In Proceedings of the IEEE Computer Society Conference on Computer Vision and Pattern Recognition, Seattle, WA, USA, 13–19 June 2020; pp. 10545–10554. Available online: https://arxiv.org/abs/2004.03572v1 (accessed on 31 July 2021).
185. Redmon, J.; Farhadi, A. YOLOv3: An Incremental Improvement. 2018. Available online: https://arxiv.org/abs/1804.02767v1 (accessed on 31 July 2021).
186. Bochkovskiy, A.; Wang, C.-Y.; Liao, H.-Y.M. YOLOv4: Optimal Speed and Accuracy of Object Detection. 2020. Available online: https://arxiv.org/abs/2004.10934v1 (accessed on 31 July 2021).
187. Venkatasubramanian, V.; Rengaswamy, R.; Yin, K.; Kavuri, S.N. A review of process fault detection and diagnosis: Part I: Quantitative model-based methods. *Comput. Chem. Eng.* **2003**, *27*, 293–311. [CrossRef]
188. Seifried, P. Fault Detection and Diagnosis in Chemical and Petrochemical Processes, Bd. 8 der Serie "Chemical Engineering Monographs". Von D. M. Himmelblau, herausgegeben von S. W. Churchill, Elsevier Scientific Publishing Company, Amsterdam—New York 1978. 1. Aufl., X, 414 S., 137 Abb., 66 Tab., DM 145,-. *Chem. Ing. Tech.* **1979**, *51*, 766. [CrossRef]
189. Amherst, S.; Collingwood, L.; Wilkerson, J. Tradeoffs in Accuracy and Efficiency in Supervised Learning Methods. Available online: https://scholarworks.umass.edu/jitpc2011/4/ (accessed on 24 January 2023).
190. Hassan, N.M.H.; Elshoky, B.; Hassan, N.M.H.; Elshoky, B.R.G.; Mabrouk, A.M. Quality of performance evaluation of ten machine learning algorithms in classifying thirteen types of apple fruits. *Indones. J. Electr. Eng. Comput. Sci.* **2023**, *30*, 102–109. [CrossRef]
191. Yaacob, M.R.; Fahmi, F. Study on speed and accuracy in measuring people flow rate using computer vision. In Proceedings of the Mechanical Engineering Research Day 2022, Moratuwa, Sri Lanka, 27–29 July 2022; pp. 143–144. Available online: https://youtu.be/Xc625PpsGrU (accessed on 23 January 2023).
192. Colbrook, M.J.; Antun, V.; Hansen, A.C. The difficulty of computing stable and accurate neural networks: On the barriers of deep learning and Smale's 18th problem. *Proc. Natl. Acad. Sci. USA* **2022**, *119*, e2107151119. [CrossRef] [PubMed]
193. Ilyas, A.; Santurkar, S.; Tsipras, D.; Engstrom, L.; Tran, B.; Madry, A. Adversarial Examples Are Not Bugs, They Are Features. *Adv. Neural Inf. Process. Syst.* **2019**, *32*, 1–12. [CrossRef]
194. Moosavi-Dezfooli, S.-M.; Fawzi, A.; Frossard', P.F.; Polytechnique, F.; de Lausanne, F. DeepFool: A Simple and Accurate Method to Fool Deep Neural Networks. In Proceedings of the IEEE Conference on Computer Vision and Pattern Recognition 2016, Las Vegas, NV, USA, 27–30 June 2016; pp. 2574–2582. Available online: http://github.com/lts4/deepfool (accessed on 17 February 2023).
195. Szegedy, C.; Zaremba, W.; Sutskever, I.; Bruna, J.; Erhan, D.; Goodfellow, I.; Fergus, R. Intriguing properties of neural networks. *arXiv* **2013**, arXiv:1312.6199.
196. Su, J.; Vargas, D.V.; Sakurai, K. One Pixel Attack for Fooling Deep Neural Networks. *IEEE Trans. Evol. Comput.* **2019**, *23*, 828–841. [CrossRef]
197. He, L.; Li, H.; Chow, W.T.; Zeng, B.; Qian, Y. Increasing the interlayer strength of 3D printed concrete with tooth-like interface: An experimental and theoretical investigation. *Mater. Des.* **2022**, *223*, 111117. [CrossRef]

198. Kulkarni, A.; Chong, D.; Batarseh, F.A. Foundations of data imbalance and solutions for a data democracy. In *Data Democracy: At the Nexus of Artificial Intelligence, Software Development, and Knowledge Engineering*; Academic Press: Cambridge, MA, USA, 2020; pp. 83–106. [CrossRef]
199. Grandini, M.; Bagli, E.; Visani, G. Metrics for Multi-Class Classification: An Overview. *arXiv* **2020**, arXiv:2008.05756. [CrossRef]
200. Boughorbel, S.; Jarray, F.; El-Anbari, M. Optimal classifier for imbalanced data using Matthews Correlation Coefficient metric. *PLoS ONE* **2017**, *12*, e0177678. [CrossRef]
201. Daskalaki, S.; Kopanas, I.; Avouris, N. Evaluation of classifiers for an uneven class distribution problem. *Appl. Artif. Intell.* **2006**, *20*, 381–417. [CrossRef]
202. Clark, A.F.; Clark, C. Performance Characterization in Computer Vision. Available online: http://peipa.essex.ac.uk/benchmark/ (accessed on 18 February 2023).
203. Chai, J.; Zeng, H.; Li, A.; Ngai, E.W.T. Deep learning in computer vision: A critical review of emerging techniques and application scenarios. *Mach. Learn. Appl.* **2021**, *6*, 100134. [CrossRef]
204. Galarreta, J.F.; Kerle, N.; Gerke, M. UAV-based urban structural damage assessment using object-based image analysis and semantic reasoning. *Nat. Hazards Earth Syst. Sci.* **2015**, *15*, 1087–1101. [CrossRef]
205. Sapirstein, P. Accurate measurement with photogrammetry at large sites. *J. Archaeol. Sci.* **2016**, *66*, 137–145. [CrossRef]
206. Yastikli, N. Documentation of cultural heritage using digital photogrammetry and laser scanning. *J. Cult. Herit.* **2007**, *8*, 423–427. [CrossRef]
207. Braun, A.; Borrmann, A. Combining inverse photogrammetry and BIM for automated labeling of construction site images for machine learning. *Autom. Constr.* **2019**, *106*, 102879. [CrossRef]
208. Qi, C.; Weiss, J.; Olek, J. Characterization of plastic shrinkage cracking in fiber reinforced concrete using image analysis and a modified Weibull function. *Mater. Struct.* **2003**, *36*, 386–395. [CrossRef]
209. Ma, Y.; Tan, M.; Wu, K. Effect of different geometric polypropylene fibers on plastic shrinkage cracking of cement mortars. *Mater. Struct.* **2002**, *35*, 165–169. [CrossRef]
210. Wang, W.-C.; Chen, L.-B.; Chang, W.-J. A Machine Vision Based Automatic Optical Inspection System for Measuring Drilling Quality of Printed Circuit Boards. 2017. Available online: https://www.researchgate.net/publication/317843301_A_Machine_Vision_Based_Automatic_Optical_Inspection_System_for_Measuring_Drilling_Quality_of_Printed_Circuit_Boards (accessed on 30 March 2021).
211. Nemati, K.M.; Stroeven, P. Stereological analysis of micromechanical behavior of concrete. *Mater. Struct.* **2001**, *34*, 486–494. [CrossRef]
212. Elzafraney, M.; Soroushian, P. Assessment of microcrack development in concrete materials of different strengths. *Mater. Struct.* **2004**, *37*, 724–731. [CrossRef]
213. Maraveas, C.; Bartzanas, T. Sensors for Structural Health Monitoring of Agricultural Structures. *Sensors* **2021**, *21*, 314. [CrossRef]
214. Roopa, A.K.; Hunashyal, A.M.; Venkaraddiyavar, P.; Ganachari, S.V. Smart hybrid nano composite concrete embedded sensors for structural health monitoring. *Mater. Today Proc.* **2020**, *27*, 603–609. [CrossRef]
215. Merzbacher, C.I.; Kersey, A.D.; Friebele, E.J. Fiber optic sensors in concrete structures: A review. *Smart Mater. Struct.* **1996**, *5*, 196. [CrossRef]
216. Strangfeld, C.; Johann, S.; Bartholmai, M. Smart RFID Sensors Embedded in Building Structures for Early Damage Detection and Long-Term Monitoring. *Sensors* **2019**, *19*, 5514. [CrossRef]
217. Dong, W.; Li, W.; Tao, Z.; Wang, K. Piezoresistive properties of cement-based sensors: Review and perspective. *Constr. Build. Mater.* **2019**, *203*, 146–163. [CrossRef]
218. Sam-Daliri, O.; Faller, L.M.; Farahani, M.; Zangl, H. Structural health monitoring of adhesive joints under pure mode I loading using the electrical impedance measurement. *Eng. Fract. Mech.* **2021**, *245*, 107585. [CrossRef]
219. Dong, W.; Li, W.; Shen, L.; Sheng, D. Piezoresistive behaviours of carbon black cement-based sensors with layer-distributed conductive rubber fibres. *Mater. Des.* **2019**, *182*, 108012. [CrossRef]
220. Ubertini, F.; D'Alessandro, A. Concrete with self-sensing properties. In *Eco-Efficient Repair and Rehabilitation of Concrete Infrastructures*; Woodhead Publishing: Cambridge, MA, USA, 2018; pp. 501–530. [CrossRef]
221. Han, B.; Zhang, L.; Ou, J. *Smart and Multifunctional Concrete Toward Sustainable Infrastructures*; Springer: Singapore, 2017. [CrossRef]
222. Konsta-Gdoutos, M.S.; Aza, C.A. Self sensing carbon nanotube (CNT) and nanofiber (CNF) cementitious composites for real time damage assessment in smart structures. *Cem. Concr. Compos.* **2014**, *53*, 162–169. [CrossRef]
223. Ai, D.; Zhu, H.; Luo, H.; Wang, C. Mechanical impedance based embedded piezoelectric transducer for reinforced concrete structural impact damage detection: A comparative study. *Constr. Build. Mater.* **2018**, *165*, 472–483. [CrossRef]
224. Embedded Piezoelectric Sensors for Health Monitoring of Concrete Structures. Available online: https://www.researchgate.net/publication/279570765_Embedded_Piezoelectric_Sensors_for_Health_Monitoring_of_Concrete_Structures (accessed on 9 June 2021).
225. Park, G.; Sohn, H.; Farrar, C.R.; Inman, D.J. Overview of Piezoelectric Impedance-Based Health Monitoring and Path Forward. *Shock. Vib. Dig.* **2003**, *35*, 451–464. [CrossRef]
226. Ma, G.; Li, Y.; Wang, L.; Zhang, J.; Li, Z. Real-time quantification of fresh and hardened mechanical property for 3D printing material by intellectualization with piezoelectric transducers. *Constr. Build. Mater.* **2020**, *241*, 117982. [CrossRef]

227. Xi, X.; Chung, D.D.L. Effect of nickel coating on the stress-dependent electric permittivity, piezoelectricity and piezoresistivity of carbon fiber, with relevance to stress self-sensing. *Carbon* **2019**, *145*, 401–410. [CrossRef]
228. Wen, S.; Chung, D.D.L. Electromagnetic interference shielding reaching 70 dB in steel fiber cement. *Cem. Concr. Res.* **2004**, *34*, 329–332. [CrossRef]
229. Ozturk, M.; Chung, D.D.L. Enhancing the electromagnetic interference shielding effectiveness of carbon-fiber reinforced cement paste by coating the carbon fiber with nickel. *J. Build. Eng.* **2021**, *41*, 102757. [CrossRef]
230. Hu, J.Y.; Zhang, S.S.; Chen, E.; Li, W.G. A review on corrosion detection and protection of existing reinforced concrete (RC) structures. *Constr. Build. Mater.* **2022**, *325*, 126718. [CrossRef]
231. Živica, V. Utilisation of electrical resistance method for the evaluation of the state of steel reinforcement in concrete and the rate of its corrosion. *Constr. Build. Mater.* **2000**, *14*, 351–358. [CrossRef]
232. García, A.; Bueno, M.; Norambuena-Contreras, J.; Partl, M.N. Induction healing of dense asphalt concrete. *Constr. Build. Mater.* **2013**, *49*, 1–7. [CrossRef]
233. Sengupta, D.; Huang, Y.; Davidson, C.I.; Edgar, T.F.; Edene, M.R.; El-Halwagi, M.M. Sustainable Manufacturing Education Modules for Senior Undergraduate or Graduate Engineering Curriculum. *Comput. Aided Chem. Eng.* **2018**, *44*, 1657–1662. [CrossRef]
234. IEA. 2019 Global Status Report for Buildings and Construction. 2019. Available online: https://iea.blob.core.windows.net/assets/3da9daf9-ef75-4a37-b3da-a09224e299dc/2019_Global_Status_Report_for_Buildings_and_Construction.pdf (accessed on 20 February 2023).
235. Additive Manufacturing as an Opportunity for Supporting Sustainability through Implementation of Circular Economies. Available online: https://www.researchgate.net/publication/312626449_Additive_Manufacturing_as_an_opportunity_for_supporting_sustainability_through_implementation_of_circular_economies (accessed on 20 February 2023).
236. de Schutter, G.; Lesage, K.; Mechtcherine, V.; Nerella, V.N.; Habert, G.; Agusti-Juan, I. Vision of 3D printing with concrete—Technical, economic and environmental potentials. *Cem. Concr. Res.* **2018**, *112*, 25–36. [CrossRef]
237. W. Commission on Environment, Report of the World Commission on Environment and Development: Our Common Future towards Sustainable Development 2. Part II. Common Challenges Population and Human Resources 4. Available online: https://sustainabledevelopment.un.org/content/documents/5987our-common-future.pdf (accessed on 1 March 2022).
238. Tuladhar, R.; Yin, S. Sustainability of using recycled plastic fiber in concrete. In *Use of Recycled Plastics in Eco-Efficient Concrete*; Elsevier: Amsterdam, The Netherlands, 2019; pp. 441–460. [CrossRef]
239. Dey, D.; Srinivas, D.; Panda, B.; Suraneni, P.; Sitharam, T.G. Use of industrial waste materials for 3D printing of sustainable concrete: A review. *J. Clean. Prod.* **2022**, *340*, 130749. [CrossRef]
240. Cesaretti, G.; Dini, E.; de Kestelier, X.; Colla, V.; Pambaguian, L. Building components for an outpost on the Lunar soil by means of a novel 3D printing technology. *Acta Astronaut.* **2014**, *93*, 430–450. [CrossRef]
241. Ries, R.; Bilec, M.M.; Gokhan, N.M.; Needy, K.L. The economic benefits of green buildings: A comprehensive case study. *Eng. Econ.* **2006**, *51*, 259–295. [CrossRef]
242. Colorado, H.A.; Velásquez, E.I.G.; Monteiro, S.N. Sustainability of additive manufacturing: The circular economy of materials and environmental perspectives. *J. Mater. Res. Technol.* **2020**, *9*, 8221–8234. [CrossRef]
243. Pan, M.; Linner, T.; Pan, W.; Cheng, H.; Bock, T. A framework of indicators for assessing construction automation and robotics in the sustainability context. *J. Clean. Prod.* **2018**, *182*, 82–95. [CrossRef]

Disclaimer/Publisher's Note: The statements, opinions and data contained in all publications are solely those of the individual author(s) and contributor(s) and not of MDPI and/or the editor(s). MDPI and/or the editor(s) disclaim responsibility for any injury to people or property resulting from any ideas, methods, instructions or products referred to in the content.

Article

CISA: Context Substitution for Image Semantics Augmentation

Sergey Nesteruk [1], Ilya Zherebtsov [2], Svetlana Illarionova [1], Dmitrii Shadrin [1,3], Andrey Somov [1,*], Sergey V. Bezzateev [4], Tatiana Yelina [4], Vladimir Denisenko [2] and Ivan Oseledets [1]

1. Skolkovo Institute of Science and Technology (Skoltech), 121205 Moscow, Russia
2. Voronezh State University of Engineering Technology (VSUET), 394036 Voronezh, Russia
3. Irkutsk National Research Technical University (INRTU), 664074 Irkutsk, Russia
4. Saint-Petersburg State University of Aerospace Instrumentation (SUAI), 190000 Saint Petersburg, Russia
* Correspondence: a.somov@skoltech.ru

Abstract: Large datasets catalyze the rapid expansion of deep learning and computer vision. At the same time, in many domains, there is a lack of training data, which may become an obstacle for the practical application of deep computer vision models. To overcome this problem, it is popular to apply image augmentation. When a dataset contains instance segmentation masks, it is possible to apply instance-level augmentation. It operates by cutting an instance from the original image and pasting to new backgrounds. This article challenges a dataset with the same objects present in various domains. We introduce the Context Substitution for Image Semantics Augmentation framework (CISA), which is focused on choosing good background images. We compare several ways to find backgrounds that match the context of the test set, including Contrastive Language–Image Pre-Training (CLIP) image retrieval and diffusion image generation. We prove that our augmentation method is effective for classification, segmentation, and object detection with different dataset complexity and different model types. The average percentage increase in accuracy across all the tasks on a fruits and vegetables recognition dataset is 4.95%. Moreover, we show that the Fréchet Inception Distance (FID) metrics has a strong correlation with model accuracy, and it can help to choose better backgrounds without model training. The average negative correlation between model accuracy and the FID between the augmented and test datasets is 0.55 in our experiments.

Keywords: image augmentation; computer vision; data collection; image retrieval; image generation; few-shot learning

MSC: 65D19; 51N05; 68U05

Citation: Nesteruk, S.; Zherebtsov, I.; Illarionova, S.; Shadrin, D.; Somov, A.; Bezzateev, S.V.; Yelina, T.; Denisenko, V.; Oseledets, I. CISA: Context Substitution for Image Semantics Augmentation. *Mathematics* **2023**, *11*, 1818. https://doi.org/10.3390/math11081818

Academic Editors: Paolo Mercorelli, Oleg Sergiyenko and Oleksandr Tsymbal

Received: 28 February 2023
Revised: 4 April 2023
Accepted: 6 April 2023
Published: 11 April 2023

Copyright: © 2023 by the authors. Licensee MDPI, Basel, Switzerland. This article is an open access article distributed under the terms and conditions of the Creative Commons Attribution (CC BY) license (https://creativecommons.org/licenses/by/4.0/).

1. Introduction

Deep learning and computer vision (CV) algorithms have recently shown their capabilities in addressing various challenging industrial and scientific problems [1]. Successful application of machine learning and computer vision algorithms for solving complex tasks is impossible without relying on comprehensive and high-quality training and testing data [2,3]. CV algorithms for solving classification, object detection, and semantic and instance segmentation require a huge variety of input data to ensure robust work of the trained models [4–6]. There are two major ways to enlarge a training dataset. The first one is obvious and implies physical collection of the dataset samples in various conditions to ensure high diversity of the training data. There is a set of huge datasets that have been collected for solving computer vision problems. These datasets are commonly used as the benchmark [7–10]. One of the specifics of these datasets is that they are general-domain sets. Unfortunately, general-domain-labeled data can be almost useless for solving specific industrial problems. One of the feasible applications of such well-known datasets is that they can serve as a good basis for pre-training of neural networks (transfer learning) [11,12]. Using these pre-trained neural networks, it is possible to fine-tune them and adapt them to address specific problems. However, in some cases, even for fine-tuning, a comprehensive dataset is in high demand. Some events are rare, and it is possible to collect only a few data samples [13–15]. Thus, a second approach for enhancing the characteristics of the dataset can help. This approach is based on artificial manipulations with the initial dataset [16,17]. One of the well-developed techniques is data augmentation, where original images are transformed according to special rules [18]. Usually, the goal of image augmentation is to make the training dataset more diverse. However, augmentation can be used to deliberately shift the data distribution. If the distribution of the original training dataset differs from the distribution of the test set, it is important to equalize them as much as possible.

The agricultural domain is part of the industrial and research areas for which the development of artificial methods for improvement of training datasets is vital [19–21]. This demand appears due to the high complexity and variability of the investigated system (plant) that has to be characterized by computer vision algorithms [22]. The difficulty of the agricultural domain makes it a good candidate for testing augmentation algorithms.

There are many different plant species, and plants grow slowly. Thus, collecting and labeling huge datasets for each specific plant growing in each specific stage is a complex task [23]. Overall, it is difficult to collect datasets [24], especially for plants, and it is expensive to annotate them [25]. Therefore, we propose a method to multiply the number of training samples. It does not require many computational resources, and it can be performed on the fly. The idea behind the algorithm is to cut instances from the original images and add them onto the new backgrounds (Figure 1).

Figure 1. Context substitution showcase.

The **contribution of this study** is the following:

- we describe an efficient algorithm for instance-level image augmentation and measure its performance;
- we prove that the context is vital for instance-level augmentation;
- we propose several efficient ways to find representative background images if the test environment context is known;
- we show that it is possible to estimate which dataset variant will provide better accuracy before model training, calculating the FID between the test dataset and the training dataset variants;
- we share the dataset and generate background images and source code for augmentation.

The **novelty of this study** is as follows:

- extensive experiments with instance-level augmentation for different computer vision tasks;
- experiments with different model types;
- application of FID to choose the augmentation approach.

1.1. Image Augmentation

Computer vision models require many training data. Therefore, it becomes challenging to obtain a good model with limited datasets. Namely, a small-capacity model might not capture complex patterns, while a big capacity model tends to overfit if small datasets are used [26]. Slight changes in test data connected with surrounding and environmental conditions might also lead to a decrease in model performance [27].

To overcome this issue, we use various image augmentation techniques. Data augmentation aims to add diversity to the training set and to complicate the task for a model [28]. Among these plant image augmentation approaches, we can distinguish: basic computer vision augmentations, learned augmentation, graphical modeling, augmentation policy learning, collaging, and compositions of the ones above.

Basic computer vision augmentations are the default methods preventing overfitting in most computer vision tasks. They include image cropping, scaling, flipping, rotating, and adding noise [29]. There are also advanced augmentation methods, connected with distortion techniques and coordinate system changes [30]. Since these operations are quite generic, most popular ML frameworks support them. However, although helpful, these methods demonstrate limited use, as they bring insufficient diversity to the training data for few-shot learning cases.

Learned augmentation stands for generating training samples with an ML model. For this purpose, conditional generative adversarial networks (cGANs) and variational autoencoders (VAEs) are frequently used. In the agricultural domain, there are examples of applying GANs to *Arabidopsis* plant images for the leaf counting task [31,32]. The main drawback of this approach is that generating an image with a neural network is quite resource-intensive. Another disadvantage is the overall pipeline complexity: the errors of a model that generates training samples are accumulated with the errors of a model that solves the target task.

Learned augmentation policy is a series of techniques used to find combinations of basic augmentations that maximize model generalization. This implies hard binding of the learned policy to the ML model, the dataset, and the task. Although it is shown to provide systematic generalization improvement on object detection [33] and classification [34], its universal character as well as the ability to be performed along with multi-task learning are not supported with solid evidence.

Collaging presupposes cropping an object from an input image with the help of a manually annotated mask and pasting it to a new background with basic augmentations of each object [19]. In [35], a scene generation technique using object mask was successfully implemented for an instance detection task. It boosted model performance significantly compared with the use of only original images. The study on image augmentation for instance segmentation using a copy–paste technique with object mask was extended in [36]. The importance of scene context for image augmentation is explored in [37,38].

1.2. Image Synthesis

Graphical modeling is another popular method in plant phenomics. It involves creating a 3D model of the object of interest and rendering it. The advantage of this process is that it permits the generation of large datasets [39] with precise annotations, as the labels of each pixel are known. However, this technique is highly resource-intensive; moreover, the results obtained using the existing solutions [40,41] seem artificial. More realistic synthesis is very time-consuming. This approach is suitable when there are not many variations of the modeled object. If there are many different object types, it can be easier to collect and annotate new images.

1.3. Neural Image Generation and Image Retrieval

To gain new training images for CV tasks, one can implement GAN-based or diffusion-based models. Currently, they allow for the creation of rather realistic images and meet the demands of different domains, such as agricultural [42], manufacturing processes [43], remote sensing [44], or medical [45]. Such models can be considered as a part of an image recognition pipeline. Moreover, recent results in Natural Language Processing (NLP) offer opportunities to extend image generation applications via textual description. For instance, an image can be generated based on a proposed prompt, namely, a phrase or a word. Such synthetic images help to extend the initial dataset. The same target image can be described by a broad variety of words and phrases that lead to diverse visual results. Another way to obtain additional training images is a data retrieval approach. It supposes to search for existing images from the Internet or some database according to a user's prompt. For instance, the CLIP model can be used to compute embedding of a text and to find images that match it better based on distance in a special embedding space [46].

2. Materials and Methods

The notation that we use in this section for describing the augmentation framework parameters is listed in Table 1.

Table 1. CISA framework internal notations.

Notation	Description
n	The number of objects per scene
m	The number of output masks
p	Average packaging overhead per input object
o	Average overhead for auxiliary data storage per object
$\grave{o}$	Constant system overhead
s	Objects' shrinkage ratio
θ	Orientation coefficient (width-to-height ratio)
H	The set of objects heights
$\tilde{H}$	The set of shrinked object heights
W	The set of object heights
$\tilde{W}$	The set of shrinked object widths
$\bar{h}$	Average over all input object heights
$\bar{w}$	Average over all input object widths
$\hat{h}$	Hard height restriction
M	Average RAM (random access memory) usage

2.1. Method Development and Description

In this paper, we introduce a method of image augmentation for a semantic segmentation task. When instance-level annotation areas are available, one can apply our method for other tasks such as classification, object detection, object counting, and semantic segmentation. Our method takes image–mask pairs and transforms them to obtain various scenes. Having a set of image–mask pairs, we can place many of them on a new background. Transformation of input data and background, accompanied by adding noise, gives the possibility for us to synthesize an infinite number of compound scenes.

This section first describes the overall augmentation pipeline and then describes the tested approaches for background image generation.

We distinguish between several types of image masks:

- **Single (S)**—single-channel mask that shows the object presence.
- **Multi-object (MO)**—multi-channel mask with a special color for each object (for each plant).
- **Multi-part (MP)**—multi-channel mask with a special color for each object part (for each plant leaf).
- **Semantic (Sema)**—multi-channel mask with a special color for each type of object (leaf, root, flower).
- **Class (C)**—multi-channel mask with a special color for each class (plant variety).

A single-input mask type allows us to produce more than one output mask type. Hence, multiple tasks can be solved using any dataset, even the one that was not originally designed for these tasks (see Table 2 for the possible mask transitions).

For example, an image with a multipart mask as input enables us to produce: the *S* mask, which is a Boolean representation of any other mask, the *MO* mask with unique colors for every object, the *MP* mask with a unique color for each part across all the present objects, and the *C* mask that distinguishes the classes (Figure 2). Additionally, for every generated sample, we provide bounding boxes for all objects and the number of objects of each class.

Note that we assume that each input image–mask pair includes a single object. Therefore, we can produce the *MO* mask based on any other mask. To create the *C* mask, information about input objects must be provided.

Table 2. Possible mask transitions.

Input Mask Type	S	MO	MP	Sema	C
S	+	+	-	-	+
MP	+	+	+	-	+
Sema	+	+	-	+	+

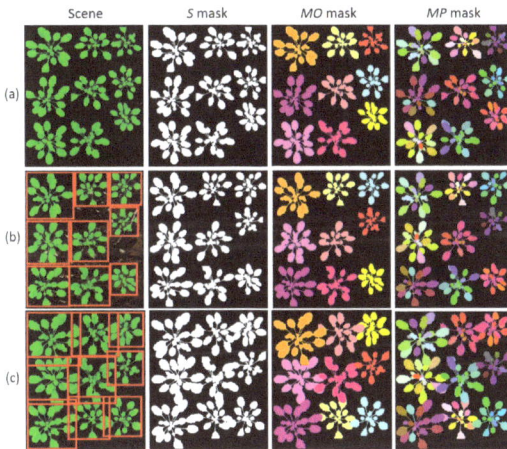

Figure 2. A MultiPartAugmentor-generated scene. (**a**) Without noise. (**b**) With added noise, blurring, and bounding boxes. (**c**) With added noise, blurring, bounding boxes, and $s = 0.1$.

2.2. System Architecture

The library with the code will be shared as an open source code with the community. The core of the presented system is the *Augmentor*. This class implements all the image and mask transformations. Such transformations as flipping or rotating are mutual for both the image and the mask. We add noise for images only.

From the main *Augmentor* class, we inherit *SingleAugmentor*, *MultiPartAugmentor* and *SemanticAugmentor* classes, helping to apply different input mask types and to treat them separately. To be more precise, *SingleAugmentor* is exploited for *S* input mask type, *MultiPartAugmentor* is for *MP* mask type, and *SemanticAugmentor* is for *Sema* mask type.

The described above classes are used in the *DataGen* class, which chooses images for each scene and balances classes if needed. Two principal ways of new scene generation are offline and online. We implement them in *SavingDataGen* and *StreamingDataGen* accordingly. Both of the classes take the path to images with corresponding masks as input. The offline data generator produces a new folder with created scenes while the online generator can be used to load data directly to a neural network.

Offline generation is more time-consuming because of additional disk access operations; at the same time, it is performed in advance and thus does not affect model training time. It also makes it easier to manually look through the obtained samples to tune the transformation parameters.

Meanwhile, the online data generator streams its results immediately to the model without saving images on the disk. Furthermore, this type of generator allows us to change parameters on the fly: for instance, the model is trained on easy samples, and then, the complexity may be manipulated based on the loss function.

2.3. Implementation Details

The present section discusses the main transformation pipeline (Figure 3).

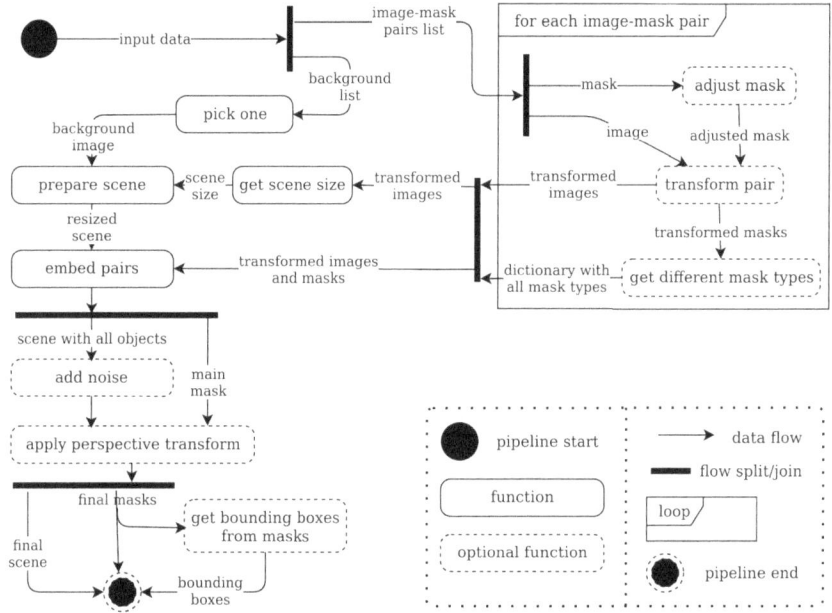

Figure 3. Transformation pipeline activity diagram.

The first step is to select the required number of image–mask pairs from a dataset. By default, we pick objects with repetitions that enable us to create scenes with a larger number of objects than present in the input data.

After that, we prepare images and masks before combining them into a single scene. The procedure is as follows:

- adjust the masks to exclude large margins;
- perform the same random transformations to both the image and mask;
- obtain all required mask types and auxiliary data.

Once all the transformations are performed and we know the sizes of all objects, the size of the output scene is calculated. Note that input objects can have different sizes and orientations; therefore, we cannot simply place objects by grid because it will lead to inefficient space usage. It is also not a good idea to place objects randomly in most cases because it will lead to uncontrollable overlapping of objects.

Within the framework of our approach, the objects are packed using the Maximal Rectangles Best Long Side Fit (MAXRECTS-BLSF) algorithm. It is a greedy algorithm that is aimed at packing rectangles of different sizes into a bin using the smallest possible area. The maximum theoretical packaging space overhead of the MAXRECTS-BLSF algorithm is

0.087. The BLSF modification of the algorithm tries to avoid a significant difference between side lengths. However, similar ot other rectangular packing algorithms, this one also tends to abuse the height dimension of the output scene, yielding a column-oriented result.

In order to control both overlapping of the objects and the orientation of output scenes, we introduce two modifications to the MAXRECTS-BLSF algorithm.

Control of the overlapping is achieved via substituting the objects' real sizes with the shrinked ones when passing them through the packing algorithm. The height and width are modified according to Equation (1):

$$\widetilde{H} = (1-s)H; \widetilde{W} = (1-s)W, \qquad (1)$$

where s ranges from 0 to 1 inclusively.

The bigger the shrinkage ratio, the smaller the substituted images. It is applied to both height and width and to all of the input objects. The real overlapping area in practice will vary depending on each objects' shape and position. To perceive the overlap percentage, see Figure 4. Here, we consider the case where all input objects are squares without any holes. In other words, it is the maximum possible overlap percentage for the defined shrinkage ratio. We show this value for an object in the corner of a scene, an object on the side, and an object in the middle, separately.

We recommend choosing s between 0 and 0.3; however, taking into consideration sparse input masks, it can be slightly higher.

To control the orientation of the output scene, we set a hard limit of the scene height for the packing algorithm. Assuming that input objects will have different sizes in practice, we cannot obtain optimal packing with the fixed output image size or width-to-height ratio. To calculate the hard height limit, we use Equation (2).

$$\hat{h} = max\left(maxH, \theta \frac{\sum_{i=1}^{n} \widetilde{H}_i}{\lceil \sqrt{n} \rceil}\right) \qquad (2)$$

The fraction in Equation (2) estimates the required value of height to make a square scene. We choose a maximum between it and the biggest objects' height to ensure that it is enough space for any input object. The orientation coefficient θ can be treated as the target width-to-height ratio. It will not produce the scenes with the fixed ratio, but with many samples, the average value will approach the target one. $\theta = 1$ will try to obtain square scenes. $\theta > 1$ will generate landscape scenes. In our experiments, we set θ to 1.2 to obtain close to square images with landscape preference. The average resulting width-to-height ratio over ten thousand samples was 1.1955.

To adjust the background image size to the obtained scene size, we resize the background if it is smaller than the scene or randomly crop it if it is bigger.

We generate the required number of colors, excluding black and white, and find their Cartesian product according to Algorithm 1 for coloring the MO and MP masks.

Algorithm 1: Color generation.

Input: Number of objects n;
Output: The set of colors C;
$L = \lceil \sqrt[3]{n+2} \rceil$
$s = \frac{1}{L}$
for $l = 0, ..., L-1$ **do**
    $T \leftarrow 1 - (s*l)$
end
return $C = \{(c_1, c_2, c_3) | c_1, c_2, c_3 \in T\}$

To preserve the correspondence between the input objects and their representation on the final scene, we color the objects in order of their occurrence.

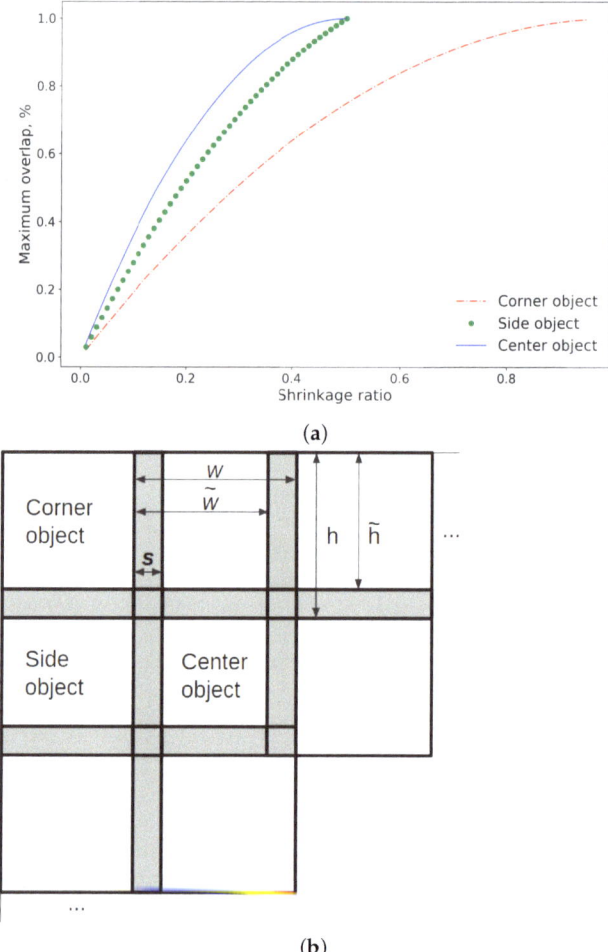

Figure 4. Shrinkage ratio effect illustration. (**a**) The dependency of maximum object overlap on shrinkage ratio. (**b**) Simplified scene generation example.

2.4. Time Performance

In this section, we measure the average time that is required to generate scenes of various complexity. For this experiment, we use Intel(R) Core(TM) i7-7700HQ CPU 2.80 GHz without multiprocessing. The average height of objects in the dataset is 385 pixels; the average width is 390 pixels. The results are averaged on a thousand scenes for each parameter combination and are reflected in Figure 5a for *MultiPartAugmentor* and Figure 5b for *SemanticAugmentor*.

SA (the red bar on the left) stands for *Simple Augmentor* with one type of output mask; *NA* (the blue bar in center) means adding noise and smoothing to scenes; *NMA* (the green bar on the right) means adding noise, smoothing, calculating bounding boxes, and generating all possible types of output masks. To recall possible mask types for each augmentor, refer to Table 2. The filled area in the bottom shows the time for loading input images and masks from disks. The shaded area in the middle shows the time for actual transformation. The empty area in the top shows the time for saving all the results to the disk. If every bar is accumulated with all the bars below it, the top of the shaded bar will show the time for *StreamingDataGen*, and the top of the empty area will show the time for *SavingDataGen*.

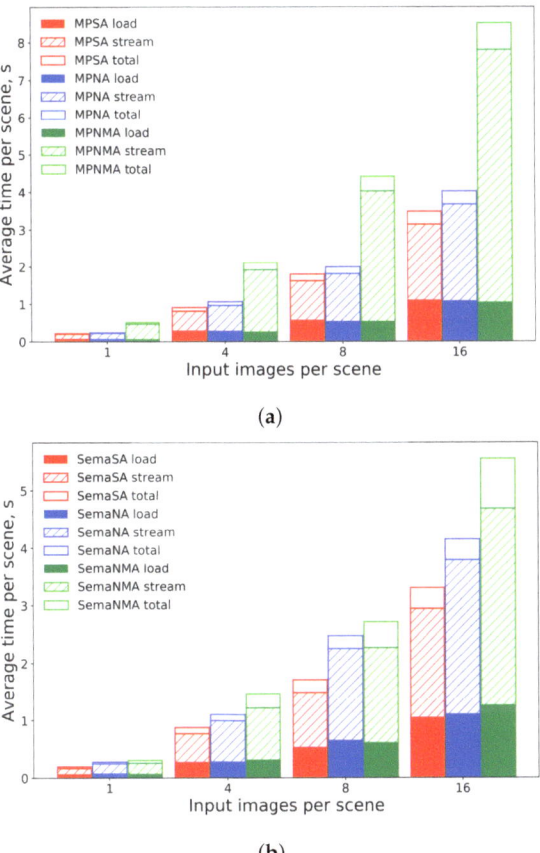

Figure 5. Average scene-generating time with (**a**) *MultiPartAugmentor* and (**b**) *SemanticAugmentor*.

From the bar plots, you can see linear dependence between the number of input objects and the time for generating a scene.

2.5. System Parameters

Two main classes of the system where we can choose parameters are *Augmentor* and *DataGen*, or classes inherited.

The *Augmentor* parameters that define the transformations are shown in Table 3.

Table 3. Augmentor transformation parameters.

Operation	Description	Range	Default Value
Shrinkage ratio	See Figure 4 for details	[0...1]	0
Rotation	The maximum angle of image and mask rotation	[0...180]	180
Flip probability	The probability to flip the image and mask horizontally	[0...1]	0.5
Smooth	The size of the Gauss kernel applied for image smoothing	1, 3, ...	1
Perspective transform	The share of added width before perspective transform	[0...3]	0

The rest of the *Augmentor* parameters define output mask types, bounding box presence, and mask preprocessing steps.

The data generator parameters define the rules to pick samples for scenes: the number of samples per scene, picking samples for a single scene from the same class or randomly, class balancing rule, the input file structure, the output file structure.

2.6. Background Image Choosing

Making many augmented copies of objects is a very powerful tool used to increase dataset variability. However, many previous works underestimate the role of image context. The role of the context in an image plays a role in its background. In this paper, we show that the proper choice of a background is vital. For this, we experiment with methods that produce images that are similar to the test set backgrounds.

In the test set, we have five types of background. It includes: grass, floor tiles, wooden table, color blanket, and shop shelves. Therefore, we want to obtain suitable images that represent every surrounding type. The corresponding text prompts are:

- **grass**: grass, green grass, grass on the Earth, photo of grass, grass grown on the Earth;
- **floor tiles**: tile, ceramic tile, beige tile, grey tile, metal, photo of metal sheet, metal sheet, tile on the floor, close photo of tile, close photo of grey tile;
- **wooden table**: wood, wooden, wooden table, dark wooden table, light wooden table, close photo of wooden table, close photo of table in the room;
- **color blanket**: veil, cover, blanket, color blanket, dark blanket, blanket spread, bed linen, close photo of veil (cover, blanket), blanket on the bed, towel, green towel, close photo of towel on the table;
- **shop shelves**: shelves, shop shelves, close photo of shop shelves, white shop shelves, shop shelves close, table in shop, empty shelves in the shop, table with scales in front of shop shelves, scales in the shop.

We also split backgrounds into easy: wooden table, floor tiles; and complex: grass, color blanket, shop shelves. This split is manual and serves to demonstrate the difference in performance between more and less realistic images. More precisely, complex backgrounds are ones where visual augmentation looks unrealistic. Various background properties are significant not only in the agriculture domain, they represent different environmental conditions in the remote sensing domain and can be considered to boost model performance through geographical regions [47]. Background complexity in CV tasks for self-driving cars depends on urban area complexity and lighting conditions and has to be taken into account to develop robust algorithms [48]. To capture observed scenes for aerial vehicle navigation, surrounding properties are also crucial [49].

We use the described above text prompts with ruDALL-E [50] and stable diffusion [51] models to generate similar images, and with the CLIP [52] model to retrieve similar images from the LAION-400M [53] dataset. There are 100 collected backgrounds for each prompt.

For the comparison, we also add the worst-case and the best-case backgrounds. As the worst case, we propose to use random pattern images. The best case is to have real images from the same place, where a CV model will be inferenced.

Dataset

To verify the proposed approach, we conduct experiments using a set of images of various fruits and vegetables. We collect a unique dataset that comprises the following species: apple, cabbage, grape, tomato, pepper sweet, and onion. The dataset has hierarchical structure where each species includes three varieties, as is depicted in Figure 6. All species and varieties are presented in Table 4. Overall, each individual fruit or vegetable variety is represented by 150 images gained in different environmental and lighting conditions. We create a manual instance segmentation annotation for the images. Each image contains several fruits or vegetables of a single variety. Therefore, instance segmentation markup can be easily automatically converted into image classification labels. We can also obtain bounding boxes for object detection based on instance segmentation masks. Hence, we create annotations for three CV tasks, namely, semantic segmentation, image classification, and object detection. For each task, the dataset is split into training and testing in an 80/20 ratio.

Figure 6. The hierarchical structure of the collected dataset.

Table 4. Species and varieties presented in the dataset.

Species	Varieties
Apple	Granny, Red delicious, Golden
Cabbage	Cauliflower, Peking, White
Grape	Black, Green, Pink
Tomato	Bull heart, Pink, Slivka
Pepper sweet	Green, Red, Yellow
Onion	Yellow, White, Purple

Figure 7 depicts generated images using the original dataset with instance segmentation masks.

Figure 7. Example of generated images using CISA instance-level augmentation.

2.7. Experiments

The experiment setup is as follows. We have to test the stability of our approach under various conditions. For this, we experiment with three CV tasks:

- image classification;
- semantic segmentation;
- object detection.

For each task, we compare:

- easy 6-species setup;
- complex 18-varieties setup.

For the classification task, we also compare different type of models:

- convolutional model (ResNet50 [54]);
- transformer model (SWIN [55]).

As well as models with different capacities:

- medium (ResNet50);
- small (MobileNetv3 [56]).

We set the following hyperparameters: For the ResNet50 training, we choose: a learning rate of 10^{-3}, cross-entropy loss function, SGD optimizer, exponential learning rate decay with gamma set to 0.95, and weight decay 2×10^{-3}.

For the MobileNetv3 training, we choose: a learning rate of 10^{-2}, cross-entropy loss function, SGD optimizer, exponential learning rate decay with gamma set to 0.95, and weight decay 3×10^{-4}.

For the SWIN training, we choose: a learning rate of 5×10^{-4}, cross-entropy loss function, Adam optimizer, cosine annealing learning rate decay, and weight decay 10^{-5}.

For the UNET++ training, we choose: a learning rate of 3×10^{-5}, binary cross-entropy with logits loss function, Adam optimizer, cosine annealing learning rate decay, and weight decay 10^{-5}. Images were resized to 512×512 px.

For YOLOv8 training, we choose: a learning rate of 10^{-3}, SGD optimizer, exponential learning rate decay with gamma set to 0.95, and weight decay 5×10^{-4}. Images were resized to 640×640 px.

We explicitly compare convolutional [57] and transformer [58] models. These are the two most popular types of computer vision models today. They differ in receptive field. Convolutions operate locally (Equation (3)), while transformers look at the greater scale (Equation (4)). The success of augmentation with one model type does not guarantee success with another.

$$O[x,y] = (I * K)(i,j) = \sum_{j=1}\sum_{i=1} I[x-i, y-j]K[i,j], \qquad (3)$$

where O is the resulting feature map; K is a kernel.

$$A(Q, K, V) = softmax(\frac{QK^T}{\sqrt{d_k}})V, \qquad (4)$$

where Q, K and V are weight matrices; d is the dimensionality of an attention head.

In each experiment, we measure the model performance using five-fold cross-validation. We use early stopping to terminate model training; therefore, the number of training epochs for different models varies. Classification models are pre-trained on the ImageNet dataset. Segmentation and detection models are pre-trained on the COCO dataset.

We compare several ways to find backgrounds that match the context of the test set, including Contrastive Language–Image Pre-Training (CLIP) [52] image retrieval, VQGAN (ruDALL-E [50]) image generation, and diffusion (Stable Diffusion [51]) image generation.

In each experiment excluding the baseline, we first pre-train a model on the CISA-augmented dataset and then fine-tune the original dataset.

2.8. Evaluation Metrics

To determine the suitability of the training dataset prior to the training procedure, we propose to use the Fréchet Inception Distance (FID) metrics [59]. It is a commonly used choice to evaluate the performance of GAN models. FID measures distance between the distribution of generated images and the original natural samples. However, in our case, the idea behind FID computation is to determine the similarity and feasibility of the generated training samples and test data. A low FID value depicts the better case when we manage to obtain an artificially realistic dataset close to the original test dataset distribution. To compute FID, we use Equation (5).

$$FID = ||\mu_r - \mu_g||^2 + T_r(\sum_r + \sum_g - 2\sqrt{(\sum_r \sum_g)}), \quad (5)$$

where r and g indexes denote real and generated datasets, correspondingly; μ is the mean of the Inceptionv3 model [60] features of a dataset; $\sum_{dataset}$ is the variance matrix of a dataset; T_r is the trace operator.

For assessing classification results, we use accuracy, because the dataset is balanced.

To evaluate semantic segmentation, we calculate pixel-wise intersection over union (IoU, Equation (6)).

$$IoU = \frac{TP}{TP + FP + FN}, \quad (6)$$

where TP is the number of true positive samples; FP is the number of false positive samples; FN is the number of false negative samples.

To evaluate object detection results, we calculate $mAP@0.5$ (Equation (7)). It means that for the prediction, we use the threshold $IoU = 0.5$.

$$mAP@0.5 = \frac{1}{\#classes} \sum_{c \in classes} \frac{TP(c)}{TP(c) + FP(c)}, \quad (7)$$

To measure the statistical significance of our results, we calculate the Spearman rank-order correlation coefficient (Equation (8)). We choose Spearman's over Pearson's correlation because the relation between the FID and accuracy is monotonous but non-linear.

$$\rho = 1 - \frac{6 \sum d_i^2}{n(n^2 - 1)}, \quad (8)$$

where ρ is the Spearman's correlation coefficient; d_i is the distance between two ranks of each observation; n is the number of observations.

3. Results

The results of the experiments are shown in Tables 5–14.

In Table 5, one can find the results of the classification of six species with the ResNet50 model. CISA with stable diffusion backgrounds shows a 2.3% relative percentage change compared with the baseline.

In Table 6, one can find the results of the classification of 18 varieties with the ResNet50 model. CISA with stable diffusion backgrounds shows a 14.2% relative percentage change compared with the baseline.

In Table 7, one can find the results of the classification of six species with the MobileNetv3 model. CISA with stable diffusion backgrounds show a 1.2% relative percentage change compared with the baseline.

Table 5. Classification results for ResNet50 model on test images for six species.

Source of Augmentation Background	Prompts	Pre-Training Accuracy ↑	Fine-Tuned Accuracy ↑	FID ↓
Baseline	—	—	95.2 ± 0.7	—
Patterns	—	93.5 ± 1.2	94.7 ± 0.8	12.93
CLIP	easy	95 ± 0.9	97 ± 0.6	10.76
	complex	95 ± 1	96.6 ± 0.7	10.92
	all	95 ± 1	96.7 ± 0.7	9.6
ruDALL-E	all	94 ± 0.9	95.5 ± 0.8	11.1
Stable Diffusion	easy	95 ± 0.9	**97.4 ± 0.5**	9.43
	complex	94.9 ± 1	97.1 ± 0.6	9.81
	all	95 ± 1	97.3 ± 0.6	8.7
Natural backgrounds	easy	95.8 ± 0.7	98 ± 0.4	7.15
	complex	95.1 ± 0.8	97.8 ± 0.4	7.9
	all	95.3 ± 0.8	98 ± 0.4	6.14

The bold value depicts the best model, excluding models that are trained with natural backgrounds.

Table 6. Classification results for ResNet50 model on test images for 18 varieties.

Source of Augmentation Background	Prompts	Pre-Training Accuracy ↑	Fine-Tuned Accuracy ↑	FID ↓
Baseline	—	—	50 ± 2.3	—
Patterns	—	48 ± 2.5	54.9 ± 2.3	12.93
CLIP	easy	49.5 ± 3	56.4 ± 2.2	10.76
	complex	49 ± 2.7	56.1 ± 2.3	10.92
	all	49.3 ± 2.9	56.3 ± 2.1	9.6
ruDALL-E	all	49 ± 3	56 ± 2.4	11.1
Stable Diffusion	easy	50.5 ± 2.8	**57.1 ± 1.9**	9.43
	complex	50 ± 3.1	56.9 ± 2	9.81
	all	50.2 ± 2.9	**57.1 ± 1.8**	8.7
Natural backgrounds	easy	50.8 ± 2.2	57.4 ± 1.7	7.15
	complex	49.6 ± 3	56.8 ± 1.9	7.9
	all	50.1 ± 2.4	57.2 ± 1.8	6.14

Table 7. Classification results for MobileNetv3 model on test images for six species.

Source of Augmentation Background	Prompts	Pre-Training Accuracy ↑	Fine-Tuned Accuracy ↑	FID ↓
Baseline	—	—	90 ± 1.3	—
Patterns	—	88 ± 2.2	89.9 ± 1.1	12.93
CLIP	easy	90 ± 1.7	90.9 ± 1.1	10.76
	complex	89.1 ± 1.9	90.7 ± 1.2	10.92
	all	89.7 ± 1.9	90.9 ± 1	9.6
ruDALL-E	all	89 ± 2	90.8 ± 1.2	11.1
Stable Diffusion	easy	90 ± 1.5	**91.1 ± 1**	9.43
	complex	89.4 ± 1.8	90.9 ± 0.9	9.81
	all	89.8 ± 1.6	91 ± 0.9	8.7
Natural backgrounds	easy	90 ± 1.6	91.3 ± 0.9	7.15
	complex	88.9 ± 2	90.8 ± 1	7.9
	all	89.8 ± 1.4	91.2 ± 1	6.14

In Table 8, one can find the results of the classification of 18 varieties with the MobileNetv3 model. CISA with stable diffusion backgrounds show a 6.6% relative percentage change compared with the baseline.

Table 8. Classification results for MobileNetv3 model on test images for 18 varieties.

Source of Augmentation Background	Prompts	Pre-Training Accuracy ↑	Fine-Tuned Accuracy ↑	FID ↓
Baseline	—	—	38 ± 3.1	—
Patterns	—	36.5 ± 2.8	39.5 ± 2.3	12.93
CLIP	easy	37 ± 3	39.8 ± 2.7	10.76
	complex	36.8 ± 2.7	39.6 ± 2.5	10.92
	all	37 ± 2.9	39.8 ± 2.8	9.6
ruDALL-E	all	37.2 ± 3.1	39.9 ± 2.5	11.1
Stable Diffusion	easy	37.9 ± 3	40.4 ± 2.6	9.43
	complex	37.3 ± 3.2	40 ± 2.7	9.81
	all	37.7 ± 2.9	**40.5 ± 2.6**	8.7
Natural backgrounds	easy	38 ± 2.4	40.9 ± 2.1	7.15
	complex	37.2 ± 2.8	40.4 ± 2.4	7.9
	all	37.9 ± 3	40.8 ± 2.3	6.14

In Table 9, one can find the results of the classification of six species with the SWIN model. CISA with stable diffusion backgrounds show a 1% relative percentage change compared with the baseline.

Table 9. Classification results for SWIN model on test images for six species.

Source of Augmentation Background	Prompts	Pre-Training Accuracy ↑	Fine-Tuned Accuracy ↑	FID ↓
Baseline	—	—	96.8 ± 0.5	—
Patterns	—	92.8 ± 1.1	95.9 ± 0.7	12.93
CLIP	easy	93.9 ± 1	97.5 ± 0.6	10.76
	complex	94.2 ± 0.8	97.6 ± 0.5	10.92
	all	94.1 ± 0.9	97.6 ± 0.6	9.6
ruDALL-E	all	93 ± 1	96.6 ± 0.5	11.1
Stable Diffusion	easy	94.1 ± 0.8	97.7 ± 0.6	9.43
	complex	94.2 ± 0.9	97.7 ± 0.5	9.81
	all	94.3 ± 0.8	**97.8 ± 0.4**	8.7
Natural backgrounds	easy	94.7 ± 0.8	98.1 ± 0.5	7.15
	complex	94.9 ± 0.6	98.2 ± 0.4	7.9
	all	94.9 ± 0.7	98.2 ± 0.3	6.14

In Table 10, one can find the results of the classification of 18 varieties with SWIN model. CISA with stable diffusion backgrounds show a 6.4% relative percentage change compared with the baseline.

In Table 11, one can find the results of the semantic segmentation of six species with the UNET++ model. CISA with stable diffusion backgrounds show a 2.7% relative percentage change compared with the baseline.

In Table 12, one can find the results of the semantic segmentation of 18 varieties with the UNET++ model. CISA with stable diffusion backgrounds show a 6% relative percentage change compared with the baseline.

In Table 13, one can find the results of the object detection of six species with the YOLOv8 model. CISA with stable diffusion backgrounds show a 2.2% relative percentage change compared with the baseline.

In Table 14, one can find the results of the object detection of 18 varieties with the YOLOv8 model. CISA with stable diffusion backgrounds show a 6.8% relative percentage change compared with the baseline.

Table 10. Classification results for SWIN model on test images for 18 varieties.

Source of Augmentation Background	Prompts	Pre-Training Accuracy ↑	Fine-Tuned Accuracy ↑	FID ↓
Baseline	—	—	51.4 ± 2	—
Patterns	—	47.5 ± 2.6	52 ± 2	12.93
CLIP	easy	48.8 ± 2.7	53.9 ± 1.8	10.76
	complex	49.1 ± 2.5	54 ± 2	10.92
	all	49 ± 2.4	54 ± 1.9	9.6
ruDALL-E	all	48.4 ± 2.8	53 ± 2.1	11.1
Stable Diffusion	easy	49.8 ± 2.7	54.5 ± 1.8	9.43
	complex	49.9 ± 2.9	**54.7 ± 1.7**	9.81
	all	49.9 ± 2.6	54.6 ± 1.6	8.7
Natural backgrounds	easy	50.2 ± 2.1	55.1 ± 1.8	7.15
	complex	50.3 ± 2.3	55 ± 1.8	7.9
	all	50.4 ± 2.2	55.1 ± 1.6	6.14

Table 11. Segmentation results for UNET++ model on test images for six species.

Source of Augmentation Background	Prompts	Pre-Training IoU ↑	Pre-Training Accuracy ↑	Fine-Tuned IoU ↑	Fine-Tuned Accuracy ↑	FID ↓
Baseline	—	—	—	89.5 ± 0.3	95.4 ± 0.25	—
Patterns	—	85 ± 0.6	91.7 ± 0.5	91.2 ± 0.6	96.3 ± 0.3	12.93
CLIP	easy	87.3 ± 0.3	93.2 ± 0.2	93.5 ± 0.3	**98.2 ± 0.1**	10.76
	complex	86.9 ± 0.4	92.9 ± 0.4	93.4 ± 0.2	98.1 ± 0.1	10.92
	all	87.2 ± 0.4	93.1 ± 0.3	93.6 ± 0.3	98.1 ± 0.1	9.6
ruDALL-E	all	86.4 ± 0.6	92.2 ± 0.4	91.9 ± 0.5	97.7 ± 0.2	11.1
Stable Diffusion	easy	88.3 ± 0.3	94.1 ± 0.3	94.5 ± 0.2	98 ± 0.2	9.43
	complex	86.9 ± 0.5	93.8 ± 0.3	93.8 ± 0.2	97.9 ± 0.2	9.81
	all	88.2 ± 0.3	94.1 ± 0.2	94.4 ± 0.3	98 ± 0.2	8.7
Natural backgrounds	easy	88.8 ± 0.3	94.6 ± 0.3	95.3 ± 0.1	98.2 ± 0.15	7.15
	complex	88.6 ± 0.4	94.3 ± 0.2	94.8 ± 0.3	98.2 ± 0.15	7.9
	all	88.8 ± 0.4	94.5 ± 0.3	95.2 ± 0.2	98.2 ± 0.15	6.14

Table 12. Segmentation results for UNET++ model on test images for 18 varieties.

Source of Augmentation Background	Prompts	Pre-Training IoU ↑	Pre-Training Accuracy ↑	Fine-Tuned IoU ↑	Fine-Tuned Accuracy ↑	FID ↓
Baseline	—	—	—	74.5 ± 0.5	85.6 ± 0.5	—
Patterns	—	70.2 ± 0.9	81.9 ± 0.8	73.2 ± 0.6	85.8 ± 0.6	12.93
CLIP	easy	72 ± 0.5	84.7 ± 0.5	78.1 ± 0.4	89.8 ± 0.5	10.76
	complex	71.9 ± 0.8	84.6 ± 0.5	77.3 ± 0.3	89.6 ± 0.4	10.92
	all	72.1 ± 0.7	84.7 ± 0.6	77.5 ± 0.4	89.9 ± 0.4	9.6
ruDALL-E	all	71.6 ± 0.6	84.3 ± 0.7	76.1 ± 0.5	89.2 ± 0.5	11.1
Stable Diffusion	easy	72.9 ± 0.5	85.5 ± 0.35	80 ± 0.3	90.5 ± 0.4	9.43
	complex	71.4 ± 0.7	84.8 ± 0.4	78.9 ± 0.4	89.6 ± 0.5	9.81
	all	72.5 ± 0.5	85.4 ± 0.4	80.2 ± 0.4	**90.7 ± 0.4**	8.7
Natural backgrounds	easy	73.9 ± 0.6	85.5 ± 0.4	81.7 ± 0.2	91.8 ± 0.3	7.15
	complex	71.8 ± 0.7	84.6 ± 0.5	80.9 ± 0.3	91.6 ± 0.4	7.9
	all	73.5 ± 0.6	85.5 ± 0.4	81.5 ± 0.3	91.9 ± 0.3	6.14

Table 13. Object detection for YOLOv8 model on test images for six species.

Source of Augmentation Background	Prompts	Pre-Training mAP ↑	Fine-Tuned mAP ↑	FID ↓
Baseline	—	—	57.9 ± 0.5	—
Patterns	—	54.9 ± 0.4	58.2 ± 0.4	12.93
CLIP	easy	55.6 ± 0.4	59 ± 0.3	10.76
	complex	55.7 ± 0.5	58.9 ± 0.4	10.92
	all	55.6 ± 0.6	58.9 ± 0.3	9.6
ruDALL-E	all	55.2 ± 0.6	58.9 ± 0.5	11.1
Stable Diffusion	easy	55.7 ± 0.4	59.1 ± 0.3	9.43
	complex	55.5 ± 0.5	59 ± 0.5	9.81
	all	55.7 ± 0.3	**59.2 ± 0.4**	8.7
Natural backgrounds	easy	56.1 ± 0.6	60.1 ± 0.3	7.15
	complex	56.2 ± 0.4	60.2 ± 0.4	7.9
	all	56.2 ± 0.5	60.1 ± 0.3	6.14

Table 14. Object detection for YOLOv8 model on test images for 18 varieties.

Source of Augmentation Background	Prompts	Pre-Training mAP ↑	Fine-Tuned mAP ↑	FID ↓
Baseline	—	—	38.3 ± 1.1	—
Patterns	—	35.6 ± 1.2	39.2 ± 0.6	12.93
CLIP	easy	36.1 ± 0.9	40.2 ± 0.8	10.76
	complex	35.9 ± 1.2	40 ± 0.8	10.92
	all	36.1 ± 1.1	40.2 ± 0.9	9.6
ruDALL-E	all	36.2 ± 1.1	40.5 ± 1	11.1
Stable Diffusion	easy	36.7 ± 0.7	40.7 ± 0.9	9.43
	complex	36.8 ± 0.9	**40.9 ± 0.7**	9.81
	all	36.7 ± 0.8	40.9 ± 0.8	8.7
Natural backgrounds	easy	37 ± 1	41.4 ± 0.7	7.15
	complex	37.1 ± 1	41.3 ± 0.7	7.9
	all	37 ± 0.9	41.4 ± 0.6	6.14

Figure 8 shows the segmentation model predictions on the test images. The source of augmentation background for this model training is stable diffusion.

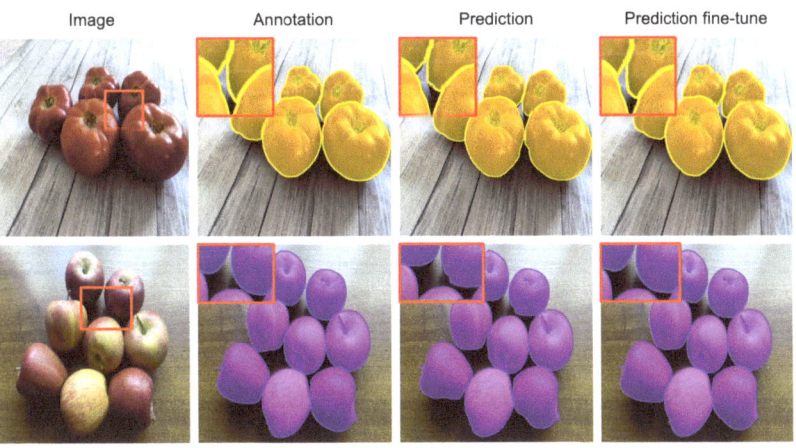

Figure 8. Example of model predictions.

4. Discussion

4.1. CISA Efficiency

Our experiments show that CISA instance-level augmentation provides a stable improvement for all of the tested CV tasks. This works both for convolutional and transformer models. The major observation is the importance of the context. Note that with random patterns, augmentation sometimes works worse than the baseline.

The best choice is to use a natural background from the location where the CV system will be used. This is possible when the camera is stationary. If there are multiple camera locations, it is better to collect background images from all of them. Recall that background images do not require any manual annotation.

Any other approach to collect similar images gives substantial improvement in comparison with other augmentation approaches. Both image retrieval and image generation show promising results. In our experiments, stable diffusion beats all other approaches for the majority of cases.

For more complex tasks, the boost is higher. The natural training dataset is still required for fine-tuning. The results from the approach without the fine-tuning are worse than the baseline.

Table 15 as well as Figures 9 and 10 show the correlation between the model performance and FID. One can see that if an augmented training set is similar to the test set, it will result in higher accuracy. It allows for choosing a better set of backgrounds without model training. For more complex tasks, the correlation seems to be lower. For segmentation and detection tasks, the correlation is very high.

Table 15. Correlation.

Model	Task	#Classes	Correlation	p Value ↓
ResNet50	classification	6	−0.64	4×10^{-13}
ResNet50	classification	18	−0.27	10^{-3}
MobileNetv3	classification	6	−0.2	2×10^{-1}
MobileNetv3	classification	18	−0.18	4×10^{-2}
SWIN	classification	6	−0.65	2×10^{-10}
SWIN	classification	18	−0.37	8×10^{-3}
UNET++	segmentation	6	−0.94	2×10^{-25}
UNET++	segmentation	18	−0.95	2×10^{-26}
YOLOv8	detection	6	−0.75	3×10^{-11}
YOLOv8	detection	18	−0.57	6×10^{-11}

The importance of context for image augmentation has been previously demonstrated in [37], where the authors created an additional neural network to select a proper location on a new background to paste the target object. In turn, we focus on the retrieval and generation of an extensive dataset using various sources of background images. Although the proposed approach does not involve additional generative models for dataset augmentation, it is a simple and powerful way to adjust recognition model performance. CISA instance-level augmentation extends the pioneering research on image augmentation [35] and recent studies [36], and it allows one to estimate dataset suitability before model training based on FID measures between original and generated datasets.

4.2. Limitations

The proposed image augmentation scheme can be used when we have masks for input images. The system can work with instance segmentation masks and semantic segmentation masks. However, if there are no instance masks available, one can try to generate pseudo-segmentation masks.

The system's primary usage involves generating complex scenes from simple input data; however, the scene can include a single object if needed. The key feature of the system is its ability to generate a huge amount of training samples even for the task for which the original dataset was not designed. For instance, having only an image and a multi-part mask as input, we can produce samples for instance segmentation, instance parts segmentation, object detection, object counting, denoising, and classification. The described system can also be beneficial for few-shot learning when the original dataset is minimal.

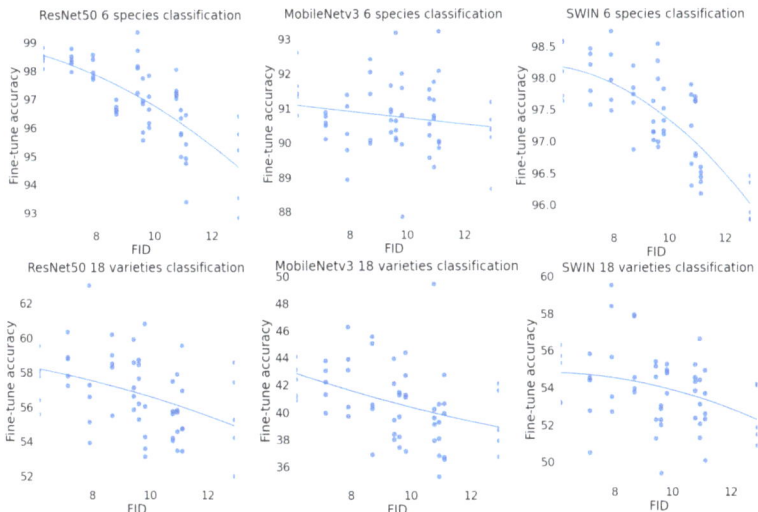

Figure 9. Relation between FID and accuracy in the classification task.

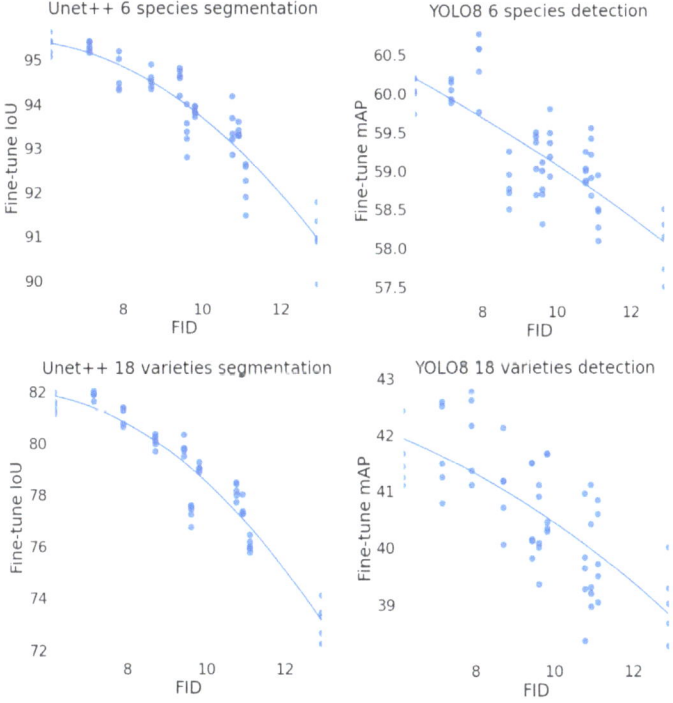

Figure 10. Relation between FID and IoU in the segmentation task and mAP in the object detection task.

To apply the proposed augmentation scheme successfully, the dataset should not be exceedingly sensitive to scene geometry, since such behavior can be undesirable in some cases. For example, if you use a dataset of people or cars, the described approach by default can place one object on top of the other. Nevertheless, we can add some extra height limitations or use perspective transformation in these cases.

Another point is that we should find appropriate background images that would fit some particular case. Retrieval-based approaches used to generate new training samples using CLIP can be significantly impeded, in particular, domains such as medical or remote sensing. For instance, in [43], the authors aimed to generate thermal images, with defective areas occurring due to the manufacturing process. It is a more complex task to retrieve such unique backgrounds using CLIP. However, there are various special data sources that do not contain annotated data but are useful as backgrounds for new samples. Another possible limitation is that if it is not possible to know the test set context, we may expect a slight performance drop.

Further study on CISA application for images derived from different sensors on different wavelengths should be conducted. Multispectral and hyperspectral data, radiography, and radar scanning have their own properties. Their artificial generation is currently under consideration in a number of works [61]. However, it is vital to take into account the nature of data, because image augmentations should not break any physical law of the studied objects.

Recall that it is important to fine-tune the model on natural images to increase the performance.

The time for scene generation is close to linear when we have enough memory to store all objects and overhead for a scene. To estimate the average required RAM per scene, we use Equation (9)

$$M = 3n\bar{h}\bar{w}[(1+m)p + o + 2] + 'o \tag{9}$$

In this equation, we can neglect the overhead, $'o < o << M$, because it is considerably smaller than the data itself.

Although GAN-based image augmentation approaches are capable of providing more realistic images under certain conditions, the proposed CISA approach does not require computational resources to train an additional generative model.

5. Conclusions

In this article, we introduce an image augmentation technique for few-shot learning. The presented framework allows for generating large training datasets using only a few input samples. It also provides training data for the tasks, including instance segmentation, semantic segmentation, classification, object detection, and object counting, even if the original dataset contains annotations for the instance segmentation task only. To show our method's advantage, we compared the model performances on the tasks with different difficulties, we checked the models of different types and different capacities, and we showed the substantial improvement for all of the listed cases. The average percentage increase in accuracy across all the tasks on the fruits and vegetables recognition dataset is 4.95%. Moreover, we extensively explored approaches to collect background images, and we showed an efficient method used to choose the best background dataset without model training. WE showed that the Fréchet Inception Distance (FID) metrics has a strong correlation with model accuracy, and it can help to choose better backgrounds without model training. The average negative correlation between model accuracy and the FID between The augmented and test datasets was 0.55 in our experiments.

Author Contributions: Conceptualization, S.N.; methodology, S.N. and A.S.; software, I.Z.; validation, S.N. and S.I.; formal analysis, S.N. and I.Z.; investigation, I.Z. and S.N.; resources, S.V.B. and T.Y.; data curation, I.Z. and S.N.; writing—original draft preparation, S.N. and S.I.; writing—review and editing, A.S. and S.V.B.; visualization, S.N. and S.I.; supervision, A.S., V.D. and I.O.; project administration, S.N. and D.S.; funding acquisition, S.V.B. and T.Y. All authors have read and agreed to the published version of the manuscript.

Funding: This research received no external funding.

Data Availability Statement: The code is available at https://github.com/NesterukSergey/segmentation_image_augmentation, accessed on 27 February 2023. Data are shared at https://disk.yandex.com/d/VeTwxns9ncOqGA, accessed on 27 February 2023.

Conflicts of Interest: The authors declare no conflict of interest.

Abbreviations

The following abbreviations are used in this manuscript:

CISA	Context Image Semantics Augmentation framework
CLIP	Contrast Language-Image Pre-Training model
FID	Frechet Inception Distance
CV	Computer Vision
GAN	Generative Adversarial Network
cGAN	Conditional Generative Adversarial Network
VQGAN	Vector-Quantized Generative Adversarial Network
VAE	Variational Autoencoder
ML	Machine Learning
NLP	Natural Language Processing
RAM	Random Access Memory
MO	Multi-Object
MP	Multi-Part
MAXRECTS-BLSF	Maximal Rectangles Best Long Side Fit algorithm
SGD	Stochastic Gradient Descent
Adam	Adaptive Momentum Optimizer
IoU	Intersection over Union
mAP	Mean Average Precision

References

1. Kwon, O.; Sim, J.M. Effects of data set features on the performances of classification algorithms. *Expert Syst. Appl.* **2013**, *40*, 1847–1857. [CrossRef]
2. Sbai, O.; Couprie, C.; Aubry, M. Impact of base dataset design on few-shot image classification. In *Proceedings of the European Conference on Computer Vision*; Springer: Berlin/Heidelberg, Germany, 2020; pp. 597–613.
3. Zendel, O.; Murschitz, M.; Humenberger, M.; Herzner, W. How good is my test data? Introducing safety analysis for computer vision. *Int. J. Comput. Vis.* **2017**, *125*, 95–109. [CrossRef]
4. Barbedo, J.G.A. Impact of dataset size and variety on the effectiveness of deep learning and transfer learning for plant disease classification. *Comput. Electron. Agric.* **2018**, *153*, 46–53. [CrossRef]
5. Zheng, S.; Song, Y.; Leung, T.; Goodfellow, I. Improving the robustness of deep neural networks via stability training. In Proceedings of the IEEE Conference on Computer Vision and Pattern Recognition, Las Vegas, NV, USA, 27–30 June 2016; pp. 4480–4488.
6. Hendrycks, D.; Basart, S.; Mu, N.; Kadavath, S.; Wang, F.; Dorundo, E.; Desai, R.; Zhu, T.; Parajuli, S.; Guo, M.; et al. The many faces of robustness: A critical analysis of out-of-distribution generalization. *arXiv* **2020**, arXiv:2006.16241.
7. Deng, J.; Dong, W.; Socher, R.; Li, L.J.; Li, K.; Fei-Fei, L. Imagenet: A large-scale hierarchical image database. In Proceedings of the 2009 IEEE Conference on Computer Vision and Pattern Recognition, Miami Beach, FL, USA, 20–25 June 2009; pp. 248–255.
8. Lin, T.Y.; Maire, M.; Belongie, S.; Hays, J.; Perona, P.; Ramanan, D.; Dollár, P.; Zitnick, C.L. Microsoft coco: Common objects in context. In *Proceedings of the European Conference on Computer Vision*; Springer: Berlin/Heidelberg, Germany, 2014; pp. 740–755.
9. Xia, G.S.; Bai, X.; Ding, J.; Zhu, Z.; Belongie, S.; Luo, J.; Datcu, M.; Pelillo, M.; Zhang, L. DOTA: A large-scale dataset for object detection in aerial images. In Proceedings of the IEEE Conference on Computer Vision and Pattern Recognition, Salt Lake City, UT, USA, 18–22 June 2018; pp. 3974–3983.

10. Caba Heilbron, F.; Escorcia, V.; Ghanem, B.; Carlos Niebles, J. Activitynet: A large-scale video benchmark for human activity understanding. In Proceedings of the IEEE Conference on Computer Vision and Pattern Recognition, Boston, MA, USA, 7–12 June 2015; pp. 961–970.
11. Tan, C.; Sun, F.; Kong, T.; Zhang, W.; Yang, C.; Liu, C. A survey on deep transfer learning. In *Proceedings of the International Conference on Artificial Neural Networks*; Springer: Berlin/Heidelberg, Germany, 2018; pp. 270–279.
12. Lemikhova, L.; Nesteruk, S.; Somov, A. Transfer Learning for Few-Shot Plants Recognition: Antarctic Station Greenhouse Use-Case. In Proceedings of the 2022 IEEE 31st International Symposium on Industrial Electronics (ISIE), Anchorage, AL, USA, 1–3 June 2022; pp. 715–720. [CrossRef]
13. Vannucci, M.; Colla, V. Classification of unbalanced datasets and detection of rare events in industry: issues and solutions. In *Proceedings of the International Conference on Engineering Applications of Neural Networks*; Springer: Berlin/Heidelberg, Germany, 2016; pp. 337–351.
14. Nesteruk, S.; Shadrin, D.; Pukalchik, M.; Somov, A.; Zeidler, C.; Zabel, P.; Schubert, D. Image compression and plants classification using machine learning in controlled-environment agriculture: Antarctic station use case. *IEEE Sensors J.* **2021**, *21*, 17564–17572. [CrossRef]
15. Wang, Y.; Yao, Q.; Kwok, J.T.; Ni, L.M. Generalizing from a few examples: A survey on few-shot learning. *ACM Comput. Surv. (CSUR)* **2020**, *53*, 1–34. [CrossRef]
16. Illarionova, S.; Nesteruk, S.; Shadrin, D.; Ignatiev, V.; Pukalchik, M.; Oseledets, I. Object-based augmentation for building semantic segmentation: Ventura and santa rosa case study. In Proceedings of the Proceedings of the IEEE/CVF International Conference on Computer Vision, Montreal, BC, Canada, 11–17 October 2021; pp. 1659–1668.
17. Illarionova, S.; Shadrin, D.; Ignatiev, V.; Shayakhmetov, S.; Trekin, A.; Oseledets, I. Augmentation-Based Methodology for Enhancement of Trees Map Detalization on a Large Scale. *Remote. Sens.* **2022**, *14*, 2281. [CrossRef]
18. Shorten, C.; Khoshgoftaar, T.M. A survey on image data augmentation for deep learning. *J. Big Data* **2019**, *6*, 60. [CrossRef]
19. Kuznichov, D.; Zvirin, A.; Honen, Y.; Kimmel, R. Data Augmentation for Leaf Segmentation and Counting Tasks in Rosette Plants. In Proceedings of the Proceedings of the IEEE/CVF Conference on Computer Vision and Pattern Recognition (CVPR) Workshops, Long Beach, CA, USA, 15–20 June 2019.
20. Fawakherji, M.; Potena, C.; Prevedello, I.; Pretto, A.; Bloisi, D.D.; Nardi, D. Data Augmentation Using GANs for Crop/Weed Segmentation in Precision Farming. In Proceedings of the 2020 IEEE Conference on Control Technology and Applications (CCTA), Montreal, QC, Canada, 24–26 August 2020; pp. 279–284.
21. Wu, Q.; Chen, Y.; Meng, J. DCGAN Based Data Augmentation for Tomato Leaf Disease Identification. *IEEE Access* **2020**. [CrossRef]
22. Nesteruk, S.; Shadrin, D.; Kovalenko, V.; Rodriguez-Sanchez, A.; Somov, A. Plant Growth Prediction through Intelligent Embedded Sensing. In Proceedings of the IEEE 29th International Symposium on Industrial Electronics (ISIE), Delft, The Netherlands, 17–19 June 2020; Volume 2020, pp. 411–416. [CrossRef]
23. Nesteruk, S.; Illarionova, S.; Akhtyamov, T.; Shadrin, D.; Somov, A.; Pukalchik, M.; Oseledets, I. XtremeAugment: Getting More From Your Data Through Combination of Image Collection and Image Augmentation. *IEEE Access* **2022**, *10*, 24010–24028. [CrossRef]
24. Nesteruk, S.; Bezzateev, S. Location-Based Protocol for the Pairwise Authentication in the Networks without Infrastructure. In Proceedings of the 2018 22nd Conference of Open Innovations Association (FRUCT), Jyvaskyla, Finland, 15–18 May 2018; pp. 190–197. [CrossRef]
25. Ching, T.; Himmelstein, D.S.; Beaulieu-Jones, B.K.; Kalinin, A.A.; Do, B.T.; Way, G.P.; Ferreo, E.; Agapow, P.-M.; Zirtz, M.; Hoffman, M.M.; et al. Opportunities and obstacles for deep learning in biology and medicine. *J. R. Soc. Interface* **2018**, *15*, 20170387. [CrossRef] [PubMed]
26. Feng, R.; Gu, J.; Qiao, Y.; Dong, C. Suppressing Model Overfitting for Image Super-Resolution Networks. In Proceedings of the Proceedings of the IEEE/CVF Conference on Computer Vision and Pattern Recognition (CVPR) Workshops, Long Beach, CA, USA, 15–20 June2019.
27. Illarionova, S.; Nesteruk, S.; Shadrin, D.; Ignatiev, V.; Pukalchik, M.; Oseledets, I. MixChannel: Advanced augmentation for multispectral satellite images. *Remote. Sens.* **2021**, *13*, 2181. [CrossRef]
28. Zeiler, M.D.; Fergus, R. Visualizing and Understanding Convolutional Networks. In *Proceedings of the Computer Vision—ECCV 2014*; Fleet, D., Pajdla, T., Schiele, B., Tuytelaars, T., Eds.; Springer International Publishing: Cham, Switzerland, 2014; pp. 818–833.
29. Krizhevsky, A.; Sutskever, I.; Hinton, G.E. ImageNet Classification with Deep Convolutional Neural Networks. *Commun. ACM* **2017**, *60*, 84–90. [CrossRef]
30. Buslaev, A.; Parinov, A.; Khvedchenya, E.; Iglovikov, V.I.; Kalinin, A.A. Albumentations: Fast and flexible image augmentations. *Information* **2020**, *11*, 125. [CrossRef]
31. Zhu, Y.; Aoun, M.; Krijn, M.; Vanschoren, J.; Campus, H.T. Data Augmentation using Conditional Generative Adversarial Networks for Leaf Counting in Arabidopsis Plants. In Proceedings of the BMVC, Newcastle, UK, 3–6 September 2018; p. 324.
32. Valerio Giuffrida, M.; Scharr, H.; Tsaftaris, S.A. ARIGAN: Synthetic Arabidopsis Plants Using Generative Adversarial Network. In Proceedings of the Proceedings of the IEEE International Conference on Computer Vision (ICCV) Workshops, Venice, Italy, 22–29 October 2017.

33. Zoph, B.; Cubuk, E.D.; Ghiasi, G.; Lin, T.; Shlens, J.; Le, Q.V. Learning Data Augmentation Strategies for Object Detection. *arXiv* **2019**, arXiv:1906.11172.
34. Lemley, J.; Bazrafkan, S.; Corcoran, P. Smart Augmentation Learning an Optimal Data Augmentation Strategy. *IEEE Access* **2017**, *5*, 5858–5869. [CrossRef]
35. Dwibedi, D.; Misra, I.; Hebert, M. Cut, paste and learn: Surprisingly easy synthesis for instance detection. In Proceedings of the IEEE International Conference on Computer Vision, Venice, Italy, 22–29 October 2017; pp. 1301–1310.
36. Ghiasi, G.; Cui, Y.; Srinivas, A.; Qian, R.; Lin, T.Y.; Cubuk, E.D.; Le, Q.V.; Zoph, B. Simple copy-paste is a strong data augmentation method for instance segmentation. In Proceedings of the IEEE/CVF Conference on Computer Vision and Pattern Recognition, Online, 19–25 June 2021; pp. 2918–2928.
37. Dvornik, N.; Mairal, J.; Schmid, C. On the importance of visual context for data augmentation in scene understanding. *IEEE Trans. Pattern Anal. Mach. Intell.* **2019**, *43*, 2014–2028. [CrossRef]
38. Su, Y.; Sun, R.; Lin, G.; Wu, Q. Context decoupling augmentation for weakly supervised semantic segmentation. In Proceedings of the IEEE/CVF International Conference on Computer Vision, Montreal, BC, Canada, 11–17 October 2021; pp. 7004–7014.
39. Flores-Fuentes, W.; Trujillo-Hernández, G.; Alba-Corpus, I.Y.; Rodríguez-Quiñonez, J.C.; Mirada-Vega, J.E.; Hernández-Balbuena, D.; Murrieta-Rico, F.N.; Sergiyenko, O. 3D spatial measurement for model reconstruction: A review. *Measurement* **2023**, *207*, 112321. [CrossRef]
40. Barth, R.; IJsselmuiden, J.; Hemming, J.; Henten, E.V. Data synthesis methods for semantic segmentation in agriculture: A Capsicum annuum dataset. *Comput. Electron. Agric.* **2018**, *144*, 284–296. [CrossRef]
41. Ward, D.; Moghadam, P.; Hudson, N. Deep Leaf Segmentation Using Synthetic Data. *arXiv* **2018**, arXiv:1807.10931.
42. Lu, Y.; Chen, D.; Olaniyi, E.; Huang, Y. Generative adversarial networks (GANs) for image augmentation in agriculture: A systematic review. *Comput. Electron. Agric.* **2022**, *200*, 107208. [CrossRef]
43. Liu, K.; Li, Y.; Yang, J.; Liu, Y.; Yao, Y. Generative principal component thermography for enhanced defect detection and analysis. *IEEE Trans. Instrum. Meas.* **2020**, *69*, 8261–8269. [CrossRef]
44. Illarionova, S.; Shadrin, D.; Trekin, A.; Ignatiev, V.; Oseledets, I. Generation of the nir spectral band for satellite images with convolutional neural networks. *Sensors* **2021**, *21*, 5646. [CrossRef] [PubMed]
45. Chen, Y.; Yang, X.H.; Wei, Z.; Heidari, A.A.; Zheng, N.; Li, Z.; Chen, H.; Hu, H.; Zhou, Q.; Guan, Q. Generative adversarial networks in medical image augmentation: A review. *Comput. Biol. Med.* **2022**, 105382. [CrossRef]
46. Beaumont, R. Clip Retrieval: Easily Compute Clip Embeddings and Build a Clip Retrieval System with Them. 2020 Available online: https://github.com/rom1504/clip-retrieval (accessed on 27 February 2023).
47. Illarionova, S.; Shadrin, D.; Tregubova, P.; Ignatiev, V.; Efimov, A.; Oseledets, I.; Burnaev, E. A Survey of Computer Vision Techniques for Forest Characterization and Carbon Monitoring Tasks. *Remote. Sens.* **2022**, *14*, 5861. [CrossRef]
48. Agarwal, N.; Chiang, C.W.; Sharma, A. A study on computer vision techniques for self-driving cars. In *Proceedings of the Frontier Computing: Theory, Technologies and Applications (FC 2018) 7*; Springer: Berlin/Heidelberg, Germany, 2019; pp. 629–634.
49. Lindner, L.; Sergiyenko, O.; Rivas-López, M.; Ivanov, M.; Rodríguez-Quiñonez, J.C.; Hernández-Balbuena, D.; Flores-Fuentes, W.; Tyrsa, V.; Muerrieta-Rico, F.N.; Mercorelli, P. Machine vision system errors for unmanned aerial vehicle navigation. In Proceedings of the 2017 IEEE 26th International Symposium on Industrial Electronics (ISIE), Edinburgh, UK, 19–21 June 2017; pp. 1615–1620.
50. Shonenkov, A. Ai-Forever/RU-Dalle: Generate images from texts. (In Russian)
51. Rombach, R.; Blattmann, A.; Lorenz, D.; Esser, P.; Ommer, B. High-resolution image synthesis with latent diffusion models. 2022 IEEE. In Proceedings of the CVF Conference on Computer Vision and Pattern Recognition (CVPR), New Orleans, LA, USA, 18–24 June 2022; pp. 10674–10685.
52. Radford, A.; Kim, J.W.; Hallacy, C.; Ramesh, A.; Goh, G.; Agarwal, S.; Sastry, G.; Askell, A.; Mishkin, P.; Clark, J.; et al. Learning Transferable Visual Models From Natural Language Supervision. In *Proceedings of the 38th International Conference on Machine Learning*; Meila, M., Zhang, T., Eds.; PMLR: New York, NY, USA, 2021; Volume 139, pp. 8748–8763.
53. Schuhmann, C.; Kaczmarczyk, R.; Komatsuzaki, A.; Katta, A.; Vencu, R.; Beaumont, R.; Jitsev, J.; Coombes, T.; Mullis, C. LAION-400M: Open Dataset of CLIP-Filtered 400 Million Image-Text Pairs. In Proceedings of the NeurIPS Workshop Datacentric AI. Jülich Supercomputing Center, Virtual, 13 December 2021; number FZJ-2022-00923.
54. He, K.; Zhang, X.; Ren, S.; Sun, J. Deep residual learning for image recognition. In Proceedings of the IEEE Conference on Computer Vision and Pattern Recognition, Las Vegas, NV, USA, 27–30 June 2016; pp. 770–778.
55. Liu, Z.; Lin, Y.; Cao, Y.; Hu, H.; Wei, Y.; Zhang, Z.; Lin, S.; Guo, B. Swin transformer: Hierarchical vision transformer using shifted windows. In Proceedings of the IEEE/CVF International Conference on Computer Vision, Montreal, BC, Canada, 11–17 October 2021; pp. 10012–10022.
56. Howard, M.; Sandler, M.; Chu, G.; Chen, L.C.; Chen, B.; Tan, M.; Wang, W.; Zhu, Y.; Pang, R.; Vasudevan, V.; et al. Searching for mobilenetv3. In Proceedings of the IEEE/CVF International Conference on Computer Vision, Seoul, Korea, 27 October–2 November 2019; pp. 1314–1324.
57. Goodfellow, I.J.; Bengio, Y.; Courville, A. *Deep Learning*; MIT Press: Cambridge, MA, USA, 2016. Available online: http://www.deeplearningbook.org (accessed on 27 February 2023).
58. Dosovitskiy, A.; Beyer, L.; Kolesnikov, A.; Weissenborn, D.; Zhai, X.; Unterthiner, T.; Dehghani, M.; Minderer, M.; Heigold, G.; Gelly, S.; et al. An image is worth 16x16 words: Transformers for image recognition at scale. *arXiv* **2020**, arXiv:2010.11929.

59. Bynagari, N.B. GANs trained by a two time-scale update rule converge to a local Nash equilibrium. *Asian J. Appl. Sci. Eng.* **2019**, *8*, 25–34.
60. Szegedy, C.; Vanhoucke, V.; Ioffe, S.; Shlens, J.; Wojna, Z. Rethinking the inception architecture for computer vision. In Proceedings of the IEEE Conference on Computer Vision and Pattern Recognition, Las Vegas, NV, USA, 27–30 June 2016; pp. 2818–2826.
61. Gao, S.; Dai, Y.; Xu, Y.; Chen, J.; Liu, Y. Generative adversarial network–assisted image classification for imbalanced tire X-ray defect detection. *Trans. Inst. Meas. Control.* **2023**, 01423312221140940. [CrossRef]

Disclaimer/Publisher's Note: The statements, opinions and data contained in all publications are solely those of the individual author(s) and contributor(s) and not of MDPI and/or the editor(s). MDPI and/or the editor(s) disclaim responsibility for any injury to people or property resulting from any ideas, methods, instructions or products referred to in the content.

Article

Neural Network Based Control of Four-Bar Mechanism with Variable Input Velocity

R. Peón-Escalante, Manuel Flota-Bañuelos, Roberto Quintal-Palomo *, Luis J. Ricalde, F. Peñuñuri, B. Cruz Jiménez and J. Avilés Viñas

Faculty of Engineering, University of Yucatan, Mérida 97000, Mexico; rpeon@correo.uady.mx (R.P.-E.); manuel.flota@correo.uady.mx (M.F.-B.); lricalde@correo.uady.mx (L.J.R.); francisco.pa@correo.uady.mx (F.P.); braulio.cruz@correo.uady.mx (B.C.J.); javiles@correo.uady.mx (J.A.V.)
* Correspondence: roberto.quintal@correo.uady.mx

Abstract: For control applications, the angular velocity of the drive crank of a four-bar mechanism is traditionally assumed to be constant. In this paper, we propose control of variable velocity of the drive crank to obtain the desired output motions for the coupler point. To estimate the reference trajectory for the crank velocity, a neural network is trained with data from the kinematic model. The control law is designed from feedback linearization of the tracking error dynamics and a Proportional–Integral–Derivative (PID) controller. The applicability of the proposed scheme is validated through simulations for three variable speed profiles, obtaining excellent results from the system.

Keywords: four-bar mechanism; variable input-velocity; trajectory tracking; PID neural network controller

MSC: 70E60

1. Introduction

When an electric motor is coupled in a four-bar mechanism, a periodically time varying torque, produced by the changing inertia of the mechanism during its rotation, is applied as an external load to the motor [1]. Different control techniques have been studied to regulate the crank angular velocity fluctuations introduced by the inertia of the rotor and the rotating bars in four-bar linkages. Among applied controllers that address this issue, are proportional–integral–derivative (PID) [1], proportional–derivative (PD) [2–4], nonlinear PD [5], model reference adaptive control [6], fuzzy [7], type-2 fuzzy sliding mode [8], adaptive fuzzy sliding mode [9], robust fuzzy [10], PID Fuzzy [11], PID neural network [12], PD and neural adaptive [13], moving sliding mode [14], robust backstepping control [15], and fuzzy logic controller combined with grey system modeling approach [16]. In [17], several control schemes are investigated (filtered proportional–integral–derivative, filtered sliding mode, filtered fuzzy, and filtered genetic-based reinforcement neuro-controller). In reference [18], experimental data were used to develop parametric models for a four-bar mechanism driven by a geared DC motor by employing artificial neural networks. In reference [19], PID linear control was used to control a micro-aerial-vehicle that has four flapping wings (four-bar mechanisms). In [20], the gains of a PID controller for the four-bar mechanism are optimized via evolutionary algorithms. Recently, in [21], an indirect adaptive control based on online multi-objective optimization for the velocity regulation of the four-bar mechanism was proposed. Other advanced control schemes for trajectory tracking in mechanical systems consider sliding modes [22] and Linear Matrix Inequalities (LMI) approaches [23], which are both applied for docking mechanisms. Furthermore, optimal sliding mode control has been applied in quick-return mechanisms [24]. On the other hand, fuzzy-based controlled schemes for trajectory tracking have been recently developed with applications on mobile robots with promising results [25–27]. In reference [25], the design of a highly efficient path-following scheme for wheeled mobile robots is proposed. Here the

authors present a new controller constructed by the type-3 (T3) fuzzy logic systems (FLS) and a predictive compensator where the stability of the complete system is validated with the Lyapunov methodology. Furthermore, this scheme is tested with good performance in a chaotic generated path.

The main topic of this work is to integrate computational intelligence methods to solve the inverse kinematics problem to control a four-bar mechanism for trajectory tracking in the coupler point; this trajectory requires a variable angular velocity of the drive crank. This control scheme is defined as variable input velocity control. There are few reports of simulation studies on cases of trajectory tracking where the problem of variable input velocity control is addressed [2,3,6,15,28–30]. In [6], a model reference adaptive controller for the velocity regulation of a four-bar mechanism is designed. In reference [2], motion control of four-bar mechanism driven by a brushless servo motor is applied where simulation and experimental results were validated for different crank motion profiles. In [3], a PD control algorithm is employed for trajectory tracking in a four-bar mechanism which is redesigned by applying a new mass-distribution scheme. In reference [28], an integrated approach for variable input velocity servo four-bar linkages is designed in order to satisfy the kinematic requirements, reduce the shaking force and moment, improve the velocity trajectory tracking performance, and minimize the motor power dissipation where dimensions of the links, counterweights, input-velocity trajectory and controller parameters are considered as design variables simultaneously. In [15], a robust backstepping controller is designed and tested in simulation for a four-bar linkage mechanism that is driven by a DC motor, without a priori knowledge of the model parameters where five cases were examined. In reference [29,30], the problem of trajectory tracking by controlling the angular velocity of the input link is investigated in a four-bar mechanism to fulfill moving the coupler point with a constant velocity. A vision controller for regulation of the velocity of the coupler point in a four-bar mechanism was implemented in [30], where the desired trajectory for the coupler point of the mechanism is achieved by controlling the angular velocity of the crank using a feedback linearization algorithm for the error dynamics and a PID controller.

For a four-bar mechanism, the characteristics of the output movement depend on the crank's input movement. Then, it is necessary that the designed control fulfills the mechanism desired input velocity profile in order for the output motion to follow the desired trajectory. In this work, the problem of trajectory tracking is considered; the variable input velocity control is designed to ensure that the coupler point follows a constant velocity reference. To obtain the reference for the crank velocity and to reduce the computational burden for the synthesized control, a neural network is implemented. Neural networks have been widely applied to aid the control design process for mechanisms due to their simple design and easy implementation. In [12], a feed-forward neural network is applied to predict the reference model used by a PID controller for the constant velocity of the crank.

The structure of this work is presented as follows: Section 2 explains the kinematic model for the four-bar mechanism, the DC motor and mechanical coupling mathematical models are developed, and the overall dynamic model is presented. In Section 3, the Artificial Neural Network and PID control scheme are synthesized. Section 4 presents the path for the coupler point in the mechanism, and simulation results for several cases of trajectory tracking are discussed. In Section 5, the conclusions are summarized.

2. Mathematical Model for a Motor-Driven Four-Bar Mechanism System

2.1. Dynamics of the Four-Bar Linkages

A general four-bar linkage is presented in Figure 1, where link L_2 (crank) is driven by an electrical motor, and it is able to perform a complete rotation. The link L_3 (coupler) performs a general motion in the plane, and it transmits the movement to link L_4 (rocker), which executes an oscillatory motion, and the link L_1 (ground) is fixed with respect to the reference frame. The kinematic model of the four-bar mechanism is defined with respect to the global reference system $\{X - Y\}$. The local reference system $\{x_r - y_r\}$ is assigned with the origin coinciding on the pivot O_2 of the mechanism and is specified the direction

x_r along of the link L_1. Thus, the relation between the local reference system with respect to the global $\{X-Y\}$, is defined by the translation r_0 and orientation α.

The parameters in Figure 1 required to develop the dynamical model of the mechanism are summarized in Table 1. Each link has a mass of m_i, a mass moment of inertia with respect to the centroid J_i, and L_i is the length of the link i. The angular positions of each link with respect to the x_r axis of the base frame are denoted by ϕ_2, ϕ_3, and ϕ_4. The position vector of the center of mass for each link i is displayed by a dark circle and their locations are described by r_i and θ_i. A torsional spring with a stiffness constant k_s and a torsional damper with a damping constant c are attached to the rocker link to represent a general loading situation.

Table 1. Parameters of four-bar mechanism.

Parameter	Description for Each Link
L_i	length of the link i
ϕ_i	angular position for link i with respect to the axis x_r
m_i	mass of link i
J_i	mass moment of inertia
r_i and θ_i	location of the center of mass for each link i
r_{cx} and r_{cy}	location of point Q on link 3

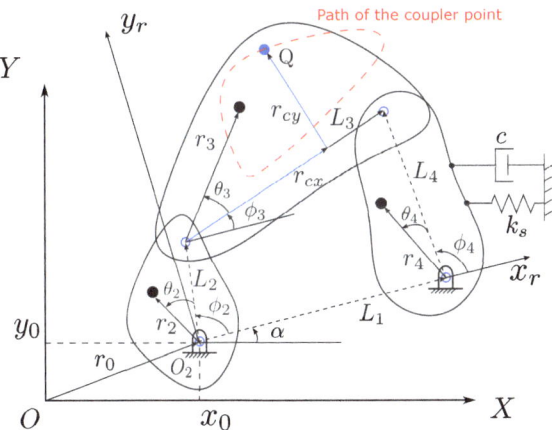

Figure 1. Schematic of four-bar linkage.

Applying the Euler–Lagrange modeling methodology [1,31], the equation of motion for the mechanism, by using the crank angle ϕ_2 as the generalized coordinate, is given by

$$\frac{d}{dt}\left(\frac{\partial K}{\partial \dot{\phi}_2}\right) - \frac{\partial K}{\partial \phi_2} + \frac{\partial P}{\partial \phi_2} + \frac{\partial D}{\partial \dot{\phi}_2} = T \quad (1)$$

where K, P, and D denote the kinetic, potential, and dissipative energies, respectively, and T is the applied external torque. The dissipation term can be neglected in the mechanism, since the damping is relatively small.

The kinetic energy of the mechanism is defined as

$$K = \sum_{i=2}^{4}\left[\frac{1}{2}m_i(V_{ix}^2 + V_{iy}^2) + \frac{1}{2}J_i\dot{\phi}_i^2\right] \quad (2)$$

where V_{ix} and V_{iy} represent the components of velocity at the mass center in X and Y of the link i, and $\dot{\phi}_i$ is the angular velocity of the link i.

According to the scheme in Figure 1, the kinetic energy can be expressed as

$$K = \frac{1}{2} A(\phi_2) \dot{\phi}_2^2 \tag{3}$$

where $A(\phi_2)$ is defined as,

$$A(\phi_2) = C_0 + C_1 \gamma_3^2 + C_2 \gamma_4^2 + C_3 \gamma_3 \cos(\phi_2 - \phi_3 - \theta_3) \tag{4}$$

and

$$C_0 = J_2 + m_2 r_2^2 + m_3 L_2^2$$
$$C_1 = J_3 + m_3 r_3^2$$
$$C_2 = J_4 + m_4 r_4^2$$
$$C_3 = 2 L_2 r_3 m_3$$

From the four-bar linkage kinematics analysis position, the functions for the angular position of the coupler link, ϕ_3, and the oscillator link, ϕ_4, are determined.

The angle ϕ_3, corresponding to the orientation for coupler link, L_3, is defined from

$$\phi_3(\phi_2) = 2 \arctan\left(\frac{-k_b \pm \sqrt{k_b^2 - 4 k_a k_c}}{2 k_a} \right) \tag{5}$$

where

$$k_a = -l_1 + (l_2 + 1) \cos \phi_2 + l_3,$$
$$k_b = -2 \sin \phi_2,$$
$$k_c = l_1 + (l_2 - 1) \cos \phi_2 + l_3,$$

and the constants l_1, l_2, and l_3 are

$$l_1 = \frac{L_1}{L_2}$$
$$l_2 = \frac{L_1}{L_3}$$
$$l_3 = \frac{L_4^2 - L_1^2 - L_2^2 - L_3^2}{2 L_2 L_3}$$

The angle ϕ_4, corresponding to the orientation for oscillator link L_4, is defined from

$$\phi_4(\phi_2) = 2 \arctan\left(\frac{-k_b \pm \sqrt{k_b^2 - 4 k_d k_e}}{2 k_d} \right) \tag{6}$$

where the coefficients k_d and k_e are

$$k_d = -l_1 + (1 - l_4) \cos \phi_2 + l_5,$$
$$k_e = l_1 - (l_4 + 1) \cos \phi_2 + l_5,$$

and the constants l_4 and l_5 are

$$l_4 = \frac{L_1}{L_4}$$
$$l_5 = \frac{L_2^2 - L_3^2 + L_4^2 + L_1^2}{2 L_2 L_4}.$$

From four-bar linkage kinematics analysis, the functions for the angular velocity of the coupler link, $\dot{\phi}_3$ can be expressed as

$$\dot{\phi}_3 = \gamma_3 \dot{\phi}_2 \tag{7}$$

where γ_3 is defined as

$$\gamma_3 = \frac{L_2 \sin(\phi_4 - \phi_2)}{L_3 \sin(\phi_3 - \phi_4)}$$

and the angular velocity of the rocker link, $\dot{\phi}_4$ is

$$\dot{\phi}_4 = \gamma_4 \dot{\phi}_2 \tag{8}$$

where γ_4 is defined as

$$\gamma_4 = \frac{L_2 \sin(\phi_3 + \phi_2)}{L_4 \sin(\phi_3 - \phi_4)}$$

It is important to notice that from (7) and (8), both $\dot{\phi}_3$ and $\dot{\phi}_4$ are functions of the crank link-driven velocity $\dot{\phi}_2$, which is the time derivative of the generalized coordinate.

The first term of the Euler–Lagrange movement equation is

$$\frac{d}{dt}\left(\frac{\partial K}{\partial \dot{\phi}_2}\right) = \frac{dA(\phi_2)}{d\phi_2}\dot{\phi}_2^2 + A(\phi_2)\ddot{\phi}_2 \tag{9}$$

Then, the second term of (1), yields

$$\frac{\partial K}{\partial \phi_2} = \frac{1}{2}\frac{dA(\phi_2)}{d\phi_2}\dot{\phi}_2^2 \tag{10}$$

In order to determine $\frac{dA(\phi_2)}{d\phi_2}$, it is necessary to calculate $\frac{d\gamma_3}{d\phi_2}$ and $\frac{d\gamma_4}{d\phi_2}$

The term $\frac{d\gamma_3}{d\phi_2}$ can be obtained from

$$\frac{d\gamma_3}{d\phi_2} = \frac{L_2}{L_3}\left[\frac{D_1 + D_2}{\sin^2(\phi_3 - \phi_4)}\right] \tag{11}$$

where

$$D_1 = (\gamma_4 - 1)\cos(\phi_4 - \phi_2)\sin(\phi_3 - \phi_4)$$
$$D_2 = (\gamma_4 - \gamma_3)\sin(\phi_4 - \phi_2)\cos(\phi_3 - \phi_4)$$

The term $\frac{d\gamma_4}{d\phi_2}$ is expressed as

$$\frac{d\gamma_4}{d\phi_2} = \frac{L_2}{L_4}\left[\frac{D_3 + D_4}{\sin^2(\phi_3 - \phi_4)}\right] \tag{12}$$

where

$$D_3 = (\gamma_3 - 1)\cos(\phi_3 - \phi_2)\sin(\phi_3 - \phi_4)$$
$$D_4 = (\gamma_4 - \gamma_3)\sin(\phi_3 - \phi_2)\cos(\phi_3 - \phi_4)$$

Using the expressions (11) and (12), we can rewrite $\frac{dA(\phi_2)}{d\phi_2}$ as

$$\frac{dA(\phi_2)}{d\phi_2} = \frac{L_2}{L_3}\left[\frac{D_1+D_2}{\sin^2(\phi_3-\phi_4)}\right][2C_1\gamma_3+C_3\cos(\phi_2-\phi_3-\theta_3)]+2C_2\gamma_4\frac{L_2}{L_4}\left[\frac{D_3+D_4}{\sin^2(\phi_3-\phi_4)}\right]$$
$$+C_3\gamma_3[-\sin(\phi_2-\phi_3-\theta_3)(1-\gamma_3)] \quad (13)$$

To obtain the term $\frac{\partial P}{\partial \phi_2}$, let us consider that the potential energy from the four-bar mechanism can be expressed as
$$P = P_g + P_s \quad (14)$$
where P_g indicates the potential energy caused by gravity and P_s is the potential energy stored in the torsional spring. The potential energy due to gravitational forces can be expressed as
$$P_g = [m_2 r_2 \sin(\theta_2+\phi_2) + m_3(L_2\sin\phi_2 + r_3\sin(\theta_3+\phi_3))$$
$$+ m_4(L_1\sin\theta_1 + r_4\sin(\phi_4+\theta_4))]g$$

Now, taking the time derivative of the potential energy with respect to ϕ_2, it follows
$$\frac{\partial P_g}{\partial \phi_2} = [m_2 r_2 \cos(\theta_2+\phi_2) + m_4(r_4\gamma_4\cos(\theta_4+\phi_4))$$
$$+ m_3(L_2\cos\phi_2 + r_3\gamma_3\cos(\theta_3+\phi_3))]g \quad (15)$$

The potential energy stored in the torsional spring can be written as
$$P_s = \frac{1}{2}k(\phi_4 - \phi_{4,0})^2 \quad (16)$$
and the dissipation energy is given by
$$D = \frac{1}{2}c\dot{\phi}_4^2 \quad (17)$$

Differentiating Equation (16) with respect to ϕ_2, and (17) with respect to $\dot{\phi}_2$, and using (8) we have
$$\frac{\partial P_s}{\partial \phi_2} = k_s \gamma_4(\phi_4 - \phi_{4,0}) \quad (18)$$
$$\frac{\partial D}{\partial \dot{\phi}_2} = C\gamma_4^2 \dot{\phi}_2 \quad (19)$$

To this end, the motion equation can be written by employing (9), (10), (15), (18), and (19) as
$$A(\phi_2)\ddot{\phi}_2 + \frac{1}{2}\frac{dA(\phi_2)}{d\phi_2}\dot{\phi}_2^2 + k\gamma_4(\phi_4-\phi_{4,0}) + c\gamma_4^2\dot{\phi}_2 + [m_2r_2\cos(\theta_2+\phi_2)$$
$$+m_4(r_4\gamma_4\cos(\theta_4+\phi_4))m_3(L_2\cos\phi_2+r_3\gamma_3\cos(\theta_3+\phi_3))]g = T \quad (20)$$

2.2. Mathematical Model of the Electric Motor and Transmission

In Figure 2, a schematic diagram of the electric motor is presented. The transmission ratio is
$$n = \frac{T_b}{T_a} = \frac{\omega_a}{\omega_b} \quad (21)$$
where ω_a and T_a are the angular speed and the torque at the shaft a, respectively, ω_b is the angular velocity of the shaft b. T_b is the system-delivered torque and is equal to T in Equation (1).

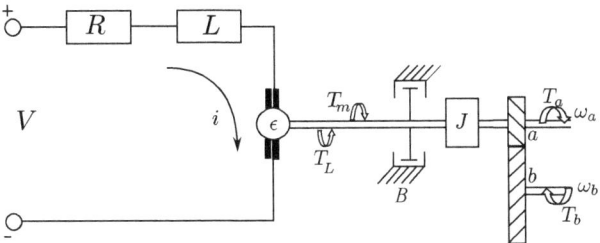

Figure 2. Schematic diagram of the motor and transmission.

By using Kirchoff's voltage law we obtain

$$V_a = Ri(t) + L\dot{i}(t) + e \quad (22)$$

where V_a is the input voltage to the motor–gear system, R is the motor's armature resistance, L is the motor inductance, $i(t)$ is the current, and e is the electromotive force generated by the motor. The applied torques in the motor and gear are expressed as

$$T = n(T_m - T_L - B\omega_a - J\dot{\omega}_a) \quad (23)$$

where T_m represents the motor electromagnetic torque and n is the transmission ratio defined in Equation (21).

The magnetic torque and the back electromotive force are defined as

$$T_m = K_m i(t) \quad (24)$$
$$e = K_g \omega_a \quad (25)$$

where K_m and K_g represent the torque and voltage parameters of the motor.

Since the shaft b gives propulsion to the crank mechanism, (21) can be written as:

$$\omega_a = n\omega_b = n\dot{\phi}_2 \quad (26)$$

From (22)–(26), the mathematical model of the motor is obtained as

$$\dot{i}(t) = \frac{1}{L}(V_a - Ri(t) - nK_g\dot{\phi}_2) \quad (27)$$
$$T = nK_m i(t) - nT_L - n^2 B\dot{\phi}_2 - n^2 J\ddot{\phi}_2 \quad (28)$$

2.3. Dynamic Model of the System

The potential and dissipative energies can be neglected in the mechanism since they are relatively small and the terms related to potential energy and due to the orientation of the mechanism. In this way, combining (20) and (28), the nonlinear equation of the system movement is

$$A(\phi_2)\ddot{\phi}_2 + \frac{1}{2}\frac{dA(\phi_2)}{d\phi_2}\dot{\phi}_2^2 = nK_m i(t) - nT_L - n^2 B\dot{\phi}_2 - n^2 J\ddot{\phi}_2 \quad (29)$$

From (27) and (29), it is possible to present the complete system model in state space as

$$\frac{d}{dt}\left(\frac{d\phi_2}{dt}\right) = A_0\left[A_1\left(\frac{d\phi_2}{dt}\right)^2 + A_2\frac{d\phi_2}{dt} + nK_m i + A_3\right] \quad (30)$$

$$\frac{di}{dt} = \frac{1}{L}\left(V_a - Ri - nK_g\frac{d\phi_2}{dt}\right) \quad (31)$$

where

$$A_0 = \frac{1}{A(\phi_2) + n^2 J}$$
$$A_1 = -\frac{1}{2}\frac{A(\phi_2)}{\phi_2}$$
$$A_2 = -n^2 B$$
$$A_3 = -n T_L$$

3. ANN-Based PID Control Scheme

The control scheme described in this work consists of two stages. The first one obtains the current reference (i_a), which is a virtual control signal as a function of the velocity error. The second stage determines the armature voltage applied to the motor (v_a), which is necessary to achieve the desired coupler point velocity. Linearization via feedback and a PID controller are applied in both control loops to assure the correct velocity regulation in the coupler point. It is important to highlight that for each point of the trajectory, it is necessary to solve the kinematic model for the crank velocity for the coupler point motion to reach the desired speed. A neural network estimator is used for this task as a variable velocity drive estimator. The complete control scheme is presented in Figure 3.

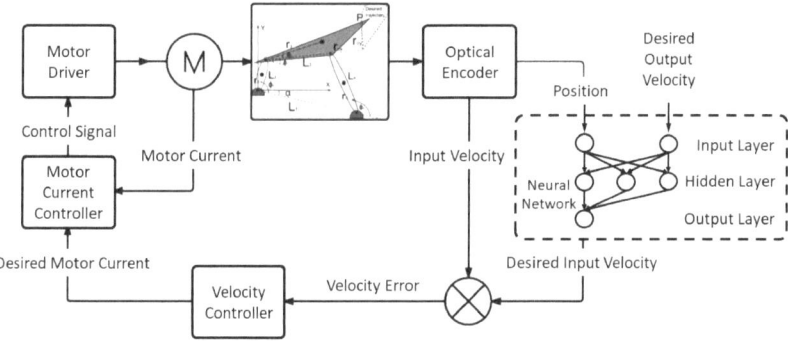

Figure 3. ANN-based control scheme for variable input velocity tracking of four-bar mechanism.

3.1. Current Control Loop

To synthesize the control law for the motor current, the tracking error is defined as $e_i = i - i^*$. Taking into account (31), the error dynamics $\frac{de_i}{dt}$ can be written as

$$\frac{de_i}{dt} = \frac{1}{L}(V_a - R i - n k_g \dot{\phi}_2) - \frac{di^*}{dt}. \tag{32}$$

From (32), a linearizing PID control signal can be proposed as follows:

$$V_a = R i + n k_g \dot{\phi}_2 + L \frac{di^*}{dt} - L\left(k_p e_i + k_i \eta + k_d \frac{de_i}{dt}\right) \tag{33}$$

where

$$\frac{d\eta}{dt} = e_i$$

Introducing the control law (33) into the error dynamics (32), we obtain

$$\frac{de_i}{dt} = -k_p e_i - k_i \eta - k_d \frac{de_i}{dt}$$
$$= -\frac{k_p e_i + k_i \eta}{1 + k_d} \tag{34}$$

where the error dynamics can be globally asymptotically stable if the gains k_p, k_i, and k_d are adequately selected.

3.2. Velocity Control Loop

As can be noted, the control law (33), includes the current reference (i^*) and its time derivative. To calculate this reference signal, we design the second control loop where we must consider the velocity tracking error, defined as $e_v = \dot{\phi}_2 - \dot{\phi}_2^*$, where $\dot{\phi}_2^*$ is the reference velocity. Considering (30), the velocity error dynamics can be written as

$$\frac{de_v}{dt} = A_0 \left(A_1 \dot{\phi}_2^{\,2} + A_2 \dot{\phi}_2 + n K_m i + A_3 \right) - \frac{d}{dt} \dot{\phi}_2^*. \tag{35}$$

Replacing i with $e_i + i^*$,

$$\frac{de_v}{dt} = A_0 \left(A_1 \dot{\phi}_2^{\,2} + A_2 \dot{\phi}_2 + n K_m (e_i + i^*) + A_3 \right) - \frac{d}{dt} \dot{\phi}_2^*. \tag{36}$$

Taking into account that the first control loop ensures that $e_i \to 0$ in short time, (36) is reduced to

$$\frac{de_v}{dt} = A_0 \left(A_1 \dot{\phi}_2^{\,2} + A_2 \dot{\phi}_2 + n K_m i^* + A_3 \right) - \frac{d}{dt} \dot{\phi}_2^*. \tag{37}$$

As i^* is considered a virtual control signal, it can be proposed as

$$i^* = -\frac{1}{n k_m} \left(A_1 \dot{\phi}_2^{\,2} + A_2 \dot{\phi}_2 + A_3 + \frac{k_{p2} e_v + k_{i2} \zeta + k_{d2} \frac{de_v}{dt} - \frac{d}{dt} \dot{\phi}_2^*}{A_0} \right), \tag{38}$$

where

$$\dot{\zeta} = e_v.$$

Then, replacing the control law (38) into the velocity error dynamics (37), we obtain

$$\begin{aligned} d\frac{e_v}{dt} &= -k_{p2} e_v - k_{i2} \zeta - k_{d2} d\frac{e_v}{dt} \\ &= -\frac{k_{p2} e_v + k_{i2} \zeta}{1 + k_{d2}}. \end{aligned} \tag{39}$$

To verify the stability of the complete closed loop system, a Lyapunov candidate function is proposed as

$$W(z) = z^T K z > 0 \tag{40}$$

where

$$z = [e_i, e_v, \eta, \zeta]^T$$

and

$$K = \begin{bmatrix} 1 + k_{d2} & 0 & 1 + k_{d2} & 0 \\ 0 & 1 + k_d & 0 & 1 + k_d \\ 1 + k_{d2} & 0 & k_{p2} + k_{i2} & 0 \\ 0 & 1 + k_d & 0 & k_p + k_i \end{bmatrix}$$

Selecting $k_p + k_i > 1 + k_d > 0$ and $k_{p2} + k_{i2} > 1 + k_{d2} > 0$, we can guarantee that the matrix K is positive definite.

Then, if $\dot{W}(z) < 0 \,\forall z \in \mathbb{R} - \{0\}$, the global and asymptotically stability condition of the system is demonstrated. So, this time derivative can be written as follows:

$$\begin{aligned} \dot{W}(z) &= \dot{z}^T K z \\ &= -(k_{p2} - k_{d2} - 1) e_i^2 - (k_p - k_d - 1) e_v^2 - k_{i2} \zeta^2 - k_i \eta^2 \end{aligned}$$

The above result satisfies the stability condition if $k_p > 1 + k_d$, $k_{p2} > 1 + k_{d2}$, $k_i > 0$, and $k_{i2} > 0$, then the origin of the error dynamics of the complete closed loop system is the unique stability point, and is global and asymptotically stable.

It is important to remark that in the stability proof, the error $e_i = i - i^*$ was not explicitly included because it is identical to the variable ξ.

3.3. Variable Input Velocity Generator with Artificial Neural Networks (ANNs)

To determine the velocity reference $\dot{\phi}_2^*$ at which the crank must rotate so that the coupler point Q reaches the desired velocity, we first establish a kinematics model for the four-bar mechanism.

The description of the position of $^O\mathbf{Q}$ with respect to the global reference system $\{X - Y\}$, from Figure 1, is given by

$$^O\mathbf{Q} = \mathbf{r}_0 + R(\hat{z}, \alpha)^r\mathbf{Q} \tag{41}$$

where $^r\mathbf{Q}$ represents the position of the point Q measured with respect the local reference system, $\mathbf{r}_0$ represents the translation, and $R(\hat{z}, \alpha)$ corresponds to the canonical rotation matrix of an angle α around the $\hat{z}$ axis, between the local reference system $\{x_r - y_r\}$ and the global $\{X - Y\}$. This can be expanded as

$$^O\mathbf{Q} = \begin{bmatrix} ^0Q_x \\ ^0Q_y \end{bmatrix} = \begin{bmatrix} x_0 + L_2 \cos(\phi_2 + \alpha) + r_{cx}\cos(\phi_3 + \alpha) - r_{cy}\sin(\phi_3 + \alpha) \\ y_0 + L_2 \sin(\phi_2 + \alpha) + r_{cx}\sin(\phi_3 + \alpha) + r_{cy}\cos(\phi_3 + \alpha) \end{bmatrix} \tag{42}$$

The linear velocity of the point $^O\mathbf{Q}$ is obtained from the derivate of Equation (42) as

$$^O\mathbf{V}_Q = \begin{bmatrix} ^0V_x \\ ^0V_y \end{bmatrix} = \begin{bmatrix} -L_2 \sin(\phi_2 + \alpha)\dot{\phi}_2 - r_{cx}\sin(\phi_3 + \alpha)\dot{\phi}_3 - r_{cy}\cos(\phi_3 + \alpha)\dot{\phi}_3 \\ L_2 \cos(\phi_2 + \alpha)\dot{\phi}_2 + r_{cx}\cos(\phi_3 + \alpha)\dot{\phi}_3 - r_{cy}\sin(\phi_3 + \alpha)\dot{\phi}_3 \end{bmatrix} \tag{43}$$

The function of the linear input velocity profile is defined as

$$\|^O\mathbf{V}_Q\| = \sqrt{^0V_x^2 + ^0V_y^2} \tag{44}$$

The desired angular velocity profile function is given by

$$\dot{\phi}_2 = \frac{\sqrt{^0V_x^2 + ^0V_y^2}}{\lambda} \tag{45}$$

where

$$\lambda^2 = L_2^2 + r_{cx}^2 \gamma^3 + r_{cy}^2 \gamma^3 + 2 L_2 \gamma_3 [r_{cx} \cos(\phi_2 - \phi_3) + r_{cy} \sin(\phi_2 - \phi_3)]$$

To reduce the computational burden in the numerical solution of (45), when estimating $\dot{\phi}_2^*$ we train an artificial neural network feed with the measured crank angular position ϕ_2 and the desired output velocity $^O\mathbf{V}_Q$. Computational intelligence methods have been successfully integrated with control schemes to relax the requirement of knowledge of the system model, consider uncertainties, and incorporate performance criteria. In particular, Artificial Neural Networks (ANNs) are attractive due to their nonlinear function approximation capabilities and simplicity of design and implementation.

A neural network generates a function approximation through a training process. The ANN is composed of an input layer with m inputs, a hidden neurons layer with N neurons, and an output layer with one single neuron as shown in Figure 4. Each hidden neuron is fully connected to the inputs and neurons in the output layer via the adaptable weights w_{Ok} and $w_{I(k,m)}$, and b_m and b_O are the bias terms for each neuron. The function φ is known as the activation function and is usually a sigmoid. In feedforward networks, the learning algorithm is based on retro-propagation of the approximation error which adapts each weight in the network [32].

$$y = \sum_{k=1}^{N} \left[w_{Ok} \cdot \varphi \left(\sum_{m=1}^{M} w_{I(k,m)} \cdot x_m + b_m \right) + b_O \right] \quad (46)$$

$$\varphi(x) = \frac{1}{1 + e^{-x}}$$

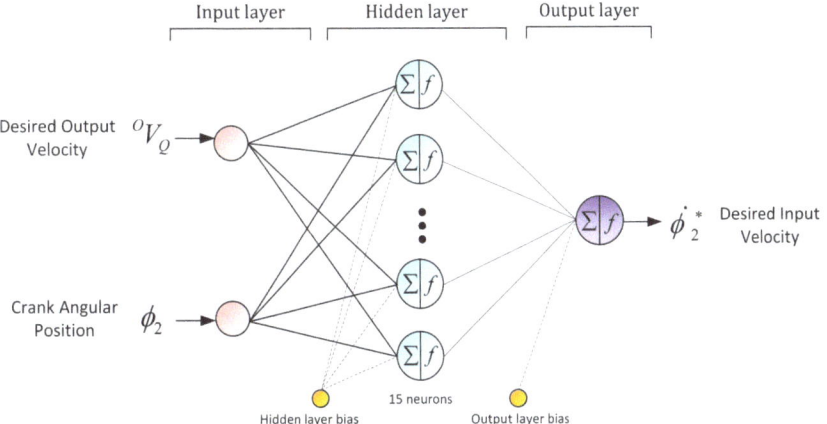

Figure 4. Neural network estimator for the input velocity Feedforward architecture.

In this study, a two-layer feed-forward neural network with fifteen neurons in its hidden layer was designed. The data to build the neural net were taken by turning the crank at various velocities; the velocity, the coupler point velocity, and the angular position of both were recorded. To adjust the neural network, the crank's angular position and the coupler point's velocity are used as input data; the output data point is the crank velocity. Of the 46 simulation runs under different velocity profiles, 16,560 samples constituted the data set where 70% was used for training, 15% for validation, and 15% for testing. The training algorithm used was Bayesian regularization and the number of epochs is fixed at 1000, with a fitness calculated as $R^2 = 99.99\%$ and a medium square error $MSE = 0.000372$ as displayed in Figure 4.

4. Simulation Results and Discussion

To verify the performance of the proposed control scheme, several simulations in closed-loop were performed. The first simulation applies the state space model of the four-bar mechanism with a PID controller and constant crank velocity. The second test presents the proposed control scheme with a variable input velocity to obtain a constant output velocity at the coupler point. The third experiment presents the proposed control scheme with a variable input velocity, but in this case, it generates two different output velocities at the coupler point. These tests are intended to demonstrate the advantages of the proposed control scheme compared with [28].

4.1. Servo-Controlled Four-Bar Mechanism Simulation Parameters

The parameters of the simulated servo-controlled four-bar mechanism are detailed in Tables 2 and 3. The resulting path of the coupler point for this mechanism is shown in Figure 5. As can be seen, this path has two linear sections followed by two curved segments, the upper one is smooth and the lower one is more demanding. This behavior demonstrates that the relationship between the velocity of the crank and the velocity of the coupler point is nonlinear since the displacements are different, even if the angular movement is the same. Hence, some points the trajectory generated by the coupler point of the four-bar mechanism have a complex geometric trajectory that will cause abrupt changes in the velocity direction. Therefore, one complex trajectory and the required constant speed profile of the coupler point during the whole trajectory, and limit positions for the output link, evidently will generate speed fluctuations that the controller has to overcome in order to fulfil the task.

Table 2. Mechanism Parameters.

Parameter	Value
L_1 (m)	0.3972
L_2 (m)	0.0588
L_3 (m)	0.2351
L_4 (m)	0.22716
r_{cx} (m)	0.403779
r_{cy} (m)	0.093921
J_2 (kg·m^2)	2.76×10^{-5}
J_3 (kg·m^2)	3.5468×10^{-3}
J_4 (kg·m^2)	3.8779×10^{-4}
m_2 (kg)	0.04234
m_3 (kg)	0.2586
m_4 (kg)	0.08156
α (rad)	5.83047

Table 3. Motor Parameters.

Parameter	Value
R (Ω)	2
L (H)	1
K_m (N·m/A)	0.260
K_g (V·s)	0.260
J (kg·m^2)	0.011
T_L (N·m)	0.28
B (N·m·s)	0

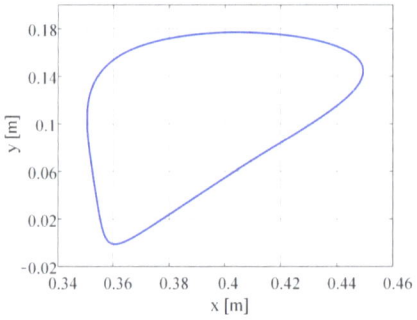

Figure 5. Path of the coupler point of the mechanism.

4.2. Constant Crank Velocity

The test consists of regulating the crank angular velocity of the mechanism at 5 rad/s (47.74 rpm) by means of the PID controller presented in [29]. The controller gains are given in Table 4. As observed in Figure 6a, the crank angular velocity is regulated with a maximum error of 0.02 rad/s, and the convergence time is 0.05 s (at 15°). In addition, Figure 6b shows that the velocity of the coupler point is variable all the time during the trajectory of the mechanism. As previously mentioned, this is the traditional control task for this mechanism; however, the coupler point is where the work is performed, so it is important to control its velocity at a desired value.

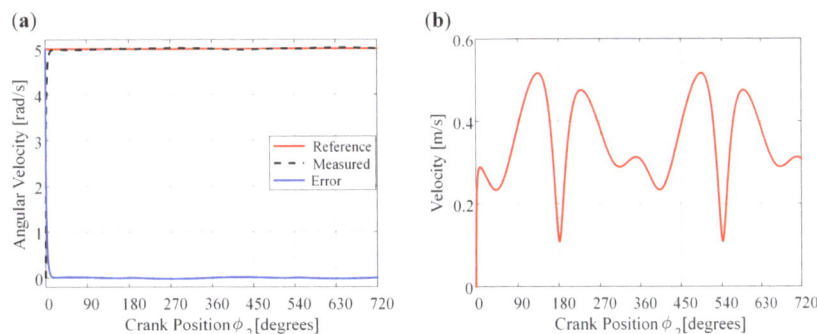

Figure 6. Simulation results of constant crank velocity with PID Control. (**a**) Crank angular velocity. (**b**) Coupler point velocity.

Table 4. Controller Gains.

Parameter	Value
K_p	3000
K_d	200
K_i	50
K_{p2}	10.8
K_{d2}	0
K_{i2}	100

4.3. Variable Input Velocity for Obtaining a Constant Output Velocity at the Coupler Point

This test is carried out to show that the proposed control scheme allows for indirect regulation of the velocity of the coupler point by fulfilling two requirements. Firstly, the reference crank velocity, obtained through the developed neural network, is close to the real value; additionally, the proposed control tracks this reference with minimal error. In this case, a velocity of 0.2 m/s is imposed for the coupler point. In Figure 7a it is noted that there is an excellent tracking of the desired trajectory, since the convergence time is 0.02 s (at 8°) and the maximum error is 0.07 rad/s. The previous result makes it possible to regulate the velocity of the coupler point at the desired value, as shown in Figure 7b. Note that the coupler point velocity error is less than 0.003 m/s and the convergence time is 0.02 s, which is consistent with that of the angular velocity of the crank presented in Figure 7a.

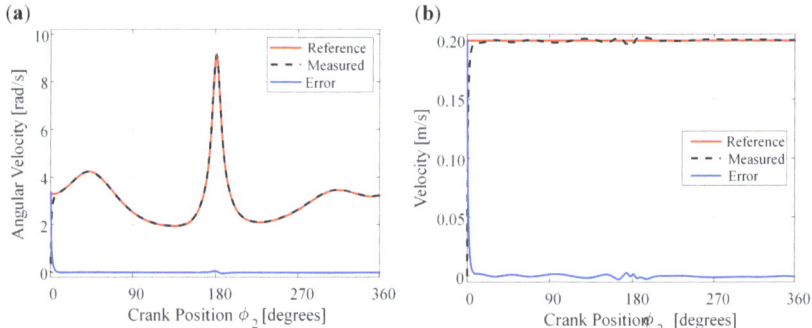

Figure 7. Variable input velocity for obtaining a constant output velocity at the coupler point. (**a**) Crank angular velocity. (**b**) Coupler point velocity.

4.4. Variable Input Velocity for Generating Two Different Output Velocities at the Coupler Point

In real applications, the coupler point is not required to carry out its entire travel with a constant velocity, but rather to have a specific velocity in the segment in which it performs the work and a different velocity for the return. For this reason, the experiment is carried out when a more complex velocity profile is imposed on the coupler point. As displayed in Figure 8a, the angular crank velocity reference has abrupt changes at 90° and 270°. These are needed to regulate the coupler point velocity to the conditions

$$V_Q = \begin{cases} 0.2 \text{ m/s} & 90° \leq \phi_2 < 270° \\ 0.1 \text{ m/s} & \text{otherwise.} \end{cases} \tag{47}$$

In Figure 8b, the coupler point velocity error is less than 0.003 m/s and the convergence time is 0.02 s, which are the same as the presented in Section 4.3 for the coupler point.

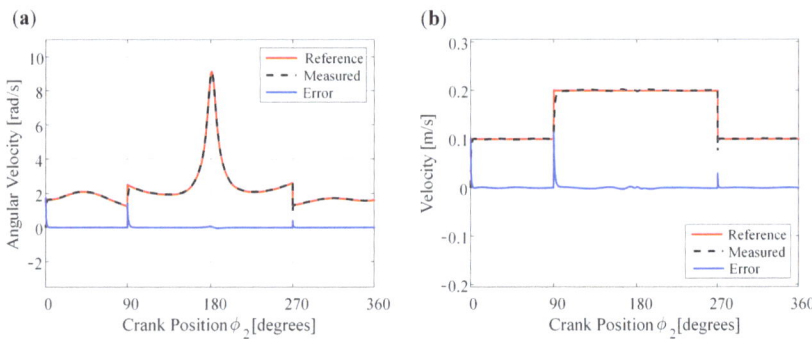

Figure 8. Variable input velocity for generating two different output velocities at the coupler point. (**a**) Crank angular velocity. (**b**) Coupler point velocity.

A more severe test is the one that implies that the velocity changes of the coupler point are where the control is most demanded, this happens when $\phi_2 = 180°$, which is where the most abrupt change would occur. In this test, the velocity profile that is imposed on the coupler point is

$$V_Q = \begin{cases} 0.2 \text{ m/s} & 180° \leq \phi_2 < 360° \\ 0.1 \text{ m/s} & \text{otherwise.} \end{cases} \tag{48}$$

Figure 9a shows the tracking of the crank velocity reference, this is fast and with minimum error. In Figure 9b, the change of velocity at the coupler point is presented. In this case, the convergence time is 0.0266 s (at 20°) and the maximum error is 0.03 m/s. It can be emphasized that this would be the worst case for this mechanism; in spite of that, the system is controlled at the desired velocity at the specified points.

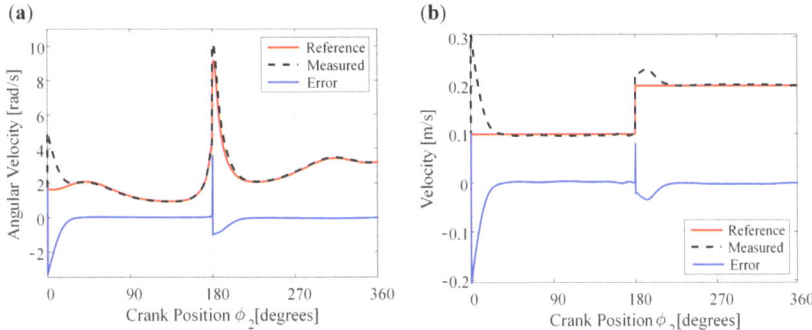

Figure 9. Variable input velocity for generating two different output velocities at the coupler point. (**a**) Crank angular velocity. (**b**) Coupler point velocity.

It is important to indicate that the saturation function was used in the simulation to prevent V_a from increasing to values that could cause some damage to the system; however, it was observed that in all the cases presented, such voltage did not reach the saturation limits. To exhibit this performance, Figure 10 shows the input voltage to the motor corresponding to the input profiles defined by (47) and (48), and the results are shown in Figures 8 and 9.

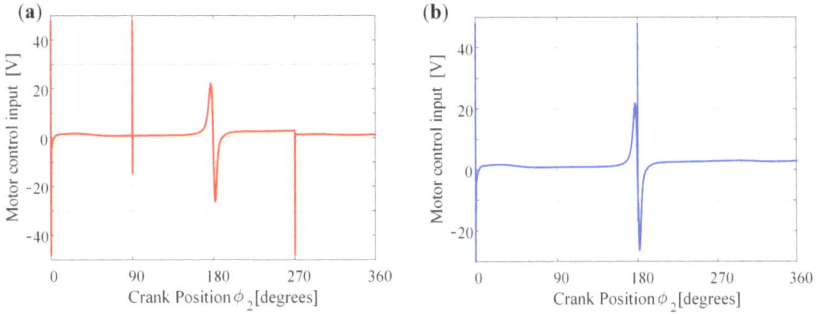

Figure 10. Variable input velocity for generating two different output velocities at the coupler point. (**a**) V_Q described in Equation (47). (**b**) V_Q described in Equation (48)

In summary, the designed controller achieved trajectory tracking with good performance both on tracking error and transient response. The proposed control scheme has a simple structure and low computational burden for real-time applications. In the case when more demanding performance is required, then the computational intelligence methods can be integrated with other high-performance algorithms such as the type-2 fuzzy presented in [25–27] which can deliver exact responses and robustness.

5. Conclusions

In this work, the problem of controlling a four-bar mechanism for the case of variable velocity of the crank is considered. To obtain the desired output motions for the coupler point, an indirect control is designed to estimate the reference values for the motor current to achieve trajectory tracking for each crank velocity profile. Furthermore, a neural network is introduced in the control scheme to solve the kinematic model of the mechanism to obtain the velocity reference. The controlled system is tested through simulations under several trajectories, obtaining excellent results. Further research will implement the four-bar mechanism with the proposed controller using an optical encoder and or computer vision for the position feedback.

Author Contributions: Conceptualization, R.P.-E. and R.Q.-P.; methodology, J.A.V. and M.F.-B.; software, M.F.-B. and B.C.J.; validation, F.P., L.J.R. and B.C.J.; investigation, R.P.-E.; writing, R.P.-E. and L.J.R.; supervision, J.A.V., R.Q.-P. and M.F.-B. All authors have read and agreed to the published version of the manuscript.

Funding: This research received no external funding.

Data Availability Statement: Data available with the corresponding author.

Conflicts of Interest: The authors declare no conflict of interest.

References

1. Tao, J.; Sadler, J. Constant speed control of a motor driven mechanism system. *Mech. Mach. Theory* **1995**, *30*, 737–748. [CrossRef]
2. Dulger, L.; Uyan, S. Modelling, simulation and control of a four-bar mechanism with a brushless servo motor. *Mechatronics* **1997**, *7*, 369–383. [CrossRef]
3. Li, Q.; Tso, S.; Guo, L.; Zhang, W. Improving motion tracking of servomotor-driven closed-loop mechanisms using mass-redistribution. *Mech. Mach. Theory* **2000**, *35*, 1033–1045. [CrossRef]
4. Wu, F.X.; Zhang, W.J.; Li, Q.; Ouyang, P.R. Integrated Design and PD Control of High-Speed Closed-loop Mechanisms. *J. Dyn. Syst. Meas. Control* **2002**, *124*, 522–528. [CrossRef]
5. Su, Y.; Sun, D.; Zheng, C. Nonlinear trajectory tracking control of a closed-chain manipulator. In Proceedings of the Fifth World Congress on Intelligent Control and Automation (IEEE Cat. No. 04EX788), Hangzhou, China, 15–19 June 2004; Volume 6, pp. 5012–5016. [CrossRef]
6. Lin, M.C.; Chen, J.S. Experiments toward MRAC design for linkage system. *Mechatronics* **1996**, *6*, 933–953. [CrossRef]
7. Gündoğdu, Ö.; Erentürk, K. Fuzzy control of a dc motor driven four-bar mechanism. *Mechatronics* **2005**, *15*, 423–438. [CrossRef]
8. Koca, G.O.; Akpolat, Z.H.; Özdemir, M. Type-2 Fuzzy Sliding Mode Control of A Four-Bar Mechanism. *Int. J. Model. Simul.* **2011**, *31*, 60–68. [CrossRef]
9. Hwang, C.L.; Kuo, C.Y. A stable adaptive fuzzy sliding-mode control for affine nonlinear systems with application to four-bar linkage systems. *IEEE Trans. Fuzzy Syst.* **2001**, *9*, 238–252. [CrossRef]
10. Koca, G.O.; Akpolat, Z.H.; Özdemir, M. Development of robust fuzzy control methods and their applications to a mechanical system. *Turk. J. Sci. Technol.* **2014**, *9*, 47–56.
11. Ren, Q.; Bigras, P. Design and implementation of model-free PID fuzzy logic control on a 4-bar parallel mechanism. In Proceedings of the 2015 IEEE International Conference on Advanced Intelligent Mechatronics (AIM), Busan, Republic of Korea, 7–11 July 2015; pp. 1647–1652. [CrossRef]
12. Zhang, Y.; Feng, C.; Li, B. PID Control of Nonlinear Motor-Mechanism Coupling System Using Artificial Neural Network. In *Advances in Neural Networks—ISNN 2006, Proceedings of the Third International Symposium on Neural Networks, Chengdu, China, 28 May–1 June 2006*; Wang, J., Yi, Z., Zurada, J.M., Lu, B.L., Yin, H., Eds.; Springer: Berlin/Heidelberg, Germany, 2006; pp. 1096–1103.
13. Lungu, R.; Sepcu, L.; Lungu, M. Four-Bar Mechanism's Proportional-Derivative and Neural Adaptive Control for the Thorax of the Micromechanical Flying Insects. *J. Dyn. Syst. Meas. Control* **2015**, *137*, 051005. [CrossRef]
14. Çakar, O.; Tanyıldızı, A.K. Application of moving sliding mode control for a DC motor driven four-bar mechanism. *Adv. Mech. Eng.* **2018**, *10*, 1687814018762184. [CrossRef]
15. Salah, M.; Al-Jarrah, A.; Tatlicioglu, E.; Banihani, S. Robust Backstepping Control for a Four-Bar Linkage Mechanism Driven by a DC Motor. *J. Intell. Robot. Syst.* **2019**, *94*, 327–338. [CrossRef]
16. Erenturk, K. Hybrid Control of a Mechatronic System: Fuzzy Logic and Grey System Modeling Approach. *IEEE/ASME Trans. Mechatronics* **2007**, *12*, 703–710. [CrossRef]
17. Al-Jarrah, A.; Salah, M.; Banihani, S.; Al-Widyan, K.; Ahmad, A. Applications of Various Control Schemes on a Four-Bar Linkage Mechanism Driven by a Geared DC Motor. *WSEAS Trans. Syst. Control* **2015**, *10*, 584–597.
18. Tutunji, T.A.; Salah, M.; Al-Jarrah, A.; Ahmad, A.; Alhamdan, R. Modeling and Identification of a Four-Bar Linkage Mechanism Driven by a Geared DC Motor. *Int. Rev. Mech. Eng.* **2015**, *9*, 296–306. [CrossRef]
19. İşbitirici, A.; Altuğ, E. Design and Control of a Mini Aerial Vehicle that has Four Flapping-Wings. *J. Intell. Robot. Syst.* **2017**, *88*, 247–265. [CrossRef]
20. Mohseni, S.A.; Duchaine, V.; Wong, T. A comparative study of the optimal control design using evolutionary algorithms: Application on a close-loop system. In Proceedings of the 2017 Intelligent Systems Conference (IntelliSys), London, UK, 7–8 September 2017; pp. 942–948. [CrossRef]
21. Rodríguez-Molina, A.; Villarreal-Cervantes, M.G.; Aldape-Pérez, M. Indirect adaptive control using the novel online hypervolume-based differential evolution for the four-bar mechanism. *Mechatronics* **2020**, *69*, 102384. [CrossRef]

22. Shi, K.; Liu, C.; Sun, Z.; Yue, X. Coupled orbit-attitude dynamics and trajectory tracking control for spacecraft electromagnetic docking. *Appl. Math. Model.* **2022**, *101*, 553–572. [CrossRef]
23. Liu, C.; Yue, X.; Shi, K.; Sun, Z. *Spacecraft Attitude Control: A Linear Matrix Inequality Approach*; Elsevier: London, UK, 2022. [CrossRef]
24. Perrusquía, A.; Flores-Campos, J.A.; Yu, W. Optimal sliding mode control for cutting tasks of quick-return mechanisms. *ISA Trans.* **2022**, *122*, 88–95. [CrossRef]
25. Hua, G.; Wang, F.; Zhang, J.; Alattas, K.A.; Mohammadzadeh, A.; The Vu, M. A New Type-3 Fuzzy Predictive Approach for Mobile Robots. *Mathematics* **2022**, *10*, 3186. [CrossRef]
26. Xu, S.; Zhang, C.; Mohammadzadeh, A. Type-3 Fuzzy Control of Robotic Manipulators. *Symmetry* **2023**, *15*, 483. [CrossRef]
27. Mohammadzadeh, A.; Sabzalian, M.H.; Ahmadian, A.; Nabipour, N. A dynamic general type-2 fuzzy system with optimized secondary membership for online frequency regulation. *ISA Trans.* **2021**, *112*, 150–160. [CrossRef]
28. Yan, H.S.; Yan, G.J. Integrated control and mechanism design for the variable input-speed servo four-bar linkages. *Mechatronics* **2009**, *19*, 274–285. [CrossRef]
29. Peón-Escalante, R.; Flota-Bañuelos, M.; Ricalde, L.J.; Acosta, C.; Perales, G.S. On the coupler point velocity control of variable input speed servo-controlled four-bar mechanism. *Adv. Mech. Eng.* **2016**, *8*, 1687814016678356. [CrossRef]
30. Flota-Bañuelos, M.; Peón-Escalante, R.; Ricalde, L.J.; Cruz, B.J.; Quintal-Palomo, R.; Medina, J. Vision-based control for trajectory tracking of four-bar linkage. *J. Braz. Soc. Mech. Sci. Eng.* **2021**, *43*, 5. [CrossRef]
31. Goldstein, H.; Poole, C.; Safko, J. *Classical Mechanics*; Pearson Education: London, UK, 2011.
32. Haykin, S.S. *Neural Networks and Learning Machines*; Prentice Hall: London, UK, 2016.

Disclaimer/Publisher's Note: The statements, opinions and data contained in all publications are solely those of the individual author(s) and contributor(s) and not of MDPI and/or the editor(s). MDPI and/or the editor(s) disclaim responsibility for any injury to people or property resulting from any ideas, methods, instructions or products referred to in the content.

Article

Mathematical Methods for an Accurate Navigation of the Robotic Telescopes

Vadym Savanevych [1], Sergii Khlamov [2,*], Oleksandr Briukhovetskyi [3], Tetiana Trunova [2] and Iryna Tabakova [2]

[1] Department of Systems Engineering, Kharkiv National University of Radio Electronics, Nauki Ave., 14, 61166 Kharkiv, Ukraine; vadym.savanevych1@nure.ua
[2] Department of Media Systems and Technologies, Kharkiv National University of Radio Electronics, Nauki Ave., 14, 61166 Kharkiv, Ukraine; tetiana.trunova@nure.ua (T.T.); iryna.tabakova@nure.ua (I.T.)
[3] Western Center of Radio Engineering Surveillance, National Space Facilities Control and Test Center, Kosmonavtov Str., 896112 Mukacheve, Ukraine; oleksandr.briukhovetskyi@gmail.com
* Correspondence: sergii.khlamov@gmail.com

Abstract: Accurate sky identification is one of the most important functions of an automated telescope mount. The more accurately the robotic telescope is navigated to the investigated part of the sky, the better the observations and discoveries made. In this paper, we present mathematical methods for accurate sky identification (celestial coordinates determination). They include the automatic selection of the reference stars, preliminary and full sky identification, as well as an interaction with international databases, which are a part of the astrometric calibration. All described methods help to receive accurately calculated astrometric data and use it for the positional calibration and better navigation of the automated telescope mount. The developed methods were successfully implemented in the Collection Light Technology (CoLiTec) software. Through its use, more than 1600 small solar system objects were discovered. It has been used in more than 700,000 observations and successful sky identifications, during which, five comets were discovered. Additionally, the accuracy indicators of the processing results of the CoLiTec software are provided in the paper, which shows benefits of the CoLiTec software and lower standard deviation of the sky identification in the case of low signal-to-noise ratios.

Keywords: mathematics; image processing; sky identification; astrometric reduction; celestial coordinates; robotic telescopes; calibration; navigation

MSC: 68U10; 68U05; 97M50

Citation: Savanevych, V.; Khlamov, S.; Briukhovetskyi, O.; Trunova, T.; Tabakova, I. Mathematical Methods for an Accurate Navigation of the Robotic Telescopes. *Mathematics* 2023, 11, 2246. https://doi.org/10.3390/math11102246

Academic Editor: Ivan Lorencin

Received: 31 March 2023
Revised: 24 April 2023
Accepted: 29 April 2023
Published: 11 May 2023

Copyright: © 2023 by the authors. Licensee MDPI, Basel, Switzerland. This article is an open access article distributed under the terms and conditions of the Creative Commons Attribution (CC BY) license (https://creativecommons.org/licenses/by/4.0/).

1. Introduction

The requirements for accurate navigation of ground-based robotic telescopes have become more and more strict. In the common case, such accuracy depends on two main factors: instrumental error (telescope mount navigation error) [1] and sky identification error [2]. The second one means that the robotic telescope was not calibrated properly and the coordinates of the center field of view (FOV) [3] are incorrect in comparison with real celestial coordinates in sky. The FOV of a robotic telescope is directly related to its aperture (diameter), its objective (mirror or primary lens, which collects and focuses the light), and its light-gathering power. It depends on the focal length, which is related to the objective's area and an angular resolution. Thus, the FOV is a true angular size of the investigated area of the sky, which is seen through the eyepiece of a telescope.

All astronomical images are made by the charge-coupled device (CCD) [4] or other cameras/sensors. Thus, a resolution of the output images made by the robotic telescope also depends on the CCD-matrix resolution [5]. In this case, the accuracy of the sky identification is in direct ratio with the selected pixel or sub-pixel Gaussian model for the detection of astronomical objects in the CCD-frame [6,7].

There are different research projects [8,9] and organizations, including the National Aeronautics and Space Administration (NASA), that work on improvements to automated navigation systems [10]. The main goal of their research is to minimize instrumental errors [11] during telescope navigation by the development of modern hardware modules or the improvement of the software used for the automated telescope's mount [12].

In paper [13], the authors suggest automated determination of the reference point as part of the calibration. Several such reference points are selected from the FOV and can be useful for their purposes only, but in the scope of sky identification, it will not be accurate because there are a lot of artifacts in the astronomical images, which can cause false detection. Thus, such reference points will not be related to the real reference objects, such as stars that are fixed in the sky.

Another proposal from the authors of paper [14] is related to the alignment procedure to avoid the intrinsic coma of the secondary mirror of the telescope. However, there is a more improved approach which uses inverse median filter in combination with master frames (Bias, Dark, Flat), applied as described in paper [15].

All of the above-described approaches and methods have a main disadvantage regarding the current purpose of automated navigation of robotic telescopes. They are not very effective at accurate sky identification, which allows reception of the real celestial coordinates of the FOV. In this case, the automated telescope's mount with the implemented navigation software in it cannot guarantee which exact part of the sky is being navigated.

In the current research, we propose using especially developed mathematical methods for accurate sky identification (celestial coordinates determination) as well as navigation of the robotic telescopes. Such methods include the automatic selection of the reference stars [16], preliminary and full sky identification, as well as an interaction with the international databases [17,18], which are the part of the full astrometric calibration process [19].

The theoretic results, in view of the developed methods, have a very wide background for practical usage, such as implementation in modern image processing softwar, autonomous identification services for astronomical images/videos, and software for automated mount navigations for both amateur and professional robotic telescopes. Additionally, as a contribution to the state of the art, it will be helpful for the recognition of constellations and galaxies using augmented reality for real-time image processing. One more point is that it can be a cheaper approach to improve the accuracy of the software in comparison with the development of special hardware and embedded microcontrollers.

The developed mathematical methods were successfully implemented in the Collection Light Technology (CoLiTec) software [20]. Using it, more than 1600 small solar system objects were discovered. It has been used in more than 700,000 observations and successful sky identifications, during which, five comets were discovered. Additionally, the accuracy indicators of the processing results of the CoLiTec software are provided in the paper.

2. Materials and Methods

Sky Identification is one of the common functions of an automated telescope mount. Such an approach is related to the determination of celestial coordinates to calibrate an image's center and its verification with the etalon or navigation coordinates [21]. In this case, the automated telescope's mount with implemented navigation software in it can recognize what exact part of the sky is navigated to. Thus, a high accuracy of the telescope's navigation to the investigated part of the sky is required, which allows better observations and discoveries to be made.

To avoid inaccurate automated navigation of the robotic telescope's or even low-altitude mobile robots [22], the authors propose using specially developed mathematical methods for sky identification. Such computational methods include the following stages of the full astrometric calibration process or reduction [23]:

1. Preliminary sky identification in the CCD-frames in a series, which allows finding the consistency between all objects in such CCD-frames in a series.

2. Full sky identification for the initial approximation determination when identifying object measurements in CCD-frames [24] with the reference stars from the international star catalogs/databases [18].
3. Automatic selection of the reference astronomical objects (stars) [25] in the CCD-frame, which have fixed positional celestial coordinates in the sky.

2.1. Preliminary Sky Identification

One of the cases of identification significant for practice is the case of mutual identification of frames of a series formed at approximately the same time on the same telescope by one CCD-camera without changing the angle of its rotation. For this, it is necessary to find the initial approximation of the parameters of pairwise correspondence (matching) between two sets of measurements formed in two frames and corresponding to the same region of the celestial sphere. The position of celestial objects in frames formed in this way, as a rule, differs only in the shift parameters (rotation parameters are near-zero [26], and the scale is unchanged from frame to frame). Shift parameters are common for all measurements of two frames and characterize the mutual arrangement of frames relative to each other on the celestial sphere, being the desired matching parameters between two sets of measurements.

With a preliminary sky identification of the measurements of digital frames of one series, it is advisable to avoid a global enumeration of matching measurements of these frames. To do this, it is necessary to consider the invariability of the shift parameters from pair to pair. In this case, it is possible to solve the problem of preliminary sky identification by putting forward (sorting out) hypotheses about the belonging of the measurements of different frames to the same object. Each such matching hypothesis corresponds to shift estimates conditional on the hypothesis of correspondence to the same object of the "measurement–measurement" pair for one measurement of each frame [27]:

$$\Delta_{xi} = x_{1(i)} - x_{2(i)}; \tag{1}$$

$$\Delta_{yi} = y_{1(i)} - y_{2(i)}, \tag{2}$$

where, $x_{1(i)}, y_{1(i)}, x_{2(i)}, y_{2(i)}$ are the coordinates of measurements of the same i-th object (estimates of the object's coordinates) on the first and second identified frames in the coordinate system of the base frame of the series.

At the same time, the conditional estimate that corresponds to the hypothesis of a combination of pairs of measurements from different frames with the highest weight can be considered an unconditional estimate of the shift parameters between measurements of the position of the same object on different frames. As the weight of these hypotheses, the number of acknowledgments N_{ack} was used. The number of acknowledgments is the number of acknowledgment circular areas (strobes) to which at least one measurement of another frame belongs (associated). The acknowledgment circular area (strobe) has a predetermined radius R_{rej} and center with the measurement coordinates of the first frame with the shift values (1), (2) added to them. In the general case, frames are quite rarefied and diverse in the sense that their individual parts are not like each other. Under this assumption, it is not possible to test all hypotheses about the combination of measurements of two frames. It is enough to find the first hypothesis, in which the number of acknowledgments will be higher than the predetermined allowable number of acknowledgments N_{min_ack} (Figure 1).

One of the necessary requirements for the method of preliminary sky identification is its that it be resistant to various kinds of destabilizing factors [28]. First, the possible presence of a bright track of an artificial earth satellite in one of the frames. When a bright satellite [29] enters the frame, its image can illuminate the frame, forming many false measurements (Figure 2a). Second, the effect of charge flow when images of the brightest stars in frame lead to a decrease in the accuracy of the estimation of their position, which makes them undesirable candidates for reference stars (Figure 2b). To ensure the stability of results of the preliminary sky identification, the CCD-frame is divided into a predetermined number of regions of the same size $M_{reg} \times M_{reg}$. From each such area, the same predetermined number of the brightest objects is selected N_{mea_reg}. Thus, the selected measurements will be evenly distributed over the frame, which will help to minimize the probability of errors in the preliminary sky identification. Such a selection of measurements will allow, for example, to exclude from consideration many bright false measurements caused by the charge flow of a large star or a bright satellite track.

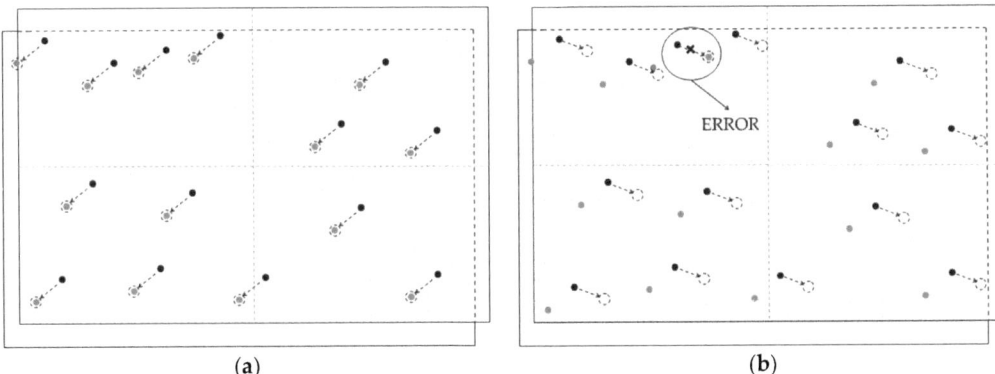

Figure 1. Determining the shift parameters between measurements in frame (gray dot) and catalog or other frame (black dot): (**a**) Correct identification; (**b**) Wrong identification.

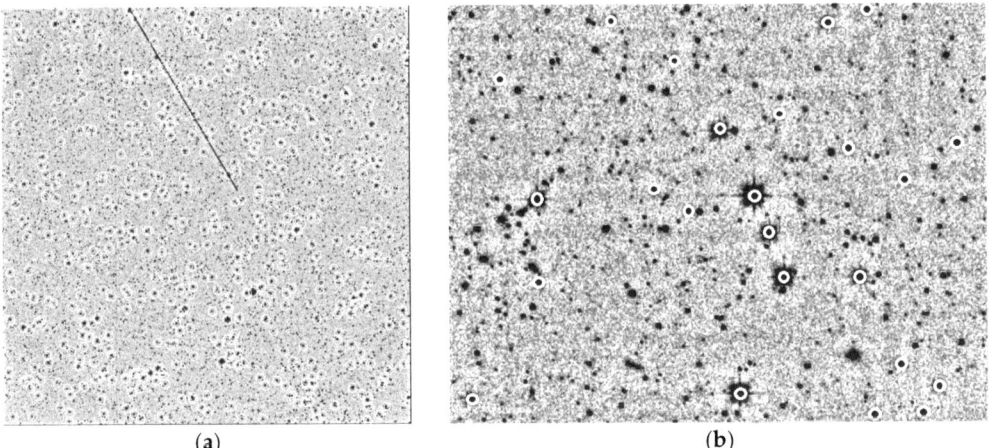

Figure 2. Various kinds of destabilizing factors in CCD-frame: (**a**) bright track of the satellite; (**b**) charge flow in images of the brightest stars.

Since the positions of objects in each frame are determined with errors, the parameters of frame shift relative to each other can be determined more precisely. This is achieved by averaging the shift parameters in each separate pair of object images in two frames:

$$\bar{\Delta}_x = \sum_{i=1}^{N_{ident}} \Delta_{xi} / N_{ident}; \qquad (3)$$

$$\bar{\Delta}_y = \sum_{i=1}^{N_{ident}} \Delta_{yi} / N_{ident}, \qquad (4)$$

where, N_{ident} is the pair number used in estimating frame shift parameters relative to each other.

Thus, the preliminary sky identification stage includes the following sequential steps.

1. The frame is divided into a set of equal regions $M_{reg} \times M_{reg}$. Sets of the brightest measurements in frame are formed based on an equal predetermined number N_{mea_reg} of measurements with the highest brightness estimates corresponding to the hypothetical objects selected from each region.
2. Selecting of the next measurement from a preselected set of the brightest measurements in the first frame. There should be no more than three such measurements. If, during the process, this step is reached for the fourth time (trying to select the fourth measurement), an emergency exit is performed with a message about identification failure. This is usually associated with large errors in estimating the anchoring coordinates of center in the identified frame.
3. The investigated measurement of the first frame is put in correspondence with the next measurement of the second frame from a preselected set of measurements of the second frame (a cycle is organized according to the investigated measurements of the second frame). For this, a conditional estimate of the shift parameters is preliminarily calculated by the pair hypothesis, according to Equations (1) and (2).
4. For each selected pair (steps 2 and 3), the weight of the next hypothesis about the correspondence of pairs of measurements of the first and second frames (measurement of the frame and the star catalog) to the same object is estimated. For this, each measurement of the first frame is compared with each measurement of the second frame. Additionally, the shift parameters (1) and (2) are added to the measurement coordinates of the first frame. Based on the deviations between the measurements of the first and second frames, a fact that the measurements of the second frame fall into the acknowledgment area (strobe) is determined.
5. If a sufficient number of measurements of the second frame fell into the strobe, then it is considered that the hypothesis about the combination of pairs of measurements of the first and second frames is confirmed (go to step 6). If not, then the hypothesis about the shift parameters is considered false and a transition is made (to step 3) to the next measurement of the second frame. When the preselected set of measurements of the second frame is exhausted, a transition is made to the next measurement of the first frame (to step 2). If this set is also exhausted, a message is displayed about the impossibility of identifying the measurements of the first and second frames.
6. The final estimate of the shift parameters (3) and (4) is calculated.

2.2. Full Sky Identification

For the full sky identification with the star catalog, it is enough to have three points (stars) in a frame and their corresponding pairs in the star catalog. The coordinates of three stars include six parameters (x and y positional coordinates for each star). In this regard, a calculation of the plate constants by three points is the finite statistical method. It does not use the redundant data. Using such a method, it is impossible to eliminate or reduce the errors contained in the position estimates of stars in the catalog and frame. However, the finite method makes it possible to obtain an initial approximation with minimal computational costs.

The initial data for obtaining the plate linear constants by the finite statistical method are, on the one hand, the positions of three stars in the identified frame in the coordinate system (CS) of this CCD-frame (Figure 3). On the other hand, the ideal coordinates of the corresponding catalog stars. To obtain the ideal coordinates of the catalog stars from their equatorial coordinates, it is sufficient to have some approximation of the equatorial coordinates of the frame's optical center. The points in Figure 3 correspond to three stars used, and their coordinates are indicated as $A(x_1, y_1)$, $B(x_2, y_2)$, $C(x_3, y_3)$. The catalog equatorial coordinates of these stars correspond to the ideal coordinates $A(\xi_1, \eta_1)$, $B(\xi_2, \eta_2)$, $C(\xi_3, \eta_3)$, respectively. The ideal coordinates of an object with its coordinates in the CS of the CCD-frame are related by the reduction equation [30]:

$$\begin{bmatrix} a_0 \\ a_1 \\ a_2 \end{bmatrix} = \begin{bmatrix} 1 & x_1 & y_1 \\ 1 & x_2 & y_2 \\ 1 & x_3 & y_3 \end{bmatrix}^{-1} \begin{bmatrix} \xi_1 \\ \xi_2 \\ \xi_3 \end{bmatrix}; \quad (5)$$

$$\begin{bmatrix} b_0 \\ b_1 \\ b_2 \end{bmatrix} = \begin{bmatrix} 1 & x_1 & y_1 \\ 1 & x_2 & y_2 \\ 1 & x_3 & y_3 \end{bmatrix}^{-1} \begin{bmatrix} \eta_1 \\ \eta_2 \\ \eta_3 \end{bmatrix}. \quad (6)$$

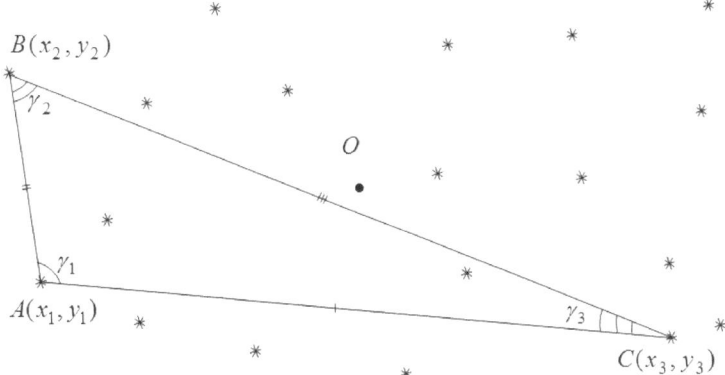

Figure 3. Formation of triplets of the preliminary sky identification, where * is a star in frame.

An inverse reduction equation is also possible, which relates the coordinates of an object in the CS of the CCD-frame (x, y) with its ideal coordinates (ξ, η) [31]:

$$\begin{bmatrix} a'_0 \\ a'_1 \\ a'_2 \end{bmatrix} = \begin{bmatrix} 1 & \xi_1 & \eta_1 \\ 1 & \xi_2 & \eta_2 \\ 1 & \xi_3 & \eta_3 \end{bmatrix}^{-1} \begin{bmatrix} x_1 \\ x_2 \\ x_3 \end{bmatrix}; \quad (7)$$

$$\begin{bmatrix} b'_0 \\ b'_1 \\ b'_2 \end{bmatrix} = \begin{bmatrix} 1 & \xi_1 & \eta_1 \\ 1 & \xi_2 & \eta_2 \\ 1 & \xi_3 & \eta_3 \end{bmatrix}^{-1} \begin{bmatrix} y_1 \\ y_2 \\ y_3 \end{bmatrix}. \quad (8)$$

To obtain the plate linear constants, it is necessary to have at least three stars in frame (three measurements) and their corresponding pairs—stars from the catalog. This matching can be called the primary identification triple. Obviously, this triple is not unique, but none of them are initially unknown. Each triple corresponds to the hypothesis of "primary identification" about the correspondence of frame and catalog triples. Selection of the first point of any triple is made without conditions. As such, all elements of the set of measurements Ω_{bl50} are used in turn. For the triple of measurements with coordinates $(x_{1(k)}, y_{1(k)})$, $(x_{2(k)}, y_{2(k)})$, $(x_{3(k)}, y_{3(k)})$ in the CS of the CCD-frame to form a triangle, which covers a significant part of the frame, for the other two points of the triple, the following conditions are experimentally introduced. The second point of the triple must be no closer than k_h of the frame's angular size R_{CCD} from the first one:

$$r_{(1)(2)} = \sqrt{(y_{2(k)} - y_{1(k)})^2 + (x_{1(k)} - x_{2(k)})^2} \geq 0.5 k_h \left(R_{CCD(x)} + R_{CCD(y)} \right). \quad (9)$$

A condition for the third point of the triple is the selection of such a measurement in the frame, which corresponds to the point from which the perpendicular r_{trian} can be dropped to the straight line passing through the first and second points of the primary identification triple.

The equation for finding the perpendicular length r_{trian} is derived based on the definition of the modulus of the cross product of two vectors [32]. Using the property of the cross product of two vectors, it can be determined whether the vector drawn through the third point of the triple is perpendicular to these vectors. Additionally, the module of the cross product of the two corresponding vectors will be equal to the length of the perpendicular r_{trian} [33]:

$$r_{trian} = \left| x_{1(k)} y_{2(k)} - x_{2(k)} y_{1(k)} \right|. \tag{10}$$

Thus, the sine and cosine of an angle γ_1 of the triple (Figure 3) can be found by equations:

$$\sin \gamma_1 = \left(\frac{x_{2(k)} y_{3(k)} - y_{2(k)} x_{3(k)}}{\sqrt{x_{2(k)}^2 + y_{2(k)}^2} \cdot \sqrt{x_{3(k)}^2 + y_{3(k)}^2}} \right); \tag{11}$$

$$\cos \gamma_1 = \left(\frac{x_{2(k)} x_{3(k)} + y_{2(k)} y_{3(k)}}{\sqrt{x_{2(k)}^2 + y_{2(k)}^2} \cdot \sqrt{x_{3(k)}^2 + y_{3(k)}^2}} \right). \tag{12}$$

With known sine and cosine of the angle, its unique finding is trivial. Similarly, to Equations (11) and (12), the values of the sines and cosines of the angles γ_2 and γ_3 can also be found using the following equations accordingly:

$$\sin \gamma_2 = \left(\frac{x_{1(k)} y_{3(k)} - y_{1(k)} x_{3(k)}}{\sqrt{x_{1(k)}^2 + y_{1(k)1}^2} \cdot \sqrt{x_{3(k)}^2 + y_{3(k)}^2}} \right); \tag{13}$$

$$\cos \gamma_2 = \left(\frac{x_{1(k)} x_{3(k)} + y_{1(k)} y_{3(k)}}{\sqrt{x_{1(k)}^2 + y_{1(k)}^2} \cdot \sqrt{x_{3(k)}^2 + y_{3(k)}^2}} \right); \tag{14}$$

$$\sin \gamma_3 = \left(\frac{x_{1(k)} y_{2(k)} - y_{1(k)} x_{2(k)}}{\sqrt{x_{1(k)}^2 + y_{1(k)}^2} \cdot \sqrt{x_{2(k)}^2 + y_{2(k)}^2}} \right); \tag{15}$$

$$\cos \gamma_3 = \left(\frac{x_{1(k)} x_{2(k)} + y_{1(k)} y_{2(k)}}{\sqrt{x_{1(k)}^2 + y_{1(k)}^2} \cdot \sqrt{x_{2(k)}^2 + y_{2(k)}^2}} \right). \tag{16}$$

According to [34], the CS of a CCD-frame is parallel to the plane of ideal astrophotography. Therefore, it is possible to use the plane of ideal astrophotography to calculate the angles of vertices of the triple of primary identification from the catalog side. For this, the tangential coordinates of stars of the used catalog are determined in the plane of ideal astrophotography with given equatorial coordinates (α_0, δ_0) of the optical center, according to the equations:

$$\tilde{\zeta}_{j(k)} = \frac{\cos \delta_{j(k)} \cdot \sin(\alpha_{j(k)} - \alpha_0)}{\cos \delta_0 \cdot \cos \delta_{j(k)} \cdot \cos(\alpha_{j(k)} - \alpha_0) + \sin \delta_0 \cdot \sin \delta_{j(k)}}; \tag{17}$$

$$\eta_{j(k)} = \frac{\cos \delta_0 \cdot \cos(\alpha_{j(k)} - \alpha_0)}{\cos \delta_0 \cdot \cos \delta_{j(k)} \cdot \cos(\alpha_{j(k)} - \alpha_0) + \sin \delta_0 \cdot \sin \delta_{j(k)}}, \tag{18}$$

where, $\alpha_{j(k)}, \delta_{j(k)}$ are the angular coordinates of the $j(k)$-th object in the star catalog.

Based on the obtained tangential (ideal) coordinates, by analogy with Equations (11)–(16), the angles of the next triangle are determined, corresponding to the triple of primary identification from the catalog side.

Thus, the full sky identification stage includes the following sequential steps.

1. For a set of measurements of a CCD-frame, when forming the triplets of primary sky identification, the following sequence of operations is performed.

    a. Formation of a set Ω_{bl50} of the brightest measurements in a CCD-frame, consisting of N_{bl50} applicants when choosing triplets of primary identification. To ensure a stability of the identification results, the frame is divided into M_{reg}^2 parts. The specified number of frame measurements N_{bl50} is divided by the number of frame fragments, and in each such fragment, the brightest frame measurements N_{bl50}/M_{reg}^2 are selected.

b. Formation of an additional set Ω_{bl100} of the brightest measurements in a CCD-frame, consisting of N_{bl100} elements evenly distributed in a frame (by analogy with 1a). The set Ω_{bl100} is used to confirm the hypotheses of primary identification (formation of a weight of the next hypothesis about the correspondence of triples in frame and the astronomical catalog).

2. For a set of measurements of the astronomical catalog, when forming the triplets of primary sky identification, the following sequence of operations is performed.

   a. Formation of a set $\Omega_{star100}$ of catalog measurements, considering the uniform distribution of stars in the investigated area of the sky.
   b. Formation of an additional set $\Omega_{star200}$ of catalog measurements, consisting of $N_{star200}$ elements, which are used to confirm the hypotheses of primary identification.

3. Enumeration and confirmation of hypotheses of the primary sky identification.

   a. Enumerating the measurements of a set Ω_{bl50} as elements of triples of the primary sky identification. The measurements that make up the triple of the primary sky identification must satisfy the conditions (9) and (10).
   b. Enumeration of a set $\Omega_{star100}$ of catalog measurements as elements of triples of the primary sky identification from the astronomical catalog side.
   c. Comparison of triples of measurements for the primary sky identification from the frame and catalog sides based on the corresponding angles of triangles, the values of which are calculated according to Equations (11)–(16).
   d. Confirmation of the hypothesis about the parameters of frame and catalog identification, which corresponds to the considered triplets of the primary sky identification. The hypothesis is recognized as true if during the identification process of the sets Ω_{bl100} and $\Omega_{star200}$ the formed admissible pairs exceed the predefined value v_{min_ident}. When the identification hypothesis is confirmed, further enumeration stops.

2.3. Automatic Selection of the Reference Stars

The methods for the preliminary (Section 2.1) and full (Section 2.2) sky identification make it possible to obtain the plate linear constants $(a_{pl1}; b_{pl1}; c_{pl1})$ and $(a_{pl2}; b_{pl2}; c_{pl2})$, which determine the relationship between the tangential (ideal) coordinate system and the coordinate system of a CCD-frame [35]:

$$\begin{cases} \xi = a_{pl1} \cdot x + b_{pl1} \cdot y + c_{pl1}; \\ \eta = a_{pl2} \cdot x + b_{pl2} \cdot y + c_{pl2}. \end{cases} \tag{19}$$

The plate linear constant makes it possible to obtain estimates of the equatorial coordinates of objects in frame using the following equation [36]:

$$\begin{cases} \alpha = \alpha_0 + \arctg\left(\frac{-\xi}{\cos\delta_0 - \eta\sin\delta_0}\right); \\ \delta = \arcsin\frac{\eta\cos\delta_0 + \sin\delta_0}{\sqrt{1+\xi^2+\eta^2}}, \end{cases} \tag{20}$$

The uniform distribution of the identified pairs in a CCD-frame helps to avoid cases corresponding to the presence of a large number of the "bright" measurements/stars in one area of the frame (Figure 4).

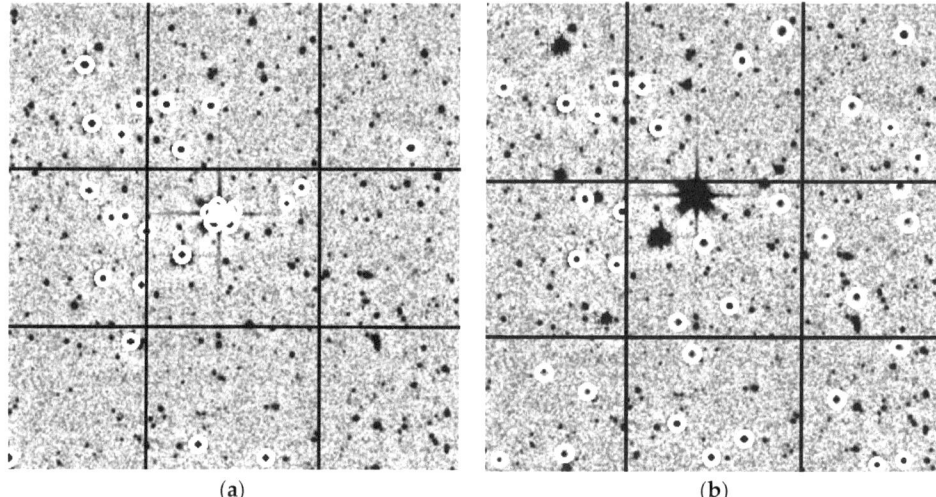

Figure 4. (a) The brightness measurements in a frame; (b) Uniform distribution of the reference stars in a frame.

To improve the accuracy of the plate constant estimates, after solving the identification task, a significant number of identified pairs are rejected. The decisive statistic for rejecting the identified pairs is the total deviation $\Delta_{\alpha\delta ijk}$ between estimates of the equatorial coordinates in such a pair:

$$\Delta_{\alpha\delta ijk} = \sqrt{(\alpha_{catj(k)} - \alpha_{meanfr(k)})^2 + (\delta_{catj(k)} - \delta_{meanfr(k)})^2}. \tag{21}$$

The pair is rejected if the value $\Delta_{\alpha\delta ijk}$ exceeds the critical value:

$$\Delta_{\alpha\delta ijk} > K_{rej}\hat{\Delta}_{\alpha\delta}, \tag{22}$$

where, $\hat{\Delta}_{\alpha\delta}$ is an average deviation modulus of the identified pair in the equatorial coordinates; K_{rej} is a coefficient of the rule for rejecting pairs from a set of reference stars.

The average deviation modulus $\hat{\Delta}_{\alpha\delta}$ is determined using the following equation:

$$\hat{\Delta}_{\alpha\delta} = \sqrt{\frac{1}{N_{count}}\left(\sum_{k=1}^{N_{count}}(\alpha_{catj(k)} - \alpha_{meanfr(k)})^2 + \sum_{k=1}^{N_{count}}(\delta_{catj(k)} + \delta_{meanfr(k)})^2\right)}, \tag{23}$$

where, N_{count} is a count of the identified pairs;

$\alpha_{catj(k)}$, $\delta_{catj(k)}$ are estimates of the right ascension and declination of an object from the j-th measurement in the astronomical catalog;

$\alpha_{meanfr(k)}$, $\delta_{meanfr(k)}$ are estimates of the right ascension and declination of the i-th measurement in the n_{fr}-th CCD-frame;

k is an index of the identified pair.

Thus, a stage for the automatic selection of the reference stars includes the following sequential steps.

1. Frame fragmentation for uniform distribution of the reference star candidates in a CCD-frame.
2. Selection of measurements from the frame and catalog for their mutual identification.
3. Rejection of candidates for the reference stars:
    a. objects whose images do not have peaks;
    b. catalog stars if they belong to the star clusters;

c. objects whose measurements have an intersection with the satellite track (Figure 2a);
   d. catalog stars that are close to each other (Figure 2b).
4. Identification of the selected measurements from the frame and catalog with the formation of identified pairs.
5. Calculation of the plate constants (19) (at each next step with a higher degree model).
6. Rejection of identified pairs by the total deviation $\Delta_{\alpha\delta ijk}$ (21) between estimates of equatorial coordinates in an identified pair (22).
7. Final calculation of the plate constants.
8. The UML-diagram of the developed mathematical methods for the sky identification is presented in Figure 5.

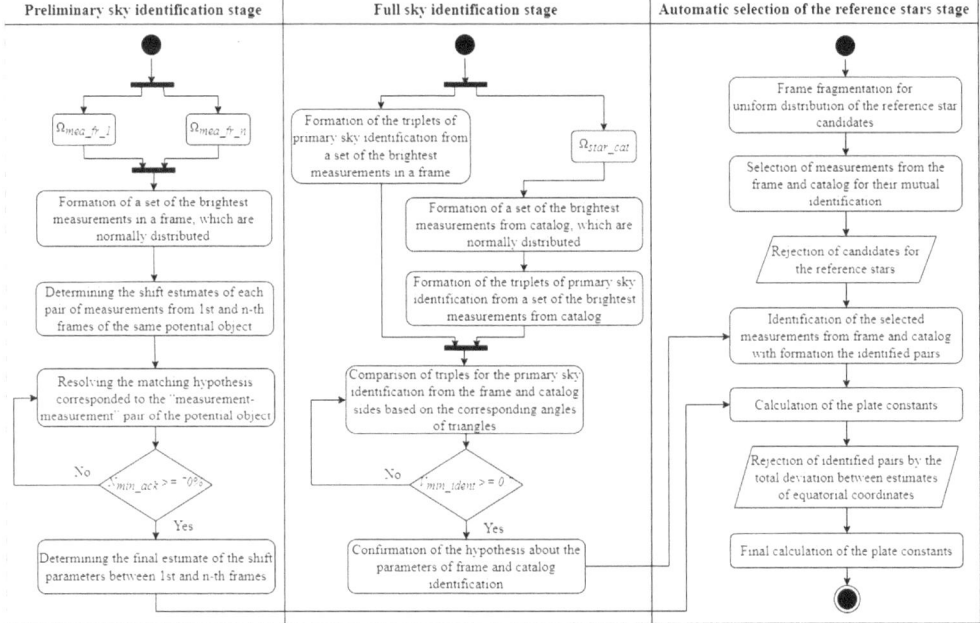

Figure 5. UML-diagram of the mathematical methods for the sky identification.

2.4. Accuracy Indicators of Estimates of the Angular Position and Brightness of the Reference Stars

The research of an accuracy indicators of estimates of the angular positions of reference stars in CCD-frames can be very useful for upgrading the software used by observatories equipped with the automated ground-based robotic telescopes, thereby increasing the accuracy of observations of the celestial objects.

Deviations between measurements from the frame and catalog of estimates of the equatorial coordinates (right ascension and declination) [37] and brightness [38] of the reference stars are determined using the following equations:

$$\Delta_{\alpha i} = \left(\alpha_{j1(i)} - \alpha_{j2(i)}\right) \cdot \cos\delta_{j1(i)}; \quad (24)$$

$$\Delta_{\delta i} = \delta_{j1(i)} - \delta_{j2(i)}; \quad (25)$$

$$\Delta_{mi} = m_{j1(i)} - m_{j2(i)}, \quad (26)$$

where, i is a index of the identified pair;

$\alpha_{j1(i)}, \alpha_{j2(i)}, \delta_{j1(i)}, \delta_{j2(i)}$ are right ascension and declination of j_1-th measurement from a frame and j_2-th measurement from a catalog, forming the i-th identified pair;

$m_{j1(i)}$, $m_{j2(i)}$ are brightness estimates of j_1-th measurement from a frame and j_2-th measurement from a catalog, forming the i-th identified pair;

j_1 is an index of the measurement from a frame in the internal numeration;

j_2 is an index of the measurement from a catalog in the internal numeration.

Estimation of the mean deviation (mathematical expectation of deviations) of estimates of the equatorial coordinates (24)–(25) and brightness (26) of the reference stars are determined using the following equations [39]:

$$\hat{\Delta}_\alpha = \sum_{i=1}^{N_{mea}} \Delta_{\alpha i} / N_{mea}; \qquad (27)$$

$$\hat{\Delta}_\delta = \sum_{i=1}^{N_{mea}} \Delta_{\delta i} / N_{mea}; \qquad (28)$$

$$\hat{\Delta}_m = \sum_{i=1}^{N_{mea}} \Delta_{mi} / N_{mea}, \qquad (29)$$

where, N_{mea} is the number of measurements used to analyze the accuracy of estimates of the angular position of objects.

Estimation of the standard deviation of estimates of the coordinates by right ascension and declination, as well as brightness of the reference stars, are determined using the following equations [40]:

$$\hat{\sigma}_\alpha = \sqrt{\sum_{i=1}^{N_{mea}} \left(\Delta_{\alpha i} - \hat{\Delta}_\alpha \right)^2 / (N_{mea} - 1)}; \qquad (30)$$

$$\hat{\sigma}_\delta = \sqrt{\sum_{i=1}^{N_{mea}} \left(\Delta_{\delta i} - \hat{\Delta}_\delta \right)^2 / (N_{mea} - 1)}; \qquad (31)$$

$$\hat{\sigma}_m = \sqrt{\sum_{i=1}^{N_{mea}} \left(\Delta_{mi} - \hat{\Delta}_m \right)^2 / (N_{mea} - 1)}, \qquad (32)$$

3. Results

3.1. Real Astronomical Data Sources

All studies were carried out using the CCD-frames formed at the different times of year, on different telescopes and CCD-cameras. Below is a list of these observatories and some technical characteristics of the telescopes and CCD cameras used. All such observatories have the special code [41] from the Minor Planet Center (MPC) from the International Astronomical Union (IAU) [42].

The ISON-NM observatory (MPC code "H15") is located on Mount Joy (Mayhill, NM, USA). This observatory uses a 40-cm SANTEL-400AN telescope as an observation tool with focal length f = 1197.37 mm and CCD-camera FLI ML09000-65 (3056 × 3056 pixels, pixel size is 12 microns) [43]. The exposure time of the studied frames was 150 s.

The Cerro Tololo observatory (MPC code "807") is located 80 km from the city of La Serena (Chile). La Silla Observatory uses a 46-cm PROMPT-8 telescope with focal length f = 4201.035 mm and CCD-camera E2V (2048 × 2048 pixels, pixel size is 13.5 microns) [44]. The exposure time of the studied frames was 10 s.

The Vihorlat Observatory in Humenné (MPC code "Humenne") is in a remote branch of the Astronomical Observatory on the Kolonitsky saddle between the Vihorlat and Bukovske Vrhi mountain ranges, 38 km from the city of Humenne (Slovakia). The observatory uses the Vihorlat National Telescope (VNT), a Cassegrain telescope with a main mirror diameter of 1 m with focal length f = 8958.50 mm and CCD-camera FLI PL1001E (512 × 512 pixels, pixel size is 4.8 microns) [15]. The exposure time of the studied frames was 60 s.

The Mayaki observing station (MPC code "583") is a section of the Astronomical Observatory Research Institute of I. I. Mechnikov Odessa National University. The station uses the AZT-3 reflector telescope with a main mirror diameter of 0.48 m with focal length f = 2025 mm and CCD-camera Sony ICX429ALL (795 × 596 pixels, pixel size is 12 microns) [37]. The exposure time of the studied frames was 150 s.

3.2. Reference Data Sources

To calculate the measurement deviations, it is necessary to obtain the reference coordinate values of the reference stars.

As reference values of the angular positions of the reference stars, we used data from the UCAC 4.0 astrometric catalog [45]. Its average density is over 2000 stars per square degree. The catalog contains data on more than 113 million stars and covers the sky in brightness up to 16 of magnitude. The position error of any object does not exceed 20 arc milliseconds. The error of the proper motion of each object is from 2 to 8 arc milliseconds per year.

As reference values of a brightness of the reference stars, we used data from the USNO B1.0 photometric catalog [46]. The catalog contains estimates of the angular positions and brightness of more than one billion objects, which were formed based on 3.6 billion individual measurements.

3.3. Accuracy of the Developed Mathematical Methods for the Sky Identification

During research the following statistical accuracy indicators [47] of estimates of the angular position and brightness of the reference stars were used:

1. Mean deviation (27)–(29);
2. Max. deviation module;
3. Min. deviation module;
4. Standard deviation of estimates (30)–(32).

The main parameters of deviations of the angular positions and brightness of the observed reference stars are presented in Table 1. In total, 30,391 measurements were processed under research.

Table 1. The main parameters of deviations of the angular positions and brightness of the observed reference stars.

Processed Measurements	30,391	28,872	27,352
Rejection percentage of the worst measurements, %	0	5	10
Mean deviation of RA, arcsec	0.003	0.002	0.001
Mean deviation of DE, arcsec	0.002	0.001	0.001
Mean deviation of brightness, mag.	0.03	0.03	0.03
Max. deviation module of RA, arcsec	0.32	0.15	0.13
Max. deviation module of DE, arcsec	0.33	0.14	0.12
Min. deviation module of brightness, mag.	0.002	0.001	0.001
Max. deviation module of brightness, mag.	3.51	0.51	0.36
Standard deviation of RA, arcsec	0.08	0.08	0.07
Standard deviation of DE, arcsec	0.07	0.07	0.06
Standard deviation of brightness, mag.	0.38	0.38	0.37

Figure 6 shows histograms of the distributions of deviations of the equatorial coordinates in right ascension (RA) and declination (DE) of the reference stars. The x-axis shows the deviation values for the appropriate equatorial coordinate (RA/DE), and the y-axis shows the number of measurements.

All specific parameters for the mathematical methods and their values, which were used under research, are described in Appendix A.

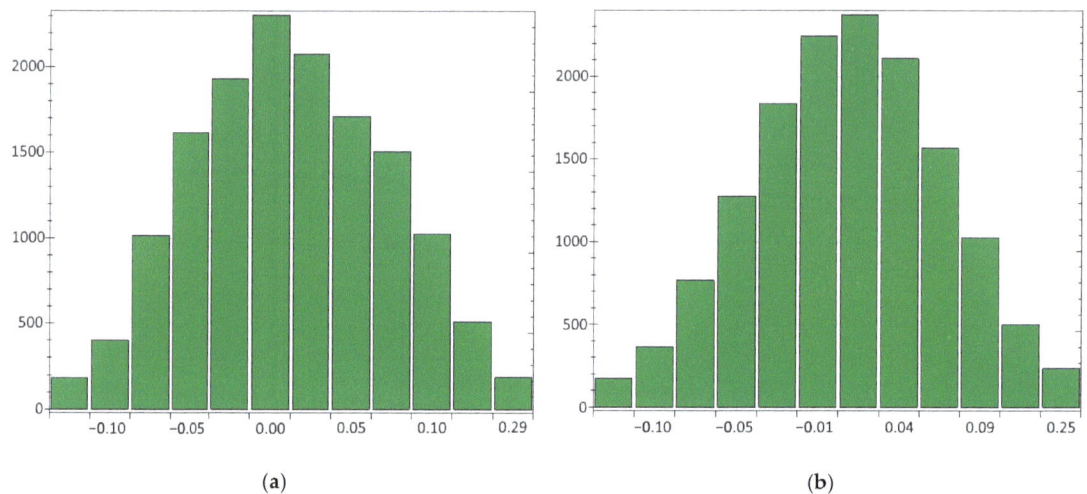

Figure 6. Histograms of the distributions of deviations of the equatorial coordinates of the reference stars in: (**a**) right ascension; (**b**) declination.

3.4. Implementation in the CoLiTec Software

The developed mathematical methods were successfully implemented in the Collection Light Technology (CoLiTec) software [48]. More details about the architecture are described in this paper [49]. It also implements modern data mining [50] and knowledge discovery in database [51] approaches.

The special module for the identification of measurements was created as a part of the CoLiTec software (Figure 7). It implements the developed mathematical methods. Its main goal is to perform accurate sky identification based on the measurements received from the module for intraframe processing and measurements of stars from the stellar catalogue.

The input for the module for the identification of measurement is a set of raw measurements, which includes estimates of the positional coordinates and the brightness of each detected but not identified object in a series of frames.

The output of such a module is a set of measurements related to the already identified real known objects (stars), including their positional coordinates and the brightness of in each frame in the series. Additionally, the celestial coordinates of each frame's center are determined, which makes it possible to navigate the automated mounts of the robotic telescopes using the special celestial coordinates.

Using the CoLiTec software, more than 1600 small solar system objects were discovered. It has been used in more than 700,000 observations and successful sky identification, during which five comets were discovered.

The accuracy of processing results of the CoLiTec software shows benefits and low standard deviation of the sky identification in the case of low signal to noise ratios. That is why the CoLiTec software was recommended for all members of the Gaia-FUN-SSO network [52] as a tool for the faint astronomical object detection in a series of frames. Additionally, the CoLiTec project belongs to the Ukrainian Virtual Observatory (UkrVO) project [53].

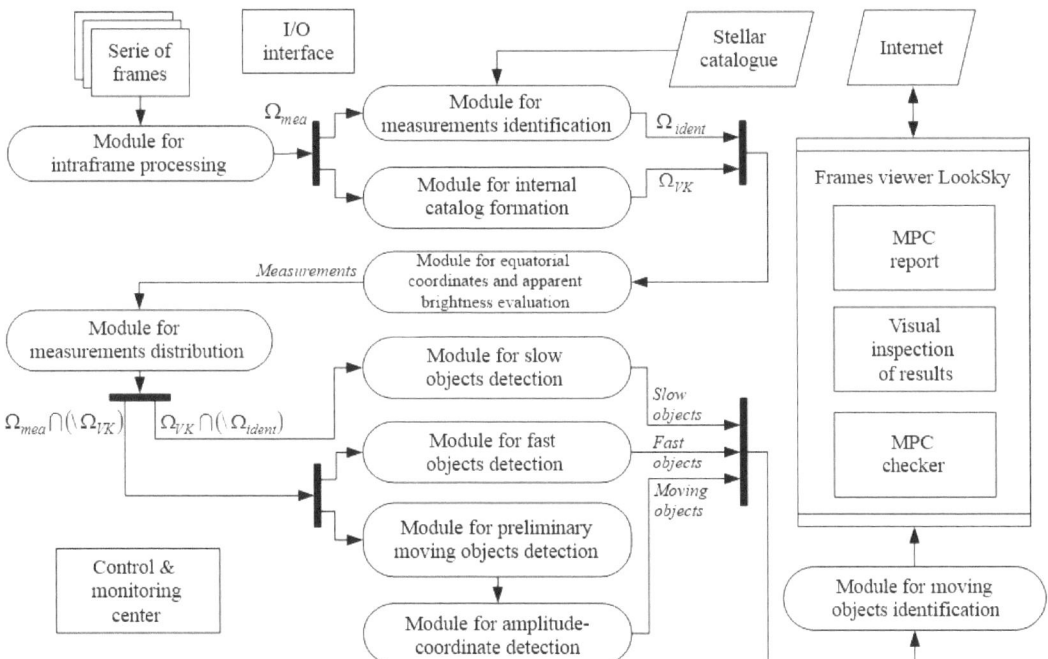

Figure 7. The CoLiTec software architecture.

4. Discussion

During the preliminary sky identification stage, the initial approximation of the parameters of pairwise correspondence (pairing) between two sets of measurements formed in the two nearest frames in a series and corresponding to the same region of the celestial sphere is performed. With its help, the shift estimates of each pair of measurements from the first and n-th frames of the same potential object were determined. After this, the matching hypothesis corresponded to the "measurement–measurement" pair of the potential object was resolved. This stage helps to determine the final estimates of the shift parameters between each frame in an input series of frames.

The full sky identification stage is used to find the initial approximation when identifying frame measurements with catalog stars under conditions of significant uncertainty in the identification parameters. With uncertainty about all six identification parameters, namely, about the parameters of the frame shift, camera rotation angle, and pixel scale, as an initial approximation, it is necessary to obtain six parameters of plate linear constants. For this, it is enough to have three points (stars in a CCD-frame), which make up a triangle of the primary identification. Proceeding from this, the stars are sorted as the vertices of the identification triangles in a CCD-frame and in the astronomical catalog. Each such pair of triangles corresponds to the "primary identification" hypothesis, within which, conditional estimates of the identification parameters are determined. After this, the comparison of triples for the primary sky identification from the frame and catalog sides based on the corresponding angles of triangles is performed. This stage helps to confirm the hypothesis about the parameters of frame and catalog identification.

The preliminary and full sky identification stages provide the necessary information (shift estimates, parameters of frame and catalog identification, and others) for the next stage. The automatic selection of the reference stars stage is based on using the cubic reduction model (plate constants) that defines the relationship between the ideal (tangential) and equatorial coordinate systems and a small number of the identified "measurement–star" pairs.

The main steps from this last stage are the rejection of candidates for the reference stars from the astronomical catalog as well as the rejection of identified pairs by the total deviation between estimates of equatorial coordinates. This allows for a uniform distribution of the reference points with almost the same magnitude and improving the set of measurements and identified pairs without large outliers in accuracy.

That is why the developed methods are resistant to various types of artifacts and errors that occur during the formation of a digital image. This is one of the main advantages of the developed computational mathematical methods.

Additionally, as a result of the research, the number of parameters of the developed method used to maximize the accuracy indicators for determining the angular position of objects was significantly reduced, and the range of their allowable values was significantly narrowed.

As shown in Table 1, a total of 30,391 measurements were processed under research and the main parameters of deviations of the angular positions and brightness of the observed reference stars were calculated. As results showed, the mean deviations of the angular coordinates (RA and DE) are 0.003 and 0.002, accordingly. If the rejection threshold is increased to reject 10% of bad measurements, the mean deviations of both coordinates become 0.001 arc seconds or 1 arc millisecond. In comparison with the known position error of any astronomical object from catalog, which does not exceed 20 arc milliseconds, this is a very high accuracy. Additionally, in comparison with an error of the proper motion of each object, which is from 2 to 8 arc milliseconds per year, this is a very exponential accuracy.

Further research is planned to adapt the developed method for the multi-robot systems based on real-time [54]. To obtain the best accuracy indicators of determining the angular position of objects, research of the influence on the accuracy of some parameters of the method is planned. They are the maximum allowable distance between neighboring stars of a group of objects r_{star_group}, the number of fragments into which the frame is divided along each coordinate when selecting the reference stars M_{reg}, and the maximum allowable distance between neighboring measurements of a group of pixels r_{mea_group}.

To prepare the wider comparison statistics, a different approach will also be applied as the Wavelet [55] and time-series analysis [56], as well as computer vision techniques [57] and machine learning [58]. However, for the last one, the set of measurements should be extremely large for the training model preparation; therefore, the collection of such test data requires a wide time frame.

5. Conclusions

Special computational mathematical methods were developed for the full astrometric calibration process. They include the preliminary and full sky identification in the CCD-frames in a series with the further automatic selection of reference stars from the international star catalogs/databases [18].

The developed methods were tested using real astronomical data from the different sources and observational conditions of telescopes. The main accuracy indicators, such as mean, minimal, maximum, standard deviation, were calculated. The results showed a high accuracy in comparison with the known position error or proper motion error of any astronomical object. The developed methods are resistant to various types of artifacts and errors that occur during the formation of a digital image because of the list of rejection rules for the raw measurements as well as reference star selection rules. During the research, a lot of processing parameters were carefully empirically selected for the best accuracy.

Limitations of the developed methods are only related to the processing time and required calibration stage for the automated mount of the robotic telescope. Such a calibration stage includes the preparation of a small series of at least three frames and processing the received measurements by the developed methods to get the accurate celestial coordinates of the FOV center for the further automated navigation. Additionally, the international star catalogs/databases can be used in two modes: online, using the Internet (if connection is available), or offline, using the downloaded catalogs on hardware.

The developed methods were implemented into the CoLiTec software [20] in the module for measurement identification. The processing results of the CoLiTec software, with the help of successful sky identification, is presented in Table 2.

Table 2. Processing results of the CoLiTec software.

Processing Results	Number
Astronomical observations	>700,000
Discoveries of the Solar System objects (SSOs)	>1600
Discoveries of the Comets	5
Discoveries of the Near-Earth objects (NEOs)	5
Discoveries of the Trojan asteroids of Jupiter	21
Discoveries of the Centaurs	1

The accuracy of processing results of the CoLiTec software shows benefits, even in case of low signal-to-noise ratios. Additionally, the CoLiTec software was recommended for all members of the Gaia-FUN-SSO network [52] as a tool for moving faint object detection, including sky identification at the pre-processing stage.

Author Contributions: Conceptualization, V.S. and S.K.; methodology, V.S.; software, O.B.; validation, V.S. and I.T.; formal analysis, V.S.; investigation, I.T. and T.T.; resources, O.B.; data curation, O.B.; writing—original draft preparation, S.K.; writing—review and editing, S.K.; visualization, T.T.; supervision, V.S.; project administration, V.S. All authors have read and agreed to the published version of the manuscript.

Funding: This research received no external funding.

Informed Consent Statement: Informed consent was obtained from all subjects involved in the study.

Data Availability Statement: Data sharing not applicable.

Conflicts of Interest: The authors declare no conflict of interest.

Appendix A

The appendix contain all specific parameters for the developed mathematical methods and their values, which were used under research. They are:

1. Radius R_{rej} of the acknowledgment circular area (strobe) is R_{rej} = 20 pixels;
2. Minimum allowable number of acknowledgments N_{min_ack} = 70%;
3. Number of equal regions $M_{reg} \times M_{reg}$, on which frame is divided into is $M_{reg} \times M_{reg} = 4 \times 4$;
4. Number N_{mea_reg} of measurements with the highest brightness estimates in frame is $N_{mea\_reg} = N_{mea}/M_{reg}^2 = 3$;
5. Number N_{bl50} of measurements (candidates) in frame for the role of elements of triplets (vertices of triangles) of the primary sky identification is N_{bl50} = 50;
6. Number N_{bl100} of elements of the set Ω_{bl100} of measurements in frame used to confirm the hypotheses of the primary sky identification is N_{bl100} = 100;
7. Ratio of the number of elements of the sets Ω_{bl100} and Ω_{bl50} of measurements in frame was assumed to be equal to $k_{blob} = N_{bl100}/N_{bl50} = 2$;
8. Number of regions M_{reg}, on which frame is divided into is M_{reg} = 4;
9. Number $N_{star100}$ of stars (candidates) in astrometric catalog for the role of elements of triplets (vertices of triangles) of the primary sky identification is $N_{start100}$ = 100;
10. Number $N_{star200}$ of stars of the set $\Omega_{star200}$ of measurements in astrometric catalog used to confirm the hypotheses of the primary sky identification is $N_{star200}$ = 200;
11. Ratio of the number of elements of the sets $\Omega_{star200}$ and $\Omega_{star100}$ of measurements in frame was assumed to be equal to $k_{star} = N_{star200}/N_{star100} = 2$;

12. Maximum allowable minimal distance between the second and first points of the triple of the primary sky identification, expressed in the angular measurements of a CCD-frame is $k_h = 0.1$;
13. Under the condition of a rectangular (not square) frame, to determine the minimum distance between the second and first points of the triple, the value k_h is multiplied by the average value of the frame size for both coordinates;
14. Maximum allowable deviation of values of the corresponding angles of the triangles (from a CCD-frame and the astrometric catalog sides) of the primary sky identification is $\Delta^\gamma = 60'$.
15. Limiting maximum value of the distance between the elements of an identified pair, at which it is considered valid is $\Delta r_{ident} = 10$ pixels;
16. Minimum allowable ratio of the number of allowed pairs to the set Ω_{bl100} size is $v_{min\_ident} = 0.7$.

References

1. Ackermann, M.; Ajello, M.; Albert, A.; Allafort, A.; Atwood, W.B.; Axelsson, M.; Baldini, L.; Ballet, J.; Barbiellini, G.; Bastieri, D.; et al. The Fermi large area telescope on orbit: Event classification, instrument response functions, and calibration. *Astrophys. J. Suppl. Ser.* **2012**, *203*, 4. [CrossRef]
2. Savanevych, V.E.; Briukhovetskyi, A.B.; Ivashchenko, Y.N.; Vavilova, I.B.; Bezkrovniy, M.M.; Dikov, E.N.; Vlasenko, V.P.; Sokovikova, N.S.; Movsesian, I.S.; Dikhtyar, N.Y.; et al. Comparative analysis of the positional accuracy of CCD measurements of small bodies in the solar system software CoLiTec and Astrometrica. *Kinemat. Phys. Celest. Bodies* **2015**, *31*, 302–313. [CrossRef]
3. Schroeder, D.J. *Astronomical Optics*; Elsevier: Amsterdam, The Netherlands, 1999.
4. Smith, G. Nobel Lecture: The invention and early history of the CCD. *Rev. Mod. Phys.* **2010**, *82*, 2307–2312. [CrossRef]
5. Adam, G.K.; Kontaxis, P.A.; Doulos, L.T.; Madias, E.-N.D.; Bouroussis, C.A.; Topalis, F.V. Embedded microcontroller with a CCD camera as a digital lighting control system. *Electronics* **2019**, *8*, 33. [CrossRef]
6. Mykhailova, L. Method of maximum likelihood estimation of compact group objects location on CCD-frame. *East.-Eur. J. Enterp. Technol.* **2014**, *5*, 16–22.
7. Savanevych, V.; Briukhovetskyi, O.B.; Sokovikova, N.S.; Bezkrovny, M.M.; Vavilova, I.B.; Ivashchenko, Y.M.; Elenin, L.V.; Khlamov, S.; Movsesian, I.S.; Dashkova, A.M.; et al. A new method based on the subpixel Gaussian model for accurate estimation of asteroid coordinates. *Mon. Not. R. Astron. Soc.* **2015**, *451*, 3287–3298. [CrossRef]
8. Hale, S.J.; Chaplin, W.J.; Davies, G.R.; Elsworth, Y.P. A next generation upgraded observing platform for the automated Birmingham Solar Oscillations Network (BiSON). In *Software and Cyberinfrastructure for Astronomy VI*; SPIE: Bellingham, WA, USA, 2020; Volume 11452.
9. Singha, J.; Basu, A.; Krishnakumar, M.A.; Joshi, B.C.; Arumugam, P. A real-time automated glitch detection pipeline at Ooty Radio Telescope. *Mon. Not. R. Astron. Soc.* **2021**, *505*, 5488–5496. [CrossRef]
10. Roberts, W.T.; Antsos, D.; Croonquist, A.; Piazzolla, S.; Roberts, L.C.; Garkanian, V.; Trinh, T.; Wright, M.W.; Rogalin, R.; Wu, J.; et al. Overview of Ground Station 1 of the NASA space communications and navigation program. *Free. Space Laser Commun. Atmos. Propag. XXVIII* **2016**, *9739*, 97390B.
11. Tarasov, S.M. A Study on the Effect Produced by Instrumental Error of Automated Astronomical System on Landmark Azimuth Accuracy. *Gyroscopy Navig.* **2021**, *12*, 178–185. [CrossRef]
12. Gayvoronsky, S.V.; Kuzmina, N.V.; Tsodokova, V.V. High-accuracy determination of the Earth's gravitational field parameters using automated zenith telescope. In Proceedings of the 24th Saint Petersburg International Conference on Integrated Navigation Systems (ICINS), Saint Petersburg, Russia, 29–31 May 2017; pp. 1–4.
13. Lösler, M.; Eschelbach, C.; Riepl, S. A modified approach for automated reference point determination of SLR and VLBI telescopes: First investigations at Satellite Observing System Wettzell. *Tech. Mess.* **2018**, *85*, 616–626. [CrossRef]
14. Hampson, K.M.; Gooding, D.; Cole, R.; Booth, M.J. High precision automated alignment procedure for two-mirror telescopes. *Appl. Opt.* **2019**, *58*, 7388–7391. [CrossRef] [PubMed]
15. Parimucha, Š.; Savanevych, V.E.; Briukhovetskyi, O.B.; Khlamov, S.V.; Pohorelov, A.V.; Vlasenko, V.P.; Dubovský, P.A.; Kudzej, I. CoLiTecVS—A new tool for an automated reduction of photometric observations. *Contrib. Astron. Obs. Skaln. Pleso* **2019**, *49*, 151–153.
16. Savanevych, V.; Akhmetov, V.; Khlamov, S.; Dikov, E.; Briukhovetskyi, A.; Vlasenko, V.; Khramtsov, V.; Movsesian, I. Selection of the reference stars for astrometric reduction of CCD-frames. *Adv. Intell. Syst. Comput.* **2020**, *1080*, 881–895.
17. Akhmetov, V.; Khlamov, S.; Dmytrenko, A. Fast coordinate cross-match tool for large astronomical catalogue. *Adv. Intell. Syst. Comput.* **2019**, *871*, 3–16.
18. Vavilova, I.; Pakuliak, L.; Babyk, I.; Elyiv, A.; Dobrycheva, D.; Melnyk, O. Surveys, catalogues, databases, and archives of astronomical data. In *Knowledge Discovery in Big Data from Astronomy and Earth Observation*; Astrogeoinformatics; Elsevier: Amsterdam, The Netherlands, 2020; pp. 57–102.

19. Akhmetov, V.; Khlamov, S.; Khramtsov, V.; Dmytrenko, A. Astrometric reduction of the wide-field images. *Adv. Intell. Syst. Comput.* **2020**, *1080*, 896–909.
20. Khlamov, S.; Savanevych, V. Big astronomical datasets and discovery of new celestial bodies in the Solar System in automated mode by the CoLiTec software. In *Knowledge Discovery in Big Data from Astronomy and Earth Observation*; Astrogeoinformatics; Elsevier: Amsterdam, The Netherlands, 2020; pp. 331–345.
21. Khlamov, S.; Savanevych, V.; Briukhovetskyi, O.; Oryshych, S. Development of computational method for detection of the object's near-zero apparent motion on the series of CCD–frames. *East. Eur. J. Enterp. Technol.* **2016**, *2*, 41–48. [CrossRef]
22. Tantsiura, A. Evaluation of the potential accuracy of correlation extreme navigation systems of low-altitude mobile robots. *Int. J. Adv. Trends Comput. Sci. Eng.* **2019**, *8*, 2161–2166. [CrossRef]
23. Savanevych, V.; Khlamov, S.; Akhmetov, V.; Briukhovetskyi, A.; Vlasenko, V.; Dikov, E.; Kudzej, I.; Dubovsky, P.; Mkrtichian, D.; Tabakova, I.; et al. CoLiTecVS software for the automated reduction of photometric observations in CCD-frames. *Astron. Comput.* **2022**, *40*, 15. [CrossRef]
24. Savanevych, V.; Khlamov, S.; Vlasenko, V.; Deineko, Z.; Briukhovetskyi, O.; Tabakova, I.; Trunova, T. Formation of a typical form of an object image in a series of digital frames. *East.-Eur. J. Enterp. Technol.* **2022**, *6*, 51–59.
25. Yeromina, N.; Tarshyn, V.; Petrov, S.; Samoylenko, V.; Tabakova, I.; Dmitriiev, O.; Surkova, K.; Danylko, O.; Kushnierova, N.; Soroka, M.; et al. Method of reference image selection to provide high-speed aircraft navigation under conditions of rapid change of flight trajectory. *Int. J. Adv. Technol. Eng. Explor.* **2021**, *8*, 1621–1638.
26. Khlamov, S.; Savanevych, V.; Briukhovetskyi, O.; Pohorelov, A. CoLiTec software-detection of the near-zero apparent motion. *Proc. Int. Astron. Union* **2016**, *12*, 349–352. [CrossRef]
27. Akhmetov, V.; Khlamov, S.; Tabakova, I.; Hernandez, W.; Hipolito, J.I.N.; Fedorov, P. New approach for pixelization of big astronomical data for machine vision purpose. In Proceedings of the IEEE International Symposium on Industrial Electronics, Vancouver, BC, Canada, 12–14 June 2019; pp. 1706–1710.
28. Zhilenkov, A.; Chernyi, S.; Sokolov, S.; Nyrkov, A. Algorithmic approach of destabilizing factors of improving the technical systems efficiency. *Vibroeng. Procedia* **2017**, *13*, 261–265. [CrossRef]
29. Akhmetov, V.; Khlamov, S.; Savanevych, V.; Dikov, E. Cloud computing analysis of Indian ASAT test on March 27, 2019. In Proceedings of the IEEE International Scientific-Practical Conference: Problems of Infocommunications Science and Technology, Kyiv, Ukraine, 8–11 October 2019; pp. 315–318.
30. Branham, R.L., Jr. Astronomical data reduction with total least squares. *New Astron. Rev.* **2001**, *45*, 649–661. [CrossRef]
31. Burger, W.; Burge, M. *Principles of Digital Image Processing: Fundamental Techniques*; Springer: New York, NY, USA, 2009.
32. Sommerville, D.M.Y. *Analytical Geometry of Three Dimensions*; Cambridge University Press: Cambridge, UK, 2016.
33. Fischer, G. *Complex Analytic Geometry*; Springer: New York, NY, USA, 2006; Volume 538.
34. Legault, T. *Astrophotography*; Rocky Nook, Inc.: San Rafael, CA, USA, 2014.
35. Khlamov, S.; Vlasenko, V.; Savanevych, V.; Briukhovetskyi, O.; Trunova, T.; Chelombitko, V.; Tabakova, I. Development of computational method for matched filtration with analytic profile of the blurred digital image. *East.-Eur. J. Enterp. Technol.* **2022**, *5*, 24–32.
36. Gonzalez, R.; Woods, R. *Digital Image Processing*, 4th ed.; Pearson: New York, NY, USA, 2018.
37. Kwiatkowski, T.; Koleńczuk, P.; Kryszczyńska, A.; Oszkiewicz, D.; Kamiński, K.; Kamińska, M.K.; Troianskyi, V.; Skiff, B.; Moskowitz, N.; Kashuba, V.; et al. Photometry and model of near-Earth asteroid 2021 DW1 from one apparition. *Astron. Astrophys.* **2021**, *656*, A126. [CrossRef]
38. Starck, J.-L.; Murtagh, F. Astronomical image and data analysis. In *Astronomy and Astrophysics Library*, 2nd ed.; Springer: Berlin/Heidelberg, Germany, 2007.
39. Steger, C.; Ulrich, M.; Wiedemann, C. *Machine Vision Algorithms and Applications*; John Wiley & Sons: Hoboken, NJ, USA, 2018.
40. Lehmann, E.; Romano, J.; Casella, G. *Testing Statistical Hypotheses*; Springer: New York, NY, USA, 2005; Volume 3.
41. The Minor Planet Center (MPC) of the International Astronomical Union. Available online: https://minorplanetcenter.net (accessed on 1 March 2023).
42. List of Observatory Codes: IAU Minor Planet Center. Available online: https://minorplanetcenter.net/iau/lists/ObsCodesF.html (accessed on 1 March 2023).
43. Molotov, I.; Agapov, V.; Kouprianov, V.; Titenko, V.; Rumyantsev, V.; Biryukov, V.; Borisov, G.; Burtsev, Y.; Khutorovsky, Z.; Kornienko, G.; et al. ISON worldwide scientific optical network. In Proceedings of the Fifth European Conference on Space Debris, Darmstadt, Germany, 30 March–2 April 2009; ESA: Paris, France, 2009; Volume 7, p. SP-672.
44. Li, T.; DePoy, D.L.; Marshall, J.L.; Nagasawa, D.Q.; Carona, D.W.; Boada, S. Monitoring the atmospheric throughput at Cerro Tololo Inter-American Observatory with aTmCam. *Ground-Based Airborne Instrum. Astron. V* **2014**, *9147*, 2194–2205.
45. Zacharias, N.; Finch, C.T.; Girard, T.M.; Henden, A.; Bartlett, J.L.; Monet, D.G.; Zacharias, M.I. The fourth US naval observatory CCD astrograph catalog (UCAC4). *Astron. J.* **2013**, *145*, 44. [CrossRef]
46. Luo, X.; Gu, S.; Xiang, Y.; Wang, X.; Yeung, B.; Ng, E.; Bai, J.; Fan, Y.; Xu, F.; Cao, D.; et al. Active longitudes and starspot evolution of the young rapidly rotating star USNO-B1.0 1388−0463685 discovered in the Yunnan–Hong Kong survey. *Mon. Not. R. Astron. Soc.* **2022**, *514*, 1511–1521. [CrossRef]
47. Shvedun, V.; Khlamov, S. Statistical modelling for determination of perspective number of advertising legislation violations. *Actual Probl. Econ.* **2016**, *184*, 389–396.

48. Khlamov, S.; Savanevych, V.; Briukhovetskyi, O.; Pohorelov, A.; Vlasenko, V.; Dikov, E. CoLiTec Software for the Astronomical Data Sets Processing. In Proceedings of the 2018 IEEE 2nd International Conference on Data Stream Mining and Processing (DSMP), Lviv, Ukraine, 21–25 August 2018; Volume 8478504, pp. 227–230.
49. Khlamov, S.; Savanevych, V.; Briukhovetskyi, O.; Tabakova, I.; Trunova, T. Data Mining of the Astronomical Images by the CoLiTec Software. *CEUR Workshop Proc.* **2022**, *3171*, 1043–1055.
50. Borne, K. Scientific data mining in astronomy. In *Data Mining and Knowledge Discovery Series*; Chapman and Hall/CRC: Boca Raton, FL, USA, 2008; pp. 115–138.
51. Zhang, Y.; Zhao, Y.; Cui, C. Data mining and knowledge discovery in database of astronomy. *Prog. Astron.* **2002**, *20*, 312–323.
52. Gaia Follow-Up Network for Solar System Objects. Available online: https://gaiafunsso.imcce.fr (accessed on 1 March 2023).
53. Vavilova, I.B.; Yatskiv, Y.S.; Pakuliak, L.K.; Andronov, I.L.; Andruk, V.M.; Protsyuk, Y.I.; Savanevych, V.E.; Savchenko, D.O.; Savchenko, V.S. UkrVO astroinformatics software and web-services. *Proc. Int. Astron. Union* **2016**, *12*, 361–366. [CrossRef]
54. Ivanov, M.; Sergiyenko, O.; Mercorelli, P.; Hernandez, W.; Tyrsa, V.; Hernandez-Balbuena, D.; Rodriguez Quinonez, J.C.; Kartashov, V.; Kolendovska, M.; Iryna, T. Effective informational entropy reduction in multi-robot systems based on real-time TVS. In Proceedings of the 2019 IEEE 28th International Symposium on Industrial Electronics (ISIE), Vancouver, BC, Canada, 12–14 June 2019; Volume 8781209, pp. 1162–1167.
55. Baranova, V.; Zeleniy, O.; Deineko, Z.; Bielcheva, G.; Lyashenko, V. Wavelet Coherence as a Tool for Studying of Economic Dynamics in Infocommunication Systems. In Proceedings of the IEEE International Scientific-Practical Conference Problems of Infocommunications, Science and Technology, Kyiv, Ukraine, 8–11 October 2019; pp. 336–340.
56. Kirichenko, L.; Alghawli, A.S.A.; Radivilova, T. Generalized approach to analysis of multifractal properties from short time series. *Int. J. Adv. Comput. Sci. Appl.* **2020**, *11*, 183–198. [CrossRef]
57. Klette, R. *Concise Computer Vision*; Springer: London, UK, 2014.
58. Kirichenko, L.; Zinchenko, P.; Radivilova, T. Classification of time realizations using machine learning recognition of recurrence plots. *Adv. Intell. Syst. Comput.* **2021**, *1246 AISC*, 687–696.

Disclaimer/Publisher's Note: The statements, opinions and data contained in all publications are solely those of the individual author(s) and contributor(s) and not of MDPI and/or the editor(s). MDPI and/or the editor(s) disclaim responsibility for any injury to people or property resulting from any ideas, methods, instructions or products referred to in the content.

Article

Distributed Finite-Time Coverage Control of Multi-Quadrotor Systems with Switching Topology †

Hilton Tnunay [1,*], **Kaouther Moussa** [2,3], **Ahmad Hably** [4] **and Nicolas Marchand** [4]

1. KU Leuven, Faculty of Engineering Technology, 9000 Ghent, Belgium
2. UPHF, CNRS, UMR 8201 - LAMIH, F-59313 Valenciennes, France
3. INSA Hauts-de-France, F-59313 Valenciennes, France
4. Univ. Grenoble Alpes, CNRS, Grenoble INP, GIPSA-lab, 38000 Grenoble, France
* Correspondence: hilton.tnunay@kuleuven.be
† This paper is an extended version of our paper published in IECON 2022—48th Annual Conference of the IEEE Industrial Electronics Society, Brussels, Belgium, 17–20 October 2022; pp. 1–6.

Abstract: This paper studies the distributed coverage control problem of multi-quadcopter systems connected with fixed and switching network topologies to guarantee the finite-time convergence. The proposed method modifies the objective function originating from the locational optimization problem to accommodate the consensus constraint and solves the problem within a given time limit. The coverage problem is solved by sending angular-rate and thrust commands to the quadcopters. By exploiting the finite-time stability theory, we ensure that the rotation and translation controllers of the quadcopters are finite-time stable both in fixed and switching communication topologies, able to be implemented distributively, and able to collaboratively drive the quadcopters towards the desired position and velocity of the Voronoi centroid independent of their initial states. After carefully designing and analyzing the performance, numerical simulations using a Robot Operating System (ROS) and Gazebo simulator are presented to validate the effectiveness of the proposed control protocols.

Keywords: coverage control; finite-time stability; distributed control; quadcopter; multiagent systems; robotic sensor network

MSC: 93D15

1. Introduction

The robotics community has shown interest in the coverage control problem of robotic sensor networks (RSNs). There have been real-world issues motivating the rising attention to this problem, such as agriculture, search and rescue, wireless communication, and nuclear decommissioning, where sensor placement with a prdefined number of sensor determines the quality of the measured data [1,2]. For example, in precision agriculture, different color distribution in an agricultural farm may correspond to water stress, fertilizer shortage, or disease [3,4]. In order to capture and analyze the temporal information of this issue, unmanned aerial vehicles (UAVs) can be equipped with relevant sensors and be deployed to the farm. From the optimization point-of-view, finding the optimal position of the UAVs and the sensors becomes one of the main tasks of an RSN in order to maximize the coverage of the deployed sensors.

The existing literature shows extensive work to address the coverage control problem. Locational optimization, having its roots in the field of operations research, has been suggested as a method for determining the optimal agent locations based on an interest function. Centroidal Voronoi tessellation has emerged as a widely recognized approach for addressing this problem, as referenced in [5–8]. By adopting the locational optimization problem, a simple proportional controller was initially developed [8,9]. This algorithm is

improved to tackle the time-varying density coverage on a group of nonholonomic mobile robots in [10]. Different approaches to coverage control have been explored in [11–15] to alleviate the constraints related to unlimited, isotropic, and homogeneous sensing ranges, as well as convex environments. Solving the optimal coverage control problem of multiple robots can offer improved coverage, energy efficiency, robustness, and scalability, among other benefits. Nonoptimal approaches may be simpler to implement and require fewer computational resources but may not achieve the same level of performance as the optimal approach. Adaptive coverage control to estimate the information density function has been studied in [16–18]. Regarding the communication topology, the result in [19] includes a dynamically routing communication algorithm while optimizing the coverage control problem. The coverage control problem on a circle with unknown terrain roughness and time-varying communication delays has been studied in [20]. The mobile sensors cooperatively estimate the roughness function and are driven to their optimal positions using proposed control laws under some delay constraints. A reinforcement learning approach has also been studied to tackle the area coverage problem of networked UAVs in [21]. However, the coverage algorithm of multiple quadcopters from the control system perspective that guarantees timely convergence in a finite time for both fixed and switching communication topology has not been investigated among the existing strategies.

In various applications, such as postdisaster evacuation and nuclear decommissioning, the importance of timeliness has grown to prevent deteriorating situations [2]. In control theory, timeliness refers to the settling or convergence time of an autonomous system starting from initial values and reaching the origin. The research presented in [22] introduced the concept of finite-time stability analysis in control systems by demonstrating the dependence of convergence time on initial states. This finite-time strategy was applied to achieve finite-time consensus among teams of agents with different dynamics in [23–25], and also used for spacecraft pose synchronization based on dual quaternions in [26]. However, these results are dependent on initial values, causing longer convergence times when agents are initially separated by a large distance. To address this issue, [27] proposed a finite-time consensus controller that ensures convergence within a specified settling time boundary regardless of the initial states. Subsequently, [28] extended this result to the consensus of multiagent systems with double-integrator dynamics. Additionally, this approach was applied to design a finite-time consensus controller for networked systems with time delays in [29].

In this article, a distributed coverage control algorithm for a sensor network consisting of multiple quadcopters is introduced. The algorithm ensures finite-time stability in both fixed and switching communication topologies. This study builds upon our previous research that focused on the finite-time stability of the coverage control problem using a fixed communication topology [30]. The contributions of this work are highlighted as follows. Firstly, it differs from existing approaches by simultaneously addressing the locational optimization and consensus problems. This approach focuses on maintaining the position, velocity, and formation shape of the agents' Voronoi centroids. Secondly, the study leverages finite-time stability theory to ensure timely attainment of desired positions, velocities (i.e., Voronoi centroids), and attitudes in switching communication networks. Thirdly, since quadcopters are used as agents, the algorithm accounts for their nonlinear dynamics, which involve coupled translational and rotational motions. The algorithm guarantees stability of both translational and rotational motions within a specified time limit.

The structure of this paper is organized as follows. Section 2 briefly reviews the concepts of graph theory, locational optimization, and quaternions. Section 3 states the main problem addressed in this paper. Following that, the main algorithms for achieving finite-time coverage control of the quadcopter flock are presented in Section 4. Finally, numerical simulations validating the proposed algorithm are provided in Section 5, followed by concluding remarks in Section 6.

2. Preliminaries

2.1. Graph Theory

A graph, denoted as $\mathcal{G}(\mathcal{V}, \mathcal{E})$, is a collection of n vertices $\mathcal{V} = \{v_1, v_2, \ldots, v_n\}$ connected by a set of edges $\mathcal{E} \subseteq \mathcal{V} \times \mathcal{V}$. If an edge $(v_i, v_j) \in \mathcal{E}$ exists, it means that vertex v_i can receive information from vertex v_j. When both (v_i, v_j) and (v_j, v_i) exist in $\mathcal{E}$, the graph is referred to as undirected. The neighbor of vertex v_i, denoted as $v_j \in \mathcal{N}_i \subset \mathcal{V}$, with $v_j \neq v_i$, is defined as a vertex connected to v_i through the edge $(v_i, v_j) \in \mathcal{E}$.

2.2. Locational Optimization

Consider the deployment of n robots within a convex environment represented by the set $\mathcal{Q} \subset \mathbb{R}^d$. The positions of all robots are denoted by the set $\mathcal{P} = p_{i=1}^n \subset \mathcal{Q}$, where p_i denotes the position of robot i.

The sensing unreliability function, denoted as $g : \mathcal{Q} \times \mathcal{Q} \to \mathbb{R}_+ : (x, p_i) \mapsto g(x, p_i)$, provides quantitative information about the sensing performance of agent i at position p_i when sensing point $x \in \mathcal{Q}$. In our context, we assume the sensing unreliability function to possess the following properties: isotropy, increasing, and convexity. An isotropic function exhibits a value that is independent of its direction. Therefore, we can redefine the function $g(x, p_i)$ as a norm-based function $f : \mathbb{R} \to \mathbb{R}_+$, such that $g(x, p_i) = f(\|x - p_i\|)$, where $i \in 1, 2, \ldots, n$.

The density function, or information distribution function, denoted by $\phi : \mathcal{Q} \to \mathbb{R}_+ : x \mapsto \phi(x)$, represents the spatial distribution of information within the environment. This function quantifies the importance of measuring a specific quantity at a particular point x in the set $\mathcal{Q}$.

After providing the definitions of the sensing unreliability function and density function, we introduce the locational optimization problem. Generated by the sensor positions at time t, $\mathcal{P}$, we are able to use the Voronoi tessellation of $\mathcal{Q}$ given by

$$V_i(p_i) = \{x \in \mathcal{Q} : \|x - p_i\| \leq \|x - p_j\|, \forall p_j \in \mathcal{P}, j \neq i\}. \tag{1}$$

In the following discussion, we use V_i conveniently to refer to $V_i(p_i)$. With this Voronoi partitions, the objective function of the locational optimization is formulated as

$$H(\mathcal{P}) = \sum_{i=1}^n \int_{V_i} g(x, p_i) \phi(q) dx. \tag{2}$$

With the defined conditions of the sensing unreliability function and density functions, the following lemma states the convexity of the objective function of the locational optimization.

Lemma 1 (Sensing Unreliability Function [30]). *Assume that the sensing unreliability function is isotropic, increasing, and convex in $p_i \in \mathcal{P}$, for all $i \in \{1, 2, \ldots, n\}$. Then, for a positive density function, the cost function H in (2) is convex.*

In this work, we make use of the quadratic sensing unreliability function defined as $f(\|x - p_i\|) = \|x - p_i\|^2$. By employing this quadratic function, we can incorporate the concept related to rigid body motion. This includes considering the mass, moment of inertia, and centroid of the i-th Voronoi region, which can be expressed as

$$M_{V_i} = \int_{V_i} \phi(x) dx, \quad \mathcal{I}_{V_i} = \int_{V_i} x \phi(x) dx, \quad \text{and } C_{V_i} = \frac{\mathcal{I}_{V_i}}{M_{V_i}}, \tag{3}$$

respectively. Therefore, applying the parallel-axis theorem of rigid-body motion [31] to the cost function (2) leads to an equivalent expression given by

$$\min_{p \in \mathcal{P}} H(p), \text{ with } H(p) = \sum_{i=1}^n \mathcal{I}_{V_i} + \sum_{i=1}^n M_{V_i} \|p_i - C_{V_i}\|^2, \tag{4}$$

where $p = [p_1^\top, \ldots, p_n^\top]^\top \in \mathbb{R}^{nd}$ denotes the vectorized positions of the robots. The coverage control problem can be regarded as the task of designing control inputs for robots to drive them towards optimal positions, aiming to minimize the objective function of the locational optimization.

2.3. Quaternion-Based Rotation

In order to prevent singularities associated with Euler angles, the rotational movements of a rigid body are parameterized using quaternions, represented by the set $\mathbb{H} = \{q \in \mathbb{R}^4 | q^\top q = 1\}$. A quaternion $q_1 \in \mathbb{H}$ can be utilized to express the rotation from frame $\mathcal{W}^b$ to frame $\mathcal{W}^a$. The element-wise expression of this quaternion is given by $q_1 = \begin{bmatrix} \eta_1 & \bar{q}_1^\top \end{bmatrix}^\top = \begin{bmatrix} \cos\frac{\vartheta_1}{2} & k_1^\top \sin\frac{\vartheta_1}{2} \end{bmatrix}^\top$, where ϑ_1 is the rotation angle around the unit vector k_1. The quaternion conjugate is denoted by a superscripted asterisk, that is, $q_1^* = [\eta_1 \ -\bar{q}_1^\top]^\top \in \mathbb{H}$. In this paper, the dot operator represents the quaternion multiplication of quaternions, for example,

$$q_3 = q_1 \cdot q_2, \text{ for } q_1, q_2 \in \mathbb{H}. \tag{5}$$

A function $T : \mathbb{H} \to \mathbb{R}^{4\times 4}$ is defined as

$$T(q_1) = \begin{bmatrix} \eta_1 & -\bar{q}_1^\top \\ \bar{q}_1 & \eta_1 I + S(\bar{q}_1) \end{bmatrix}, \tag{6}$$

where the cross-product between two vectors $v_1, v_2 \in \mathbb{R}^3$ is represented using a skew-symmetric matrix operator $S \in \mathbb{R}^{3\times 3}$ such that $v_1 \times v_2 = S(v_1)v_2$. Utilizing this function, expression (5) becomes

$$q_3 = T(q_1)q_2. \tag{7}$$

The angular velocity of frame $\mathcal{W}^a$ with respect to frame $\mathcal{W}^b$, as observed from frame $\mathcal{W}^b$, is defined as $\omega_1 \in \mathbb{R}^3$. The connection between the time derivative of quaternion q_1 and the angular velocity ω_1 is expressed by

$$\dot{q}_1 = \frac{1}{2} q_1 \cdot \begin{bmatrix} 0 \\ \omega_1 \end{bmatrix} = \frac{1}{2} T(q_1) \begin{bmatrix} 0 \\ \omega_1 \end{bmatrix} = \frac{1}{2} \tilde{T}(q_1)\omega_1, \tag{8}$$

where $\tilde{T} = [-\bar{q}_1 \ (\eta_1 I + S(\bar{q}_1))^\top]^\top$ because the first column of $T(q_1)$ vanishes.

A rotation matrix can be created using quaternions through the application of Rodrigues' formula. The rotation matrix representing a rotation from frame $\mathcal{W}^b$ to $\mathcal{W}^a$ can be formulated as

$$R_1 = I + 2\eta_1 S(\bar{q}_1) + 2S^2(\bar{q}_1). \tag{9}$$

3. Problem Formulation

Consider a robotic sensor network comprising n quadcopters deployed in a convex space $\mathcal{Q} \subseteq \mathbb{R}^d$, and their connection topology is represented by a connected undirected graph $\mathcal{G}_n = (\mathcal{V}_n, \mathcal{E}_n)$. In this study, we investigate two cases: static and switching communication topology. For the static topology, we generate an undirected connected graph among the agents before deployment. In the switching case, we employ Delaunay triangulation to generate the communication graph in each new step, as indicated by Equation (1). The corresponding Laplacian of these graphs is denoted by $\mathcal{L}_n \in \mathbb{R}^{n \times n}$.

The locational optimization with consensus performance index in the coverage control problem can be constructed from (2) into

$$\min_{p \in \mathcal{P}} \tilde{H}(p), \text{ with } \tilde{H}(p) = H(p) + \frac{1}{2}(p - C_V)^\top \hat{\mathcal{L}}_n (p - C_V), \tag{10}$$

where $\hat{\mathcal{L}}_n = \mathcal{L}_n \otimes I_d \in \mathbb{R}^{nd \times nd}$, $p = [p_1^\top, \ldots, p_n^\top]^\top \in \mathbb{R}^{nd}$ and $C_V = [C_{V_1}^\top, \ldots, C_{V_n}^\top]^\top \in \mathbb{R}^{nd}$.

Quadcopter $i \in \mathcal{V}_n$ within the network possesses position, velocity, attitude, and angular rate denoted by $p_i \in \mathcal{Q}$, $v_i \in \mathbb{R}^3$, $q_i^c \in \mathbb{H}$, and $\omega_i^c \in \mathbb{R}^3$, respectively. The coordinate frames are illustrated in Figure 1, where we adhere to the ENU coordinate convention. The motions of a quadcopter can be categorized into two components: translation and rotation. The translational motion is determined by the attitude and the total thrust of the propellers. In the inertial frame, the quadcopter's translational dynamics, normalized by its mass, are governed by

$$\ddot{p}_i = q_i^c \cdot \bar{f}_i \cdot q_i^{c*} - \bar{g} = R_i^c \bar{f}_i - \bar{g}, \quad (11)$$

where $q_i^c \in \mathbb{S}^3$ is the unit quaternion denoting the current attitude of the quadcopter, $\bar{g} = [0\ 0\ g]^\top$ is the gravitational vector, with g being the gravitational acceleration, and $\bar{f}_i = [0\ 0\ f_i]^\top$ is the thrust control input, with f_i being the total thrust input. Following (8), the rotational motion of the quadcopter is governed by

$$\dot{q}_i^c = \frac{1}{2} q_i^c \cdot \begin{bmatrix} 0 \\ u_i^\omega \end{bmatrix} = \frac{1}{2} \bar{T}(q_1) u_i^\omega, \quad (12)$$

where, in this paper, the control input for the rotational motion is the angular rate u_i^ω.

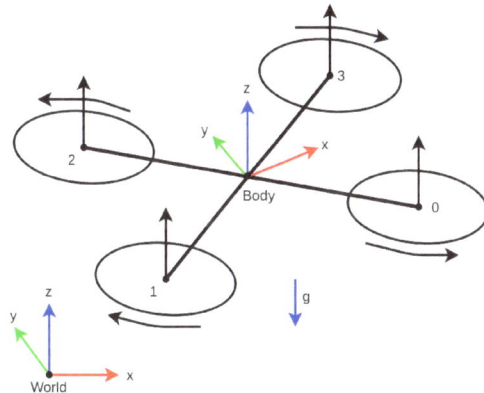

Figure 1. Coordinate frame of a quadcopter, adapted from our previous work in [30].

Using the transformed constrained optimization problem and the defined quadcopter dynamics in Equations (11) and (12), the objectives of this work are to design the quaternion-based attitude and distributed coverage controllers that guarantee convergence within a given settling time, regardless of the initial values, in both fixed and switching communication topologies.

4. Finite-Time Control Design
4.1. Translation Control with Fixed Topology

In the following control design, we tackle our first scenario: the coverage control problem with finite-time stability using a fixed communication topology. We introduce a distributed coverage controller that ensures the attainment of the optimal position and velocity within a finite duration, regardless of the initial positions, relying solely on information obtained from neighboring agents.

Let the performance index of the coverage problem be as defined in (10). The corresponding optimal point of this optimization is given by $p^\star = C_V - \frac{1}{2} M_V^{-1} \hat{\mathcal{L}}_n \tau_v$ for some vector $\tau_v \in \mathbb{R}^{nd}$. Given a fixed connected graph, it follows that the last term vanishes due to the zero eigenvalue of the Laplacian matrix $\hat{\mathcal{L}}_n$ such that $(p_1 - C_{V_1})^\star = \ldots = (p_n - C_{V_n})^\star$.

In other words, we can assert that the objective function $\tilde{H}(p)$ is at its optimum when the robots' positions converge to the optimal point $p^\star = C_V$ and consensus is reached. The velocity reaches its optimal value as $v^\star = \dot{C}_V$.

For all agent $i \in \mathcal{V}_n$, consider the following errors: $\tilde{\zeta}_i = [\tilde{p}_i^\top \ \tilde{v}_i^\top]^\top$ and $\tilde{\zeta}_{ij} = [\tilde{p}_{ij}^\top \ \tilde{v}_{ij}^\top]^\top$, where $\tilde{p}_i = p_i - C_{V_i}$, $\tilde{p}_{ij} = \text{sgn}(\tilde{p}_i - \tilde{p}_j)|\tilde{p}_i - \tilde{p}_j|$, $\tilde{v}_i = v_i - \dot{C}_{V_i}$, and $\tilde{v}_{ij} = \text{sgn}(\tilde{v}_i - \tilde{v}_j)|\tilde{v}_i - \tilde{v}_j|$. Since there are two terms to optimize in (10), by employing these errors, we design a controller consisting of centroid stabilizer and the consensus stabilizer. The controller responsible for driving the robots toward the centroids is proposed as

$$u_i^g = -\kappa_g \text{sgn}(\tilde{\zeta}_i)(|\tilde{\zeta}_i|^{\frac{m_v}{n_v}} + |\tilde{\zeta}_i|^{\frac{p_v}{q_v}}), \tag{13}$$

with $\kappa_g = [k_{gp} \ k_{gv}]^\top$, for $k_{gp}, k_{gv} > 0$, as well as some positive odd integers m_v, n_v, p_v, q_v, for $m_v > n_v$ and $p_v < q_v$. Similarly, with adjacency matrix $A = [a_{ij}]$, for $i \neq j$ and $i, j \in \mathcal{V}_n$, the consensus stabilizer to maintain the formation is given by

$$u_i^c = -\kappa_c \sum_{j=1}^n a_{ij} \text{sgn}(\tilde{\zeta}_{ij})(|\tilde{\zeta}_{ij}|^{\frac{m_v}{n_v}} + |\tilde{\zeta}_{ij}|^{\frac{p_v}{q_v}}), \tag{14}$$

with $\kappa_c = [k_{cp} \ k_{cv}]^\top$ and $k_{cp}, k_{cv} > 0$. Hence, the augmented controller reads

$$u_i^f = u_i^g + u_i^c + \bar{g}. \tag{15}$$

The following lemmas are useful for analyzing the performance of the designed control protocol.

Lemma 2 ([27]). *Let $x_1, x_2, \ldots, x_n \geq 0$. Then,*

$$\sum_{j=1}^n x_j^a \geq \left(\sum_{i=1}^n x_j\right)^a, \text{ for } a \in (0,1).$$

Lemma 3 ([27]). *Let $x_1, x_2, \ldots, x_n \geq 0$. Then,*

$$\sum_{j=1}^n x_j^a \geq n^{1-a}\left(\sum_{i=1}^n x_j\right)^a, \text{ for } a > 1.$$

Lemma 4 ([27]). *The equilibrium point of the scalar system*

$$\dot{x} = -\alpha x^{\frac{a}{b}} - \beta x^{\frac{c}{d}}, \ x(0) = x_0,$$

where $\alpha, \beta > 0$, and a, b, c, d are positive odd integers satisfying $a > b$ and $c < d$, which are finite-time stable with the settling time given by

$$T < T_{\max} := \frac{1}{\alpha}\frac{b}{a-b} + \frac{1}{\beta}\frac{d}{d-c}.$$

Remark 1. *It is worth noticing that this lemma guarantees the finite-time convergence independent of the initial value of the system.*

In the subsequent theorem, we introduce our first result regarding the finite-time convergence of the suggested coverage control protocol for the fixed-topology situation, which is adapted from our conference paper [30].

Theorem 1 (Convergence of Finite-time Coverage Controller with Fixed Topology [30]). *Let a group of n agents be connected via a fixed undirected connected graph $\mathcal{G}_n = (\mathcal{V}_n, \mathcal{E}_n)$ with agent* dynamics defined in (12) and (11). Let two adjacency matrices corresponding to this graph be denoted by $A_\alpha = [a_{ij}^{2n_v/m_v+n_v}] \in \mathbb{R}^{n \times n}$ and $A_\beta = [a_{ij}^{2q_v/p_v+q_v}] \in \mathbb{R}^{n \times n}$, respectively, with m_v, n_v, p_v, q_v being positive odd integers satisfying $m_v > n_v$ and $p_v < q_v$. Let the corresponding Laplacians $\mathcal{L}_\alpha$ and $\mathcal{L}_\beta$ have the smallest nonzero eigenvalues λ_2^α and λ_2^β, respectively. Then, there exist some constants $\kappa_1, \kappa_2 > 0$ such that the finite-time coverage problem can be solved by employing the coverage control protocol (15) with settling time expressed as

$$T_f < T_{\max}^f := \frac{1}{\kappa_1} \frac{n_v}{m_v - n_v} + \frac{1}{\kappa_2} \frac{q_v}{q_v - p_v}. \tag{16}$$

Proof. Using the translational controller (15), the translational dynamics of the quadcopter can equivalently be expressed as

$$\dot{\tilde{\zeta}}_i = A\tilde{\zeta}_i + Bu_i^f = \begin{bmatrix} 0 & 1 \\ 0 & 0 \end{bmatrix} \tilde{\zeta}_i + \begin{bmatrix} 0 \\ 1 \end{bmatrix} u_i^f. \tag{17}$$

Define a Lyapunov function:

$$V^f(\tilde{\zeta}(t)) = \frac{1}{2} \sum_{i=1}^n \tilde{\zeta}_i^2(t). \tag{18}$$

With the system dynamics in (17), the time derivative of the candidate function is given by

$$\dot{V}^f(\tilde{\zeta}) = \dot{V}^g(\tilde{\zeta}) + \dot{V}^c(\tilde{\zeta}). \tag{19}$$

The centroid stabilizer in the first term of (19) can be expanded into

$$\dot{V}^g(\tilde{\zeta}) \leq -\lambda_{\min}^g \sum_{i=1}^n \tilde{\zeta}_i \text{sgn}(\tilde{\zeta}_i)(|\tilde{\zeta}_i|^{\frac{m_v}{n_v}} + |\tilde{\zeta}_i|^{\frac{p_v}{q_v}}), \tag{20}$$

in which we already utilize the smallest eigenvalue of $A - B\kappa_g$ denoted by $\lambda_{\min}^g$. By using the fact that $|\tilde{\zeta}_i| = \tilde{\zeta}_i \text{sgn}(\tilde{\zeta}_i)$, along with Lemmas (2) and (3), the centroid stabilizer term could be written as

$$\dot{V}^g(\tilde{\zeta}) \leq -\lambda_{\min}^g \left(n^{\frac{n_v-m_v}{2n_v}} \left(\sum_{i=1}^n \tilde{\zeta}_i^2 \right)^{\frac{m_v+n_v}{2n_v}} + n^{\frac{q_v-p_v}{2q_v}} \left(\sum_{i=1}^n \tilde{\zeta}_i^2 \right)^{\frac{p_v+q_v}{2q_v}} \right)$$
$$= -\lambda_{\min}^g \left(n^{\frac{n_v-m_v}{2n_v}} (2V^f)^{\frac{m_v+n_v}{2n_v}} + n^{\frac{q_v-p_v}{2q_v}} (2V^f)^{\frac{p_v+q_v}{2q_v}} \right). \tag{21}$$

Similarly, the inequality of the consensus stabilizer from the second term of (19) can be expressed as

$$\dot{V}^c(\tilde{\zeta}) \leq -\lambda_{\min}^c \sum_{i=1}^n \tilde{\zeta}_i \sum_{j=1}^n a_{ij} \text{sgn}(\tilde{\zeta}_{ij})(|\tilde{\zeta}_{ij}|^{\frac{m_v}{n_v}} + |\tilde{\zeta}_{ij}|^{\frac{p_v}{q_v}}), \tag{22}$$

where $\lambda_{\min}^c$ is the smallest eigenvalue of $A - B\kappa_c$. By utilizing the property of the adjacency matrix and also the fact that $|\tilde{\zeta}_{ij}| = \tilde{\zeta}_{ij} \text{sgn}(\tilde{\zeta}_{ij})$, the consensus stabilizer term could be written as

$$\dot{V}^c(\tilde{\zeta}) \leq -\frac{\lambda_{\min}^c}{2}\sum_{i=1}^n\sum_{j=1}^n a_{ij}((\tilde{\zeta}_{ij}^2)^{\frac{m_v+n_v}{2n_v}} + (\tilde{\zeta}_{ij}^2)^{\frac{p_v+q_v}{2q_v}})$$
$$+ (a_{ij}^{\frac{2q_v}{p_v+q_v}}\tilde{\zeta}_{ij}^2)^{\frac{p_v+q_v}{2q_v}})$$
$$\leq -\frac{\lambda_{\min}^c}{2}(n^{\frac{n_v-m_v}{2n_v}}(\sum_{i=1}^n\sum_{j=1}^n a_{ij}^{\frac{2n_v}{m_v+n_v}}\tilde{\zeta}_{ij}^2)^{\frac{m_v+n_v}{2n_v}}$$
$$+ n^{\frac{q_v-p_v}{2q_v}}(\sum_{i=1}^n\sum_{j=1}^n a_{ij}^{\frac{2q_v}{p_v+q_v}}\tilde{\zeta}_{ij}^2)^{\frac{p_v+q_v}{2q_v}}) \tag{23}$$

where the last inequality is obtained by employing Lemmas 2 and 3.

To analyze the graph, consider two adjacency matrices of connected undirected graphs $\mathcal{G}_\alpha$ and $\mathcal{G}_\beta$, denoted by $A_\alpha = [a_{ij}^{2n_v/m_v+n_v}] \in \mathbb{R}^{n\times n}$ and $A_\beta = [a_{ij}^{2q_v/p_v+q_v}] \in \mathbb{R}^{n\times n}$, respectively. The corresponding Laplacians are given by $\mathcal{L}_\alpha$ and $\mathcal{L}_\beta$. It follows that the inequality of the consensus stabilizer can equivalently be expressed as

$$\dot{V}^c(\tilde{\zeta}) \leq -\frac{\lambda_{\min}^c}{2}(n^{\frac{n_v-m_v}{2n_v}}(2\tilde{\zeta}^\top \mathcal{L}_\alpha \tilde{\zeta})^{\frac{m_v+n_v}{2n_v}}$$
$$+ n^{\frac{q_v-p_v}{2q_v}}(2\tilde{\zeta}^\top \mathcal{L}_\beta \tilde{\zeta})^{\frac{p_v+q_v}{2q_v}}), \tag{24}$$

with $\tilde{\zeta} = [\tilde{\zeta}_1^\top,\ldots,\tilde{\zeta}_n^\top]^\top \in \mathbb{R}^{nd}$. Applying the Courant–Fischer theorem of the Laplacian matrices, $\tilde{\zeta}^\top \mathcal{L}_\alpha \tilde{\zeta} \geq \lambda_2^\alpha \|\tilde{\zeta}\|^2$ and $\tilde{\zeta}^\top \mathcal{L}_\beta \tilde{\zeta} \geq \lambda_2^\beta \|\tilde{\zeta}\|^2$ for $1_{nd}^\top \tilde{\zeta} = 0_{nd}$, leads (24) to

$$\dot{V}^c(\tilde{\zeta}) \leq -\frac{\lambda_{\min}^c}{2}(n^{\frac{n_v-m_v}{2n_v}}(4\lambda_2^\alpha V^f)^{\frac{m_v+n_v}{2n_v}}$$
$$+ n^{\frac{q_v-p_v}{2q_v}}(4\lambda_2^\beta V^f)^{\frac{p_v+q_v}{2q_v}}). \tag{25}$$

By adding (21) and (25), followed by some rearrangements, the time derivative of the Lyapunov function can be written as

$$\dot{V}^f(\tilde{\zeta}) \leq -\frac{1}{2}n^{\frac{n_v-m_v}{2n_v}}(2\lambda_{\min}^g + \lambda_{\min}^c(2\lambda_2^\alpha)^{\frac{m_v+n_v}{2n_v}})(2V^f)^{\frac{m_v+n_v}{2n_v}}$$
$$- \frac{1}{2}n^{\frac{q_v-p_v}{2q_v}}(2\lambda_{\min}^g + \lambda_{\min}^c(2\lambda_2^\beta)^{\frac{p_v+q_v}{2q_v}})(2V^f)^{\frac{p_v+q_v}{2q_v}}. \tag{26}$$

By denoting $\xi = \sqrt{2V^f}$ and $\dot{\xi} = 2\dot{V}^f/\sqrt{2V^f}$ for $V^f(\tilde{\zeta}) \neq 0$, we have

$$\dot{\xi} \leq -\frac{1}{2}n^{\frac{n_v-m_v}{2n_v}}(2\lambda_{\min}^g + \lambda_{\min}^c(2\lambda_2^\alpha)^{\frac{m_v+n_v}{2n_v}})\xi^{\frac{m_v+n_v}{n_v}}$$
$$- \frac{1}{2}n^{\frac{q_v-p_v}{2q_v}}(2\lambda_{\min}^g + \lambda_{\min}^c(2\lambda_2^\beta)^{\frac{p_v+q_v}{2q_v}})\xi^{\frac{p_v+q_v}{q_v}}. \tag{27}$$

Choosing positive odd integers m_v, n_v, p_v, q_v satisfying $m_v > n_v$ and $p_v < q_v$ and employing Lemma 4 with the Comparison Principle [32] yields the boundary of the settling time, expressed as

$$T_f < T_{\max}^f := \frac{1}{\kappa_1}\frac{n_v}{m_v-n_v} + \frac{1}{\kappa_2}\frac{q_v}{q_v-p_v},$$

with

$$\kappa_1 = \frac{1}{2}n^{\frac{n_v-m_v}{2n_v}}(2\lambda_{\min}^g + \lambda_{\min}^c(2\lambda_2^\alpha)^{\frac{m_v+n_v}{2n_v}}), \text{ and}$$
$$\kappa_2 = \frac{1}{2}n^{\frac{q_v-p_v}{2q_v}}(2\lambda_{\min}^g + \lambda_{\min}^c(2\lambda_2^\beta)^{\frac{p_v+q_v}{2q_v}}).$$

It can be observed that the system is finite-time stable, i.e., $\lim_{t \to T_{\max}^f} V^f(\tilde{\zeta}) = 0$, implying that $\lim_{t \to T_{\max}^f} \|\tilde{\zeta}\| = 0$. □

In the the quadcopter model, we may obtain the thrust via $f_i = (u_i^f)^\top R_i^c [0\ 0\ 1]^\top$ utilizing the translational control input in (15).

4.2. Translation Control with Switching Topology

In this section, we address the second scenario examined in this research paper, which pertains to the finite-time coverage problem with a switching communication topology. The subsequent control design showcases a proposed controller that ensures the finite-time convergence of the robots' trajectory towards the optimal position and velocity, regardless of their initial positions, using only information from neighboring agents.

By employing similar performance index of the coverage problem defined in (10), this optimization problem has an optimal point given by $p^\star = C_V - \frac{1}{2} M_V^{-1} \hat{\mathcal{L}}_n \tau_v$ for some vector $\tau_v \in \mathbb{R}^{nd}$. As long as the time-varying undirected graph is connected, the last term vanishes due to the zero eigenvalue of the Laplacian matrix $\hat{\mathcal{L}}_n$ such that $(p_1 - C_{V_1})^\star = \ldots = (p_n - C_{V_n})^\star$. The objective function $\tilde{H}(p)$ is optimal when the position of the robots converge to the optimal point $p^\star = C_V$ and the consensus is achieved. The optimal value of the velocity is denoted by $v^\star = \dot{C}_V$.

In this switching topology scenario, the proposed centroid stabilizer, responsible for driving the robots toward the centroids, is formulated as

$$u_i^g = -\kappa_g \text{sgn}(\tilde{\zeta}_i)(|\tilde{\zeta}_i|^{\frac{m_v}{n_v}} + |\tilde{\zeta}_i|^{\frac{p_v}{q_v}}), \tag{28}$$

with $\kappa_g = [k_{gp}\ k_{gv}]^\top$, for $k_{gp}, k_{gv} > 0$, as well as some positive odd integers m_v, n_v, p_v, q_v, for $m_v > n_v$ and $p_v < q_v$. Similarly, utilizing the adjacency matrix $A = [a_{ij}]$, for $i \neq j$ and $i, j \in \mathcal{V}_n$, the consensus stabilizer to maintain the formation is given by

$$u_i^c = -\kappa_c \sum_{j=1}^n a_{ij} \text{sgn}(\tilde{\zeta}_{ij})(|\tilde{\zeta}_{ij}|^{\frac{m_v}{n_v}} + |\tilde{\zeta}_{ij}|^{\frac{p_v}{q_v}}), \tag{29}$$

with $\kappa_c = [k_{cp}\ k_{cv}]^\top$ and $k_{cp}, k_{cv} > 0$. Combining the centroid and consensus stabilizers, the augmented controller is

$$u_i^f = u_i^g + u_i^c + \tilde{g}. \tag{30}$$

After formulating the controller, we present our second result for the finite-time convergence of the proposed coverage control protocol for the switching communication scenario extended from our previous result [30].

Theorem 2 (Convergence of Finite-time Coverage Controller with Switching Topology). *Let a group of n agents have the agent dynamics defined in (12) and (11). Let these agents be connected via a switching connected Delaunay graph $\mathcal{G}_n(t) = (\mathcal{V}_n, \mathcal{E}_n(t))$ for all time $t > 0$. Let two adjacency matrices correspond to this graph, denoted by $A_\alpha = [a_{ij}^{2n_v/m_v+n_v}] \in \mathbb{R}^{n \times n}$ and $A_\beta = [a_{ij}^{2q_v/p_v+q_v}] \in \mathbb{R}^{n \times n}$, respectively, where m_v, n_v, p_v, q_v are positive odd integers satisfying $m_v > n_v$ and $p_v < q_v$. Let the corresponding Laplacians $\mathcal{L}_\alpha$ and $\mathcal{L}_\beta$ for every time t have the smallest nonzero eigenvalues for all time $t > 0$ be $\lambda_2^{\alpha*} = \min_t \lambda_2^\alpha(\mathcal{L}_\alpha(\mathcal{G}_n))$ and $\lambda_2^{\beta*} = \min_t \lambda_2^\beta(\mathcal{L}_\beta(\mathcal{G}_n))$, respectively. Then, there exist some constants $\kappa_1, \kappa_2 > 0$ such that the finite-time coverage problem can be solved by employing the coverage control protocol (30) with settling time given by*

$$T_f < T_{\max}^f := \frac{1}{\kappa_1} \frac{n_v}{m_v - n_v} + \frac{1}{\kappa_2} \frac{q_v}{q_v - p_v}. \tag{31}$$

Proof. Using the translational controller (30), the translational dynamics of the quadcopter can equivalently be expressed as

$$\dot{\tilde{\zeta}}_i = A\tilde{\zeta}_i + Bu_i^f = \begin{bmatrix} 0 & 1 \\ 0 & 0 \end{bmatrix}\tilde{\zeta}_i + \begin{bmatrix} 0 \\ 1 \end{bmatrix}u_i^f. \tag{32}$$

Define a Lyapunov function:

$$V^f(\tilde{\zeta}(t)) = \frac{1}{2}\sum_{i=1}^n \tilde{\zeta}_i^2(t). \tag{33}$$

With the system dynamics in (32), the time derivative of the candidate function is given by

$$\dot{V}^f(\tilde{\zeta}) = \dot{V}^g(\tilde{\zeta}) + \dot{V}^c(\tilde{\zeta}). \tag{34}$$

The centroid stabilizer in the first term of (34) can be expanded into

$$\dot{V}^g(\tilde{\zeta}) \leq -\lambda_{\min}^g \sum_{i=1}^n \tilde{\zeta}_i \mathrm{sgn}(\tilde{\zeta}_i)(|\tilde{\zeta}_i|^{\frac{m_v}{n_v}} + |\tilde{\zeta}_i|^{\frac{p_v}{q_v}}), \tag{35}$$

in which we already utilize the smallest eigenvalue of $A - B\kappa_g$ denoted by $\lambda_{\min}^g$. By using the fact that $|\tilde{\zeta}_i| = \tilde{\zeta}_i \mathrm{sgn}(\tilde{\zeta}_i)$ along with Lemmas (2) and (3), the centroid stabilizer term could be written as

$$\dot{V}^g(\tilde{\zeta}) \leq -\lambda_{\min}^g \left(n^{\frac{n_v - m_v}{2n_v}} \left(\sum_{i=1}^n \tilde{\zeta}_i^2\right)^{\frac{m_v + n_v}{2n_v}} + n^{\frac{q_v - p_v}{2q_v}} \left(\sum_{i=1}^n \tilde{\zeta}_i^2\right)^{\frac{p_v + q_v}{2q_v}}\right)$$

$$= -\lambda_{\min}^g \left(n^{\frac{n_v - m_v}{2n_v}} (2V^f)^{\frac{m_v + n_v}{2n_v}} + n^{\frac{q_v - p_v}{2q_v}} (2V^f)^{\frac{p_v + q_v}{2q_v}}\right). \tag{36}$$

Similarly, the inequality of the consensus stabilizer from the second term of (34) can be expressed as

$$\dot{V}^c(\tilde{\zeta}) \leq -\lambda_{\min}^c \sum_{i=1}^n \tilde{\zeta}_i \sum_{j=1}^n a_{ij}\mathrm{sgn}(\tilde{\zeta}_{ij})(|\tilde{\zeta}_{ij}|^{\frac{m_v}{n_v}} + |\tilde{\zeta}_{ij}|^{\frac{p_v}{q_v}}), \tag{37}$$

where $\lambda_{\min}^c$ is the smallest eigenvalue of $A - B\kappa_c$. By utilizing the property of the adjacency matrix and also the fact that $|\tilde{\zeta}_{ij}| = \tilde{\zeta}_{ij}\mathrm{sgn}(\tilde{\zeta}_{ij})$, the consensus stabilizer term could be written as

$$\dot{V}^c(\tilde{\zeta}) \leq -\frac{\lambda_{\min}^c}{2}\sum_{i=1}^n\sum_{j=1}^n a_{ij}\left((\tilde{\zeta}_{ij}^2)^{\frac{m_v + n_v}{2n_v}} + (\tilde{\zeta}_{ij}^2)^{\frac{p_v + q_v}{2q_v}}\right)$$

$$+ (a_{ij}^{\frac{2q_v}{p_v + q_v}}\tilde{\zeta}_{ij}^2)^{\frac{p_v + q_v}{2q_v}})$$

$$\leq -\frac{\lambda_{\min}^c}{2}\left(n^{\frac{n_v - m_v}{2n_v}}\left(\sum_{i=1}^n\sum_{j=1}^n a_{ij}^{\frac{2n_v}{m_v + n_v}}\tilde{\zeta}_{ij}^2\right)^{\frac{m_v + n_v}{2n_v}}\right.$$

$$\left. + n^{\frac{q_v - p_v}{2q_v}}\left(\sum_{i=1}^n\sum_{j=1}^n a_{ij}^{\frac{2q_v}{p_v + q_v}}\tilde{\zeta}_{ij}^2\right)^{\frac{p_v + q_v}{2q_v}}\right) \tag{38}$$

where the last inequality is obtained by employing Lemmas 2 and 3.

Using the relationship between Laplacian and adjacency matrices, it follows that the inequality of the consensus stabilizer can equivalently be expressed as

$$\dot{V}^c(\tilde{\zeta}) \leq -\frac{\lambda^c_{\min}}{2}(n^{\frac{n_v - m_v}{2n_v}}(2\tilde{\zeta}^\top \mathcal{L}_\alpha \tilde{\zeta})^{\frac{m_v + n_v}{2n_v}} + n^{\frac{q_v - p_v}{2q_v}}(2\tilde{\zeta}^\top \mathcal{L}_\beta \tilde{\zeta})^{\frac{p_v + q_v}{2q_v}}), \tag{39}$$

with $\tilde{\zeta} = [\tilde{\zeta}_1^\top, \ldots, \tilde{\zeta}_n^\top]^\top \in \mathbb{R}^{nd}$. Using the properties of the Laplacian matrices, $\tilde{\zeta}^\top \mathcal{L}_\alpha \tilde{\zeta} \geq \lambda_2^\alpha \|\tilde{\zeta}\|^2 \geq \lambda_2^{\alpha*} \|\tilde{\zeta}\|^2$ and $\tilde{\zeta}^\top \mathcal{L}_\beta \tilde{\zeta} \geq \lambda_2^\beta \|\tilde{\zeta}\|^2 \geq \lambda_2^{\beta*} \|\tilde{\zeta}\|^2$ for $1_{nd}^\top \tilde{\zeta} = 0_{nd}$, leads (39) to

$$\dot{V}^c(\tilde{\zeta}) \leq -\frac{\lambda^c_{\min}}{2}(n^{\frac{n_v - m_v}{2n_v}}(4\lambda_2^{\alpha*} V^f)^{\frac{m_v + n_v}{2n_v}} + n^{\frac{q_v - p_v}{2q_v}}(4\lambda_2^{\beta*} V^f)^{\frac{p_v + q_v}{2q_v}}). \tag{40}$$

By adding (36) and (40), followed by some rearrangements, the time derivative of the Lyapunov function can be written as

$$\dot{V}^f(\tilde{\zeta}) \leq -\frac{1}{2} n^{\frac{n_v - m_v}{2n_v}}(2\lambda^g_{\min} + \lambda^c_{\min}(2\lambda_2^{\alpha*})^{\frac{m_v + n_v}{2n_v}})(2V^f)^{\frac{m_v + n_v}{2n_v}} \\ -\frac{1}{2} n^{\frac{q_v - p_v}{2q_v}}(2\lambda^g_{\min} + \lambda^c_{\min}(2\lambda_2^{\beta*})^{\frac{p_v + q_v}{2q_v}})(2V^f)^{\frac{p_v + q_v}{2q_v}}. \tag{41}$$

By denoting $\xi = \sqrt{2V^f}$ and $\dot{\xi} = 2\dot{V}^f/\sqrt{2V^f}$ for $V^f(\tilde{\zeta}) \neq 0$, we have

$$\dot{\xi} \leq -\frac{1}{2} n^{\frac{n_v - m_v}{2n_v}}(2\lambda^g_{\min} + \lambda^c_{\min}(2\lambda_2^{\alpha*})^{\frac{m_v + n_v}{2n_v}})\xi^{\frac{m_v + n_v}{n_v}} \\ -\frac{1}{2} n^{\frac{q_v - p_v}{2q_v}}(2\lambda^g_{\min} + \lambda^c_{\min}(2\lambda_2^{\beta*})^{\frac{p_v + q_v}{2q_v}})\xi^{\frac{p_v + q_v}{q_v}}. \tag{42}$$

Choosing positive odd integers m_v, n_v, p_v, q_v satisfying $m_v > n_v$ and $p_v < q_v$ and employing Lemma 4 with the Comparison Principle [32] yields the boundary of the settling time expressed as

$$T_f < T^f_{\max} := \frac{1}{\kappa_1} \frac{n_v}{m_v - n_v} + \frac{1}{\kappa_2} \frac{q_v}{q_v - p_v},$$

with

$$\kappa_1 = \frac{1}{2} n^{\frac{n_v - m_v}{2n_v}}(2\lambda^g_{\min} + \lambda^c_{\min}(2\lambda_2^{\alpha*})^{\frac{m_v + n_v}{2n_v}}), \text{ and}$$

$$\kappa_2 = \frac{1}{2} n^{\frac{q_v - p_v}{2q_v}}(2\lambda^g_{\min} + \lambda^c_{\min}(2\lambda_2^{\beta*})^{\frac{p_v + q_v}{2q_v}}).$$

It can be observed that the system is finite-time stable, i.e., $\lim_{t \to T^f_{\max}} V^f(\tilde{\zeta}) = 0$, implying that $\lim_{t \to T^f_{\max}} \|\tilde{\zeta}\| = 0$. □

Similar to the the previous scenario, we may compute the thrust via $f_i = (u_i^f)^\top R_i^c [0\,0\,1]^\top$ by employing the translational control input in (30).

4.3. Rotation Control

Due to the interdependence of translational and rotational motion, it is necessary to develop an attitude controller that ensures finite-time stability.

Given the current and desired attitudes of the i-th quadcopter, denoted by $q_i^c = [\eta_i^c \ \bar{q}_i^{c\top}]^\top$ and $q_i^d = [\eta_i^d \ \bar{q}_i^{d\top}]^\top$, respectively, the error quaternion can be obtained via

$q_i^e = q_i^{c*} \cdot q_i^d = T(q_i^{c*})q_i^d = [\eta_i^e \ \bar{q}_i^{e\top}]^\top$. For controller analysis, an error vector is also defined as follows:

$$e_{q_i^e} = \begin{bmatrix} 1 \mp \eta_i^e \\ \bar{q}_i^e \end{bmatrix}. \tag{43}$$

Differentiating this error yields the error dynamics expressed as

$$\dot{e}_{q_i^e} = \frac{1}{2}\bar{T}(q_i^e)u_i^\omega. \tag{44}$$

In this attitude control scheme, by employing the error vector, the angular-rate control command is defined as

$$u_i^\omega = -\kappa_\omega \text{sgn}\left(\tilde{e}_{q_i^e}\right)\left(|\tilde{e}_{q_i^e}|^{\frac{m_w}{n_w}} + |\tilde{e}_{q_i^e}|^{\frac{p_w}{q_w}}\right) \tag{45}$$

with $\tilde{e}_{q_i^e} = [\bar{T}(q_i^e)]^\top e_{q_i^e}$ and $k_\omega > 0$.

The following theorem states our next result on the attitude controller of a quadcopter.

Theorem 3 (Convergence of Finite-time Rotational Controller). *Let the attitude dynamics of a quadcopter be given by (12) and the error vector between the current and desired attitudes be given by (43). Then, given the control protocol (45), there exist some positive constants k_ω such that the equilibrium point of the error vector is finite-time stable with settling time given by*

$$T_a < T_{\max}^a := \frac{1}{\kappa_\omega}\left(\frac{n_w}{m_w - n_w} + \frac{q_w}{q_w - p_w}\right), \tag{46}$$

where m_w, n_w, p_w, q_w are positive odd integers satisfying $m_w > n_w$ and $p_w < q_w$.

Proof. Define a Lyapunov function:

$$V^a(e_{q_i^e}) = \frac{1}{2}e_{q_i^e}^\top e_{q_i^e}. \tag{47}$$

Taking the derivative of the Lyapunov function yields

$$\dot{V}^a(e_{q_i^e}) = -\kappa_\omega \frac{1}{2}\tilde{e}_{q_i^e}^\top \text{sgn}\left(\tilde{e}_{q_i^e}\right)\left(|\tilde{e}_{q_i^e}|^{\frac{m_w}{n_w}} + |\tilde{e}_{q_i^e}|^{\frac{p_w}{q_w}}\right), \tag{48}$$

where $\tilde{e}_{q_i^e} = [\bar{T}(q_i^e)]^\top e_{q_i^e}$, and the error dynamics with the proposed control command have been utilized. Since $\left|\tilde{e}_{q_i^e}\right| = \tilde{e}_{q_i^e}\text{sgn}\left(\tilde{e}_{q_i^e}\right)$, (48) can be expressed as

$$\dot{V}^a(e_{q_i^e}) = -\kappa_\omega \frac{1}{2}\left(\left(\tilde{e}_{q_i^e}^2\right)^{\frac{m_w + n_w}{2n_w}} + \left(\tilde{e}_{q_i^e}^2\right)^{\frac{p_w + q_w}{2q_w}}\right) \tag{49}$$

Substituting $2V^a = \tilde{e}_{q_i^e}^2$ to (49) leads to

$$\dot{V}^a(e_{q_i^e}) = -\kappa_\omega \frac{1}{2}\left((2V^a)^{\frac{m_w + n_w}{2n_w}} + (2V^a)^{\frac{p_w + q_w}{2q_w}}\right). \tag{50}$$

By taking $\varrho = \sqrt{2V^a}$ and $\dot{\varrho} = 2\dot{V}^a/\sqrt{2V^a}$ for $V^a > 0$, (49) can equivalently be rewritten as

$$\dot{\varrho} = -\kappa_\omega \varrho^{\frac{m_w}{n_w}} - \kappa_\omega \varrho^{\frac{p_w}{q_w}}. \tag{51}$$

Therefore, utilizing the Comparison Principle [32] and Lemma 4 with some positive odd integers m_w, n_w, p_w, q_w, for $m_w > n_w$ and $p_w < q_w$, we may conclude that the settling time of the attitude system can be expressed as

$$T_a < T_{\max}^a := \frac{1}{\kappa_\omega}\left(\frac{n_w}{m_w - n_w} + \frac{q_w}{q_w - p_w}\right),$$

and the system is finite-time stable, i.e., $\lim_{t \to T_{\max}^a} V^a(e_{q_i^e}) = 0$, implying that $\lim_{t \to T_{\max}^a} \|e_{q_i^e}\| = 0$. □

Based on Equations (16) and (46), the computation of the boundary of the settling time of this coverage controller is indeed dependent on some controller parameters and the algebraic graph topology but independent of the initial values. Furthermore, the quadcopters will reach the optimal position and velocity within the settling time $T_{\text{sys}} = T^a + T^f < T_{\max}^a + T_{\max}^f$.

To obtain the desired quaternion, given translational control input (15) or (30) and desired heading ψ_i^d, let a heading vector $x_i^c = [\cos\psi_i^d \ \sin\psi_i^d \ 0]^\top$. Then, we may have a rotation matrix $R_i^d = [x_i^d \ y_i^d \ z_i^d]$ composed of $z_i^d = u_i^f/\|u_i^f\|$, $y_i^d = z_i^d \times x_i^c/\|z_i^d \times x_i^c\|$, and $x_i^d = y_i^d \times z_i^d/\|y_i^d \times z_i^d\|$. Accordingly, the desired quaternion can easily be obtained using a rotation matrix and quaternion relationship, such that $q_i^d = \text{rotmatToQuaternion}(R_i^d)$, as documented in [33].

5. Simulation Results

In this section, a series of numerical simulations are conducted to validate the proposed control protocols. The simulations are performed using the PX4 Autopilot software-in-the-loop (SITL) on the Gazebo simulator and the Mavros controller package integrated with the Robot Operating System (ROS) [34,35]. This simulation platform provides a highly realistic environment that closely emulates the behaviors and characteristics of real quadcopters equipped with the PX4 flight controller. The PX4 flight controller incorporates control input saturation in the low-level actuator controllers. The simulations are run on a computer with a Linux-based operating system, a 3.2-GHz processor, and 16-GB RAM. Figure 2 displays a screenshot of the simulator.

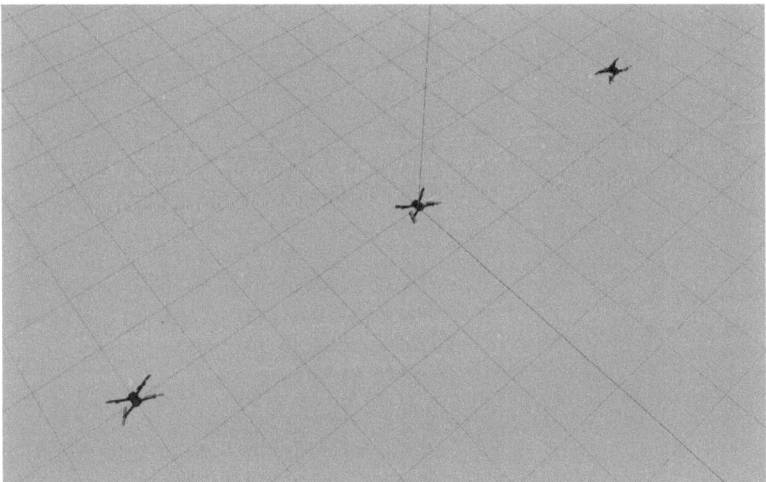

Figure 2. Quadcopters on Gazebo simulator, adapted from our previous work in [30].

Two scenarios are examined in this simulation: coverage control with fixed topology and coverage control with switching topology.

In the fixed topology scenario, nine quadcopters are randomly deployed within a bounded planar space defined by the coordinates (0,0), (0,1), (1,1), and (1,0). The quadcopters have constant altitude and adjust only their position and velocity in the $x - y$ plane. The distribution of information in this scenario is uniform. The controller parameters used are $m_v = m_w = 5$, $n_v = n_w = 3$, $p_v = p_w = 3$, $q_v = q_w = 5$, $\kappa_\omega = 0.8$, $\kappa_g = 0.5$, and $\kappa_c = 0.4$. The communication topology is represented by a complete graph among the nine agents, with the smallest nonzero eigenvalue being $\lambda_2 = 0.16$. Theoretical analysis (Theorems 1 and 3) suggests an estimated maximum settling time of $T_{sys} = 23.850$.

Applying the control protocols described in Equations (15) and (45) to the quadcopter dynamics modeled by Equations (11) and (12), the resulting trajectories of the robots and the corresponding Voronoi partition are shown in Figure 3a. Additionally, Figure 3b displays the objective function, and Figure 3c illustrates the convergence trajectory of the error $\|p_i - C_{V_i}\|$. The control inputs of the agents are depicted in Figure 3d [30].

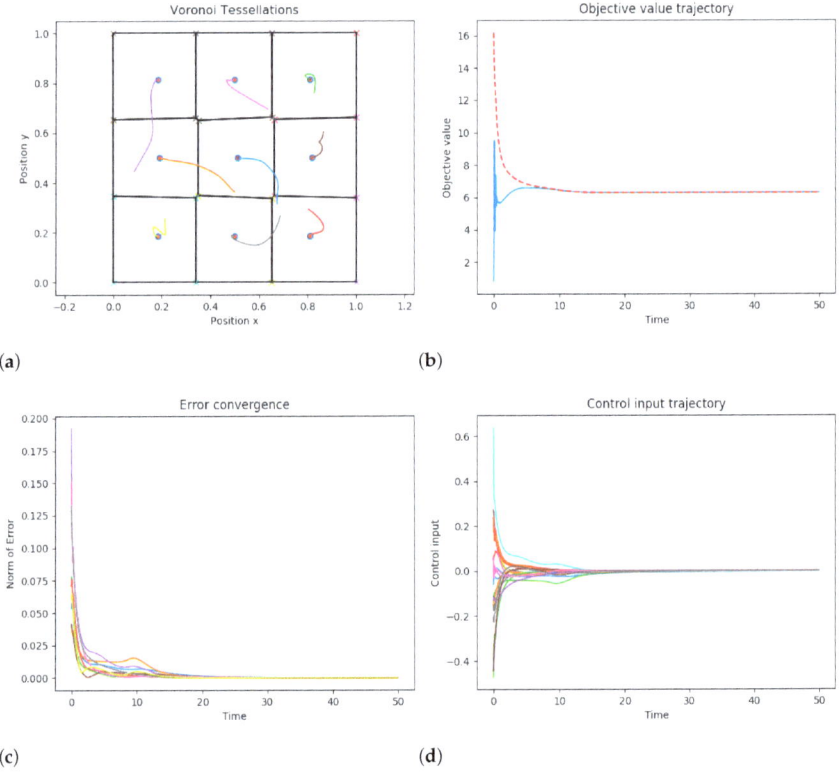

Figure 3. Finite-time coverage control simulation with fixed communication topology and uniform information distribution: (**a**) Trajectories and optimal Voronoi regions; (**b**) Objective function convergence, red-dashed line refers to the true objective function, blue line refers to the objective function computed by the agents in every iteration; (**c**) Trajectory errors; (**d**) Control inputs. Different colours in Subfigures (**a**), (**c**) and (**d**) refer to different trajectories of the quadcopters.

In the switching topology scenario, ten quadcopters are randomly deployed within a bounded planar space defined by the coordinates (0,0), (0,1), (1,1), and (1,0). Similar to the fixed topology case, the quadcopters have constant altitude and adjust only their position and velocity in the $x - y$ plane. However, the information distribution in this scenario exhibits two peaks. The controller parameters used are $m_v = m_w = 5$, $n_v = n_w = 3$, $p_v = p_w = 3$, $q_v = q_w = 5$, $\kappa_\omega = 0.8$, $\kappa_g = 0.5$, and $\kappa_c = 0.4$. The communication topology is represented by a Delaunay graph among the ten agents, with the smallest nonzero eigenvalue being $\lambda_2 = 0.4615$. Theorems 2 and 3 suggest an estimated maximum settling time of $T_{\text{sys}} = 20.298$.

Applying the control protocols described in Equations (30) and (45) to the quadcopter dynamics modeled by Equations (11) and (12), the resulting trajectories of the robots and the corresponding Voronoi partition are shown in Figure 4a. Additionally, Figure 4b displays the objective function, and Figure 4c illustrates the convergence trajectory of the error $\|p_i - C_{V_i}\|$. The control inputs to drive the agents are plotted in Figure 4d.

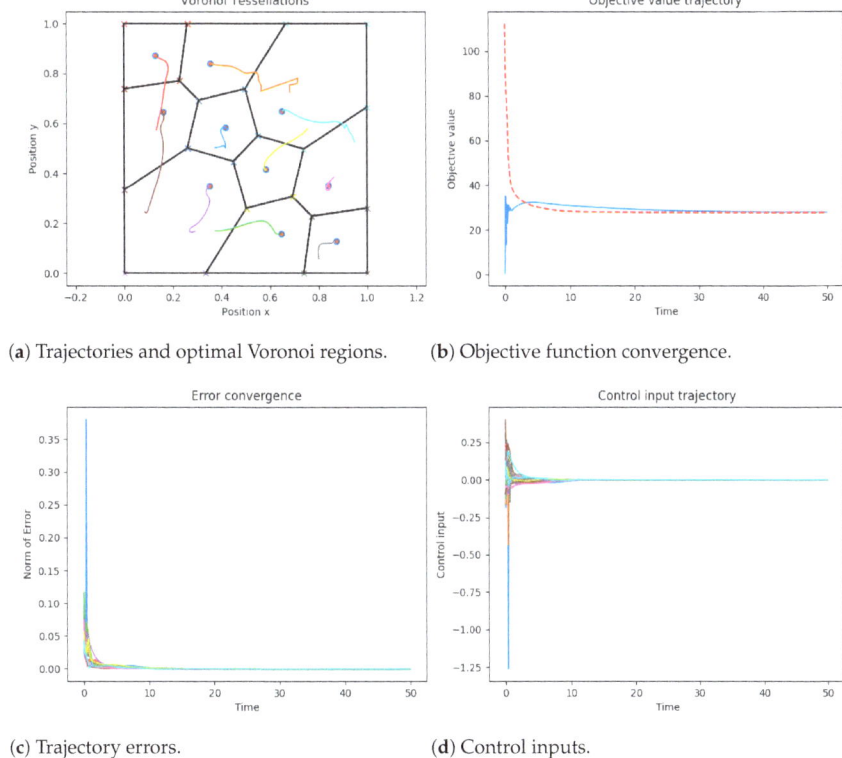

(a) Trajectories and optimal Voronoi regions.

(b) Objective function convergence.

(c) Trajectory errors.

(d) Control inputs.

Figure 4. Finite-time coverage control simulation with switching communication topology and diagonal-peak information distribution: (**a**) Trajectories and optimal Voronoi regions; (**b**) Objective function convergence, red-dashed line refers to the true objective function, blue line refers to the objective function computed by the agents in every iteration; (**c**) Trajectory errors; (**d**) Control inputs. Different colours in Subfigures (**a**), (**c**) and (**d**) refer to different trajectories of the quadcopters.

Figures 3 and 4 demonstrate the successful execution of the controllers, resulting in the alignment of the robots' positions with their respective centroids. In the first scenario, where the density function within the boundary is uniform, the distribution of robots per unit area appears similar. However, in the second scenario, quadcopters tend to cluster around the diagonal peaks. The error plots in Figures 3c and 4c confirm that the position error relative to the optimal position is minimized before the expected settling time $T_{\max}$. Additionally, Figures 3b and 4b illustrate the convergence of the objective function towards an optimal value once the centroids are reached.

Based on these results, it can be observed that the quadcopters, guided by the attractive coverage controller, move towards the optimal points from their initial positions. At certain time instances $t = t_2$ (where $t_2 > 0$), some quadcopters exhibit higher convergence errors compared with earlier time $t = t_1$ (where $t_2 > t_1$). However, analyzing the objective function curves, it can be inferred that this behavior arises because, at time $t = t_2$, the algorithm has found a more efficient way to minimize the total objective function, i.e., moving a few quadcopters is easier than adjusting the others. These simulation results further validate that the protocols (15) and (30) successfully address the coverage control problem, enabling the quadcopters to converge close to the optimal positions within a finite time.

There remains the task of theoretically analyzing the proposed finite-time coverage control protocol under constrained control inputs to account for real quadcopter systems, where the control inputs may have bounds. This aspect will be investigated in future research, which will involve the utilization of actual quadcopters to validate the analysis.

6. Conclusions

In this paper, we studied the distributed coverage control problem of quadcopter sensor networks and ensured their finite-time stability both in fixed and switching communication topologies. The control protocols were classified into two schemes according to the motions: translation and rotation. By employing the reformulated locational optimization problem, a translational control protocol was developed to guide the quadcopters in tracking the position and velocity of the Voronoi centroid derived from the coverage control problem. Subsequently, the translational control command was fed into the rotational controller to determine the desired attitude of the quadcopter. Since the planar translation of the quadcopter was coupled with its attitude, we also proposed a rotational control protocol for each quadcopter based on quaternion to follow the desired attitude. The proposed translational and rotational protocols were carefully analyzed using the finite-time stability theory to ensure that the quadcopters' position and velocity converge to the Voronoi centroid position and velocity within a designed settling time, independent of the initial values, both in fixed and switching communication networks. Through simulations on the Gazebo simulator with ROS, we validated the performance of the proposed control protocols, where the centroids were reached within the expected duration. In future work, a number of experiments with real quadcopter systems with constrained control inputs will also be carried out at the GIPSA lab to verify the effectiveness of the algorithms.

Author Contributions: Conceptualization, H.T., K.M. and A.H.; Methodology, H.T., K.M. and A.H.; Validation, H.T. and K.M.; Formal analysis, H.T.; Investigation, K.M. and N.M.; Writing—original draft, H.T.; Writing—review & editing, H.T., K.M. and A.H.; Supervision, A.H. and N.M.; Project administration, N.M.; Funding acquisition, A.H. and N.M. All authors have read and agreed to the published version of the manuscript.

Funding: This research was supported by the TAMOS (TActical Multi-Objective Swarming UAVs) project.

Data Availability Statement: Data available with the corresponding author.

Conflicts of Interest: The authors declare no conflict of interest.

References

1. Carron, A.; Zeilinger, M.N. Model Predictive Coverage Control. *IFAC-PapersOnLine* **2020**, *53*, 6107–6112. [CrossRef]
2. Mei, Y.; Lu, Y.H.; Hu, Y.C.; Lee, C.S. Deployment strategy for mobile robots with energy and timing constraints. *Proc.-IEEE Int. Conf. Robot. Autom.* **2005**, *2005*, 2816–2821. [CrossRef]
3. Tsouros, D.C.; Bibi, S.; Sarigiannidis, P.G. A Review on UAV-Based Applications for Precision Agriculture. *Information* **2019**, *10*, 349. [CrossRef]
4. Zhang, J.; Tnunay, H.; Wang, C.; Lyu, X.; Ding, Z. Distributed Coverage Optimization and Control with Applications to Precision Agriculture. In Proceedings of the 2018 37th Chinese Control Conference (CCC), Wuhan, China, 25–27 July 2018; pp. 6836–6841. [CrossRef]
5. Okabe, A.; Suzuki, A. Locational optimization problems solved through Voronoi diagrams. *Eur. J. Oper. Res.* **1997**, *98*, 445–456. [CrossRef]
6. Okabe, A.; Boots, B.; Sugihara, K.; Chiu, S.N. *Spatial Tessellations: Concepts and Applications of Voronoi Diagrams*, 2nd ed.; Wiley Series in Probability and Statistics; Wiley: New York, NY, USA, 1995; Volume 26, p. 79. [CrossRef]

7. Pavone, M.; Arsie, A.; Frazzoli, E.; Bullo, F. Distributed Algorithms for Environment Partitioning in Mobile Robotic Networks. *IEEE Trans. Autom. Control* **2011**, *56*, 1834–1848. [CrossRef]
8. Cortes, J.; Martinez, S.; Karatas, T.; Bullo, F. Coverage Control for Mobile Sensing Networks. *IEEE Trans. Robot. Autom.* **2004**, *20*, 243–255. [CrossRef]
9. Salhi, S. Facility Location: A Survey of Applications and Methods. *J. Oper. Res. Soc.* **1996**, *47*, 1421–1422. [CrossRef]
10. Lee, S.G.; Diaz-Mercado, Y.; Egerstedt, M. Multirobot Control Using Time-Varying Density Functions. *IEEE Trans. Robot.* **2015**, *31*, 489–493. [CrossRef]
11. Cortés, J.; Martínez, S.; Bullo, F. Spatially-distributed coverage optimization and control with limited-range interactions. *ESAIM-Control. Optim. Calc. Var.* **2005**, *11*, 691–719. .:2005024. [CrossRef]
12. Pimenta, L.C.; Kumar, V.; Mesquita, R.C.; Pereira, G.A. Sensing and coverage for a network of heterogeneous robots. In Proceedings of the IEEE Conference on Decision and Control, Cancun, Mexico, 9–11 December 2008; pp. 3947–3952. [CrossRef]
13. Gusrialdi, A.; Hatanaka, T.; Fujita, M. Coverage control for mobile networks with limited-range anisotropic sensors. In Proceedings of the IEEE Conference on Decision and Control, Cancun, Mexico, 9–11 December 2008; pp. 4263–4268. [CrossRef]
14. Parapari, H.F.; Abdollahi, F.; Menhaj, M.B. Coverage control in non-convex environment considering unknown non-convex obstacles. In Proceedings of the 2014 2nd RSI/ISM International Conference on Robotics and Mechatronics, ICRoM 2014, Tehran, Iran, 15–17 October 2014; pp. 119–124. [CrossRef]
15. Kantaros, Y.; Thanou, M.; Tzes, A. Distributed coverage control for concave areas by a heterogeneous Robot-Swarm with visibility sensing constraints. *Automatica* **2015**, *53*, 195–207. [CrossRef]
16. Schwager, M.; Slotine, J.J.; Rus, D. Decentralized, adaptive control for coverage with networked robots. In Proceedings of the IEEE International Conference on Robotics and Automation, Rome, Italy, 10–14 April 2007; pp. 3289–3294. [CrossRef]
17. Martinez, S. Distributed interpolation schemes for field estimation by mobile sensor networks. *IEEE Trans. Control Syst. Technol.* **2010**, *18*, 491–500. [CrossRef]
18. Schwager, M.; Vitus, M.P.; Powers, S.; Rus, D.; Tomlin, C.J. Robust adaptive coverage control for robotic sensor networks. *IEEE Trans. Control Netw. Syst.* **2017**, *4*, 462–476. [CrossRef]
19. Kantaros, Y.; Zavlanos, M.M. Distributed communication-aware coverage control by mobile sensor networks. *Automatica* **2016**, *63*, 209–220. [CrossRef]
20. Wang, P.; Song, C.; Liu, L. Coverage Control for Mobile Sensor Networks with Unknown Terrain Roughness and Time-varying Delays. In Proceedings of the 2022 41st Chinese Control Conference (CCC), Hefei, China, 25–27 July 2022; pp. 1–6. [CrossRef]
21. Tamba, T.A. Optimizing the Area Coverage of Networked UAVs using Multi-Agent Reinforcement Learning. In Proceedings of the 2021 International Conference on Instrumentation, Control, and Automation (ICA), Bandung, Indonesia, 25–27 August 2021; pp. 197–201. [CrossRef]
22. Bhat, S.P.; Bernstein, D.S. Finite-time stability of continuous autonomous systems. *SIAM J. Control Optim.* **2000**, *38*, 751–766. [CrossRef]
23. Xiao, F.; Wang, L.; Chen, J.; Gao, Y. Finite-time formation control for multi-agent systems. *Automatica* **2009**, *45*, 2605–2611. [CrossRef]
24. Khoo, S.; Xie, L.; Man, Z. Robust finite-time consensus tracking algorithm for multirobot systems. *IEEE/ASME Trans. Mechatron.* **2009**, *14*, 219–228. [CrossRef]
25. Du, H.; Yang, C.; Jia, R. Finite-time formation control of multiple mobile robots. In Proceedings of the 6th Annual IEEE International Conference on Cyber Technology in Automation, Control and Intelligent Systems, IEEE-CYBER 2016, Chengdu, China, 19–22 June 2016; pp. 416–421. [CrossRef]
26. Wang, J.; Liang, H.; Sun, Z.; Zhang, S.; Liu, M. Finite-time control for spacecraft formation with dual-number-based description. *J. Guid. Control. Dyn.* **2012**, *35*, 950–962. [CrossRef]
27. Zuo, Z.; Tie, L. A new class of finite-time nonlinear consensus protocols for multi-agent systems. *Int. J. Control* **2014**, *87*, 363–370. [CrossRef]
28. Zuo, Z. Nonsingular fixed-time consensus tracking for second-order multi-agent networks. *Automatica* **2015**, *54*, 305–309. [CrossRef]
29. Wang, C.; Tnunay, H.; Zuo, Z.; Lennox, B.; Ding, Z. Fixed-Time Formation Control of Multirobot Systems: Design and Experiments. *IEEE Trans. Ind. Electron.* **2019**, *66*. [CrossRef]
30. Tnunay, H.; Moussa, K.; Hably, A.; Marchand, N. Distributed Finite-time Coverage Control of Multi-quadrotor Systems. In Proceedings of the IECON 2022—48th Annual Conference of the IEEE Industrial Electronics Society, Brussels, Belgium, 17–20 October 2022; pp. 1–6. [CrossRef]
31. Abdulghany, A.R. Generalization of parallel axis theorem for rotational inertia. *Am. J. Phys.* **2017**, *85*, 791–795. [CrossRef]
32. Khalil, H.K. *Nonlinear Systems*, 3rd ed.; Prentice-Hall: Upper Saddle River, NJ, USA, 2002.
33. Brescianini, D.; Hehn, M.; D'Andrea, R. *Nonlinear Quadrocopter Attitude Control*; Technical Report; ETH Zürich, Departement Maschinenbau und Verfahrenstechnik: Zürich, Swizerland, 2013; pp. 1–21. [CrossRef]

34. Meier, L.; Honegger, D.; Pollefeys, M. PX4: A node-based multithreaded open source robotics framework for deeply embedded platforms. In Proceedings of the 2015 IEEE International Conference on Robotics and Automation (ICRA), Seattle, WA, USA, 26–30 May 2015; pp. 6235–6240. [CrossRef]
35. Lim, J. Mavros_CONTROLLERS—Aggressive Trajectory Tracking Using Mavros for PX4 Enabled Vehicles. 2019. Available online: https://scholar.google.co.kr/citations?view_op=view_citation&hl=en&user=NOdnT3EAAAAJ&citation_for_view=NOdnT3EAAAAJ:zYLM7Y9cAGgC (accessed on 10 January 2023). [CrossRef]

Disclaimer/Publisher's Note: The statements, opinions and data contained in all publications are solely those of the individual author(s) and contributor(s) and not of MDPI and/or the editor(s). MDPI and/or the editor(s) disclaim responsibility for any injury to people or property resulting from any ideas, methods, instructions or products referred to in the content.

MDPI AG
Grosspeteranlage 5
4052 Basel
Switzerland
Tel.: +41 61 683 77 34

Mathematics Editorial Office
E-mail: mathematics@mdpi.com
www.mdpi.com/journal/mathematics

Disclaimer/Publisher's Note: The title and front matter of this reprint are at the discretion of the Guest Editors. The publisher is not responsible for their content or any associated concerns. The statements, opinions and data contained in all individual articles are solely those of the individual Editors and contributors and not of MDPI. MDPI disclaims responsibility for any injury to people or property resulting from any ideas, methods, instructions or products referred to in the content.

www.ingramcontent.com/pod-product-compliance
Lightning Source LLC
LaVergne TN
LVHW072320090526
838202LV00019B/2322